A History of Philosophy

A History of Philosophy

MARTIN J. WALSH

GEOFFREY CHAPMAN

LONDON

A Geoffrey Chapman book published by
Cassell Publishers Ltd
Artillery House, Artillery Row,
London SW1P 1RT

First published 1985
Reprinted 1987

British Library Cataloguing in Publication Data

Walsh, Martin J.
    A history of philosophy.
    1. Philosophy—History
    I. Title
    190'.9   B72

ISBN 0 225 66360 0

Printed and bound in Great Britain by
Biddles Ltd, Guildford and King's Lynn

Contents

Preface

For several years past it has been difficult to obtain a compact textbook or concise reference book to assist the busy teacher and student of the history of philosophy. Textbooks written even ten or fifteen years ago may be partly out of date and are often no longer in print.

For the history of philosophy some short introductory books are widely available but these do not give adequate coverage for the more serious student. Fr Copleston's splendid multi-volumed work is still available but many students, especially those for whom English is a second language, find that sixteen volumes present too great a challenge. Bertrand Russell's history is available in a one-volume paperback edition but it is now widely recognized that this work presents a highly personal reaction to selected aspects of different philosophers' systems of thought rather than an objective presentation of the philosophers' actual thought. It is eminently readable but not really reliable as a comprehensive history.

The present text was originally the basis of lectures to philosophy students in universities, colleges and seminaries. The text has been revised repeatedly in use with students in different years of philosophical studies. The questions raised by students helped constantly in the clarification of language and reformulation of various passages. I have sought to improve the text not so much by the use of any simplified vocabulary but rather in the frequent use of explanatory synonyms and phrases which help to clarify the original thought.

The students for whom the present textbook is written will probably be students who are making their first acquaintance with the study of philosophy in general. They may study the history of philosophy along with courses in the introduction to philosophy, philosophical anthropology, philosophy of nature, epistemology, logic, ethics, the philosophy of being and many other subjects. In these courses it is usually accepted that philosophy is a body of natural knowledge, methodically acquired and ordered, which undertakes an investigation of the fundamental problems concerning knowledge, being, nature and values, and endeavours to attain the fundamental explanation of all things. The history of philosophy is seen in this context as that aspect of the study of philosophy in general which considers the contributions to human thought made by the most original systematic thinkers, through the course of time, who have addressed their thinking to the study of these fundamental problems. The philosophical contribution of each of these thinkers is at once a creative extension of the horizons of understanding and a critical evaluation of earlier thought. For these various reasons I have usually chosen not to introduce my own critical evaluations. The overall evaluation of particular contributions and emphases is best 'placed' in the wider 'mosaic' of the *philosophia perennis* presented in courses of epistemology, psychology and philosophy in general. The different history courses or units are then seen as having a particular and important place within the wider framework of the study of philosophy.

A history of philosophy, however, is something more than a chronology of past thought. A pure chronology would present past assertions and events without any principle of selection or evaluative judgement. Such a chronology would present little more than a diary of un-co-ordinated and unevaluated assertions and opinions. A conscientious historian, on the other hand, while always striving for objective presentation of past thoughts and events, selects for special consideration and arranges in intelligible sequence, those events and thoughts which have had special significance in the advance of human history and thought.

Different historians of philosophy make use of different schools of thought to guide their intelligent choices and arrangement of facts. Thus, for example, a historian who is a convinced rationalist, or idealist, or positivist, or empiricist, will write a history in which his emphases on the important movements of history will reveal his principle of selection. These differences of viewpoint may be divided fundamentally into three. It is recognized, almost universally, that there are two basic aspects of human knowledge, or thought: the aspect of receptivity or experience, and the aspect of spontaneity, the creative, *a priori* element. All forms of empiricism emphasize the first aspect. Idealism and rationalism emphasize the second aspect. Realism, or the philosophy of being, tries to reconcile the two elements. Some historians, in this light, place special emphasis on those philosophical movements of the past which made a significant contribution to the understanding of the empirical aspect of human knowledge. Others emphasize the importance of those historical thinkers who understood the special significance of the spontaneity and *creativity* of human thought. I am convinced that these two partial viewpoints need to be reconciled in the higher viewpoint of the philosophy of being. The implications of this 'realist' viewpoint are explicated at length in Aristotle's philosophy of being and *energeia* (see pp. 50-52 of the text below), in Aquinas's philosophy of *esse* (pp. 126-128) and in the final chapter on the philosophy of being. It is this 'realist' viewpoint which provides the principle of selection for the choices, the emphases, and the general arrangement of the present text.

A general history of philosophy necessarily relies for much of its material on the research and scholarship of previous historians who have specialized in particular areas of study. A general historian who did not make ample use of the insights of these scholars would leave himself open to serious criticism indeed. He does not necessarily accept their opinions with uncritical dependence, nor does he ignore their findings. He approaches their work as welcome sources of enlightenment and as constant challenges to further thought. In this spirit I willingly acknowledge my indebtedness to the useful work done by A. E. Taylor, W. D. Ross, J. Burnet, A. P. Armstrong, E. Gilson, F. Van Steenberghen and other authors mentioned in the Bibliography. I am indebted also to the editors and authors of the valuable *Encyclopedia of Philosophy* (Macmillan Inc.), and to Fr Frederick Copleston for his widely respected and critically acclaimed *History of Philosophy* (Search Press, London/Paulist Press, New York). It was this latter work, more than any other, which inspired the author to write a new, independent, and concise textbook to assist readers similar to those to whom Fr Copleston's monumental work is addressed. The student will find in the Bibliography below constant reference to a more extensive treatment of parallel and similar themes in the different volumes of Copleston's *magnum opus*.

Finally, it is perhaps necessary to explain that the words 'man' and 'men' will usually refer to human beings in general, without regard to sex.

The author wishes to express grateful acknowledgement also to the students whose queries called attention to passages which required further elucidations, and to Peter Oke, Kevin Ori, Michael Elue and other students for their help with typing. All those have given me constant encouragement by their quiet and implicit reassurance that we have been working together daily on a project which serves a worthwhile cause. Lastly, I would like to thank John

Stockdale, then Cassell's International Editor, for the patient prompting which persuaded me to undertake this work, and Fiona McKenzie, whose careful editing has made its publication possible.

October 1984   M. Walsh, SMA
                                 St Paul's College and Seminary
                                 Gbarnga
                                 Monrovia, Liberia

Abbreviations

b.   born
Bl. Blessed
c.   circa, about (e.g. *c.* 150 B.C.)
d.   died
fl. *floruit*, flourished (e.g. *fl.* 150 B.C.)
St   Saint

PART ONE

ANCIENT GREEK AND ROMAN
PHILOSOPHY

1 The pre-Socratic philosophers

1. The rise of the Cretan-Grecian civilization   2. The
Milesian cosmologists: Thales, Anaximander,
Anaximenes   3. The Pythagorean school
4. Heraclitus   5. The Eleatic school: Xenophanes,
Parmenides, Zeno, and Empedocles of Acragas
6. Anaxagoras   7. The atomists: Leucippus and
Democritus   8. The cosmologists in general: a critique

Out in the wine-dark sea there lies a land called Crete, a rich
and fair land, begirt with waves on every side. Therein are
many people innumerable and nine cities. Their several tongues
are mixed, one blending in with another. Here there are
Achaeans and proud native Cretans; here there are Cydonians,
three clans of Dorians and noble Pelasgians. One of their cities
is the mighty city of Cnossus. Here King Minos, nine years,
ruled and enjoyed the friendship of almighty Zeus.

(Homer, *Odyssey*, Book XIX)

1. The rise of the Cretan-Grecian civilization. Western
philosophy came to birth twenty-five centuries ago in the flourishing
Greek commercial cities of the eastern half of the Mediterranean Sea.
In these centres of prosperous trade and international dialogue,
Thales, Anaximander, the Pythagoreans and other philosopher-
scientists began to speculate rationally and freely about the nature of
our universe. They attempted to give a reasoned explanation, instead
of the existing religio-mythological explanations, of the origin, the
basic 'construction material' and the fundamental structures of our
physical world.

The Ionian civilization which provided the home or cradle in which
this original form of speculation was born had its roots in the highly
artistic maritime civilization which had existed among the Minoans in
Crete, the 'rich and fair land... out in the wine-dark sea', a thousand
years earlier.

The Minoan civilization flourished from *c.* 3000 B.C. until the

1

devastating eruption of the volcanic island of Thera (or Santorin) which destroyed many of the Minoan cities and their fleets *c*.1450 B.C. The most powerful of these cities was 'the mighty city of Cnossus... where King Minos ruled'.

Knossos (Cnossus) was the metropolitan seat of a widespread commercial empire in the islands to the west and east of Greece and in the many cities and coastal settlements of North Africa, Asia Minor, Cyprus, Greece, southern Italy and Sicily. This metropolis had a mixed population of perhaps 80,000 people, 'their several tongues... blending in with one another'. They were seamen, farmers, fishermen, smiths, potters, craftsmen, artists and traders. They utilized imported copper ingots from Cyprus, tin from Asia Minor, diorite from Egypt, elephant tusks from Syria and many other staple commodities.

At the Herakleion Museum in Crete today one can see specimens of Minoan carved jewels, frescoes, delicately thin pottery, paintings and carvings, as well as the many products of their cottage industries. At Knossos, Mallia, Zakros, Phaistos and Akrotiri the excavated ruins of Minoan palaces show evidence of multistoreyed complexes of spacious halls, numerous rooms, terracotta plumbing and highly advanced drainage systems. Minoan town-house architecture shows that these people had made major advances in architecture, art and sophisticated urban living.

About 1450 B.C. the volcano of Thera, seventy miles north of Crete, erupted and collapsed into the sea. Volcanic ash and tidal waves damaged the great fleets and farmlands and cities of the Minoans. Soon afterwards the warlike Mycenaeans of mainland Greece invaded Crete.

The Mycenaeans, the 'Sea-Kings of the Aegean', immortalized by Homer as the Achaeans, assumed power in the eastern Mediterranean after the decline of the Minoans. Mycenaean trading posts were spread far and wide during the three centuries which followed, in particular to the coast and offshore islands of western Asia Minor. The Mycenaeans drew heavily upon the Cretans' skills in forging their own civilization. Their language was a dialect of Hellenic (Greek; cf. M. G. F. Ventris, 'Evidence for Greek Dialect in the Mycenaean Archives', *Journal of Hellenic Studies* [1953]), but their whole culture was deeply influenced by the Minoan culture.

Mycenaean power was weakened by warfare. The Mycenaeans, a Bronze Age people, succumbed to the Dorians when these Greek-speaking conquerors invaded Greece with iron swords about the eleventh century B.C. Refugees from mainland Greece reinforced the settlements in Asia Minor; the most important group, the Ionians, gave their name to the area known as Ionia (as they did to the Ionian Sea between Greece and Italy).

At this time supremacy at sea passed to the Phoenicians, who are ranked as the greatest seamen of the ancient world. They called themselves Canaanites; Homer called them Sidonians (Cydonians). Their ships traversed not only the Mediterranean, but also the Red Sea and the eastern shores of the Atlantic. They had learnt the art of writing from the Egyptians and the Babylonians, but they themselves invented the idea of a phonetic alphabet. From the Phoenicians the Greeks learnt the alphabet and the practical science of navigation.

In the wealthy maritime cities in Ionia and in southern Italy and Sicily the Grecian culture revived and flourished. In Ionia the Greeks adopted coinage from the Lydians, just as previously they had adopted practical rules of arithmetic, geometry and navigation from the Egyptians, the Babylonians and the Phoenicians. It was in these same maritime cities that the Greeks themselves now made contributions of a qualitatively new kind to civilization. It was here that the foundations of the deductive, theoretical sciences of mathematics, physics, history and philosophy were laid and probed. It is in this sense that these cities are the birthplace of the deductive sciences and the cradle of Western thought.

It was in a commercially prosperous urban civilization of this kind that Thales, Anaximander and other early Greek philosopher-scientists abandoned the explanations and teachings of the mythology and poetry and traditional religions which had been handed down from an earlier pastoral and agricultural civilization. They sought to attain instead a rational, urbane and 'scientific' explanation of the visible world around them. Their 'wondering' and probing, and their tentative answers, transformed the whole of the pre-existing world of theologico-mythological thought and exercised a profound influence on the direction which all future 'scientific' thought would take.

2. The Milesian cosmologists: Thales, Anaximander, Anaximenes. Miletus, like Ephesus and Clazomenae, was one of the twelve important Greek settlements across the Aegean Sea in Ionia. It was situated on the south bank of the river Maeander (Menderes), near the sea, and was an important trading centre with links with Chaldea and Egypt. Thales, Anaximander and Anaximenes were citizens of Miletus who lived in the sixth century B.C. They were especially interested in Nature, the cosmos, and for this reason they are often called the Milesian cosmologists. They are also called philosopher-scientists because they raised cosmological problems in an age when philosophy and the mathematico-physical sciences were not yet separated as distinct branches of knowledge.

These pre-scientific philosopher-scientists were struck by the fact that Nature is an organized physical system governed by law. Nature, the cosmos, is the thing, the being, that it is. It is forever rearranging and changing and renewing itself in a patterned way. What precisely is it that is renewing itself, yet still continuing to be what it was and what it is? What is it made of? The seasons, vegetation, and things in general, come and go and come back again renewed. The universe continues to be the being that it is, despite change, or becoming. What then is its basic being made of? What is the original material of the universe? What kind of thing is it, in the universe of existing beings, that is constantly renewing itself? What or which reality is the fundamental, real 'ultimate reality' which is continually coming to be and yet continuing to be basically what it always is?

Thales of Miletus (*c.* 640-550 B.C.) suggested that the fundamental reality or being which is forever changing yet still renewing and being itself is the reality present in what we call water. Unfortunately, we know little else about Thales' thought. However, we may perhaps assume that Thales, as a child of his own time, viewed the surrounding universe as so many of his contemporaries did. The earth, like the islands, is surrounded by water. The waters above the dome of the heavens break through in torrential downpours. The waters beneath the foundation of the earth support the earth and gush upwards in springs and fountains and river sources. Water evaporates. It becomes air. Alternatively it can become solid, as ice. In the process of evaporation it leaves something of itself behind in sediments and solids. The liquidity of water allows it to appear in many different shapes and guises. The seeds of all things have a moist nature. Life is everywhere. 'Everything is full of gods.' It is perhaps the matter within these divine living waters, then, that is the primeval 'stuff' or construction material which is forever changing itself and recycling and renewing itself in Nature.

Thales holds an important place in the history of philosophy because of the philosophical question he raised rather than because of the answer which he proposed. In effect, what he had said was: Things come and go, yet, nevertheless, everything is one. This problem would be rephrased later in terms of the problem of being and becoming. He was famous in his own time for having foretold the total eclipse of the sun which took place on 28 May 585 B.C. He showed also how one can calculate the height of a pyramid from the length of its shadow, and how one can estimate the distance of a ship at sea from various measurements taken at two points on land.

Anaximander (*c.* 611-546 B.C.) was an 'associate' of Thales. He held that the primal substance from which all things come is *to apeiron*, the 'unbounded', the 'untraversable', the 'indeterminate'. It is ageless, everlasting, imperishable reality. Indeterminate Reality is not particularly this nor particularly that. It is not any definite substance such as earth, air, fire or water. It is the amorphous compound of all contrary elements. It is neutral in the cosmic strife which exists between the elements (i.e. earth, air, fire, and water). All things originate from it and return to it. Within *to apeiron* there are innumerable other worlds besides the world known to us. Our own world came forth from the *apeiron* as a whirling vortex in consequence of the 'eternal motion'. Within this vortex, flame (hot and dry) separated away from, and encircled, the cold, misty air (cold and wet) at the core. In time the mist separated into air and watery mud. In a later stage of evolution, the solids separated from the water and became dry earth under the rays of the outer circle of heat. Thus our world has the earth at its centre, with water partly surrounding the earth, and air surrounding both. The three are enclosed within the outer shield of heat. Distant heavenly bodies are themselves rings of heat enclosed in cylinders of mist.

Anaximander, like Thales, blends together philosophic speculation and scientific hypotheses. He seems to have regarded existing bodies as recent formations of much older, primeval matter (ancient cosmic dust) which was originally amorphous, formless, indeterminate matter. His doctrine of *to apeiron* or indeterminate reality may be regarded as an early philosophic probing into the 'going on in being' and the 'coming into being' which are evident in the reality or the being of the universe. These early philosophers raised philosophical problems which Aristotle tried to solve, 200 years later, in his investigation into the reality of being and becoming, and in his doctrine of actual being and potential being.

Anaximenes (*c.* 588-524 B.C.) suggested that the fundamental, boundless, self-changing substance is air. His chief concern, however, was not to answer the question concerning what the world is made of, but rather to give an explanation of how the world came to be what it now is. All things are formed from air through the processes of condensation and rarefaction (it may be noted that contemporary astronomers speak of our universe as originating in hot gases). The earth itself was formed through the condensation, or 'felting' (matting together) of air. Air is the principle of life. Life is warm breath. 'Just as our soul, which is air, integrates us, so breath and air surround the whole cosmos.' Our soul is air; it holds us together. Breath and air surround the whole universe and hold it together. Air (or gas) can take any form by condensation or expansion.

The emphasis in this theory is on quantity. All qualities can be explained in terms of condensation and rarefaction, that is, in terms of quantity. This theory had an important influence on a number of subsequent thinkers, including several members of the Pythagorean school. Anaximenes' theory on how the world came to be as it is can be called a (pre-scientific) scientific theory or hypothesis in the wide sense, namely, that it is an imaginative model, a 'bold conjecture' (cf. Sir Karl Popper) which attempts to correlate a large number of single observations.

The Milesian cosmologists are important not because of their achievements or solutions but because of the major problems their speculations raised concerning the kind of being that this world of ours continues to be even in the midst of the flow of its becoming continually different.

3. The Pythagorean school. *Pythagoras* (c. 580-497 B.C.) came from the Ionian city of Samos, about twenty miles north-west of Miletus. The island of Samos fell under the despotic rule of Polycrates, and Pythagoras emigrated to Croton (Crotone), a Dorian Greek colony in Italy on the shores of the Ionian Sea. Here, near the settlement of the colonists, he founded his own ascetic, religious community or brotherhood. The aims of the Pythagorean community were religious, philosophical and partly political. The central interest which held them together as a brotherhood was their felt need of personal salvation. Pythagoras and his immediate followers left no writings as far as we know. However, the teachings and the influence of this early Pythagorean brotherhood lived on for 700 years in the disciples of this school. These teachings combined a spirit of religious renewal and purification with an intellectual, scientific spirit interested in the pursuit of truth.

The Pythagoreans adopted the religious teachings of the Orphics. Orphism taught the doctrine of transmigration of souls. The soul is divine but imprisoned in the body. The soul can be purified and refined. It can be prepared for nobler reincarnation and for eventual liberation from the cycle of reincarnation, the wheel of birth. One of the greatest forms of purification and liberation of spirit is found in the mental delight of mathematics, philosophy and disinterested science. Here we approach a world of knowledge which is uplifting, ideal, and more certain and exact than the everyday world of disordered distractions. The emphasis is on form rather than on matter.

The philosophy of the Pythagorean school was predominantly a mathematico-metaphysical philosophy. They were impressed by the harmonious proportions of things and by the order and regulation of movement in the universe. They discovered that musical sounds (e.g. on the lyre) can be reduced to and expressed by numbers. They were interested in astronomy and measurement and geometrical figures. They wondered if perhaps all things are intrinsically measured and numbered. The limited beings in our limited cosmos are surrounded by the unlimited or boundless cosmos, *to apeiron*. Within our cosmos, the unlimited, from which all things come to be, is limited, numbered. 'All things are numbers.' All things are made of numbered points, lines and surfaces. These numbers give the measure of the very being of each thing. Numbers (as principles of limitation) can account for the wide range of different natures of different things. The order and harmony of the universe is explainable in terms of number. Numbers constitute the essences of things. Number is the key to Nature (Descartes and Galileo, in the seventeenth century A.D., spoke of the mathematical structure of Nature considered as a system of bodies in motion).

The doctrine that 'all things are numbers' is one which is difficult, at first acquaintance, to understand or accept. We may well wonder what precisely was the insight which the Pythagorean philosophers found to be so mentally exciting and which they struggled to express and communicate.

They relished the joy they experienced in mathematical discoveries (e.g. the Pythagorean proposition, Euclid I. 47). This was an achievement of the second level, that is, the mathematical or quantitative level, of abstraction. They probed further, on this same level, for a solution to the problem of how the unlimited, *to apeiron*, from which all things come, can be in some way limited differently in the limited things of our cosmos. The problem which baffled them is that of the 'limit' placed on the 'unlimited' (in limited beings). Subsequent philosophers saw this problem as one which could be answered only on a higher level of abstraction than that of number. Meanwhile, however, the Pythagoreans had raised an intriguing question in philosophy's ongoing 'pursuit of wisdom'.

4. Heraclitus (*fl.* 504 B.C.) was an aristocratic nobleman in the city of Ephesus, some thirty miles north of Miletus. He became famous in antiquity because of his 'message' expressed in pithy, obscure and oracular statements. One such statement attributed to him is the famous 'all things pass, everything flows on and nothing remains' (*panta rhei kai ouden menei*). Aristotle tells us Heraclitus taught that 'nothing steadfastly is'. Plato says he taught that 'nothing ever is; everything is becoming'. Everything is in a state of flux.

'The sun is new every day.' You can never step twice into the same river waters. All is becoming. Matter is forever moving, changing and developing. Dynamic activity, energy, strife and opposition are the very life of the world.

Over a hundred fragments from Heraclitus' writings are extant today. These show a profound interest in *genesis* or coming into being, and *phthora* or passing away. The cosmos, or ordered universe, '... ever was and is and shall be ever-living fire' (compare the parallel but totally independent line of thought concerning the 'flame of fire' in Exodus 3:2). The hearer can understand this urgent message (*logos*) only if he allows himself to be inspired through a contemplative inspiration or inbreathing of the divine word (*Logos*) of knowledge from a divine source. All things come into being through the Logos. Those who have 'inhaled' the Logos agree that all things are one. There is a purpose that governs all things. One can understand what this purpose is only through awareness, wakefulness, humble contemplation, and 'dryness'.

Heraclitus tells us that his fundamental word, or inspired message (*logos*) is that 'all things are one'. There is unity in diversity, identity in difference. The cosmos is 'an ever-living fire', a perpetual dynamic activity, 'kindled in measure and quenched in measure'. All things come into being and pass away through strife. There is a constant mingling of opposites. 'That which is at variance agrees with itself. It is an attunement of opposite tensions.' '... God is day and night, winter and summer, war and peace, surfeit and hunger.' The One exists only in the tension of the opposites. The tension is essential to the unity and to the being of the One. Within Reality all tensions are reconciled and harmonized. The One is the immanent ordering principle of all things. Man's reason is but a moment in Universal Reason, the Logos.

Heraclitus was acutely aware of the dynamic activity (the tension, strife and expenditure of energy, the *genesis* and *phthora*) evident in the world around us. But he asserts that it is only an awakened mind, docile to the power of the Logos, which can discern that all things in flux are at root One. The diverse beings of our universe are all in being; they are in Being. And being, like fire, is ever active. All things are One, and all things are becoming. Later philosophers would express this in terms of the state of 'being-in-becoming'.

Heraclitus accepted the fact that there is a plurality of interdependent beings in the universe and that the whole of reality is both one and many. Reality changes. It becomes *other*; but it does not change into *another*. Reality always is what it is: reality. There is, then, unity in the diversity just as there is diversity in the unity. (One might paraphrase this by saying that there are beings in being just as there is being in beings.) This is the word or 'message' (*logos*) of Heraclitus.

5. The Eleatic school: Xenophanes, Parmenides, Zeno, and Empedocles of Acragas. *Xenophanes* (*fl.* 540 B.C.) was the patron of the Eleatic school in Elea (modern Velia) in southern Italy. He denounced and rejected the Homeric anthropomorphic deities. He conjectured that there is one god who is the greatest among gods and men. This one god is not like mortals either in form (body) or mind; he does not move but he moves all things by the thought of his mind. But Xenophanes asserts that all of this is conjecture because there is no man who really knows about the gods or about reality. Mortals know only the appearances of things. We know little more than this about Xenophanes' thought; only a few fragments from one of his poems have survived. Aristotle maintained that Xenophanes was the originator of the attempt to reduce the whole world to a One who was god. It is likely, then, that this One of Xenophanes is a monistic One rather than a theistic One.

Parmenides (*c.* 515-448 B.C.) was a native of Elea. Plato in the *Sophist* speaks of him as the 'great Parmenides' from whom the young Socrates learnt much when he interviewed him. Parmenides in turn had been influenced by the teachings of the Pythagoreans. He presented his own doctrine in a poem *On Nature* (*Peri physeōs*). He says that Nature (or all that is) is uncreated and imperishable. Being is abiding being. It did not come to be out of that which is not, nor will it pass away into that which is not. Being never varies from being the same reality it always is. Non-being (or the Void) is not. Nature or Being *is* and always is. One cannot say of *is* that it was or will be; *is* (being) always is. It is immovable. It does not change. It cannot be added to. Where could any addition come from? Non-being is not. The *is* (being) is always completely what it is. It is the one that it is, and it is all at once. It cannot be-come. There is no coming-into-being. (There is no coming-into-is.) And it is one. It is not plural.

Plurality of being is, then, an illusion, just as be-coming too is an illusion. Being is, and it is One, and it is evenly distributed. 'It cannot be more here, less there.' But being is not unlimited. It is bounded and limited on every side. What is is spherical, continuous and evenly distributed. There is nothing beyond these bounds. There is no such thing as absolutely empty space beyond the bounds of what is. And within these bounds, differentiation of the real can never occur.

Parmenides evidently conceives 'what is' in spatial terms. He speaks of Nature as being held in bonds or fetters by Justice (or Fate or Necessity). Being is limited being, held firmly by Justice 'within the bonds of limits that keep it back on every side' (the governing power of 'Justice' is taken for granted and not analysed further). His conception of being is that it is material and motionless. His doctrine, then, is a doctrine of Materialistic Monism. It discards the illusory way of sense-appearances in its quest to know the real world of abiding being.

Plato found much that he liked in the doctrines of the 'great Parmenides'. He identified Parmenides' world of abiding Reality with the world of the eternal forms, the world of Truth, Beauty and Goodness. In this way he transformed a doctrine of materialistic monism into that of Platonic idealism.

Parmenides' probings into the philosophy of being raised issues which stimulated the thought of Plato and Aristotle. His teachings were propounded and supported by Melissus, Zeno and other students of the Eleatic school.

Zeno of Elea (*fl.* 464 B.C.) presented a series of *reductio ad absurdum* arguments to support Parmenides' doctrines on the impossibility of motion and plurality, and to refute the Pythagorean doctrine of plural units and number.

Being is motionless. Motion is illusory. If anyone wished to traverse a racecourse he would have to traverse an infinite number of points in a finite time; and this is impossible. If Achilles were to give a head-start to a tortoise in a race, then, while Achilles was moving forward towards the tortoise's position A, the tortoise would have moved on further to position B; and while Achilles moved forward towards the tortoise's position B, the tortoise meanwhile would have advanced on to position C, and so on *ad infinitum*. Thus, sense experience of motion and of plurality is illusory. Reality is a continuum, a plenum. In brief, thought shows that Being is One, motionless, and material.

The Pythagoreans had emphasized number, plurality; the Eleatics emphasized the oneness of being. Heraclitus was understood to have stressed change, becoming (*panta rhei*); the Eleatics stressed abiding being. Two questions therefore arose: (1) Is being one or is it many? and (2) Is being abiding or is it changing? These became known as the problem of the one and many, and the problem of being and becoming. Both Plato and Aristotle gave their attention to these problems.

Empedocles (*c.* 484-424 B.C.) was a native of Acragas in Sicily (modern Agrigento; Sicily and southern Italy were regarded in those days as part of 'Greater Greece'). Like Parmenides, Empedocles wrote a poem *On Nature*. He held that there are four eternal and different kinds of 'realities': earth, air, fire and water. These are ultimate, unchangeable, indestructible, and irreducible to each other. At the beginning of any circular periodic world-cycle these four 'elements' are completely separate, held apart by Hate (or forces of repulsion). As the cycle advances, Love (or forces of attraction) enters in, and different particles intermingle together in different proportions and combinations. The different objects of our concrete world come to be and then pass away through these minglings and separations in an unending cyclic process. In the part of the cycle which produced man there were different stages. Separate parts of plants and animals appeared first. Later these parts began to intermingle in multiple different chance formations. Some of these formations assumed viable forms which persisted through reproduction. This hypothesis obviously anticipates aspects of later scientific hypotheses.

6. **Anaxagoras** (*c.* 500-428 B.C.) came from Clazomenae in Ionia. He was invited by Pericles to settle in Athens around the time of the second Persian War in 480-479 B.C. At that time Athens became the predominant partner in an alliance of the Greek city-states against Persia. Under the leadership of Pericles, Athens flourished. It became the outstanding centre of architecture, sculpture, drama, history, literature and philosophy in the Hellenic world. Anaxagoras introduced philosophy to Athens. Thirty years later, however, he was prosecuted by Athenian politicians for impiety towards the traditional gods: he was accused of describing the moon as a material body shining by reflected light, and the sun as a red-hot material body bigger than the whole of the Peloponnese (southern Greece). He returned to Ionia and founded a school there.

Anaxagoras taught that there are many ultimate units or wholes. He may have had in mind minerals such as gold, silver, iron and tin, and organic materials such as wood, ivory, cotton, and so forth.

These wholes or units, when cut into parts, become merely smaller units qualitatively the same as the original units. In any concrete object of our experience there is an intermingling together of many qualitatively different particles or units but with one particular kind of particle (e.g. silver in a silver bracelet) predominating. 'There is a mixture of all things in everything.' New products are merely new mixtures or combinations of the pre-existing ultimate units. Changes in the world can be explained in terms of the intermingling and separating of these indestructible materials or particles.

In *Phaedrus*, Plato tells us that Anaxagoras was 'a scientific man... who attained to a knowledge of the true nature of intellect and folly'. Anaxagoras said that there is present in the universe an entity called *Nous* or Mind and that it is omniscient. It was Mind (and not blind necessity) which initiated the formation of the cosmos by setting the mixtures in motion. Mind controls the formation of all living things. It controls the rotary motion which separates materials partially from each other; there still remains a portion of everything in everything.

The emphasis in Anaxagoras is not on blind Necessity but on Mind. Reason of some kind underlies the movements of the cosmos. He says that Nous is 'infinite' and that it is 'self-ruled'. It is 'the finest and the purest of all things'. It has 'all knowledge about everything'. It is present in all living things and is the same in all. Socrates regarded this as an exciting new emphasis in philosophy but he was also deeply disappointed that Anaxagoras applied his doctrine of Mind only to 'air, and aethers, and other strange things'. Anaxagoras failed to make further meaningful use of the principle.

7. The atomists: Leucippus and Democritus. *Leucippus* of Miletus (*c.* 440 B.C.) was a member of the school of Parmenides and a disciple of Zeno, according to Theophrastus and Diogenes. *Democritus* (*c.* 460-371 B.C.) was a native of the Ionian colony of Abdera, a seaport in Thrace on the northern shores of the Aegean Sea. Their thought and writings are now mingled inseparably in the philosophic-scientific thought of the Atomist school. They held that all things are made of atoms. The *atoma* are 'uncut', and 'uncuttable' or physically indivisible. They were not created, and they are indestructible. Each physical object is an aggregation of several different atoms, invisibly minute.

The cosmos originated in a chaotic whirl or random movement of atoms, akin to the movement of motes in a sunbeam. In this random whirl, 'like sought like', collisions and interlockings occurred, and vortices or whirling spirals of atoms were formed. These vortices generated bodies and worlds. The further development of physical objects is explained in a way similar to the explanation which had been given earlier by Anaxagoras. The theory of the atomists however eschews any teleological explanations or explanations by final causes; it is a determinist and mechanistic explanation. Democritus argued against and rejected the *nous* of Anaxagoras. He was a committed materialist and determinist.

According to Democritus, perception, both sense-perception and intellectual perception, is an entirely physical process. Each type of perception depends totally on the thing perceived. There are certain objective qualities such as hardness, density and weight which are objectively present in the object. There are other sense-qualities such as taste, colour and warmth which are sense-reactions in the sense-organs. Perception of every kind is to be explained ultimately in terms of contact between atoms.

In the different doctrines of the pre-Socratic philosopher-scientists or 'cosmologists' (Gaston Milhaud [see below, Chapter 28, section 7] termed them 'philosopher-geometers', *philosophes géomètres*) we find a certain tendency to present 'scientific' hypotheses of various kinds as possible solutions to problems which are frequently philosophical problems about the constitutive principles of being and becoming. Some of the solutions proposed may be classified as 'sensual' or sensory solutions. Others are semi-mathematico-sensory solutions. Leucippus and Democritus brought solutions of this nature to their logical conclusions.

They proposed a materialistic mechanistic solution to the philosophic problem concerning the nature of being as presented by the different, if not conflicting, insights of Heraclitus and Parmenides. Heraclitus had emphasized the dynamic, ever-diverse oneness of being; Parmenides had emphasized unchanging abiding being. Leucippus and Democritus presented a deterministic account of the changes occurring in our abiding universe in terms of a random mechanical intermingling, interlocking and separating of different kinds and sizes of abiding material atoms. This solution is the logical outcome of the various pre-Socratic attempts to solve what later Aristotelians would call 'metaphysical' problems in terms of (non-metaphysical) 'physical' theories. Later Greek thinkers, such as Plato and Aristotle, would attempt to give more strictly 'philosophical' answers to these mainly philosophical problems.

8. The cosmologists in general: a critique. Aristotle spoke of the pre-Socratic philosophers as 'physicists' who concerned themselves primarily with the 'material cause' of the universe. He assessed the importance of their contribution to cosmology in reference to his own theory of causes (viz. material, formal, efficient and final causes). If this view is interpreted as implying that the pre-Socratic philosophers were not genuine philosophers but were merely forerunners of the physical science of cosmology, then this assessment does not do justice to the contribution which these thinkers made to philosophy. Aristotle saw them as 'physicists' (Greek *physis*, nature) in the sense that they concentrated on Nature viewed as an organized cosmos. Their emphasis is certainly on Nature rather than on man or morals or the many other problems of philosophy. Aristotle (*Metaphysics* 983b18) spoke of Thales as the initiator or original architect (*archēgos*) of philosophy. And in this context, Aristotle saw his own system as the culmination and crown of all the philosophical speculation which had gone on before his own time.

The pre-Socratics were interested in knowing about the 'material cause' of the universe. But more simply and more basically still they were interested in understanding what is, namely, Reality. They saw that the universe is a cosmos; it is an ordered universe. Outside the bounds of all that is there can only be the 'void'. Our universe, Reality, is here; the void is 'out there'. In the light of any comparison with non-being or the void, being or reality is very distinctly what it is. The problem then arose as to what it is. It changes. It becomes. Yet still it abides as what it is. What then is it? What is this reality of being that continues to abide as it is in spite of obvious change?

In the works which we know today as the *Metaphysics*, Aristotle presents his own system of philosophy as one which gives a satisfactory, final answer to the questions and probings of the pre-Socratics. The answer of the *Metaphysics* is a 'metaphysical' answer. We do an injustice to the original questioners if we fail to see that their questions, like the answer, were basically 'metaphysical' questions demanding a 'metaphysical' answer.

The questions and problems of the pre-Socratics centred on (1) an understanding of Reality (vis-à-vis non-being, the Void), or the oneness of Reality or Being despite the plurality of different beings; and (2) on an understanding of change, becoming, or coming-into-being and passing away. These problems can be called cosmological problems, but more radically they are ontological or metaphysical problems. In raising questions about philosophical cosmology, they were also raising questions which were ontological questions.

These pre-scientific philosopher-scientists attempted to give answers to the problems raised by their own partial insights into the nature of being and becoming. Their attempted answers seldom rose above the first level of abstraction (e.g. physics) or the second level of abstraction (e.g. mathematics). (Even here one must make an exception for certain aspects of thought of Heraclitus and Parmenides, and perhaps that of Anaximander and Anaxagoras.) But the fact that many of their answers were sensual or physical answers does not take away from the fact that their questions are questions which are ontological. Their 'wonder' and probing is a quest for a deeper understanding of their own metaphysical insights into the nature of being and becoming.

Students who wish to read further about early Greek philosophy will find the books given in the Bibliography (for Chapter 1) informative and helpful. See below, p.573.

2 The Sophist and Socratic period

1. The Sophist movement   2. Some prominent
Sophists   3. Socrates

1. The Sophist movement. In the fifth century B.C., the city-states of Greece formed an alliance to drive back the Persian armies and fleets from the mainland of Greece and from Ionia and the Aegean islands; they defeated the Persian king Darius at Marathon (490), and again defeated the Persian king Xerxes with the Greek fleet (480) and on land at Plataea (479). In the alliance some city-states chose to contribute the cost of a specified number of ships rather than to present the ships themselves. This is one reason among others why Athens acquired naval supremacy over the other city-states, and became a rich and prosperous metropolis.

Pericles (494-429 B.C.), the Athenian leader, made Athens the centre of the intellectual life of the Greek world. The economic prosperity and the intellectual life of Athens attracted to the metropolis the lecturers, educators, travelling teachers, polymaths, dilettanti and encyclopaedists who taught by profession or for payment in the different city-states. These 'professors' were called 'Sophists'. Their profession brought them honour as well as financial reward. They did not represent a school of thought. They represented, rather, a movement or a trend in the intellectual life of the times. In an age which was noted for democratic institutions in many city-states and for political ambition, the Sophists instructed the Athenian youth in politics, economics, speech-making, ethics, poetry, philosophy, law, grammar, rhetoric and eristic. They taught the various methods for ensuring success in law courts.

The term *sophistēs* was applied to earlier thinkers such as Solon, Pythagoras and the Seven Wise Men, who were held in high esteem. But many of the later 'Sophists', who looked on science merely as a means to power and as a practical source of gain for themselves and for their students, brought the words 'sophism' and 'sophistry' into disrepute. It was said of them that they believed in higher education and knowledge but not in truth. What they taught was the art of success.

The Sophists mistrusted the conflicting hypotheses and cosmologies of the earlier Greek philosophers. They noted their contradictions and they abandoned the attempt to understand the

16

nature of the universe. Their own interest was subjective. Their emphasis was on man and on the relatively different ways of human living. Their criticisms were often negative and destructive; and their teachings showed a tendency towards scepticism and relativism in reference to the human quest for truth.

The more outstanding teachers among the Sophists offered to their students a broadening 'higher' education. Hippias of Elis and others taught a doctrine of 'natural law' common to the laws of all countries and constituting the basic foundation of all laws. They were passionately interested in 'progressive' ideas and in moral standards. This often led to conflict with the more tradition-conscious people of their day.

2. Some prominent Sophists. *Protagoras* of Abdera (*c.* 480-410 B.C.) was invited to Athens by Pericles. Protagoras was the author of the well-known dictum: 'Man is the measure of all things, of those things that are that they are, of those things that are not that they are not'. It is possible for different interpreters to interpret this dictum in different ways, since the word 'man' can mean (1) 'each individual man', or (2) 'man as a species'. (1) In the first sense it could be interpreted as meaning that each man's experience is the criterion of what is true for himself. This would imply that there is no objective truth, and that all opinions are equally worthy (and perhaps equally unworthy) of consideration and respect. Protagoras affirmed: 'About any one thing two contradictory statements may be made', and again 'truth is what appears to each one'. The deceitfulness of the senses provides a basis for a doctrine of theoretical scepticism. (2) The dictum can be interpreted, however, in a different sense, namely, that man (as a species) is the yardstick or criterion for the evaluation of the merit or demerit of everything in the scale of beings. The emphasis is then on human nature as the criterion of value.

Protagoras taught that when one state follows one practice and another state follows a different practice, then it is the function of the wise man, the Sophist, to substitute 'better' practices for unwise practices. The individual may be uncertain about the existence of the gods and about the wisdom of certain laws and practices, but, socially, as a citizen he should abide by the social conventions and traditions and codes of behaviour for as long as these are still operative in the community. The 'wise' will help to ameliorate and transform many of these traditions, but only gradually and at the correct pace. Protagoras taught his students to try to see the merits and demerits of different debatable viewpoints, and to practise the art of defending first one of the viewpoints, and then later the opposite viewpoint. Some of his followers specialized in eristic, an art which aims at victory in disputation rather than at the discovery of the truth.

Prodicus of Ceos specialized in linguistic studies and in the use of persuasive rhetorical language. Plato implies (in *Theaetetus*) that Socrates sometimes recommended his less philosophically inclined students to go to Prodicus in order to learn a different art from him. Prodicus fell out of favour with the Athenian elders because of his doctrine that prayer is inefficacious and superfluous. He taught that primitive man elevated into gods those beneficent forces of nature which were the sources of food and fertility. Then, subsequently, men elevated and worshipped as gods the human inventors of the different arts and crafts (e.g. the 'god' of iron, the 'god' of wine, and so forth).

Hippias of Elis emphasized the idea of unwritten laws (*agraphoi nomoi*). Particular laws which varied from city-state to city-state seem to be excepted from the number of basic unwritten laws. The laws of all nations recognize certain basic (natural) human rights. He held that some laws in Greek city-states were violating these natural rights by trying to force men into doing things contrary to the unwritten (natural) law. Laws of this particular kind are merely tyrannical laws in so far as they go against basic rights.

Antiphon of Athens denounced all forms of distinctions which brought inequality of any kind among human beings. All men are born as men, and as equals. All men are equal. *Alcidamas* condemned slavery. God made all men free; Nature made no man a slave.

Thrasymachus of Chalcedon is reported to have held that, in practice, all real rights are the rights of the stronger! Might is right! Thus, the Athenian invaders (as reported by the historian Thucydides) said to all the men of Melos before they murdered them: 'If you were as strong as we are, you too would do what we now do'.

Gorgias of Leontini in Sicily (*c.* 475-375 B.C.) used arguments similar to those of Zeno and Melissus of Elea in order to prove the absurdity of Eleatic philosophy. He then abandoned philosophy and devoted himself to a study of rhetoric, practical psychology, drama and the art of persuasion. In a work called *On Not-Being* (*mē ontos*) *or Nature* (*physeōs*) he used dialectical arguments of different kinds in support of his threefold assertion:

(1) Non-being is real, and being is not. He attempted to prove this as follows: Non-being *Is* certainly non-being. Therefore it *Is*. Therefore it really exists. Non-being Is, and it is opposed to being; therefore

being is not. Therefore, Non-being is real, or Nothing is real; and what is, is not.

(2) If anything is, it cannot be known. Why? Things are in flux; thought is fixed. Things in flux cannot be fixed (in thought). And again, if being were known then there could never be any error, which is absurd.

(3) If anything is known, it cannot be expressed or imparted. Why? Words are fugitive and can be heard; thought is stable and is unheard. Thus, words cannot express thought. And again, since two people are different, how could the same representation of a thing be in two people at once? For these and other similar reasons, Gorgias decided to renounce philosophy and to refuse to answer questions concerning truth and morality.

The Sophists in general played their own (minor though vocal) part in the atmosphere of intellectual ferment which characterized the great days of the Periclean age in Athens. Many of them sought not truth but rather greatness and honour through their learning. Plato called them 'shopkeepers with spiritual wares'. They tended in general towards scepticism, relativism and destructive criticism concerning traditional values. They raised problems magisterially and articulately even though they had no satisfactory intellectual solutions for the doubts and questions which they were content merely to raise. They sought to impress, to astound and to win rather than to contemplate humbly all that is in being.

They fostered a climate of relativism, intellectual confusion and negative criticism against which Socrates and Plato reacted. In this oblique way they made a partial, though indirect contribution to the growth of philosophic thought.

3. Socrates (470-399 B.C.) was active in Athens in the great days of the Periclean age. The dramatists Aeschylus, Sophocles, Euripides and Aristophanes were his contemporaries. As a young man, Socrates served with distinction as a hoplite (foot-soldier) in the Peloponnesian War; in the camp at Potidaea, and on other occasions later in his life, he was reported to have stood in a trance for several hours in intense mental concentration.

His thought was deeply influenced by Anaxagoras' insight concerning the presence of Mind in the universe. It was influenced also by Parmenides' conviction that Being is eternal and abiding; and by Pythagoras' various teachings concerning the importance of the human soul, and contemplation, and the soul's humble quest of wisdom.

His thought was also influenced deeply by a reply given by the Delphic oracle. One of his friends, Chaerephon, had learned from the oracle that there was no man living who was wiser than Socrates. Socrates interpreted this as meaning that his wisdom consisted in a recognition of his lack of knowledge and in his humble openness to those special insights which come through contemplation and through docility to enlightened instruction. He was convinced of the working of Mind in the universe and of its working within himself. He spoke of a *daimōn* (or, perhaps, 'Mind', or 'Conscience') within him which warned him and prohibited him with regard to actions which would be wrong.

Socrates left no writings. He saw his reforming mission as one of seeking wisdom for both himself and those with whom he conversed in the streets of Athens. We know of his doctrines, activities and methods mainly through Xenophon's *Memorabilia* and Plato's dialogues.

He sought to combat the intellectual confusion of his times. Wisdom could be attained not through mental confusion but through mental clarity and rational (ethical) action. For this reason he induced his students and those whom he met to assist him to attain clear and distinct definitions and concepts of Justice, Piety, Friendship, Temperance, Courage, Truth and other such ideas of importance for ethical behaviour. He saw these as stable fixed concepts capable of being defined precisely in universal definitions.

The Socratic method took the form of a dialectic or dialogue which proceeded by question and answer. Sophists such as Hippias of Elis were prepared to lecture on any subject. Socrates enticed such men into displaying their knowledge of true friendship, true justice or similar subjects. He himself professed ignorance in these matters. He then requested a definition of the subject or concept under discussion. An initial definition (e.g. of piety) was frequently found to be not fully adequate. By means of this form of 'Socratic irony', and by further inductive argument, the conversation proceeded through less adequate definitions towards the formulation of more adequate definitions. It became known as the method of Socratic maieutic or 'midwifery', the method which enabled the student's mind to conceive and give birth to new or deeper insight into ethical ideals and ethical behaviour.

Plato, who was a student of Socrates, saw in the doctrine of stable universal fixed concepts the foundations for his own doctrine of subsistent Forms or Ideas. In many of his subsequent dialogues Plato used Socrates as a central figure and spokesman for some of Plato's own cherished doctrines. Aristotle informs us, however, that Socrates himself did not teach the doctrine of subsistent Ideas or Forms.

Socrates saw his mission in life as that of persuading men 'to seek virtue and wisdom'. And for him virtue and wisdom are one. He was convinced that any wise man who knows what is right, and who is deeply convinced that it is right, will also do what is right. Any man who is deeply convinced that a certain action will genuinely promote his own true happiness, will certainly perform that action. A virtuous life and an enlightened life are one and the same thing. The virtuous man is one who knows moral goodness: the man of wisdom. It is for this reason that insight is so important in the life of every human being.

Aristotle pointed out that this doctrine of 'ethical intellectualism' neglected to take account of moral weakness in man. For right living, both intellectual virtue and moral virtue are required. However, Aristotle agreed with Socrates in his teaching that the good life for man is the examined life; it is good for man that he live in a characteristically human way, that is, rationally, wisely, intelligently. The truly happy life is the beautifully human life; and the specifically human life is the intelligent life.

Socrates thought at length on Anaxagoras' doctrine concerning the presence of Mind in the universe. He concluded that the knowledge of the gods is not a limited knowledge; they know everything that happens in every place. Universal Mind or Intelligence is present in the gods even more so than it is present in man. They know what is for the best. There is always purpose in all that the gods do in the universe. When man prays he should pray for whatever the gods know to be for the best. Man's reason is part of universal Reason and it should always endeavour to be at one with universal Reason or Mind at work in the world.

Socrates applied this same line of thought to politics. Political leaders should be wise, competent men. The ship of state should be entrusted only to wise and competent pilots. Democracy as conducted under the guidance of Athenian speech-makers and arrogant rhetoricians did not lead in practice to the choice of good public officials. Even the war minister and the generals for the army or navy were chosen either by lot or by a count of the raised hands of the inexperienced multitude. This special application of his teaching aroused the hostility of several existing office-holders.

In the year 399 B.C., when he was about seventy years old, Socrates was tried, condemned to death and executed. He was regarded as a pernicious character who was undermining the influence and power of the social leaders and politicians who held office. He acknowledged publicly at his trial that he had resisted the democracy at a time when the authorities tried illegally to impeach eight generals as a group for their collective negligence during a thunderstorm at the sea battle of Arginusae. At a later stage he had likewise resisted the demand of the Thirty Tyrants (who seized power at Athens after the disastrous end of the Peloponnesian War) that Leon of Salamis be arrested and tried, and his property confiscated. Socrates had resisted the authorities and now he stood condemned. In both cases the authorities were acting illegally. At the instigation of Anytus, a democratic politician, Socrates was publicly accused of not worshipping the gods which the Athenian state worshipped, and furthermore of corrupting the young by his teachings. In his defence at the trial, Socrates refused to ask clemency for crimes he had not committed. He asked his judges to listen instead to censure of their own evil lives and to improve themselves rather than disable others. He was condemned, by a relatively small majority of the (500) jury members, to drink hemlock. This he did, in compliance with the decision of the court. We are told that he drained the cup of poison as cheerfully as if it were wine.

After his death, Plato said of him that he was 'the best (man) of all his time that we have known, and moreover the most wise and just'.

The thought of Socrates influenced not only his two great disciples, Plato and Aristotle, but also many secondary schools of thought. These schools (the minor Socratics) remained attached to the ethical views of Socrates.

The three principal minor Socratic schools are: (a) The Cynics. This school was founded by *Antisthenes* in the Kynosarges Gymnasium. Socrates' renunciation of earthly pleasures and possessions became their central ideal. *Diogenes* flouted conventions. Their stress on independence as an ideal inspired the ethic of Stoicism at a later date. (b) The Cyrenaics. This school was founded by *Aristippus* of Cyrene (b. 435 B.C.). It included *Theodorus* the Atheist, *Hegesias*, *Anniceris* and their followers. They taught that knowledge derives from sensation alone, and that the end of human conduct is to obtain pleasurable sensations. Their original doctrine of hedonism was developed by Epicureanism. (c) The school of Megara was founded by Euclid of Megara. This school, and also the associated Elis-Eretrian school, placed emphasis on disputation and dialectics. This tendency developed at a later date into Scepticism.

(These three themes, Stoicism, Epicureanism and Scepticism, will be treated in Chapter 7.)

3 Plato (I)

1. Life and writings   2. Plato's theory of knowledge
3. Plato's later doctrine of Forms

1. Life and writings. Aristocles (*c*. 428-348 B.C.) who was
called *Plato* (because of his broad forehead) was born on the island of
Aegina (Aiyina) near Athens. His family was an aristocratic one
which was critically aware of the lack of responsible leadership in the
period of the democracy. Plato studied under Cratylus, a Heraclitean
philosopher who taught that the world of sense perception is a world
of flux (*panta rhei*). At the age of twenty, after he had become
acquainted with Socrates, he decided to devote his life to philosophy.
Eight years later, after the death of Socrates, he emigrated and stayed
with Euclid at Megara. He travelled to Egypt where he studied
astronomy, and to Italy and Sicily where he studied the doctrine of
the Pythagoreans. About 387 B.C., at Athens, he opened a school of
philosophy 'for the worship of the Muses' in the public gardens
dedicated to the hero Academus. It became known as the 'Academy'
(hence the word), and it continued as a school of Platonic philosophy
for over 900 years.

Plato was convinced of the necessity of producing wise statesmen,
men whose principles and ideals would be founded on eternal truths.
He himself travelled, on invitation, to Syracuse in Sicily to supervise
the education of the young ruler Dionysius II. Plato had hopes that
this young man would be a model philosopher-king. Dionysius II,
however proved to be a self-centred, reckless tyrant, and Plato
returned to the Academy.

No notes of Plato's academic lectures were ever published. But his
'popular' dialogues (for educated people) were published. These
dialogues are beautifully written literary works. In several of the
dialogues, Socrates is the central character who articulates doctrines
which, at times, are probably Plato's own doctrines.

Among the most important of Plato's writings we may list the
following: *Apology*, on the trial and defence of Socrates; *Euthyphro*,
on piety and impiety; *Crito*, on Socrates' reasons for refusing to
attempt to escape from prison and from his death sentence;
Protagoras, on the unity of the virtues; *Meno*, on virtue; *Gorgias*, on
rhetoric; *Symposium*, on love and beauty; *Phaedo*, on Ideas and
immortality; *Republic (Politeia)*, on justice and the ideal state;

Phaedrus, on love and love of beauty; *Theaetetus,* on knowledge; *Parmenides,* on the doctrine of Ideas; *Sophist,* on Being and on the art of persuasive discourse; *Statesman (Politicus),* on statesmanship; *Philebus,* on pleasures and wisdom; *Timaeus,* on universal nature; *Laws (Nomoi),* on government, the purpose of legislation and on the rule of law.

Plato died at the age of 81 in the first days of the war in which Philip of Macedonia brought Athens and Greece under his dominion. He had lived through the latter days of Athens' greatness, and its subsequent decline and fall.

2. Plato's theory of knowledge. Plato was impressed by the arguments of Heraclitus and Parmenides that our five senses present us with a world which is merely a sensed world, unstable, imperfect, changing and decaying. (Thus, for example, in the river Jordan, the immediate knowledge which a fish has of John the Baptist and his activities is a sensed or animal form of knowledge. The fish knows John and his activities not as John is, but as the fish is. Similarly, the immediate sense-knowledge of the infant mind knows beings not as they are, but as the infant mind is.) Human knowledge, on the other hand, presents us with forms of being, realities, and definitions which are stable and perfect.

Thus, reality as sensed (by an animal or rational animal) is not reality as reality really is. Being is always distinctly what it is, and it is totally all that is. It is this world of ongoing being, intelligible, capable of being understood, that is the real world. The human mind struggles to grasp this real intelligible world, through its concepts and definitions of, for example, 'goodness', or 'beauty', or other such stable and intelligible forms of being.

Plato concluded, for example, that the imperfect circular objects which we sense bring to mind an intelligible form of circularity which is not-imperfect. The sensed (imperfect) circular is known as circular because it partakes in the general idea of perfect circularity. The same can be said of 'goodness', or 'justice' or 'straightness' or other forms or ideas. Perfect squareness, perfect whiteness, perfect beauty and other such ideal forms of being exist as universal concepts; they are unchanging universals having their own reality independently of sensation which is necessarily imperfect and fleeting.

In *Meno,* Plato tells the story of how Socrates asks certain geometrical questions of Meno's slave boy. The boy has had no training in mathematics. By asking appropriate questions about a given diagram Socrates finds that the boy gives the correct answer.

The boy seems to have a knowledge that he did not know he possessed. Could it be that this slave boy had already acquired such knowledge in a previous intelligent life before birth? His knowledge might be explained as a recall (*anamnēsis*) of a knowledge of forms of being acquired before birth. How otherwise could he have had such knowledge of ideal forms of being?

Plato makes an important distinction in *Meno* between knowledge (*epistēmē*) and everyday belief (*doxa*) or opinion. If a man has already travelled along the road to Larissa (Lárisa in Thessaly), then he *knows* the way there. If a second man who has not been to Larissa has been told about the route, then he may have a correct opinion or *belief* about the way to Larissa. The knowledge of the first man is more firmly based than the belief of the second man.

In the *Republic*, Plato argues that rational, universal, real knowledge and the type of inferior 'belief' which is based on hearsay or sensation pertain to separate levels of human awareness, having different objects. Sense-knowledge, like hearsay knowledge, is merely representational, believed 'knowledge'. The two are closely connected in actual practice; but real knowledge is of the realm of universal and intelligible forms of being, while belief or opinion is of the animal-like world of hearing and sensation. Knowledge is of the intelligible archetypes; sense-beliefs are merely sensed opinions based on mirror images, shadows, reflections (as in a stream), or anthropomorphic copies of the intelligible archetypes. Sensed material objects are inferior copies which imitate and partake of the ideal archetype. Just as the sun is the source of physical illumination and of life on earth, so also the Good is the source of knowledge, mental enlightment, and existence in the world.

In Book VII of the *Republic* Plato presents his well-known allegory of 'the Cave', which attempts to depict the progressive stages of human education and enlightenment. We are asked to imagine some lifelong prisoners chained to a wall in an underground cave where they can see only shadows on the opposite wall. The shadows are cast by various dispersed statues, vessels and figurines on an unseen parapet behind, where a fire burns. Now, if a prisoner were to free himself and actually see the artificial figurines in the flickering firelight, he would then be in the world of belief concerning realities. If he were to escape into the sunlight outside the cave he would be dazzled on seeing the real world of true realities, analogous to the realm of forms. Here he would feel tempted to dwell forever. But if he were to return to his chained companions they would throw scorn on his explanations, just as the sensists scorn explanations of the doctrine of real understandable forms of being. The philosopher-educator has to be patient in his efforts to uplift and educate his students. Through education, the young can be brought gradually to behold and to cherish eternal and absolute truths and values.

One of the finest of Plato's dialogues is *Theaetetus*, which dates from Plato's middle period. Theaetetus, a young mathematical student, is conversing with Socrates on the nature of knowledge. When Socrates asks Theaetetus for a definition of *knowledge* he replies that it is nothing but *perception* (or sensation). Socrates, through his customary question-and-answer technique, questions whether this Protagorean view implies that the world of perception is a world which is private and different in each sense-organ of each particular perceiver. It is apparent that perceptions are always in flux. Knowledge, however, is stable. We know remembered things that we no longer perceive. We know of 'non-existence', and of tomorrow, and mathematical conclusions, by reflection rather than by bare sensation. It would appear then that knowledge and perception cannot be equated. Knowledge involves a mind which interprets the presentations of sense; uninterpreted sense-experience cannot possibly be knowledge. In the light of these objections, Theaetetus is induced to formulate a new definition of knowledge.

Theaetetus proposes next that knowledge is 'true opinion'. This definition too is found to be inadequate. One might judge, or opine or believe, that some fact is the case (e.g. this witness is telling the truth) without definitely knowing that it is the case; the pronounced judgement might perhaps happen to be a correct or true judgement though one did not definitely know it to be correct. Thus true belief is not the same thing as knowledge. Theaetetus then proposes that knowledge is true belief accompanied by a reason or correct explanation. This implies that to true belief there is added an enumeration of known or knowable parts (or details), or else some particular distinguishing characteristic of the matter which is believed. But no mere enumeration of details of itself gives scientific knowledge of the whole; and no notion can be called a correct notion unless the distinguishing characteristics are already included in the notion. Thus I cannot transform a true belief into knowledge by adding on something already contained in the belief. Furthermore, to assert, even implicitly, that knowledge is a true opinion actually known to be true is a circular definition and therefore not acceptable. Theaetetus is asked therefore to reflect more deeply on the nature of knowledge before he can truly say that he knows what it is.

In the background of this dialogue, there is for both Plato and Socrates the unspoken conviction that all knowledge is absolute, stable and infallible knowledge of universal forms of being, principles and values capable of being grasped in clear and scientific definitions. True knowledge is knowledge of the universal (e.g. of 'goodness', 'courage' and so forth), and the universal always has an objective reference to the realm of reality. The different degrees of progression through belief towards knowledge are illustrated in the simile of 'the Line'. The human mind can progress along a 'line' from an initial state of ignorance through intermediary imperfect stages (along the line) to a final state of true knowledge of universal first principles and ideas (*Republic* 509-511).

Plato presents three intermediary, imperfect stages in human progression along the 'line' towards true knowledge. (1) The lowest stage of opinion is that of shady, sophistic opinions or judgements about reality. The specious arguments of eristic rhetoricians who try to persuade the law courts that their clients' questionable conduct is really legal and moral are of this type. Their opinions constitute neither knowledge nor belief but merely shades or caricatures of belief (*eikasia*). (2) The second stage of opinion (*doxa*) or judgement is that of genuine belief (*pistis*) in the existence of particular sense-objects in the world of nature and art. Each object of nature or art is an imperfect copy or realization of the perfect archetypal model from which it derives whatever partial degree of 'imitative' reality there is within it. Belief about sense-particulars and individuals is of this kind. (3) The third stage of progression towards perfect knowledge is a stage of knowledge in which the knower knows and concerns himself with *intelligible particular* entities such as individual mathematical figures and numbers. These are unique individual entities in themselves, and not imperfect copies or images of perfect reality. The mathematician attains a form of knowledge (*epistēmē*) which is a particular understanding (*dianoia*) of the particular objects or entities of the world of mathematics. He can make, for example, a few diagrams which illustrate the several entities (e.g. multitudinous different triangles) which he can understand and 'see only with the eye of thought' (*Republic* 511c-d). His knowledge gives him a particular understanding (*dianoia*) of these intelligible particulars. *Dianoia* is a form of knowledge which is inferior to *noēsis* or *nous*, that is, pure knowledge, which is concerned with the originals or archetypes (*archai*). Pure knowledge or pure reason (*nous*) ascends to the level of the exemplars of all things, the first principles or forms.

3. Plato's later doctrine of Forms.

Plato accepted the Socratic theory that we have knowledge of matters, or forms of things, which are permanent, unvarying and sufficiently defined to be intelligible to us. These objects known to us retain their identity down through successive generations of speakers and thinkers. They are stable and unvarying in their nature. Objects of this kind cannot be found anywhere in the stream (world) of sensations where everything is in flux. They must therefore belong to an intelligible world of abiding forms of being superior to the evanescent experiential objects and forms perceived in a flickering shadow-like way by the senses. Our knowledge of those abiding realities is therefore a knowledge of intelligible forms of things or 'Ideas' (*eidē*) and not a knowledge of sensible forms or images. (Note that when Plato speaks of the intelligible 'Ideas' or Forms, he uses the Greek word *eidos* [plural *eidē*] which means the 'kind' or 'species' or 'form' [of being]. In this context, he does not use the Greek word *idea* or 'concept'.)

Plato was quite aware that the doctrine concerning the reality of the Intelligible Forms of being gave rise to several difficulties. He presented a number of these difficulties in one of the later dialogues, *Parmenides*. In this dialogue the old and venerable Parmenides asks the young Socrates a number of penetrating questions which force Socrates to reconsider the theory of Ideas or Forms, in its undeveloped state, as a solution to the problem of the one and the many. Socrates has asserted to Parmenides and Zeno that there are absolute Ideas (*eidē*) of likeness, unity and plurality, and of the just, the beautiful, the good and such matters. He is not certain however that there are absolute Forms of man, fire and water; and he is quite certain that there are no absolute Forms of vile materials such as mud, hair and dirt. There does, however, seem to be an Idea of Everything, and if so, then mud, hair and dirt would partake of this perfect Idea. Parmenides points out the difficulty in the claim that many things can partake of a single absolute nature or Idea. A sail-cloth spread out over many men covers each man with only parts of itself. If an Idea such as the Idea of equality covers things with only parts of itself, then, for example, particular things which partake of equality would in fact be partaking not of equality but of less than equality (or, only a part of equality).

Two problems, therefore, have been raised so far with regard to the theory of the Forms: Are there Forms of everything? How are the

Forms and particulars related? *Parmenides* then proceeds to raise further problems: Are the Forms thoughts (universals) in the mind or do they exist independently of the mind? And are these ideal patterns or Forms cut off or sundered (by a *chōrismos*) from the sensed world? Are the two worlds parallel? Is the ideal world a reduplication of the world of sensations? How are the Ideas related to each other and what is their relation to individuals? The individual thing may perhaps be seen as a participation (*methexis*) in the Idea, or as an imitation or copy or resemblance (*mimēsis*) of the Idea or pattern or exemplar (*paradeigma*). The different presentations of the doctrine of Forms are then shown to give rise to serious difficulties. The Idea cannot be spoken of as an object like other individual objects, and its relationship to individuals is entirely different from the relationship between individuals themselves. The young Socrates is finally advised by Parmenides to think further and more deeply about the whole matter before trying to retrieve his original position.

The discussion in the *Sophist* dialogue centres on class concepts. Here Plato makes use of the technique of classification, or division, in which he proceeds from the more general or generic terms to the more specific in his efforts to describe the nature of, for example, a 'sophist'. Through the use of this technique of 'division', a suggested definition of 'sophist' emerges: 'one who practises the art of purifying the soul of a false belief in its own wisdom by education'. In this instance, explicit knowledge of the sophist's nature consists in apprehending this class concept in a definition which employs genus and difference; e.g., when 'man' is defined as 'a rational animal', the term 'animal' expresses the genus, and the term 'rational' expresses the difference within the genus (of animal).

One of the ways in which the forms of being intercommunicate, or in which they are related among themselves, resembles the interconnections of the parts of a pyramidal or hierarchical structure. A higher form ('animal') embraces a number of subordinate forms ('horse', 'dog', 'mole'). A definition maps out the position of the form which is being defined in its place within the pyramid or world of forms. All forms of being are subordinate to the highest and all-pervading 'Idea', Being, the One, at the top of the hierarchy of forms.

At the base of the pyramid there are the *infimae species*, the *atoma eidē*, that is, the lowest forms of being, those which admit of no further division into subordinate specific classes. The form of Man, for example, cannot be divided further into lower species. These lowest forms of being in the pyramid are on the border of the sensible sphere. But the *Sophist* does not bridge the chasm or *chōrismos* between the lowest, intelligible 'atomic forms' and sensed individuals or sense particulars of the sensible world which are impenetrable to reason (*logos*) and which cannot correctly be said to be.

The *Sophist* calls attention to the philosophical battle going on between the Gods (or the idealists) and the Giants (the materialists) concerning the nature of reality. The Gods maintain that sensible reality is 'not real being, but a sort of moving process of becoming' (246c). The Giants maintain that 'whatever they cannot squeeze between their hands is just nothing at all' (247c). The stranger from Elea (probably representing Plato himself) then makes a suggestion which he hopes may help to resolve the conflict. He points out that certain things which have body and other things which are bodiless (such as wisdom, justice, or soul) are all regarded as 'real'. He then suggests a description of the real which he hopes 'reformed' Giants may find acceptable: 'I suggest that anything has *real being* that is so constituted as to possess any sort of *power* (*dynamis*) either to affect anything else or to be affected, in however small a degree, by the most insignificant agent, though it be only once. I am proposing as a mark to distinguish *real things* that they are nothing but *power*' (*Sophist* 247e). A variation on this doctrine of power to change or to be changed (*dynamis*) was to play a significant role at a later date in the philosophical thought of Plato's disciple Aristotle.

In the *Timaeus*, Socrates asks Timaeus, an enthusiastic Pythagorean astronomer, to give an account of the generation of the world. Timaeus commences his account by distinguishing between, on the one hand, the form of being which is apprehended by intelligence and reason and is always in the same state, and on the other hand, the sensed particular (This) 'which is conceived by opinion without reason, and *always in a process of becoming and perishing* and never really is'. There is in the universe a non-intelligible, non-deducible, 'chaotic' element (that is, the merely particular), which exists alongside of the intelligible world; and there is also Space, 'the home-nurse of all created things'. Timaeus then speaks in pictorial language of how the 'Demiurge' introduced order among the disordered, discordant sense-particulars, within the Receptacle (Space), taking the intelligible realm of forms as his model in building up the universe. The non-logical, non-deducible element is simply an unintelligible and unexplainable factor which one finds in the universe. One can simply say of it that it is not non-being.

Here once again Plato faced the problem of the relationship between the intelligible forms of being and sense-knowledge of the individual. He did not discover a solution to the problem of individuation in being; but, then, neither did any other philosopher present an adequate solution, during several subsequent centuries.

Plato, like Heraclitus and Parmenides, regarded the world of being as a world which is obviously real, and which is also, in some sense, one. Being *is*. The human mind tries to grasp this real world of being in its different 'shapes' or 'kinds' or 'forms' (*eidē*) of being. It attempts to express these 'forms' of being in human concepts and definitions. An object which is a sensed particular 'this' is impervious to understanding in so far as it is a mere sensed 'this'. But if a certain particular 'this' is said to be a 'horse' or 'large', or so forth, then we can understand something of its reality through the forms of being (namely, the form or the nature of 'being horse' or 'being large') in which its being is realized. Thus, a knowledge (or 'science') of being or beings is a knowledge of the forms of being which limit or define the ways in which different beings are realized. Plato's philosophy is therefore a quest for a deeper knowledge of these forms of being.

Aristotle asserted that Plato introduced a *chōrismos*, a crevasse, or separation between the world of forms and the concrete world of natural things. He was convinced that this was the logical consequence of Plato's approach to understanding reality. However, we have no evidence from Plato's own writings that Plato himself ever wished to introduce any such *chōrismos* between the particular being that is sensed and the form of being in which that being is realized. Aristotle's assessment may possibly be seen as an indirect assertion of the evident superiority of the Peripatetic school of philosophy to that of Plato.

Plato does make a distinction between perceived phenomena and knowledge of reality. For Plato, it is 'being' that is real, and not flickering sense-experiences. The many beings that we encounter are given to us as beings of different forms or 'kinds' (*eidē*) or natures. The human mind lays hold of these natures or essences and thereby comes to know the exemplars or archetypes of different kinds of beings. They are not invented by the mind. They are discovered; they are real. They are objective essences, real natures or, in brief, 'forms', forms of being in which beings participate.

A careful reading of the dialogues, and especially of the later dialogues, will convey a strong impression that Plato saw the forms of being as archetypes or exemplars which exist in the mind of the One, the Good, the True, Beauty its very self, absolute Being itself. At the same time it is not anywhere stated explicitly, in so many words, that the source of the forms is the mind of God. After the shameful treatment of Socrates, Plato stated that there were certain themes on which he was not prepared to write explicitly (*Letter* 2, 314); one may well infer from Plato's writings that this theme was one of them.

In his *Letters* (cf. *Letter* 6), Plato speaks of 'the god who is the captain of all things present and future,' and he also speaks of 'the Father of that captain and cause'. In *Timaeus* (28c) he asserts that it is impossible to speak of 'the maker and father of the universe'. In the second *Letter* (312e), though the authenticity of this letter is sometimes disputed, there is a similar assertion that no human predicates can apply to 'the king of the universe'. Plato speaks, then, of certain matters in figurative and hypothetical language. He uses allegory and myth. The figurative 'Demiurge' or Maker is said to make use of the forms of being in his task of bringing order into the primeval disorder. One may question whether the figurative 'Demiurge' is the same as the figurative 'maker and father', or not. Is the Demiurge the 'captain and cause'? And is the 'king of the universe' the 'father' who is the 'father of the captain and cause'? The language is figurative, and Plato avoids being more explicit.

Aristotle tells us (*Eudemian Ethics* 1218a24) that Plato identified the Good and the One; and Aristoxenus informs us that Plato gave a discourse to an audience on, among other things, the identity of the Good and the One. Plotinus identified the One or the Good with the 'Father' who transcends all positive predicates and human concepts.

There are good grounds, then, for the view that, in Plato's philosophy it is the One, the Supremely Real, the Absolute Exemplary Cause, that is the source of the forms, even though Plato himself does not explicitly say so.

We are now in a position to make a brief assessment of the different layers of probings of Plato's thought. Plato was aware of the profound difference that exists between sense-perception and intellectual perception. Sense-perception does not attain to the inner reality of the thing perceived. Intellectual perception is a knowing of the being, the reality, of the thing known. The being or thing known is known as being this individual kind or particular form of being. However, a study of the different kinds or forms of things reveals their bewildering variety. Some kinds of beings seem to be capable of being defined, while others are not so. Some things are perceived to be immutable and timeless; others not so. There are particular kinds of things, and there are universals. There are individuals, species, genera, and transcendental archetypes. All are different forms of being. Being is itself perceived to be simply the one that it is. All limited beings may be thought of as having their source in the One transcendent reality. Some systematized schema of all the distinctions, divisions and subdivisions of the forms of being seems, therefore, to be required. Several of the Platonic dialogues end on the note that the bewildering variety of the forms or kinds of being warrants still further investigation. A major advance had already been made, however, in the Platonic insight that intellectual perception (intellectual knowing) is a knowing of being (or reality) and its different forms.

In his later years, Plato devoted much of his attention to trying to rationalize the forms of reality further by trying to mathematize the forms. Aristotle says in his *Metaphysics* (I, 6) that Plato thought of the forms as numbers and thought of things as existing by participation in numbers. For Plato, mathematical entities (*ta mathēmatika*) constitute a class of intelligible particulars which are intermediaries (on the 'line') between sensible particulars and intelligible universals. They are known by understanding (*dianoia*), which lies between opinion (*doxa*) and pure reason (*noēsis*). The Demiurge conferred geometrical and mathematical patterns upon the unordered primary elements within Space, taking the forms of being as his model. This order in the world may then be understood better through an understanding of *ta mathēmatika*. These particular or individual mathematical entities, in turn, participate in the forms, which are themselves numbers or principles of order.

The forms of being are many, even though being itself (or 'Is') is one. These forms of being are rational, or understandable. But in the material beings which exist there is an element which is irrational, namely, their unanalysable particularity or materiality. Each is simply a 'this' that is in flux. This non-analysable irrational element is similar to the element of irrationality which we find in the endlessness perceived in the continued fraction, or in the non-terminating decimal. Nevertheless, the irrational, non-terminating, sensed 'this' that is in a state of flux, participates in the One (in Being), and from this participation comes its 'form' of being, or its 'number'. Thus Aristotle in his *Metaphysics* (987b21-22) can assert that, according to Plato, 'from the great and the small' (or from the more and the less), that is, from the non-terminating irrational factors, 'by participation in the One, come the forms, i.e. the numbers' (cf. A. E. Taylor, 'Plato' in *Encyclopædia Britannica* and articles in *Mind* [1926-27]). Different limited forms of being arise from different degrees of participation in being.

The student may perhaps be allowed to approach the doctrine more simply as follows: In the world of our perceptions, particular sensed beings, which are in a state of flux, forever coming into being and taking on new forms of being, are similar to irrational numbers such as non-terminating decimals (e.g.$\pi \backsimeq 22/7$ or $3.1415926...$). Their unceasing 'flux' cannot be apprehended in stable 'shapes' or forms. However, there is present within every unstable particular being: (1) its *being*, or its non-rational, non-conceptual, endlessly 'flowing' singularity or *particularity* which, through participating in the One being, gives rise to (2) its *form* of being, its 'number', or its principle of limitation in being.

Thus, in reference to each particular being, we can speak of (1) its principle of *perfection* in being, that is, its principle of ongoing, endlessly flowing, singular richness in being, and (2) its principle of *suchness* or form or limitation in being. Plato seems to have felt that the key to the eventual understanding of each thing's limitation in being and singularity in being might possibly be found in a mathematizing of these principles of being; the modern physicist, for example, endeavours to understand the 'natures' of different chemical substances through measurement techniques and pointer readings which give arithmetic numbers related to particular boiling points, densities, specific gravities, atomic weights, and numbered chemical tables. However, having said this one must be careful not to say that this was clearly and explicitly asserted by Plato himself or by Aristotle in reference to Plato. It is, rather, a schema which may help the student to schematize the probing tendencies latent within Plato's efforts to 'mathematize' his doctrine concerning the different kinds or natures or forms of beings.

Plato aimed to train philosopher-statesmen who would see clearly that everything in existence, everything in being, in society or in the universe, participates in Being, in the One, in Justice, Truth, Beauty, transcendent Reality. The student philosopher-statesmen must apprehend more clearly the values, objectives and ideas which are operating in our universe in order to lead society towards a greater actualization of these operative Ideals. The enlightened statesman will help society to pursue more intelligent and rational patterns of human conduct in conformity with the world of pure Archetypal Ideas, the exemplary forms of being, which (appear to) have their ultimate source in the transcendent One, Reality its very self.

In his theory of forms of being, Plato proposed a new synthesis of all that was valuable in the philosophies of Socrates, Parmenides, Heraclitus and the pre-Socratics in general. It was a new, Platonic synthesis which constituted a prodigious advance in the ongoing history of philosophic thought.

4 Plato (II)

1. Plato's physics: cosmogony and cosmology. Plato asserts that no scientifically exact account of the origins of the universe is possible. One can merely suggest or put forward physical theories that are 'likely' or possible. The *Timaeus* dialogue presents a 'scientific' theory of this kind.

Timaeus, the dominant speaker in the dialogue, gives an account of the origins and nature of the universe in terms of mainly Pythagorean ideas. In the early stages of the dialogue the question as to whether the world did or did not have a beginning is settled quickly in the light of the Platonic distinction between constant (intellectually known) reality and the 'unreal' world of inconstant sense-perceptions. This latter world is not constant and so it is not abiding or eternal. It must have come into being. Now, whatever comes into being must have a cause; and the cause or 'artificer' (or 'Demiurge') of the whole universe must surely have been the best of all artificers or causes. A 'craftsman' of this kind could not possibly be satisfied with a product which would be imperfect, dis-ordered, inanimate or unintelligent. He would certainly wish to model his product on perfect plans or forms of being.

Within the great 'Receptacle' of Space, godlike Intelligence, or Mind, arranged ordered patterns of behaviour and bodies in and from un-co-ordinated, minute (dust) elements, to create a universe which, without Mind, would have been a disorganized chaos of purposeless particles existing by mere chance or 'necessity'.

The Demiurge, using the eternal designs or forms as models, arranged the disarranged primary elements (the different 'atoms', for example, which Democritus and Leucippus had spoken of previously) into three-dimensional, geometrical atomic shapes to form various combinations such as those which we call salt or copper or other such substances.

The Demiurge has shaped the universe in the form of a globe. It revolves in a circle. It has life and therefore soul within it. Within the living globe there are seven planets circling in different orbits. Stars were placed in each of these orbits. The stars in their orbits brought time into being as an image of the eternal.

Within the seven orbits, the Demiurge formed a great fire, the sun, to light up the heavens. Through observation of the sun and of the stars of the heavens in their courses men and animals can learn to adjust their lives according to the seasons and according to the measures of motion. In this way man himself acquires knowledge of time and of numbers and of philosophy.

The universe, as we find it, then, is an ordered body having life within it. It is a unitary animated whole with life, intelligence and soul. The world-soul, like all other embodied immortal souls, participates, at one and the same time, in both the eternal intelligible world and the changing perceptual world.

In brief, Plato presents the figurative 'Demiurge' not as creating out of nothing but as arranging in order the (Democritean) elements or atoms present within space as a receptacle; this arranging or ordering was done in accordance with the eternal *eidē* (forms, shapes, plans, natures). In this way the ordered universe came to be what it is.

Some of Plato's followers interpreted this figurative explanation in a very literal way. They accepted that the Demiurge is a divine artificer who is a lower god (or spirit) subordinate to the 'king' spoken of in the letters of Plato and in *Philebus*. This is one possible interpretation of Plato's thought. However, it is not the only possible interpretation. It is possible also to interpret Plato's figurative and mythological narratives in a less poetical and more philosophical sense. Plato views the universe as one which evidences finality. It is the handiwork of the One, that is, absolute Being its very self. It is a material, corporeal world. But it is not merely sensible, it is also intelligible. It is corporeal, but it gives evidence of the workings of mind within it. It is therefore both sensible and intelligible. Man himself partakes of both these worlds. He is an entity having both body and soul. He participates in both the sensible world and the intelligible world. In this sense, man, as the ancients have always said, is a microcosm of the macrocosm.

2. Plato's psychology. In Book X of the dialogue called the *Laws*, the Athenian Stranger (who is thought by some scholars to represent Plato himself) asserts that the spiritual nature of the soul is the same as that of the gods. The soul is prior to the body. The soul is a 'self-moving' principle which is identified with life. It is defined, in essence, as that power or source which can initiate self-movement. It is the source of motion in all things. The human body, like all bodies, is essentially inert; it has no moving power of its own. The soul is the initiator of movement in and of the body. Soul is also the author or initiator of movement in and of all bodies, including, for example, even the movement of the heavenly planets. The soul or spirit is superior to, and prior to, that which is moved by it. It is superior to the body. The soul alone possesses intelligence (*Timaeus* 46; the global, corporeal world is itself a living body endowed by providence with soul and intelligence, according to Plato's Timaeus—the original Timaeus was a Pythagorean astronomer). The soul must rule the body.

In *Phaedo*, Plato's Socrates reminds his followers Simmias and Cebes of the difference between the unstable body which is subject to dissolution and the immortal soul which 'is in the very likeness of the divine'. The soul is destined to enter into the blissful company of the gods. It is shackled to the body, deceived by the senses, and enslaved by its own desires. Philosophy offers release from this deception. Simmias reminds Socrates of the Pythagorean conception of the soul as a sort of (mere) harmony or attunement of the elements of the body, akin to the harmony of a lyre, Socrates then points out that the soul as governor of the body is sometimes out of harmony with the body. It is superior and prior to the body. It existed before the body and will continue to exist after the body. It renders the body alive. It has an essential relation to life and so it cannot admit to itself its opposite, which is death; it is spiritual and immortal. It must take command over the rebellious desires of the body. Some souls allow themselves to be enthralled by love of sensual pleasures and by evil passions. They become weighed down by the corporeal and they may, later, be reincarnated in animals. The soul must control the body; the body can exercise an enslaving influence on the soul as in the case of vicious habits, bad music, physical training, diseased heredity and unenlightened upbringing. After death, the mind will be wholly freed from the enslaving influence of the body.

Plato taught that the soul has three principles of action, or three groups of functions. The lowest group of functions comprises sensations and appetencies or sensual desires. The intermediary group of functions is that which is guided by opinion or belief (*doxa*) concerning what is beautiful and good; it inspires spirited and courageous behaviour in the overcoming of obstacles. It is prone to error, however, and must be controlled by the superior soul (cf. *Timaeus* and *Phaedo*). The highest group of functions of the soul is the immortal group (*nous*). This group is found in the rational and volitional part (*to logistikon*) of the soul which is associated with the head. In this highest group of functions we find wisdom, scientific knowledge and human will (*boulē*). These higher functions are simple and immortal. The lower functions or principles of action are mortal and perishable.

The immortal soul (*to logistikon*) seems to go through an eternal cycle of incarnation, death and successive reincarnations. The quality of life of each reincarnation depends on the quality of ethical conduct in the previous state of incarnation. The soul itself is a spiritual principle which participates in the Form of life. There is no intrinsic composition within the soul and so it is not subject to any dissolution of composition. It is simple, spiritual, god-like, immortal, uncreated, indestructible and unchanging in its nature (cf. *Gorgias, Phaedo, Phaedrus* and the *Republic*).

There can be conflict within the soul between its 'spirited' principle of action and the soul's lower 'appetitive' functions. The immortal group of functions (*to logistikon*) must rule, like a charioteer, over the two lower groups, which are like two chariot-horses. The lower groups, like horses, must be controlled and kept in line so that they will work together (cf. *Phaedrus*). The quality of one's life in the next life will depend largely on the quality of one's ethical control and conduct in this life.

What Plato says concerning reincarnation and the soul's escape from the cycle of reincarnations is presented in his myths and allegories. One may well wonder whether Plato meant every detail of these pictorial teaching aids to be taken literally and seriously. The central emphasis is on the soul's survival in a state of life the quality of which will depend on one's present pattern of behaviour. The emphasis and the interest throughout this whole treatment is seen, then, to be ethical primarily, and psychological secondarily.

3. Moral theory. Plato accepted Socrates' moral theory. Thus, all men desire only what is good. No man desires to do wrong; and if a man actually does wrong then he does so unwillingly. All men desire to bring about what is good; that is, they desire virtue. Virtue is entirely dependent on knowledge of what is good. Each particular virtue aims at what is good in particular circumstances. And since all virtues depend on knowledge of what is good, then all virtues are ultimately one. Plato accepted this moral theory, but he was aware that the Socratic theory raised a number of difficulties and problems. He dealt with several of these problems in *Protagoras, Gorgias*, the *Republic, Theaetetus* and *Philebus*. In doing so he developed and improved the Socratic moral theory.

Protagoras is one of the early dialogues. It raises the problem as to whether or not goodness can be taught; and it concludes that virtue is knowledge and can be taught. In the course of the dialogue a question arises concerning whether or not the wise man is the good man. Is knowledge identical with goodness, that is, with justice or right-eousness? It is argued that ordinary men believe that one always acts so as to increase the ratio of pleasure over pain for oneself. But men also say that sometimes they are 'overcome by pleasure' and that they do not do the good that they should. Now, if men always seek their own pleasure, and if whatever is good is also pleasant, then, to be 'overcome by pleasure' and 'not do the good they should' can only mean that they have chosen a lesser instead of a greater ratio of pleasure over pain. To act at a time when one is 'overcome by pleasure' implies that one has acted out of ignorance (at the time) of what the good is. The agent has chosen not a long-term pleasure but a short-term pleasure. He has failed to estimate the future conse-quences or returns properly. To make a proper estimation of the long-term consequences of one's acts is a matter of knowledge. It is for this reason then that the wise man is the good man.

Plato, like Socrates before him, sought in philosophy the secret of man's happiness. What is the highest good for man? Is happiness to be found in pleasure or in wisdom, or in a mixture of both? This question provides the central theme in the *Philebus* dialogue. Pleasure alone, in a creature that has neither mind nor memory nor knowledge nor anticipation, has little value. A pleasurable life without knowledge would be reduced to the kind of existence that an oyster has. Alternatively, a life of wisdom without pleasure would be an unsatisfactory life.

Thus a 'mixed' life of both pleasure and wisdom is a superior way of life; it is the good life, the happy life. But which of these two elements, pleasure or wisdom, is primary in rendering the mixed life good? The answer to this question as it emerges from the dialogue is that wisdom contributes more to the good life than pleasure does, for, by wisdom, order and harmony are achieved; and order and harmony are the essential features of the good.

True happiness, *eudaimonia*, or the good life, can be found only where there is measure and proportion in man's life. The highest good (*summum bonum*) for man consists in the harmonious well-being of his whole personality. This harmonious well-being can be attained and retained only in the life of the temperate man. The happy life is one in which intellectual activity and pleasant satisfaction are intermingled together in due proportion. The good life is the temperate, beautifully human life. The archetypal pattern of man's happiness is divine happiness. Happiness of this kind can be attained only by the pursuit of virtue. The truly virtuous man, then, is the temperate and prudent man; and the temperate man is truly good and happy. Man must become 'like the divine' so far as he can; he must 'become righteous' with the help of wisdom (*Theaetetus* 176; *Republic* 613). Wisdom unites man to the immutable forms. It unites him particularly to the form of the Good which is the compound of all the forms. And true happiness is to be found in the unending enjoyment of the Good.

4. Plato's corporate theory of the state. Man, according to Plato, is essentially social, and he can find true happiness only in society. This conviction leads Plato to try to discover the nature of the Ideal State. The philosopher-statesman should know what the state ought to be if he wishes to lead his society towards what society ought to be.

The ideal state must obviously be the 'just' state, the state that exhibits justice. This is the theme of the *Republic*. In this dialogue, Thrasymachus points out that society actually 'honours' corrupt men of power who dissolve contracts with impunity and who never pay taxes.

Socrates asserts that Thrasymachus is actually challenging the whole conduct of living.

He points out that any art, whether it be that of medicine, piloting a ship, or governing, is practised for the sake of those (patients, passengers or the governed) who are to receive its benefits. The art is not practised for the sake of its practitioner. The 'just' practitioner of an art rules both himself and others. The unjust, intemperate man rules neither himself nor others.

Men are not self-sufficient. They cannot individually supply themselves with all the necessities of life. They are social. They pool their resources. They specialize as weavers, traders, tutors, musicians and so forth. In this way, through their services to others, they provide food, shelter, and clothing for themselves. On this basis, the city-state can expand and flourish. This gives rise to growing expectations and to luxurious wants. The state expands its army to protect its expanding interests. Success in warfare leads to an accumulation of booty. The trained soldiers of the state are required then to be like watchdogs, gentle to the citizens and fierce towards all enemies. The state needs also rulers or guardians. These are to be carefully selected and specially trained.

The guardians of the state should censor literature, such as that of Hesiod and Homer, which portrays the gods and heroes as deceitful, lustful, brutal, petty and venal. These degrading tales are responsible to some degree for the decline of morality in the city-state.

The guardians will find it necessary to persuade and convince the citizens that they must be loyal to, and not overstep, their position and their duties within the social structures of the state. They will instruct the citizens that men have been moulded by the gods to be either natural rulers (guardians), or auxiliaries to the rulers (soldiers), or artisans. Men differ naturally, just as gold, silver and bronze differ by nature. Those who are notably wise are marked for leadership; those who are courageous and spirited will be soldiers; and those who are not endowed with these virtues are naturally selected to be the artisans of the city-state. Each class does the task for which it is best suited. In this way justice and temperance will be attained in the state.

If the ideal state is to be established in any place it can be achieved in 'three waves'. These are discussed in Book V of the *Republic*. In the first wave, the rulers, men and women, are to be selected from among those who show the proper aptitudes. In the second wave, communal life, in which spouses and children will be held in common, must be shared by the ruling class. In this way the class of rulers and guardians will become a veritable brotherhood. In the third wave the ideal to be striven for is that philosophers be the kings, or the kings be philosophers. Political power and intellectual wisdom combine. Justice can then prevail. This is the ideal. It is unlikely to be realized in detail in any existing city-state. But if, as a minimum, power can be vested in even any one philosopher-king, then an approach towards the partial establishment of the ideal state will become possible.

Plato states that a study of history reveals, in practice, that there are periods when a state of justice is temporarily established in the state only to be followed later by a decline in the practice of justice. The perfect state, that is, the aristocratic state, can turn into a timocracy when there arise property qualifications for office holders. Timocracy turns into plutocracy when only a few wealthy property holders command political office. The wealthy reduce the citizenry to a status close to slavery. When the citizens finally revolt and expel the rich, the multitude establishes democracy. Demogogues arise who know how to appeal cunningly to the passions of the mutinous multitude and how to win popularity. The leading 'champion of the people' gradually assumes power until finally he can throw away his pretence and establish despotic, tyrannic power-control. The state then becomes the worst and most unhappy of all states. The tyrant is controlled by his appetites. He is master of nothing and is the most miserable of men. He lives in fear and pain.

The *Statesman* dialogue is likewise an essay in political philosophy. The problem confronting the Athenian Stranger (Plato perhaps) and Socrates is how one should define the ideal statesman. Statesmanship is an art. It is in a certain sense, in fact, the art of all arts. Special training is required for the art of governing just as it is required for the art of navigation or piloting. The statesman or king is a member of the class of producers who direct human action. He initiates directives which unify and shepherd the citizenry. The true statesman, as opposed to the tyrant, has his 'tending' freely accepted by the free herd or groups; he is accepted willingly by the subjects.

There are three major types of states. In a monarchical state there is rule by one. This may be exemplified by a constitutional monarch, or alternatively by a tyrant. In the oligarchic state a few wield power, as, for example, in an 'aristocracy' where the best citizens rule, or alternatively in a 'plutocracy' where only the wealthy rule. In the democratic state, there is weak government by the many, as, for example, when the majority controls power either by consent or by force. It is the lowest form of lawful government and it is the best form of all lawless governments. It is weak government, unable to do any great good, just as it is unable to do any great evil. However, the art of statesmanship does not depend essentially on the kind of state to be governed. A gifted statesman can govern wisely in any form of government. Laws are certainly important, but the ruler is more important than the laws. In many cases the wise ruler must be a good judge of cases in which the laws do not apply. The statesman, like a royal weaver, must develop the best out of the conflicting natures of his subjects. He must use good judgement in deciding whether the generals are to fight or whether friendly settlement is possible. He frames the laws which the honest judges can interpret and apply in the courts. In this way wise statesmanship is the art of arts just as the good is the form of forms.

The *Laws* is probably Plato's last dialogue and its concern is with the rule of law. The Athenian Stranger questions Megillus about the adequacy of the Spartan programme in training the young to be courageous, without preparing them for resisting flattery and improper pleasures. The form of character-training in Sparta is based on prohibition rather than on the virtue of temperance.

Ancient society began on a simple, pastoral level. Man merely followed the customs of the 'olden days'. Laws were initiated later when broader communities merged together and sought to attain a fixed uniformity of custom. Some societies failed, either because ignorant lack of wisdom triumphed over wisdom, or because intemperate licence defeated temperance in freedom. Other communities in history, however, have been successful. Some combined democracy with constitutional monarchy. They became well-governed states, characterized by friendship, wisdom and freedom.

Legislation should be designed to assure freedom, promote harmony and foster understanding within the framework of a sanctioned constitution. Any state where the laws are above the transient rulers enjoys the possibility of salvation, and among rulers the best ruler is the one who can enforce the (constitutional) laws by persuasion and command.

Owners of private property should be taught that they owe the stability of their possession to the state, and that basically all property belongs to the whole citizenry. The laws of the state should allow censorship of disturbing and improper kinds of music, dancing, poetry, eulogies and drama. Where licence in these areas becomes excessive and relativity of etiquette and morality is allowed to take over, there reverence is lost and authority is ignored. Soon, both rulers and laws are ignored and disobeyed.

Legislation must make provision for the punishment of criminals. Punishment is to be regarded as a form of rehabilitation. It is designed to cure or to improve the criminal, since no man does wrong knowingly.

Plato sought to discover the basic principles which lie at the foundations of political society. He saw the role of the political community as one which rendered possible and promoted the temporal welfare and the good life of man. Society is necessary for man if man is to reach his goal, which is happiness. Society exists, then, by right of nature. (It does not depend, for example, on some artificial social contract.) It was on these foundations that Plato built his philosophical theory of the state.

Plato thought of the state in terms of the small Greek city-state. In the *Laws* he speaks of the state as one in which there are about 5,000 families or houses. Nevertheless his treatment of the nature of the ideal state in general is one which applies to all political societies as such, and not merely to the small, ancient city-state. In the ideal *polis* or state, each citizen is called upon to play his own personal and significant role in shouldering his share of the burden of community responsibility. Each is called upon to be politically active. He must be politically conscious of his duties, rights and responsibilities within the political community which is his bigger self. Aristotle and Aquinas based their philosophical theory of the state on similar foundations.

However, in his deductions of the practical implications of his social theory Plato can justifiably be regarded as having overemphasized the importance of the collective social concern of the corporate state (the 'bigger self') at the expense of the dignity and freedom of the individual person. He advocates, for instance, that the marriages of the (military) auxiliaries and guardians should be entirely under the control of the magistrates; they should marry the women prescribed for them, so that the best possible offspring can be obtained for the good of the state. He tends to emphasize the 'public good', the rights of the collectivity or state, rather than the human rights of the human being. In the political thought of Aquinas a synthesis of these various rights, held in delicate balance, is achieved; the elements of merit in the corporate theory of the state are combined with the elements of merit in the later, liberal, *laissez-faire* idea of the state and the rights of the individual. In the political thought of Plato, however, a disproportionate emphasis is placed upon the corporate aspect of political society, so that personal human rights are overlooked and neglected. There is little consciousness in practice of the fact that the state is for man, not man for the state.

5. Influence. The whole corpus of Plato's writings proved to be epoch-making in the history of philosophy. Plato's thought had a profound effect on several generations of philosophers who succeeded him and continued to study him.

The disciples of Plato continued to teach various aspects of Platonic thought in the Academy until the closure of the Academy by the emperor Justinian in the year A.D. 529. After Plato's death, his disciples and associates in the old Academy taught the philosophy of their master. They emphasized particularly the Pythagorean elements of Platonism. Speusippus and Xenocrates simplified Platonic thought by equating the forms with *ta mathēmatika* and by their doctrine that all reality consists in mathematical numbers.

Aristotle himself expressed his profound respect for Plato as a human being and as an outstanding thinker, even though, on several issues, he found it necessary to disagree with the thought of his teacher and mentor.

Plotinus and the Neo-Platonists found in Plato almost all the basic material they needed to make a new synthesis of philosophic thought based on the descent and ascent of all things from and to the eternal One. Later, through the medium of Neo-Platonism, Plato's thought inspired Augustine and the great Augustinian current of philosophy in medieval times. Plato was the father or the original inspiration of 'spiritualist' forms of philosophy and of different forms of objective idealism. He raised philosophic thought to summits that had hitherto been unsuspected. He became widely regarded as the progenitor and founder of natural theology. His writings have inspired a multitude of religious, idealistic, ethical, political, logical, epistemological and metaphysical thinkers down through the ages and into our own times.

5 Aristotle (I)

1. Life and writings   2. Formal logic   3. Philosophy of
nature   4. Psychology

1. Life and writings. *Aristotle* was born in 384 B.C. at Stagira
in Macedonia in northern Greece. His father Nicomachus was a privy
councillor and physician at the king's court. When Aristotle was
eighteen he became a member of Plato's Academy, where he studied
for eighteen years until Plato's death in 347 B.C. He then spent three
years at Assos and two years at Mitylene teaching and studying
biology and philosophy. At Assos he married Pythias, the niece of
Hermeias, the governor. Subsequently, for a period of three or four
years, he became the tutor of the young prince Alexander (the Great)
of Macedonia. In 335 he went to Athens and set up a school of
philosophy at the Lyceum or the Peripatos. The members of the
school were known as the *peripatetikoi* because of their covered
ambulatory (*peripatos*) in the Lyceum. Aristotle taught there for
twelve years. In 323, after the death of Alexander the Great, Aristotle
was indicted in Athens for 'impiety'. He placed the Lyceum in the
care of his pupil Theophrastus, withdrew from Athens and went to
his mother's estate at Chalcis, where he died in the following year at
the age of 62.

Aristotle's early writings, during the years he spent at the
Academy, were relatively close in content and general form to the
writings of Plato, his teacher and friend. The lost *Eudemus* (on the
soul) and *Protrepticus* (on the joy of active reasoning) and the early
parts of Aristotle's extant *Physics, De Anima,* and logical works were
probably composed in Athens while Plato was still alive.

After Plato's death, Speusippus became head of the Academy.
Special emphasis was given to the mathematical and Pythagorean
aspects of Platonic thought. Aristotle's writings now became more
independent and critical of the teachings of the Athenian Academy.
In the lost dialogue *On Philosophy*, Aristotle criticized the Platonic
theory of forms as numbers. The first draft of the *Metaphysics* is
thought to have contained an attack on the doctrines of Speusippus.
The original *Politics* criticized utopian theories of the ideal State.

Aristotle's finest work dates from the days when he was active in
teaching and research work in the Lyceum (335-323 B.C.). Different
lectures given by Aristotle were collected together, probably in many

instances by Aristotle's disciples and collaborators, and then given classificatory titles. Among the most important of these compilations there survive: (1) the *Organon* or *Logical Works*: the *Categories, On Interpretation,* the *Prior Analytics,* the *Posterior Analytics* and the *Topics*; (2) the *Physics, On Generation and Corruption, Meteorology, On the Heavens, De Anima* or *On the Soul,* books on natural history and the generation of animals, and the *Parva Naturalia*; (3) the *Nicomachean Ethics,* the *Magna Moralia,* the *Eudemian Ethics,* the *Politics* and the *Poetics* (parts of which have been lost); and (4) the twelve books of different lectures or sections of *Metaphysics.*

The general style and outlook of these pedagogical lecture notes differ noticeably from the literary style and inspirational perspective of the Platonic dialogues. Plato's writings are suffused with poetic imagery, myth and literary grace. Aristotle, too, wrote dialogues of this genre, which were praised by Cicero for 'the sweeping force and the fascinating grace of his [Aristotle's] style'. But these Aristotelian dialogues are no longer extant. The compiled lecture notes, on the other hand, eschew imagery, myth and stylistic embellishment. Terms are used with utmost precision. Shades of meaning are delicately distinguished. The manner of presentation is pedagogical, didactic and demonstrative. The approach is empirical and carefully founded on physical facts, and the method is both inductive and deductive. The notes are concise and 'scientific'. The overall aim is to produce a vast body of human knowledge synthesized in terms of the different categories of intelligible being. The imposing structure reveals a philosophy of Nature and Reality which is firmly based in the world of factual research, observation and experience.

2. Formal logic. Logic as a science was founded by Aristotle. He is the 'Father of Logic' (in the historic sense of the word 'logic'), though he himself called it the science of 'analytics'. The six treatises in which his logical works are presented were given the title of *Organon* ('instrument') by one of his ancient commentators. These treatises are: the *Categories,* which treats of terms; *On Interpretation,* which treats of propositions; the *Prior Analytics,* which treats of syllogisms; the *Posterior Analytics,* which treats of problems of inference; the *Topics,* which treats of dialectical arguments; and the *Sophistical Refutations,* which treats of fallacious arguments.

The *Categories* presents ten ultimate genera or classes of predicates which people use in everyday speech. They are listed as: substance, quality, quantity, relation, action, affection (or passion), place, time, position and state (or endowments). Among those, substance or reality is presupposed by the remaining nine which are properties or characteristics of substances. These categories or predicaments are a classification of predicates but they represent the real modes of being in the world of reality outside the mind. They are ontological as well as logical categories.

Realities are divisible into primary and secondary realities. A primary reality, such as a living individual man or an individual horse, is neither 'predicable of' nor 'present in' a subject. (One cannot use '*this* individual' as a predicate 'P' present within or predicable of a subject 'S'.) Secondary realities (such as the species of 'man' or of 'horse') are the species of which the primary realities are members. Primary realities or individuals come first; they are the 'entities which underlie and are the subjects of' everything else. Individuals come first; what is said (predicated) of them comes second.

Aristotle expounded his formal logic as a science of deductive proof in the *Prior Analytics*. He studied in special detail the assertoric syllogism. He invented certain concepts and techniques which made further development of formal logic possible. Thus, he used letters of the alphabet (A,B,C...) to represent variables in stating his syllogistic forms of implication. For example, 'If A is present in all B, and if B is predicable of all C, then A is present in all C', or, more simply, 'If all B is A, and all C is B, then all C is A'. (If all men are mortal, and all Greeks are men, then all Greeks are mortal; in this process one passes from a consideration of the intension to a consideration of the extension of the middle term.) This introduction of variables into logic made it possible to develop logic into a science with general laws instead of a mere collection of different examples.

The Aristotelian syllogism has a major premiss, a minor premiss and a conclusion that follows necessarily from the premisses. It has three and only three terms (A, B and C). 'I call that term the major in which the middle term (B) is contained and that term the minor which comes under the middle' (*Prior Analytics* 26a21). If one focuses one's attention, as Aristotle does, on subject-predicate sentences 'affirming or denying one thing of another', then four types of premisses are possible, namely, universal affirmative, universal negative, particular affirmative and particular negative: either 'All S is P', or 'No S is P', or 'Some S is P', or 'Some S is not P'.

There are four possible arrangements of 'figures' or schemata which emerge from the order in which the terms (A,B,C; or S,M,P) may occur. (1) If the middle term (M) is predicated of one extreme (S) while the other extreme (P) is predicated of the middle term, then the syllogism is a syllogism in the first figure. The first figure is represented by the letters PMS. This figure is assumed as basic or axiomatic. The other figures can be regarded as theorems which are derived from the first figure and which can be reduced to it. (2) If the middle term is predicated of both major and minor, the syllogism (MPS) is in the second figure. (3) If the major and the minor are both predicated of the middle, then the syllogism (PSM) is in the third figure. The fourth figure ('If P is M and M is S, then S is P') is seen as a variation of the first figure (PMS).

Aristotle then established that there are fourteen valid forms (or 'moods') of the first three figures and a further five valid forms in the fourth figure. (In the thirteenth century, William of Shyreswood and Petrus Hispanus gave individual names to each of these nineteen moods: Barbara, Celarent, Darii, Ferio, and so forth. A fuller treatment of these traditional moods may be found in any textbook of logic.) Each of these is established as valid, one by one, in the first book of the *Prior Analytics*. In this way Aristotle systematized a fundamentally important part of the science of logic.

Aristotle did not investigate the logic of propositions, and his system of logic is incomplete by modern standards. The Stoics, the medieval logicians, and logicians of the nineteenth century made significant further discoveries in the science of logic, but all of these logicians continued to revere Aristotle as the 'Father' of the science.

3. Philosophy of nature. The *Physics* is the name given to eight separate Aristotelian treatises or lectures on Nature (Greek *physis*). The science of physics is understood as the philosophy of nature or natural philosophy. It studies 'those realities that exist by nature' such as 'animals, plants and simple bodies like earth, fire, air and water'. Each of these realities has in itself a source of motion and rest; and nature is the principle and cause of this motion and rest (cf. *Physics* II, 1).

For Aristotle, the first unmoved (undeveloping) mover, namely God, *is* his act, whereas the world must develop its act through motion. Physics studies the problems and principles of realities which contain within themselves a principle of motion. Motion, then, is the proper subject-matter of physics.

Motion (*kinēsis*) or process 'is thought to be a sort of activity, but incomplete'. 'It cannot be classed simply as a potentiality or as an activity' (*Physics* III, 2, 201b). It is an incomplete activity in the sense that it is not finished at once. Thus, for example, a wound in the process of healing has not yet attained its end state of being completely healed. Healing, learning, and building are processes or actions whose completed ends are not present in the act. The entity has not been fully realized in the respect in which it is potential. Motion or change is the activity of what is in power. It is the activity of the potential as potential. 'Motion is the possession of the end of what is in power as such' (*Physics* III, 2, 201b).

Aristotle therefore explains motion, or coming-into-being, in terms of activity and power, or act and potency. In speaking of potency, he used the word *dynamis* ('power', 'faculty', 'ability'); this term was a common term in current use. However, in speaking of its correlative, 'act', Aristotle coined two new words, *energeia* and *entelecheia*, which he then used as interchangeable synonyms. The word *energeia* means 'an internal doing' or 'inner activity'; and the word *entelecheia* means 'to be ended' 'to be fulfilled' or 'complete', or 'possessing its end within itself'. The *entelecheia* is the primary act, the basic present *perfection* going on in being within the individual being.

In several passages of the *Physics, Generation and Corruption*, and the *Metaphysics*, Aristotle shows his keen interest in the constant developing and changing of all natural things. He thinks of all living things, such as seeds, as both 'buildable' and as being now 'abuilding', becoming, in motion, evolving. It is in this sense that he understands living *motion*, the 'becoming' of the ongoing being of each living thing.

'Motion (*kinēsis*) is the possession of the end (*entelecheia*) of what is in power (*dynamis*) as such... (Thus) when the buildable has its end in itself (*entelecheia*) it is being built, and this is construction.... Each thing can be active at some times and not at others, such as the buildable—and the activity (*energeia*) of the buildable as buildable is construction.... Construction is the activity (*energeia*); and construction is a kind of process' (*Physics* III, 1, 201a). In this passage, as also in several other similar passages, Aristotle used the term for 'inner possession of the end' as completely interchangeable with the term 'inward activity'. In his later writings, Aristotle made less and less use of the term 'inner possession of the end' and used the term *energeia* ('inward activity') more frequently instead. This latter term, *energeia* or activity, connotes in his writings the first primary 'activity' of any entity, that is, the (energetic) activity of going on in being, or existing. In this sense the process of healing, for example, is the ongoing 'activity' of the inner power of healing as a real power. It is the ongoing activity (*energeia*) of a power (*dynamis*). When a power of this kind exists merely in power alone, then there is no motion because there is no activity of the power as a power.

The student who approaches for the first time Aristotle's under-standing of 'inner activity' or *energeia* may find it helpful to attain an experiential knowledge of *energeia* in the following way. If one closes one's eyes, for example, one can concentrate with ease on one's personal inner experience of being alive. 'I experience myself as living now; and I am going on *living* now, and now, and now.' Similarly, one experiences one's own *existing* now and now. Again, one experiences oneself in the same way as *'be-ing'* in each and every now. The reality experienced in living or existing or being is one and the same reality. It is the inner reality of my being or my going on in being now. This inner activity of going on in being is also going on within every blade of grass, every existing thing. Aristotle speaks of it as the being's *energeia*, or primary inner 'working', or, in other words, its primary activity of going on in being in every moment of its existing. Furthermore, every developing being, going on in being, is also coming into being, becoming. Each is be-ing, and in a state of becoming. In brief, each is a developing, 'evolving' being, a being in becoming. Each living thing, for example, is always becoming other, even though it is not becoming another. In nature, in the universe, every ongoing being is a being-in-becoming.

All natural beings are in motion (evolving). They have their own natural activity originating from a internal principle of activity. They are beings which are in motion, coming to be and passing away. Motion in its general sense of 'be-coming' is of two kinds, a coming into being or a passing out of being. Motion in its narrower sense of change or transition is of three kinds: qualitative change, quantitative change, and locomotion.

Coming into being, and change, can also be explained in terms of the material cause or the 'matter', and the formal cause, or the 'form' of being of the natural reality. The material being of the entity and the formal being of the entity (e.g. an animal, or plant, or simple natural entity) are merely two different aspects of the same entity. The material aspect is the aspect of the power or capacity (*dynamis*), whereas the form of being is the actual activity of being (*energeia*). Matter is 'power'; form is the 'activity' of this power. Potentiality means having its end outside itself; activity means having its end ongoing within itself. Everything becomes what it is from what it used to be potentially.

Aristotle's theory of matter and form, traditionally known as the hylomorphic theory, was destined to play an important role in the subsequent thought of several schools of philosophy. The theory was interpreted in various ways, and this makes it all the more important to understand Aristotle's own presentations of the theory. Aristotle's treatment of these principles of being has, invariably, metaphysical overtones. Matter and form are regarded as intrinsic constitutive principles of material being, while efficient and final causes are extrinsic causes of purely material things. The union of prime matter and the essential nature, or form, is seen as a union of a radical 'capacity of becoming' (*dynamis*) and a radical, limited 'act of ongoing being' (*energeia*), a being 'such', going on within the embodied being. Thus, for example, Aristotle regarded the limited, specific 'act of living', going on within each living being, as the living being's primary 'act of being' now emerging from the primary (primeval) capacities of a particular kind of living matter which is 'abuilding', coming into being, growing, evolving, changing, becoming other, but abiding and not becoming another.

Aristotle's word for 'matter' (Greek *hylē*) literally means wood or timber as raw material. Matter is the raw material empowering a specific form of activity. It is the underlying (*hypokeimenon*) power that persists through change in things that have a principle of movement in themselves (*Physics* II, 1). The form of being is that ongoing activity of being which is empowered by the potentiality of the being.

Physical (natural) beings are therefore regarded as ongoing activities which are in a state of becoming. They are happenings and occurrings rather than inert material 'objects'. They are ongoing beings that are also changeable; they are beings-in-becoming. They are beings that can become what they are not. The ongoing being of any particular entity is the activity of certain powers of that entity, and the entity has still further (latent) powers for further activation. This applies to every being other than the undeveloping first 'mover' (or bringer-into-being). Physical reality is therefore not made of elemental inert building blocks; it is made of ongoing beings which are in a state of becoming.

According to Aristotle, if we wish to understand any particular entity and if we wish to understand how it has come to be what it is, then we must try to discover the causes which have made it to be what it is. And there are four main types of causes.

The *material* cause or raw material (*hylē*) of any particular being is the power (*dynamis*) within the physical entity empowering its primary activity of being. The *formal* cause is the activity of being (*energeia*) which is energetically going on within the particular reality or entity. The *efficient* cause is the agent that initiates a transition from an inner activity of one kind to a new and changed activity of another kind; thus, certain juices added to wine will change the wine into vinegar. The *final* cause is the goal-directed cause of a natural being's development. 'When a thing is produced by nature, the earlier stages in every case lead up to the final development... . The operation is directed by a purpose... . Hence, if it is by nature and also for a purpose that the swallow makes her nest, and that plants make leaves for the sake of the fruit,... it is clear that causality is at work in things that come about or exist in the course of nature... . That nature is a cause, then, and a goal-directed cause, is above dispute' (*Physics* II, 8, 198b-199b). It is for this reason that nature is amenable to intelligence, and that a knowledge of nature ('Physics') is possible.

In Book III, nature is seen as a sensible magnitude. It is a numerable quantity. It is not actually infinite. An infinite body, bounded by its own surface, is impossible. Like time and the number of time, nature is in a process of coming to be. It is an infinite which is potential, never actual.

Is the world in any *place*? The place of a thing is separable from the thing itself. It differs from the thing's form or shape. Place is the innermost motionless boundary of the surrounding containing body. The universe is not contained within any containing body. Thus, it is not in 'place'.

What is *time*? It is not movement. Yet it is not independent of movement. It is the numerable or countable aspect of change or movement. Time is the number of motion in respect to before and after. The movement of the sun is uniform. It is a natural medium for enumerating time. Time will exist so long as anything in motion exists. Things which change and become are in time. Things which always are cannot be in time.

In Book VII of the *Physics* we have a presentation of Aristotle's thought on the existence of an 'unmoved' (undeveloping) mover of all that is in motion. Anything which did not exist and yet actually came to be could not have brought itself to be (since it did not exist). It must have been brought to be by another. A series of beings every member of which was brought into being is neither self-sufficient nor self-explanatory. Each and all are dependent for their very being on something outside themselves. Each and all can be explained only in terms of a mover (that is, a bringer into being) which does not itself belong to the series of movers.

This argument for the existence of an unmoved mover is an argument which is grounded on the very nature of motion (or coming-into-being) itself. The whole universe and each thing within it is in *motion*. The ultimate source of motion, bringing all into being, must (itself) be in being and unmoved; it is an unmoved mover, a first principle of motion. A first unmoved mover of this kind cannot have any magnitude. It is indivisible and without parts.

Locomotion is evident in the universe. Locomotion is either rotary or rectilinear or a combination of the two. Aristotle thought that there cannot be a continuous rectilinear motion that is eternal. Cosmic locomotion is eternal, and so this eternal locomotion of the universe must be a rotary locomotion.

According to Aristotle, all natural motion, including locomotion, is directed towards an end. There is an active tendency within the totality of nature to develop from a state of potentiality to a state of actuality. There is an inner tendency in nature for new actual *forms* of immanent activity to develop from, or be educed from, the potentiality of *matter*. There appear to be all-pervasive ends present everywhere in nature. Nature evolves and develops in a way which seems to indicate that there is teleological activity inherently at work within nature its very self. Aristotle accepts that this is so without delving further into the matter. He does not speak of any 'world-soul' nor of any consciously operating and organizing principle at work within nature in general. Again, he does not treat of the relation of nature to God. His teleological view seems to have its basis in the undeveloped implications of his general theory concerning the activity of the unmoved mover.

The collection of treatises called the *Physics* presents, then, an outline of Aristotle's philosophy of nature. In these works Aristotle focused his thought on several basic principles and fundamental concepts concerning physical nature. He attempted to enumerate and define these first principles and concepts. Down through the centuries these treatises on the philosophy of nature (or cosmology) have been regarded as classics because of their insights into issues which are fundamental for all physical enquiry.

4. Psychology. Aristotle's philosophical psychology is presented mainly in the three books *On the Soul* (usually known by the Latin title *De Anima*). In these works concerning living matter, Aristotle speaks of the *entelecheia* or the soul as the *energeia*, namely the ongoing activity of existing, the primary activity, of the correlative potency, the matter, or *dynamis*. Each living reality is an abiding activity of a potency, a power to change and be changed. Thus, being a living reality is being an abiding happening, actively, energetically *be-ing*. The soul, then, is that activity of existing, living, being, which is going on within every specimen of living matter. In brief, the soul is the *energeia*, the abiding activity of be-ing, occurring within each living reality.

Aristotle defines the soul as 'reality in the sense of the form of any natural body that has the power of life; and reality in this sense is in fact the inward possession of the end. The soul then is the (first) entelechy of a (natural) body of this kind.... The soul may be defined as the first entelechy (or inward activity) of a natural body potentially possessing life; and a body of this kind must in fact be such that it possesses organs' (II, 1, 412a). The soul is the energetic reality or inward activity of the living organism (cf. *Metaphysics* 1043a35). It is the form of being, or activity of being, in virtue of which individuality is directly attributed (II, 1, 412a6). The soul can therefore be said to be the principle of individuation. The *matter* of the composite being is potentiality and the *form* is inner activity (414a)... 'and since the composite is an animate thing, the body cannot be the activity of a soul, but rather the soul is the activity of some body... for the activity of each thing is naturally inherent in its potentiality, that is, in its own proper matter. From all of this it is clear that the soul is the activity or form (of being) of that (natural reality) which has the capacity of having a soul' (*De Anima* 414a).

Suppose, for example, that the eye, the organ of sight, were an independent organism: 'If the eye were an animal, its soul would be eyesight' (414a). Sight is the entelechy or inner end of the organ of sight. It is the first immanent activity of that potency. Similarly the soul is the first immanent activity of any natural being possessing the power of being alive. It is the immanent 'activity-of-being' empowered by its corresponding 'power-of-being'. Thus, a plant or an animal is not just an entity which performs certain activities. Rather, it is an activity, a living activity of a living power. Life, or, rather, living, is the activity of 'be-ing' of living things; and it is this primary activity of living which is the source and principle of other secondary activities of the living being.

Living plants have within themselves the powers of nourishment, growth and reproduction 'in order that, as far as their nature allows, they may partake in the eternal and divine. That is the goal towards which all things strive, and it is the purpose of all their natural activities' (II, 4). All things, plants included, strive towards fullness of being.

Living animals have the powers of nourishment, growth, reproduction, locomotion, sensation and desire. Man has all these powers and he is endowed furthermore with the power of thinking (*nous*), a power which is separable from the powers of the body and is immortal.

Thus one can speak of the vegetative soul of plants, the sensitive soul of animals and the rational soul of man.

In Book III of *De Anima* Aristotle treats of perception and thought. His thesis is that in the activity of sensing, as also in the activity of knowing, the activity of the perceived being's being perceived is one and the same activity even though there is a distinction between perceiving and the perceived. 'The activity of the sensible and that of the sense are one and the same, but the distinction between them remains' (425b).

Any sensible reality (*aistheton*) is itself a happening or an activity, empowered by its inner power to be what it is. It is a sensible reality capable of being sensed. It has within itself a power rendering it capable of being sensed. The activity of sensing is, at one and the same time, the activity of that power of being sensed and the activity of the power of sensing. Thus, the activity of perceiving is the activity of the perceived being's being perceived. The activity is just one activity 'excited' in the perceiver by the form of being of the perceivable being (II, 5, 417b). The activity of the sensible being excites the activity of seeing in the perceiver's power of sight and the activity of smelling in the power of smell, and other similar activities in the other sense powers of the perceiver.

Mind (*nous*) is 'that part of the soul with which it knows and thinks' (III, 4, 429a). Mind assimilates all things. It thinks all things. It is not mixed with the body and it has no organ. It is 'potentially identical with the objects of thought but is actually nothing, until it thinks' (430a). Knowledge is not what the mind builds up, or does; it is what the mind is. All beings are intelligible beings. Mind, or knowing, is conscious being being conscious of intelligible beings of various kinds. Various realities, each of them an 'activity' (of being), excite the power of the knower to know. Knowing is the activity of the conscious being's being conscious of the intelligible. It is an activity (*energeia*) of a power (*dynamis*); it is the activity of the power of the knower to know and of the intelligible to be known. It is the activity of intelligible being being understood. The power of the knower to know differs from the power of the intelligible reality to be understood, but the activity of the knower in knowing is one and the same as the activity of the intelligible reality's being known. The activity of knowing is the activity (*energeia*) of the intelligible.

Aristotle asserts that 'mind in the passive sense... becomes all things', but mind in the active sense (like light) 'makes all things'.

'Mind in this (active) sense is separable, impassive and unmixed (with body) since it is essentially an activity.' It is 'immortal and ever-lasting' (430a).

Aristotle's doctrine concerning the Active Intellect is not precise and clear. It has given rise to different interpretations. Some interpreters have identified Aristotle's Active Intellect with God, even though Aristotle says elsewhere that God knows only himself. Some say that, for Aristotle, the Active Intellect is particular in each individual man, though Aristotle asserts that in its separate existence it does not remember its previous activity. Other interpreters say that the Active Intellect is an essentially active principle which is identical in all men: it functions within men (like light), and it survives the deaths of individual men. The formulation of Aristotle's teachings as presented in *De Anima* concerning the immortality of man's active intellect leaves itself open therefore to different interpretations. 'When it (Mind, *Nous*) has been separated it is its true self and nothing more, and this alone is immortal and everlasting' (*De Anima* III, 5, 430a).

6 Aristotle (II)

1. The *Metaphysics*   2. Ethics   3. Politics   4. Aesthetics
5. Plato and Aristotle

1. The *Metaphysics*. The *Metaphysics* is a collection of lecture notes put together by Aristotle's students and then placed in the collection of his writings *after* (*meta*) the treatise on *Physics*. Metaphysics was thought of as coming after physics. It is the science of first principles or first causes; these principles provide the basis for the special sciences such as the science of natural philosophy, which studies the principles of natural movement alone.

Book Alpha (I) of the *Metaphysics* presents a brief review of the theories of the pre-Socratics and Plato; it gives a critical appraisal of the merits and demerits of these theories.

The book begins with the famous dictum: 'All men by nature desire to know'. Aristotle then goes on to say that there are different degrees of *knowledge*. There is the form of knowledge which men and animals acquire by experience. Then there are the arts, such as the art of medicine, in which the mind advances from a knowledge of particulars to a knowledge of universals and of the causes of things. This latter kind of knowledge is scientific knowledge. The sciences were invented in those places where men had leisure. 'Thus the mathematical sciences originated in the neighbourhood of Egypt, because there the priestly class were allowed leisure.'

The highest degree of knowledge, wisdom, aims at apprehending the ultimate causes of all things, the first principles of reality. This highest form of science, based on fewer and ultimate principles, is the most exact of the sciences and the hardest for man to grasp. Its subject is those things which are the most universal and furthest removed from the senses. Nevertheless it is the science which is the most instructive of all, and the most knowable of all, since it is the science of first principles and causes. This supreme science began in *wonder*, wonder 'about the changes of the moon and the sun, about the stars and the origin of the universe' (982b). It is a science which is divine; none is more excellent. It seeks to know the ultimate *causes* of all things.

'Now there are four recognized kinds of cause... one is the essence or essential nature (being such and such) of the thing... another is the matter or abiding substrate; the third is the source of motion; and the fourth is... the purpose or good' (983b). In other words, the *four causes* are: the formal cause, the material cause, the efficient cause and the final cause. The mind desires to know the truth about things, and it can discover this truth through a grasp of the causes of things. These causes are not indefinite or infinite in number; their number is limited to four.

Book Gamma (III) commences with the famous definition of metaphysics as the 'science which studies being *qua* being, and the properties inherent in it by virtue of its being itself'. It studies *being* generally *qua* being, and it seeks to discover the first principles and the most ultimate causes as elements or properties of beings in general or being as such. The philosopher must develop a grasp of the basic principles, such as the principle of non-contradiction, which lie behind all demonstration. The starting-point of all forms of demonstration cannot be a matter of demonstration; it must be certain basic axioms beyond proof yet accepted as true in themselves. This starting-point is to be found in the principles of being itself.

'Knowledge is principally concerned with that which is primary, i.e. that upon which all other things depend, and from which they get their names.' And it is being in the category of substance (i.e. reality) that is primary. Things are either substances (i.e. realities) or modifications or negations or privations or affections or qualities of substance. 'If, then, substance is primary, it is of substances that the philosopher must grasp the first principles and causes' (1003b).

Now, to be existent (being) and to be a unity are the same. Being and unity are one. Thus, for example, 'one man' and 'man', and 'existent man' and 'man', are the same thing; to say 'he is a man and an *existent* man' gives no fresh meaning (1003b). Unity, then, is an essential attribute of being. Unity, like being, is found in all the categories. Being and unity are not confined to any one category. They are not mere genera. Being and unity can be predicated of all categories, all genera, specific differences, existent things and all parts of existent things. (Later philosophers would call ideas of this kind transcendental ideas.)

Book Delta (IV) of the *Metaphysics* presents an analysis of various common meanings given to some important philosophic terms. It presents a list of several possible meanings of crucial terms such as being, substance, cause, nature, necessity, unity, potency, quality, relation, limit, privation, accident, genus and other key words for philosophy. Aristotle's definitions of these and other philosophical terms present us with an outline of his views on the world's basic structure.

The term 'being' has as many senses or meanings as there are ways of predication. Since some predicates indicate what a thing is, and others its quantity, quality, relation, activity or passivity, place, time, to each of these (categories) there corresponds a sense of 'being' (1017a).

'Substance' or reality or 'primary being' has a double meaning: it signifies the ultimate subject which cannot be further predicated of something else, e.g. any individual particular being; and it signifies the different sources of actual existence. The essence or essential nature of the composite, and the form or activity of the potency is of this kind (1017b and 1042a29).

Now, 'if there is some eternal, immovable and independent being' then the first science (metaphysics) will seek to know this being. 'For it is clear that if the divine belongs anywhere it belongs inherently to the theological (or divine) branch of philosophy, the supreme philosophy being the theory of the supreme kind of being' (1026a). However, Aristotle attends to the question of the existence and nature of an eternal unmovable first mover only at a later stage (Book XII, Lambda) of his *Metaphysics* (cf. below).

For a comprehensive understanding of the different basic tenets and facets of Aristotle's thought one must consult the books of the *Physics* as well as those of the *Metaphysics*. These treaties present his doctrines on change, act and potency, four causes, abstraction, essence or form, matter, individuation, immanent finality and God. We shall now deal briefly with each of these themes.

Motion (*kinēsis*) or becoming is an evident datum in the world around us. A small seed grows into a large tree. This involves a passage from a starting-point (a *terminus a quo*) to a finishing-point (a *terminus ad quem*). It involves a passage from a state of potentiality (*dynamis*) to a state of actuality (*energeia*). All the things of our experience are in a state of constant change; they are 'mobile' beings. They are capable of changing into innumerable other things. Each thing has a potency or power to change (in time) into almost anything else. From within its own potency to become other than it is now, new forms of being or 'activities' are educed. The entity becomes other than it was. Older forms of being pass away; yet the entity is not entirely annihilated. New forms of being are educed; yet the new reality is not a totally new creation. There is always a substrate of some kind which remains throughout the whole process of change. In the new, second subject or entity there still remains a primary something which has come down to this present subject from the many prior subjects from which it has evolved or emerged. This abiding 'matter' or power which still continues to be, despite the innumerable changes of the past, Aristotle calls primary power or primary matter. It is the abiding substratum of change. It is that which is in potentiality to the eduction of innumerable new forms of being or 'activities' in innumerable changes still possible in the future.

Book Theta (IX) of the *Metaphysics* presents Aristotle's mature thought on the doctrine of act and potency. He starts by saying 'let us now explain *dynamis* and *entelecheia*', or in other words, 'power' and 'fulfilment' or immanent possession of the end. From that point onwards he equates *entelecheia* with *energeia* (inner activity), and then proceeds to discuss *dynamis* (power) and *energeia* (activity) throughout the remainder of the book. He says: 'The word *energeia* (activity within) which is combined with *entelecheia* (inner fulfilment) has a meaning which is extended from its chief meaning of "work" to other uses; for activity (*energeia*) in the strict sense is to be understood as a "doing" or movement' (Book Theta, 1047a30-32). This inner activity is present within any thing when that thing is not what we call 'in power' (1048a32). Thus, seeing is the activity of the organ of sight, whereas closed eyes are merely 'in power' (1048b1); and living is the activity of any natural body possessing the power of being alive. 'Activity is related to potentiality in some cases in the way that movement (coming-to-be) is related to the power to become; and in other cases it is related as a reality (a substance) is related to its matter' (1048b8). In this latter case, we see that, for Aristotle, a reality or substance is fundamentally an activity. The individual form of being is the individual activity of being. Form is what matter (power) is energetically being.

It is the form of being, or in other words the nature or essence of a thing, that is knowable. Thus, we know, by abstraction, the 'humanness' of a human being. The potential or matter of the same being is unknowable. Matter is unknowable in itself. And since matter is unknowable, no composite individual is ever fully knowable (*Metaphysics* 1034a and 1039b).

The individual beings or substances of our experience are composite beings made of matter (*dynamis*) and form (*energeia*). They are individuals of a certain kind of specific essence. Each has within itself its own immanent form of being or immanent 'activity' or nature. The substantial form of the individual is the objective foundation of the subjective form or universal idea. The mind frees the substantial forms of things from the individuating conditions of matter and conceives these forms as universal ideas. The specific object of our intelligence is being.

Beings change. Older forms give way to newer forms. A lump of bronze is turned into a bronze sphere. An acorn turns into an oak. 'What can explain how what was potentially becomes actual except the effective agent?' (1045a30). An efficient cause, that is, an agent, external or internal, is required to explain the movement or process of change in which new forms of being are educed from the potentiality of matter. 'Any movement involves an immediate agent, a thing moved, a time of change, a starting-point and a culmination' (1067b7).

Aristotle speaks of the *final cause* as the 'wherefor' or the 'good' or the 'end of any generation or change' (983a32). A movement or action may be directed to an end outside itself and not yet present, as for example in the process of healing or building or dieting. Another movement or action may have its end inhering in itself, as in the action of seeing or thinking; thus, he who is knowing is in possession of knowledge (1048b25). 'Everything that is produced proceeds according to its principle, for its wherefor is its principle and at the same time its coming into being is directed by the end; hence the "activity" is the end, and it is thanks to it that a power is possessed; for animals do not see in order that they may have the power of sight, but they have the power of sight that they may see... . Hence, as teachers consider that they have attained their end when they have exhibited their students actually performing their learning, so it is with nature... . The work is the end; and the activity is the work. And so even the word "activity" is used in reference to action and points to "the internal possession of the end"' (1050a). Aristotle's emphasis is on immanent activity, internal finality. Beings strive towards fulfilment. Things strive to attain that perfection of development of which their natures are capable. This finality is present within their forms, their formal cause. The form of the seed tends towards the full actualization or realization of the final plant.

Aristotle does not list the 'exemplary cause' in his list of causes (for example, an architect's plan or idea provides a pattern or exemplar which may be listed as one of the 'causes' why the finished product assumes the form that it does). He identified it with the intrinsic formal element which constitutes the essence of things. He regarded the doctrine of exemplary causality as an aspect of the doctrine of the ideal forms of being. He was adamant, in his polemic against the Ideas, to make the world of 'forms' an integral part of the world of nature. Moreover, his views on the providence of the unmoved mover did not require any Platonic doctrine of exemplarism.

Plato had argued that his doctrine of *'ideas'* or *forms* of being explained how scientific knowledge of universal matters is possible. Aristotle argued against the Platonists that, while science is of the universal, nevertheless the universals do not subsist separately (*chōris*) or apart from individual things. The specific essence or substantial form of an individual thing is *abstracted from* the object by a process in which we come to know the nature of the individual object in a *universal* idea. The universal, then, is simply a mental transposition of the nature or form of the individual thing.

Aristotle presented several arguments and objections against the Platonic 'doctrine of Ideas' and the closely associated 'doctrine that numbers are themselves primary beings (which) explain all things'. 'How could the ideas, if they are the primary being of concrete things, be in isolation (*chōris*)?' he objected (1080a1-12). And again, 'what sort of number would man-himself or animal-itself or any other general form be?' (1081a9).

The Platonic doctrine of forms or Ideas postulates a purposeless doubling of visible realities, and these 'doubles' are useless for our knowledge of the visible universe, he asserts. The forms do not explain the notion of beings which are in a state of becoming, since these forms are motionless (cf. 990a-991a). The theory is both useless and impossible. It must be held to be 'impossible that a primary being (a substance) and that whose primary being it is, be dissociated'. 'To say that the ideas are patterns and that other things participate in them is to use empty words and poetical metaphors' (1079b25-38).

In these passages Aristotle uses the word 'separately' (*chōris*) or 'independently' in the sense of 'apart from' and 'in isolation'. Plato himself did not think of the forms of being as existing in isolation or apart from the world of the knower. For Plato the world of comprehensive human experience is a world of images, a world produced by the interaction of perceiver and perceived, knower and known. It is within this world that forms of being, kinds, or *eidē* are discovered. The philosopher then attempts to define them through patient and painstaking analysis.

Aristotle's emphasis and thought focuses on the immanent *substantial form* and the doctrine of abstraction. His standpoint is that of the anatomist and physiologist who is a philosophical psychologist. His interest is in the immanent substantial form, the 'first entelechy of the potentially alive' (*De Anima* 412b). From this viewpoint the doctrine of forms and numbers appeared to contribute nothing to our knowledge of the nature of organisms. In rejecting this doctrine, however, Aristotle rejected also exemplary causality in general. It was left then to later philosophers to develop the more comprehensive doctrine of the five causes.

Book XII (or Lambda) of the *Metaphysics* treats of *Divine Being*. 'Everything that changes is something that is changed by something into something. That by which it is changed is its first mover; what is changed is its material; and that into which it is changed is its form. Now there would be an infinite regress if when some brass becomes a sphere, not only that brass sphere, but also brass and spheres then came into being; therefore this coming into being must stop somewhere' (1070a). 'There must be a principle such that its very nature is to be in act' (1071b20). A primary being of this kind must be 'without material' (immaterial), eternal, changeless and ever actual. It is an unmoved mover, being eternal, primary and in act (1072a25). It is 'a necessary being' (1072b10), 'purely actual', 'always at its best' and 'knowing what is inherently best' (1072b). 'It cannot have magnitude, but is without parts and indivisible' (1073a). In summary, 'we maintain, therefore, that the divine (*ho theos*) is the eternal best living being, so that the divine is life unending, continuous and eternal' (1072b30).

Chapter 8 of Book Lambda (XII) of the *Metaphysics* seems strangely out of tune with previous and subsequent chapters. Some commentators regard it as a later additon to the original *Metaphysics*. In chapter 8, Aristotle speaks of those traditions 'in mythical form' handed down by 'our ancestors and forerunners' about the 47 or 55 celestial bodies whose movements are induced by 'gods in the form of men or animals' (1074b6). Each of these is a primary being who is an unmoved (or undeveloping) mover. However, 'it is evident... that one of them is first and another is second according to the order of the stellar movements' (1073b). This 'unmoved first mover is one in both definition and number' (1073b39).

The unmoved first mover 'knows what is most divine and most honourable' (1074b26). The '*divine mind* knows itself, since it is the supreme excellence; and its thinking is a thinking on thinking (*noēsis noēseōs*)' (1074b35). God knows his own thought, and his thought is about thought itself. It would seem to be implied that this Aristotelian 'God' knows little about the physical world or the human beings who dwell in it. He is not a provident, loving God but a supreme Thinker who thinks about Thought itself. 'The first mover's living activity (*energeia*) is enjoyable, even as we too, most enjoy being awake, conscious, and thinking.... . This knowing, by its very nature, concerns what is inherently best.... . (His) intellect finds its fulfilment in being aware of the intelligible... or essential being.... . It is the activity of intellectual vision that is most pleasant and best.... . It is in this better state that the divine has its being and its life at its eternal best. We maintain, therefore, that the divine is the eternal best living being, so that the divine is life unending, continuous and eternal' (1072b13-30). Aristotle's God is, in brief, conscious Being being conscious.

It is this 'first being or first principle' that 'induces the first eternal and single movement' (1073a25). The *unmoved first mover* induces the first eternal movement from potency towards actuality. The unmoved mover is the final cause, that is, the cause of causes, the good or the 'wherefor' of this ongoing movement, or coming-to-be, which is happening in the universe. The first mover is the 'end' or 'good' of generation and change. 'Everything that is produced proceeds according to its principle, for its wherefor is its principle, and at the same time its coming into being is directed by the end' (1050a7-9).

In this way, God, who is pure act, fullness of being, the object of desire, moves the universe not as an efficient physical cause but as the Final Cause of all things. Under the influence of the Final Cause everything is 'drawn' immanently towards the completion of its being. The object of desire moves without being moved. It produces motion as being loved or desired. The Good then is the final cause, the cause of causes.

Aristotle's notion of God, and his 'theoretical divine science' or theodicy in general, are not fully adequate or satisfactory. Later philosophers, however, found Aristotle's thought stimulating. They enriched his metaphysics with treatises on God as creator, 'mover', law-giver and supreme rewarder, and with treatises on God's knowledge, liberty, exemplarism and providence. In some of these areas, Plato's thought was closer to the truth than that of Aristotle. Aristotle's polemic against the Platonic theory of Forms led him to abandon several valuable insights which were either suggested or explicitly taught in Plato's works.

2. Ethics. Aristotle's *ethics* is closely allied to his metaphysics and to his speculative study of man. The *Nicomachean Ethics* is a version of Aristotle's lectures as recorded by his son Nicomachus. The *Eudemian Ethics*, a version recorded by Aristotle's pupil Eudemus, supplements the *Nicomachean Ethics*.

For Aristotle, all things in the universe (man included) are to be understood in terms of the ends toward which they tend. These ends are immanent in the forms of different beings; they are integral to their natures. Aristotle's view is therefore a teleological view of all that is in being.

The 'good', or the 'end' is 'that at which all things aim'. The final good for man is man's well-being or happiness. Men desire other goods for the sake of happiness; they never desire happiness for the sake of some further good. And what is happiness or well-being for man? It is the realization of man's essential nature in a life lived intelligently and wisely. The end for man is that man become an integral complete man, just as the end or *telos* of the acorn is that the acorn become a fully realized oak tree. The potentialities become actualized; the essential nature becomes fulfilled.

The virtue or excellence of a thing is the full development of the potentialities of its essential nature or form. Man is essentially a rational animal. The good, then, for man is activity of his (human) nature in accordance with right reason and accompanied by right reason. The good for man is that he be a rational rational-animal.

The end of man is to be found then in his form, that is, in his soul, his first 'activity' or entelechy or perfection. This form has various 'powers' or faculties. Reason has no direct control over human vegetative functions, and it has only a partial 'guiding' control over human appetitive functions. Nevertheless, the good for man is that the activity of his entire nature be in accordance with reason; only thus can man be seen at his human best.

The striving to be human, that is, to be rational, must be habitual. Goodness of character and disposition is developed only through repeated good acts. In this way good habits of behaviour are acquired. Good habits, or virtues, give rise to the good disposition. Hence the importance of virtuous education in childhood and adolescence.

Now, to act in accordance with reason, to be virtuous, generally involves a choosing of a certain mean between extremes of conduct. Thus for example, courage (in facing a danger of death) is a mean between rashness, a vice of excess, and cowardice, a vice of defect. Similarly, temperance is a mean between self-indulgence and insensibility. This *mean* is variable. The proper amount of food for a labourer would be too much for a secretary. Ordinary practical wisdom will determine the mean relative to ourselves. Virtue or excellence lies in constantly acting rightly in relation to time, manner, motives, objects and people.

Some kinds of actions are intrinsically bad, such as hate, adultery or murder. In cases of this kind the doctrine of the mean does not apply; there can be no mean or right ways of performing such actions. The virtuous mean is always an excellence; it is not an aberration, and it is not a mediocrity.

Though there is a mean for most forms of human behaviour, Aristotle points out, the theory of the mean does not apply in quite the same way to the virtue of justice. (Thus one cannot claim that, in all cases, virtue is always a mean.)

Justice in its 'universal' or Platonic sense comprehends all other virtues. As a particular virtue, however, it comprehends what is 'fair and equal'. It involves the sharing of external goods such as money or honour. The sharing involved in *distributive justice* is a (geometrical) proportional relation between persons (e.g. A and B) and goods (e.g. C and D) or burdens apportioned to them. (Thus, A:B::C:D.) *Remedial* or *rectificatory justice* involves the righting of wrongs, as in a lawcourt. *Commercial* or *commutative justice* governs transactions of exchange in which each is given his due, article for article and coin for coin, in arithmetical equivalence. Particular justice is a demand of man's social nature so that social life may be possible. Equity in a particular case is a type of justice superior to legal justice, which can legislate only for general cases.

The *Ethics* is, in the main, a treatise or a portrait of the good and happy man. Aristotle sums up his thought in the figure of the *megalopsychos*, the magnanimous or great-souled man, the man who is rightly proud of his rationality and his humanity. The great-souled man is a high-minded man. He is courageous, noble, honourable and honoured. He is wise, temperate, liberal, dignified yet unassuming, disdainful of the petty, frank in expressing his loves and hatreds, a man of few but great deeds. He is a man whose friends are themselves virtuous men.

Friendship is necessary for the good life. The highest and rarest form of friendship is that between similarly virtuous men loved because of their goodness. 'In its essence friendship seems to consist more in giving than in receiving affection... affection seems to be the mark of a good friend... . Good men neither err themselves nor permit their friends to err.' The friend is a second self (*Nicomachean Ethics* 1169a30).

There is a high form of 'self-love' in which one seeks that which is most fitting to one's highest nature—the just, the temperate, and the noble. If all men sought their highest good, then true self-love would ensure the greatest common welfare.

In addition to the moral virtues the good man also needs intellectual virtue. Theoretical wisdom (*sophia*) contemplates the truth of the highest and most precious things, as in the case of philosophy and mathematics. This form of wisdom is 'a combination of demonstrative science and intuitive reason directed to the noblest objects in creation'. It contemplates the truth *per se*. Practical wisdom (*phronēsis*) is a virtue which gives one 'a true and reasoned disposition towards action with regard to things that are good or bad for man' (1140b6). Practical wisdom is the intellectual virtue most closely connected with moral virtue. It is concerned with the recognition of the end and the choice of the best means to the good life. It presupposes intuitive speculative reason which grasps first principles, universals, and ultimate general facts in the light of which practical wisdom then does its own work. Practical wisdom is a function of the practical or productive intellect which can command and often indirectly control the irrational soul, the feelings and desires. In this way it prepares the way for the functioning of theoretical or philosophical wisdom.

Man's highest happiness consists in theoretical contemplation, *to theōrēsai*. The exercise of contemplative reason expresses the divine element in man. Contemplation (as, for example, in the case of absorbing and satisfying research work) is not just something directed towards the highest human good, it *is* the highest human good. It is the highest human activity. It makes man happy. It is the actualized end, the highest degree of human happiness, not just as a feeling but rather as a state of being. It is the state of being in which man is most like God.

In the closing lines (1249b20) of his *Eudemian Ethics* (an earlier and more 'Platonic' work), Aristotle defined the ideal contemplative life in terms of the worship (or service) and contemplation of God.

Aristotle's emphasis on contemplation had a profound influence on Arabic, Jewish and Christian Aristotelians. St Thomas Aquinas, for example, in his commentary (*Expositio*) on the *Nicomachean Ethics*, says it is clear that Aristotle places the supreme happiness of man in the operation of wisdom (2135). He adds, however, that perfect happiness cannot be found in this mortal life (2136). 'And since a natural desire is not inane, it can rightly be thought that perfect beatitude is reserved for man after this life' (202). Man's supreme happiness, then, is to be found in his beatific vision of God in heaven (*Summa Theologica* Ia, 26, 2). This approach transforms the whole concept of contemplation. It supplements, or supplies what is lacking in, the *Nicomachean Ethics*. It gives new meaning and life to the

Ethics, while respecting the essentials of Aristotle's structure. (Cf. A. H. A. Armstrong, *An Introduction to Ancient Philosophy*, chapter X.)

3. Political theory. In the *Politics* Aristotle applies his basic ethical and philosophical principles to the life of man in the *polis* or city-state. He saw the city-state of his times as a natural conglomerate of families united by community of race and language, and of civilized groupings of families mutually assisting each other for the purpose of making possible in a practical way the acquiring of happiness for each and all.

There are eight separate treatises bound together in the volume called the *Politics*. They deal with a variety of special topics. Their central theme is summed up in Aristotle's well-known saying: 'Man is by nature a political animal', that is, man is by his nature adapted for life in a *polis* or city-state. 'Every state is a sort of partnership, and every partnership is formed in order to attain some good' (*Politics*, Book I, opening lines). The state is that highest community in and through which people attain to physical, moral and intellectual perfection. For this reason Aristotle places special emphasis on the importance of human political activity and of the proper education of the community's citizens. Responsible political activity gives expression to the whole range of virtuous human actions insofar as man, a political animal, must live in associations and devote attention to the family and to the commonweal.

Good citizenship cannot be exercised in a vacuum. It is exercised in some actually existing state; and there are many different kinds of states and state-governments. There is, for example, the state of Sparta which is geared towards conducting war; there is the Cretan state, ruled in the interests of the rich; and the Carthaginian state, which relies on a policy of emigration to keep down domestic insurrection.

There are three broad types of political partnerships or states and each of these three types may be either good or bad. The good states are monarchies, aristocracies and (constitutional) polities. The corresponding bad states are tyrannies, oligarchies, and radical democracies (or mob-rule). In a society where there are free men of excellent character, aristocracy is better than monarchy. In the contemporary state, however, polity may be the most expedient form of state. Aristotle had in mind a state ruled, under constitution, by the propertied classes, both the rich and the not-so-rich combined. Those polities which lean toward the democratic form of government possess the greatest stability and are least liable to revolutions. In democratic polities of this kind, offices rotate frequently and there is a relatively wide personal participation in government on the part of the citizens. The citizenry or citizen-body did not include the 'slaves and mechanics', that is, the servants, manual workers and artisans, in the day and age in which Aristotle lived.

The final end at which government aims is the general happiness or well-being of the body politic. This can be achieved, in any type of state, only through the practical wisdom of the sound statesman. Responsible statesmen must apply their knowledge of principles, common sense, and sound judgement to specific situations.

The most humanly satisfying life for man is the life which combines action and contemplation. The political philosopher is one who must refine his practical wisdom through a constant rediscovery of the practical applicability of rules evolved in the history of political communities. Political power can never stand as the highest good; yet political activity is not degrading. The statesman's natural capacities, developed under the guidance of right reason, can lead to his attaining the philosopher's ideal of wisdom.

The legislative body of the state is responsible for the education of the citizens in the spirit of the constitution. Citizenship is a full-time occupation. The good citizens will devote their lives to the service of the state, as soldiers when they are young, as assembly members and jurymen in middle age, and as priests of the state when they are old. Citizenship, or full membership of the state and its government, must therefore be confined to the leisured classes. It is these classes alone who will have time to take a direct and personal share in the business of law-making in the assembly.

The city will prosper when individual persons attain their proper end as moral human beings. The state is for man, not man for the state. The state exists for the good life for its members. It is the same things that are best for both individuals and states. In this, Aristotle disagreed with the theory propounded in Plato's *Laws* that all private concerns must be subordinated to the good of the community as a whole. For Aristotle, the end of the state is the happiness of the individual citizen.

4. Aesthetics. Aristotle's *Poetics* is a treatise on aesthetics. Only half of the original volume has been preserved, and this segment analyses the poetic art of the tragedy and epic poetry of his day.

Poetry and drama, like fine art in general, present an artistic imitation of human life in its universal aspects. They are modes of imitation of character, emotion and action. They differ, however, from one another in three respects—the *means* of imitation (such as the rhythm, language and melody), the *manner* of imitation (as acted, or narrated, or sung), and the *objects* of imitation (that is, men, represented as either better or worse than in real life, or as they are). The distinction that marks off tragedy from comedy is this, that 'comedy aims at representing men as worse, tragedy as better than in real life'. In both cases there is an artistic imitation of human life and human nature. 'And, indeed, every one feels a natural pleasure in things imitated.'

'Tragedy is an imitation of an action that is serious, complete, and of a certain magnitude; in language embellished with each kind of artistic ornament, the several kinds being found in separate parts of the play; in the form of (dramatic) action, not of narrative; through pity and fear effecting the proper purgation (*katharsis*) of these emotions.' The effect which is aimed at in tragedy is the relief or purging of the soul from the tensions aroused by distressing pity, sympathy and dread, by means of a harmless and pleasurable venting of these emotions through the medium of dramatic art.

The principal character in a great tragedy is neither a perfectly virtuous man nor a depraved villain. The tragic hero is a man who is better than most men but who nevertheless brings about his own downfall because of some tragic error in judgement or some tragic flaw (*hamartia*) of character.

The three most important moments in a great dramatic tragedy are (a) the *peripeteia* or reversal of fortune, when a complication develops in the plot, (b) the *anagnōrisis*, the recognition or discovery of the critical fact which hastens the denouement, the unravelling of the plot, and (c) the pathetic suffering and final submission of the hero to fortune.

In the action of the drama the incidents which happen should be able to speak for themselves without verbal explanation. Similarly, the speeches should directly produce the effect desired by the speaker without extraneous aid.

The diction of poetry is made specially effective by the use of metaphor. Metaphor is the transference of a name from one thing to another—from a genus to a species of it, or from a species to a genus, or from species to species, or by analogy or proportion. In the case of metaphor by proportional analogy, the second term is related to the first as the fourth term is to the third. Thus, the metaphor 'the evening of life' implies that old age is to life as evening is to day.

In the *Poetics*, Aristotle made a permanent, classical contribution to the philosophy of literature and language. In doing so he answered

Plato's criticism that tragedy had a demoralizing effect on the citizens. As in the case of his other philosophical treatises, Aristotle once again gave the key, central place in the discussion to the discovery of the end, or purpose, of tragedy. Tragedy assists human nature to remove excess amounts of distressing sympathy and dread. This explanation is closely associated to the theory that virtue lies in the mean. The soul of tragedy is to be found in its action or plot. The action must be a complete action, just as the life of the happy man is one which is complete. All natural things tend naturally towards their fullness of being. The great drama is an imitation of nature. It is an artistic unity, a work of genius, which brings us closer to universal human nature.

5. Plato and Aristotle. The pre-Socratics were, in the main, philosopher-scientists who 'wondered' about the nature of the organized *cosmos*. The early Sophists and Socrates and Plato were more interested in *man* and ethical values than in the workings of the cosmos. Socrates devoted most of his attention to ethical analysis. Plato focused his thought on those abiding forms of being which would explain the stable, invariable world of necessary truth. Aristotle abandoned the quest for abiding forms and probed into the physical world of changing forms, that is, the dynamic world of experience, the world of beings which are in a state of becoming or change.

It cannot be too often emphasized that the world which Plato is preoccupied with is not the world of concepts and ideas but rather the world of *eidē*, that is, forms or kinds or species of being. The different forms of being have their own part to play within the world of comprehensive human experience, the world of *doxa* or images, or everyday beliefs. The known cosmos, the world of experience, is a world, a 'whole' which arises from the interaction of the knower and the known. In this experienced world, several factors are involved: the intellect or soul, the receptacle, the senses, natures or forms of being, memories, images, phenomena and so forth. The product of the interaction is the world of everyday experience, *doxa*. Forms of being have their own role to play within that world of everday 'images', and these forms are accessible to the philosopher who seeks them out from that 'whole' that is experienced.

The process of philosophizing is a process of thinking out and sifting out forms of being or 'natures' that become partly visible in the world of everyday beliefs. The philosopher strives towards intel-lectual perception of the types or forms of all things, rather than towards sense-perceptions and sense-impressions of the external appearances of all things. The Platonic dialogues are themselves a depiction of the process of philosophizing in action, a process in which two voices (sometimes within oneself) ask and answer questions until a final affirmation or judgement is reached. (For a description of the process of thinking, see *Theaetetus* 189e-190a.) In this way the philosopher sifts through the world of conflicting experiences and opinions in his effort to discover the realities which are accessible in and to this world of *doxa* or belief. In later ages, this Platonic doctrine gave rise to different, subjectivist theories which asserted that physical existents are not knowable in themselves and that it is the phenomenal alone that is known. For Plato himself, however, the forms of being are present within the world of experience, a world which tells us as much about the knower as about the known. (Later philosophers would express this view in the dictum: 'The known is present in the knower according to the nature of the knower'.) Are these forms of being real, and if so, in what way? Plato's explanation was not really adequate. But then, no fully satisfactory theory concerning the problem of the different forms of being (and the problem of the universals) would emerge until nearly fifteen hundred years later (cf. below, Peter Abelard [1079-1142]).

Aristotle brought philosophical enquiry back to nature, *physis*, as the object of investigation. Philosophy is not primarily concerned with the 'separate', subjective world of private experience. Mental activity is not the only activity which takes place in the act of knowing. Natural things are ongoing beings or 'activities' which have a principle of change within themselves. Physical objects are capable of both intrinsic change and transitive activities which effect changes in each other. The mind is capable of receiving such activities within itself. It is because it is both receptive and active that it is capable of inquiring into nature itself.

According to Aristotle, each natural reality is an abiding 'activity', ongoing in being. Its form of inner activity in being is its immanent essence or formal principle, its substantial form, which is the source of its further specific activities. This immanent essence or nature is the intelligible principle in the object. In the act of perceiving, it is the individual form of the thing perceived which is received within the perceiver. The reality known is a reality received; it is not an object actively produced or generated. In the process of abstraction there is a natural, 'physical' apprehension of the datum.

In these areas Aristotle made a profoundly significant contribution to the history of philosophic thought. But in his attempt to show the eminent superiority of his own system of thought over that of his teacher, Plato, he discarded aspects of Plato's thought which would have complemented and enhanced his own doctrines. He discarded, for example, the doctrine of exemplary causality and the doctrine of Divine Mind immanently and providently at work in the universe. The Neo-Platonists saw the need of a higher synthesis of the insights of Plato and Aristotle. Neo-Platonism proved to be one attempt among several other attempts in the history of philosophy which sought to achieve this wider synthesis.

7 Hellenistic and Roman philosophy

1. The Academy 2. Peripateticism 3. The Hellenistic period 4. Stoicism 5. Epicureanism 6. Scepticism and eclecticism 7. Neo-Platonism

1. The Academy. After the deaths of Plato and Aristotle, there came a certain change in the points of emphasis in the systems of philosophy taught at the Academy and at the Lyceum.

Speusippus, a nephew of Plato, and his successor as Scholarch of the Academy, taught that the forms of being and the mathematical entities were one and the same. The old Academy then continued to teach the mathematical aspect of the Platonic tradition. Speusippus was sceptical about the traditional accounts of the traditional gods. He regarded these gods as natural, physical forces. *Xenocrates* of Chalcedon, who succeeded Speusippus, attempted to show how the many, the mathematical numbers, were derived from the One and its double, that is, from 'the father and the mother of the gods'. *Eudoxus* taught that the forms belong inherently to the things which participate in them (cf. Aristotle, *Metaphysics* 1079b19). In this matter he may well have been elucidating the doctrine of Plato himself. *Crantor* (c. 300 B.C.) and other Platonists handed on the master's teachings and wrote some commentaries on the Platonic dialogues.

The outlook of the movement called the 'New Academy' was profoundly different, however, from that of Plato and his immediate successors. *Arcesilaus* (315-241 B.C.) attacked the Stoic doctrine of apprehensive presentations or intuitions. He taught that, though theoretical knowledge is impossible and no one can ever be certain, nevertheless if a man wishes to know how he should behave, he should be told to behave in accordance with what appears to be reasonable. *Carneades* (213-129 B.C.), following the scepticism of Arcesilaus, taught that there was nothing within any experience that could assure one that it was veridical or the reverse. All judgements, therefore, are always fallible. There is no criterion of truth. Human action can be guided by probability alone. Some forms of so-called knowledge or appearances are merely probable; some appearances are probable and confirmed; and some are probable, confirmed and tested. But none is immune to correction. *Antiochus* of Ascalon (d. 68

B.C.), his disciple and subsequent rival, became an eclectic who held that there was no real difference between the Academy, the Lyceum and the Stoa. *Cicero* (see below, section 6) said that in his day all the schools differed only in words.

2. Peripateticism.

In the Lyceum or Peripatos, *Theophrastus of Eresus* (d. 287 B.C.) succeeded Aristotle as the head of the Peripatetic school. He emphasized the trend towards empirical observation already apparent in Aristotle's work. He wrote works which outlined his studies in botany and zoology, and studies on the history and nature of religion. He also wrote a history of philosophy. His disciple *Demetrius of Phaleron* was instrumental in the foundation of the library and school of Alexandria in the early part of the third century B.C. *Strato of Lampsacus*, who was known as 'the Physicist', was head of the Peripatetic school about 287-269 B.C. He was interested in astronomy, mechanics and medicine, and in physical science in general. He attempted to mechanize the Peripatetic system in terms of the atomic theory of Democritus and to give a completely mechanical account of all things. He identified God with the unconscious forces of nature, and attempted to explain all physical activities in terms of motion.

Andronicus of Rhodes was the tenth Scholarch; he was head of the school about 70-50 B.C. Andronicus, aided by the grammarian Tyrannion, compiled the first complete edition of the pedagogical works of Aristotle. He reassembled the connected fragments, investigated their authenticity, arranged them in order, titled the different works, and then accompanied this whole task with a commentary on the logical treatises and on several other works. Many others also undertook the task of writing commentaries on the works of Aristotle. The most famous of these was *Alexander of Aphrodisias*, who lectured at Athens at the close of the second century A.D.; he has frequently been called the 'second Aristotle'. Alexander attempted to add new clarity and precision to Aristotle's thought on points which seemed obscure. He proposed a number of contestable views which were developed further by the Arabic philosophers of the Middle Ages. In his interpretation of Aristotle's remarks on mind in *De Anima*, Alexander said that the active intellect was identical in all men, and identified it with pure actuality. The implication then would be that it is Mind that thinks in us whenever we think; there would therefore be no basis for any doctrine of personal immortality. Other Peripatetics of the third and fourth centuries A.D. inclined more and more towards eclectic theories which combined the doctrines of the Neo-Platonists with those of Peripateticism. They can be called 'Peripatetics' only in a loose sense of the term. The school became almost indiscernible from that of Neo-Platonism.

3. The Hellenistic period is usually accepted as having begun with the death of Alexander the Great in 323 B.C. and to have ended with the establishment in power of Augustus Caesar in 30 B.C. However many features of the period persisted into the days of the Roman empire.

Alexander the Great (356-323 B.C.) was encouraged at an early age by his parents, King Philip II and Olympias, to carry out their plan of uniting the Greek states under Macedonia (in northern Greece) and to carry out further conquests of nearby territory. Alexander conquered and united the Greek city-states while still in his teens, and then moved on to the conquest of a great empire in Europe, Asia and North Africa. He established local government; he broke down the barriers between Greek and barbarian. Many Persians and others rose to high ranks in his army. He founded new cities and promoted education. He strove to unite all races and factions into one great cosmopolitan people. Greek ideas and Hellenic forms in art, literature and philosophy, modified by Oriental and Egyptian influence, became widespread throughout these areas during the last three centuries B.C. The period has become known as the Hellenistic period, the age of classical civilization.

The Hellenistic period was a time of political, social and religious upheaval. It was for this reason that philosophy now took on a new practical importance. People saw themselves as part of a much larger whole. The good life for the citizen was no longer seen as being necessarily tied to the small home-town community. The educated individual saw himself as cosmopolitan and as freed from many of the ancient traditional practices. The emphasis was on the cosmopolitan individual and the cosmopolitan Hellenistic civilization.

All over the Hellenistic world, Greek models in architecture, art, statuary and coinage were followed, from Sicily and Italy in the west to the river Jaxartes on the border of India. In the new cities, Greek town planning emphasized public structures such as temples, the theatre, the gymnasium and the agora (market) rather than private homes. In the capital cities there arose libraries, museums and scientific institutes. In these research and study centres a new emphasis was placed on specialization in literary and philological research, and in medical, physical and mathematical studies.

Philosophy too began to specialize, or rather to concentrate on the new-felt needs of the insecure cosmopolitan-minded individual who now felt cut adrift from the security of the small, self-sufficient, traditional community. Philosophers concentrated on the individual, on character, ethics, codes of conduct and personal behaviour. Popular philosophy was called on to satisfy the religious and moral needs of individuals seeking personal salvation and sure standards for life and conduct. This, then, was the background and setting in which Stoicism, Epicureanism and Neo-Platonism came to birth.

4. Stoicism. The founder of the Stoic school was *Zeno* of Citium (336-264 B.C.), a disciple of Socrates' disciple Crates the Cynic. Zeno's followers became known as Stoics, a name derived from the beautiful colonnaded porch (*Stoa Poikilē*) in Athens where Zeno gave his lectures.

Zeno, his successor *Cleanthes*, and *Chrysippus* (282-204 B.C.), a powerful dialectician, preached a doctrine of *apatheia*, that is, apathy in the sense of freedom from all human passions. The good life, as the Stoics saw it, could be obtained only by energetic, rational self-discipline coupled with complete independence of external goods. This doctrine, in practice, implied the observance of the four cardinal Stoic virtues: (1) prudence, in the sense of wisdom or moral insight and good judgement in the choice of means towards rational ends; (2) justice, in the sense of having due regard for the rights of others; (3) courage, or fortitude and endurance; and (4) temperance, in the sense of sobriety and self-control. Through the practice of these virtues, the wise man conforms to the rhythm of universal life. Every passion is irrational and evil. The wise man aims constantly to extirpate passion. Ascetic effort or 'straining' is necessary if one is to attain untroubledness of soul, that is, peace and happiness. Apathy can be attained solely in the reasonable life, a life in which one lives in accord with one's rational nature. One must 'follow nature'; and Nature is rational. Affections are to be controlled, and sufferings calmly endured. The goal of life is virtue as the only source of that peace or apathy of spirit which is true human happiness.

For the Stoics, philosophy has three interdependent parts, namely ethics, physics (or cosmology), and logic (including gnosiology); and in Stoic philosophy it is ethics which has the first place of honour.

The Stoic principle 'follow nature' has its source in a monistic and materialistic view of man and the universe. The universe is animated by a universal soul who is one, intelligent and wise. This soul, which is Logos or Reason, organizes the universe into a harmonious hierarchy. It is 'Seed-bearing Reason'; it generates the order, beauty and goodness of the universe. It is corporeal and material 'fire' (dynamic change, energy), the most subtle body; and it is intelligent, provident fire, immanent in all things. Each being of nature is a part or particular member of the great, divine body. The soul of man is at the peak of the hierarchy of beings; it is a god-like spark of the divine fire. It has descended from the divine fire and it will return to the divine fire on the day of universal conflagration when once again a cycle of palingenesis or regeneration will recommence in the universe. In the meantime, man's happiness each day lies in his being at one with universal Logos.

Logic is the art and science which assists man to attain a knowledge of the Logos. A knowledge or science of the Logos is the first means of identification with him. Since all reality is corporeal, sensation is the only knowledge which is possible. Our concepts of reality are simply common names which group together individuals which appear more or less similar.

Perfect scientific knowledge arises from the gathering together as a unified bundle of sensations which are closely knit. The acquisition of scientific knowledge, through unification and synthesis of this kind, like the acquisition of virtue, requires effort and 'straining' on the part of man. In this instance, there is the effort involved in re-checking back to the physical objects before judgement can be pronounced; there is the effort of sifting through memories and traces of previous sensations; and there is the effort of reason in its attempt to synthesize a multitude of associated facts under one law or principle of order. Effort, or intense preoccupation of mind, is necessary if one is to attain truth, happiness and untroubledness of soul in a life lived according to reason.

Stoic logic was influenced by the germinal logical theories of Euclid of Megara, a contemporary of Plato, even more than by the logic of Aristotle. The Megarian school attempted to formulate the principles of a logic that was propositional, that is, concerned with propositions rather than with predicates or terms; Philo and Diodorus Cronos, two Megarian logicians, became involved in some widely reported disputes on the analysis of hypothetical propositions, and the analysis of modal (apodeictic, and problematic) propositions. Stoic logic concerned itself in a special way with the relations between 'incorporeal' propositions, that is, propositions whose analysis was concerned with the truth and falsity of the relations between the propositions, without regard to their content. It attempted to formulate and formalize argument-schemata or inference-patterns in which symbols would be substituted for actual propositions (thus, 'If p then q; but p, therefore q'). In this work, they anticipated the medieval theory of *consequentiae* or the drawing of conclusions, and the contemporary theories of modern symbolic logic.

The Stoic philosophers of the third and second centuries B.C. tended towards eclecticism. Their form of philosophy came to be known later as that of the Middle Stoa. The two major figures in this period were *Panaetius* of Rhodes (180-110 B.C.) and *Poseidonius* of Apameia (128-44 B.C.). Panaetius mitigated the Stoic cult of the wise man, and the doctrine of apathy. The goal of life for the ordinary man is the rational perfection of his human nature. This humanistic form of Stoicism became acceptable to Cicero and to the Roman Stoics. Poseidonius, a disciple of Panaetius, was Cicero's teacher. He taught that the human being, a composite of body and soul, is a bridge between all that is mortal and the immortal in the great cosmic system governed by Providence. The passions are an essential aspect of human nature. Human nature would not be human if it had no passions. Nevertheless, these passions must be kept under control if human nature is to be rational.

Stoicism succeeded in attracting a great number of learned and aristocratic followers, especially in the Roman world. The Stoicism of the Later Stoa became more and more a practical philosophy or a way of life.

Lucius Annaeus Seneca of Cordoba (A.D. 5-65), tutor and adviser of the emperor Nero, advocated the practice of the virtues and benevolence towards one's fellow-man. He also advocated the use of daily self-examination, and the conquest of the passions as a way of salvation from the general evils of the time.

Epictetus of Hierapolis (*c.* A.D. 65-*c.* 135) was a freedman of Epaphroditus, who in turn was a freedman of Nero's. His disciple Arrian compiled the *Discourses*, the *Life* and the *Manual* of Epictetus. Epictetus was a professional philosopher who taught that the good life is a life of inner tranquillity. This comes from conforming to nature, that is, to reason or to truth. To achieve a life of inner serenity, a man must master his desires, perform his duties, and think carefully and truthfully concerning himself and the world. Epictetus recommended daily self-examination, and taught that all men have God (Zeus) for their father. Thus, every man has God-given dignity. Each is a citizen of the world; and each has a duty to others. All men are brothers. If my brother uses me unjustly, and if I think of the injustice, I cannot bear it, but if I think of him as a brother, I can. If my brother says to me 'I am richer than you are, therefore I am better than you', the inference is invalid. The correct inference is merely 'I have more possessions than you'. Each man, rich or poor, shares human dignity.

Marcus Aurelius Antoninus (A.D. 121-180), emperor and philosopher, made a personal record of his thoughts in his *Meditations*. He found a strengthening faith in the way of Nature, the way of God or Reason. Virtue is the highest good; it consists in being in harmony with the way of Nature. Death and the misfortunes of life are not evil. They are according to nature and 'nothing that is according to nature can be evil'. In a world in which all events are determined by the great ordering breath of God, which pervades all Nature, man's freedom lies in his power to assent to or dissent from the course of events. The man who consents to Reason controls himself in those respects in which control is possible, that is, in desiring, believing and responding to the way of Nature. 'Meditate often upon the connection of all things in the world; and upon the mutual relation that they have one unto another. For all things are after a sort folded and involved one within another, and by these means all agree well together' (*Meditations*, Book V). True manhood is made possible by reflection on God's ways in Nature and by the calm acceptance of God's will in all circumstances.

5. Epicureanism. *Epicurus* of Samos (341-270 B.C.) was the founder of the Epicurean school in Athens. Only a few fragments from his voluminous works have survived. However, Diogenes Laertius preserved forty extracts of the *Principal Doctrines* of Epicurus, and also his *Letter to Menoeceus*, and we also have Lucretius' *De rerum natura* ('On the Nature of Things': see below).

Epicurus' central teaching was that 'pleasure is the beginning and end of the life of blessedness'. Pleasure is the standard by which every right action and every good is to be judged.

Pleasures vary in intensity and duration, but if one sets these secondary factors aside, all pleasures are basically of the same kind; and no pleasure is in itself bad. The feeling of pleasure is the good in life, and it is always simple and immediate.

Epicurus maintained that pleasures may be: natural and necessary, natural and not necessary, or neither natural nor necessary. The last kind of pleasure is to be avoided, and the first is to be made the primary object and goal of human living. The three natural and necessary pleasures, or natural and necessary needs, of man are: equanimity (*ataraxia*, or freedom from care), bodily health and comfort, and the sustenance of life. Fortunately, few things are necessary for bodily health and for sustenance of life. Thus, man's main concern is with the preservation of peace of mind (*ataraxia*).

To preserve peace of mind, Epicurus recommended two means. Firstly, the cultivation of virtues, and particularly the virtue of prudence; and secondly, the study of philosophy. The man of prudence will accustom himself to simple meals and to plain surroundings as a means towards becoming independent of desire. He will also retire from the world of business and political affairs which disturb serenity of soul. Life is made pleasant by sober contemplation and by the study of philosophy.

Epicurus found the philosophic views of Leucippus and Democritus suited to his own view of nature. All things have been formed by the accidental collision of atoms falling through empty space. Theories involving creator gods and teleology are unnecessary. The gods live in calm tranquillity. Man should therefore free himself from baseless religious scruples and dreads concerning the gods and the heavenly bodies. Similarly, man should free himself from the fear of death and of an afterlife. At death, the atoms of the soul are separated and dispersed through space. 'So long as we exist, death is not with us; but when death comes, then we do not exist.' Death therefore is nothing, and nothing is not to be feared.

Every sensation or perception is true, according to Epicurus, and this is the sole source of knowledge. Atoms given off by objects come in contact with sense organs and give rise to immediate sensation. Mistakes concerning perceptions arise only through one's judgement. Concepts, or memory images of past sensations, are stored up in the mind. Knowing or perceiving consists both in the receiving of a sensation and in its alignment with similar memory images. From these primary ideas, processes of reasoning then build up secondary ideas, as for example in the case of our inferences concerning the distant stars.

The *De rerum natura* of *Titus Lucretius Carus* (*c*. 98-55 B.C.) is a Latin didactic poem which gives an exposition of Epicurus' philosophy. Nature consists of tiny 'seeds' or 'beginnings' (or atoms) moving in the void. These atoms are of many different shapes and the number of atoms of each shape is infinite. In their natural downward movement, collisions occur and atoms 'swerve' off the determined course. A similar phenomenon is seen in the undetermined movement of free will among the subtle atoms which compose the human soul. The soul's atoms are dispersed at death, and all consciousness ceases. Hence fears of hell and of the afterlife are foolish. 'Death, therefore, is nothing to us.' Fear of the gods is likewise foolish. The gods are blessed, untroubled beings. It is a mistaken notion that such blessed beings ever trouble themselves about humans, or even know of their existence. Human blessedness consists in making one's own life, as far as possible, like the untroubled life of the gods.

The Cyrenaic school, following the doctrines of its founder Aristippus, had taught that the end of human conduct is to obtain pleasurable sensations. This doctrine of hedonism was refined by the Epicureans. The form of pleasure which is the end of life is not gross sensual pleasure but rather intellectual pleasure in which the untroubled soul enjoys serenity and tranquillity. To achieve this, one must live calmly, moderately and virtuously. The emphasis is on calm, tranquillity, and effortless equilibrium. The Stoic ethic, by way of contrast, emphasized the effort or 'straining' which is necesssary if one is to live rationally and virtuously and in accordance with the divinely appointed order of the universe. The Stoic ethic appealed to those who sought heroic nobility of character. The Epicurean ethic appealed to those who sought the happiness which derives from equanimity and moderation in all things.

6. Scepticism and eclecticism. Philosophical scepticism is a doctrine which admits the existence of feelings of certitude as an internal, subjective reality; but it denies that the objective validity of any speculative judgment is ever demonstrable. It teaches therefore that one can never obtain an objectively founded certitude which is infallibly true. All certitude is subjective.

Pyrrho (362-270 B.C.), a citizen of Elis, founded a school of sceptical philosophy in Elis after the death of Alexander the Great (323). According to his disciples, Pyrrho taught that things can be known only as they seem to be, and not as they actually are. Objective knowledge is impossible. The philosopher who wishes to achieve mental tranquillity should happily suspend judgement and not attempt to evaluate any proposition or doctrine. The resigned philosopher can then live at peace with himself and his neighbours. This doctrine of universal or philosophical scepticism became known as Pyrrhonism. Arcesilaus, founder of the Middle Academy, and Carneades, founder of the New Academy, were influenced by this doctrine. They asserted that in many philosophical discussions one should concede merely that some opinions are more probable than others. This became known as the doctrine of Probabilism.

Aenesidemus of Knossos (*fl. c.* first century B.C.) codified the system of philosophical scepticism in his teachings and writings at

Alexandria. *Agrippa* listed five persuasive motives for absolute doubt. *Sextus Empiricus* (*c*. A.D. 250) made a comprehensive collection of all the objections of his Sceptic predecessors. He held that one cannot attain objective knowledge from syllogisms, causal arguments, or theology, and that all opinions and judgements are relative and subjective.

The Eclectics were influenced by the arguments of the Sceptics. However, they would not accept that truth is impossible to attain. They held that there is no philosophical system that can synthesize within itself the sum-total of truths that are to be found in the multiple philosophical systems already formulated. They sought, then, to revise and reconcile various earlier opinions by choosing and collecting what each judged to be true and valuable in these different systems of thought.

The Eclectic school in Alexandria (*c*. 20 B.C.) was actually known as the 'Selective Choice school' (*eklektikē hairesis*). It combined Peripatetic and Stoic teachings. Other Eclectic schools combined Platonic, Aristotelian, Stoic, Cynic and Pythagorean elements. *Cicero* (106-43 B.C.; better known as a Roman statesman and orator) adopted those doctrines which he judged to be most in conformity with 'common sense': the Stoic doctrine of remembrances or impressions, Plato's doctrines on the soul and God, and the Peripatetic theories about law and politics. *Plutarch* of Chaeronea (*c*. A.D. 50-*c*.120) was influenced by the thought of Plato, Aristotle, the Stoics and the Neo-Pythagoreans. He taught that there are intermediary beings (demons, powers, or dominations) in the hierarchy of beings between God and man. God is the author of good, and Matter with its World-Soul is the author of evil. Plutarch presented a religious syncretism of elements borrowed from Egyptian and Greek cults combined with a doctrine of Oriental dualism. This and other similar doctrines incorporating a philosophy of religion, e.g. the Jewish-Hellenistic philosophy of Philo of Alexandria (*c*. 35 B.C. -*c*. A.D. 40), and the Gnostic movement of the first and second centuries A.D., helped to prepare the way for Neo-Platonism.

7. Neo-Platonism. The philosophical system known as Neo-Platonism was first proposed at Alexandria, by *Ammonius Saccas* (A.D. 175-242), and first expounded as a system by his student Plotinus. Neo-Platonism was the last great philosophical system to come from the philosophers of the ancient world.

Plotinus (203-269), who came from Egypt, founded a school in Rome where he taught his devoted disciples, male and female, for twenty-five years (244-269). Porphyry (see below), a disciple of Plotinus, edited and rearranged the writings of his master. He arranged them, mainly by subject-matter, into six books of nine chapters each, which were entitled the *Enneads* (from the Greek word *ennea*, 'nine').

Plotinus' Neo-Platonism combined the insights of Platonic philosophy with elements of Pythagorean, Aristotelian and Stoic thought, and included some religious and mystical ideas derived from Oriental thought. In this unified system, philosophical speculation, at its summit of development, was seen as pointing beyond itself to a higher plane of mystical union with Divine Being.

For Plotinus, 'the One', which is Pure Act, in opposition to all multiplicity and distinction, is the First Reality, the highest perfection. The transcendent One produces the multiple without losing anything of its fullness and without suffering any change. All the lower gradations of unity are derived from the ineffable, incomprehensible One which is the Good; and they depend upon the Good for their continuance in existence.

The procession of multiplicity out of the ultimate Divine Unity is mediated by a gradation of beings which issue (or proceed, or emanate) from God by necessity. This emanation of beings could not have been by free creation out of nothing, since creation would involve change in God. It is therefore an emanation 'according to necessity of nature'. It is a succession or procession which is timeless, and so the world as a whole is eternal.

In the cosmos there are two forms of procession or movement. The primary cosmic movement is that in which the various levels of reality are being eternally brought into being. It is an out-going emanation, a *procession of descent*. The other cosmic movement is one of return or ascent; it is one in which the pilgrim soul ascends through all the stages of being to final union with the One or the Good. This latter movement is the movement of the spiritual life. Thus the One is both the first principle of the cosmos and the final goal of the spiritual life. For Plotinus, then, philosophy provides both a speculative systematization of cosmic reality and a religious pathway to personal salvation.

From the absolutely simple One, which is beyond all thought and beyond all reality (and which Plotinus sometimes calls 'the Father'), there emanates, firstly, Thought, Mind, or Nous, whose content is the world of Forms or Being. This emanation or radiation can be partially understood in terms of an imperfect analogy with the radiation of heat and light from the sun or from fire, or with the

diffusion of scent from a flower. The emanation, however, is eternal
and spontaneous; and it leaves the all-perfect source undiminished
and unchanged. Emanation occurs because perfection is necessarily
diffusive of itself.

Nous or Thought in its first 'moment' of out-going is Thought-in-
potency. In its second 'moment', it is Thought-in-action turning
back to contemplate its source; and in doing so it becomes informed
Thought, filled with content. The two moments or movements are
timeless and simultaneous. The world of *Nous* is the world of
Beauty. It is the world of the Forms of Being which are a manifold
image of the One. These Forms or archetypes include the Forms of
individual things in all their particularity as well as the Forms of
classes; and all are contained indivisibly and inseparably in Divine
Thought.

Universal Soul, one of the Forms of Being, proceeds from Nous
and becomes a link or bridge-principle between the intelligible world
and the corporeal universe. Universal Soul, in turn, contemplates
Mind, and becomes informed Soul. It gives being and life to the
corporeal universe. It is the universal principle and source through
which bodies are informed. From the Universal Soul there emanate
(1) World-Soul, that is, the soul of the organic universe, Nature, and
(2) individual souls which, by the law of the Universal Soul, occupy
and administer those bodies to which they are appointed.

The human soul is destined by nature to contemplate transcendent Soul and then to ascend beyond this to find mind's rightful
place within Mind Itself. It can also descend into the engrossing
corporeal concerns of the body. It can become the prisoner of the
body's demands if it fails to control the body, and in this way it can
become isolated and alienated from its high destiny.

Nature produces the immanent forms of all natural bodies. It
imposes these forms on matter, which is formless negation. Matter is
the principle of negation and darkness; in this sense it is the
principle of evil. It resists the activity of the informing soul. However, the visible matter of the material universe is *informed* matter
and this is not evil. The universe is an ensouled living being. It
manifests order and harmony in spite of tension and conflict. The
tension and suffering present in the world are not at all unnatural;
they are a simple and necessary consequence of embodiment. The
wise man knows this and can accept it and rise above it. The one who
is unwise engrosses himself in the corporeal, the brutal. His lonely
anguish is then a consequence of his own previous choices; it is of his
own making. He has turned away from his proper destiny.

Man's living body proceeds from his *psychē*, or reasoning soul, and this in turn proceeds from his *nous*, his intuitive intelligence (or spirit, or mind). These three elements in man are not separable; they proceed one from the other and are intimately present to each other. The human psyche possesses a faculty of reasoning by which it can distance itself from bodies and ascend towards Mind; it also has lower faculties by which it organizes the body. The human spirit or mind (*nous*) has the power of contemplation by which it can ascend to an intuition of the ideal world, and by which it can ascend higher still to the One, in ecstasy.

Within every being, that is, every effect, man included, there is an inner natural desire (*erōs*) to return to its perfect cause so that it may find there its proper perfection and its happiness. This desire, in man, is the principle of his ascent towards Beauty Itself. The beauty which we see in the things of nature reminds us that these things are descendants of higher orders. The beauties of nature are an expression of higher principles. For the wise man they are a deeply stirring phenomenon. They give a simple foretaste of the realm beyond being which the soul, the lover, seeks.

The first stage of *man's ascent*, prompted by inner desire, consists in a process of purification (*katharsis*) in which the soul is radically separated from materiality and sensuality, and becomes proficient in the practice of the cardinal virtues. The second stage of ascent is that in which the mind occupies itself with philosophy and science. It rises above the level of perception in total abstraction from matter. It develops its reasoning power at the expense of sensations in order to discover the true nature of mind and soul. The scientific research work of which Aristotle spoke contributes towards this result. The third stage of ascent is one in which the mind rises above the reasoning processes of the soul and in which the intuitive intelligence is actuated. The mind partakes in the divine intelligence, truth is seen in one glance, and the soul becomes capable of practising, in an eminent fashion, all the virtues. This stage of union with Nous is preparatory to the final stage in which the human spirit is re-united, mystically and ecstatically, with the One. To attain this sublime union, the soul must have already acquired a state of complete silence of the senses, of reasoning processes, and even of intuitions. The spirit can then touch the infinite and can be enraptured by the One in unspeakable ecstasy.

The thought and emphasis in the system of Plotinus is much more closely akin to that of the Pythagorean school, and that of Plato and the Orphic cults, than it is to the philosophy of Aristotle. The world to which human beings really belong is the world which is 'beyond'. The emphasis is on intellectual contemplation, and the quest is for personal salvation through union with distant Reality Itself. Plotinus offered to the spiritually insecure Hellenist world a philosophic way of human salvation which appealed to the intellectual elite of the third and fourth centuries A.D. His system of philosophy and his philosophy of religion did not have the widespread appeal of the Greco-Oriental mystery religions, but they appealed to those minds who sought for a naturalistic and rationalist form of contemplation and piety in an age when Christianity still appeared suspect and uncouth to the educated classes of the time. They also appealed to Augustine and the early Christian thinkers, giving them philosophical insights and a vocabulary which enabled them to make an intellectual statement of Christian thought and Christian theology in the Patristic age. In this way the Neo-Platonism of Plotinus had a lasting influence on Patristic and early Scholastic philosophy.

Porphyry of Tyre (232-305) succeeded Plotinus as head of the school in Rome, and kept close to the doctrines of his master. He also wrote several commentaries on the works of Plato and Aristotle. The most influential of these was his *Isagoge* or introduction to Aristotle's *Organon,* which was translated into Latin by Boethius and became famous in the Middle Ages.

Iamblichus the Syrian (d. *c.* 330) succeeded Porphyry in Rome. Later in life he transported the school to Pergamon and then to Alexandria. New centres of Neo-Platonism sprang up in Syria, Egypt, Greece and the Latin West. The Academy itself became Neo-Platonist in the fifth century, and it continued to teach Neo-Platonism until its closure by the emperor Justinian in 529. Iamblichus and his successors developed and transformed the doctrine of Plotinus. Some minor and secondary aspects of the teachings of Plotinus were developed at length and given a new emphasis. Iamblichus multiplied the numbers of angels, heroes, demons and intermediary beings between the One above the One who is the good and ordinary human beings. *Aedesius* of Pergamon and the emperor *Julian* (322-363), an apostate Christian, developed an interest in theurgy, magic, and the revival of polytheism. Two Athenian Scholarchs, *Plutarch* (d.*c.*431) and *Syrianus* (d.*c.*430), wrote Neo-Platonist commentaries on Aristotle's *De Anima* and *Metaphysics.*

Proclus (410-485), an Athenian Scholarch, wrote several influential works which included commentaries on Plato's dialogues, and a systematic textbook of Neo-Platonism, the *Elements of Theology.* He became known as the greatest scholastic of antiquity because of his masterly skills in dialectics and in complex systematization. It was largely through Proclus that Neo-Platonism was handed down to posterity. Proclus regarded matter as part of the universal order of being (and therefore good) and regarded evil as the absence or deficiency of good. This doctrine was taken up later by Augustine and the Scholastics. To show that all reality with all its multiplicity is a continuum, Proclus postulated a series of subordinate triads of hypostases. Plotinus had spoken of the One, the Intellect and the Soul. Proclus then spoke of the Intellect as a triad of being, life and mind, each of which is subdivided into its own triad. He developed this form of dialectical systematization through triadic development down through the whole range of the various orders of being. In each triad he distinguished the moment of remaining in the principle, the moment of proceeding out of the principle, and the moment of turning back towards the principle (Hegel [1770-1831] made use of a similar dialectical process of 'thesis, antithesis and synthesis'). Proclus, like his teacher Syrianus, also taught the doctrine of the Divine Henads (Units, individuals or Gods). Just as the many minds and many souls in the universe are subordinate to Universal Mind and Universal Soul, so too there are many Ones (henads) subordinate to the Supreme One. Each henad is responsible for a hierarchy of subordinate entities extending downwards to all the lower levels of reality. In this way, Proclus attempted to explain how the many can proceed from the ultimate Absolute Unity.

Christian Neo-Platonists found the syntheses of Plotinus and Proclus rich storehouses of academic thought. However, they found that these syntheses lacked any theory of omnipotent free 'creation out of nothing', and so were lacking in any meaningful theory of finite existence. The notion of creation and the notion of the absolute and continuous dependence of the multiple finite beings on the Infinite would have helped the pagan Neo-Platonists solve the problem of the One and the Many. Neo-Platonism drew on many Orphic, Pythagorean, Socratic, Platonic and Stoic themes in its endeavour to present philosophy as a highly intellectual way of salvation, an imposing and sublime structure. The Christian Neo-Platonists regarded Neo-Platonic thought as a preparation for Christianity, a *preparatio evangelica*, which made the Greco-Roman world ready for the true (Christian) way of salvation. They regarded philosophy, then, as academically helpful but non-salvational.

8 Early Christian philosophy

1. The Patristic period   2. St Augustine   3. Pseudo-Dionysius   4. The age of transmission

1. The Patristic period. The thought and works of the ancient Christian writers exercised a deep influence on the Christian philosophers of the Middle Ages. This is true especially of the writings of Gregory of Nyssa, Augustine, and the Pseudo-Dionysius, and to a lesser extent of those of the early Greek and Latin apologists (Aristides, Justin Martyr, Minucius Felix, Tertullian, St Irenaeus), the catechetical school of Alexandria (Clement, Origen), and the Greek and Latin Fathers of the Church.

It was an age in which these writers felt called upon to present a rational explanation of their views on God, man and the universe, as opposed to the views of the Roman imperial authorities who were their adversaries and persecutors. They drew on several aspects of Platonic, Stoic and Neo-Platonic philosophy to show how these schools of thought achieved a gradual, providential preparation of the world for the unique wisdom (*sophia*) of the Christian vision of the universe.

St Justin Martyr (100-164) had studied the doctrines of the Stoics, the Peripatetics, the Pythagoreans and the Platonists before his discovery of Christianity. In his *Dialogue with Trypho*, as a Christian convert, and in his *Apologies*, Justin used the vocabulary of his philosophical training to show how the thought of Socrates, Plato and the Stoics prepared the civilized world for its eventual acceptance of the wisdom of the Logos of God who became incarnate.

Minucius Felix, about the end of the second century A.D., argued that the unity and wisdom of God can be known by reason from the unity and finality seen to be present in cosmic order. Plato himself had spoken of God as the Maker and Father of all things; and the Stoics had recognized the pervading presence of divine providence at work in the universe. The ancient Greeks had discovered these and several other truths by the unaided light of human reason.

Tertullian (c. 155-c. 230) spoke disparagingly of pagan wisdom as contrasted with Christian wisdom and its revealed mysteries. He said that reason cannot be the judge of divinely revealed doctrine. The believer is one who hears and accepts; he separates himself from the deaf: '*Credo quia ab-surdum est*'. Tertullian's skill in formal Latin, disputation, rhetoric, and legal practice, enabled him to create a technical vocabulary for the presentation of the Christian philosophy, or wisdom, which became the standard vocabulary of the Patristic age. Towards the end of his life, however, he joined the rigorous Montanist sect and dedicated his energies to combating what he regarded as the growing secularization of Christianity.

Origen (*c*. 185-*c*. 253), head of the catechetical school in Alexandria, established a school at Caesarea in Palestine. In his various writings he attempted to reconcile the teachings of Platonic and Neo-Platonic philosophy with the teachings of Christianity. He himself, like Plotinus, had been a student of Ammonius Saccas, the reputed founder of Neo-Platonism. Origen's *De principiis* commenced with a discussion on the attributes of God and then went on to present a vast scheme which included all created beings in an account of the origin and the end of the universe. God is the 'Good' which is beyond final human comprehension. He is an incorporeal intellectual being, who is the light, the truth and the good. The divine Intelligible-World, or Nous, is personal in nature, eternal, and co-equal with the divine Thinker. Nous contains the seeds and forms of all things; it is the source of our natural order. Pagan philosophy had known about Nous, but it did not know about the personal Holy Spirit. Christianity's unique contribution to the philosophy of religion is its doctrine of the divine, personal Spirit of Love. All creation came forth eternally from God by a necessity of Love, and all creatures, even the fallen demons, will be finally 'straightened up', restored and re-established in the final reunion of all things with their ultimate principle. Doctrines of this kind exposed Origen to charges of heterodoxy, if not heresy, in the early Councils of the Church.

St Gregory of Nyssa (*c*. 330-*c*. 395), born at Caesarea in Cappadocia, became Bishop of Nyssa about 372. He maintained that truths such as the existence of God, discovered by reason, provide a useful preamble to the acceptance of revealed truth. He made use of several themes and expressions of Plato, Plotinus, and the Jewish-Hellenistic philosopher Philo of Alexandria in his systematized exposition of the insights of Christian 'wisdom'. He held that the universal plans of all things exist in the divine mind and that these universals are then partially expressed or realized in the many particular individuals created by God. The exemplar of man, for instance, as existing in the divine mind, is neither male nor female, but it is expressed partially and differently in the singular embodiments of this idea. (This interpretation of the 'Platonist' doctrine of forms was adopted and developed by John Scotus Eriugena in the ninth century.) Reality itself is immaterial. Each corporeal entity is composed of principles (of being) which are themselves immaterial. Finite beings are created totally out of nothing. Corporeal beings are sensible and sensed entities which are symbols or appearances or epiphanies of immaterial reality. The pilgrim soul in its ascent to mystical union with God is drawn by God to rise above all forms of sensation into a world of 'dark' contemplation where it is finally transformed in a state of ecstatic love. Gregory of Nyssa's systematization of the stages of the soul's ascent to mystical union with God inspired further developments of this theme on the part of the Pseudo-Dionysius and the Christian mystical philosophers of the Middle Ages.

No clear distinction was made in the Patristic age between philosophy and theology. Many, though not all, of the early writers and Fathers of the Church saw ancient Greek and Roman 'wisdom' (*sophia*), or philosophy, as a precursor of Christian *sophia*. They drew largely on the Platonic, Stoic and Neo-Platonic traditions in their attempts to express clearly the implications of Christian revelation and the Christian philosophy of religion. Their formulations of Christian philosophy and theology exercised a notable influence on the Christian philosophers of the Middle Ages. In the case of Augustine, his influence became widespread and profound.

2. St Augustine (354-430) was born in Tagaste in the province of Numidia in North Africa. He did his early studies in grammar and arithmetic in his home town, and then went to the city of Carthage to study rhetoric. For nine years he became an auditor (or catechumen) of the Manichaean religious movement and converted some of his friends to its doctrines. Manes, the founder of Manichaeanism, taught, among other things, that there dwell in man a light-soul which emanates from the cosmic principle of light and a body-soul which emanates from the evil principle of darkness (matter), and that these two are in a constant state of conflict. In 384 Augustine obtained a chair of rhetoric at Milan. He listened to St Ambrose's sermons on the Scriptures; and in 386 he was reconverted to the faith of his mother St Monica. In 388 Augustine returned to Tagaste where he opened and established a monastery. In 391 he was ordained priest; and in 395 he became Bishop of Hippo. He preached frequently, and wrote several treatises against the Manichaeans, the Donatists, the pagans, the Pelagians, and the Arians. His numerous writings include the following works: *Contra Academicos* (386), *De immortalitate animae* (387), *De libero arbitrio* (388–396), the *Confessions* (publ. 400), *De civitate Dei* (publ. 426), and *De anima et eius origine*

(419). He died during the Vandal siege of Hippo in August 430.

Augustine sought truth with his whole soul; and this, for him, was a seeking for God. 'O Truth, O Truth, the very intimate parts of my soul long for Thee.' 'Thou hast made us for Thyself, and our heart is restless until it rest in Thee' (*Confessions* I, 1, 1). The outstanding trait of his philosophy is an impassioned love and quest of Truth, Wisdom. His faith sought ever deeper understanding. His quest for Truth helped him to transform Platonic and Neo-Platonic thought in a powerful new intellectual interpretation of God, man and the universe. He did not distinguish philosophy and theology in his writings, but his philosophy is nevertheless easy to separate from his strictly theological thought.

Augustine's philosophy can be treated under three main sections: (1) The existence of Truth (God); (2) The creative work of Truth (Creation); and (3) The beatifying possession of Truth (the soul's ascent). We shall adopt this schema in the following paragraphs.

(1) For Augustine, the affirmation of scepticism on the part of the New Academicians entails that scepticism itself is self-destructive by its very affirmation. The sceptic affirms that it is wise and true to affirm that there is no truth and no criterion of truth. There must therefore be a criterion of truth by which this singular truth (viz. that there is no truth) can be affirmed to be wise and true! Scepticism is, from every viewpoint, self-destructive. The sceptic, like everyone else, is certain about his subjective impressions, as when he says 'I certainly feel cold'. He is certain of his own existence because he, like every human being, has an experiential knowledge of his own existing and living and understanding. Everyone, the sceptic included, is certain of the principle of contradiction, and of mathematical truths, as, for example, that five and three do actually make eight. Even if he makes a miscalculation, he knows he is existing at the time that he is miscalculating: '*Si fallor, sum*'.

For Augustine, the intuition of our own thinking self (e.g. 'If I am doubting, if I am dreaming, I am alive') is merely one particularly striking example of our intellectual ability to grasp certain truths, in their fullest sense, and independently of physical sensations. We have intellectual intuition of our own existence and of our thoughts. We discover within ourselves an intelligible world which establishes its own existence through immediate evidence independently of the senses. Truth is superior to man. It is divine Wisdom. It imposes itself on man.

Augustine's proof for the existence of the intelligible world of truth is closely allied with his proof for the existence of God. The one is a continuation of the other. The truth sought by the soul is discovered, not in the world of sense, but within the soul, in the necessary and changeless truths which transcend it and rule its thought. These eternal truths reflect and reveal the Ground of all truth, the eternal and all-perfect Being, who is Truth itself. They participate in the immutable and eternal; and participation in the immutable and eternal supposes the existence of a Source possessing, in itself and absolutely, immutability and eternity.

The existence of God can be proved from 'the very order, disposition, beauty, change and motion of the world and of all visible things' (*De civitate Dei* 11, 4). The creative source of the beauty and perfections of the universe is Absolute Beauty and Supreme Perfection itself. The whole human race confesses the one God as 'something than which nothing more excellent or more sublime exists' (Anselm's *a simultaneo* argument for the existence of God developed Augustine's line of thought). But Augustine prefers to regard all these proofs as connected stages in one long process of complete proof in which everything in the sensible world and in the inner world of consciousness points to the one God as the Creative Source of all things.

God is, then, Subsisting Truth, in whom all perfections are included and identified. He is the supreme Truth, the source of the logical truth of all forms of knowledge and the ontological truth of all forms of perfections present in the world. In him all perfections are identified. He is eternal, self-existent, infinite, immutable, simple, spiritual, incomprehensible Perfection its very self. Within the divine intelligence the archetypal forms or essences are present eternally and without change. In 'one eternal, immutable and ineffable vision', God knows these exemplars of all things as they are in himself. Existing things are external and finite reflections of his divine essence. Creatures have ontological truth in so far as they exemplify or embody the model in the divine mind which is Truth its very self. (This doctrine became known as the Augustinian doctrine of exemplarism.)

(2) It is a basic principle for St Augustine that every reality in the universe is totally dependent on subsistent Truth for the continuous creation of its entire being. God, Truth, is the explicative cause, the source, the principle of emanation of all that is in being. Each created thing possesses its being, its unity, truth and goodness by participation in the subsisting Truth in which all these perfections are realized in their absolutely pure state. God created the entire being of each reality *ex nihilo*. Creation involves no change in God, since God is not circumscribed by time. The measurement of time arises only from a certain measurement of creatures. All things are present to God in his

immutable, everlasting now. Time, like movement, is one of his creatures. God himself is in eternity, unchangeable, and unchanged in the emanation of the world in time. Furthermore, this continuous creation of all things is accomplished by God through an act of absolute freedom. The divine volition is not determined or caused by anything superior to itself since there is no being superior to God. The explicative cause of creation is to be found, then, in the free, self-diffusive and gratuitous Love which God bears towards all the works of his creation. He wills the goodness of his work, and he wills it with an efficacious will through communicating himself by means of creation. Everything emanates from God, and so goodness is spread through all things. Subsisting Truth is the conscious and benevolent source of order, justice and goodness in the world. In this sense, it is necessarily Providence.

Evil, in general, is a privation of being, of substance or of good. 'There is no efficient cause of evil, but merely a deficient one, for evil is not effected, but a defection' (*De civitate Dei* 12, 7). Physical evil is the privation of physical good; it has its source in the limitation, the finiteness, of creatures. Moral evil, or sin, is a privation of right order in the created free will. The evil consists in the turning away of the will from the infinite Good. It is the human agent who is exclusively responsible for this form of evil, that is, for turning oneself away from God.

All of creation, the work of the Creator, is arranged in a harmonious hierarchy. It is a hierarchy of beings each of which depends for its entire being on the subsistent Truth. At the summit of the sensible universe there is the human being in whom soul and body are joined by nature. For Augustine, as also for Plotinus, the study of man is primarily the study of the soul.

Soul and body together constitute one human being, but nevertheless the soul is a substance in its own right. It is an incorporeal, immaterial principle whose fundamental activity is that of animation. It vivifies and moves its body. An inanimate body is incapable of sensation. Sensation is, then, an activity of the soul using the body as an instrument. In sensation, the external world makes impressions on the animated body. The soul actively gathers these impressions and produces within itself a representative image of the external world. This representative image produced by the soul is an image which pertains to the conscious and spiritual order of reality. Intellectual activity frees man from the concrete limitations of the body. Intellection is an immediate participation in the Light of the subsisting Truth. Man comes to possess the truth through an active illumination of his intellect by divine Truth. Illumination is the continuous work of the Divine Intelligence. It is through *divine illumination* that man acquires wisdom, which is a knowledge of realities in so far as they partake of the eternal, immutable Ideas of the Logos, the Word. Human intellection is not its own source. It is an activity which is truly human, but an activity which is totally dependent on God.

Human liberty, similarly, receives its full human perfection as liberty through the immediate influence of God. Liberty is the power to cause one's actions and to be master of one's own life. It is not merely freedom-of-will, it is freedom-of-judgement-and-choice (*liberum arbitrium*). It is sovereign judgement and decision. Thus, it is a property of the will enlightened by reason. Human activity, like human intellection, is entirely free only through a positive motion of God which perfects it as human activity. 'It is within each man's will to consent to the call from God or to resist it' (*De spiritu et littera* 34, 60). The divine movement which occurs within us when we freely consent to the call of the Good gives rise to 'the victorious enjoyment of the good'. The source of the movement in which we resist the call of Good is concupiscence; concupiscence furnishes the victorious pleasure of evil. In this light, Augustine asks 'What would be more free than free judgement-and-choice if it were unable to serve sin?' (*De correptione et gratia* 32). This implies that the power to choose between good and evil is not essential to liberty. The ability to sin is not a perfection; it is a deficiency of free judgement-and-choice. Free judgement-and-choice is more free as it is more healthy; and it is more healthy the more subject it is to the call of the Good.

The human soul is immaterial, and it is a substance in its own right. These qualities alone assure the immortality of the soul. The soul participates in Life. It apprehends indestructible truth. It has a natural desire for perfect happiness, beatitude. Each of these factors argues likewise for its immortality.

Augustine asserted clearly that the soul of the first man was created directly by God at the moment that the soul animated the body. He hesitated about applying this same view, however, to the origin of individual souls and to the manner in which they come from God. He inclined rather to the view of 'spiritual traducianism'. According to this view the soul proceeds by propagation from the parents according to a certain kind of spiritual emanation, 'as a light is lit by another light... and comes from it' (cf. *Letters* 156 and 190). Thomas Aquinas pointed out effectively that any traducianist view (i.e. that the soul is 'handed on' by the parents) is irreconcilable with the doctrine of the immaterial and spiritual nature of the soul.

The corporeal world, too, depends for its entire being on the continuous creative activity of the subsistent Truth. Corporeal beings are characterized by continual transformation. This continual transformation of corporeal beings is explained by Augustine in terms of two principles, namely, passive matter and active 'seminal reasons' (*rationes seminales*).

Matter is a potential reality, a passive, receptive substrate of all forms; it is itself absolutely deprived of any form or determination. (This concept is closely allied to Aristotle's concept of prime matter and Aquinas' concept of pure potentiality.) In the hierarchy of beings, matter is the last reflection of subsisting Truth. It is almost nothingness because it is wholly lacking in form, but it is the receptive substrate of all forms, and the source of movement and time. It is a created, finite, determinable reality which came to be at the time that the first form determined it. It is a passive principle of being, a principle of potentiality, a principle of determinability. It is not repugnant to reason that a principle of this kind may perhaps be present in human souls and in pure spirits as a certain 'quasi-matter' of the spiritual order, and thereby exempt from quantity (*De Genesi ad litteram* 7, 6, 9; the Augustinian theory of spiritual matter was developed further by Augustine's followers in the Middle Ages). Even pure spirits are determinable. God alone is unchangeable, pure perfection.

The continual transformation of corporeal being requires, in addition, an active principle or active principles of change, the *rationes seminales*. When the Creator first created all of creation, he created many things in a seminal way, in germ. Various species unfolded in time from these invisible, seed-like, active virtues or potentialities. In this way, Divine Providence placed in the world the active principles of its subsequent ordered development. 'He that liveth forever created all things together' (Ecclesiasticus 18:1). All of creation was accomplished in the first instant of time. Plants and animals came into being on the face of the earth later at the providential appointed moment. 'As mothers are heavy with foetuses, so the world is heavy with the causes of things to be born' (*De Trinitate* 3, 9, 16). The seminal natures are therefore immanent forces of expansion implanted in the universe by the Creator; they are forces which, under the aegis of Divine Providence, are capable of unfolding ever further new forms of being on the earth and in the universe.

(3) The Divine Truth is the unique and perfect cause not only of the descent of all beings from the Divine Truth but also of the ascent of the purified soul to the beatifying possession of the Truth. Our desire

for happiness is a natural urge of our created nature which makes us restless until we find repose in subsisting Goodness its very self. In his creative act, God made his own subsisting Goodness to be the supreme object and natural goal of all our voluntary activity. It is for this reason that all human activity tends irresistibly, by nature, towards supreme happiness, that is, towards the beatifying, loving vision and possession of the subsisting Truth, God himself. 'The desire of beatitude is therefore the striving after God; the attainment of God is beatitude itself' (*De moribus ecclesiae* 9, 11, 18). For this reason Augustine's ethic or moral theory is based on the dynamism of love, the natural dynamism of the will, aided by Providence, in its quest for happiness and repose in subsisting goodness; and happiness is joy in the Truth.

Man's progress and ascent towards the possession of Truth is facilitated by the acquisition of *virtue*. Reason tells us to conform all our activity habitually to the order of creation. Constancy in virtuous behaviour facilitates this conforming of our activity to the order of creation. Virtue is the perfection of the reasonable life; it is the reign of reason and love in human life. If one grows to love the Good truly, then one will always do the good: 'Love and do what you will', or 'Love and do what you please' (*In Epistolas Joannis* 7, 8).

Virtue does not suppress love; rather, it makes our love to be rightly ordered love. Virtue enables us to establish right order among our values and right orientation in our lives. It detaches us from the sensible order in such a way that every creature then becomes a signpost, a means leading us onwards towards our goal, beatifying Goodness itself.

The virtuous life is the perfection of the reasonable life in which the virtuous man conforms himself to the order of creation. This order has been established by the Divine Reason, united to the Divine Will. God determines and preserves the natural order, and he prevents this order from being disturbed. Virtue therefore enables us to conform ourselves rationally to the order which the Divine Reason and Will obliges us to preserve. Thus, the man who abandons the way of virtue, morality and happiness is guilty not only of folly but also of sin in as far as he has violated the Law of God obliging that right order be preserved in all of creation.

The ultimate foundation of moral obligation lies in the supreme Eternal Law at work in the continuous creative activity on which every creature depends for its very being. This law is universal and invariable throughout all of creation. Every being partakes in its own particular way in the eternal law. Providence moves each being towards its own destiny. This particular form of participation in the eternal law is called the natural law for that particular being. In human society, human law is a more precise application of the natural law to details of social life.

All mankind can be divided into two fundamental camps or 'cities', according to the character of their dominant love. Those who love God and prefer God to self belong to the City of Jerusalem; those who prefer self to God belong to the City of Babylon. On the face of the earth they mingle together in body, but in heart they are separated. The history of mankind is a history of the dialectic and conflict of these two 'loves'. One can see vestiges of it, for example, in the conflict between the Church and the pagan State; nevertheless, the identification is not complete. Thus, a State official whose conduct is governed by justice and the love of God belongs spiritually and morally to the City of Jerusalem, and a Church official whose conduct is governed by self-love is in fact a citizen of the terrestrial City of Babylon. The idea of the 'terrestrial city' is a moral and spiritual idea; it should not be confused or identified with the different idea of the 'temporal state'. Those who belong in heart to the City of God must try to permeate society, like spiritual leaven in the mass, with the moral and spiritual principles of the City of God. They will be a constant encouragement to all men to make a common effort towards God-centred, moral ends. In this way they will influence and uplift all of civil and social life in the temporal state.

3. Pseudo-Dionysius. The pseudonym 'Dionysius the Presbyter' was used at the close of the fifth century by the unknown author of the writings on the *Divine Names*, the *Mystical Theology*, the *Celestial Hierarchy* and the *Ecclesiastical Hierarchy*. The author, now known as the *Pseudo-Dionysius*, or as Denis the pseudo-Areopagite, may possibly have been the Syrian mystical theologian Stephen Bar Sadaili (*c.* 500) or a contemporary of his. These writings were widely esteemed in the Eastern Church and in the West as being by St Paul's disciple, Dionysius the Areopagite. The writings incorporate several of the Neo-Platonist ideas of Proclus and attempt to reconcile these ideas with the teachings of Christianity.

The Pseudo-Dionysius distinguished between an affirmative and a negative knowledge or science of God. Affirmative theology makes statements about God based on God's effects in the order of creation, and attributes many 'positive' names to him. Thus God is called super-essential Goodness, super-essential Life, the super-essential One, Beauty, Intelligence, Wisdom, Light, and Power, even though

God himself transcends the content of all such names. Negative theology, on the other hand, rises to a different kind of knowledge of God by way of negation, or exclusion from God of the imperfections of creatures. God is the infinite and nameless One who is above all determinations and anthropomorphic conceptions. The human soul which rises in prayer towards union with God is blinded by the excess of light, and God reveals himself to the soul in a silence and darkness which is introductory to his revelation of his infinite mysteries.

God is the principle or source of all things. He is Goodness which is ever overflowing. Creatures are the out-going emanations or effusions of this Goodness; but they are finite and really distinct from God. They are created by God through the archetypal forms or ideas which exist in him.

God is the finality of all things. He attracts all things back to himself, their source and end. All creatures are deified in the Divine Goodness from which they descended and to which they return. Man's deification is achieved through grace, love and ecstasy.

Evil has no positive being. It is a deprivation or an absence of a good that ought to have been present. Even the fallen angels have the goodness of their very being; they are called evil because of their deprivation of their proper virtues. All creation is good, and it comes from one Cause; evil arises from many partial deficiencies.

The writings of the pseudo-Areopagite exercised a great influence on the philosophy of religion and mysticism of the Middle Ages. This influence is particularly noticeable in the case of John Scotus Eriugena, Hugh of St Victor, Denis the Carthusian, Meister Eckhart, Nicholas of Cusa, and the several writers of commentaries on the works of 'the saintly Dionysius, the personal disciple of St Paul'.

4. The age of transmission. The sixth and seventh centuries may well be regarded as an age of compilation and transmission. It was an age in which several of the ideas of the philosophers of ancient Greece and Rome were retained and passed on to the later philosophers of the Middle Ages. In 410, Rome was sacked by the Visigoths, under their chief Alaric. Central government in the Western Empire collapsed. The pastoral, nomadic tribes of Goths, Huns, Vandals and others, with their great herds of cattle, crossed the frontiers of the old empire and swept in a great torrent into Gaul, Spain, Italy and North Africa. Many of the cities and their institutions, including the institutions of learning, crumbled. Political organization became decentralized, and life became predominantly rustic. The Latin language degenerated, and literary culture all but perished except in the schools and monasteries of Ireland (a country where the Romans had never set foot) and to a lesser extent in the growing monastic settlements at Lérins, Marmoutier, Monte Cassino, Bobbio and other centres of prayer, study and missionary activity.

In this age of transmission, *Boethius* (480-525), like the Pseudo-Dionysius, deserves special mention as an important transmitter of the ancient philosophy to men of learning in the Middle Ages. He was a philosopher with a Hellenistic education who became a consul under Theodoric, the leader or king of the Ostrogoths. Boethius attempted to establish a literary and intellectual atmosphere in the court of the Ostrogoth king. He translated into Latin and wrote commentaries on the *Isagoge* of Porphyry, and the *Organon* of Aristotle; this latter work, however, was lost, being recovered only in the twelfth century. He also wrote some original treatises on logic, as well as his famous work written in prison before his death, *De consolatione Philosophiae* (*On the Consolation of Philosophy*).

Boethius transmitted several aspects of Aristotelian thought to the early Middle Ages, such as the doctrine of matter and form, act and potency, substantial change, the ten categories and the Aristotelian logic. Until the new translations of the thirteenth century, Aristotle was known in the West only through the works of Boethius.

He also formulated several definitions among which the following became specially notable among the Scholastics: *eternity* is *'interminabilis vitae tota simul et perfecta possessio'* ('the total, simultaneous and perfect possession of unending life'); *person* is 'an individual substance (*hypostasis*) of rational nature'; *happiness* is 'a state perfected by the junction of all goods'. Even though his writings, for the main part, show little originality, these same writings had nevertheless a profound influence in the formation of Scholasticism in the early Schools of the Middle Ages.

Cassiodorus (477-570), a pupil of Boethius, became a senator and chancellor to Theodoric the Great at the Ostrogoth court. In his *De Anima* he stated that he wished to transmit to others a summary of what he had learned from earlier writers. He achieved this primarily in his *Institutiones*, a compendium of the 'divine and secular' arts and sciences. In this work he divided the seven liberal arts into two groups, namely, grammar, dialectic and rhetoric, which came to be known as the Trivium, and arithmetic, geometry, music and astronomy, which came to be known as the Quadrivium. This compendium of the seven liberal arts became a widely used textbook in the Schools of the early Middle Ages.

St Isidore of Seville (560-636), St Bede the Venerable (675-735) and other compilers similarly played their own role in handing on the learning of the ancient writers.

PART TWO

MEDIEVAL PHILOSOPHY: THE SCHOLASTIC SYNTHESES
(seventh to seventeenth centuries)

---

9 The formation of Scholasticism

1. The Carolingian renaissance   2. John Scotus Eriugena
3. The problem of universals: Realists and Anti-Realists
4. St Anselm   5. Medieval Islamic and Jewish philosophy

1. The Carolingian renaissance. Charlemagne or Charles the Great (742-814) was crowned emperor of the Frankish empire in 800. He invited to his court (at Aix-la-Chapelle, or Aachen) the leading scholars of his day: Alcuin of York, Theodulf, Peter of Pisa, Dungal, Angilbert, Paul the Deacon, Eginhard and others. Provision was made for the construction of schools at the royal palace and near the monasteries and cathedrals of the empire. Many manuscripts were recopied in these schools, in a clear, artistic script called the Caroline minuscule. A new intellectual and cultural revival was initiated, which has become known as the Carolingian renaissance.

Alcuin (*c.* 730-804) was the first master or director in 782 of the royal Palatine or Palace School, where Charlemagne with his family followed the courses of organized instruction. Alcuin built up the Palatine School library, improving the method of emending and copying manuscripts. He also founded a school at Tours.

Two of Alcuin's most renowned successors at the Palatine School were Rabanus Maurus and John Scotus Eriugena. They gave special attention to the School teaching staff and the School library, and widened and deepened the curriculum to cover several courses in theology, exegesis, and the Trivium and Quadrivium courses of the seven liberal arts. In this way the Palatine School set a standard for the cathedral or capitular schools and the monastery schools which had been founded at Reichenau, St Gall, Corbie, Corvey, Fulda, Mainz and other centres. Rabanus Maurus became Abbot of the monastery at Fulda, and later Archbishop of Mainz; he showed a stimulating enthusiasm for learning and a deep concern for the education of the clergy, even though his own writings show very little, if any, originality. John Scotus Eriugena, on the other hand, was a profoundly original thinker whose system of philosophy merits special consideration and study.

2. John Scotus Eriugena (*c.* 810-*c.* 877) was born in 'Erin' (Ireland) and studied in one of the many flourishing Irish monasteries, where he acquired his knowledge of the Greek language. He accepted an invitation to teach in the Palatine School, and found there the Greek texts of the works of the Pseudo-Dionysius and Gregory of Nyssa, which he translated and on which he wrote commentaries. He also took inspiration from them for his own principal work, *De divisione Naturae*. In this work Eriugena produced an original system of philosophical speculation which can rightly be called the first great system of philosophy of the Scholastic Middle Ages.

The term 'Nature', as used in *De divisione Naturae*, denotes being-in-general, or the totality of all reality. In this totality, God and creatures are clearly affirmed to be distinct, even though they can also be said to form a totality or universe of being. Nature, or being-in-general, can best be understood in terms of the different *species* or stages of providential emanation of all things from the Creator. Eriugena presents four stages of this kind.

(1) *Natura Increata Creans*, 'Nature which creates and is not created', is God, the uncaused and transcendent first cause who created all things from nothing. The Divine Nature is unknowable in itself. It is wisdom, and yet not wisdom, since it is super-wisdom. It is essence, yet not essence, since it is super-essential. It transcends all predicables and categories. It made all things, and yet did not make all things since its being is in all things as 'increate Nature creating'. In this sense, created beings are a created theophany or manifestation of 'Nature creating'. Nevertheless, positive concepts, derived from creatures, of 'Nature creating', have value solely as metaphors or analogies. Negative theology provides the only knowledge which is remotely worthy of the absolutely ineffable and transcendent.

(2) *Natura Creata Creans*, 'Nature which is created and creates', is God's eternal projection of himself in the ideal world of the *Logos* where the perfection of his being is reflected in an intelligible manner in the *praedestinationes* or the primordial exemplary causes. Eriugena calls it the 'created Nature creating' because he sees it as referring to the eternally 'generated' Word, or Logos, or Thought of God in whose divine ideas all creatures participate.

(3) *Natura Creata non Creans*, 'Nature which is created and does not create', consists of *created beings*. They are theophanies, or

self-manifestations, of Creating Being. All of creation is a descensive emanation of beings from Being Itself. Eriugena defended himself vigorously against pantheistic interpretations of his doctrine, but he continued to use Neo-Platonic expressions which carried obscure and pantheistic overtones for all his contemporaries. Thus, the world is created 'within God'; there is nothing outside God. The Divine Nature 'contains within Itself all that it created and creates, in such a way, though, that It is one superessential thing Itself, different from that which It creates in Itself' (*De divisione Naturae* III, 17). Eriugena appealed to a higher, intuitive knowledge for a deeper understanding of the ineffable ways of God.

(4) *Natura nec Creata nec Creans*, 'Nature which neither creates nor is created', is Nature as *final* end, loving and attracting all creation to return to its Source. In this cosmic return, every creature attains its fullness of perfection and happiness in a certain type of 'deification' or transformation of the creature in God. Thus human nature, after its resurrection, will attain full perfection in that state of original innocence which it had before its fall. The fallen angels, too, like all the rest of God's creation, will return to God and be perfected in God. The perverse will, of perverse men and angels, was not made by God. Its eternal punishment must consist in God's eternal prevention of the will's tendency to focus itself on the goods of God rather than upon God who is Goodness Itself. Those who had been perverse shall experience the joy of full possession of natural happiness in God. Those who are the elect will enjoy 'deification'. In this final stage, God will be all in all.

Eriugena quoted extensively from Gregory of Nyssa, 'St Dionysius', St Paul, St Ambrose and Augustine. He considered that his system of thought was well grounded in the Scriptures and Tradition. He pointed out that where the Fathers suggest different opinions, then we are free to choose that opinion which 'appears to reason to agree better with the sense of the divine words'. It is in this sense that one can speak of the 'rationalism' of Eriugena.

He constructed a coherent, systematic metaphysics, a general explanation of the universe: a remarkable achievement in an age of compilation and transmission. However, its tendency to assert startling, absolute formulas which lacked refining nuances of thought left it open to unintended interpretations. Berengarius of Tours (1009-88) disregarded all authorities and dialecticians and subordinated reason to blind faith, quoting Eriugena in support of his views. Amalric of Bène (d.1206) interpreted Eriugena in a pantheistic sense, shielding his own pantheistic views behind the patronage of

Eriugena. The Albigensians similarly appealed to the *De divisione Naturae*. The Council of Sens forbade the reading of the book, and Pope Honorius III condemned it in 1225.

Eriugena had considerable influence on several philosophers who succeeded him: Remigius, Anselm, Gerbert, Alan of Lille, Hugh of St Victor, and others. He helped to perpetuate the Neo-Platonic pattern of thought. His metaphysical system stands out in a century which was otherwise notably unoriginal in thought.

3. The problem of universals: Realists and Anti-Realists.

The Latin translation by Boethius of Porphyry's *Isagoge* was used as a manual in dialectic by the teachers in the Schools of the tenth, eleventh and twelfth centuries. In these Schools dialectical problems became dominant, and in particular the *problem of the universals*. Are the universals real? What is the relation between the individual object and the general concept? This problem was posed by Porphyry at the end of his *Isagoge* or introduction to the categories of Aristotle. Are genera and species real, or are they merely concepts? Boethius called attention to the problem and pointed out that Plato and Aristotle had differed in their solutions to this problem. Aristotle suggested that genera and species subsist (as substantial forms) in sensible things, and that our concepts of these genera and species are universal ideas formed by abstraction. But Boethius added that he did not think it proper to decide between Plato and Aristotle. This comment gave rise to the proposal of different solutions to the problems concerning the reality of the universals in the Schools of the early Middle Ages. One group regarded the universals as subsisting realities. This group came to be known as the 'Realists'. Different members of the group gave various kinds of explanations concerning the reality of ideas and the relationship between mind and reality. A separate group, called the 'Anti-Realists', raised objections taken from philosophical psychology against the views of the 'Exaggerated Realists'.

(1) The Realist doctrine was regarded as the 'ancient doctrine' until the twelfth century. It had been accepted implicitly in a number of the 'ancient' schools, such as the monastery school at Tours, and in the writings of John Scotus Eriugena, Remigius of Auxerre (*c*. 840-908) and Odo of Tournai (d.1113). They held implicitly that the two worlds of mind (or logic) and reality are in exact correspondence with each other. The universals are among things existing apart from man, extra-mentally. They are subsistent realities, such as 'Humanity', or 'Animality', in which individuals participate and share. Is 'humanness' not something present within Peter, James and John,

and is it not something real in which each of them shares? Eric of Auxerre and other early medieval theologians favoured this view as one which also allowed a relatively simple explanation of the doctrine of the transmission of original sin, and of the doctrine of a trinity of Persons in one nature in the Godhead.

William of Champeaux (1070-1120) was accoladed a master at the cathedral school of Notre Dame in Paris about 1100. For some years he taught the 'ancient doctrine' of realism, until the questions and objections of his student Peter Abelard caused him to modify his doctrine and to retire from the school; in 1113 he became Bishop of Châlons-sur-Marne.

According to Abelard, William maintained, first, the theory that each species or essential nature, as for example human nature, is wholly present in each individual of that species. Individuals, such as Socrates and Plato, would therefore differ not substantially but only accidentally. In fact, it must follow from a theory of this kind that 'if Socrates be whipped, then every substance is whipped'. William then modified his previous *theory of identity* and taught instead the *theory of indifference* or resemblance, a theory which tended towards the view of moderate realism. Only the individual members of the same species are real subsistent entities. However, they do share an element (e.g. humanness) which is common and *indifferent* (in the sense of 'not different' in essence) towards each and all. Their natures are not numerically the same; the unity of their nature is one of similitude rather than of identity. This similitude is the foundation of the common concept which applies indifferently to each and every member of the species. In this way William abandoned (exaggerated) realism and tended towards what came to be called the doctrine of moderate realism.

The school of Chartres, founded in 990 by St Fulbert, specialized in humanistic studies. Several of its masters attempted to solve the problem of the universals with the help of Platonism.

Bernard of Chartres (d.1130) and his brother *Theodoric of Chartres* (d.1155) were Platonists. They attempted to resolve the opposition between the concrete and the universal. Individuality derives from disordered matter created out of nothingness. The universal (genus and species) derives from the eternal exemplary ideas. The generic and specific perfections are created by God as 'native forms' within matter, and in this way these perfections or forms are multiplied in individuals. *Gilbert de la Porrée* (1076-1154), a disciple of Bernard, and his successor at Chartres, held likewise that the 'native forms' are distinct copies of the divine ideas and that they are multiplied in individuals. These forms when compared among themselves are seen to have a conformable element which reason is somehow able to abstract; this constitutes the genus or species. He called this theory the theory of conformity. This theory, like the theory of indifference, tended towards the theory of moderate realism.

Bernard of Tours or Bernardus Silvestris (*fl. c.* 1153) maintained the Platonic theory of the World-Soul. He regarded Nature as one great organism. *Amalric of Bène* (d.1206) developed the doctrine of realism into a doctrine of pantheism. 'All things are one, because whatever is, is God.' All things are one through participating in God. Sin is unreal. Every man is divine. The absolute formulas of exaggerated realism tended logically towards a doctrine of monism or pantheism. *David of Dinant* (*fl. c.* 1205) identified God with the potentiality, or prime matter, of all things. Bodies, souls and eternal substances are simple indivisibles; they are all one and the same since they are all one in being, one in substance, and, thus, they are all one and the same in God. These views were condemned at the Council of Paris in 1210. They are views which derive logically from the implications of the doctrine of ultra-realism.

(2) *Roscelin* (*c.* 1050-1120) was regarded in his own times as the first defender of anti-realism, and as 'the first who, in our times, stabilized the meaning of words' (cf. Otto of Freising, *Gesta* I, 47). William of Champeaux and Abelard were his pupils. Roscelin's anti-realism was primarily negative and critical. Universals are not things. They are not concrete individuals. They do not exist in things. Only individuals exist. The universal with which logic is concerned is the *universal term*; it is a sound, an utterance of voice (*flatus vocis*). Roscelin was not concerned to develop this viewpoint further; he was concerned primarily to refute realism.

Peter Abelard (1079-1142) was a famous teacher who attracted thousands of students to the school of St Geneviève in Paris in the twelfth century. He was an outstanding dialectician, whose application of dialectics to theology prepared the way for the Scholastic systematization of theology in the next century. On the problem of the universals he gathered together and systematized the principal elements of the solution of moderate realism. The concept differs from the concrete word (*vox*) or name. It is not a subsistent thing. The concept is a universal. It is a *sermo*, a discourse, which expresses the common nature immanent to similar concrete individuals. It expresses the common reality or nature and neglects the individual traits through the abstractive action of the mind. The *sermo* signifies the word as related to the logical content. In predication it is this logical content, expressed by the universal name, which is predicated.

This Abelardian doctrine was expressed more clearly still in an anonymous work *De intellectibus*, written probably by one of Abelard's students at the end of the twelfth century. The universals are not things. Only the individual exists. The universals are spiritual ideas which are expressive of the real. The word is the symbol for the spiritual idea which is abstracted from individuals. In this process of abstraction the mind considers only the nature that is alike in the different individuals. The nature as truly expressed in the idea is abstract and universal, or spiritual, in the mind. The exemplary idea of the Creator is the model for the concrete individual essence in the thing, and this concrete essence is abstracted in the universal concept in the mind. (These were called the *universale ante rem*, the *universale in re*, and the *universale post rem*, respectively.) This solution given by 'moderate realism' to the problem of the universals was unanimously accepted by the Scholastics.

4. St Anselm. *Anselm of Canterbury* (1033-1109) came from Aosta in Piedmont, and was the Benedictine Abbot of Bec in Normandy before he became Archbishop of Canterbury. Anselm adopted Augustine as his master, and his thought in general is Augustinian. He held that one must believe in order to understand: '*Crede ut intellegas*'. Faith is an immediate and infallible knowledge of truth. However, faith is obscure, and this obscurity is to be dissipated by an effort of reason to find the 'necessary reasons' underlying the doctrine accepted in faith (it is only in this restricted sense that one can speak of the 'rationalism' of Anselm). His 'rationalist' approach to the doctrines of his faith, such as the doctrines of the Trinity and the Incarnation, led some of his admirers to characterize Anselm as the first of the Scholastics.

Anselm's chief work is his *Monologion*, a scientific exposition of knowledge of God. He added to this work a smaller *Proslogion* in which he presented his well-known 'ontological' or *a simultaneo* argument for the existence of God: to know what God is is to know that he is.

In the *Monologion*, Anselm argues *a posteriori* from the observed degrees of perfection found in creatures to God's existence as cause of these perfections. The source of the goodness and reality, or being, of things in this world must be Goodness and Being itself, and not merely something that possesses goodness and being from another. God is Goodness and Being by his very essence. He is absolutely simple and immutable, since any composition in being, or any radical change, would have to come from a superior cause. God is super-eminently Perfect, the perfect and self-explanatory source of the perfections with which he has filled the world.

Anselm's 'ontological' argument given in the *Proslogion* proceeds *a simultaneo* from the idea of God to God as necessarily being. God is conceived as absolute perfection. He is uniquely 'that than which nothing greater can be conceived'. If such a being were merely to exist in the understanding alone, then it would not be the greatest conceiveable being. A being that exists in reality as well as existing in the understanding is greater than a being which exists in the understanding alone. 'That than which nothing greater can be conceived' must exist in reality as well as in the understanding. The unique idea of God as absolute perfection is necessarily the unique idea of Perfection existing extra-mentally as well as mentally. Therefore God, absolute Perfection, exists, not only in idea, mentally, but also extra-mentally. To know what God is is to know that he is.

This argument met opposition from the monk Gaunilo in his work *In Behalf of the Fool, Against Anselm*. If this mode of argument were sound we could then prove other things. The most beautiful island possible might be said to exist just because we conceive it. However, Anselm, in reply, denied the parity, and justly so. The idea of an all-perfect Being is a unique idea; it is the idea of a Being that is necessarily existent. The idea of a beautiful island is not an idea of something that necessarily exists. One may speak without contradic-tion of a beautiful island which is a mere possibility. But the idea of a necessarily existent being is the unique idea of a Being that necessarily exists. If the idea of a unique Being of this kind involves no contradiction, that is, if the idea of God is the idea of a possible being, then this unique Being must exist, since it would involve a contradiction in terms if one were to speak of a Being which is necessarily existent but merely possible.

This *a simultaneo* argument was rejected by the Scholastics in general as an argument which made an illicit transition from the ideal (or possible) order to the real order. Bonaventure, Duns Scotus, Descartes and Leibniz tried to re-phrase and amend the argument, but without notable success. The main objection to Anselm's argument is this: an inability on our part to see any contradiction (or impossibility) inherent in the idea of a necessarily existent Being does not really show that there is no actual contradiction in the idea. One must first show, by an *a posteriori* argument, that the necessarily existent Being is, before one can know assuredly and positively that there is no contradiction in the idea of such a Being. One must present not a 'negative' possibility but a 'positive' possibility in arguing from the idea of God as the idea of a possible Being to the idea of God as the idea of the One who Is. (The phrase 'I don't see why not', for example, expresses a 'negative' possibility; it does not present any proof that the matter which is under consideration is positively, or actually, possible.) One must therefore first present an *a posteriori* argument for God's existence in order to know that one is dealing with a possibility which is 'positive'.

If the necessarily existent Being is positively possible, then that Being necessarily Is. But Anselm's *a simultaneo* argument does not show that this Being is positively possible.

5. Medieval Islamic and Jewish philosophy. The writings of Plato, Aristotle, Plotinus, Proclus and other ancient writers were translated into Arabic at Baghdad in the ninth century. At the time of the formation of Islamic philosophy, a Neo-Platonic interpretation of Aristotelianism had become popular among Islamic philosophers and commentators.

Alfarabi (d. 950) of Baghdad made use of Aristotle's arguments from 'motion' and from contingency to argue to the existence of a first Mover, and necessary Being, God. He re-developed the Neo-Platonic doctrines of divine emanation and divine illumination in a way which was acceptable to the tenets of Sufi mysticism.

Avicenna or Ibn Sina (980-1036) endeavoured to reconcile the thought of Plato and Aristotle with the revelation of the Koran. Each and every man (including even a 'flying' spaceman) acquires the notion of being through consciousness and affirmation of his own existence. Limited, contingent beings are seen to be composed of matter and form, potency and act, essence and existence. They are caused beings. Matter is their principle of individuation. God alone is necessary Being, Pure Act, and first mover. He is the only one in whom essence is identical with existence. The concentric spheres of the heavens flow from God through creature participation. At the summit of this celestial hierarchy is the perfect first Intelligence which produces the first sphere. It produces also a second, separated Intelligence, which produces a third, and this in turn produces the fourth. Thus there is a gradual descent to the tenth separated Intelligence, the Active Intellect, the 'giver of forms'. This tenth Intelligence functions as the active intellect in man. It illuminates each human mind and enables each mind to grasp the natures or essences of things. When Avicenna's writings were translated into

Spanish and then into Latin in the twelfth century, several of the Latin Scholastics attributed the doctrine of Avicenna to Aristotle himself. The writings of Avicenna were widely criticized in the Latin West, but his thought was nevertheless influential in the development of Scholastic philosophy.

Algazel (1058-1111) in his treatise on the *Tendencies of Philosophers* gave a summary of the philosophy of Alfarabi and Avicenna. In another work, entitled *Destruction of Philosophers,* he criticized these philosophers and attempted to show the inconsistencies present in their thought. He was a spiritual writer and Sufi mystic, protesting against the rationalistic tendencies of Islamic philosophers of religion. His own thought emphasized the absolute freedom and 'absorptive causality' of God's creation of both the being and the activity of creatures. This emphasis involves a certain type of fatalism, occasionalism and predestinationism which is also found in several subsequent Muslim writings.

Averroes or Ibn Rushd (1126-98) of Cordoba in Spain had a profound esteem for Aristotle and composed a number of paraphrases and commentaries on Aristotle's works. His philosophical views are similar to those of Avicenna. God, Pure Act, created the ten Intelligences, who are associated with the celestial spheres. The Creator educes material forms from potency of prime matter (pure potentiality), which is co-eternal with God. In the case of the human being, God gave each individual a passive intellect which is activated by a separate and unitary active intellect shared by the human species. At death each person is absorbed into this universal, immortal and common intelligence. Here there is immortality but not personal immortality. Averroes then attempted to harmonize these views with the teachings of Mohammed. The Islamic theologian presents hidden, mystical interpretations of the Koran. The philosopher presents the true meaning with the help of reasoned, scientific demonstration. If the text of the Koran differs from the discoveries of reason, then the text is to be interpreted allegorically. This view came to be known later as 'the theory of the two truths'. It aroused the hostility of Islamic traditionalists against the study of Greek philosophy.

Avicebron or Salomon Ibn Gabirol (1021-70), a Jewish philosopher in Spain, wrote his chief work, *Fons Vitae,* in Arabic. This work advocates a generalized hylomorphism. All things emanate successively from the will of God, the simple and ineffable Being. The Soul of the Universe, or Cosmic Spirit, composed of universal matter and of a universal form, is the first in this series of emanations. Then proceed the angels and spiritual souls, composed of spiritual matter and spiritual forms. Finally, corporeal beings emanate from God; these are composed of prime matter and a corruptible form. These views were widely discussed by the Scholastics of the Middle Ages.

Moses Maimonides (1135-1204), of Cordoba and Alexandria, attempted to reconcile Aristotelian philosophy with Jewish orthodoxy. He presented *a posteriori* arguments (from creatures) for the existence of God, the first Mover, necessary Being and first Cause of all things. God, who is one, Pure Spirit, transcendent and provident, has a special providence for the just. The passive intellects of philosophers and saints will be endowed with immortality; the philosophers are those who actually attain science, and the saints are those who lift themselves to the contemplative life.

Each of these different philosophers, Islamic and Jewish, endeavoured to reconcile Greek philosophy with the doctrines of their different faiths. In each of their systems of thought there is evidence of a more or less powerful resurgence of Aristotelianism even in spite of the Neo-Platonic infiltrations which are equally evident in their views. The Latin translations of these Islamic and Jewish writings played a notable part in the overall formation of Scholasticism, which is basically a Christian re-thinking of Peripateticism.

10 The thirteenth-century Scholastics: pre-Thomistic thought

1. The translations   2. The universities   3. Peripatetic Augustinians   4. St Bonaventure   5. St Albert the Great

1. The translations. The Scholastics were not acquainted with many of the works of Aristotle before the twelfth and thirteenth centuries; they had access only to Aristotle's treatises as translated and commented upon by Boethius. The writings of ancient Greece, and those of the Islamic and Jewish philosophers, came to the Latin West through the Crusades and through Christian contact with Islamic civilization in Spain. At Toledo in Spain, Archbishop Raymond (1126-51) established a college of scholars who translated into Latin the works of Aristotle, Ptolemy, Galen and the Islamic and Jewish philosophers. In Sicily, scholars at the courts of Frederick II (ruled 1198-1250) and Manfred (ruled 1258-66) translated the works of Euclid, Ptolemy, Proclus and Averroes. Robert Grosseteste (see below) translated and wrote commentaries on some of Aristotle's works. William of Moerbeke (d.1286), a Dominican Archbishop of Corinth, at the request of Thomas Aquinas, made a new Latin translation, directly from the Greek, of the principal works of Aristotle, Alexander of Aphrodisias, Themistius, Proclus, Hippocrates, Galen, Archimedes and others. This influx from the ancient world of new ideas in philosophy, medicine, astronomy, chemistry and mathematics gave rise to what has been called the great Doctrinal Renaissance of the thirteenth century.

2. The universities. At the end of the twelfth century the episcopal schools of Paris, with their large numbers of masters and scholars, began to unite into associations modelled on the trade guilds of the Middle Ages. They acknowledged the jurisdiction of the chancellor of the cathedral of Paris. The statutes of their union as a university were sanctioned by the Cardinal legate Robert de Courçon in 1215. Other universities similarly received their charters about this time: Oxford (1214), Bologna (*c.* 1220), Toulouse (1233), Cambridge (*c.* 1241), Salamanca (1248), and Montpellier (1289).

These charters, received from the Pope, king or emperor, empowered the universities to become independent, privileged corporations exempt from local taxation and military service, and entitled them to confer the official licence to teach the liberal arts and the sacred sciences.

In Paris, the students were grouped according to their various nations: French, Norman, English, Spanish, etc. They were free to choose their courses but were obliged to be attached to a master of their own choice. This frequently occasioned rivalries between groups, and between masters. The masters at first were all seculars, that is, secular clergy or diocesan priests. After the foundation of the Franciscans (1214) and the Dominicans (1217), these religious orders set up their own study-centres, which became incorporated into the universities a few years later. The Cistercians, Augustinians and Carmelites then opened their own colleges for the formation of their students. The religious orders, with their large numbers of religious aspirants, scholars and teachers, soon took over the intellectual leadership of the new movements and ferments of thought in the philosophy and theology of the Doctrinal Renaissance.

3. Peripatetic Augustinians. Aristotle was known as 'the Philosopher' by the Scholastics of the thirteenth century. His vast, scientific synthesis of thought, especially as interpreted by the commentaries of the Islamic philosophers, was seen at first as confronting the wisdom of Christianity. It was only in the second quarter of the thirteenth century that certain Platonizing forms of Aristotelianism began to be taught by Christian thinkers as doctrines which did not seriously endanger the traditional Augustinian world-view of Christian wisdom. Among the representatives of this Peripatetic Augustinian eclectic movement were: William of Auxerre (d.1231), Peter of Spain (*c.* 1271; see below, Chapter 14), and William of Auvergne, who were seculars; Roland of Cremona (*c.* 1244), Hugh of St Cher (d. 1264), Thomas of Cantimpré (*c.* 1232), Richard Fishacre (*c.* 1248) and Peter of Tarentaise (1225-76), who were Dominicans; and Alexander of Hales, John de la Rochelle (1200-45) and Bonaventure, who were Franciscans; several of these philosophers and theologians later became bishops, Cardinals or Popes.

These writers made frequent use of the writings of Aristotle, but they endeavoured in different ways to correct Aristotle by means of the teaching of Augustine. All truth, whether natural or supernatural, philosophical or theological, is explained in terms of a special illumination received through immediate contact with God. Moral goodness of will is regarded as the most important prerequisite for divine illumination of this kind. Emphasis is placed on the primacy of love, freedom, goodness and will over wisdom, science, mind and truth. Primary matter was regarded either as endowed with its own active principles of development ('seminal reasons') or as incomplete actuality. This view was then developed into the doctrine of generalized hylomorphism: there is spiritual matter in the composition of the angels and in human souls. The soul is endowed with its own substantial form and it is individualized independently of body. Thus, in the human being, there is a plurality of substantial forms which explain the diversity of operations in man.

William of Auvergne, Bishop of Paris (d. 1249), is regarded as the first great Scholastic of the thirteenth century. His *Magisterium divinale* is a treatise on God, the world, the human soul and ethics; this work makes much use of the new translations of Aristotle and the Islamic and Jewish philosophers, even though the basic outlook is that of traditional Augustinianism. William of Auvergne was one of the first writers to make extensive use of the Scholastic method for teaching and writing. In this method, the first procedural step is the *lectio*: an ancient text is read and explained, as, for example, an ancient text on the eternity of the world. (A copious source of texts was Peter Lombard's *Libri quattuor Sententiarum* [*c.* 1148-52], known as the *Sentences*.) This gives rise to the *quaestiones*, and to the *disputationes*. The disputations are regulated according to set rules for speeches and rebuttals. The reasons *for* a particular point of view (e.g. the eternity of the world) are presented, and then the reasons *against* this point of view. These reasons are normally based on the (inherited) writings of the established authorities. A definitive solution is then proposed, developed and established. Finally, answers are given to objections which might be raised against this solution to the original question.

Using this School or Scholastic method, William taught that God alone is pure *esse*. God's creatures are finite beings composed of essence and *esse*. Creatures have *esse* by participation; God is *esse* itself. The word *esse*, or being, is used analogously of all beings. The universe was created not through intermediaries but directly, and not from eternity but in time. Hylomorphic composition applies only to sensible substances. There is only one substantial form, that is, one soul, in man. In the activity of perceiving and understanding, it is the soul itself which engenders its ideas, with sensation as an occasion. In this activity the soul is passive to God's impression upon it of the intelligible forms of sensible objects. In this way, William attempted to incorporate several of the insights of the new translations into a system of thought which was fundamentally Augustinian.

Robert Grosseteste (1175-1253), chancellor of Oxford and Bishop of Lincoln, utilized a number of Aristotelian themes in presenting a traditional Augustinian system of thought. He was also interested in the empirical sciences and wrote works on the stars, comets, light, colour, sound, heat and other scientific themes. The human mind perceives the truth pertaining to all such matters in the light of the divine illumination. The writings of Robert Grosseteste excited the interest and admiration of his pupil Roger Bacon, one of the leading figures of British philosophy.

Alexander of Hales (1180-1245) was the first holder of the chair of theology granted to the Franciscan order by the university of Paris. His major, and uncompleted, work is the *Summa universae theologiae*. This work utilized Aristotelian themes to develop further the traditional lines of thought as found in Augustine and Anselm. Alexander defended the hylomorphic make-up or composition of every creature, man and angels included. The 'matter' within every creature is its principle of potentiality. The rational soul, independently of the body, is itself a substance with its own matter and form. Man's knowledge of the corporeal world can be explained in terms of Aristotle's doctrine of abstraction, and his knowledge of the spiritual world is to be explained in terms of Augustine's doctrine of divine illumination.

In all of these writers, Aristotelian thought is used extensively whenever it is seen to harmonize with the traditional Augustinian school of thought. This is true also of the writings of Bonaventure, whose philosophy merits special consideration now in a section by itself.

4. St Bonaventure, or Giovanni Fidanza (1221-74) of Tuscany, was a Franciscan who studied at Paris under Alexander of Hales. He and Thomas Aquinas pronounced their inaugural lectures at Paris as Doctors on the same day. Bonaventure wrote his *Breviloquium* before becoming Minister General of the Franciscans in 1257. He also wrote a *Commentary on the four Books of Sentences* (*c.* 1248-55), *Itinerarium mentis in Deum* (1259), *Collationes in Hexaemeron* (1273) and other works. He became Bishop of Albano and Cardinal in 1273, and died at the Council of Lyons in 1274.

Bonaventure's philosophical work is an original and profound synthesis of Augustinian thought in which he adopted several Aristotelian ideas in his presentation of an updated or 'modernized' Augustinianism. In this work of Christian wisdom, man is always seen as having, in actual fact, a supernatural vocation. The most important aim in life, then, is communion with God in Christ. In the light of this Christian viewpoint, the metaphysical philosophy of Aristotle was seen as partly helpful but fundamentally deficient since it lacked Christian wisdom and the light of faith. Thus, according to Bonaventure, it is not to be wondered at that Aristotle denied divine foreknowledge, creation, providence and divine knowledge of particulars, and that his merely natural philosophy fell inevitably into error. Bonaventure respected Aristotle as a philosopher of nature and used several of the insights of Aristotelianism; but the inspiration of his own philosophical thought derives from his deep immersal in the sources of Augustinianism.

The fundamental theory and unifying viewpoint of St Bonaventure's system of thought is the doctrine of Exemplarism; that is, that all things are intelligible through their explicative source, the exemplary Ideas of God. Through the medium of this doctrine Bonaventure attempted to rise up towards the overall viewpoint of God himself. The whole hierarchy of distinct forms of being in creation is seen as a multiple, diffused reflection and expression of a divine plan which human reason rediscovers when it contemplates God's creation in the light of divine illumination.

Human reason can rise to the contemplation of God in various ways. It can contemplate the beauty, order and perfection of sensible things, and from a knowledge of these effects it can attain an *a posteriori* knowledge of the first, necessary Being as Cause. But, better still, each human being can contemplate explicitly and profoundly on his own implicit, virtual awareness of God's activity within himself. Each person has a natural orientation towards the Good, a natural desire for perfect happiness. Each one is implicitly aware of the finitude of the whole sensible world, and of his own personal finitude and dependency in being. This virtual knowledge of God contained in the experience of dependency can become explicit knowledge of God through interior reflection. There is present in every thinking mind a positive idea of perfect Being, an idea formed in the soul in the light of divine illumination. It is the idea of a perfect, necessary Being, incapable of not existing since it is of the very essence of perfect Being to exist. Bonaventure represented Anselm's *Proslogion* proof: 'For God, or the highest Truth, is Being itself, than which nothing better can be thought of;

hence, he cannot not-exist, nor be thought of as not existing' (*In I Sent.* 8, 1, 1). Being is, and cannot even be thought of as not existing.

God himself is the exemplar, the Truth-source, of all things. He radiates himself in creation. His infinite number of Ideas express all actual things and all possibles inasmuch as he is capable of producing all of them. The Divine Ideas establish the ontological truth of each thing by establishing each thing according to its degree of participation in the divine perfection. The divine Word produces each thing not only in its specific perfection but also in its concrete reality as an existent individual. All things are reflections, then, of the divine Word; and all things are eternally present to the eternal Word as external mirrorings of the divine essence. The creative act drew each and all out of nothingness (*non ex aliquo*), and it did so in time. No creature can have been from eternity without ever having been in nothingness: the very idea involves a contradiction. God created the world in time and produced it as a work of art for his own glory. He manifested his glory in pouring out his own goodness in creation and in leading each thing towards happiness.

All creatures (*exemplata*) resemble God, their Exemplar. Sensible things are vague images (*vestigia, umbrae*) or epiphanies of God in the world. The rational creature is God's image and likeness (*imago Dei*) in a special sense: its spiritual power can help it to become ever more conformed to God. This resemblance between creatures and their Exemplar, and between creatures themselves, is the foundation for the doctrine of the community in being of all that is. It is a community in being which is expressed by analogy, since analogy allows for likeness and difference. There is an analogy of exemplarity between creatures and God, and an analogy of proportionality between beings of different genera. Sensible things resemble God only remotely, and man must not attach himself to them. The ascent of the soul to God requires a turning away from these sensible images (*umbrae*) towards the interior reflection of God in the soul and finally towards the contemplation of God in himself. This is the way of spiritual ascent, through asceticism, to mystical life with God, our supreme end and happiness.

Bonaventure made use of Aristotle's physical theory of matter and form to unify a variety of Augustinian propositions pertaining to the created universe. He enlarged and deepened Aristotle's (physical) theory by interpreting it as a metaphysical theory concerning the constitutive principles of finite being. Every contingent (or finite) being is a composition of co-relative constitutive co-principles of (1) *matter*, in the sense of potentiality or determinability, and (2) *form*, in the sense of determination or suchness. These co-principles are to be found in all contingent beings, corporeal or spiritual. Spiritual beings, such as angels and the human soul, are composed beings too, composed of spiritual matter and spiritual form. They can be numerically multiplied because it is matter which is their principle of individuation. Individuation arises from the union of matter and form. The prime matter which is present and realized in the individual is matter having an exigency for a determined form as complement. In this sense prime matter can be said to be endowed with a beginning of actuality. It is endowed with diverse virtualities, or 'seminal reasons', which allow it to be successively actualized by diverse forms, as in the case of successive substantial changes. The diverse forms which are individuated in existing individuals constitute a hierarchy of forms having different degrees of perfection in being. Within any one substance there can be a plurality of accidental and substantial forms. The lower forms (such as the corporeal form, the vegetative form, and the sensitive form) present in a substance predispose the substance for the reception of higher forms or perfections. They are incomplete beings, dominated by the final, specific form which imposes its unity on them.

The human soul is a spiritual substance created directly by God and endowed with a natural inclination to inform a body. It is present wholly in every part of the body as the form and moving principle of the body. It is the principle of intellection and the principle of sensation. As a spiritual substance it has been made in the image and likeness of God. It has been endowed with a natural desire to possess the Supreme Good, perfect happiness, God himself. It is capable of subsisting apart from the body since it is spiritual and therefore immortal. Furthermore, its immortality is personal. Experience and reason affirm that human souls, minds and thoughts are not merged in any kind of impersonal, shared, collective unit substance; rather, they are individual, personal and different in each human being.

The soul's spiritual faculties of intellect and will are 'consubstantial with the soul' in the 'total positive content of their being' and yet they are distinct from the soul itself in as far as they are faculties or powers of the soul. The human soul also has vegetative and sensible faculties, as Aristotle taught in his *De Anima*. On this basis Bonaventure integrated the Augustinian doctrine of illumination with the Peripatetic doctrine of abstraction by means of the unifying power of the theory of exemplarism.

Our intellectual knowledge has two distinct orders of complementary operations. We acquire a knowledge of the nature and laws of sensible things through the abstractive ability of the intellect to disengage the intelligible species from the sensible image. This abstractive operation is performed by 'inferior reason'. We acquire a higher vision of necessary, immutable and eternal truths through an immediate divine intervention in which God illuminates human reason by uniting it with divine reason and allowing it in this way to participate in the Truth. The proper object of this divine illumination is the spontaneous apprehension of the first principles in their universality, as, for example, in the case of the principle that the whole is greater than the part. The divine illumination enables the mind also to see certain unchanging and supertemporal essences (such as unchanging justice, charity, beauty and goodness) with reference to which it can pass judgements on changeable sensible objects.

In the light of the divine illumination, the soul has a direct intuitive knowledge of itself without recourse to abstraction. By interior reflection on its own nature and orientations, it is capable of knowing God and spiritual realities without recourse to sense-perceptions. Our Creator and Illuminator is intimately present within the soul, 'even more closely than the soul is to itself'. Our intelligence grasps his presence indirectly but infallibly in every eternal truth which it grasps and affirms. One can call this knowledge a quasi-intuitive knowledge of God, or a contuition of God.

Just as the divine ideas are the source and explanation of man's intellectual life, so, too, they are the source of his moral life. God illuminates the mind with the first principles of the moral life, the principles of the natural law (or *synderesis*). The natural law itself merely reflects the eternal laws of the divine plan. In this way God directs the rational will indirectly by illuminating it. But furthermore, God also places within the rational will an inborn predisposition towards goodness and virtue; and in this way he influences the rational will directly by informing it.

The divine illumination, therefore, enlightens the soul both in the speculative order, that it may acquire wisdom, and in the practical order, that it may live the good life. Under the guidance of the divine light and the assistance of divine providence the soul is enabled to pass through stages of upward ascent from sensible creatures (*vestigia Dei*), through reflection on the image of God (*imago Dei*) in one's interior life, and through contemplation of the Good, God as he is in himself, to eventual beatific vision of God in the happiness of heaven.

Bonaventure's view of the life of the soul is one in which reason and faith, philosophy and theology, blend together in a unified Christian wisdom which is seen as a reflection of the Wisdom of the Divine Mind, the Exemplar of all things. His followers looked on Bonaventure as a master of Christian mysticism. In the Franciscan order, this spiritual and mystical approach to the philosophy of religion perpetuated itself as a tradition.

5. St Albert the Great (1206-80), a German Dominican, Bishop of Regensburg, was a prolific writer who had a gifted and encyclopedic interest in all branches of learning. He aimed in a special way to make all aspects (physical, mathematical and metaphysical) of Aristotelian thought available to his Latin-speaking contemporaries. He wrote several paraphrases of different works of Aristotle, and commentaries on the books of the Pseudo-Dionysius and the *Sentences* of Peter Lombard. In his scientific writings, such as *De vegetalibus* and *De animalibus*, he presented his own observations and descriptions of different plants, comets, minerals, medicines, rainbows, migrating birds and several other such themes, insisting on the necessity of observation and experiment in these matters. Roger Bacon tells us that Albert was called 'the Great' even during his lifetime.

As Dominican Provincial Superior, Albert encouraged among his disciples and followers the study of philosophy as an independent science distinct from theology. Thomas Aquinas was one of his pupils in Paris, and became his assistant lecturer afterwards in Cologne.

Albert's doctrine is Aristotelian in all its fundamental principles: potency and act, matter and form, substance and accidents, sensation, abstraction and ideogeny. But in the practical application of these fundamental propositions of Peripateticism he sometimes introduced Augustinian or Neo-Platonic solutions. Thus, for example, he adopted the theory of 'seminal reasons', the theory of the permanence of anterior forms throughout substantial changes, and the theories that the soul is not the essential form of the body, and that pure spirits are multiplied in some numerical way.

The overall trend of Albert's thought, however, in all his commentaries and personal paraphrases, is fundamentally Aristotelian. He speaks of God as first unmoved mover and Pure Act, whose very essence is its own existence (*esse*). Each man has his own individual *esse*, and so each must have his own individual rational soul. The (spiritual) operations of the human soul transcend matter; and this may be regarded as the reason for and the proof of the individual's personal immortality.

Albert's teachings and writings, in general, represent a further and notable step in the gradual process of adaptation of Aristotelian principles to the subsequent Scholastic synthesis of philosophical and Christian thought as we find it pre-eminently in the work of his pupil and assistant Thomas Aquinas.

11   St Thomas Aquinas

1. Life and works   2. Faith and reason   3. The
metaphysical order of finite beings   4. *Quinque
viae*   5. God   6. Continuous creation
7. Psychology   8. Knowledge of reality
9. Ethics   10. Political theory   11. Concluding
comments

1. Life and works. *Thomas Aquinas* (1224/25-74), of the
family of the Counts of Aquino, was born at the castle of Roccasecca
near Naples in the winter of 1224-25. He received his early education
at Monte Cassino and the university of Naples. He joined the
Dominican friars when he was nineteen, and studied under Albert
the Great in Paris for three years. From 1248 to 1252 he collaborated
with Albert in the foundation of a Dominican institute of general
studies in Cologne. In 1252 he returned to Paris to continue his
studies. Subsequently he lectured as Dominican professor in Paris
until 1259. He summarized those lectures in his first work, *De ente et
essentia (On Being and Essence)*, a work in which the fundamentals of
his philosophical synthesis were already established even at this early
stage of his career. He was then called to lecture at the papal court in
Italy, where he met William of Moerbeke, the translator. He lectured
again in Paris from 1268 to 1272 at a time of polemical opposition
from the seculars, the Latin Averroists and the traditionalist
Augustinians (see Chapter 12). He was then called and appointed to
lecture at the new general house of studies in Naples from 1272 to
1274, the year of his death.

Among his writings we may mention the following works as having
a special place in the history of philosophy: commentaries on the
Sentences (1256); *De principiis naturae, De ente et essentia, De veritate,
Quaestiones quodlibetales, Summa contra Gentiles, De potentia, De
regimine principum*; commentaries on Aristotle's *Metaphysics, Physics,
Nicomachean Ethics, De Anima* and *Politics; De aeternitate mundi, De
unitate intellectus, De Malo, De spiritualibus creaturis, Quaestio
disputata de anima*; commentaries on *De causis, De coelo* and *De
generatione et corruptione; Summa Theologica* (or *Summa Theologiae*;
1265-73) and a *Compendium Theologiae* which he was unable to
complete before his death.

In these works Aquinas was openly Peripatetic. He not only separated the true Aristotle from the Arabic interpretations but also in some instances corrected Aristotle by a profound application of Aristotle's own principles. Thus, for example, in his commentary on the *Metaphysics* (XII), Aquinas shows clearly that God knows not only himself but the world also, since 'by knowing himself, God knows all things'. He absorbed, deepened and transformed the thought of Aristotle, and in this way achieved a revolutionary change of thought in the Christian philosophy and theology of the thirteenth century.

Aquinas sees God as *subsistent Being, ipsum esse subsistens,* and he sees every created thing as receiving its limited *esse* from subsistent *Esse*. The human being, in the act of knowing beings of different kinds, first experiences them as beings and then develops this experience in an immanent conceptual transposition which assimilates and possesses the beings which are known. It is being that is grasped in every experience. It is always being which is the *primum notum*. Everything is intelligible through being. It is being which dominates intelligence and specifies it. The immediate object of the human intellect is being and the modalities of being. 'Whatever can be, can be understood' (*Summa contra Gentiles* II, XCVIII). Metaphysics is the science of being. It studies being as being. Aquinas's philosophy can therefore be said to be simply the philosophy of being.

2. Faith and reason. At the beginning of the *Summa Theologica* (Ia, 1, 1) Aquinas points out that the sacred science of theology and the philosophical sciences are formally distinct. There are occasions when theology and philosophy may happen to deal with the same theme, or 'material objects', as for example when they consider man's end, or again, God's act of creation. Nevertheless the two sciences differ generically in their different 'formal objects', that is, in their different formal viewpoints and in their approaches to the themes which they consider. Theology considers 'objects as known by the light of divine *revelation*', whereas philosophy considers objects 'as they are knowable by the light of *reason*'. Thus, for example, philosophy studies man's final end as knowable by reason, while theology studies man's final end as known through divine revelation. In actual fact, man's final end is supernatural beatitude, but no philosopher can divine by reason alone that man is called to a supernatural beatitude transcending the powers of human nature. The philosopher (e.g. Aristotle) can discover by reason alone (unaided by faith) that man's final end is human happiness. This conclusion is true even though it does not present all that can be known (from reason and revelation combined) about man's end.

Faith and reason have their own respective juridical domains. Nevertheless they do not contradict each other. Truths of faith and truths of reason derive from the same origin, God, Truth itself. The truths of the two domains are fundamentally in accord and they can be used harmoniously, either directly or indirectly, in the construction of a Christian philosophy and theology.

Faith renders a valuable service to reason by healing, liberating and elevating the mind in its natural functionings. Grace does not destroy reason but rather perfects it. Reason, in turn, renders a valuable service to faith by the role which it plays in apologetics, in theology, and in polemics, or the refutation of objections raised against the truths of faith. It is only necessary then that the Christian philosopher and theologian keep the truths of the two domains functioning and collaborating together in delicate, harmonious balance.

3. The metaphysical order of finite beings. The science of Metaphysics or First Philosophy is concerned with being as being. It commences with our experience of being. Among the immediate and undeniable data of our everyday experience we encounter everywhere and continually a *multiplicity* of different kinds of *individual* beings: persons, animals, plants, and inanimate beings. Each individual (such as myself, for example) shows certain characteristics: unity, autonomy, complexity and dependency on others. Each individual is 'being' and each is 'being *such*'; each is one and multiple at the same time. This experience of the multiple modes of reality leads to the discovery that each such being is composed of a constitutive co-principle of perfection (*esse; quo est*) 'in virtue of which a substance is called a being', and a constitutive co-principle of limitation (*essentia; quo est tale*) 'in virtue of which it is such-and-such a being'. These principles of being are objectively distinct and yet they are incapable of existing apart. Thomas points out that this composition in being applies to all finite beings, that is, to all beings which are limited to being 'such-and-such' a particular kind of being.

It is also an immediate and undeniable datum of experience that beings *change*. They become other than they were. How do we reconcile being and becoming? What is becoming? What is coming-to-be? When flint and iron are struck together near dry grass, a spark and a fire come to be. Later, they cease to be. Living things die and their whole being, or substance, undergoes a radical modification and change. The experience of change, substantial or accidental, leads to the mind's discovery of a distinction in objects between substance and accidents of different kinds, and to the discovery of the hylomorphic composition of every material substance.

Some objects change in accidental ways (e.g. in colour, or position) while remaining substantially the same objects. Some objects change radically or substantially; yet there remains in the process of change an underlying indeterminate substrate of change, which Aristotle called 'prime matter'. In this case, one substantial form gives way to another substantial form which informs the 'prime matter'. This reveals a composition for becoming in beings which are capable of change. The being which changes, and becomes other than it was, must have within itself a principle of determinability (*potentia*) which is essentially correlative to its principles of determination (*esse*, and *esse tale*). The new form is educed out of the potentiality of the being which becomes other, under the action of some external efficient cause. The principle by which a thing is such-and-such (*quo est tale*) is individuated by the matter (*potentia*), according to Thomas. In material things, this principle of determinability is a principle of quantitative determinability, or *materia quantitate signata*; and any form which is quantified is thereby a form which is individuated. In this conception there is a vestige of the Platonic way of thinking of 'forms' as being 'universal' and as therefore requiring individuation. The theory would seem to require, rather, that it is the *esse* which is the principle of individuation, and that it is the combined principles of *esse* and *tale* which constitute the individual.

Aquinas maintained that it is in accordance with reason that there be in the hierarchic gradation of beings, and in between the human being and God, a distinct class of finite, incorporeal, spiritual forms, such as 'angels', or intelligences. Each of these incorporeal beings is composed of a constitutive co-principle of perfection (*quo est*), and a constitutive co-principle of limitation or 'suchness' (*quo est tale*). Beings of this kind have no primary matter and, hence, no principle of individuation within a species. Each angel, then, is totally its own species, differing in kind from others. Each angel can change accidentally (but not substantially) and so it has within it a principle of accidental determinability, or *potency* for new secondary, accidental determinations.

The finite beings of the universe, such as human persons, animals, plants and inanimate beings, appear to us as a universe, or order, of finite individuals each of which is wholly 'being' and wholly 'being such' at the same time. They constitute an order of finite or limited or composed beings. They are beings which are similar to each other by virtue of their principle of perfection (*esse*), and different from each other by virtue of their principle of limitation (*esse tale; essentia*). They constitute an order or a family of being in which each individual member of the family of being is *similar* by its whole being to every other member of the family. This similarity is not self-explanatory. The quest for an explanation of this similarity in being leads to the discovery of the ultimate cause of the whole family of finite being, namely, absolute, self-explanatory Being itself (*Ipsum Esse Subsistens*).

4. *Quinque viae*. Aquinas points out that while the proposition 'God is', or 'Absolute Being is', is one which is self-evident in itself (since the predicate is included in the subject), nevertheless it is one which is not self-evident to us. There is therefore a need of proof. Anselm's *a priori* argument does not present us with evident proof. The human intellect is unable to discern, in an *a priori* way, the positive possibility of the supremely perfect Being whose essence is existence itself. The human intellect must first come to know in an *a posteriori* way the fact that perfect Being is. It can do this only in an *a posteriori* way, that is, in an argument which proceeds from effect to cause.

The intellect abstracts the idea of being from any experience of any being whatsoever. It is an idea whose extension is unlimited and transcendental. In this transcendental idea of being the mind attains a confused but adequate possession of all that is, the totality of being. Now the totality of all reality cannot depend on anything outside itself, since there is nothing outside itself. It must therefore suffice for itself; that is, it must be independent, absolute and unconditioned. Therefore, absolute (non-dependent) being *is*. This is the metaphysical insight which underlies each of the '*Quinque viae*' of Aquinas, that is, the five ways in which the mind can proceed from a knowledge of limited beings as effects to absolute, infinite Being as their cause.

The *Quinque viae*, given in the *Summa Theologica* (Ia, 2, 3, c) and in the *Summa contra Gentiles* (I, 13; see also *Compendium Theologiae* I, 3; *De Potentia* III, 5, c) can be presented summarily as follows: (1) The first way proceeds from our experience of *motio* or passive coming-to-be. We experience that things are 'moved', that is, they are continually and passively coming-to-be, in the sense of being brought to be or being brought to be other than they were. Now nothing can come to be, or be brought into being, except by the agency of something already in act, and that agent, in turn, cannot be now coming into being except by yet another agent. There must therefore be an 'unmoved mover', that is, a being bringing things into being but not itself brought into being, 'and all understand that this is God'. (2) The second way is based on our experience of the existence in the sensible world of an order of active efficient causes, or agents, dependent one on another for their being. We find nothing here that is the total cause of itself. (Any such being would have to be in being before bringing itself into being.) The existence of efficient causes of this kind leads the mind to the conclusion that there is a first efficient cause which is itself uncaused; and this cause 'all men call God'. (3) The third way is based on our experience of contingent, un-necessary beings, of uncertain occurrence: they come to be; they cease to be. This leads the mind to conclude that there must be a necessary being which is the reason why contingent things actually do come to be, since, otherwise, nothing at all would be in being. (4) The fourth way proceeds from our experience of limited degrees of being, beauty, goodness, truth and other perfections in the limited corporeal beings around us. (Thus, one being may be said to be better or more beautiful than another.) This implies that there is in these beings a constitutive composition of a co-principle of perfection and a co-principle of limitation. The composition for 'limited perfection' is not the self-explanatory source either of the principle of perfection or of the principle of restriction in the composed being. Such perfection necessarily implies a self-explanatory source of perfection, that is, absolute Perfection itself, as the ultimate cause of the limited perfection present in every limited being; '*et hoc dicimus Deum*', 'and this we call God'. (5) The fifth way proceeds from our experience of immanent order and universal immanent purposiveness in being which we discover in the beings of the universe. The inner nature of each thing is the principle of its natural tendencies and activities. Each has within itself its purposiveness in being. Universal intelligible order in being, or purposiveness in being, reveals to the mind the presence of intelligent, provident Being itself as the source of the immanent ordering and directing of all natures towards their ends. Immanent order in being can be effected only by Being itself; '*et hoc dicimus Deum*'.

The insight which lies at the heart of each of these five ways may be stated thus: The totality of being is non-dependent (on anything outside); therefore absolute (self-sufficient) Being is; and all dependent beings are dependent for their being on Absolute Being.

The 'five ways', taken in conjunction, lead the intellect *a posteriori*, from experienced effects to a knowledge of (1) Being itself, the supreme 'mover' who is not 'moved', (2) the supreme efficient cause which is uncaused, (3) Necessary Being, the bringer into being of all contingent beings upheld in being, (4) infinite perfection in being, cause of all limited perfections in being, and (5) supreme intelligent author of the co-operation and immanent order in all beings. And this supreme Being 'we call God'.

5. God. In the *Summa Theologica*, after having discussed the question 'whether God exists' (Ia, q. 2, art. 3), Aquinas then proceeds at once to a consideration of the essence or nature of God. 'Now because we cannot know what God is, but rather what he is not, we have no means for considering how God is, but rather how he is not... (and) it can be shown how God is not, by removing from him whatever does not befit him – viz., composition, motion and the like. Therefore, first, we must discuss his simplicity, whereby we remove composition from him' (Ia, q. 3, art. 3). In this way, Aquinas introduced the *via negativa* of early Christian Neo-Platonists, and the consideration of 'simplicity' as the divine attribute which was most highly prized and stressed by these thinkers. God's simplicity is protected in an absolute denial that he can be a body in any sense. Anything corporeal is by its nature subject to division and contains potentiality, whereas God is simple, full actuality. God is not corporeal because he is much more than body. He cannot be assigned to any particular genus because he 'superexceeds' all genera and species. He is not composed because he is Being itself, Pure Act. He transcends all limitations, imperfections, finitude, change and temporality because he is Pure Act, subsistent *Esse*.

Created beings mirror, in an imperfect way, Absolute Being (*Ipsum Esse*). This 'mirroring' allows us to affirm certain positive predicates of God in a supereminent way. Thus God is Being, Cause, Truth, Wisdom, Goodness, Love, Actuality, Perfection, Unity, Immanence, and so forth, *'secundum modum altiorem'*. These positive predicates can be applied to creatures and to the Creator not in a univocal sense nor again in an equivocal sense, but rather in an analogical sense and in a supereminent way. Analogy expresses simultaneously both similarity and difference.

Aquinas uses several types of analogies in his various works (cf. G. P. Klubertanz, *St Thomas Aquinas on Analogy*, Chicago, 1960). In his commentary on the *Sentences* (*In I Sent.* 19, 5, 2, ad 1) he described three main sorts of analogy: one in which a given perfection is specifically present in one item but merely attributed (extrinsically) to another; one in which one perfection exists (intrinsically) in a somewhat different way in two or more items; and one in which there is implied a remote resemblance or community between two items which have no identity either in existence or in signification. 'In this last way', Aquinas says, 'truth and goodness, and all things of this kind, are predicated analogously of God and creatures.' In other works (cf. *De veritate* 2) he introduced the notion of proportionality. Thus, there is a resemblance of proportion between God and his intellectual activity and man and his intellectual activity. The act of being in an animal is proportional to the act of being in a man as the nature of the animal is proportional to the nature of man; and this analogy applies similarly to the act of being in God as related to the nature of God. Later philosophers who were influenced by Aquinas renamed these forms of analogy as the analogy of (intrinsic) attribution (Suárez), and the analogy of proportion or proportionality (Cajetan). The predication of a name or predicate analogously to both God and creatures has a foundation in the total dependence in being of the created being upon Being Itself and in the similarity of being (*esse simile*) which exists between all members of the family of being created by Being Itself.

Being Itself (*Ipsum Esse*) is the very essence of God. He is pure actuality. In him there is no distinction between the act of being (*esse*) and essence. His most appropriate name, according to Aquinas, is *Qui est*, He who is. He is the source of all that is in being. Creatures have existence; he is. He created all things according to the exemplary idea or plan in his mind. This exemplary idea is identical with the simple divine essence. It is imitable outside itself in a multiplicity of creatures, and, in terms of human language, in a plurality of ideas embodied in these creatures. In one simple act of knowing himself, God knows all that is. He establishes the plan (*ratio*) by which all creatures are kept in order. He executes this plan through continued governance of the world (*Summa contra Gentiles* III). The attribute of God by which he intelligently orders all things and events in the universe is divine providence. This attribute is not really distinct from the attribute of divine goodness, or justice or intelligence or mercy. The human mind can enrich its knowledge of the real and the modalities of the real by means of conceptual dissection and predication; but it also knows that, in God, the attributes of God are identical, and not separated, in the infinitely rich and absolutely simple divine essence.

6. Continuous creation. The universe exists in a state of continuous dependency in being upon God, Absolute Being. Each and every contingent being is produced by God in an act of free continuous creation without the help of any pre-existent material (*creatio ex nihilo*). Creation occurs without potentiality and without change. It is not a temporal happening, though time can commence with it. The act of creation is an inner act of the divine will. It is intelligent and free and identified with the divine essence. It brings about no internal change in God even though its external efficacy results in the world as his effect. It is an act which proceeds from the power over existence as such; and this power belongs to God alone, the first cause, Being itself.

According to Aquinas, the purpose of creation must be God's already existing infinite perfection insofar as he wishes to communicate it through finite participation. God diffuses his own goodness to beings outside himself, and his infinite perfection manifests itself in the universe in a finite fashion. All of creation attains its own end by representing or manifesting the divine goodness.

The world could possibly have been dependent in being from eternity upon the act of continuous creation. There is no intrinsic contradiction in the idea of a series without a beginning or in the idea of creation from eternity. God is eternal and he is free to will to create either in time or from eternity. That he actually created the world in time can be known from revelation alone.

In *De Malo*, Aquinas asserts that evil, as Plotinus and Augustine had seen, is a privation of goodness, of perfection, in being or in action. Evil is real (Jacques Maritain, in presenting the Thomistic doctrine, says that evil is like a wound in being). It occurs, and, like any defect, such as blindness or a painful deprivation, it is important by reason of what is lacking. In willing this universe God did not positively will the physical privations contained in it. He can be said to have caused them *per accidens* in willing that the natures of things be as they are in our universe. However, he did not will moral evil, or sin, in any manner, either *per se* or *per accidens*. He merely permitted the possibility of moral disorder in willing that human nature be able to respond, with free 'response-ability', to the call of the good. Many physical evils, as for example many physical injuries, arise from human immoral behaviour. God does not will these but merely permits them for the sake of greater good.

7. Psychology. In the creation of the human being, the human soul is created in direct relation to the prime matter which it individualizes. It is the one and only substantial form in the unity of the composite human substance. It is the principle of all man's rational, sensitive and vegetative operations.

The human composite has several faculties or powers of operation. It has the vegetative powers of nutrition, growth and reproduction, and also the sensitive powers of the external and internal senses, the power of locomotion and the power of sensitive appetite. These are powers which the human being has in common with other living beings and animals. The internal estimative sense, which enables the animal to apprehend that things are useful or harmful to its well-being, is a power which is called the cogitative power in the case of the human being. The sensitive appetite, common to men and animals, is the inner sense by which particular objects are desired.

The highest human power is the faculty of intellection. It is grounded in the nature of the human soul or spirit. In as far as it is restricted to the particular conditions of the substantial form of the human body, it is dependent on sense-experience for knowledge. Nevertheless, it is a spiritual faculty not intrinsically dependent on the body. Its proper object is the real and the modalities of the real. The proper object of the intellectual appetite, the will, is the good in general, happiness or beatitude. Man necessarily desires happiness, but he enjoys free judgement and choice (*liberum arbitrium*) with regard to particular goods, that is, particular objects seen as good.

These faculties, of intellection and will, are not substances. They are powers of acting which are in potentiality to their own acts. They are really distinct from each other, and really distinct from the soul. They are distinct powers inhering in the soul, and they remain in the soul even when the soul is separated from the body.

In Aquinas's day, the Latin Averroists held that the intellect is a substance distinct from the soul and common to all men. Aquinas pointed out that the intellectual lives and activities of different men differ from one man to another and that the functioning of the intellect is totally under the control of the individual human being. Again, different men have different intellectual capacities. Thus, each person has his own active and passive intellect and his own individual control over his own intellectual activity. The intellect is a faculty or power of the soul and not a separated substance. It is the soul which is the form of the body, and it is the individual soul which is the principle of its own intellectual operations.

The human soul is a subsistent form whose powers are not exhausted in informing the body. The soul has a natural aptitude to inform a body, but it is not intrinsically dependent on the body for its subsistence. It is an immaterial, spiritual, subsistent form which is capable, for example, of immaterial self-reflection. It is capable of knowing supersensible, spiritual and transcendent realities. It is simple and spiritual in essence and it is therefore incorruptible and immortal by nature. It has a natural desire for perpetual persistence in being. A natural appetite of this kind, implanted in it by God the Author of its nature, cannot be in vain (*Summa contra Gentiles* II, 79). The human soul is by nature a self-subsistent form, an intellectual substance, having being (*esse*) by virtue of itself; and it is impossible for such a form to cease to exist (*Summa Theologica* Ia, q. 75, art. 6). It is, in brief, simple, spiritual, incorruptible and immortal.

8. Knowledge of reality.

The Thomistic theory of knowledge is a realist theory. It plays an integral part in his general metaphysics, or philosophy of being. For Aquinas, knowledge is knowledge of the real; it is knowledge of being and of the modalities of being. The human being obtains his knowledge of being or reality through his experiences of the data of reality.

Corporeal realities obtrude themselves upon the sense organs of the human composite. They are sensed and imaged as particular beings. Aquinas calls the imaged, particular representation of the object the 'expressed sensible species' or the phantasm. The interior human senses (that is, the common, imaginative, memorative and cogitative powers) work to unify, to localize and place in time, to represent and store away, and to evaluate as helpful or harmful, the various phantasms through which particular realities are directly known in human sensory knowledge.

Man's higher cognitive functions (those of abstracting, understanding, judging and reasoning) have as their objects the universal meanings that arise out of man's sense-experience of particular beings. The active intellect operates on the being that is imaged by 'illuminating' it and abstracting from it its 'intelligible species', or universal intelligible form. This intelligible species is impressed (as *species impressa*) in the passive intellect which reacts to it and receives it as the *species intelligibilis expressa*, that is, the universal concept. Thus, from the particular being that is imaged, its universal element (the nature, or essence) is isolated, and the *verbum mentis*, or concept, is formed as an abstracted or essential likeness of the particular being. This essential 'likeness' is a means for knowing the particular being both as being and as being such-and-such. Thus, it is the particular being that is known (*id quod intelligitur*) and not the idea; the idea is only the instrument of knowledge (*id quo intelligitur*).

All our experiences, whether objective or lived experiences, are experiences of being; they are experiences of something real (*aliquid*; 'this' thing). We express our experiences in affirmations which express our experiential and conceptual knowledge of reality. Thus, for example, we say: this thing exists, the totality of reality exists, this thing is hard, and so forth. Our experience of the particular being gives us an experiential knowledge of reality. Our concepts, abstracted from the experienced being, give us a 'universal' knowledge either of being itself or of its modalities (as being this or that kind of being) abstracting from particularity. The intellect then by a turning back or a 'conversion' to the phantasm (the being as imaged) obtains an indirect reflexive knowledge of the individual reality itself. In brief, the abstracting mind obtains direct knowledge of being and its modalities, and it obtains indirect knowledge of individual objects in their particularity.

Human knowledge of one's own particular self is likewise dependent on the subject's sense-knowledge of his activities and lived experiences. It is only through a 'conversion' to these imaged, lived experiences (the *phantasmata*) that one obtains an indirect reflexive knowledge of one's own self.

Metaphysical knowledge of God (*Ipsum Esse subsistens*) is possible because the intellect is the faculty or power of apprehending being and its modalities. Whenever we know anything, it is always something (some being) that we know. Being is the *primum notum*. Being or the real is the first and in a certain sense the only content of every experience of being. In as far as Being Itself (God) is manifested in and through the beings of the sensible world, as the necessary source with which these beings have a relationship of dependency in being, the embodied human intellect is capable of proceeding beyond sense to know this source as non-dependent, non-conditioned, absolute Being Itself. This metaphysical knowledge of absolute Being (God) is knowledge of Being (*Ipsum Esse*) as having within itself its own reason or explanation for being. Our knowledge is a conceptual knowledge which gives us an objective possession of Being itself through the transcendental concept of being, an abstract representation which is vague and confused but adequate and completely objective. We express this knowledge when we say: 'Being is' or 'Absolute Being is'.

God is known, then, by the embodied human intellect through the transcendental concept of being and through the relationship of causal dependency in being of all contingent beings upon absolute Being itself. He is known positively and analogically as Being and cause by means of the anagogical *via affirmativa, per excessum, modo eminentiori*. He is also known by the anagogical *via negativa* as absolute and infinite. These positive concepts of being and cause, and the negative concepts of infinite and absolute can be developed further by a development of what is implied in these attributes. Thus he can be known further as immutable, incorporeal, simple, unique, eternal, transcendent, goodness, truth, wisdom, love, intelligent, free, benevolent, provident and so forth. This analogical knowledge of God has manifold imperfections. It is finite, indirect, imperfect and incomplete; but nevertheless this knowledge has rich consequences for philosophy in general and for the application of a general philosophy of being to moral behaviour, political life and other areas.

9. Ethics. The moral theory of Aquinas has its roots in philosophical psychology and in metaphysics. It has its roots (or its foundation) specifically in the theory of rational voluntary appetite, which, in turn, is rooted in the metaphysical notions of the good and of final and efficient cause.

Each being tends towards or seeks its proper good, its full actuation or perfection. This applies to the human being too. Man is capable of knowing the universal aspect of good, and his rational appetite is necessarily drawn towards the possession of the true good, though he remains free in judging and choosing the particular means which lead towards the attainment of his full actuation and happiness.

Aristotle, in his *Nicomachean Ethics*, maintained that man's final goal is the attainment of happiness; and he asserted that this can be attained primarily in philosophic contemplation of the highest objects, and especially so in the contemplation of God, the unmoved Mover. Aquinas added that man's perfect happiness can be attained only in man's permanent and secure possession of the transcendent good, God himself, by way of knowledge and love in the beatifying contemplation of God, the supreme good. Human reason's intellectual appetite can have no rest until its desire for union with the beatifying good is satisfied, permanently, that is, in the next life.

Human actions are the means by which the human being progresses towards or regresses away from the full actuation or perfection of his human nature. No human deliberate act is amoral or morally indifferent. Each deliberate act is either good or bad in so far as it is in accordance or not with the attainment of the end, beatitude, which perfects man as a rational being.

Deliberate actions, by repetition, engender new principles of actions, called habits (either virtues or vices), which permit man to act with facility and pleasure. There are virtues of the intellect and virtues of the will. The virtues of the intellect, such as skill in judging, facility in reasoning, wisdom, prudence and so forth, perfect man with regard to the knowledge of the truth. The moral virtues, or virtues of the will, such as courage, justice and temperance, dispose the human will to be in a constant state of readiness to carry out what the intellect points out as right.

Moral obligation arises from the fact that there are certain good actions which have an essential relationship to happiness, a relationship of such a kind that one cannot omit these actions without renouncing one's final goal. It is practical reason which declares that a particular action or a particular means is necessary to attain the end; and it is practical reason therefore that is the foundation of obligation. 'The good must be done and pursued, and evil must be avoided.' The declaration of practical reason constitutes law. Natural moral law is based on human nature; it obliges those things which are necessary for human nature to attain its last end. Some precepts, called primary precepts, of the natural law are universally known and absolutely necessary for the good of man. Other precepts are secondary precepts. Men may be ignorant of these latter precepts because of human prejudice or passion. The formation of conscience through the virtue of prudence governs the practical application of these precepts to particular actions. It is Divine Reason, Wisdom itself, which is the ultimate and supreme rule of morality. The declaration of Divine Reason is called eternal law. Eternal law as applied to man and as reflected in human nature is called natural moral law. The moral law is promulgated by the light of human reason, and is declared as obligatory by practical reason with the help of man's practical moral sense (*synderesis*) in relation to particular acts which are to be either performed or avoided.

Thus, it is human reason, functioning as moral conscience, which is the immediate and proximate rule of morality.

Aquinas's ethical theory, or theory of the moral life, has a philosophical basis which is similar to that of Aristotle. It differs noticeably from the theory of the Augustinians, who proposed that the ultimate basis of morality and obligation is the Will of God. Aquinas deepened and broadened the Aristotelian ethical theory and supplied it with a further theological basis which was lacking in Aristotle's theory. In this way, Aquinas went on further still to develop this philosophical ethic into a profound synthesis of moral theology.

10. Political theory. Aquinas wrote his *De regimine principum* or *De regno* (1265-69) for the education of Hugh II, King of Cyprus. It opens with an exposition of the nature of political society, and the necessity and reason for authority; it then gives a detailed code of the duties of rulers. In this work, as also in his commentary on the *Politics* and in the *Summa Theologica* (Ia IIae), Aquinas stresses that the purpose of the State is to provide for temporal peace and welfare.

Man is by nature a social being. Society, and therefore social government or the State, is natural to man. Men attain their rational end through co-operation. This is evidenced in men's use of language and in their division of labour. Human society disintegrates if there is no ruling power to direct human activities towards the attainment of the common good. The necessity for authority in society is based, then, on the social nature of man. It is God who is the author and creator of human nature; and so it is God himself who is the author of the exigency in human nature for sovereign social governance and leadership. Governance and leadership are necessities for man's attainment of temporal peace and welfare; and temporal peace and welfare are necessities in view of man's attainment of his final end. The State is for man, not man for the State.

The human need for sovereign governance and leadership lies in the community of human beings, that is, 'the people', seeking to organize for the common good. Sovereign leadership is indispensable, but the mode of designation of the rulers of the State is undetermined and depends upon the community itself in its particular circumstances. The mode of designation of the different rulers accepted by different communities may be by election or through heredity or other means.

The State is a natural society in the sense that man's nature demands it. It is also a 'perfect' society (like the Church) in the sense that it possesses all the means and powers for providing for the social nature of man and for the necessities that the family cannot take care of. Its immediate goal is the common good; and so it is also called a commonwealth or republic (*res publica*). One of its principal functions is to add precision to applications of the natural law in the interests of distributive justice. It achieves this through the construction of a code of human positive laws. It promotes the common good of the common man by maintaining peace, by giving unity of direction to the community's activities, and by providing for basic human needs. It has at its disposal those means, such as the judiciary and armed force, which are necessary for the protection of the common good against internal or external agents of disintegration.

The human legislators and leaders of the State are themselves human beings who are subject to the natural moral law. If any sovereign ruler abuses his power for his private good and not for the common good he becomes a tyrant. Deposition of a tyrant is legitimate. However, murder or assassination of a tyrant is immoral and must be condemned. Again, revolt and rebellion often lead to worse consequences. It is therefore preferable that the power of the sovereign be tempered in advance by constitution.

The form of government which seemed preferable to Aquinas himself, against the background of his own times, was that of a limited monarchy, or that kind of State which Aristotle had called the *politeia*. In this particular form of government there is one ruler whose power is moderated, controlled and assisted through a social organization of some kind. However, Aquinas points out that this is merely one form of legitimate State leadership and sovereignty. There are many others. In political matters the emphasis is placed on right reason, moderation and the use of the enlightened estimative or cogitative sense in the interests of the common good. Being political is a particular modality of being social and rational or, more simply, of being human, integrally human. For Aquinas, political philosophy, like moral philosophy, has its roots in metaphysical anthropology and in the philosophy of Being itself.

11. Concluding comments. The original and profound synthesis of thought achieved in the written work of Thomas Aquinas is the product of a brilliant philosopher-theologian. It is a synthesis which is a Christian synthesis. In this, it resembles, but surpasses, the syntheses of Christian wisdom produced in the Patristic period and in the works of Augustine, Anselm, Albert, Bonaventure and the 'Augustinian' philosopher-theologians. The basic attitude is that of Christian 'faith seeking deeper understanding' of Christian Wisdom (*fides quaerens intellectum*). This Christian attitude stands in stark contrast to that of the radical Aristotelians, or *philosophi*, and the Ockhamists of the thirteenth and fourteenth centuries, for whom philosophy was not only distinct from but also at variance, sometimes, with traditional Christian thought. Augustine and the Fathers of the Church adapted Neo-Platonic themes to their exposition of a Christian philosophical-theological world-view. Aquinas adapted the insights of the newly-translated Aristotelian and other Greek and Arabic texts to his own exposition of a Christian philosophical-theological world-view. In doing so he provided all the material for a separate, autonomous, and complete philosophy of being, even though his own ideal was that of a Christian philosophical-theological synthesis.

The Thomistic philosophy of *esse* (being) is a rich philosophical synthesis in which we find harmonized together the major insights and doctrines of the Platonic, Aristotelian and Neo-Platonic lines of thought. The various doctrines of act and potency, being and becoming, exemplary forms of being, participation in being, substantial forms of being and other related doctrinal themes are blended and synthesized together in a philosophy which is a philosophy of *esse*, of *esse tale* and of *Ipsum Esse subsistens*.

12 Thirteenth-century cross-currents

1. Doctrinal struggles and condemnations   2. The Latin Averroists   3. The seculars   4. The regulars   5. Roger Bacon

1. Doctrinal struggles and condemnations. In November 1268, at a time of strife and controversy in the university of Paris, Thomas Aquinas was asked by his religious superiors to leave the school attached to the papal court and take up a chair of theology as a teaching master in Paris. In Paris, he encountered a triple form of opposition: from the seculars, from the radical Aristotelians or 'Averroists', and from the Augustinians.

The controversy with the secular masters had arisen during Aquinas's first sojourn as a teacher at Paris (1252-59). The courses given by Aquinas, Bonaventure and other religious masters were popular and well attended by the students, who deserted the courses given by the secular masters. A dispute arose about the right of regulars (religious) to teach in the university, and in 1256 the secular masters went on strike. The dispute about rights later developed into a theological quarrel about the value and place of the religious life in the life of the Church. William of St Amour (d. 1272), one of the seculars, addressed to Pope Clement IV *A Book on Antichrist and his Ministers*. Gerard of Abbeville (d. 1271) attacked the regulars in his *Against the Adversaries of Christian Perfection*. Bonaventure, John Peckham and Aquinas wrote in defence of the 'state of perfection'; Nicholas of Lisieux and others wrote in defence of the 'secular' clerical state. The struggle was carried on in public disputations in the university halls.

At the same time among the young masters of arts a number of the seculars who were enthusiastic philosophers followed the radical (Averroistic) Aristotelian teachings (see section 2 below) of Siger of Brabant, Boethius of Dacia, Bernier of Nivelles and other philosophers in the university faculty of arts. About a sixth of the philosophers, especially those in the Picard and Norman groups, followed this trend. It lead to open conflict with the papal delegate, Simon of Brie. In 1270 some of these Averroistic doctrines were condemned, and though Averroism continued to have its partisans, these doctrines were no longer officially taught at the university of Paris.

141

Aquinas accepted the truth of the fundamental Aristotelian principles and, with his genius for systematization, built on these principles a masterly and comprehensive synthesis of philosophical and theological thought. Thus, he accepted the Aristotelian doctrines of act and potency, being-in-becoming, analogy, hylomorphism, the four causes, substance and accidents, the categories and predicables, and other doctrines; and he then went beyond Aristotle in re-thinking, developing and applying these doctrines and principles in a more profound, metaphysical way to the whole order of being, finite and infinite.

In his interpretation of certain obscure Aristotelian passages (as for example on God's knowledge of individuals, and on human immortality) Aquinas used Aristotle's own principles to show how the logical application of these principles leads to evident conclusions which harmonize with Christian philosophical and theological thought. In doctrinal areas of subtle and delicate tensions between the viewpoints of reason and revelation, the natural and the supernatural, philosophy and theology, Aquinas achieved a brilliant and balanced (but precarious) synthesis which was capable of being disrupted when philosophy eventually made its declaration of independence from supernatural revelation.

Aquinas achieved this balanced synthesis in spite of, and in the midst of, the academic and religious strife and struggles in which he himself became necessarily involved. In an age when the Averroistic interpretation of Aristotle was seen as undermining the traditional teachings of the Fathers of the Church, and even the teachings of revelation itself, Aquinas's adoption of Aristotle was bitterly attacked by the Augustinians and traditionalist thinkers of his day. He was accused, even by members of his own Dominican community, as teaching 'temerarious novelties' which were dangerously out of tune with the revered traditional doctrines of the ancient Christian wisdom.

In 1277, Bishop Stephen Tempier of Paris, with the help of the faculty of theology at Paris, listed 219 propositions which were condemned under pain of excommunication. Some of these propositions had been defended by both Aquinas and Siger of Brabant. In the same year at Oxford, the Dominican Archbishop of Canterbury Robert Kilwardby, and in 1284 his successor John Peckham drew up a similar list of condemned propositions which Peckham declared to be heretical. However, these events did not stop the rise of Thomism. The Dominican order defended Thomism at different chapters, in 1278, 1279 and subsequently. Thomas Aquinas was canonized in 1323; and the Bishop of Paris withdrew the condemnations in 1325.

2. The Latin Averroists. *Siger of Brabant* (1235-82) was the leader of the 'Latin Averroists'. He was a canon at St Martin in Liège and a teacher in the faculty of arts of the national group of Picards at the university of Paris. In his *De aeternitate mundi, Quaestiones... de Anima, De Anima intellectiva* and other works he presented a synthesis of Aristotelian thought as interpreted by Averroes and other Islamic writers.

The term '(Latin) Averroism' was coined by Aquinas to describe a radical Arabic interpretation, taught at Paris between 1260 and 1265, of an obscure answer which Aristotle gave on the nature of the human mind. Siger, and the Latin Averroists, taught that there is only one rational soul shared in common by all men, and that the human intellect (both active and passive) is one and the same in all men. It is this unitary intellect which survives at death. Thus there is immortality but not personal immortality; and there are no sanctions in the afterlife. This doctrine of monopsychism, and also the Averroist doctrines of determinism and denial of divine providence, were attacked vehemently by Bonaventure and the Augustinian theologians at Paris. Many of the theologians came to regard the whole corpus of Aristotelian writings as fundamentally tainted with heresy.

Aquinas published his *De unitate intellectus contra Averroistas* in 1270. He pointed out that, according to Aristotle himself, the soul is the first actuality of a physically organized body. In the human being, the intellect is one of the powers (a spiritual power) of the human soul. Thus the human soul partakes in the nature of spiritual and of corporeal beings in such a way that it is at once both joined to and separated from the body according to its diverse faculties. Human experience testifies that in the act of comprehension it is the individual person who comprehends; and so each person must possess his own faculty of intelligence. The existence of certain items of knowledge in some men and its exclusion from others, as well as the fact of various errors in various men, demand that each individual person has his own mind. (See above, section 7 of Chapter 11.)

Siger of Brabant, in his later writings, made some important modifications in his views (cf. F. van Steenberghen, *Siger de Brabant* [in Bibliography]). In his last group of writings he held that the intellective soul is the substantial form of the body and is independent of the human body in the higher human operations. It is multiplied numerically with each human being. It is subsistent and immortal. These views are similar to those of Aquinas.

However, Siger continued until the close of his life to teach his doctrine concerning the eternity of the celestial spheres as devolving necessarily and eternally from Pure Actuality. God, the Creator, operates mediately through emanating intelligences in creating the world from eternity. Under the control of the eternal intelligences the cyclic movements of the heavenly bodies determine the eternal recurrence of terrestrial events. These doctrines of 'independent' philosophy, as well as the doctrine of monopsychism, were condemned by the ecclesiastical authorities in 1270, and again in 1277. Averroism then ceased to be taught officially at Paris, though it continued to have its partisans.

3. The seculars.

The secular masters in the universities played their own role in the doctrinal struggles which culminated in the condemnations of 1270. In general they were traditionalists. They regarded Aquinas, for example, as an innovator who defended several of the fundamentally Averroistic-Peripatetic propositions which were so alien to the teachings of the Fathers of the Church.

Henry Bate of Malines (1246-1310) in his *Speculum divinorum et quorumdam naturalium* attempted to blend several of the teachings of Aristotle into the traditional outlines of Augustinian thought. He accused Aquinas of an exaggerated attachment to Aristotelianism.

Godfrey of Fontaines (d. 1303) published the text of sixteen *Quaestiones Quodlibetales* which he had disputed. In these he showed himself as opposed to Aquinas on the question of the real distinction between essence and existence and on the question of individuation through matter.

Peter of Auvergne (d. 1304) also published some *Quaestiones Quodlibetales* which he had disputed between 1296 and 1302. He defended the view that the human soul unites itself to the body after the body has been endowed with its own bodily form. He defended the doctrine of plurality of substantial forms.

Stephen Tempier (d. 1279) was an avowed anti-Averroist and anti-Peripatetic who became Bishop of Paris in 1268. He condemned not only the doctrines of monopsychism, determinism, denial of divine providence and denial of personal immortality, but also the theories of the necessary unicity of the world, of the individualization of angels and their relation to the world, and of matter as the principle of individuation. He regarded all of these theories as contrary to traditional doctrine and dangerous to the tenets of the true faith.

Henry of Ghent (d.1293) was an archdeacon of Tournai and a lecturer at Paris. He wrote a *Summa Theologica*, fifteen *Quodlibets*, and other works. He selected different strands of thought from Aristotle, Augustine and Avicenna and blended these into a system of thought which is predominantly Platonic.

Henry maintained that metaphysics differs from physics in that metaphysics considers essences whereas physics considers singular objects. Singular objects are experienced as existents which differ from each other simply by existing. They are actualized essences. Metaphysics is concerned with intelligible essences rather than with existing individuals. Individuals are not intelligible in themselves as singular. They are merely experienced as lacking intrinsic division and as lacking identity with any other beings. They are intelligible only as contained in the essence, the 'truth', of the object. The intelligible essences of things are reflections of the Idea in God. God knows directly the specific essence, and in and through the specific essence he knows singular things. Metaphysics seeks to know the 'truth', the 'idea', of the object and to apprehend its relation to the unchanging truth. It attempts to understand objects in terms of essence; and it seeks to discover how the intelligible essences can be arranged under the notion of being.

Scotus and Ockham made extended criticism of the ideas propounded by Henry of Ghent. This may be regarded as a certain measure of his considerable influence in his own age. Henry rejected the Thomist theory of individuation. He also rejected the doctrines of plurality of forms and universal hylomorphism. He emphasized the divine freedom and the superiority of the free will to the intellect. He minimized the intelligibility of individual beings while placing a new emphasis on concrete particularity. In so doing he helped to prepare the way for the transition from the constructive systematization which characterizes thirteenth-century thought to the critical analysis and tendency to simplification which is characteristic of fourteenth-century thinking.

4. The regulars. The religious masters, or the 'regulars', in the schools and universities in the later part of the thirteenth century tended to divide into two broad schools of thought: those who attempted to develop the doctrinal current initiated by Bonaventure, and those who developed the current of thought initiated by Thomas Aquinas.

John Peckham (*c.* 1225-92) was a Franciscan who studied under Bonaventure. He and his disciples Matthew of Aquasparta, Roger

Marston and Vital du Four made a selective use of Greek and Arabic sources in their presentation of the thought of Augustine. They held that creatures are entirely dependent upon the First Cause not only with regard to their continuance in existence but also with regard to their natural activities. Furthermore, the First Cause can readily bypass the active agency of the creature and intervene to produce the natural effect immediately. Thus, for example, Peckham held that prime matter is capable of existing autonomously without any form.

Matthew of Aquasparta (c. 1240-1302) expounded again the theories of *rationes seminales, forma corporeitatis* and Bonaventure's doctrine of universal hylomorphic composition. He held that the intellect, with the assistance and concurrence of the divine illumination, knows singular things intuitively, or directly in themselves, by means of *species singulares*. The intellect apprehends the individual, and from the singular object apprehended it then abstracts the universal notion.

Robert Kilwardby (d. 1279) was an English Dominican who held resolutely to the doctrine of plurality of forms and to the theory of seminal reasons. He used all his influence as Archbishop of Canterbury to banish Thomism from Oxford.

Peter John Olivi (1248-98), a Franciscan philosopher and theologian, anticipated some of the theories of Duns Scotus and William of Ockham. He made a sharp distinction between the ontological order and the conceptual order. From the multiplicity of concepts one must not deduce that there is a corresponding multiplicity in the realm of reality. 'Entities are not unnecessarily multiplied.' Some entities are really distinct. Some concepts are merely logically distinct. Between these two groups there is a place for logical distinctions which are grounded in reality. Thus, there is a *ratio realis* which grounds the distinction between essence and existence, being and its attributes, and general and specific concepts. Man is composed of matter and spirit, and these are really distinct. In man, as also in all corporeal beings, there is a plurality of forms. The *forma corporeitatis* actualizes the body before its union with the soul. The soul is a unity even though it has three partial forms, namely, the vegetative, the sensitive and the rational principles. The body is informed directly by the vegetative and sensitive principles but not by the immortal rational principle. The rational principle moves the lower principles only through the mediation of spiritual matter; it does not inform the body directly. This view was condemned by the Council of Vienne.

Richard of Mediavilla or Middleton (d. *c*. 1300) was a Franciscan scholar in the tradition of Bonaventure and John Peckham. However, he replaced some of the Augustinian views with theories which were more sympathetic to the Thomistic school of thought. He maintained that knowledge comes by way of abstraction, not by way of divine illumination, and that all proofs of God's existence must be *a posteriori* proofs. His modified Augustinianism represents an ongoing stage in the development of the Franciscan-Augustinian doctrine from that of Bonaventure to that of Duns Scotus.

Ramon Lull (1232-1316), a Franciscan from Palma de Mallorca, studied Arabic in order to combat Averroism and to convert the Muslims. He made use of the Muslim (*hadras*) and Jewish (*sephiroth*) teachings concerning the divine attributes or 'dignities' as a basis for dialogue with the Muslim and Jewish scholars of his day. He wrote many works in Catalan, Arabic and Latin. In his *Ars combinatoria* he invented a new logical method called the Great Art (*Ars Magna*) in which he attempted to reduce all created things to the divine attributes or 'dignities'. These Dignities, such as goodness, greatness, eternity, power, wisdom, will, virtue, truth, and glory, are principles of knowing as well as principles of being. They are the causes and archetypes of all created perfection and they are the instruments of God's creative activities. They are the absolute predicates. Now, particular things can be compared together, in the light of the Dignities, by means of other predicates which are relative predicates, such as difference, or agreement, contrariety, beginning, middle, end, majority, minority or equality. The combination of these absolute and relative predicates give rise to the fundamental ideas and self-evident principles common to all the sciences. These predicates and principles can be combined and interconnected in circular figures, such as those used by Isidore of Seville and the Spanish Jewish cabbalists, where letters (B, C, D) are substituted for their names. The letter B can be substituted for 'goodness', and so forth. In this way one may be able to expose and explain the principles and truths of philosophy and the particular sciences. This technique and schematism anticipated Leibniz's ideal, some centuries later, of constructing an algebra of logical symbols which would facilitate the exposition and explanation of new and known truths in philosophy and the sciences.

Giles of Rome, or Aegidius Colonna Romanus (*c*. 1247-1316), was a member of the Augustinian order of hermits, and a pupil of Aquinas in Paris. In 1280 he wrote a commentary on the *Liber de Causis* of Proclus, in which his thought focuses on the universe of intelligible beings. From this viewpoint he saw *esse* and *essentia* not in terms of Aquinas's constitutive principles of being but as distinct intelligible beings (*res*). Intelligible essences possess their own mode of being. They are in potentiality to existence, that is, to becoming actually existing essences, or actual essences. The *esse* (existence) present in an actual essence is a received created participation of the divine *esse*. The doctrine is seen as safeguarding the doctrine of the creature's total dependence on God. Matter and form are intelligible essences. So are mass and volume, and body and soul. They are distinct and separable modes of being. If matter, which is the principle of individuation, were to be separated from form, then all members of that species (form) would be one. 'The same quiddity, considered in things, is particular, and considered in the mind, is universal.' Giles interested himself in scientific questions concerning the two kinds of quantity (mass and volume), the accelerated speed of falling bodies, movement through a medium and movement in a vacuum, and other similar problems. He, like Roger Bacon, was one of the forerunners of the scientific inquiry which is characteristic of the fourteenth century.

The members of the Dominican order were quick to rally to the defence of Thomas Aquinas after his death in 1274. Albert the Great interposed at Paris to have the condemnations reversed. Pierre of Conflans and Giles of Lessines remonstrated with Archbishop Kilwardby, and Richard Clapwell, a prior at Oxford, maintained Thomism against Archbishop Peckham. The English and French Dominicans at successive chapters adopted the teachings of Aquinas. John of Paris, Thomas Sutton, Raymond Martin, William of Macclesfield and several other noteworthy teachers taught Thomism. Towards the close of the thirteenth century, Thomism became preponderant in several of the schools of France, England, Spain, Italy and Germany.

5. Roger Bacon (*c.* 1215-92), known as Doctor Mirabilis, Franciscan philosopher and scientist, studied under Robert Grosseteste at Oxford, and later taught at Paris and Oxford. He showed a lively interest in the experimental sciences, in philosophy, mysticism, logic and semantics. In an age when he saw that preference was shown to the more orthodox Augustinian theologians, Bacon made incessant criticisms of the secular masters and of Scholastics who did not share his views on the importance of experimental work for the discovery of the secrets of nature. He came to be regarded as an irascible friar of biting invective who dabbled in astrology and who needed to be silenced because of his 'suspected novelties'. He was forbidden by his Superior General, Jerome of Ascoli, to circulate his writings outside the Franciscan order. Nevertheless he composed his *Opus Maius, Opus Minor, Opus Tertium* and several other works before he died in 1292.

Bacon's *Opus Maius* presents a plan for reform in university education. He outlines, in seven different sections, his views on the contemporary causes of error, on philosophy, the study of languages, mathematics, optics, experimental science and moral philosophy. He says that the principal causes of failure to attain truth are: the current worship of unworthy authorities (such as living theologians), the baneful influence of custom and habit, widespread popular prejudices, and, above all, the technical display of apparent wisdom on the part of the less talented masters who strive vigorously to conceal their own ignorance. He claimed that philosophy and all speculative science should be ordered to (or culminate in) moral philosophy, which aims to lead men to the knowledge and service of God. He advocated a scientific study of language as a means to the correct interpretation and translation of the sacred scriptures and of Greek and Islamic philosophers. A study of mathematical science is a prerequisite for the study of the natural sciences, such as astronomy.

The term 'experimental science', as used in the *Opus Maius*, signifies experiential knowledge. Sense-perception is a necessary basis for knowledge, but it is not from this basis that certainty is derived. Certainty cannot be attained without divine illumination. God, as active intellect, concurs with the human mind in its activities and enlightens the mind of the individual. In this way certain 'experimental science' is attained.

The main part of the *Opus Maius* is devoted to optics, mathematics and moral philosophy. Bacon made use of the recent translations of Alhazen and Alkindi to develop further Grosseteste's theories concerning the tides, the rainbow, heat, sound, double refraction, and the transmission of light in pulses or waves not instantaneously but over a time-interval. He applied this latter theory to vision and to the working of the eye as well as to refracting lenses and parabolic mirrors. He attempted to explain how these lenses can magnify things that are small, and can make faraway objects appear near. He pointed out how further research work could perfect powders having awesome effects and craft that could travel on land, sea and air. Research and induction are necessary in addition to deduction if scientific advance is to be made.

Bacon was a Scholastic who was deeply attached to his faith and his religious vocation and to the spirit of the ancient Augustinian school. He was a complex personality who extolled the method of scientific research as a potent medium and occasion of (Augustinian) divine illumination. He was fascinated by the study of nature as one means among others towards attaining the state of mysticism. All truth and all creatures come from God. All sciences should be interrelated in such a way as to constitute a unique science which would express the fullness of truth. His views were for the main part ignored, and his name was seldom mentioned in the history of philosophy until Samuel Jebb published his edition of the *Opus Maius,* nearly 500 years later, in 1733.

13 Duns Scotus

1. Writings and viewpoint   2. Theory of knowledge
3. Metaphysics   4. Natural theology   5. Psychology
6. Ethics and political philosophy   7. General comment

1. Writings and viewpoint. *John Duns Scotus* (*c.*
1266-1308), who was born in Scotland, entered the Franciscan order
in 1290. He studied at Oxford at a time when the anti-Thomistic
influence was prevalent in the university. He lectured at Cambridge
(*c.* 1298), Oxford (*c.* 1300) and Paris (1302-03 and 1304-07). In 1307
he lectured in Cologne, where he died in 1308. His main work was
his monumental commentary on the *Sentences* which was known as
the *Opus Oxoniense* and came to be known later as the *Ordinatio*. He
also wrote *Quaestiones Quodlibetales, Quaestiones subtilissimae in
Metaphysicam, Tractatus de primo principio* and other shorter works.
These writings present a constructive system of philosophy which is
one of the great syntheses of the thirteenth century. They are the
product of an independent and original thinker who is nevertheless
faithful, in the main, to the Franciscan-Augustinian tradition. In an
intellectual climate which accepted that Aquinas had made too great
a concession to Aristotelian thought, Scotus undertook to correct
and to complete the work of synthesis which Aquinas had initiated.
The Thomist emphasis was seen as excessively humanist and
rationalist. It put an over-optimistic emphasis on the competence of
human reason, rather than on the creature's utter dependence on the
Creator. It relied dangerously on argument by analogy, and thereby
left itself open to the destructive counter-arguments of agnostics and
sceptics. The Augustinian emphasis, in contrast, centred on the
divine elevating and remaking of human nature (corrupted since the
Fall) and the uplifting and transforming of the will and the affections. Man's ultimate end consists in love of God rather than in
knowledge of God. It is the will, then, which has primacy over the
intellect, and not vice versa. Scotus criticized a number of the
positions held by Aquinas and the Averroists and Henry of Ghent.
He sought to safeguard the objectivity of human knowledge against
the sceptical strains which he thought to be inherent in these
systems, and to safeguard the objective character of natural theology
from the agnostic tendencies inherent in their doctrines. The
elements of critical analysis and voluntarism present in Scotus'

writings were given a new central importance in the movement of thought in the fourteenth century.

In the Prologue to the *Ordinatio*, Scotus entered into lengthy discussions on the nature of theology and its relationship with philosophy. Philosophy, even though it is limited where questions of man's nature and actual destiny are concerned, is a work of reason unaided by faith. It is an autonomous discipline and enjoys a competence of its own. Theology is a practical science, not a speculative science as Aquinas had asserted. It is a science or form of knowledge whose necessary truths and first principles derive from God's own divine science. It is a practical science of faith, will and love rather than a science dependent on reason and theoretic contemplation. It reveals to us man's utter dependence on the love of God, God's infinite grace. Thus, it is a science which has its own safeguards against undue reliance on merely rational speculations. It deals with revealed truths, necessary truths, necessary in themselves even if not self-evident to us. Its principles are accepted on authority and faith. The harmonious balance between faith and reason which Aquinas had sought was regarded as being intrinsically too precarious. Theology has a certainty of its own which is not necessarily tied to the various lines of reasoning of the different schools of human thought. Its certainty is the certainty of faith. Reason can be of valuable assistance, however, in defending, explaining and deepening that faith.

2. Theory of knowledge. For Scotus, as for Aristotle, being as being (*ens in quantum ens*) is the object of the human intellect. It is entities, realities, things that the mind knows. In this present life, the mind knows created sensible things. The emphasis here is on *ens* and *entia*, or things, rather than on *esse* (the process of going on in being) as in the thought of Aquinas. The intellect has a confused but direct intuition of singular things apprehended by the senses as existents. They are apprehended and intuited as 'this' and 'that' or 'these' data immediately present to consciousness. From these singular things the intellect abstracts its universal ideas directly. There is no need to postulate further theories of innatism or illuminationism, nor any *conversio ad phantasmata*, as some of the earlier Schoolmen had done. The mind has both experiential knowledge and abstract knowledge. It has a simple, non-judgemental awareness of individual objects as existing, and it has universal ideas of the essences of objects considered in abstraction from existence.

Our natural knowledge of first principles and the conclusions necessarily entailed by them arises from our understanding and combining of simple ideas abstracted as universals from sensible objects. Necessary truths of this kind (such as that the 'whole' is greater than the 'part') assert a universal and necessary connection or disconnection between universal concepts that is independent of the particular source of the concepts. The necessary connection of the terms or concepts depends only on a knowledge of the concepts, not on the particularity of the sources through which we attained the concepts. In this way certainty of judgement is possible without any special illumination.

Certainty is attainable also in regard to internal states of mind or actions which we experience. When one says that one feels such and such, or doubts or wills such and such, these are primary contingent propositions of which one is absolutely certain. They arise from a simple awareness of the existential situation that verifies the proposition. They are experiential facts which can be known with a degree of certainty which is equal to the certainty of the first principles or to the conclusions which the first principles entail.

Certainty is attainable, thirdly, in many propositions of natural science such as those which express certainty concerning natural causes. The method of induction enables the scientist to know by the experience of a sufficient number of observed instances, that a certain natural event proceeds as a necessary effect from a certain natural cause, and that this is invariably and necessarily so. There are several areas of knowledge, then, where the human mind is capable of attaining certitude without any additional divine enlightenment.

3. Metaphysics. Metaphysics, for Scotus, is an autonomous science which is concerned with being as being and its transcendental attributes. A transcendental notion is one which is applicable to reality but is not included in Aristotle's ten categories. It is a supercategory. The concept of being is an irreducibly simple, indefinable concept which designates any subject whose existence implies no contradiction. The three attributes 'one', 'true', and 'good' are interconvertible with being and with one another. There are other attributes such as 'infinite-or-finite', 'necessary-or-contingent', 'act-or-potency', 'cause-or-caused' which Scotus calls disjunctive transcendentals. They are co-extensive with being only in conjunction. There are also transcendental predicates, such as wisdom, knowledge, truth, beatitude, freedom and benevolence, which are pure or unqualified perfections. Their definition contains no implication of limitation. They can be ascribed univocally to God or to creatures.

All our general notions are formed by abstraction from sensible things. Some notions, in as far as they are notions of beings, apply to both sensible and supersensible beings. The transcendentals are notions of this kind. They are univocally predicable of both the sensible and supersensible. If these notions were merely analogical or equivocal, then all knowledge of God and spiritual things would be either suspect or impossible. The univocal concept of being applies to God and creatures in common, and to substance and accidents in common. People can be certain that God is a being, even though some may remain in doubt as to whether this divine being is infinite or finite. This shows that the notion of being is a common notion which can be qualified and perfected further to express spiritual and even infinite being itself. It transcends the level of sensible phenomena. The same can be said of other transcendental notions such as goodness, truth, freedom of will and so forth. The mind is capable of forming concepts of perfections which are proper to God. It does so by taking a common univocal transcendental notion, such as 'wisdom' or 'being', and combining with it other simple, univocal conceptual elements, by affirmation, denial and interrelation, in such a way that a composite concept, such as 'infinite wisdom', is constructed. This composite notion of a perfection of God can then be regarded as analogous to its created similitude, even though the basic conceptual element ('wisdom') in the composite notion is a univocal concept.

The common univocal concept of being (*ens*) denotes distinction or determination (in existence: 'is') as opposed to the non-distinction of sheer nothingness. It is a univocal concept which possesses a unity in the logical order prior to the division of being into infinite and finite being in the real order. It is a mental construct, a logical concept, but it has an objective foundation in real things. It is founded on particular sensible beings and is abstracted from these objective beings, but it is a logical or mental construct which does not formally express any one particular existent, finite or infinite. It expresses only the common element of 'distinction' (or 'is') as opposed to nothingness. It is therefore a logical or mental construct of a particular kind, in so far as it has an objective foundation in the particular beings from which it was abstracted. Thus it is not a purely subjective construction. Scotus was convinced that it is possible to attain objective knowledge of God in this life; and it was through this theory of univocity that he tried to safeguard our objective knowledge of God against theories of agnosticism and scepticism.

The transcendental attributes and predicates transcend all definite genera. The 'one', the 'true' and the 'good' are interconvertible with being and with one another. How, then, do they differ from each other? Again, the divine attributes, such as wisdom, knowledge and love, are inseparable from the divine nature even though they must be distinct formalities of the divine nature. How do they differ from each other? The distinction between God's Mercy and God's Justice is not a real distinction of distinct entities such as the real distinction existing between Peter and Paul. Nor is it a purely mental distinction such as the merely conceptual distinction which is made between the morning 'star' and the evening 'star' (both of which are identically the planet Venus). God's Mercy, for example, is one of the several formalities or attributes of God. It is an intelligible aspect or formality or real feature of God which is formally distinct from God's Wisdom or Justice. The distinction, then, is a distinction between different formalities present objectively in the nature of God. Scotus called this distinction an objective formal distinction (*distinctio formalis a parte rei*); and he made extensive use of this distinction throughout his entire system of philosophy. Thus, for example, in man, human sensation is not human intellection. These are intelligible aspects or features of the human being, giving a partial insight into particular powers which are objectively present within the human being. They are different modes of being, or formalities, present within the human being. Thus one can say that there is an object-oriented formal distinction between the different formalities or objective features of the individual entity (or subject) which is being studied. The distinction is an objective formal distinction. It is a distinction of this kind, namely, an objective formal distinction, which exists similarly between the 'essence' and the 'existence' in each finite individual. Essence and existence are inseparable, but nevertheless distinct, objective formalities of the composite particular being in which they are discovered.

Scotus made use of the objective formal distinction to explain also how the mind can form universal conceptions of individuals. Various individuals, such as different human beings, share an intelligible feature or *ratio* by which each resembles the other. This common intelligible characteristic or nature (*natura communis*) is individualized in numerically distinct ways in the different individuals. Thus, for example, 'humanness' is individualized con- cretely in Socrates, and it is individualized through the agency of

Socrates' principle of individuation, namely his own unique 'Socreity' or his own unique 'thisness' (haecceity), a unique formality which characterizes him alone. This individuating difference of Socrates, by which he differs from all other individuals, is the unique formality by which he is known distinctly by God. It is a unique formality which is inseparable from, and yet also distinct from, the specific (human) nature of Socrates. The distinction between them is an objective formal distinction. It is from the specific nature of Socrates that the human mind abstracts the common nature. This common nature, when reflexively analysed and conceived in its predicability, is the logical universal or concept (e.g. of 'man' or 'humanness') which is predicated of Socrates and other similar human beings.

The individual beings of our experience are corporeal beings, composed of matter and form. The prime matter which is the correlative of form is a real subjective potency, that is, a real potency or capacity within the subject. Matter is not identified with the form, nor indeed with any of the different forms with which it can correlate. As a real subjective potency it must have some minimal actuality of its own, apart from the actuality of the different forms which inform it; it is in some sense a separable positive entity. God could give it existence apart from any form, if he so wished. It is a separable entity.

(This doctrine was subject to critical query by the 'nominalists' of the fourteenth century. Is a stone, for example, a specific petrifying of actual prime matter, and an elephant an elephantizing of prime matter, and a human being a specific humanizing of prime matter? And is Socrates a unique Socratizing of the specific humanizing of actual prime matter? These questions derive from an over-simplification of Scotus' thought. Nevertheless, the philosophical system of Scotus was not sufficiently cogent to withstand the barrage of misunderstanding and criticism to which it gave rise.)

It is possible to interpret the *haecceitas* of Scotus as the equivalent of Aquinas' principle of *esse* within a composite being. In this sense, then, it is the principle of *esse* or perfection in being which is the principle of individuation. This interpretation of Scotus' theory of individuation would save it from a number of the objections which were raised against it. However it was not explicitly formulated in this way by Scotus himself. He thought of the principle of individuation as the final, actual individual entity itself as determining the being to be 'this' being by the very fact that the entity is an actual reality. Here, as elsewhere, his thought is more 'physical' than that of Aquinas.

Scotus also maintained that there is a plurality of forms in the human being. There is a distinct form of corporeity which disposes the body for the reception of the substantial form, the soul. The soul itself is a spiritual substance. It is the intellective substantial form which makes the corporeal being precisely human. It has within itself the formal perfections of both the lower vegetative soul and the animal soul. These lower forms are not really distinct parts. They are faculties or powers of the human soul; they are formally distinct from the soul and from each other.

4. Natural theology. An *a posteriori* consideration of the effects of God's work in the universe can lead the philosopher to a knowledge of the existence of God and to a knowledge of several truths about the nature of God. From creatures we are able to form univocal concepts such as being, cause, actuality, absolute, supreme, and goodness, which we can then combine to form a composite idea of God as supremely good and actual being. It is only in theology, however, and not in philosophy, that God is known as he is in his essence. Philosophical knowledge of God is unavoidably obscure, indirect, imperfect and abstract. Nevertheless, it is a knowledge which is objective, distinct, adequate and precious to the human mind.

The different proofs for the existence of God may be grouped under two general headings: the (Aristotelian-type) way of causality and the (Augustinian-type) way of eminence. Scotus himself prefered to present his own causal arguments in terms of 'possibles'. He pointed out that if a process of reasoning holds for all possible states then it holds for whatever set of states happens to be actual. He then argued: we know from experience that things can be produced, therefore something can be productive. Now an infinite regress or circularity in essentially concatenated causes in which all these essentially concatenated causes co-exist both to produce and to conserve in being their effect, is impossible. Therefore some uncaused agent must be possible. But an uncaused agent cannot be both possible and incapable of being caused if it is not actually existing. Therefore it is both possible and actual. (A similar argument can be produced concerning the possibility of a final cause, or of a most perfect nature.)

An argument parallel to that given above can be formulated in this way: Beings which come to be, and which have previously not been in being, are neither caused by themselves nor caused by nothing. They must be caused by another, which must in turn be caused by another if that other is likewise a dependent being. But one cannot proceed infinitely in a (vertical) ascending order of dependency. There must therefore be an uncaused transcendent cause on which the whole ascending series of contingent causes depend for their present being and for their continuance in being. The whole universe of contingent beings requires an actual, transcendent, uncaused cause. This first cause must be not merely possible but actual. It must be not merely able to exist but one that cannot not exist, that is, necessary being.

Scotus said of Anselm, with reference to Anselm's *a priori* argument for the existence of God, that 'his reasoning can be coloured' (*I Sent.* I, 2, q. II). He rehabilitated the argument and presented it in the following way: The supreme being, God, is the supreme intelligible (*summum cogitabile*). He is that than which, having been thought without contradiction, a greater cannot be thought without contradiction. The supreme intelligible (*summum cogitabile*) cannot be merely in the intelligence alone, for then it would be possible in as much as it is thinkable, and it would not be possible since it could not exist through another. From this it follows that the supreme intelligible must really exist. This argument, he says, does not present an *a posteriori* demonstrative proof. Rather, it presents us with an auxiliary, probable, persuasive, *a priori* argument for the existence of God as the supreme intelligible.

The univocal concept of being is predicable of both God and creatures. When we prove God to be the uncaused, non-dependent, non-finite, transcendent cause of all dependent beings we add to our previous imperfect notion of him (namely, as being); we now know him simply and *distinctly* as the being who is infinite. The concept of the infinite is the concept which signifies his intrinsic and distinct mode of being. The infinite mode of being includes 'virtually' every perfection compatible with the infinity of being; it is the infinitely perfect mode of being.

The infinitely perfect Being enjoys full, perfect *liberty*. Supreme liberty requires the presence of a power which is not arrested by anything. The power of supreme liberty is capable, consequently, of producing, beyond existing creatures, an infinity of other (known) possible creatures. This attribute of full liberty is the attribute which is proper to God. It is the attribute in fact from which one can conclude that Infinity is also proper to him. It is also the fundamental attribute from which one can conclude to the attribute of divine intelligence, since knowing is a condition of willing.

God wills rationally for an end, which is himself. He wills rationally but without having any determining reason determining his absolute freedom of choice in willing what he wills. God wills with full liberty even in his necessarily loving himself. Liberty belongs to the perfection of volition, and the divine volition is absolutely self-determining. His creative act causes contingent beings contingently, and hence freely. Contingency means that the act is dependent on the will's direction; and nothing is a principle of contingent operation except will. This is the source of Scotus' well-known doctrine of 'voluntarism'. It is the will that has primacy. Every action other than an action which is contingent upon the will is a necessary action. The creation of the natural order is an entirely contingent, and hence free, action. The contingency is in the act of willing, within the First Principle itself, God. In this way Scotus raises contingency to a central place in the divine nature itself.

5. **Psychology.** Man's exercise of intellectual activity is the exercise of an activity transcending the (sensitive) powers of his different and determinate organic sensations. This exercise of intellectual activity must be the act of the intellective *soul*, the specific or substantial form which makes the human composite human.

The human soul is the substantial form of the composite man. The soul is the principle of all of his activities, intellectual, sensitive, or vegetative. These faculties or powers are objectively distinct formalities of the substantial form of man, the rational soul.

Man is a composite being, composed of separable entities, body and soul. At death the composite is disintegrated, and body and soul separate. The body or corpse has its own perishable form of corporeity after the soul is separated from it. The doctrine of the immortality of the soul is a doctrine that cannot be proved demonstratively in philosophy. The arguments given by the Schoolmen are probable and persuasive but not demonstrative. Faith alone can bring certainty about this truth.

The intellect and the will are natural powers. But the intellect, unlike the will, is not a free power. It is determined by its nature to act in a specific way. If the truth of a principle or proposition becomes clear to the intellect, the intellect is not free to restrain its assent. The will, however, is unique among the agencies found in nature: it is free. It is not just simply an intellective appetite, as so many of the Schoolmen had asserted. It is a distinct power. It is free to act and free to refrain from acting; and it is free to act now one way and now another. It has an inborn inclination to seek what is good and shun what is evil; and it is free to follow or not follow its inclination.

The will has a more basic liberty still, according to Scotus. It is free to overcome the natural physical inclination to seek in a self-centred way the individual's own welfare and perfection, or what is personally advantageous (*affectio commodi*), and it can opt to follow, instead, man's inclination or affection for true justice (*affectio justitiae*). This is the human inclination which inclines one to love and to do justice to the intrinsic value of any being regardless of what is merely to one's own advantage. It is the affection for justice which enables us, for example, to love God, and also to love our neighbour, in himself as he is, and for his own sake. It seeks the good of the beloved, for the sake of the beloved. This form of human affection is called the love of willing-well to another (*amor benevolentiae*) or the love of friendship (*amor amicitiae*). In this form of altruistic love, the will overcomes itself as self-centred natural inclination, and it becomes the will as just and free.

6. Ethics and political philosophy. Man's free will enables him to free himself from the inclinations of his natural appetites so that he can choose to act in accord with right reason, and with 'affection for justice'. A human action is called a naturally good action if it is free, objectively good, conformable to right reason, done with a right intention and performed in the right way. An action of this kind is naturally good even though it may be an 'indifferent' act with regard to morality. If a naturally good act of this kind is, in addition, referred to God, either actually or virtually, the act then becomes a morally good action. If any requisite for a good act is lacking or defective, then that act is morally bad. Human acts may therefore be either morally good, or morally bad, or merely indifferent. (Aquinas had taught that there is no such thing as a morally indifferent act; Scotus disagreed.)

The first moral principle or ethical norm is: 'God is to be loved'. Its converse is 'God must never be hated or dishonoured'. Even God himself can never dispense from these two obligations, since love of God for his own sake can never be inordinate or unbecoming. Indifferent human acts, motivated by love or hatred of God, become morally good or morally bad. The only acts invested with intrinsic moral value, then, are love of God and hatred of God. All other actions depend upon the will of God, commanding or forbidding, for their value as good or bad actions. Thus, for example, God can dispense from the prescriptions of the natural law (e.g. permitting polygamy among the patriarchs, or disregarding the inviolability of private property) if he so wills. However, God's free will is not arbitrary since it is in itself an attribute of the divine nature. There are therefore some moral principles, pertaining to the love of God, which do not depend on the arbitrary decision of God's will, according to Scotus. William of Ockham, who was also a Franciscan, would reject this hesitant reservation, and declare, twenty years later, that the moral law in its entirety is the arbitrary creation of the absolutely free will of God. Scotus' doctrine had helped to prepare the ground, then, for the Ockhamist authoritarian theory of ethics.

All political authority, as distinct from natural parental authority, in Scotus' view, is derived from the consent of the governed. This authority must be exercised prudently, in accordance with right reason. No legislator may pass laws for mere private advantage, or laws which conflict with the divine positive law or with the natural moral law. Private property may not be administered to the detriment of the common good. The end of all legislation is the common good.

7. General comment. Scotus' philosophy may be regarded as the last of the great speculative syntheses of the Middle Ages. In spite of his moderate but constant criticism of his recent predecessors, he shared their desire to construct a speculative synthesis based on the commonly accepted principles of thirteenth-century metaphysical thought. For this reason Scotus has much more in common with Albert the Great, Thomas Aquinas and Bonaventure than he has with the logicians and critical analysts of the fourteenth century.

Scotus had a widespread influence in the universities of the later Middle Ages. He had many disciples who admired the subtlety of his thought; these disciples came to be known (by the humanists and Reformers) as 'Dunsmen' because of their relish for subtlety of expression. The relish for subtlety was frequently accompanied by a similar relish for criticism of the weakness of the opinions which were refuted. Several doctrines concerning God and men were removed by Scotus and his followers from the domain of philosophic thought to the domain of faith where the supernatural light of faith could compensate for the darkness of reason. This loss of confidence in the value of human reason, prevalent among the 'Dunsmen' or Scotists, had its origin in the critical, 'safeguarding' thought of Scotus himself.

14 The fourteenth century: William of Ockham

1. The fourteenth century   2. Some transitional thinkers
3. The *logica moderna*   4. Ockham's life and writings
5. Ockham's logic and theory of science   6. Theory of
knowledge   7. Metaphysics   8. Psychology and ethics
9. Political theory   10. Ockhamism

1. The fourteenth century. The fourteenth century was a
century of rival schools of philosophical thought: Thomist, Scotist,
Augustinian and Ockhamist. The merits of one school of thought
were matched against those of the others. Each school developed its
own conservative party line. Logical argumentation was sharpened,
but this was often at the expense of originality. Thomism was still a
minority movement; several prominent Dominican teachers did not
adhere to it. Scotism developed principally within the Franciscan
order, where it eventually replaced the older school of Alexander of
Hales and Bonaventure. Augustinianism continued to be influential,
inspiring the doctrinal teachings of several of the Schoolmen,
including those who were followers of Giles of Rome. Ockhamism
gave its primary attention to logical problems. It made a critical
analysis of philosophic terms currently in use, and endeavoured to
clarify and explain the logical function of terms, especially as used in
the previous period of constructive synthesis. The criticisms of the
Ockhamist school tended to divorce the domain of philosophy from
the domain of faith.

In the political and social fields, the fourteenth and fifteenth
centuries were times of conflict, political intrigue, heavy taxation,
scandal in the Church, plague, economic disruption, widespread
criticism, and schism in Christendom. The financing of the papal
wars against the emperor, and later of rival Popes against each other,
necessitated the imposition of heavy papal taxation throughout
Christendom. The benefice system in the Church became a source of
major scandal. National hatreds flared. The kings of France and
England extended and centralized the royal power at the expense of
the emperors in the West. The fortress-monasteries of the Templars
were plundered and destroyed for their wealth. England pillaged

France in raids which came to be known as the Hundred Years War. In the catastrophe called the Black Death (bubonic plague), forty million people died in western Europe in a period of twenty months. Half the population of England died of the plague in twelve months; monasteries and universities were affected worst of all. It was an age of turbulent individualism, nationalism and separatism; an age of disruption, disintegration and decline. Studies suffered. Entry requirements for admission to universities were lowered. Large numbers of university degrees were secured through patronage. The Schoolmen were satisfied with writing compendiums summarizing the masters. Emphasis was placed on detailed points of opposition between the different Scholastic schools of thought. It was an age of 'simplification', and of little originality.

2. Some transitional thinkers. The beginnings of the trend in philosophy to place special emphasis on the individuality of the individual existent is already apparent in certain transitional thinkers who taught in the Schools at the end of the thirteenth and the beginning of the fourteenth century. These thinkers continued to be moderate realists to some extent: they continued to speak of universal concepts, but they thought of them mainly as subjective mental constructs.

At Paris, Durandus of Saint-Pourçain (*c*. 1275-1334) and his fellow-Dominican James of Metz criticized the theories of Thomas Aquinas. Durandus rejected the reality of mental species. He rejected the distinction between agent and possible intellect, and the distinction between essence and existence in creatures. Only individuals exist. Individuals receive their individuality from their efficient cause. The intellect grasps individual existents directly and creates universal concepts by ignoring individual differences. The real nature, conceived as universal, is a nature which exists really in individual things. This view received widespread approval. At the university of Salamanca, Durandus's teachings rivalled those of Aquinas and Scotus.

Peter Aureol (*c*. 1275-1322), a Franciscan, lectured at the *studium generale* at Bologna, and at Toulouse, Naples and Paris, before becoming Archbishop of Aix in 1321. His philosophical system shows evidence of sceptical and empirical traits. He discarded several contemporary philosophical theories as useless. He held that each individual existent is individuated simply by its factual existence. Universal ideas have a form of psychic reality, but they have no objective universality outside the mind. There are certain individual things that have a qualitative similarity to each other. Each of them is capable of producing a perfect impression of itself in the intellect. The perfect impression caused by one thing is similar to the perfect impression caused by another. From this the specific concept arises as a mental construct. It is the individual thing itself which impresses itself on the intellect and which is known directly by the intellect as possessing *esse intentionale* or *esse apparens*. A problem then arose concerning man's knowledge of God, since there is no apparent common ground of being between men and God. Aureol asserted that men do in practice have a particular kind of knowledge of God; it is a knowledge which is largely dependent on the psychological dispositions of the particular individual. Views of this kind contributed to a general outlook which facilitated the widespread acceptance of Ockhamism a few years later.

Henry of Harclay (*c.* 1270-1317), chancellor of the university of Oxford, wrote a commentary on the *Sentences*, and also *Disputed Questions*. He held, against Scotus, that there are no common natures in reality; there are only individuals. Each individual has its own nature. The human mind has particular concepts of individuals distinctly conceived, and universal concepts of individuals indistinctly conceived. Thus a particular human being, Titus, indistinctly conceived, is known as a man, an animal and a body. (Ockham rejected Harclay's theory as unduly realist in character.) It was theories of this kind which facilitated the Ockhamist final breakaway from the moderate realist theory concerning the nature of universal concepts.

3. The *logica moderna*. In the early Middle Ages, the formal logic taught in the monastic and cathedral Schools had depended almost entirely on the translations and works of Boethius. It concerned itself mainly with the syntax and semantics of language and with syllogistic and topical inferences. It was used by the theologians in their commentaries on the texts of the Bible and the Church Fathers, and in their attempts to reconcile any apparent contradictions found in these texts. When the remaining books of Aristotle's *Organon* became available in the translations at the end of the twelfth century, the new discoveries in logic were called the 'new art' of logic (*ars nova*) as distinguished from the 'old art' of logic (*ars vetus*). Several commentaries and paraphrases were written on the original logical works of Aristotle. The form of logic presented in these commentaries soon came to be known, however, as the *logica antica*, the ancient logic.

Around the middle of the thirteenth century, new methods in logic and new logical problems came to the fore in the arts faculties of the universities of Paris and Oxford. New treatises and textbooks in logic were written by William of Shyreswood and Peter of Spain. This gave rise to an interest in what came to be known as the *logica moderna*, the new logic.

Some of the elements or ingredients of the *logica moderna* are to be found in earlier works, such as the logical works of Peter Abelard. Abelard had made a systematic analysis of the functions of the copula, of quantifying prefixes, of the negation sign treated as a truth function, and of conditional and disjunctive sentential connectives. Shyreswood made a complete organization of these and other elements in a new form of medieval logic.

William of Shyreswood or Sherwood (*c.* 1200-*c.* 1266), an English logician, seems to have taught logic at Paris from about 1235 to about 1250; he lectured at Oxford in 1252. In his *Introductiones in Logicam* and *Syncategoremata*, he dealt not only with the traditional Aristotelian logic but also with the logical and semantical 'properties of terms' (*significatio, suppositio, copulatio* and *appelatio*) and with the logical and semantical properties of syncategorematic words such as 'except', 'not', 'is', 'every', 'if', 'only', 'or', 'necessarily', 'some'. He made an analysis of the double general proposition (e.g. 'Every man looking into a mirror sees a man'), in which the scope of one quantifier extends to include the other. He applied this notion in his special treatment of the supposition of terms in general propositions; here, his doctrine of supposition presented an interpretation of the logic of quantifiers in terms of a theory of reference rather than in terms of a theory of meaning. This distinction between the normal referent (supposition) of a term and the meaning (signification) of the term is of fundamental importance in the 'modern logic'. Shyreswood's writings also contain the first presentation of the well-known 'Barbara, Celarent...' mnemonic verses on the moods of the categorical syllogism.

Peter of Spain, or Petrus Hispanus (*c.* 1210-77), studied logic in Paris when Shyreswood was teaching there, and subsequently became a master at the university of Paris. His logical works *Summulae logicales, Syncategoremata,* and *Tractatus maiorum fallaciarum* enjoyed widespread popularity. The *Summulae* became a standard textbook of the *logica moderna* for the next three hundred years. Peter himself became Pope John XXI in 1276, and died in a building accident eight months later. His logical works present the traditional themes and the new doctrines concerning the 'properties of terms'. They show less logical insight than the treatises of Shyreswood. Nevertheless, the simplicity of the presentation of the *Summulae* may account for the fact that this textbook survived 166 editions.

William of Ockham composed his *Summa Logicae* in or around 1326. This work inaugurated what may be called the period of maturity of the *logica moderna*. It established the general form, and much of the content, of subsequent fourteenth-century logical treatises. The central perspective now shifted from the logic of terms and predicates to the theory of supposition of terms and to the theory of implication (*consequentia*). It gave rise to the formulation and investigation of new syntactical and semantical problems, such as those connected with the Liar paradox.

4. Ockham's life and writings. *William of Ockham* (*c.* 1285-1349) was born at Ockham, in Surrey, near London. He became a Franciscan and studied at Oxford, where he qualified as an 'inceptor' or candidate for the doctorate. In 1327, at a time of conflict between the Franciscans and Pope John XXII, Ockham and other Franciscan leaders sought the protection of the emperor Louis the Bavarian. He wrote a commentary on the *Sentences, Summa totius Logicae, Quodlibeta septem* and several theological, political and polemical treatises before he died in Bavaria, a victim of the Black Death, in 1349.

In these writings, Ockham made use of the terms of the *logica moderna* in his quest for lucid simplicity. He sought earnestly to safeguard the Christian doctrines of God's freedom and omnipotence from the doctrines of determinism and necessitarianism, which arose, he was convinced, from doctrines of 'realism', whether ultra-realist or moderate realist. He saw himself as a loyal, active Franciscan leader of simple, logical Christian thought, who lived in an age when Christian simplicity and poverty were engulfed in a plethora of luxurious excrescences. In Christian life and in Christian thought, all forms of ostentatious and cluttering overgrowth needed to be trimmed back and swept away in order to reveal once again the purity and simplicity of the essential structures. In undertaking this project, he called attention to a series of unnecessarily arresting problems which arose from 'realist', essentialist theories; and he developed an original system of 'terminist' philosophy as a simple solution to these problems. This solution is based on the insight that each individual is a unique creature of God, utterly dependent on the absolutely free and omnipotent will of God. The creative will of God is in no way restricted by 'essences' or universal, limiting 'forms'. It is not restricted by 'common natures' or species or finite imitations of eternal ideas. Essentialist doctrines of this kind endanger the Christian doctrines of God's omnipotence and liberty. They must be ruthlessly swept away. They are an affront to God, free and omnipotent. Philosophy must never lose sight of the absolute liberty of the divine choice and the utter contingency of the dependent creature.

5. Ockham's logic and theory of science. Logic, according to Ockham, is a science of language, a *scientia sermocinalis*. It deals with language as a system of signs (such as terms) which are used in making statements, either true or false, about the objects (*res*) signified by those signs. Knowledge is concerned with truth, and truth is found in propositions. Propositions are free, mental combinations of concepts derived from our intuitive cognition of things. Logic is the science which concerns itself with the ways in which we put concepts together in propositions which are capable of being true or false.

Language signs can be divided into (1) categorematic signs, or terms, which can function as subjects and predicates of propositions, and (2) syncategorematic signs (such as 'not', 'some', 'every', 'if') which exercise different logical functions with respect to the categorematic signs. Categorematic signs, or 'terms', are divided into two types: terms of first intention, which signify objective things, and terms of second intention which signify language signs (namely, the descriptive signs of the metalanguage). Thus, for example, one can say (1) Socrates is a man, and (2) man is a species; but one cannot say Socrates is a species.

One must be careful in philosophy not to construe terms of second intention (such as genera and species) as terms of first intention. Terms of second intention are class-names which can be predicated of terms of first intention. One may say, for example, that 'man' is a species and 'horse' is a different species; these are class-names which are signs of signs. It was confusion over these two types of terms, Ockham maintained, which led the Schoolmen into the entanglements of the problem of universal 'shared natures' within individuals. In actual fact, universality and community are properties only of language expressions (signs) and of the acts of thought expressed by them. The problem of individuation is simply a logical problem of showing how general terms are used in propositions to refer to the individuals signified by these terms. The problem of individuation is resolved in terms of the syncategorematic determinations (such as the quantifying prefixes) of the referential use of terms in propositions.

One must distinguish the 'signification' of a term from the 'supposition' of that term in a proposition. The signification of a term connotes its meaning, its connotation, its implication. The supposition of the term in a proposition is its application, its reference, its scope or extension in that proposition.

Aristotle classified certain terms of first intention as signifying 'primary substances' or concrete individuals. Ockham called these *absolute* terms: they signify individuals alone. Aristotle classified other concrete terms, such as 'small', 'that', 'father', 'alike', 'now', 'here', as belonging to the categories of accident. Ockham called these *connotative* terms: they connote or imply some contingent factual condition determining the range of objects for which the term can stand. This distinction helps one not to lose sight of the fact that the only realities which are real entities are concrete individuals.

The term 'large', or the term 'father', does not connote some universal entity, such as 'magnitude', or 'fatherhood', which inheres in the concrete thing denoted by the term 'large' or by the term 'father', as the realists taught. Facts about individuals are not entities distinct from these individuals but inhering in them. Thus, 'fatherhood' is not an entity distinct from Abraham but inhering in Abraham. The term 'father', as applied to Abraham, is a connotative term which refers obliquely to another thing (Isaac) with respect to which the denoted thing (Abraham) stands in a contingent relation. Thus the abstract form (fatherhood) of the connotative term (father) does not connote any distinct entity. Connotative terms, whether concrete or abstract, signify no entities distinct from the individual things signified by absolute terms. They merely indicate a contingent fact or factual condition about the object or objects.

The affirmative copula in a proposition, such as 'Abraham is a father', indicates that the individual denoted by the name 'Abraham' is an individual for which the term 'father' stands and which it signifies. It does not indicate that fatherhood inheres in Abraham. Thus the truth condition of an affirmative categorical proposition is that subject and predicate denote the same referent.

Scientific knowledge is evident grasp of propositions composed of universal terms and having the properties of necessity and evidence. Real science is concerned with terms of primary intention; its terms stand for individual things. Rational science, such as logic, is concerned with terms of second intention; its terms are class-names which stand for terms. A rational science, such as logic, deals directly with signs and concepts and only indirectly with individual things through these signs and concepts.

Science makes use of indemonstrable first principles which the mind cannot but assent to as soon as the mind has grasped the meaning of the terms (*per se nota*). Science also makes use of indemonstrable premisses which are evident through experience (*nota per experientiam*; e.g. 'all heat is calefacient', 'all wood is combustible'). Scientific premisses of this kind are established by generalization from singular contingent propositions evident by intuitive cognition. The justification for scientific generalization of this kind rests on a rule of induction, namely, that all specifically similar individuals act or react in similar manner to similar conditions. The application of this rule is valid only within the general hypothesis of the 'common course of nature'. The rule of induction corresponds to the principle of the general uniformity of nature. This uniformity is not absolute. It is hypothetical, since it is still possible, by the free, omnipotent power of God, that an effect can be produced without its natural cause.

All demonstration, including scientific demonstration, is necessarily syllogistic demonstration of attributes pertaining to a subject. Real science is capable of attaining necessary truths concerning contingent things in propositions which are construed as conditionals or as propositions concerning the possible (*de eo quod potest esse*). Scientific propositions are frequently stated in the form of 'Every S is P' or 'Every contingent S possesses the property P' (e.g. 'All wood is combustible'). These propositions are necessary if they are considered as equivalent to 'if there is an S, it is P' or 'if it is true to say of something that it is an S, then it is also true to say of it that it is P'. In this case, scientific demonstration must necessarily be demonstration of an attribute of the subject. There can be no demonstration of the existence of the subject. Factual existence can only be experienced. Existence cannot be syllogistically demonstrated. Thus Ockham continued to adhere to the Aristotelian idea of demonstrative 'science'. He maintained, like the rationalists of later times, that syllogistic demonstrative 'science' is capable of telling us about the properties of reality. There is therefore a 'rationalist' as well as an 'empiricist' element in Ockham's philosophy.

6. Theory of knowledge. Ockham rejected the epistemological and ontological assumptions of medieval realism. He sought, instead, to reconstruct philosophy on the basis of a realistic empiricism. The basis of all knowledge is direct experience of individual things and particular events. The human mind can directly apprehend not only its own acts but also existent individuals and their sensible qualities.

Individuals alone exist. Abstract essences and extra-linguistic constructs must be systematically eliminated by a logical analysis of language. Ockham sought, then, in his logical writings, to make a nominalistic analysis of the semantical structure and ontological commitment of cognitive language. In so doing he made frequent use of the methodological principle of parsimony or economy: 'Plurality is not to be assumed without necessity', and 'What can be explained by the assumption of fewer things is vainly explained by the assumption of more things'. This principle came to be known as 'Ockham's razor'. It was reformulated by his followers as 'Beings are not to be multiplied without necessity'. Individual existents are the only real entities; and their adequate explanation lies solely in the fact that they are radically contingent beings utterly dependent on the omnipotent will of their Creator. Granted that this is so, the problem then arises of explaining how intuitive experience of *individual* existents can give rise to *universal* concepts and to universally quantified propositions (such as 'All S is P'). Ockham's answer to this problem of universals is contained in his doctrine of intuitive and abstractive cognition.

An intuitive cognition is an act of immediate awareness of the factual existence or non-existence of an object, or of some factual condition of the object, in virtue of which an evident judgement of contingent fact can be made. Thus one may say 'This exists' or 'This is hot' or 'I evidently know that Saul is seated'. Apprehension of this kind is caused immediately by the object and not by any intermediary. The guarantee of intuitive knowledge is immediate evidence.

Abstractive cognition is that form of intellectual apprehension in which concepts or mental universals are used as natural signs through which concrete existents are understood. It is that form of cognition in which we cannot evidently know whether the apprehended thing exists or does not exist and concerning which no evident contingent judgement can be made. We know by experience that the intellect acquires abstractive knowledge of an object or event of which it has intuitive cognition. The intellect retains this abstractive knowledge after the object or event has passed. Abstractive cognition has *signification* but it acquires *supposition* only through the formation of a proposition. It is that form of cognition of objects in virtue of which one cannot evidently judge that the object now exists or does not exist. One might perhaps think of the concept as the 'being conceived' or the 'being understood' of the external object (*eorum esse est eorum cognosci*); or, better still, one may think of the concept as merely the act of understanding the individual things of which it is said to be a concept. It is called abstractive cognition because we have abstracted from existence.

It is a fact of experience that objects are similar. Peter is similar to Paul. Both are men. They are similar not by reason of anything common or anything in which they share but simply by reason of what each individual is in itself. A concept is a single act of understanding many similar individuals in which it is the individuals themselves that are understood. The act of understanding them has no content other than the objects understood. The universal is a natural sign signifying individual things; it 'stands for' individual things in a proposition. It exists in the mind as an act of understanding things which are similar solely because of the divine choice that they be so. Ockham felt unable to clarify the matter any further. 'In the case of the universals', he said, 'nature works in a hidden manner' (*natura occulte operatur in universalibus*).

It is God, as first Cause, who produces knowledge in us, and he does so freely, in practice, by using things as secondary causes. But he is equally free not to use objects if he so wishes. He is free, for example, to give us an intuition or 'vision' of the future or the past. He has the power to cause in us, if he so wishes, the intuition of a thing (such as an apparent star) which was a non-existent object. He can produce in us the psychological and physiological conditions and effects by which we could attain knowledge. There is no absolutely necessary connection, for example, between a star and the act of seeing the star. The divine omnipotence could annihilate one and conserve the other.

Distinct things are distinct absolutes having no necessary connection with each other. A man and his son are two existent absolutes. Paternity is not a third entity linking them together. A relation between two or more absolutes is a concept in the soul, signifying several absolute things. An absolute thing can be studied in itself without reference to its relationships with other absolutes. The creature, for example, can be studied scientifically without reference to God, its creator and conserver in being. A physicist can study an object without reference to its Creator. Individuals alone are real; relationships are simply concepts in the soul.

The order of the universe, too, is conceptual. Contingent absolutes have no necessary connection with each other. They do, in fact, act on each other in a predictable way, but the Creator is omnipotent and free to will otherwise. God's choice is simply factual and not necessitated. If we wish to discover what happens factually we must study things empirically. Causal relationships cannot be deduced *a priori*. Thus, for example, fire and boiling water are two distinct absolutes. We learn by experience that when fire is posited then a certain 'effect' is posited, and if it is not posited then the 'effect' is not posited. The regularity of the sequence is simply factual. It arises solely from God's free actual choice; and he is free to will otherwise. The student of Nature, therefore, should not seek for essences; he acts rightly when he seeks to discover the simple explanations for the simple empirical facts.

Motion, place and time can be explained simply and economically and without the invocation of unobservable entities. Local motion is explained simply by the fact that a body is successively in distinct places and not at rest in any of them. Place is explained simply in terms of the surface of the surrounding body. Time signifies the before and after in motion as known by an act of the soul.

Ockham's emphasis is on the importance of experiential knowledge of observable entities, and on the need for simplicity in the presentation of explanations based on an analysis of reality. One finds this 'empiricist' element constantly present in his thought and writings. He warns philosophers against the use of nouns derived from verbs, adverbs and syncategorematic terms. Terms of this kind can be misleading. They do not signify any entities in addition to the concrete things from which they derive. The philosopher must make a nominalistic analysis of the semantical structure and the ontological commitment of the linguistic expressions which he uses; and he must then carefully eliminate all abstract extra-linguistic entities from his philosophical vocabulary. Philosophy must be reconstructed on an empiricist and nominalist basis.

7. Metaphysics.

Being is the primary subject of the metaphysical sciences from the viewpoint of priority of predication. The term 'being' in the sense in which it is equivalent to the term 'something' is predicated in the same way, indifferently, of everything there is. However, it does not signify everything in a single determinate way. It can be said to have as many meanings and denotations as there are different kinds of things; thus, for example, 'to be a horse' is not 'to be wet'. The general abstract concept of being is not an extra-mental entity. Things do not participate in it. There is no implication here of any doctrine of monism or pantheism; and so there is no need of any theory of analogy of being. Common being is simply a general concept or term which is equivalent to the concept of 'something'. The metaphysical sciences each have their own different subjects of study. They have a certain comparability with one another, like different kingdoms with different jurisdictions; but they do not constitute one science numerically. They study different entities.

In fact, Ockham's metaphysical teachings are, for the main part, a series of criticisms of the metaphysical doctrines of his thirteenth-century predecessors. The distinction between potential being and actual being, and between essence and existence in things, rests on a semantic confusion between the ways of signifying things and the things signified. There is no actual existence which is added on to an actual nonexistent. The distinction is not between things but rather between modalities of statements. One must be careful not to confuse logical and physical concepts. The term 'substance' as applied to corporeal things, for example, is best understood in terms of connotative and negative concepts expressing its referential function: 'Thing (being) such that it is not in something else', or 'thing which is the subject of sensible qualities'. This theory concerning the nature of substance anticipates and points the way to Locke's later theory of substance as the invisible substratum.

Ockham modified and simplified the traditional doctrine of the four causes. He thought of the material cause and formal cause in physical terms rather than as metaphysical principles of being. Matter is actual spatial body. Form is the form or shape or structure of the material parts. Quantity is substance itself as numerable. Efficient causality is known only experientially; it is experienced as a certain observed sequence in the pattern of behaviour of concomitant absolute things. Final causality is interpreted as a metaphor. Things which act uniformly by necessity of nature act *as if* aiming at an end; language of this kind is purely metaphorical.

It is only by intuitive cognition of an object that we can evidently judge that it exists. Now man, in this present life, does not have intuitive knowledge of God. For this reason, we cannot have any simple and proper concept of God, nor can we have any direct evidence of his existence. It is possible, however, through the use of the common concept of 'being' and the connotative or negative terms 'supremely perfect', 'uncaused' and 'non-finite', to form a descriptive concept of God as infinitely perfect being. But, then, no cogent proof of the existence of a being of this kind has ever been formulated. The embodied human intellect can give no more than a probable argument for the existence of God, the supreme intelligible reality.

The traditional 'first mover' argument concludes merely about the existence of a superior, perhaps angelic, type of being. The argument that the animate and inanimate things of the universe act for an end is a merely metaphorical argument; they act by natural necessity. The argument from efficient causality, if presented as an argument for the existence of a cause for the conservation of the universe in being here and now, can prove the existence of some conserving cause; but perhaps the celestial spheres may adequately account for this conservation of the things in the world. It is true that most people, and the philosophers of old, have believed in the existence of the unique, supreme, perfect, infinite being. But knowledge of this kind is derived not from logic but from faith.

The position is similar with regard to our knowledge of the nature and attributes of God. Here, too, certain knowledge is attained only through our acceptance on faith of God's self-revelation. There can be no logical demonstration of any divine attributes because there can be no syllogistic 'middle term' to which these concepts belong. The concept of general being can be predicated of God and creatures in common. Connotative terms such as 'absolute', 'good' and 'infinite' can be added to 'being' to give us distinct concepts of God. This knowledge is not a proper knowledge of God's essence as it is in itself. It is merely a knowledge of God through the medium of conceptual representations of the divine essence. Analyses of these representations or 'attributes' are merely analyses of theologians' concepts.

The divine intellect, will and essence are one reality in God. In him there are no 'universal' ideas of genera and so forth. In the act of creation it is the producible individual creatures that are the individuals (or 'ideas') known from eternity by God. In brief, there are no 'universals' in God and there are no universals in the act of creation.

It is the divine will, or in other words the divine essence, which is the direct and immediate cause of all things. The divine will is free and omnipotent. It can produce every possible effect, and it can do so directly without making use of any secondary cause. The divine goodness is purely spontaneous and unnecessitated. The whole of creation must be seen then in terms of its bountiful 'givenness'. The order in the universe, the regular sequence, the causal relations are all radically contingent. They are manifestations of God's omnipotence, freedom and spontaneous liberality. These are articles of faith which cannot be philosophically proved; but, once they are assumed, the world is seen in a more transparent and intelligible light.

8. Psychology and ethics. Ockham accepted as a truth of faith that man possesses a spiritual, immortal soul. But, since we experience only our acts of understanding and willing, any philosophy would reasonably conclude that these are acts of a corporeal form. 'It cannot be evidently known by reason or experience that an (immaterial and incorruptible) form exists in us, nor that the understanding proper to such a substance exists in us, nor that such a soul is a form of the body' (*Quodlibeta* 1, q. 10). Man's sensitive, corruptible body must be informed by a sensitive, corruptible soul or form, extended throughout the body and working through the different sense-organs. The sensitive soul is distinct from the intellective soul, and both are distinct from man's form of corporeity. In spite of this plurality of forms, each man experiences himself as being only one human being; and so, man's unity as a single entity is not impaired. Each person experiences himself as an intellectual, complete, whole human being; and it is the whole man that is the person. It is the whole person who thinks and the whole person who wills. For this reason, the terms 'intellect' and 'will' refer to the same subject and not to distinct entities or faculties within the subject. The whole subject simply elicits different acts.

The human being enjoys the power of freedom. This can be known evidently by experience. 'A man experiences the fact that however much his reason dictates some actions, his will can will, or not will, this act' (*Quodlibeta* 1, 16). It is because we know that we are free that we impute to people the responsibility for their deliberate actions. We are free to will, or not will, indifferently and contingently, to accept or reject, any inclinations of our sensitive appetites, and any judgement of our intellect. We can freely reject a judgement pertaining to our perfect happiness. We are free similarly to act against even long-established acquired habits formed in the power of the will through over-indulgence of the sensitive appetite. Freedom of this kind is the foundation of human dignity and the basis of moral goodness and responsibility.

The moral law is wholly contingent and totally dependent on the divine omnipotent, free and creative will. God has actually willed to establish a particular, freely chosen, moral order. He could freely have willed otherwise. If he had actually commanded men to steal and lie, then these would be meritorious acts. Evil acts are evil because they are forbidden; good acts are good because they are commanded.

Man is obliged to follow the existing ethical code established by the divine fiat. His conscience obliges him to do what he sincerely discerns and understands to be in accordance with God's command. He must do the commanded thing and he must do it for the right reason, that is, because he sincerely believes that this is what has been prescribed to be done. He must follow his conscience even if it happens to be an (inculpable, invincible) erroneous conscience. He must always do what he believes in good faith to be the commanded thing to be done. In doing so he shows that he loves and obeys God above all else.

Ockham asserted that God might freely command a man to hate him (or to disobey him). In this case, if it were God's will that a man should not do God's will, the man would do God's will if he did not do it and he would not do God's will if he did do it. The command would be impossible to fulfil. It would therefore be unreasonable, if not self-contradictory, for God to will that it should be fulfilled. This paradox points to the general tendency in Ockham's works to depreciate reason in the process of safeguarding and promoting faith and freedom.

9. Political theory. Ockham's political and polemic writings present his views on fundamental human rights and on the use and abuse of authority. These writings were occasioned by the controversies concerning the relations between Pope and emperor, or Church and State, and between Church members and the Holy See. Ockham's thesis is that the law of God is the law of liberty and not a law of coercion or oppression. Human rights and Christian liberty must be defended resolutely against absolutism in either Church or State.

In his *Opus nonaginta dierum* and *De Imperatorum et Pontificum potestate*, Ockham points out that there are certain fundamental natural rights, such as the right of private property, anterior to human conventions and dependent on the divine will alone. These human rights were justly and admittedly enjoyed even before the coming of Christ. Christ did not come into the world in order to take away from men their goods and rights; and Christ's vicar on earth has no authority or power to deprive others of their goods and rights. The Pope has no power to command anything other than those things necessary for the Christian in his quest for eternal life. The disposition of temporal thing belongs to the laity; they must be 'rendered unto Caesar' and not to the papal court. The law of the Gospels must not be turned into a law of slavery through the illegitimate assumption of tyrannical powers by holders of the papal office. Authority, religious or civil, must govern within the general framework of established custom and law.

The authority and power of the emperor, monarch, or magistrate, derives from God through the people. It is not derived from the papacy. All men enjoy a natural right to freedom and a natural right to choose and appoint their own leaders and rulers. The legitimacy of the temporal authority rests on the free acceptance of its subjects. The community can assert its freedom by deposing the monarch who betrays or abuses the trust reposed in him.

A Pope too may be deposed if he proves to be a heretic. He can be deposed by a general council of the Church. A council of this kind, having elected representatives, both lay and clerical, should be established as a means for checking and limiting the unrestrained use of papal absolute power. Legitimate papal supremacy must not be allowed to degenerate into illegitimate tyrannical supremacy. The wielding of papal power needs to be decisively limited and checked by an effective conciliar contribution. This suggestion was taken up and developed further by Jean Gerson (1363-1429), chancellor of the university of Paris, and other members of the Conciliar Movement. It was a suggestion whose implications affected also the wider arena of political power of absolute monarchs.

10. Ockhamism. William of Ockham became a guiding light in the new movement of philosophic thought which was known as the *via moderna*, or the modern way, in the fourteenth and fifteenth centuries. This movement of thought, which was also known as the philosophy of Terminism, or Nominalism, or Ockhamism, was characterized by its critical and sceptical attitude towards the tenets and arguments of traditional metaphysics and natural theology. It undermined the medieval effort to synthesize ancient philosophy and Christian theology, and fostered new mental attitudes and lines of development which paved the way for the scientific empiricism of the seventeenth century.

At Oxford and Cambridge, Adam Wodham (d. 1349) and Robert Holkot (d. 1349) used the new 'terminist' logic in arguing that Christian dogma is not a science; it is accepted by an act of will, on the authority of the teaching Church. Richard Swineshead ('the Calculator'), William Heytesbury, Richard Billingham and John Dumbleton attacked the proofs which had been offered in traditional metaphysics. They emphasized the weakness of human reason and the primacy of faith.

At Paris, John of Mirecourt and Nicholas of Autrecourt accepted Ockham's doctrines. They established a nominalist school of philosophy that spread outwards from Paris and penetrated into all the religious orders and universities of central Europe before the end of the century. They held that, in any proposition, a class-name or general term 'stands for' individual things alone. It supposes them, or supposits them. Universality belongs solely to supposital terms or class-names in their logical function. Ideas are simply supposital terms. The only propositions which are certain are analytic propositions; and these are reducible to the principle of contradiction. Statements about causal relation are not analytic; they are merely inductive generalizations, which may be probable though they are never certain. This applies to the traditional metaphysical arguments about God and immortality. Certainty about God and the immortal soul arises not from logic but from one's acceptance of the truths of faith. In the new universities of Tübingen, Heidelberg, Leipzig, Cracow, Wittenberg and other centres this *via moderna* possessed all the popular charm of modernity. It championed the fight against 'realism', which continued to be taught by the 'old-fashioned' schools of Thomism, Scotism and Augustinianism.

*John of Mirecourt (fl. c.*1345), a Cistercian, and so known as 'the white monk', was a well-known Ockhamist who lectured in Paris on Peter Lombard's *Sentences*. His views gave rise to widespread controversy and to official condemnation by the chancellor in 1347. He taught that the only propositions in which our assent is compellingly evident are those propositions which are intimately connected with the principle of non-contradiction. All other propositions rest merely on our experience of nature; and our assent to these is not a compellingly evident assent but a naturally evident assent. The only evidence available is limited natural evidence. The things of nature are radically contingent; God is absolutely free to do as he wills. For this reason there are severe limits on the range of truths known with analytical certainty. The only experience which enjoys compelling evidence is the experience of the thinking self; I should contradict myself if I were to deny or doubt that I exist. Compelling evident knowledge allows of no denial. We do not have such completely evident knowledge of the external world, or of the principle of causality, or of God. We do not know whether a higher being than God can be envisaged or not, or whether God could or could not mislead Christ and cause Christ to mislead his disciples and hate God. These present different possible points of view. There is no unquestionable certainty about their truth. If any of these viewpoints were completely evident, it would be impossible to contradict or deny them. (One can have personal certainty concerning the truth of what one believes even though this truth may not be compellingly evident to the intellect. Certainty of this kind is had with regard to those truths of faith which are firmly accepted on the authority of God revealing them.) The fundamental reason for the wide-ranging scepticism of Mirecourt's thought is the inherent uncertainty of all finite being, utterly dependent on the totally free divine choice.

Nicholas of Autrecourt (*c.* 1300- *c.* 1351), or Nicholas de Ultracuria, who lectured on the *Sentences* at Paris, was charged with teaching heresy and forced to recant many of his published statements. In his *Exigit ordo executionis* and other writings, which were discovered only in the nineteenth century, Nicholas maintained that, apart from the certitude of faith, the only certitude is that attained in propositions reducible to the principle of non-contradiction. This principle, that contradictories cannot be simultaneously true, is the only principle which manifests its own guarantee: it cannot be denied without self-contradiction. Thus, for example, in a geometric or syllogistic argument, if anyone were to affirm the antecedent and yet to deny the logical conclusion this would involve a contradiction. Similarly in the case of immediate, perceived, factual knowledge, based on external sense-perception or inner perception, the principle of non-contradiction is again the criterion of certitude. Immediate knowledge is its own guarantee.

However, from the factual existence of any one known or perceived thing it is not at all evident that the factual existence of some other different thing can be deduced where one is dealing with independent propositions whose interconnections are not reducible to the principle of non-contradiction. Thus, for example, it is logically possible to speak of a certain actual sound, or of a certain effect, while denying the existence of any non-apparent substance, or of any cause. It is logically possible, without contradiction, to deny substance and cause. It is possible to speak, for example, of acts of understanding and willing without inferring with compelling objective certainty to the objective existence of intellects or wills or souls. The existence of the spiritual soul can certainly be known with the certainty of faith without the presence of philosophical objective evidence; and, in any case, no philosophical causal argument can ever be objectively evident, demonstrative and certain. The existence of efficient causality, like the existence of substances, is indemonstrable. This applies also to natural theology and to the traditional arguments about God, his existence and nature. One existent cannot be deduced (*a priori*) from any other existent. This does not imply that its non-existence can be deduced. Existence is experienced; it is not deduced.

Probable arguments can be advanced for the existence of God and for the immortality of the soul; but they are only probable arguments, not demonstrative arguments. The degree of probability of any philosophical argument can be measured in terms of the natural evidence available at the time. One argument may be seen by the human mind to be less probable than its apparently more probable opposite, whereas it may be this less probable argument that really expresses the actual truth. One can advance a plausible argument, for example, that the world is probably eternal, and that the successive combinations of the eternal atoms of things recur in eternal successive cycles. One can argue with plausible reasons that it is probable that all change is only apparent. The apparentness or appearance of change can probably be accounted for in terms of the aggregation and separation of atomic particles. From a merely probable argument of this kind one may not conclude that the contradictory proposition is not true. One can present probable arguments for each of the debatable and opposed views; and one may finally judge that the arguments given for one view are more plausible or probable than the arguments given for the other view. It was in this spirit that Nicholas presented his own philosophical views as probable views which were more probable than their contradictories.

Nicholas of Autrecourt's denial that the existence of substance and causality is demonstrable has a certain similarity to Hume's critique of substance and causality 400 years later. Nicholas, however, did not deny that substances and causes existed; he merely denied that their existence or non-existence is demonstrable. His arguments are representative in a notable way of the radical critical attack upon traditional metaphysics which one associates with the Ockhamist movement in general. The modernity and energy of this movement drained away, in the course of time, into a barren wilderness of minutiae of terminist subtleties and 'logic-chopping'. Ockhamism was finally submerged by the combined forces of the Protestant and humanist revolts against the medieval cultural tradition. At this stage it was the Renaissance which gave a new impetus to philosophic thinking.

15 New trends and reactions in the late Middle Ages

1. Marsilius (dei Mainardini) **of Padua** (*c*. 1277-1342) was an Italian political theorist who became rector of the university of Paris in 1312, at a time when Philip (IV) the Fair was still king of France. King Philip had levied taxes on the clergy; and Pope Boniface VIII had excommunicated all who paid and all who received such taxes. A French expeditionary force invaded Italy and attempted to arrest the Pope. Subsequently, Pope John XXII (1316-34) attempted to administer the empire in the West, at a time of conflict between Louis the Bavarian and his rival Frederick of Austria. The papal forces waged a losing war in northern Italy against Louis. Many of the discontented forces in the Church, including the extremist Franciscan Spirituals, rallied to Louis' cause. Marsilius of Padua fulminated against the claims to papal supremacy in political matters as represented in the attitude of Boniface VIII and his supporters and successors. He considered that the papal claims to political control over the Italian city-states, and the papal interdicts and excommunications, were responsible for the wars, the devastated cities, the abandoned churches, the violence, hatreds and miseries of the war-torn areas, and especially those of northern Italy.

The medieval Scholastics in general had regarded the Church and the State as two 'perfect' societies, willed by God as means by which man may attain his supernatural and 'temporal' well-being. The ideal to be aimed at is a harmonious balance in which each of these two Powers will assist man to attain his final end. Pope Innocent IV, Giles of Rome and other writers had claimed that the Church is superior in dignity and value to the State and has a 'plenitude of power' since the salvation of every human creature depends on his obedience to the Pope. Marsilius, on the contrary, attempted to give a theoretical justification for the subordination of all churchmen to the authority of the people as a whole and the elected government of the people.

Marsilius and his collaborator John of Jandun (1286-1328), a leading Averroist at Paris, completed the writing of the treatise *Defensor pacis (Defender of Peace)* in 1324. They then took refuge at the imperial court of Louis in Nuremberg, where Marsilius wrote his *Defensor minor* and a treatise on the jurisdiction of the State in matrimonial matters before his death in 1342.

The *Defensor pacis* was written primarily as a critical refutation of the papalist claims to plenitude of power in temporal affairs. In the process of refuting these claims Marsilius laid down the guidelines for a new form of purely secular State and secular society under the control of a popularly elected government. He fused together three distinct themes into a unified and synthesized political theory.

The primary theme or premiss in Marsilius' political theory is the Aristotelian theme that the State is a self-sufficient community which exists for the good life, the common good. The judiciary, the government, the priestly class, and the various parts of the State, all subserve the good life of society or the State as a whole.

The second theme emphasizes the need for the existence and constant use of coercive law and government to regulate the destructive strife and conflicts which will inevitably arise in every human society. If society is to survive at all, then, State law must be 'coercive through punishment or reward in this present world'. This coercive force must apply to all rival parties and classes, priestly or otherwise, within the State. A papal party, claiming a superior 'plenitude of power', is a grave threat to civil peace. State law is not simply doctrinal or prescriptive or exhortatory, nor is it merely a dictate of right reason. It is preceptive and strengthened by sanctions applicable in this present life. It is not the same thing as justice. Justice is not a necessary condition for legal rules having coercive force. The legislative body in the State must not be a rival body in conflict with the governing body. If a society is to survive, State legislation and State government must be unitary. No society can afford to have diverse centres of coercive power.

The third theme asserts that regulations and politicians require popular consent or election before they can actually be coercive laws and government officials. This is the doctrine of republicanism. All authority derives ultimately from the people's electoral authority. Government exists by consent of the subjects; otherwise it is not government but tyrannical subjection. Freedom requires popular consent in both Church and State. The Church is an association of Christians whose leaders should serve to create the moral and spiritual climate in which the self-sufficing 'perfect society', the

State, can function in peace and tranquillity for the well-being of all.

The *Defensor pacis* was not widely circulated in the fourteenth century. In the following century, however, at the time of the Great Schism, several aspects of Marsilius' theories were developed further by the supporters of the Conciliar Movement. Other aspects of his thought were developed subsequently by the Erastians of the sixteenth century.

2. Mystical writings. The late Middle Ages are noted not only for the proud contentiousness of the unyielding rival schools of thought but also for an extraordinary flowering of mystical reflection and writings. It is the age of the Rhineland, the English, the French and the Italian mystics. These writers followed in the Christian Neo-Platonic tradition of Gregory of Nyssa, the Pseudo-Dionysius, Anselm, St Bernard, Bonaventure and others. They aimed in a practical way to deepen the spiritual life of religious people who sought for practical spiritual direction as a means towards a life of loving union with God. Many of these writers drew on the insights and vocabulary of the earlier Scholastics in their speculation upon the human experience of mystical union with God. Thus one finds in many of these writers a special working alliance of practical mysticism and Scholastic speculation.

Meister (Johannes) *Eckhart* (*c*. 1260-1327) was a Dominican who studied at Cologne and lectured at Paris. In his *Quaestiones Parisienses*, he speaks of God in a manner which combines rational speculation with an interpretation of mystical experience. The Godhead (*Deitas*) is indescribable and ineffable. It is the Ground of God (*Deus*) as manifested in the Trinity. Being manifests itself to itself in consciousness. The (undifferentiated) Godhead manifests itself to itself in God. God is Consciousness Itself. 'The nature of God is intellect, and to him, to be (*esse*) is to understand (*intelligere*).' God is above existence and existents. He is Being itself being conscious. All created existents find and receive and have their being in him and not independently or outside of him. Apart from him, creatures are pure nothing. The conscious creature has faculties, such as the will and the higher intellect, which are distinct from the 'ground', or the inner being, which is the *scintilla* or inner 'spark' of the soul. It is possible, through 'dark' contemplation, to leave aside the discursive and imaginative activities of 'clear' contemplation and to attain to the ground of one's very being. At this deeper level of contemplation one's inner being has a 'dark' experiential knowledge of Being Itself. God, in the dark inner depths, unites one's innermost being with his own Being, in an ineffable manner, in the hidden *scintilla* of the soul. God brings one's inner being into mystic union with Being Its Very Self in this mystic prayer of dark contemplation. Eckhart used many ambiguous expressions and daring antinomies in his effort to express the relations of the creature to God. These expressions gave rise to several misunderstandings on the part of the theologians, and condemnations by the Church authorities of the time. Eckhart's writings and sermons were presented in homely German vernacular, largely for the instruction and direction of the women who were members of the semimonastic order of the Beguines. There is a rich blending of Neo-Platonism and Scholasticism in all of his work.

Johann Tauler (1300-61) and Blessed Heinrich Suso (1300-65) were Dominican preachers and writers who avoided original specu-lation of the kind that brought about Eckhart's condemnation. They used Eckhartism and Neo-Platonic themes to express how the mystical union of the human will with the divine will takes place in the inner centre, the 'spark' or foundation of the soul. If the 'heart' (*Gemüt*) is permanently turned towards the inner ground of one's being, where God resides, then, God will allow the soul to become immersed in God himself while retaining its own identity. Man becomes deiform even though he remains man.

Blessed Jan van Ruysbroeck (1293-1381), a Flemish mystic, was a founder and prior of a religious community at Groenendael near Brussels. This community dedicated itself to the practice of apostolic good works suffused by the loving knowledge of God obtained in contemplative union with God. This form of apostolic and contem-plative life was known as 'the common life'. According to Ruys-broeck, man has existed from eternity within the super-essential Unity of God. The ground of the soul, man's inner being, is man's eternal archetype; and it is in this interior ground of one's being that one is capable of being elevated once again to union with God. From the Brethren of the Common Life came the pietistic movement called the *devotio moderna* of the late Middle Ages. In their school at Deventer, the Brethren of the Common Life educated Nicholas of Cusa, Erasmus, and other philosophers and theologians of the fifteenth and sixteenth centuries.

Jean de Gerson (1363-1429), chancellor of the university of Paris, was a religious reformer and writer on mysticism who lectured at Paris on the theory and practice of contemplation. He attributed the existing state of aridity in theology to the arid subtleties and neologisms of Scotist theologians theorizing proudly about the nature of God. Practical theology and dynamic religion must be liberated from formalism. Mystical theology is the crown of all speculative endeavour. In the experiential knowledge of God it is love which is at work. In affective knowledge of this kind, the human will is in total conformity with the divine will, and the highest powers of the soul are brought to fulfilment.

Nicholas of Cusa (see below) and Denis the Carthusian (1402-71) emphasized both the transcendence of God and his immanence in creation. He is transcendent and cannot be known positively through phantasms or concepts. But he can be known 'darkly' and immediately in the darkness of loving mystical union and supra-rational contemplation.

All these writers on mysticism were philosophers who placed philosophical speculation at the service of the mystical experience of union with God. Their work differs notably from the non-philosophical and basically erotic mysticism of, for example, Mechthild of Magdeburg (1212-82) and the *Frauenmystik* of the same period. In the writings of these philosophers of religion one finds a constant alliance of (de-eroticized) practical mysticism and philosophical speculation.

3. The physical sciences. In the thirteenth century, the Franciscan philosopher Peter John Olivi (see Chapter 12) advocated once again the 'impetus' theory of John Philoponus of Alexandria (sixth century A.D.) and Alpetragius or al-Bitruji (twelfth century). The theory was discussed and investigated further by Ockham, Buridan, Oresme and other Schoolmen of the fourteenth century. In this way the ground was prepared for the later scientific concept of momentum or kinetic energy and for the achievements of the Renaissance scientists.

John Philoponus, in his commentaries and books on Aristotle, Proclus and other cosmologists, criticized the Greek belief in the divine nature of the stars. There is no essential dichotomy between the matter of the heavens and the earth. As the different colours of fires on earth depend on the nature of their fuel, so too the different colours of the fire of the sun and the stars depend on their material composition. These bodies and other bodies in motion are not kept moving by the constant teleological drawing power of final causes lying ahead of them nor of the push of the air behind the bodies. They are projectiles to which an impetus or invisible kinetic force has been imparted by the projecting agent to the object thrown. When that impetus has been consumed, the object resumes its natural downward movement. Light, too, is to be explained in this way as an impetus emitted from a luminous body and following the physical and geometric laws of nature.

Scientific theorizing in the fourteenth century continued the theorizing of Grosseteste, Bacon and others in the thirteenth century on magnetism, optics, refraction, the rainbow and other phenomena of nature. But the newly discovered approach to the problem of physical motion and impetus gave a new insight into how these phenomena of the universe are to be explained.

Ockham declared that a moving body is moving simply because it is successively in distinct places and not at rest in any of them. There is no need to postulate that motion is an unobservable entity or 'quality' impressed on a projectile. *Jean Buridan* (1295-1356) declared that a projectile is not kept moving by the continuous supporting agency of the medium (air, water and so forth). The launching mover or agent imparts to the projectile moving force which is proportional to the projectile's speed and mass. This transmitted force keeps the projectile moving even after it has lost contact with its launching agent until such time as the medium progressively reduces the impetus. *Marsilius of Inghen* (d.1396), a disciple of Buridan, pointed out that even though impetus ceases when movement ceases, impetus differs from movement, and is necessarily directional. It is impetus which causes the constancy of speed in movement. It is a disposition facilitating movement, and differs from movement just as speed differs from movement. Quantity, similarly, differs from extension.

Nicholas of Oresme (c. 1325-82) was a French mathematician, philosopher and scientist who became Bishop of Lisieux in 1377. He insisted that, in problems pertaining to physical science, equally plausible alternative hypotheses may be presented as probable solutions. A view repudiated by tradition may be as tenable as the traditional opinion itself. Thus, for example, the traditional view states that the earth is stationary at the centre of the universe, and the celestial spheres undergo a daily rotation. But many arguments can be advanced for the view that the earth performs a diurnal rotation on its axis while the heavens remain stationary. Astronomical and physical phenomena can be accounted for, and 'appearances' can be 'saved', on either one or the other of these alternative hypotheses. The view that the earth rotates is not a novel theory, he states. It appears to have been propounded by Heraclides of Pontus (d. *c.* 310 B.C.) at the Academy during Plato's lifetime, and by Aristarchus of Samos, who was attacked by the Stoics for teaching such an impiety. Nicholas himself decided to accept the common view of his times, since the alternative hypothesis had not been conclusively established.

Albert of Saxony (c. 1316-90), rector of the university of Paris in

1357 and first rector of the new university of Vienna in 1365, popularized the ideas of Buridan and Oresme. He himself was not an original scientific thinker, but his publications exercised considerable influence on subsequent scientific thought. He pointed out that a greater mass generates a greater impetus and so gives rise to increased acceleration. He agreed with Oresme that the earth's centre of gravity is identical with the centre of the earth. For this reason a falling body tends towards being united with its centre of gravity in the centre of the earth; and once a moving body has acquired impetus, speed too gains increased velocity. It was ideas of this kind which paved the way for the experiments, discoveries and new theories of the scientists and astronomers of the Renaissance. In the process, physical science was gradually being separated from philosophical science.

4. Nicholas of Cusa, or Nicholas Kryfts of Kues (1401-64), revitalized Neo-Platonism as an answer to the social, political and religious unrest of his times. He was a mathematician, a philosopher, a theologian and a man of action who gave his attention to the cause of reform of the Church and the empire. On one occasion he called himself a Pythagorean. He was deeply convinced of the truth of the Pythagorean theory that the key to all truth is to be found in numbers, and in the order, proportion and harmony in multiplicity which numbers symbolize. In the Creator's Universe there is a grand unity of design which is present in the harmonious reconciliation or synthesis of opposites. In the Providence of God contradictories are reconciled. There is a *coincidentia oppositorum* or a coincidence of opposites. This is applicable, too, to the ideal of preserving unity in Christendom and federal unity in the empire. The ideal to be striven for is harmonious unity in multiplicity without suppression of differences. Nicholas himself strove to implement this ideal as a Cardinal, Bishop and papal legate in Germany.

In his treatise *De docta ignorantia*, Nicholas maintained that a man is wise only if he realizes that the human intellect never grasps any one truth with infinite precision. Human knowledge, then is learned ignorance. At best it is piecemeal conjecture. It sees things in terms of contradictories and opposites. The divine mind, however, sees that in reality all things are a unity in coincidence of what, to us, are opposites. In God, essence and existence and all oppositions and distinctions are united within his infinite transcendent unity. For this reason, we can attain only a learned ignorance of his nature.

Being transcends every maximum and every minimum. God is absolute transcendent maximum and absolute transcendent minimum in a perfect coincidence of opposites which are opposites only according to limited intellect. He is *in actu* all that is *in posse*, or he is in act all that is capable of being. He alone is *Possest*, incomprehensible *posse ipsum*, namely, absolute Power or Ability Itself.

The intellect can express its insight into God's relation to creatures in limited symbols, analogies and antinomies. Creatures mirror God; they are his theophany. He is the world's centre and the world's circumference, immanent and transcendent. He is the *complicatio* or enfolding of all things, containing all things; and he is their *explicatio* or unfolding since they come forth from him. But creature is always creature, and God is God.

God alone can be said to be positively infinite. But the universe reflects, in a 'contracted' way, this infinity of God. It has no circumference. It is boundless or undetermined; and it has no fixed centre. All things are in motion relative to the finite observer who is himself in motion. There is no fixity, and no absolute in the material universe, a universe where all bodies are composed of similar material substances.

The philosophy of Nicholas of Cusa has its roots in the thought of Proclus and the Christian medieval Neo-Platonists. His vision is theocentric and Christian. At the same time, his interests are those of the humanistic, Renaissance man. For this reason, his works were widely read for several centuries. He was held in high esteem by Giordano Bruno and other Renaissance thinkers.

5. The 'restoration of letters'. In Italy in the fourteenth century the enthusiasm of Petrarch (1304-74), Giotto (*c*. 1266-1337) and others for Greek antiquity, its art, culture and literature, inaugurated a new cultural movement which spread gradually through the rest of Europe. The writers of this period were convinced that they were witnessing the awakening of a new cultural epoch which was inspired by the rediscovery of the fine arts of ancient Greece and Rome. No particular name was given to this cultural epoch for some hundreds of years. In 1743, the historian J. J. Brucker referred to it as the era of the 'restoration of letters' (*restauratio literarum*) and the 'recovery of philosophy' (*restitutio philosophiae*). In 1787, Edward Gibbon referred to the 'restoration of the Greek letters in Italy'. In the eighteenth century, several French authors spoke of this work of restoration as a renaissance. In 1855, the French historian Jules Michelet (1798-1874) named the period *La Renaissance* and characterized it colourfully as the age of 'the discovery of the world, the discovery of man'. Subsequently, the term 'Renaissance' began to be used in a sense which seemed to disparage the presumably unawakened and unenlightened 'dark' ages of Christian theological 'supernaturalism' which had preceded it. Nevertheless, this (nineteenth-century) term is now an established term in almost all works produced by recent historians, where it no longer carries disparaging implications about the Christian 'wisdom', or the philosophers, of the previous ten centuries.

The literary renaissance inaugurated by Petrarch, Boccaccio (1313-75) and others degenerated in Italy, in the following century, into a stylized 'Ciceronianism' which frequently gave disdainful and cavalier expression to 'semi-pagan' scepticism. The emphasis was on grandiloquent literary style for the cultured, 'aristocratic' courtier who thirsted for personal glory, and on a civilized and urbane way of life, rather than on human social and moral reform. However, the growth of princely trade and wealth enabled the patrons of the humanities to purchase and copy manuscripts of the ancient classics and to finance the foundation of new libraries.

In the fifteenth and sixteenth centuries, the literary and humanistic phase of the Renaissance spread to northern Europe where it was allied with a religious, moral and educational movement for the reformation of society in general. The invention of printing (*c*. 1439) helped to make the newly discovered classics available to a wide audience. Self-education, as well as institutional education, now became a real possibility on a far wider scale than ever before. At the end of the fifteenth and the beginning of the sixteenth century, classical and literary scholars such as Erasmus, Tunstall, Grocyn, Linacre, Colet, Thomas More, St John Fisher, Melanchthon and others were influential figures in the development of humanistic education in the new educational institutions.

6. The 'recovery of philosophy'. The era of the 'restoration of letters' is also called the era of the 'recovery of philosophy'. The main stream of philosophy in the late Middle Ages, at the time of the Renaissance, continued to be Aristotelian. The problems posed, and the solutions given, are presented in the technical terms of Aristotelian philosophy. However, these Aristotelians were, for the main part, anti-Scholastic, Renaissance Aristotelians. They promoted the study of the original writings of Aristotle. Nicoletto Vernias (*fl. c.* 1490), Agostino Nipho (d. 1546), A. Achillini (d. 1512), M. A. Zimara (d. 1532) and their followers tended to interpret Aristotle in a modified Averroistic sense. Pietro Pomponazzi (d. 1525), Simon Porta (d. 1555) and others tended to interpret the 'pure'

Aristotle in terms of Aristotle's own emphasis on observable facts and empirical evidence; they paid more attention to Alexander of Aphrodisias' interpretation of Aristotle than to that of Averroes, and encouraged a 'naturalistic' outlook in their approach to philosophic questions. Melanchthon (1497-1560) endeavoured to introduce Aristotelianism into the Lutheran universities, but this suggestion encountered lively opposition from many Lutheran theologians. However, none of these writers, or other Renaissance Aristotelians, made any major or significant contribution to Peripatetic philosophy or to Renaissance science.

Several of the humanists whose interests were literary, 'cultured', and aesthetic, rather than philosophic or scientific, attacked Aristotelian logic in the process of their attack upon the Scholastic metaphysical method. Laurentius Valla (d. 1457), Rudolf Agricola (d. 1485), Luis Vives (d. 1540) and others held that rhetoric, that is, the general science of 'meaning', is the soul and principle of all the other sciences. The Ciceronian orations have a far deeper insight into human happiness and factual reality than the Aristotelian abstractions. Petrus Ramus (1515-72) held that the spontaneous natural logic of rhetorical orations and of cultured speech must replace the slavish traditional adherence to vacuous formal logic. The emphasis must be on the beauty of things rather than on the immateriality of abstractions. This emphasis may be seen as a factor in the gradual growth of the empiricist outlook in Renaissance times.

The Academy in Florence, founded by Cosimo de' Medici in the middle of the fifteenth century, became a lively centre of Platonic and Neo-Platonic studies in the late Middle Ages. The Academy, which was intentionally modelled on Plato's Academy, was placed under the guidance of the Byzantine scholar, Giorgios Pletho (d. 1452). There were similar centres of Platonic study at Pisa and Ferrara. The most renowned members of the Florentine Academy were Marsilio Ficino (1433-99), who translated the *Corpus Hermeticum* and the works of Plato, Plotinus, Proclus, Porphyry and others into Latin, and Giovanni Pico della Mirandola (1463-94) whose writings were influenced by Plato, the Pseudo-Dionysius and the Jewish Cabbala. These writers and their contemporaries John Argyropoulos, John Bessarion of Trebizon and others attempted to unite together all the valuable insights of Greco-Roman, Jewish, Christian and Islamic thought into a harmonious Neo-Platonic and Christian view of the hierarchy of being in which man is seen as linking together the spiritual world and the material. The members of the Neo-Platonic society that grouped itself around Ficino were theists and humanists who saw all of Nature as the expression of the Divinity. Their form of natural religion aimed at moral improvement; it endeavoured to bring about the full growth of the highest potentialities of the human person.

The doctrines of ancient Stoicism were revived and taught by Justus Lipsius (1547-1606) and Guillaume du Vair (d. *c.* 1621). The moral doctrine of Pomponazzi, too, was strongly influenced by the Stoic doctrine of rational self-control in accordance with the universal laws of nature, and rigorous strength of character in ethical and political action. Pierre Gassendi (see below, section 8) revived Epicurean atomism, and insisted that his Epicureanism was a Christian Epicureanism. As mentioned above, Nicholas of Cusa called himself a Pythagorean.

The works of Sextus Empiricus were first published in 1562, and from that time onwards his codification of the doctrines of Greek Scepticism exercised an important influence upon Renaissance and modern thought and literature. Michel de Montaigne (1533-92) revived the arguments for Pyrrhonic scepticism, from the relativity of sense-experience and value-judgements. Pierre Charron (1541-1603) taught that the human mind cannot discover any truth except by revelation. Theologians and atheists know no more and no less about God than the humblest artisans. The humble sceptic must empty his mind of all dubious opinions in order to receive the divine revelation on faith alone. Francis Sanchez (*c.* 1551-1623) argued at length, in his *Quod nihil scitur (Why Nothing Can Be Known)*, that the finite mind cannot even know whether or not it knew nothing. God alone has genuinely certain knowledge. One can therefore merely deal constructively with one's experience in order to attain the best information available. One must replace a probabilistic empirical study of experience for the hopeless quest for certain knowledge.

Towards the end of the sixteenth century, as the Renaissance itself drew to a close, the yearning for the revival of ancient thought began to subside. The new vogue was for 'modern' approaches and for 'new' systems of thought. Francesco Patrizi, for example, wrote his *Nova de universis philosophia* in 1591, and Francis Bacon spoke, in 1605, of replacing the 'restorations' with a 'Great Instauration' of a new scientific philosophy which would give man mastery over the natural world.

7. **Political philosophy.** The feudal society of the Middle Ages was already giving way in the thirteenth century to a new form of political consciousness which favoured the growth of political absolutism. The various wars in France, England, Spain and

elsewhere gave rise to a widespread felt need for national unity and stability. National hates were active, and national consciousness grew steadily everywhere in the latter part of the Middle Ages.

The governing authorities of the rising nation-states were naturally concerned with certain fundamental problems of political and legal theory. Their legally trained administrators tended to combine the doctrines of the older Roman *ius commune* with a political theory favouring royal absolutism. Bartolus of Sassoferrato (1314-57) held that, apart from the *ius gentium* which is immutable, the ruler is not bound by the laws of the city-state even though it is 'equitable' that he should respect them and voluntarily comply with them. Lucas de Penna (1320-90), and many of the civilian commentators on civil law, known as post-glossators, maintained that law is not an expression of the will of the community, and that the prince, whose lordship rests on divine authority, is responsible to God alone.

Niccolò Machiavelli (1469-1527) was an Italian politician and political thinker who was deeply involved in the statecraft, intrigue and power divisions of the sixteenth-century Italian city-states. He became famous for his treatise of 1513, *Il principe* (*The Prince*), and for his book of *Discourses* on the first ten books of the Roman historian Livy, which was completed in 1517. These works were written by way of advice, and proof of his personal political usefulness, to the senior officials and executives of the Florentine government at a time when he himself was unemployed and living in straitened financial circumstances.

Machiavelli admonished the prince, or head of state, to disregard any mental probings as to whether the prince's actions would be regarded as virtuous or vicious. He must above all else be efficient in the affairs of state and successful in saving the state. Cesare Borgia, for example, chose at different times cruelty, or leniency, or loyalty, or villainy, as the correct means for the attainment of the interests of the state, namely, its greater security and well-being. His choice depended entirely on the circumstances. The successful head of state is not concerned with morality, good or bad; his sole concern is with political necessity and political efficiency. In every political organization, growth and expansion is the law of life. For this reason, 'vitality' and forcefulness are an integral element in successful politics. Christian meekness generates political weakness. Political man needs *virtù* (vitality), not Christian virtues. The ancient Romans, for example, succeeded in extending their power over the entire world. The prince should make a constant study of the past to broaden his experience by means of historical experience. Political science should study not the philosophical nature of the good society but the historical political experiences of the past. Political organizations, like organic beings, grow, age and die. Those that are well organized live longer than others; but all in fact decline. Machiavelli detached himself totally from moral issues, being chiefly interested in the historical practices and political techniques which ensured political success. He sought to discover those patterns in political history which would enable him, by historical induction, to formulate the general rules which appear to govern the art and practice of successful politics.

St Thomas More (1478-1535), Lord Chancellor of England, was concerned that power-hungry governments, involved in war, statecraft and intrigue, were totally unconcerned about the social injustice and covetousness of the rich proprietors and traders who were allowed to manipulate commerce and the national economy in such a way that they could unjustly and inhumanly exploit the basic human needs and vital commodities of the small farmer, the dependent wage-earner, and the impoverished artisan. His well-known and influential *Utopia* (1516) called attention to this commercial exploitation of the small farmer; then, like Plato's *Laws* and *Republic,* it depicted an ideal communal state, Utopia, a 'best society', where all men would be assured of security and a decent means of livelihood in a casteless, co-operative, democratic society. More's attempt to establish a pattern for an ideal commonwealth inspired many other notable works in subsequent centuries, such as Bacon's *New Atlantis,* Campanella's *City of the Sun,* and Samuel Johnson's *Rasselas.*

Richard Hooker (1553-1600) wrote his *Laws of Ecclesiastical Polity* to uphold (against the Calvinist William Travers, and Protestant Puritan extremists) the establishment of Church and State as represented by the ecclesiastical and political institutions of Elizabethan England. He elaborated and adapted the implications of Thomist Aristotelianism in political and social philosophy as a rational foundation for Queen Elizabeth's conciliatory settlement policies. Book I of the 'Laws' is a compendium of Thomistic philosophy. We learn the will of God, the eternal law, by using our God-given reason to discover the dictates of the natural law. The law of nature is embodied in secular government just as the revealed law is embodied in the Church. In a Christian State, Church and State are not distinct societies. Revealed law and natural law, Church and State, are joint guides in the commonwealth. In this way Hooker upheld the establishment of Church and State.

Jean Bodin (1530-96) is chiefly known for his *Method for the Easy Comprehension of History* (1566) and *Six Books of the Republic* (1576). In these works he attempted to demonstrate that monarchy of the French type, in which the king guarantees all liberty, is the best of all possible regimes. The sovereign administrator of the republic is the head of all the families, corporations, classes and provinces acting in concert within the republic; his task is the proper government of the households composing the State. Sovereignty is the active form and personification of the absolute and perpetual power of the State. Its distinguishing mark is that of making, promulgating and repealing laws. All legislative and judicial power is concentrated in the sovereign. Sovereignty, in a monarch or in an assembly, is indivisible, inalienable and absolute. It is not limited by custom of any kind, but it is limited by the requirements of the higher law of justice and by the recognition of the legitimacy of other sovereignties in neighbouring countries. The ideal is peaceful coexistence. The source of sovereign authority lies in social law, in the law of justice. This is clearly seen in the long history of the government of France in which hereditary monarchy has always been regarded as being subject to a higher law.

Johannes Althusius (1557-1638), a German Calvinist political philosopher, was a strong opponent of Bodin's doctrine of royal absolutism. He held that sovereignty is popular sovereignty. There is a natural need in men to form natural, co-operative community groups. These build up into a universal community of civil and private corporations, called the State. This State-community makes a contract with a political officer to whom supreme administrative power is delegated. The political administrative officer, or chief of state, is to ensure that the constitution is observed. Politics is then the science and art of linking human beings to each other for a social life. The chief of state must remember that he is only a commissioner of the people. If he acts contrary to the contract between himself and the community, he may be deposed.

Hugo Grotius or Huig de Groot (1583-1645), of Delft, wrote his famous work *De iure belli ac pacis* (1625) at a time when the lawless Thirty Years War was raging in much of Europe, and when there was no prospect of re-establishing the international authority which had formerly been exercised by Popes and emperors. He pointed out that in the absence of an international sovereign authority there are certain overriding principles of the natural law which govern the relations between sovereign national states. The human nature of man and peoples is essentially rational. A binding principle binding both man and nations is '*pacta sunt servanda*': men and nations must have respect for promises given and treaties signed. This principle can be taken as a fundamental principle which binds the nations to a common standard of behaviour. Man is a rational and social animal with an impelling natural need for peaceful and organized social life. Expediency and natural justice lead to that form of association which binds nations together under a common law of nations which is 'valid alike in peace and war'. War is permissible only in cases of necessity, when there is no doubt as to its justice and only when there is no international court of arbitration. A just war might be waged, for example, against a State to prevent that State's maltreatment of its own subjects. In the conduct of any just war, the 'law of nations' must be observed, and the law of nature continues to bind all men as men. Grotius' lasting influence on the philosophy of international law may be attributed to the fact that, at a critical moment in history, he formulated and systematized a corpus of principles and ideas which were demanded by the changing needs of a changing world.

8. Philosophy of Nature. The speculative philosophers of Nature in the sixteenth and early seventeenth centuries, were prompted by their interest in scientific matters to speculate freely about Nature in general and to advance fresh hypotheses about Nature as a marvellously organized (if not positively organic) system. The majority of these speculative natural philosophers saw Nature as the external self-revelation of the divine inner mystery. They mingled together, with different emphases, empiricist theories, scientific observations, metaphysical themes and various hypotheses taken from astrology, magic and alchemy. The emphasis on one or other of these elements differed and varied, but for each of these thinkers the vision of Nature as a manifestation of divine mystery was a fascinating subject for further speculation and study.

Henricus C. Agrippa von Nettesheim (1486-1535) was a colourful Renaissance lawyer, physician, diplomat and adventurer who was also a notorious magician, cabbalist, and anti-intellectualist religious Reformer. His three volumes on occult science, *De occulta philosophia* (1510) attempted to explain Nature and the Universe in terms of a Christian interpretation of cabbalistic analysis of Hebrew letters and Pythagorean numerological symbols as related to natural phenomena. In 1515, Agrippa taught occult science at the university of Pavia. The Universe or macrocosm, like man, the microcosm, possesses a Spirit whose effluences are present in all things as vital principles or latent powers. Man can wrest these secrets from nature.

Girolamo Fracastoro (1483-1553), a papal physician, attempted to explain the movement and interactions of bodies in terms of sympathies and antipathies (or forces of attraction and repulsion) between objects. Bodies emit tiny corpuscula, or *species* (images), which enter through the pores of other bodies. This explains in a simple and naturalistic way how perception takes place.

Theophrastus Bombastus of Hohenheim (or *Paracelsus*; 1493-1541) was physician, surgeon, chemist, alchemist, pharmacologist and philosopher. He accepted the alchemist and cabbalist doctrine that decay is the beginning of all birth: Nature emerges through separations. Prime matter emerged from the immaterial, eternal, ultimate matter which was with God. Prime matter is a seed and the seed is the element of fluid, a watery matrix, which spawns nature. The three states of nature, namely combustible, vaporous, and solid, confer on material bodies their structure, corporeality and function. Nature lives through decay and separation; life eats life. The food of one is poison to another. Within every living body there is an alchemist that selects the food and rejects the poisonous. Diseases arise from poisons, positive evils. The physician uses various combinations of the fundamental elements sulphur, mercury and salt to stimulate the *archeus*, or the alchemist, in man, and to assist Nature in its healing work.

Sebastian Franck (von Wörd, 1499-1542) was a religious philosopher who saw history as a dualistic interaction between God and the external world. This interaction is reflected within man as a struggle between the Spirit and the forces which resist it, or between the Inner Word in man and the outer word of flesh and selfishness. Exterior authorities, and even the authority of the Bible itself, are external, outer words which can be truly comprehended only when 'we listen to the word of God within ourselves'. The true Church is the universal invisible Church of the Spirit. All men, Christians, Jews, Muslims or others, are equal, and all are accessible to the Holy Spirit. Religious liberty and toleration must be extended to all. In the *ecclesia spiritualis*, inward enlightenment alone is sufficient. This view was condemned by the leading Lutheran theologians; it was accepted nevertheless ardently by several believers who called themselves Franckists or Sebastianists.

Girolamo Cardano (1501-76) was a mathematician and professor of medicine at Pavia who viewed the world as a unified, law-governed organic system animated by a world-soul. In this living world system, man is the 'mean' or the microcosm. God has subjected all of Nature to the universal power of natural magic and mathematical laws. The mathematician's quest for a mathematical understanding of nature is a contemplative pilgrimage of the human mind towards an experience of union with God.

Bernardino Telesio (1509-88) attempted to explain Nature in terms of concrete, passive, inert matter and the two active forces or principles of material beings, heat and cold, which are responsible for all natural events. In his *De rerum natura* he asserted that all of nature is animated (hylozoism), and endowed with sensation in varying degrees (panpsychism). Heat is the source of life in plants and animals. It is the cause of the biological and sensitive functions in man. In both man and animals, 'animal-spirit' is generated with the body; it is a subtle material substance that emanates from the warm element. Man has in addition a 'superadded soul', an immortal 'mind', which is specially created by God and which informs both body and animal-spirit. All human activities, emotions and virtues are explained by the fundamental natural drive for self-preservation and personal well-being. Telesio pointed out that he was attempting to explain nature and the actual world as it is in its concrete reality. He was concerned only with the actual intrinsic principles of things, not with Aristotelian extrinsic causes. For this reason Francis Bacon spoke of Telesio as 'the first of the moderns' in as far as Telesio called for natural explanations based not on Peripatetic causes but on sense-experience in the study of nature.

Francesco Patrizi (1529-97) was a professor of Platonic philosophy at the university of Ferrara and later at Rome. He held that physical light is a formative principle, at work on space, warmth and fluidity, in constituting the world. He attacked forcefully the doctrines of the well-established Aristotelians. His emphasis on the mathematical study of space helped in part to prepare the ground for Galileo's new physics based on quantities, experiments and calculations.

Giordano Bruno (1548-1600), of Nola near Naples, is perhaps the most renowned of the Italian philosophers of the Renaissance. He was deeply impressed by the occult philosophy of Agrippa von Nettesheim, and by Marsilio Ficino's Neo-Platonic vision of Nature and astral magic. He regarded mathematics as a 'pedantry' which lacked the profound animist and magical insight into Nature found in the *Corpus Hermeticum* of 'Hermes Trismegistus', the ancient Egyptian source of Platonic thought. (These Hermetica or pseudo-Hermetic writings were actually written by several unknown, presumably Gnostic, authors between A.D. 100 and 300; Ficino translated a number of these texts in 1400.) These ancient writings direct attention to the occult powers at work within the cosmos. Here we have the true religion, that is, the religion of *natura* in contact with the powers of Nature. This true religion was destroyed by Christianity.

For Bruno, the living earth moves around the divine sun. Innumerable other living worlds move with a life of their own in the boundless universe. Copernicus saw only the shallow, mathematical aspect of this profound religious truth. Life is movement, and nothing in the living universe is immobile. The infinitely extended All is a living One. There are ladders of occult sympathies running through all nature. The mind of the magus can ascend these ladders to the height of the divinity where he can attain to 'the truths and secrets of nature'. From this vantage point, the philosopher-magus can formulate imaginative new doctrines about the immense living body of the cosmos. For Bruno, the hidden laws of the universe were placed there by the divine philosopher-magician, whereas for Newton they were placed there by the divine mechanic-mathematician. In this sense, Bruno's vision of the universe is analogous in certain ways to that of Newton. His theological doctrines about Christianity aroused the hostility of Catholic, Calvinist and Lutheran theologians. He was condemned by the Roman Inquisition and burned at Rome on 17 February 1600.

Tommaso Campanella (1568-1639), a Dominican from Calabria, admired and defended Telesio's *De rerum natura*. He adopted Telesio's doctrine of passive matter and active principles of heat and cold instead of the Aristotelian hylomorphic theory. Matter has a concrete reality of its own; it is inactive and formless, but (like wax) it is capable of being moulded into many forms. God placed matter in space. Space is the substratum of all things. It is the primary and incorporeal substantial receptacle having the capacity to receive all bodies. Time is matter itself considered in its successive duration; it is the successive duration of material things having a beginning and an end. Our knowledge of matter, space, time, and Nature in general must rest on empirical investigation, observation and sense-perception. We then interpret Nature (all being) on an analogy with our own being. Man is microcosm, a world in miniature, mirroring all that is in being.

Campanella asserted that the philosopher should posit a universal doubt at the beginning of his system of knowledge, and that he should then start with the principle of self-consciousness as the basis of knowledge and certitude. One's own existence is revealed in the very act of thinking or doubting about anything. This view anticipates and antedates the Cartesian method of universal methodic doubt and the Cartesian foundational truth: *cogito ergo sum*. Campanella asserted that the conscious soul is an essentially knowing nature. 'To know', or to be conscious, is 'to be' (*cognoscere est esse*). In knowing oneself as knowing, the knower *is* the known. The knowledge in this case is a knowledge of the original being of the knower. Self-knowledge of this kind can legitimately be called 'innate' knowledge. This form of knowledge differs from the knowledge that one has of anything other than oneself. Knowledge of other beings is knowledge which is inferred by reasoning; it can therefore be called 'illate' knowledge. In the case of innate knowledge (where a conscious being is being conscious of itself as being conscious), the very knowing *is* the *esse*. In the case of knowledge of the non-self, knowledge becomes intentionally the *esse* in the possession of the other, the non-self. (In other words, in the unitary act of knowing, which is necessarily a knowing of something, the subjective pole becomes one with the objective pole in the simple act of knowing or assimilating the known; the knowing of an object is one with the object as known.) Acquired, or illate, knowledge is the soul's cognition of things other than itself. Knowledge of the external world can be acquired either by (Platonic) intellectual intuition of a being in its concrete reality, or by (Aristotelian) abstract universals. In several of his doctrines, Campanella anticipated trends which became common among later thinkers. His *City of the Sun* (*Civitas Solis*) presents several germinal suggestions about social, political and educational reforms which anticipate modern theories and practices.

Jakob Boehme (1575-1624), 'the cobbler of Görlitz', combined a Germanic philosophy of Nature with a Lutheran concern for the soul's union with God. He grappled with the problem of the relation of the world to God and with the problem of evil. God is the original ground, the *Ungrund* or *Urgrund*, of all things. He is 'the Being of Beings, the Byss and the Abyss', the eternal One. Within God, incomprehensible will is a will to self-intuition; and it finds itself as the 'heart' or the eternal mind of the will. From the will and the heart of the will there emanates dynamic 'moving life'. (This triadic movement in the inner life of God is correlated with the Trinity.)

Boehme regarded the original abysmal will as needing a real object to arouse self-knowledge. For this reason the original will differentiates itself through a triadic movement in which it reveals itself externally in the visible variety of nature. It differentiates itself, firstly, by a process of contraction whereby substances become individuated; secondly, by a process of diffusion whereby things intermingle and gravitate to one another; and thirdly, by a process of oscillation or rotation which arises from the interplay of the forces of contraction and diffusion. This triadic movement is an evolutionary movement in which opposition is overcome and transformed into a harmony (the German Idealists of the nineteenth century spoke of it as a triadic movement of thesis, antithesis and synthesis). In this way the divine will reveals itself in the universe. Nature is a manifestation of God in visible variety. It is God external. It is therefore animated by an inner spiritual world, or world-spirit (*spiritus mundi*), which is the prototype of the visible exterior universe. It is the *mysterium magnum*. It reveals the goodness of God and the wrath of God. Evil is related to the wrath of God. The movement of history will end in a triumph of the good, a triumph of love.

Boehme's thought and writings were influential. In England, William Law (d. 1761) and Boehme's disciples, the Behmenists, who eventually merged with the Quakers, came under his influence. In Germany, Boehme's idea of the self-unfolding of God in triadic movements re-emerged in post-Kantian German Idealism.

Jan Baptista van Helmont (1577-1644) was a Flemish alchemist, physician and philosopher who made important discoveries in chemistry and medicine. He came under the influence of Paracelsus and the Hermetic writings. He maintained that the experimental physicist must rely on his own inner light and on the wisdom of the ancients, if he is to make genuine progress in scientific knowledge. Abstract reasoning leads only to error. Intuitive intellection derives from a divine inner illumination within the soul when the soul is introspective, prayerful and believing. He maintained that every organ within any living body had its own *archeus insitus* (or monad) which determines the special function of that organ. Each organism has a general *archeus influus*, or vegetative soul, from which the organism derives its life. Diseases of different kinds arise from disorders in these various *archei*.

Pierre Gassendi (1592-1655) devoted much thought to the doctrine of Epicurean atomism. He held that this doctrine can provide a helpful model for the data of knowledge which we acquire about the observable world. Atoms have various shapes, sizes and weights. This can account for the differences between bodies of different kinds. He described the characteristics of different atoms by way of the different sensory qualities experienced. Our knowledge of the world comes only from sensory experience. Inductions from sensory experience can never produce certainty. Inductions cannot produce certain universal propositions, since a negative instance may still be discovered at any time in the future. We can only know how things appear to us, not how things really are in themselves. We must therefore be content to make a careful examination of appearances and be cautious in our evaluations of the data derived from them. The atomist system presents the best explanatory account for the sense qualities we experience. Gassendi himself, however, did not use the atomic theory to produce any significant scientific results, since he limited his descriptions of atoms to descriptions of the sensory qualities of sense-experience.

9. Renaissance science, as represented for example in the work of Galileo and Newton, exercised a strong influence on the subject-matter, method and aims of the philosophy of the seventeenth and eighteenth centuries. The new sciences emphasized the empirical method of inquiry and the mathematical-deductive method of attaining scientific certitude. The remarkable development of these mathematico-physical sciences provided a stimulus for the growth of British empiricism, European Continental rationalism, and mechanistic philosophies as represented in the works of Descartes and Thomas Hobbes. Imaginative new schematic representations or 'models' of gravitation, matter and the universe emerged; and these changed schematic pictures gave rise to new emphases in philosophic thought.

These mathematico-physical sciences focus attention on what are called 'facts', 'laws' and (scientific) theories. The observed 'facts' of which the physicist or chemist or astronomer speaks are those observations which are expressible in measurements or pointer-readings. The scientist uses weighing scales, watches, rulers and thermometers to express the pointer-readings which are verifiable arithmetic 'facts'. These facts or measurements then provide the basis of algebraic 'laws' which express relationships between the measurements or 'facts'. Thus, for example, Boyle's 'law' states algebraically that '$PV=C$'. Scientific arithmetic 'facts' and algebraic 'laws' are based on direct observation of empirical data and are continually referred back to these data for empirical verification. Once the facts and laws are verified, the scientist then seeks an explanatory hypothesis, or model, or theory (such as the undulatory theory of light) which will serve to correlate and schematize a large number of observations and laws. The notable achievements of the Renaissance scientists were achievements of this kind.

Simon Stevin, in 1586, measured the velocity of falling leaden balls in controlled experiments on gravitation. William Gilbert, in 1600, published his experimental findings on the effects which a spherical (magnetic) loadstone, as a 'model' of the magnetic polarization of the earth, had upon magnetic compass needles.

Galileo Galilei (1564-1642), an Italian astronomer and physicist, made important contributions to the methodology of scientific investigation. He pointed out (against Telesio and Bacon) that the physicist must not rely solely on sensory evidence. In physics, mathematical relations prevail. The demands of sense-data, reason and mathematical interpretation must be satisfied simultaneously. 'The book of nature is written in mathematical characters.' He himself contrived several deliberately controlled experiments as means of verifying new explanatory hypotheses and theories. He challenged a number of the theories pertaining to floating bodies, motion, acceleration, the perfect sphericity and immutability of celestial bodies, and other theories advanced by the Aristotelian professors in the universities. He rejected authority of any kind as a criterion of truth in scientific matters. He pointed out that telescopic observations of the mountainous character of the moon presented irrefutable evidence against the Aristotelians' axiom of perfect sphericity of celestial bodies; and the variations in sunspots destroyed the axiom of immutability and perfection of celestial bodies. The analogy of terrestrial phenomena to solar phenomena provides an adequate foundation for the theory that terrestrial qualities can be attributed to celestial bodies.

Galileo himself, like many other Renaissance scientists, did not always recognize the hypothetical and replaceable character of the provisional models or theories of science. A scientific hypothesis presents an imaginative representation or model, which may prove, for some years, to be 'fruitful' for further deductions, until such time as that model is replaced by a still more fruitful model or schematization: thus, for example, in the history of atomic physics, new models of what the atom is 'like' have repeatedly replaced old models or representations of what the atom had been thought to be 'like'. Each schematic model may justifiably be recorded as good or fruitful rather than 'true'. Galileo had a naively realist conception of the 'absolute truth' of physico-mathematical models or theories. He presented his 'truth' in critical and polemical writings which frequently generated hostility rather than enlightenment. This involved him in a sad and needless conflict with Scripture scholars, theologians and Church authorities.

Galileo did realize, however, that mathematics is an indispensable practical tool and key to the scientist's understanding of the structures of the material universe. It facilitates the presentation of the physicist's view of reality in terms of mathematical formulae.

Johannes Kepler had applied mathematical reasoning to astronomy and physical science, but Kepler tended to think that numerical relationships constituted the structures of the universe in the idealist sense of transcendent Pythagorean realities. Galileo, on the contrary, tended to use mathematics to create mathematical proofs for physical theories of which he felt certain, such as the Copernican-Kepler theory of the elliptical orbits of the planets; he deemed these orbits to be certain and true even though he had no theory of gravitation by which the elliptical orbits could be adequately explained. He regarded scientific theories as true; and he regarded mathematics as both an indispensable auxiliary for buttressing the theories and a definitive test for establishing their truth with certainty. This emphasis on the deductive and mathematical aspect of the scientific method influenced the thought of the 'rationalist' philosophers of the post-Renaissance period. These thinkers sought to attain in philosophy the clarity, exactitude and certainty which the mathematical deductive method had achieved in the pre-eminently satisfactory explanations of the new physical sciences.

10. Francis Bacon (1561-1626), as Viscount St Albans and Lord Chancellor of England, continually pressed on King James I the idea of founding a great college or institute for advanced experimental science and research. He saw himself as the champion of a new experimental philosophy which would be based on a new developed method of inductive logical detection and discovery. He wrote *Of the Advancement of Learning* (1609), *Novum Organon* (1620), *De augmentis scientiarum* (1623), *New Atlantis* and other works. He decried the stagnation of the universities. 'Natural philosophy' had made no progress since ancient times. The world was entering into a new modern era. A new world had been discovered by Columbus. The earth had been circumnavigated by Magellan. A vast and mysterious universe had been discovered through the lenses of the telescope and the microscope. New discoveries in mineralogy and metallurgy had given rise to major improvements in firearms and artillery. A new world was emerging; and this great new world needed a 'Great Instauration' of an experimental science and philosophy of nature. Men must accumulate a quantity of widely dispersed data about nature; they must interpret these data judiciously; and they must conduct controlled experiments, if they are to learn the secrets of nature by carefully organized observations of its regularities. This method of approach will be the new method of the Great Instauration. Through this technique and method there will be restored to man his lost mastery over the natural world.

The modern scholar must free himself from awed bondage to the accomplishments of ancient Greece and Rome. A new spirit of adventure had fired the explorations of Sir Francis Drake and Sir Walter Raleigh. The same fiery spirit must motivate research work in the universities.

Bacon proposed a new principle for the classification of the university sciences. He drew a sharp division between human learning and divine; human reason must have its own autonomy. He then divided human learning into three main parts, paralleling the 'three parts of man's understanding': memory, imagination and reason. He regarded memory as the basis for the different branches of history, such as natural, civil and ecclesiastical history. He regarded imagination as the basis for the different branches of poesy (or literature), such as narrative, representative and allusive poesy. He saw reason as the basis for philosophy, divine, natural and human. Natural philosophy is divided into theoretical philosophy which seeks the causes of effects, and practical philosophy which tries to produce effects by applying knowledge of causes (as in the case of medicine). The theoretical part of natural philosophy is divided into metaphysics and physics; metaphysics concerns itself with first causes and formal causes, whereas physics is concerned with particular material causes and efficient causes. Bacon regarded metaphysics as theoretical physics. It is the science which studies the physical forms and physical properties of different physical and chemical substances. It studies the general natures or 'forms' of silver, gold, iron, heat, light, wind, colours and so forth. Immaterial being is relegated to the sphere of faith, liturgy, and revealed theology. Traditional philosophy must give way to the new 'naturalistic' philosophical sciences which aim to be of practical use and benefit to man.

Over and above the stagnation of learning in the universities, Bacon said that he discerned four general tendencies of the human mind that needed to be corrected if knowledge of nature is to be advanced. Certain revered falsehoods, or Idols, have taken deep root in our minds and strongly resist our efforts to study nature impartially. They are preconceptions and prejudices which must be eliminated from true science. (1) The Idols of the Tribe or Race are revered falsehoods which all mankind tend to accept and believe without questioning; thus human nature tends to hypostatize abstractions and to accept abstractions as if they were concrete realities of experience. (2) The Idols of the Cave, or immediate local environment, are narrow, self-centred 'favourite' views and biases, as, for example, that the wide world is as one sees it in one's confined cell or den. (3) The Idols of the Market-place are those errors imposed on the mind by the public misuse of currently accepted words and by the language of social control; thus, for example, certain studies are said to be taboo and others are unduly honoured. (4) Finally there are the Idols of the Theatre or the revered fictions of the unreal 'stage-plays' of the popular, traditional schools of dogmatic thought. They do not stage reality or the universe as it really is.

The new Active Science of discovery and 'inventions' must be based on patient, careful induction. There is a rash form of induction in which the mind gropes unmethodically from particular perceptions to inaccurate generalizations (as in alchemy). In the case of true induction, the mind proceeds from patient and painstaking examination of particular perceptions, of presences, absences and differences, to immediate and accurate generalizations, and thence, slowly and patiently, to more general axioms or truths. In the patient employment of this inductive method, the mind's activity must be constantly controlled by observation if it is to attain a certain knowledge of the natures or forms of concrete things.

True induction takes place when the scientist, on the basis of his carefully controlled observations, is able to educe a general axiom (or hypothesis) whose various implications can then be subjected to additional experimental tests. In order to do this the scientist must keep a notebook or calendar in which he must first draw up a table of varied instances of presences of the 'nature' (e.g. the nature of heat) which he is investigating, and a table of instances in which the form or nature is absent. Thus, Bacon recommended the systematic investigation of 'negative' as well as affirmative instances of the nature of the form which is under investigation. (Heat, for example, is present in the rays of the sun but absent from the rays of the moon.) The scientist must then draw up a third table of comparison in which the 'form' is present in varying degrees. (John Stuart Mill called these rules of method: the rule of Agreement, the rule of Difference, the joint rule of Agreement and Difference, and the rule of Concomitant Variations.) On the evidence of these tables of presences, absences and variations, the mind can make a provisional affirmation or hypothesis concerning the nature of the thing which is being investigated. This provisional affirmation, or hypothesis or theory, must then be applied to some 'privileged instances' and to further deduced experiments which will test the value of the provisional axiom or affirmation. A ladder of axioms, or scientific hypothesis, of this kind should lead automatically to scientific certainty.

By way of example, Bacon said that a scientist who is investigating the nature of heat must draw up three lists or tables of hot bodies, cold bodies, and bodies of varying degrees of heat. These lists may likely show some special characteristic always present in heated bodies, absent in cold bodies, and present in varying degrees in others. He may conclude, for example, that heat is a form of motion, that it is an expanding and restrained motion which makes its way through the smallest parts of bodies. It consists of rapid irregular motions of the tiny parts. The three different lists will manifest with certainty that this is invariably so.

Bacon strove hard to find a wealthy patron who would sponsor and finance the new institute of scientific research. He failed at the court of King James. But his *De augmentis scientiarum* (1623) became the centre-piece of a great crusade. Bacon was hailed by independent scholars as the secretary of Nature and the architect of the new learning. It was Bacon's writings which inspired the foundation in 1660 of The Royal Society of London for Improving Natural Knowledge.

Bacon's historical importance lies not in his contributions to epistemology or ontology but rather in the fact that he was the inspiration and founding father of the new scientific method in England. Diderot said of Bacon: 'he drew up the map of what men had to learn'. His writings played an historically important role in the development of inductive logic and in the history of the philosophy of science.

Nevertheless, neither Bacon nor any of his followers provided a satisfactory philosophy of induction. Bacon claimed that his tables of presences, absences and variations and his ladder of axioms would lead automatically to certainty. He failed to see the vital role of inspiration and genius (the 'eureka moment') in the formulation of new scientific hypotheses. He failed also to see the vital role of mathematics, and scientific deduction, in the achievements of the experimental scientists of his own day. He had no laboratory and made no new discoveries; he was, nonetheless, the prophet of modern science.

16 The revival of Scholasticism: Suárez

1. Scholastic philosophy in the late Middle Ages
2. Suárez's metaphysics   3. Suárez's philosophy of law

1. Scholastic philosophy in the late Middle Ages. In the fifteenth and sixteenth centuries, several of the religious orders in Europe attempted to bring about a reform in their community way of life. The Black Death, which began in 1347, had brought about a collapse of observance of community life and widespread decline of fervour in the monastic institutes and houses of study. In the case of the Order of Friars Preachers (OP) or Dominicans, this reform of observance reintroduced a renewed vitality which was especially evident in the vigorous revival of theological and philosophical studies. Under the impact of Protestantism, the Dominicans concentrated education in larger houses of study. Thomistic studies flourished especially in the colleges of St Gregory in Valladolid (1488), St Thomas in Seville (1515), St Thomas at the Minerva (Rome; 1577) and other centres. At the Council of Trent in 1545, there were 130 Dominican bishops and theologians who participated in the Council discussions. The Council inaugurated the 'Counter-Reformation' movement, and gave a powerful impetus to the renewal of Scholastic studies.

In 1540 the Society of Jesus was founded. In turn it founded numerous schools, colleges and universities, and produced eminent scholars, Toletus, Molina, Vásquez, Lessius, Bellarmine, Suárez and others, who played a significant part in the theological and philosophical discussions and controversies of the sixteenth and seventeenth centuries. These Jesuits, and their Dominican counterparts Cajetan, Ferrariensis, Vitoria, Soto, Cano, Báñez and others, played a leading role in the revival of Scholastic thought at the time of the Renaissance.

Thomas de Vio (1468-1535) was a Dominican Master General and Cardinal who was known as *Cajetan(us)* ('the one from Gaeta'). He taught philosophy at Padua and Pavia. He wrote commentaries on Aristotle, Porphyry and Aquinas. In these works he developed a special theory of analogy. He spoke of the analogy of attribution as a form of analogy in which the primary analogate is found in only one subject and is merely attributed to others. Thus, health is found in animals, and is merely attributed to medicine or urine. (It is therefore an analogy of extrinsic attribution and not an analogy of intrinsic attribution.) Cajetan preferred the analogy of proportionality as the more basic form of analogy. For example, seeing is related to the sense of sight as intellectual vision is related to the power of understanding.

This latter form of analogy is used in the case of our analogical knowledge of God. Cajetan maintained (contrary to the view of Aquinas) that the analogy of proper proportionality is the only type of analogy which obtains between the finite and the Infinite. He seemed to take it for granted that the analogy of proportionality is at the same time an analogy of intrinsic attribution. For this reason, his general treatment of this theme is obscure.

Cajetan spent much of his time in controversy with Averroists and Scotists. In doing so, he assimilated some of their viewpoints and adopted some of their terminology. Thus, for example, he thought of the *esse* of Aquinas as if it were a synonym for *existens* or *subsistens* or for the act of subsisting as a substance. This interpretation finds itself more at home in themes which deal with subsisting essence, essences, and substances, than in themes which focus on the dynamic act of going on in being (*esse*). Cajetan therefore missed the centre-point (*esse*) of Thomism. In applying this viewpoint in practice he concluded that the *quinque viae* arrive at the existence of an Absolute Being but not at a Creator, and that, furthermore, no philosopher had proved the immortality of the soul. Cajetan held that we accept these doctrines as articles of faith, and that the arguments which have been adduced are genuinely probable arguments but not demonstrative arguments.

Francisco de Vitoria (1492-1546) was a Dominican who taught at the university of Salamanca. His teachings helped in the formulation of imperial legislation with regard to the newly discovered American territories. The emergence of nation-states had brought to the forefront of legal thinking the problem of the rational foundation of international law. Vitoria is regarded by numerous scholars as the founder of international law, which he applied to the defence of the American Indians against their colonial oppressors.

Vitoria held that political society (*respublica*) is a natural society in the sense that it is required by nature and has its end set by nature. The end of society is the promotion of the common good of its citizens and the protection of the rights of its citizens. The remote origin, then, of political society is human nature. The proximate origin of political society is the will of families which transfer public authority to one or several rulers. The particular forms of government depend on the will of the citizens of the State.

All human beings belong to one, human, world community or human family; they belong to international society. International society possesses its own type of authority, immanent in the whole of humankind. Different nation-states have rights and correlative duties which derive from the international laws of universal human authority. Thus, every nation, or natural society, great or small, has the right to existence; it has the right to juridical equality; it has the right to independence; it has the right to free communication and trade; and it has the right and duty to assist in the defence of nations victimized by tyrants or by aggressor-nations. The sum of these international laws, rights and duties, forms the *ius gentium*. The *ius gentium* belongs to the natural law or is derivable from it. It consists in prescriptions for the common good of mankind. It confers rights and obligations upon the nations and upon their rulers. It is made up of (1) conclusions drawn from the principles of natural law by natural reason and (2) positive customs and treaties among nations. Vitoria was not the first philosopher who spoke of the *ius gentium*: St Isidore of Seville (*c.* 636), St Raymond of Peñafort and others had treated of it previously. Vitoria, however, developed the idea in a way which gave rise to the study of international law as it applied to the newly emerging nation-states. He applied the principles governing international conduct to the problem of colonization, to the rights of Indians, and to the problem of just and unjust inter-national wars. For this reason he is now regarded in international law associations as the founder of international law.

Dominic Báñez (1528-1604) was a Dominican professor of philosophy at the university of Salamanca (1577-81) who wrote a commentary on some of the works of Aristotle and Aquinas. In his *Scholastica commentaria*, Báñez saw the importance of the act of being (*esse*) as the constitutive principle of perfection in every being. In the finite being, the act of being (*esse*) is limited by the constitutive co-relative co-principle of limitation in being (*essentia*). This constitutive composition gives being to the finite reality and gives the finite reality a place in the community of being. It is Being Its Very Self (*Ipsum Esse*: God) which gives both the principle of being (*esse*) and the active power of operation (*agere*) to every finite being in a state of becoming. Thus God gives to the free human act of the whole human being a 'physical premotion', or ability to come to be, which enables the human being to act humanly, that is, freely.

Luis de Molina, S J (1535-1600), who taught at Coimbra and Évora in Portugal, held that the doctrine of 'physical premotion' was a disguised form of determinism. Molina's famous *Concordia* was published in Lisbon in 1588, and led to a controversy which divided the Jesuit and Dominican philosophers and theologians for nearly 300 years. The difference between the two schools was essentially a difference of views concerning the relative emphasis to be placed on divine creative causality or on human freedom. Molina and the Molinists had a 'humanistic' concern to safeguard the freedom of the human will, while also allowing for God's foreknowledge of man's contingent, free future actions.

Molina introduced a key term, *scientia media*, in an attempt to resolve the apparent contradiction between the doctrines of divine aid (*gratia*) and human freedom. God's infallible foreknowledge of what an individual will freely do in no way predetermines the free will of the individual.

God's knowledge of all that exists, or has existed, or will exist is called a knowledge of 'vision'. God's knowledge of the purely and merely possible is called a knowledge of 'simple understanding' of events which never have existed and never will exist. God's knowledge of conditional free contingent events is a 'mean' between the two; it is called *scientia media*. God foreknows, for example, from all eternity, what a certain individual will do under certain circumstances if offered divine assistance (*gratia*). This divine foreknowledge does not predetermine our free acts. God, foreknowing what the individual will do, decrees the circumstances and the grace necessary to effect the co-operative free action of the individual. The efficacy of the divine aid is due to the divine foreknowledge, the *scientia media*; it is not due to anything within the divine aid itself. All men receive sufficient divine aid (*gratia*); some men accept it, and some do not.

The Molinists (e.g. Bellarmine and Suárez) maintained the doctrine of 'Congruism'. All men receive divine assistance. When this divine assistance and the circumstances and dispositions of the individual are congruous, the divine grace enables the individual to act freely and infallibly. The divine aid can be called, in this case, efficacious grace, or congruous grace. On the other hand, when they are not congruous, then the divine aid which the individual receives may be called (merely) sufficient grace or *gratia incongrua*. God foresees in his *scientia media* that some individuals will co-operate with his grace, and God predestines those individuals to glory by offering them his grace.

The Molinists placed emphasis on the fact that the individual is free and that it is the *scientia media* which regulates the efficaciousness or inefficaciousness of divine grace. The Thomists placed emphasis on the fact that it is the universal divine causality that enables the human being not only to be, but also to be human, and to be free. It is now generally accepted by theologians and philosophers of religion alike that both viewpoints present acceptable doctrines. It is the emphases that differ.

2. Suárez's metaphysics. *Francisco Suárez* (1548-1617), 'Doctor Eximius', of Granada in Spain, was a Jesuit scholar of outstanding erudition who devoted his life to writing, study and lecturing. His many works include his well-known *Disputationes metaphysicae* (1597), which was used as a textbook in several Catholic and Protestant universities, *Tractatus de legibus* (1612) and *Tractatus de anima* (1621). These and other works were written when he was a professor at the university of Évora in Portugal from 1593 to 1616. His *Disputationes* were studied and admired by Descartes, C. Wolff, Leibniz, Schopenhauer and several other philosophers. This work shows a profound knowledge of the thought of his predecessors, and especially of the works of Aristotle and Aquinas.

For Suárez, as for Aristotle, metaphysics or first philosophy is the study of being as real being (*ens in quantum ens*). It studies being in general, the concept of being, and the different kinds of being, material or immaterial, substantial or accidental, real or conceptual being.

The word 'being', when taken as a noun (as when one speaks of a being, an *ens* or a reality), signifies a real nature or essence that can exist or does exist in reality. When taken as a participle qualifying a noun (e.g. being this or being that), 'being' refers to the act of existing as a real essence. The emphasis, therefore, is on what can really exist or what does exist in the mind or in reality.

Suárez asserted, contrary to the doctrine of Aquinas, that the distinction between *esse* (being) and *essentia* in finite beings is a mental or logical distinction and not a real distinction. He maintained that if *esse* were distinct from the essence in a real essence, then the *esse* of the real essence could be known, and to be known it would have to have its own essence, that is, an essence of existence. This argument implies that the only things that can be known are real essences, or beings. For Suárez, then, knowledge is an assimilation of beings (*entia*). For Aquinas, knowledge is an assimilation of 'be-ing' (*esse*) and the modalities of being (*esse tale*). The emphasis in Suárez is on 'existents'; the emphasis in Aquinas is on the act of existing or 'being'. Thus, for

Suárez, the actual existence and the actual essence are not really or actually distinct. Together they form one entity, *ens per se unum*. 'Existence is nothing other than essence constituted in act.' However, according to Suárez, the distinction between essence and existence has an objective foundation. The creature is actually existing as an actual essence. The intrinsic principle of limitation is the entire entity of the creature. It is limited intrinsically by what it is in itself and it is limited extrinsically or *effective* by God. The distinction between actual existence and actual essence is grounded on the creature's contingent dependent character. The distinction is therefore not a 'real' distinction but a distinction of reason with a foundation in reality.

The concept of being considers only the likeness of things as they agree in being. It is a concept of the objective similarity in being (*esse simile*) of real essences in their likeness to other real essences or natures. It is an analogical concept, not a univocal concept. It can be made more determinate by being contracted to, or focused upon, concepts of different kinds of being which are already contained in the concept of being. This analogy of being is only an analogy of attribution, and not an analogy of proportionality. 'Every creature is being in virtue of a relation to God, inasmuch as it participates in or in some way imitates the being of God.'

A concept, such as the concept of being, is a universal. It is abstracted by the mind from the likenesses of individuals. In this sense, the concept has a foundation in reality. But concepts or universals have no existence as universals either in reality or in individuals. Individuals alone exist.

The intellect has a direct knowledge of individual material objects without reflection. This is the work of the active intellect. It is the function of the active intellect, also, to make the passive intellect as similar as possible to the representation of the phantasms of the individual material objects. The passive intellect is then able to abstract the universal.

The individual is individuated by its entire entity or being. The principle of individuation in created things is the entire composite being. In the case of hylomorphic substances, the principle of individuation is the united matter and form. Scotus had said that the principle of individuation was the *haecceitas*, a unique formality which is distinct from the specific nature (and distinct from the common nature which is abstracted from the specific nature). Suárez agreed with Scotus to a limited extent: 'individuality adds to the common nature something which is mentally distinct from that nature...and which together with the nature constitutes the individual metaphysically'. There is a distinction between individuality and the specific or common nature. The distinction is not a real distinction and it is not purely logical. Suárez called it a *modal* distinction.

The distinction between a substance and its mode of being is a modal distinction. (Different substances may be, for example, corporeal, incorporeal, living, individual, possible, finite, or contingent substances.) In a created substance, subsistence denotes a determinate mode of existence. It adds to the existence of the actual essence or nature a mode or way of existing which differs modally (*modaliter*) from the nature. There is therefore within the created substance a composition of substantial mode and the actual essence or thing modified. The distinction is a modal distinction.

In material substances, matter has its own mode of partial subsistence, and form has its own mode of partial subsistence. There is also, in addition, their mode of union together. In the case of the human composite, the form, or the rational soul, when separated from the body, probably has its own positive mode of subsistence. When it is separated from the body, it is deprived simply of the positive mode of union with the body. It is then capable of subsisting separately.

In the general thought, or philosophy, of Suárez, the central metaphysical insight from which all his teachings radiate is his insight into the utter dependency of the total reality of every finite, contingent, participated being on the omnipotent free will of the Infinite Creator. Every finite entity, throughout every moment, is continually dependent for its existence upon the Supreme Being. The finite being is totally different from the Supreme Being, not because its existence is distinct from its essence, but because it is an utterly dependent being, dependent for its existence and its activity on Being Itself. Each dependent being is a being by created 'participation'. It is the continuous creative command, 'Be', that makes it and keeps it in being. The emphasis therefore in Suárez's thought is placed on the omnipotent, free and provident divine will. (The central insight of Thomas Aquinas is the intelligibility of *esse*; the Thomistic emphasis is on being as intelligible.)

Aristotle and Aquinas attempted to prove the existence of God, immaterial pure act, by an argument from 'motion' which was a physical argument, according to Suárez. This argument depended upon an uncertain principle, namely, that 'everything that moves is moved by another', Suárez held that this physical principle must be replaced by a metaphysical principle, namely, that 'everything which is produced is produced by another'. From this principle one can then argue, *a posteriori*, in the following way: Every being is either produced (made, created) or not produced. Not all beings are produced (by another, outside the series of 'all'). Therefore there must necessarily be unproduced, uncreated, self-subsistent being. Now, the nature of self-subsistent being is being itself, and it is not a common multipliable nature. It is not multipliable; hence it is one. Thus, being itself is, and it is one. God is and is one. With regard to the nature of God, his perfection, wisdom, infinitude, omnipresence, omnipotence and so forth, Suárez followed Aquinas and the common Scholastic tradition.

The relation of the dependent creature to the Omnipotent Creator is a real relation of total dependency in being. It belongs to the very essence of a created existence that it depends on the Creator. The creature cannot be conceived or exist without a transcendental relation to that on which it depends. However, this does not imply that the relation between the creature and the Creator is a two-way reciprocal relationship. The relation of the Creator to the creature is a mental relation; and a mental relation is a mental construct 'which is thought of by the mind as being, although it has no being in itself'. Its being consists in being thought of, in virtue of 'some analogy' to being; it is in some way founded on being even though it is a being of the mind (*ens rationis*).

Suárez had an extraordinary ability to bring together into synthesis a wide-ranging understanding of ancient Greek, Patristic, Scholastic and Renaissance controversy and thought. Schopenhauer regarded Suárez's *Disputationes* as 'an authentic compendium of the whole of Scholastic wisdom'. Descartes carried a copy of the *Disputationes* with him during his travels. Suárez had an extensive knowledge of previous philosophic thought; and he blended this wide spectrum of thought into a unified metaphysical synthesis which centred on the idea of the dependency of the finite existent on the omnipotent, free creative act.

Étienne Gilson, in his book *Being and Some Philosophers* (1948), contended that the metaphysics of Suárez is an 'essentialist' metaphysics which tended to reduce the Thomistic 'act of being' (*esse*) to essence. Christian Wolff and others certainly interpreted Suárez in this sense. However, the emphasis in Suárez's thought is on the 'real essence', that is, on the realized entity, the reality, rather than on the pure essence (of the entity). It is true that the emphasis is not on *esse*, as in the case of Aquinas. But it would not be true to say that the emphasis is solely on *essentia*, and Professor Gilson himself does not say this. The emphasis in Suárez's thought is on the *res*, *ens*, and on *entia*, 'existents', entities, and dependent realities of different kinds.

In a word, the emphasis is on 'existents' rather than on the act of being (*esse*). This emphasis is particularly evident in Suárez's philosophy of law where, again, every reality is seen as totally dependent on the omnipotent divine command.

3. Suárez's philosophy of law was based on the Thomist and medieval conception of law in many respects, but it was presented with a new and original understanding which proved to be profoundly influential in the general transition from the medieval to the modern conception of law.

Suárez stated explicitly that Aquinas' account of law is inadequate. It places an inordinate emphasis on reason and intellect. He sought a new definition of law to replace the Thomist definition that law is 'an ordinance of reason directed to the common good.' Reason certainly has a certain place in law, but obligation is the primary element in law, and obligation derives from an act of will. Law, therefore, can be defined as 'a common, just and stable precept which has been sufficiently promulgated' or as 'the act of a just and right will by which a superior wills to oblige his inferior to do this or that' (*De legibus* I, 12). Law (*lex*) differs from right (*ius*) even though many writers have used them interchangeably. A right (as in the case of a right to a just wage) is defined as 'a certain moral power which every man has, either over his own property or with regard to what is due to him' (*De legibus* I, 2).

Suárez, like Aquinas, distinguished between eternal law, positive divine law, natural law and human law; but he treated each of these in relation to his basic contention that law is essentially an act of will.

Eternal law is an eternal, immutable, 'free decree of the will of God, who lays down the order to be observed' in the universe. It is the universal divine providence which extends over all of creation. It is from this law that all other laws are derived. Eternal law is promulgated to rational creatures through the medium of divine and human laws which participate in and are an effect of eternal law.

Positive divine law is contained in the direct revelation of God, as in the case of the Mosaic law. The power and will of God impose on the human creature a necessity, which consists in the obligation of duty, to obey the revealed law.

Natural law is the participation of the moral nature of man in the eternal law. Thus its ultimate source is God, the supreme legislator. Natural law is *preceptive* law, ordering and prohibiting; it is not a merely demonstrative law, elucidating what should or should not be done. It is a preceptive judgement of the mind permanently retained in the mind, relating to the community of mankind, and promulgated by the natural light of reason. It commands certain acts which are seen to be intrinsically good and prohibits other acts which are intrinsically evil. It is God, the Creator of nature, who is the author of natural law. God sees that certain moral acts are in harmony with rational nature and that other acts are morally incompatible with rational nature. Thus the divine command is not arbitrary. It is in accordance with the divine reason; and it is in accordance with created nature. Human reason makes known to man what is pleasing and what is displeasing to the author and governor of nature.

The precepts of the natural law may be divided into three groups. (These have been called the primary, secondary and tertiary precepts of the natural law.) There are, firstly, general and primary principles of morality, such as 'do good and avoid evil', of which no one can be ignorant. Secondly, there are the more definite and specific principles, such as 'God must be worshipped'. Precepts and ethical propositions of this kind, according to Suárez, are self-evident. Thirdly, there are certain moral precepts which may be deduced from the self-evident principles and which are known through rational reflection, as, for example, that 'usury is unjust' and that 'lying can never be justified'. Invincible ignorance is possible with regard to these deduced moral precepts known through rational reflection.

The precept that 'good must be done and evil avoided' does not oblige us to do every good act which it is possible to do (e.g. both to marry and to vow perpetual chastity). 'Not all good acts fall under a precept.' In the general precept 'do good and avoid evil', the natural law enjoins that, in the performance of any individual human act, the free act must be in accordance with right reason and not in any way in disaccord with right reason (*recta ratio*).

This doctrine is close to the Thomistic doctrine, and yet the viewpoint is different. The Thomistic emphasis is on one's nature and one's end; the teleological understanding of natural law is fundamental. In the Suárezian doctrine of natural law, this teleological aspect is present, but the emphasis is placed on right reason and its conformity with the divine command. Hugo Grotius, Samuel von Pufendorf and Jean-Jacques Burlamaqui accepted this emphasis on right reason (*recta ratio* or *sana ratio*) and then more or less gradually abandoned the Thomistic teleological philosophy of natural law. This attenuation prepared the way for purely rationalistic interpretations of natural law, and for subsequent rationalist theories about the (presocietal) state of nature.

Human law, according to Suárez, pertains to each self-sufficing or 'perfect' society, just as natural law pertains to the community of mankind. Human law must be based on the divine law or the natural law. Human law is not derived from natural law by logical inference but by specific 'determination'; it is in a certain sense arbitrary (*De legibus* II, 20). Civil law is enacted 'more by the will than by reason'. It is a common, just and stable precept, the act of a just and right will, and adequately promulgated. Human law, to be just and binding in conscience, must be enacted for the common good (commutative justice), by a legislator having authority over his subjects (legal justice), and equitable in proportioning out its burdens (distributive justice). Positive laws that run counter to prohibitive natural laws are null and void. Positive laws (such as purely penal laws) which fall short of affirmative natural law are obligatory although not binding in conscience. Thus purely penal laws impose an obligation to accept the penalties incurred for their violation, but not to omit or perform the actions prescribed by the laws.

The 'law of nations' (*ius gentium*) is not the same thing as the natural law. The precepts of the *ius gentium* are unwritten laws established through the customs of all or nearly all nations. They are positive, human laws, somewhat like civil law. But civil laws are specific determinations of natural law, whereas the precepts of the *ius gentium* are general conclusions (not specific determinations) drawn from the principles of the natural law. Given the fact that men and States have accepted, for example, certain customary methods of avenging injuries or of negotiating international treaties, then the habitual conduct of nations has introduced certain unwritten laws concerning what is customary behaviour in these accepted methods. The rational basis for these unwritten laws is that the human race, even though divided into nations, still preserves a certain quasi-political and moral unity as the family of humanity, the human species.

The origin of political society lies in the natural needs and social nature of man. Man is by nature a social animal, having a natural desire to live in community. Nature, however, has not specified which particular political communities are to be formed. The formation of particular communities arises through the will of people who gather together by common consent. No such community could endure without a directive principle, or leader, whose function is to preserve unity and to direct the members in the attainment of the common good. A body, or community, needs a head. It is nature itself, therefore, which demands the establishment of civil magistracy or political sovereignty in the community-State; and this would still be naturally so even if there were no state of sin on earth.

The power to legislate and góvern comes from God, the creator of human nature. This power manifests itself as soon as consenting human beings form into their different political communities. Political power is not conferred without the intervention of community-will and consent. It is through human consent that political society and its human, political power arises. The State is not an artificial artifact; it is natural. The legislative power of the State is derived from the community and it exists for the good of the community. The ultimate source of this power is God, who bestows it as a natural property upon the community.

Even though political authority derives ultimately from God, nevertheless, the conferring of sovereign political authority on specified individuals depends on human agreement. Where there is no such consent, societal power cannot be justly held. If one who was an unjust usurper of power actually does, in the course of time, receive the consent of the people, then, in this case, he acquires legitimate sovereignty. An agreement or pact emerges in which the community acknowledges their existing ruler as lawful monarch.

The monarch may not be deprived of his sovereignty unless he lapses into manifest tyranny. Natural law enjoins obedience to the prince as obligatory in conscience. If the one who had been prince becomes a manifest tyrant, then 'the kingdom may wage a just war against him'. The citizens have a right to depose a tyrannical potentate who has manifestly violated his trust. In the case of a usurping tyrant, the people may legitimately resort even to tyrannicide, if the injustice is extreme and the appeal to higher authority is impossible.

Wars are not necessarily and intrinsically evil. Just and defensive wars are permissible. In order that a war may be a just war certain conditions must be fulfilled. It must be waged by the supreme sovereign. It must be for a just cause which can likely be attained but not in any other way, other than by war. It must be conducted properly, with due proportion at all times, and without intentional injury to innocent persons. The sovereign himself should make diligent inquiry into the justice of his cause by consulting 'prudent and conscientious men' concerning the justice of the cause for waging war.

These doctrines of Suárez were influential in the universities for the next two centuries. Suárez's reputation at the time of his death was unsurpassed, and his influence on other philosophers, theologians and students was profound. One can see this influence evidently at work, for example, in the philosophy of natural law and social contract of Hugo Grotius. In the seminaries and universities of Spain and Portugal, the vast renown of Suárez marked the end of further philosophical speculations for centuries. In these countries the Suárezian interpretation of Thomism reigned unchallenged down to recent times.

PART THREE

'MODERN' PHILOSOPHY
The Age of Reason: Descartes to Kant

17 Descartes

1. Life and writings   2. Aim and method   3. The
criterion of truth   4. The existence of God   5. Mind and
body   6. Extension and motion   7. General remarks

1. Life and writings. *René Descartes* (1596-1650) is frequently called the 'father of modern philosophy', though this title is
sometimes given also to Francis Bacon (1561-1626). Descartes was
born in 1596 at La Haye (now La Haye-Descartes), a small town
south of Tours in France. He was educated at the Jesuit college of La
Flèche, where his studies included courses in mathematics and
philosophy. He was impressed by the certainty and clarity of
mathematical thought as contrasted with the uncertainty and contention which held sway in contemporary philosophic thought.
Subsequently he travelled widely throughout Europe to complete his
education. He had a dream of the possibility of attaining truth in a
unified science of nature with the certainty with which truth was
attained in mathematics. He settled for a while at Breda in Holland,
where he wrote papers on mathematics, music, optics and physics.
He presented his main system of thought in his philosophical works:
Discourse on Method (1637), *Meditations on First Philosophy* (1641),
Replies to Objections (1641-44), *Principles of Philosophy* (1644) and
Passions of the Soul (1649). In 1649 he travelled to Stockholm at the
invitation of Queen Christina of Sweden to instruct her in philosophy. Within a few months he caught pneumonia and, at the age of
fifty-four, died at Stockholm in February 1650.

2. Aim and method. Descartes was preoccupied primarily
with the problem of the attainment of certainty. He sought to
overcome the current revived scepticism of the Renaissance. Montaigne, Charron and other French writers were influential in spreading
an attitude of general scepticism concerning the attainment of truth
by way of the labyrinths of traditional philosophy and metaphysics.

Descartes desired indubitable and unquestionable intellectual certainty about the nature of reality. He looked to mathematics as a model of clear and indubitable reasoning. Here the basis of intellectual certainty lay solely in the conceptual-discursive thought of man's reasoning faculties. In the mathematical sciences certainty is not attained from tradition or authority, or from sense-observations or experiments. He regarded all science and knowledge as one and interconnected. There must be one all-embracing, universal science concerning the nature of all things. There is a need for a vast system of indubitable and self-evident truths organically related to each other in such a way that the mind can move easily from one truth or principle to another just as it moves rationally and clearly in the carefully regulated field of mathematics. All knowledge must be restructured into one comprehensive scientific philosophy through the application of one universal, rational, scientific method. A comprehensive system of truth of this kind would be derivable solely from carefully regulated rational thought.

Descartes' *Discourse on Method* (Part II) presents four rules which must govern conceptual-discursive thought. One must accept nothing as true that is not clearly and distinctly recognized to be so. One must divide up (or analyse) difficulties into as many simpler parts as are requisite. One must advance from the more simple and easy to knowledge of other complex, related objects. One must ensure that nothing has been omitted. According to Descartes these four rules adequately express his method for employing aright the natural operation of the mind.

We learn from Descartes' use of the first rule that the new Cartesian method is one of universal methodic doubt. The application of methodic doubt to every proposition will enable the thinker to sift indubitable truths from the doubtful. The application of this method to empirical propositions, for example, shows that they are all based on 'adventitious' ideas derived from mere sense-experience. These are not indubitable; they remain forever doubtful. The application of universal methodic doubt to one's belief in the goodness of God or the existence of God, or to one's belief in the veracity of human impressions about the earth, or sky, or extended bodies constrains one to 'confess that there is nothing in what I formerly believed to be true that I somehow cannot doubt'. Perhaps God himself is a powerful and deceitful evil genius who has deluded me into believing, for example, that 'two and three together will always make the number five'. One must search for some proposition or propositions which one cannot conceivably disbelieve and about which one cannot conceivably be mistaken. In this way, Descartes uses what he calls methodic or 'hyperbolical' doubt and sceptical arguments as an analytic device for identifying the indubitable.

We learn also from the four rules that the Cartesian method is one of conceptual-discursive thinking. The method is applied to situations in which the thinker is confronted with problems of different kinds. The recommended method of procedure is that of resolving each difficulty into a number of constituent elements or 'truths' which point beyond themselves to further truths awaiting discovery. Descartes regarded this method of approach to new discoveries as an analytical-heuristic method. It is the method of conceptual-discursive inquiry. It enables us to discover the 'simple natures' or ultimate elements of rational thought as a solid foundation for further discursive thinking. We resolve involved propositions, for example, into 'simple natures' such as the existence, unity and duration of existing realities; the extension, figure, and corporeity of all bodies; and the willing, thinking and doubting of intelligent beings. Further thought on these simple natures leads to further discoveries and syntheses. In this way the area of our intuitive knowledge is continually enlarged.

Our human minds possess mental powers, of intuition and deduction, 'mental powers by which we are able, entirely without fear of illusion, to arrive at the knowledge of things'. It is by intuition that I know, for example, that *I desire*, that *I think*, that *I exist*, and that any two things which are equal to a third thing must be equal to one another. In intuitive perceptions of this kind there is immediate knowledge without the mediation of other knowledge contents. Intuition is a clear and distinct vision of such clarity that it dispels all doubt.

Some of our existing ideas are clear and distinct ideas. They differ from the factitious ideas of our imagination and from the adventitious ideas which arise from varied sense-experiences. Ideas which are intuitively clear and distinct 'exist naturally in our souls'...'implanted therein by nature'. They are 'eternal truths' virtually present in the mind by reason of the mind's innate constitution to think in the way that it does. In this sense they can be called innate ideas. Sense-experience merely furnishes the occasions on which the mind forms clear and distinct ideas that are drawn out of its own innate potentialities.

3. The criterion of truth. Descartes asserted that he was 'fortunate enough to find a single truth which is certain and indubitable'. It became the first principle of the new system of philosophy which he was seeking. 'I noticed that while I was trying to think everything false, it must needs be that I, who was thinking this, was something. And observing that this truth, *Je pense, donc je suis* (*Cogito ergo sum*: I am thinking, therefore I am), was so solid and secure that the most extravagant suppositions of the sceptics could not overthrow it, I judged that I need not scruple to accept it as the first principle of the philosophy that I was seeking' (*Discourse*, Part IV).

The French words '*Je pense*' and '*pensées*' are not adequately translated by the English words 'I think' and 'thoughts'. They imply rather that the one who is conscious is conscious of himself and of the manifold contents (such as feelings, doubts, images, thoughts, desires, and so forth: *Principles of Philosophy* I, 9) present in his field of consciousness. The Cartesian formula '*Je pense, donc je suis*' or its Latin equivalent '*Cogito ergo sum*' would be rendered more accurately in English by the words' I am aware, hence (of course) I exist' (or, I am). In the very act of doubting I am aware of myself as doubting and I am assured with certainty of my existence as a conscious being being conscious of my act. I intuit the objective and necessary connection between my being and my being aware.

Descartes did not develop this insight along the lines that 'being conscious' is necessarily a consciousness of being or of beings (of one kind or another). Had he done so, his philosophy would have developed into a philosophy of being. Descartes developed his insight instead in a rationalist and idealist direction through focusing his interest merely on the clarity and distinctness and certainty of his foundational idea.

The proposition 'I am aware that I am' or 'I am aware I am' contains within itself its own self-verification. It is a 'truth' which is an indubitable truth. The more one thinks about it or attempts to doubt it the more one becomes aware of the reality of one's consciousness. Descartes ascribed the indubitability of the *Cogito* to the clarity and distinctness of the idea; the criterion of truth must therefore be clarity and distinctness in ideas. In the *Discourse on Method* (4) he tells us he concluded that we 'might assume as a general rule that the things we conceive very clearly and distinctly are all true'. And in the *Principles of Philosophy* (I, 46) he tells us what he means by the terms clear and distinct. 'I call that (idea) clear which is present and *apparent* to an attentive mind'; and 'the distinct is that which is precise and *different* from all other objects'. 'The things we conceive very clearly and distinctly are all true.' The clarity and distinctness of the conception renders it indubitable. Clarity and distinctness became for Descartes the criterion of truth.

4. The existence of God. On reflection, we find within our field of consciousness a wide range of clear and distinct ideas. We know for example that a sphere has a single surface, and that three fives are fifteen, and so forth. Ideas of this kind are evident to us human beings. But are they evident and true in themselves? If we apply our universal methodic doubt to them we can begin to wonder whether or not God is an all-powerful deceiver who has succeeded completely in deceiving us that these things are so. However, if God exists and if he is not a deceiver, then the goodness and veracity of the Creator of all things (including our inborn powers of intuition and deduction) would be a guarantee of the veracity of immediately evident clear and distinct ideas. It is therefore necessary, at the very start, to establish the existence and absolute perfection of God.

We find among our ideas the idea of God. 'By the name God I understand a substance which is infinite, independent, all-knowing, all-powerful and by which I myself and everything else, if anything else exists, have been created.' I am conscious of my own imperfections only because I already possess the idea of the perfect. Now the actual perfection of this idea of the perfect cannot be produced by that which is imperfect. An actual effect of this kind must proceed from a being that actually exists. It is the Perfect alone that can be the cause of the idea of the perfect. The cause of the idea of the perfect must be the perfect being, God himself. Thus, the cause which is the cause of myself and of my powers must also be the perfect cause of my idea of the perfect. Now, 'the light of nature teaches us that fraud and deception necessarily proceed from some defect'. Defect cannot be attributed to a perfect Being. Thus, the Perfect Cause of all things is not a deceiver. The creator of all things is a Perfect Cause who created me and all my powers including my intellectual power to form clear and distinct ideas. These powers were not created by an all-powerful deceiver. The perfection of the Creator is the guarantee of the veracity of my clear and distinct ideas.

Antoine Arnauld (1612-94), a doctor of the Sorbonne, pointed out to Descartes that this line of reasoning involved Descartes in a circular argument: 'The only secure reason we have for believing that what we clearly and distinctly perceive is true, is the fact that God exists. But we can be sure that God exists only because we clearly and evidently perceive that. Therefore, prior to being certain that God exists, we should be certain that whatever we clearly and evidently perceive is true' (*Quatrièmes Objections* [1641]).

Descartes replied that 'we are sure that God exists because we have attended to the proofs which established this fact'. At the time that we are concentrating attentively on the proofs we perceive clearly and distinctly the validity and truth of the proofs. We become clearly aware that God exists. Subsequently our minds attend to other matters. In this later stage, 'afterwards it is enough for us to remember that we have (previously) perceived something clearly, in order to be sure that it is true'. The moment of insight into the validity of the proofs is also a moment of perception of the validity of the principles in this particularized application.

This reply and solution proffered by Descartes does not remove indubitably the hyperbolical doubt which he himself had raised through his fictitious hypothesis of a superhuman deceiver. If methodic doubt is to be carried to this extreme, and if consciousness is regarded not as consciousness of reality (being) but as consciousness of 'ideas', then Descartes' line of causal argumentation is one which involves itself in 'circular reasoning'.

The second argument presented by Descartes for the existence of God is a re-rendering of the *a simultaneo* (or 'ontological') argument of Anselm. We perceive clearly and distinctly that the idea of God is the idea of perfect Being. 'That which we clearly and distinctly understand to belong to the true and immutable nature of anything, its essence or form, can be truly affirmed of that thing.... We clearly and distinctly understand that to exist belongs to (God's) true and immutable nature. Therefore, we can with truth affirm of God that he exists' (*Reply to Objections* I). It is not within my power to think of a supremely perfect being devoid of a supreme perfection. It is not within my power to think of God as being without existence. 'I cannot conceive anything but God himself to whose essence existence pertains of necessity' (*Meditations* 5). For this reason the idea of God, like the idea of the *Cogito*, is also a privileged idea, holding a unique status in consciousness. 'To exist belongs to his true and immutable nature. Therefore we can with truth affirm of God that he exists' (*Reply to Objections* I).

Pierre Gassendi, a French sceptical and Epicurean philosopher (see above, Chapter 15, section 8), wrote a series of objections to Descartes' *Meditations*. He pointed out that people often think that they clearly and distinctly perceive something and then discover subsequently that they were wrong. Thus, clarity and distinctness as a criterion of knowledge needs to be based on a further criterion of true knowledge. This second criterion in turn may need to be based on a third, and so forth. Descartes regarded Gassendi's objection as the objection of objections. It implied that all knowledge is knowledge merely of matters internal to the mind. Descartes refused to take the objection seriously, since if one did then it would necessarily follow that 'there is nothing that we can in any way comprehend, conceive or imagine, that should be accepted as true'. We should have to 'shut the door completely on reason, and be content to be... parrots, and no longer men' (*Oeuvres* IXa, p.212).

Descartes recognized Gassendi's objection as the most important objection of all objections. It pointed, in effect, to the fact that if consciousness is only consciousness of the inner contents of consciousness (and is not always and necessarily a consciousness of being or reality) then there is no way in which we can verify whether or not our inner 'ideas' are 'true' in their representation of reality. Descartes was unable to present any reply to the objection other than to say that the consequences and conclusions of a subjectivist theory of knowledge are irrational. This did not redeem Descartes' theory of knowledge from its own tendency towards representationism, rationalism and idealism.

5. Mind and body. Descartes now turned his attention to our consciousness of the presence of (extended) bodies, and in particular our own personal bodies, in the contents of our consciousness. My thinking and reasoning and consciousness are unextended but in my field of consciousness my body is given to me as being an extended thing. I have clear and distinct experiences and ideas of the extension and local motions of my body and its parts. My body is clearly a thing distinct from my (unextended) awareness and thought. It is a body which is similar to other extended bodies given as present among the contents of my consciousness. These other bodies, however, are known by me only through the medium of sense-impressions such as sight, touch and smell. They are given to me as intruding on my senses and, at times, as obstructing my local motions. I have an overwhelming inclination to believe that my sense-impressions arise from the stimulation and presence of bodies exterior to my own. My sense faculties and my whole nature have been created by my Creator in this way; and the Creator is not a deceiver. If my sense-impressions were produced by causes other than corporeal objects, then God could not be defended from the accusation of deceit. 'Hence we must allow that corporeal objects exist.' Thus, I exist, God exists, my body exists, and corporeal objects exist. And, now, what is the relationship between my mind and my body?

We do not perceive substances but we do perceive their attributes, properties and qualities, according to Descartes. Now, the principal attribute of a spiritual substance is thinking, and the principal attribute of corporeal substance is extension, 'extension in length, breadth and depth'. These principal attributes are inseparable from the substances of which they are attributes.

Living bodies and animals are corporeal substances. They partake of extension, and they are part of the material world. Their operations are governed by the same mechanical laws that govern the operations of all material things. They do not think. They are not spiritual substances. The workings of their bodies, like the workings of any mechanism, can be understood in terms of the laws of physics. This applies, too, to the automatic activities (such as digestion and respiration) of the human body. Is the human being, then, two substances?

'Nature teaches me...that I am not only lodged in my body as a pilot in a vessel, but that I am very closely united to it, and, so to speak, so intermingled with it that I seem to compose with it one whole' (*Meditations* 6). Descartes did not wish to assert that body and soul are two different substances, even though his clear and distinct ideas of body and soul seemed to indicate that man is 'a spirit which makes use of a body' (*Oeuvres* VII, 103). Neither did he wish to deny interaction between body and soul, matter and spirit. He tried to localize the point of interaction in the pineal gland and the movements of its 'animal spirits'. But localization did not really solve the problem of how matter can affect spirit or how spirit can affect matter when the two are so essentially different.

6. Extension and motion. 'Extension in length, breadth and depth constitutes the nature of corporeal substance' (*Principles of Philosophy* I, 53). The size and figure of a corporeal substance are modes or variable modifications of its extension; they are objective natural phenomena which belong to the essence or nature of a corporeal substance. Perceived qualities such as colour, sound and taste are sense-reactions which arise in the perceiver on the occasion of superficial contact of the sense-organs with superficial aspects of the extended substance. Secondary qualities of this kind are, in general, subjective. The objective reality of the corporeal substance is understood in terms of its magnitude, size and figure. For this reason, Descartes and his followers, it is frequently said, attempted to geometrize physics.

The corporeal substances which we encounter in the universe are presented to us as being in a state of motion or rest according to the points of reference of the observer. Two people seated in a moving carriage, for example, are at rest relative to each other, even though they are in motion relative to the ground. Motion and rest are modes of a body; they are present objectively in the body and not just merely subjectively in the agent or in the observer. Motion can be defined as 'the transference of one part of matter or of one body from the vicinity of those bodies which are in immediate contact with it, and which we regard as being in repose, into the vicinity of others' (II, 25).

Descartes aimed to establish a universal and all-encompassing science of nature. In the preface of the French translation of his *Principia Philosophiae* he appealed for assistance in the task of achieving his programme for the sciences. He was conscious, for example, that the *Principia* lacked the proposed sections on plants, animals and man. He suggested that co-operative endeavour in the sharing of '*expériences*' would be necessary if the new philosophers of nature were to make definitive decisions on the more particular facets of nature out of a wide variety of theories and explanations that seemed equally possible. In the meantime, he continued with his own project of clarifying certain basic ideas and axioms on which the science of nature and its future progress rested. Thus, for example, he devoted special attention to the ideas of space, place, body, time, duration and the laws of motion.

Place indicates situation relative to other bodies. Space or internal place is extension in general. Body is actual extension. Time is a common measure of different durations. Duration is a mode of a thing in so far as it is considered as continuing to exist. Local motion is a mode of corporeal substance. But motion cannot be explained by extension which, of itself, is static. Motion, like matter, was created by God. 'It is none other than God who...has created matter with its movement.' God created the energy which is in the universe. The total quantity of this energy will remain for ever the same; this is so because God is constant. The laws of motion can be deduced from the immutability of God. The first law is that each thing continues in the same state of rest or motion unless changed by another. The second law states that every moving body continues its movement in a straight line. The third law states that a moving body which encounters another moving body loses as much of its movement as it gives to the other.

Descartes presented his theory of *vortices* and his doctrine of *subtle matter* in Parts III and IV of the *Principles of Philosophy*. The whirling universe is a corporeal universe. The principal attribute of corporeality is continuous extension. There are no gaps or empty spaces within continuous extension. There are no empty spaces in the universe. The heavens are filled with tiny, adaptable, indeterminate particles of subtle matter. This applies too to the 'pores' of bodies and to experimentally produced vacuums. All are actually filled with subtle matter.

Everything in the universe (except human consciousness) can be explained in terms of extension and movement. This applies, for example, to 'qualitative' entities such as colour, heat, light, weight, gravitation, attraction, virtues, powers, faculties, sensible qualities and vegetative and sensitive forms or souls. Weight is a centripetal reaction in a vortex of bodies of a certain size. Volume is quantity of matter. The concept of force is derived from a principle of inertia. The force of a body in motion is reckoned as the product of its volume and velocity.

This corpus of 'Cartesian science' won widespread acceptance among the admirers and followers of Descartes, '*les cartésiens*', in the seventeenth century. It was regarded as the product of a new and powerful method of investigating nature. Newton, however, showed that the theory of vortices was incompatible with Kepler's laws; and Leibniz showed that the Cartesian laws of motion were inconsistent with Galileo's laws. The Cartesian physics which had attracted the main attention of Descartes' early admirers soon fell into disfavour, and at this stage it was Descartes' theory of knowledge rather than his philosophy of nature which became the focus of interest.

7. General remarks. Descartes was a pioneer in the modern approach to the science of epistemology. By means of his 'methodical doubt' he placed every item of knowledge in doubt except the indubitable proposition '*Cogito ergo sum*'. On the basis of this indubitable principle, which provided him with his criterion for truth (namely, clarity and distinctness in ideas), Descartes then attempted to erect an edifice of true and certain knowledge of the whole world. However, he interpreted his 'consciousness' in a subjectivistic way. For Descartes, consciousness is a consciousness of ideas. He did not seem to realize that any awareness or knowledge of anything is necessarily an awareness of something, a consciousness of being or of beings of one kind or another. His philosophy is not a philosophy of being. It is a philosophy of representationist indirect realism.

The Cartesian criterion of truth (clear and distinct ideas) is insufficient. It presupposes that consciousness is for the main part a closed consciousness and that the objective datum is largely inaccessible. There is an excessive distrust of sensory experience, and a depreciation of the objective datum. The emphasis is placed on reason; the sensory is sacrificed in the attempt to save metaphysics. All certain knowledge is deduced from principles which are evident *a priori*, independently of the data of sensory experience. This is the approach which one associates with the philosophy of rationalism.

The influence of Descartes has been immense. French philosophy, for example, since the days of Descartes has always shown that there is a close alliance between philosophy, mathematics and the sciences. It expresses itself in clear ideas and in simple language. Thomas Reid pointed out that philosophers as diverse as Malebranche, Locke, Berkeley and Hume shared Descartes' view of the human understanding, and that to this extent they can be called philosophers of 'the Cartesian system'. Hegel saw Cartesianism as an important stage in the development of philosophy towards absolute idealism. Empiricists and positivists drew inspiration from the Cartesian explanation of the world through pure mechanism. Husserl attempted to overcome the empiricist approach by recapturing the original Cartesian approach. He saw Descartes as the forerunner of modern phenomenology. Sartre interpreted the *Cogito* (*Je pense à...*) as opening out into a world of intersubjectivity, a world in which affirmation awaits a response. In short, Descartes is considered the father of modern philosophy in the pre-Kantian period; his approach to philosophy was made use of by many later thinkers in their own philosophies.

18 Theocentric thinkers and rationalist systems

1. Pascal and *le coeur*   2. Geulincx and 'Occasionalism'
3. Malebranche and 'vision in God'   4. Spinoza
5. Leibniz

1. Pascal and *le coeur*. *Blaise Pascal* (1623-62) French mathematician, physicist, inventor, philosopher and theologian, from childhood displayed signs of outstanding intelligence. In 1642 he invented the calculating machine. His accomplishments in mathematics and science are classed among the major achievements in the seventeenth-century sciences. To help the hospitals and the poor of Paris, he invented the first 'omnibus' carriage with several seats for passenger transport, the bus revenues being bequeathed to the hospitals. In 1654, Pascal had a profound experience of union with 'God of Jesus Christ... Jesus Christ' and devoted the rest of his life to religious activities and to writings in the philosophy of religion.

Pascal maintained in *De l'Esprit géométrique* that the geometrical procedure or method provides the greatest form of certainty attainable by the limited capacities of the human mind. This method starts from primitive terms and axioms, clearly known and assumed by everyone, though unproved and indefinable. The method then proceeds to derive further propositions from these primitive principles. This is not the ideal method for discovering truth but it is the best available to the limited human mind. The set of propositions or conclusions logically derived from the primitive axioms are true if these primitive axioms themselves are true.

In *De l'Art de persuader*, Pascal said that, if we wish to avoid Pyrrhonism (scepticism) and seeing that we cannot prove our first principles, then we must recognize and constantly acknowledge that all our primitive principles are gained through basic human insight (instinct) and relevation. We must acknowledge that the total activity of the knowing human being is a many-sided activity in which we can distinguish several aspects: the cognitive activity, the affective activity (*le coeur*) and the biological activity. Total human awareness is a conscious knowing of more 'truths' than those attained by ratiocination. We must therefore admit to ourselves the important role of basic insight, and submission to God, in our quest for truth.

Pascal jotted down various notes presenting in brief outline his personal reflections as a Christian thinker and apologist. He intended to publish an *Apologie de la religion chrétienne*; but this project was not completed before his death in 1662. The collection of notes was published posthumously as the famous *Pensées* of Pascal. In these notes Pascal points out that the human way of knowing is a severely limited way of knowing. 'The heart has its reasons of which reason knows nothing: we know this in countless ways.... Is it reason that makes you love yourself?' (*Pensées* 2, 2, 423 [277]). 'We know truth not only by reason but also by the heart (*le coeur*). It is in this latter way that we know first principles; and it is in vain that reason, which plays no part in this, tries to refute them' (*ibid.* 1, 6, 110 [282]). It is by the heart, that is, intuitively, that the first principles of geometry are known. The reason then employs these immediately perceived principles to establish theorems. Thus there are two different sources of certainty and one must not foolishly expect that the second source should try to validate or establish the first.

The certainty of the rational, geometrical method does not extend outside the field of deduction and demonstration; and within that limited field it is incapable of demonstrating its own intuited principles. For this reason, the geometrical (*a priori*) method is inefficacious in all non-deductive areas of knowledge. It cannot tell us for example about the existence of a diamond, or a vacuum, or God. The deductive-demonstrative method finds little application in the acquisition of those new types of knowledge attained for instance in experimental physics, or in metaphysics.

The way of *a priori* reasoning has only a very limited role to play therefore in the vitally important field of philosophy of religion. A treatise presenting a deductive form of knowledge of God is of little use indeed to an agnostic. Real knowledge of God involves a knowledge of man's need of redemption. It involves a knowledge of God as revealed in Jesus Christ, mediator and redeemer. Man left to himself is blind, wounded and corrupted. Philosophy is unable to remedy man's existential situation. Man needs the Redeemer.

'It is the heart which perceives (feels, intuits, apprehends) God, and not the reason' (*Pensées* 2, 2, 242 [278]). The total human being attains, in 'the heart', or in the inmost centre of his being, an immediate, unreasoned, apprehension of God, Supreme Being. Man without God is wretched. Man's greatness consists in his capacity for God. 'Man is only a reed, the weakest thing in nature; but he is a thinking reed.... A breath of wind, a drop of water is sufficient to destroy him. But were the universe to crush him man would still be nobler than his slayer' (*ibid.* 1, 15, 200, H3 [347]). 'Judge of all things, feeble earthworm;...the glory and the refuse of the universe' (*ibid.* 1, 7, 131 [343]). 'The knowledge of God without that of our wretchedness makes for pride. The knowledge of our wretchedness without the knowledge of God makes for despair. The knowledge of Jesus Christ strikes the balance; for there we find both God and our wretchedness' (*ibid.* 1, 14, 192 [527]).

Pascal then sought to show in his famous 'wager argument' that it is not unreasonable to accept the existence of God and to submit to his guidance and revelation. This argument is addressed to all those who, because of their human passions and worldly attachments, are hesitating to accept revealed truth. 'Either God is or he is not.... How will you wager? Reason cannot make you choose either, reason cannot prove either wrong' (*Pensées* 2, 2, 418 [233]). You must wager. Not to wager is a choice; it is to choose against God. Heads or tails? 'If you win you win everything, if you lose you lose nothing. Do not hesitate then, wager that he does exist.... There is an infinity of infinitely happy life to be won.... There is no room for hesitation, you must give everything' (*ibid.*). The man who will actually wager for God abandons some noxious pleasures only to find that he has wagered for something certain and infinite. Once he has wagered for God, God then gives him the certainty of the light of faith; he becomes a believer who gains in every way, even in this life. He who continues to hesitate, and thereby remains an unbeliever, is taking an infinitely unreasonable risk simply by continuing to waver between the alternatives. Wager for God. 'Submit to him for your own good and for his glory' (*ibid.*).

Pascal's thought is that of an 'existentialist' religious thinker, concerned with the relation between the existent human being and God. His philosophy is a philosophy of religion in which conceptual discursive reasoning (*ratio*) is seen as merely one activity in the total knowing-activity (*intellectus*) of the whole man oriented towards God.

2. Geulincx and 'Occasionalism'. *Arnold* (Aernout) *Geulincx* (1624-69) of Louvain and Leiden was a Flemish metaphysician, doctor and moralist. In his *Metaphysics*, published posthumously in 1691, he followed the Cartesian order of procedure. Our first knowledge is knowledge of the thinking self and of the various states of consciousness. He took it to be a self-evident principle that the active self does not do what the active self does not know how to

do. Nothing can be done unless there is knowledge of how it is done. Thus, active movements of the body cannot be attributed to the mind or soul if the soul does not know how movements of the nerves and muscles and brain are initiated, or how external actions actually come about. The mind knows only its own states and is not the true cause of movements in the body. Similarly, a body does not know how to produce sensations or effects in the mind. It is obvious, therefore, that there can be no interaction between mind and body.

The agent responsible for the apparent interaction of mind and body has to be God himself. It is God who is the only real causal agent of all things, and constantly synchronizes the movements of things. Thus, a movement in one thing, such as a body, becomes an occasion on which God produces an event in another thing, such as a soul, or another body. This doctrine came to be known as the doctrine of 'Occasionalism'. It was developed further by Leibniz, who spoke of the divinely pre-established harmony between mind and body.

Geulincx also made a Cartesian distinction between corporeality, or body in general, that is, extension, and particular bodies which are merely modes of body in general. Corporeality is simple, unique, individual, infinite, and indivisible. Particular bodies are modes or limitations of infinite, unique extension. Individual minds, similarly, are modes of infinitely thinking substance, God. There are therefore only two substances, thinking substance and extended substance, matter. This view of substance is a Cartesian view which lies roughly midway between the view of Descartes himself and that of Spinoza.

3. Malebranche and 'vision in God'. *Nicolas Malebranche* (1638-1715) was an ordained member of the Paris house of the Congregation of the Oratory. He was deeply impressed by the philosophy of Augustine and the writings of Descartes and his followers. He wrote *Search after Truth* (1674-75), *Treatise of Nature and Grace* (1680), *Meditations, Christian and Metaphysical* (1683), *Dialogues on Metaphysics and on Religion* (1688) and other works. These works present a new, original synthesis of Platonic-Augustinian-Cartesian thought in which the world and human experience is interpreted in the light of a vision or viewpoint which is theocentric: 'In God we live and move and have our being'. This philosophical viewpoint was widely known as the 'malebranchiste' viewpoint at the time of his death in 1715.

In his *Search after Truth* Malebranche supported and skilfully developed several Cartesian themes: matter as extension; the elimination of faculties, qualities and forms; different bodies as different configurations of parts; animals as machines; configuration and movement as adequately explaining corporeal behaviour; the human soul as distinct and separable; mental awareness as immediate and certain; sense perception as indirect and uncertain; and knowledge of Nature as originating from clear and distinct ideas. The senses were given us by God to serve practical needs; they were not given us for the purpose of revealing the natures of things. It is our ideas which re-present to us the nature of reality. Ideas, like all other finite creatures, can be explained only as the product of that causal efficacy which is the prerogative of the Deity.

We do not see or perceive objects outside of ourselves (*hors de nous, hors de l'âme*). The soul, for instance, does not go out walking about the heavens to know the sun and the stars. It is the Creator alone who can produce such ideas. These ideas created in us by God are finite representations of the ideas or archetypes of the natures of things as present in the mind of God. God, the first being (*primum ontologicum*), is also the first known (*primum notum*) in whom we know everything else. This theory came to be known as the theory of 'ontologism'. It states, in brief, that in God we see all things: '*nous voyons toutes choses en Dieu*'.

Malebranche pointed out that this vision in God is not the same as the vision of God enjoyed by the blessed in heaven. It is simply a vision of his essence insofar as it is the exemplar of all ideas. Vincenzo Gioberti (d. 1852) attempted to refine this view further by saying that this vision in God is really a vision of being-in-itself as presented to the knower by the existent which is present; the existent, a creation of being, is known by virtue of being: 'Being creates the existent'.

One can say by way of criticism that the doctrine of 'ontologism' fails to make any distinction between our abstract, confused concept of being and Absolute Being itself. Our concept of being is a perfectly objective and adequate, though confused, representation of our experience of being. Our idea of being is an idea or concept of a very special kind. It expresses the concrete real adequately with all its differences and modes. It is a transcendental concept which expresses everything that exists. As such, it expresses absolute, unconditioned reality also. However, the *concept* of being is not itself the more primitive *experience* of being. The concept of being derives from our experience of any being. The experience is intuitive. The concept is an adequate but abstract and confused representation of the experience. The error of ontologism resides, therefore, in its confusion of our abstract knowledge of being with the infinite divine being itself which we do not directly, intuitively experience. We have no experience of any vision in God or of God. It is only through our abstract, transcendental idea of being that we know him.

According to Malebranche, God is the one and only true cause. It is God who is the true cause for example of motion in bodies; his will is their moving force. Thus, if one ball strikes a second ball, the impact is merely the *occasional* or particular cause of the movement of the second ball. It is God who is the real or true cause of that movement. Similarly, it is not the mind, but God, who is the true cause moving my arm on the *occasion* of my willing that my arm should be moved. God acts in accordance with the general laws of motion that he has enacted; he does not act at random. Accordingly, God acts in conformity with his own laws connecting our mental events and our bodily events in such a way that our bodily movements takes place on the *occasion* of our willing them to do so ('Occasionalism'). There is no interaction between mind and body; but there is a divine correspondence or psycho-physical parallelism between them. The soul itself is not united to the body; it is directly united to God alone.

The doctrines of both Geulincx and Malebranche bring to the surface the theocentric tendency latent in Cartesian thought. The further development of this tendency leads to its natural and logical growth into a doctrine of pantheism: there is only one substance or nature, namely, absolute, eternal, infinite, immutable, impersonal being. Men and things are merely modes, or determinations, or reflections of Absolute Nature. Geulincx and Malebranche arrested and held in check this pantheistic tendency latent in Cartesianism. Baruch Spinoza developed the implications of the Cartesian concepts of substance and attributes into an organized and systematized philosophy of pantheism.

4. Spinoza. *Baruch* (Benedict) *Spinoza* (1632-77) was born at Amsterdam, where his Portuguese Jewish parents had sought refuge from religious persecution. He received his early rabbinical education in the Jewish academy at Amsterdam. Later, he was initiated into the mysteries of Talmudic literature and cabbalistic philosophy by a circle of Jewish philosophers and friends. This group sought to cope with the unhappy social circumstances of the Jewish people by emphasizing the importance of asceticism, love and world-shunning contemplation, as a means of purifying the soul. The contemplative soul attained a new cosmic role in the cabbalistic reinterpretation of the messianic hope. Spinoza declined the offer of a professorship at Heidelberg in 1673, and chose the quiet, independent and humble

life of a lens grinder. His *Principles of Philosophy* was published in
1663 and his *Theological Political Treatise* in 1670. His *Opera
posthuma*, including the *Ethics*, were published shortly after he had
died of consumption, at the age of forty-five, in 1677.

Spinozism, the philosophy of Spinoza, is not Cartesianism. It is a
powerfully original creation of Spinoza's own thought. The
fundamental insight lying at the centre of this system of thought is the
identity of God, Nature and Substance in the one, infinite, unique
substance of all that is. Descartes had started with the existence of an
awareness which clearly evidences one's own existence; Spinoza
started with our awareness of all that is. For the systematic
presentation and development of the implications of this fundamental
insight, Spinoza made use of the Cartesian terminology and ideal of
method. Thus, Spinoza, like Descartes, used the geometrical method
in his attempt to achieve an exact knowledge of the whole system of
reality. With the aid of a complex interrelated set of axioms or
theorems he attempted to deduce from the fundamental idea of God
or Nature other derived ideas or 'truths' concerning the nature, the
attributes and modes of all that is in being in the cosmos.

Like Descartes, Spinoza accepted it as evident that every clear and
distinct deduction is true. Genuine knowledge is self-guaranteeing.
Reason operates infallibly. Every definition is true. 'The order and
connection of ideas is the same as the order and connection of things.'
Ideas reflect reality. The world of geometry reflects the world of
physics. The order of ideas reflects the order of causes. For this
reason Spinoza assumed that the ontological causal relation is
assimilated to the mental relation of logical entailment, and that exact
factual knowledge of reality can be attained through the use of
conceptual discursive reasoning about reality itself. An exact understanding of the nature of things can arise only through an understanding of the overall system in which these things are merely parts. A
parasitic worm living in the bloodstream does not understand the role
of the bloodstream in an organism if it is acquainted only with
individual drops of blood. One must grasp the universal system as a
whole before one can hope to grasp the role or the nature of the part.

For Spinoza, the whole of reality is a single system. It is Nature, the
Universe, God, Substance. It is non-dependent being, subsisting in
itself and of itself. This is the very definition of substance. 'Substance
is that which is in itself and is conceived through itself.' Substance or
God or Nature is 'cause of itself'. Its essence involves its existence.
Substance, or Being, 'excludes all imperfections and involves absolute perfection'. By this very fact all doubt is removed concerning the

existence of God or Nature; its existence is most certain. Reality, Substance, exists. It is what it is, and it is unique. There cannot be two of its kind since there cannot be an 'other' which lies outside of 'what is'. Substance is infinite and it is unique. It is *causa sui* and *causa omnium rerum*. It is its own total explanation of all that is.

Infinite substance possesses an infinity of infinite attributes; 'the more reality or being anything has, the more attributes it possesses' (*Ethics* I, 9). An attribute, according to Spinoza, is 'that which an intellect perceives as constituting the essence of substance'. The human intellect is capable of perceiving only two of these attributes, namely the attribute of thought and the attribute of extension. The reason for this is that 'we feel and perceive no particular things save bodies and modes of thought'. Our ideas about reality are merely different images or different ways of envisaging one and the same reality. Hence we conceive of reality as made up of separate realities or bodies. But reality, or extended substance, is not made up of parts or bodies really distinct from each other; reality, or being, is one, not many. It is infinite substance perceived as infinite thought and infinite extension. It is God or Nature, and we conceive it as expressed in various modes of thought and corporeality.

The things that we experience in the world 'are nothing else than modifications of the attributes of God, or modes by which attributes are expressed in a certain and determined manner'. These modes of being can be thought of as *natura naturata*, or 'the world'. The things of the world are modes of God's attributes. They are 'things which are in God (Nature) which without God (Nature) can neither be nor be conceived'. *Natura naturans* is substance and its attributes. *Natura naturata* is not distinct from God; it is simply God or Nature expressed in various modes of thought and extension.

The infinite and eternal attribute of extension is expressed in the world (*natura naturata*) in the immediate, infinite and eternal mode of motion-and-rest in Nature. Motion-and-rest is expressed mediately in the total system of moving bodies. Each aspect or state of this system can be explained in terms of the motion and rest of ultimate energetic units (realities) which come together into configurations of different kinds. The configurations are known to us as individual physical objects. These objects in turn are the parts of wider configurations which come together within the total configuration of the individual universe. All are parts of 'the face of the whole universe' (*facies totius universi*).

It is the whole universe that is the individual. Nevertheless, we do look upon certain parts of the universe as being individuals also.

These individuals are configurations which maintain themselves in being and possess a drive towards self-preservation (*conatus in suo esse perseverandi*). There is a hierarchy of individuals of this kind, all within 'the face of the universe'. Some are inorganic, some are vegetative, some are animal and some are human.

The infinite attribute of thought is expressed, in *natura naturata*, in the immediate, infinite and eternal mode of 'absolutely infinite understanding' in God or Nature. This infinite understanding is expressed, or appears, mediately, in the total infinite system of all minds in the universe.

Finite minds, like finite bodies, are the modal expression of the self-determination of God (Nature). They are modes or modifications of God, existing in God, and following of necessity from the divine nature (*natura naturans*). God necessarily produces his finite modes; nevertheless this production is 'free' in the sense that God (*natura naturans*) is self-determined.

The human being, mind and body, is simply a mode of infinite Being's attributes of thought and extension. The human body is simply the human being considered as a mode of the infinite attribute of extension. The human mind is simply the human being considered as a mode of the infinite attribute of thought. The mind is simply the 'idea', or the form of being of the body. They do not interact; they are not two beings. They are simply two aspects or viewpoints of one mode, the human mode, of being. The quality of the perfection of mind, in man or animal, depends on the quality of perfection of the body. This dependence of mind on body provides a basis for a valuable scientific research programme in experimental psychology.

Spinoza asserted that a scientific account of God or Nature necessarily eliminates any and every form of belief in final causality. Earthquakes and diseases and rainfall do not act for a purpose. 'Nature has no fixed aim in view....All final causes are simply fabrications of men.' For this reason all scientific knowledge and research eliminates final causality and seeks to explain nature in terms of the causal connections of efficient causality alone. This aspect of Spinoza's doctrine was commended by the naturalists and empiricists of the late seventeenth and early eighteenth centuries, who interpreted Spinozism as a system of thought which emphasized the importance of scientific research in the study of nature and the physical universe. This emphasis is certainly present in Spinozism but it is not true to say that it is the primary emphasis. Spinozism is a metaphysical system which aims to give a rational explanation of the totality of reality. Its basic, fundamental principle, from which all its deductions arise, is formulated in the assertion that reality is one substance, infinite, immutable, eternal and unique. This single substance has two names, 'God' and 'Nature'. The terms 'God', 'Nature', 'Reality', 'Being', 'Substance' are interchangeable. They express a reality which is one. For this reason historians of philosophy, in general, regard Spinozism as a particular form of pantheism. It is a philosophical system of static, impersonal pantheism; or more simply, it is a doctrine of metaphysical monism.

In the *Ethics*, Spinoza distinguished three different levels at which the mind operates. They are three levels of 'perception' or knowledge. In our attempt to understand the nature of reality we must try to move from the lowest levels of knowledge to the highest.

The lowest level of perception is that of vague or confused sense experiences. On this level we form general images (*imaginationes*) and notions which are based on the particular experiences of causal associations that our senses or bodies enter into. We pick up, by hearsay, a welter of unrelated notions about people and animals, for example; and we see that a puff of breath can quench a candle flame. Notions of this kind do not reveal the true order of causation in nature. They are fragmented, isolated, inadequate and logically unrelated, even if they do have a practical utility for daily living.

The second level is that of adequate, reasoned, scientific knowledge. The propositions and ideas of mathematics and physics, for example, rise above immediate, transitory, sensed things, in order to deal with abstract, general and common notions which reflect the common properties of bodies. Ideas of this kind are logically related; and they have within themselves their own criterion of self-evident truth. The universal idea is simply the counterpart of the *ideatum*: the mode of thought is simply the counterpart of the mode of extension. There is a hierarchy of ideas of this kind. They form a single total system of ideas embracing the whole universe in the mode of thought. Rational inquiry will always attempt to draw closer to an understanding of this ideal system of interrelated ideas.

The highest grade of perception, 'intuitive science', is the knowledge of God or Nature. It is the vision of all things in the whole system of Nature. The human mind can ascend only by degrees in its approach towards the high vantage point of this vision. The total system of ideas is the 'infinite idea of God or Nature'. Knowledge of this kind is divine. All things are seen in their essential relation to God. One discovers one's own place in the whole system of Nature. This aspect of Spinoza's thought prompted Novalis (von Hardenberg) to speak of Spinoza as the 'God-intoxicated man' (*gottbetrunkener Mensch*). However, the 'God' which is the constant focus of attention in Spinozism is not the God of Judaism or theism but rather that totality of reality which can aptly be called Being or Substance or 'God' or 'Nature'.

The human mind is capable of advancing gradually in conceiving and perceiving all things *sub specie aeternitatis*. It can see things as part of the eternal, logically connected system of infinite reality. From this vision of reality there arises a satisfaction or pleasure of the mind which Spinoza calls 'the intellectual love of God'. This understanding-love of God or Nature is 'our salvation, blessedness, or liberty'. It fills the mind and thereby makes the mind impervious to change, to pain and to circumstance.

All men, and all things, have a natural tendency or *conatus* to preserve themselves in being and to develop their powers and activities. Men experience 'pleasure' (*laetitia*) when they become conscious of heightened degrees of self-preservation and perfection. They experience 'pain' when they become conscious of a reduction of such perfection. Human actions which give rise to the 'pleasure' of heightened self-perfection are called 'good'. Those which give rise to pain are called 'bad'. The terms goodness and badness merely reflect a subjective evaluation of the experiences of pleasure and pain.

Human emotions and passions arise as reflections of bodily modifications which accompany the conscious experiences of heightened or reduced self-perfection. The person who feels constrained to follow a degrading passion, because he lacks power to moderate his emotions, falls into a state of servitude to his uncontrolled passions. It is only through a moving up to the higher levels of knowledge that a person can moderate his emotions and confine their natural tendencies to their proper places in the whole order of Nature. This is the pathway to moral excellence. It is not easy. 'All things excellent are as difficult as they are rare.' But it is the true pathway to the blessedness of intellectual love of God or Nature.

For Spinoza, Nature is determined, and man is an integral part of Nature. Is there any sense, then, in which one can meaningfully say that man is free? The man in the street feels free only because he is ignorant of all the prior causes which determine his will to desire certain things. He is not truly free at all; everything occurs necessarily. True freedom, virtue and power lie in the *conatus suo esse perseverandi*. The events of Nature are beyond our control. But it does lie within our power to strive wilfully to align our attitudes and our wills to the self-determining will of God or Nature. We attain the virtue and power of self-determination in a loving resignation to all that necessarily is and all that will be. In this way we can arrive at the highest possible mental acquiescence to the eternally perfect arrangement of all things in God or Nature. The way of knowledge and loving surrender is the way to the attainment of true peace of mind and of freedom from the servitude of the passions. This is the pathway to the happy and blessed state of intellectual love of God or Nature.

The concepts of virtue, power and self-determination, or freedom, are again the central concepts in Spinoza's political philosophy. Spinoza had read the works of Thomas Hobbes. He agreed with Hobbes's theory that in order to restrain social anarchy, and to ensure peace and survival, men enter into a social contract in which they agree to give sovereign power to a sovereign political ruler. He agreed too that politics is entirely a matter of power. But Spinoza assimilated and transformed these political theories into his own wider, metaphysical theory about man's role and man's place within the infinite individual which is God or Nature.

Every finite thing, including man, has a sovereign natural right to behave in the way in which Nature has conditioned and determined its powers and activities. Spinoza says that 'by virtue and power (*virtus*) I understand the same thing' (*Ethics* IV, Def. 8). The sovereign rights of the individual are commensurate with the individual's natural striving (*conatus*) to persist in being and to develop its powers and activities. Enlightened self-interest prompts individuals to enter into a social compact so that a social framework within which men can live securely and rationally is provided for each and all. Sovereignty is given to the State to provide the framework in which men can live rationally. For the sake of peace and security, then, sovereign power is handed over to a sovereign ruler or to a sovereign body whose right to command and rule is limited only by the limits of his (or their) own natural desires and natural powers. The sovereign has the right to do what he has the natural power (*virtus*) to do. Sovereign power is required for the control of rebellious passions and for the maintenance of peace. Within this framework of virtue and peace, the individual can then develop his own personality and power through his personal striving to attain his natural well-being. This is the way of Nature for both the State and the individual.

For almost a century after his death, Spinoza was either attacked and execrated or ignored and slighted by philosophers, theologians and literary critics alike. The influential *Dictionnaire philosophique* (1697), for example, condemned Spinoza's identification of God with Nature as a 'most absurd and monstrous hypothesis'. A century later, however, at the time of the German *Aufklärung* or Enlightenment, Jacobi, Lessing, Herder, Heine and Goethe acknowledged a certain indebtedness to the writings of Spinoza. Later still, Fichte, Schelling and Hegel regarded Spinozism as the starting point of all philosophy. Russian Marxists, such as G.V. Plekhanov, have spoken of Marxism as simply a form of Spinozism. Thus several different lines of interpretation of Spinozism have emerged in the course of history. The writings of Spinoza have had a catalytic influence on the thought of several different schools of thought, though Spinozism itself never gave rise to a single, consistent school of philosophical and political thought. As for Spinoza himself, his system of knowledge mapped out the cosmic pathway to freedom from the domination of the passions and to the attainment of true peace of mind in a world of widespread social suffering.

     5. Leibniz. *Gottfried Wilhelm Leibniz* (1646-1716), as a boy, studied Aristotelian Scholastic philosophy in his father's house library at the university of Leipzig. Later, as a student at the university, he studied modern philosophy, mathematics and jurisprudence. Subsequently, as a courtier on diplomatic missions to France and England, he conversed with several of the leading philosophers and scientists of his day. During a month spent in Amsterdam, Leibniz read as many of the Spinozan writings as Spinoza was prepared to allow him to read, and was then allowed to interview Spinoza on the material he had read. However, in order to avoid accusations levelled against Spinozist thought, Leibniz declared subsequently that his contact with Spinoza had been minimal. The voluminous writings and correspondence of Leibniz cover wide areas of interests in, and contributions to, symbolic logic, calculus, physics, mathematics, law, philosophy, theology, Christian unity, and the political alliance of Christian states. As a librarian-employee in Hanover, he had written the history of the House of Brunswick up to the year 1005 when he died unnoticed and neglected, at the age of seventy.

     Leibniz was a complex and many-sided genius who seldom re-read any of his own previous writings and never worked out a fully systematic synthesis of his own thought. However, one can say with some justification that the central idea in Leibniz's philosophy is the idea of the universal harmony, under God, of all the particular beings (or monads) which make up the system of Nature. Every single being (or monad) in the universe is explainable *a priori* in terms of its continually created being; and human knowledge is capable of attaining to a universal science, of a mathematical type, from which clear reasons and explanations can be deduced concerning each monad, or being, which exists.

Leibniz compared the universe to a configuration of several different bands of musicians and choirs, each unit playing its own notes and its own part, separate from and oblivious to the playing of the others, but in a manner which has been so prearranged that he who listens will find in them a wonderful harmony. Each unit, actively in being, is independent in its being from any other unit, and is dependent in being upon God alone. It is God who prearranges and establishes the harmonization of all. In papers written in 1695 and 1696 (in C. J. Gerhardt's ed.: [1863] II, p.298; [1890] IV, p. 468-499). Leibniz called this explanation 'the way of pre-established harmony' of all that exists.

Leibniz tells us that he was led gradually to this viewpoint, and that it came as a surprise even to himself. In 1694 and 1695 he published various articles in the *Acta Eruditorum* and other journals. Here he stressed the notion of 'inner activity', or inner existing, as essential to the notion of any individual substance. He asserted that the Aristotelian word 'entelechy' (that is, inner fulfilment or inner possession of the end) expresses the inner reality of any substance. Every existing substance is independent of others for its being and is completely self-contained. There can be no interaction between the inner being of one substance and the inner existing of another substance. Thus, there can be no interaction of matter and mind. (He did not agree, however, with Malebranche's doctrine of 'Occasionalism', which, he maintained, while stressing the omnipotence of God, seems to ignore completely the wisdom of God.) Leibniz came to the conclusion that each creature of God comes to be and to act spontaneously through its own inner being, uninfluenced in its being by any being other than God alone, and that all creation displays the varieties of received existence in a way which is harmoniously prearranged by the Creator.

The universe is a harmonious universe of different beings each gifted with its own inner finality (entelechy), or inner activity of being. Each is unique, even though the apparent differences between similar particular beings may be imperceptible. Leibniz spoke of this as the individual uniqueness or 'identity of (different) indiscernibles'. Compound substances or beings, such as bodies, exist. 'The compound is only an aggregate of simple substances.' The inner activity of existing, going on within simple organisms or bodies, does not itself possess extension or divisibility. Simple existing or simple being has no parts. These units of inner activities (of being) can be called 'monads'. (The Greek word *monas* is Euclid's term for the fundamental unit or element in the world of geometrical thought.) Each monad is a dynamic-teleologic centre of energetic being.

The extended bodies of our experience are bodies which have bodies within bodies without end; and the monads of these bodies are monads within monads without end. Each monad (or unit of active 'existing') has its own organic body. It is part of the function of a monad to express its own body. A monad without its own 'organism' (in the sense of the Greek word for a 'work-tool') would be 'a deserter from the general order' (Gerhardt [1890] VI, p. 546). Every tiny particle of matter, like every organic body, big or small, is composed of still smaller organic bodies, each having its own dominant monad. The organism or work-instrument of the monad is extended; but the unit of activity of being, that is, the monad itself, is not extended. The world is a universe of independent units of being dependent solely on the continuous creative activity of the Supreme Being. It is a universe of harmonized units of being, that is, units of 'existing'; or, more simply, it is a harmonized system of monads.

There are cases, such as that of the phenomenon of the rainbow, in which we erroneously attribute unity of being to an aggregate of 'well-founded phenomena'. The phenomenon of the rainbow, Leibniz says, is based on an aggregate of beams of light refracted from droplets of water each of which, in turn, is merely a phenomenal aggregate based on the actual units of reality, the monads. 'Bodies' without entelechies have no proper reality and are mere phenomena. The real, though indiscernible, reality is the unit of energetic being which expresses itself in its organic body.

Each corporeal substance, the human being included, has within itself not only its active principle of being, or entelechy, or substantial form, but also a passive component, a principle of potentiality, or determinability, or resistant passivity, which can be called prime matter. Prime matter is the passive, determinable or potential element of the monad. It manifests its existence in what we experience as the inertia and the impenetrability of substances. The phenomenon experienced by our senses is this impenetrable passive aspect of the innumerable active monads which form the aggregate. The energetic monads are the reality; the quasi-inert aggregate is the phenomenal, the sense-appearance.

Each unit of being, or monad, expresses and mirrors within itself the being of the whole universe, even though each one is also an island by itself, 'a world apart'. Each is a 'windowless' miniature universe, a self-contained and self-developing entity. Each receives its inner being from the Creator without further dependence on any other.

Each has its own unique position in the whole series of created beings in the universe. Together they form a continuous series which has no 'gaps'. The whole family or order of beings, some inferior, some superior, forms a continuous series in which every position is occupied. 'Nature makes no leaps.' The law which governs this state of affairs in the universe is called the law of continuity; it is the principle of general order.

Each unit of being has a primitive awareness of its own being or existing. Each mirrors within itself the being of the universe outside itself. Each has an internal principle of 'appetition' which gives rise to successive changes in the primitive contents of awareness. Thus, all monads have some degree, perhaps minimal, of perception and appetition. Some monads have a higher degree of perception than others. In the animal, the dominant monad, that is, the animal 'entelechy' or soul, enjoys a high degree of perception, accompanied by sense-memories and feelings. In the human being, the perception and appetition is of a higher level still: it is at the level of human, spiritual apperception.

The relationship between soul and body is the relationship between the highest entelechy and the organism. It is the relationship between the dominant monad and the lower organic assemblage of monads within monads. There is a divinely pre-established harmony between the immanent activities of 'existing' going on within each and all; but there is no interaction between their different ongoing, immanent activities of being. It is the divine wisdom that is the sufficient reason which explains the harmony of their independent immanent activities. Thus, while there is no interaction, there is a specific, intelligent co-ordination of action, that is, a real agreement in action, which is the effect of God's original design in establishing harmony in the universe.

Leibniz's metaphysic of substances is closely connected to his logical studies. For Leibniz there is an evident connection between the dominant ontological unit of being (as, for example, the being of Socrates) and the logical or grammatical subject expressed or understood, which 'underlies' (*sub-jectum*) every verb and every form of predication. Knowledge of the subject is knowledge of the reality, and knowledge of the reality is knowledge of the subject. Truth is the correspondence of a proposition with reality, possible or actual.

Leibniz divided propositions into those which express (logical) truths of reason and those which express experienced truths of fact (e.g. the news). A truth of reason (e.g. that A is not non-A) is a necessary truth; to deny it is to involve oneself in a contradiction. It is a truth which is concerned with the sphere of possibility, the non-contradictory. It is non-existential, except in the unique case of the proposition that 'God is'. Thus, for example, to say that 'dragons are monsters' asserts only that the class 'dragon' falls under the class 'monster'. All truths of reason are analytic and necessary, and non-existential (except the necessary proposition that God is). Truths of fact, on the contrary, are contingent, synthetic, existential propositions known *a posteriori* (e.g. James married Martha). Their truth does not follow from the laws of logic. Their truth rests not on the principles of non-contradiction but on the principle of sufficient reason. The existential fact arises from a divine free choice which is motivated but not necessitated by the divine goodness. The full and perfect reason for the existence of the contingent fact is known to God alone.

Leibniz held that, in particular propositions expressing a truth of fact (e.g. Socrates is mortal), the quality denoted by the predicate is part of the nature or the idea of the substance denoted by the subject. The predicate is already contained in the subject. The notion of an individual being (e.g. Socrates) is such that it already has within itself as a subject all the predicates attributable to it. God apprehends the notion of Socrates in every detail. He knows *a priori* from eternity every attribute and every existential fact concerning Socrates and his actions. For God, all true propositions about Socrates, such as the proposition that Socrates drank hemlock, are analytic propositions. The drinking of hemlock is an integral part of the eternal individual notion of the subject. To the divine mind, then, truths of fact, like truths of reason, are analytic and necessary propositions; the predicate is contained in the subject. Nevertheless this does not destroy the freedom of God in the divine choice concerning creation. God created the world freely and he gave to man too the power of free judgement and choice.

Leibniz presented his thoughts on the origin of the existing universe in two different and complementary series of writings. He decided to publish one series, but not the other. Antoine Arnauld, the Jansenist theologian and philosopher, had strongly objected to Leibniz's view that the individual notion of each person involves everything that the person will do and everything that is to happen to him. Leibniz aimed to promote unity of thought and belief; he had no desire to promote further polemic. Thus the second series of writings remained unpublished during his lifetime. Some historians, following Bertrand Russell, speak of the 'popular (exoteric) philosophy' in which Leibniz sought the approbation of his patrons, and the more profound 'esoteric doctrine' which remained unpublished because it would not have won popular approbation during his lifetime. The distinction is a valid distinction; but it does not necessarily carry any derogatory implication that Leibniz was some kind of insincere sycophant, as Russell seems to imply. There is no reason for doubting Leibniz's sincerity in wishing to promote (Christian) harmony rather than dissension in matters which had theological implications.

In the unpublished writings, Leibniz attempted to explain why it is that some things exist and that others, equally possible, do not. (One might ask, for example, why it is that, from among the millions of spermary seeds of the progenitor, only a small number of these possible beings become actual.) A possible being is, by definition, one that can be; it is capable of becoming actual if all the necessary requisites are operative and not obstructed. It tends by its very nature toward its entelechy, that is, towards an inward possession of its fulfilment or end. Nevertheless, not all possibles can become actual because they are not all 'compossible'. Thus, for example, a female progenitor will have only a limited number of offspring over a lifetime. 'The existent is the being which is compatible with the most things.' The actual being is the one for which the whole complex of requisites was actually operative. In this sense the actual existent is the unique, actually favoured possible, or the 'best possible'.

In the *Monadology* (1714), the *Principles of Nature and Grace* (1714), and the *Théodicée* (1710), Leibniz held that the Creator always has a sufficient reason, based in the divine reason, motivating the action of the divine will. This 'principle of sufficient reason' is complemented by the 'principle of perfection'. God acts for the objectively best. God wills freely to do all things in the best possible way. That God 'should prefer the most perfect...follows from the nature of God'. It was therefore morally necessary that he should act for the best even though it was not logically or metaphysically necessary for him to choose to create. His freedom is the freedom of self-determination. God gave man too this same kind of freedom. In the given universe it was morally necessary for Socrates to drink the hemlock even though it was not metaphysically or logically necessary for Socrates to make this choice. Moral influence of this kind does not deprive the human being of free judgement and choice. This theme, however, is one which had previously given rise to several bitter controversies in Scholastic philosophy and theology. Leibniz preferred not to add further to the fracas. This fact however provides no proof at all for the contentious assertion that Leibniz was insincere.

Leibniz's *New Essays on Human Understanding* was published posthumously in 1765. In these writings Leibniz stated that he accepted as valid the traditional proofs for the existence of God that had been presented in the past, though some of the proofs needed to be perfected. He held that the *a simultaneo* argument for the existence of God, as presented by Anselm and Descartes, needed to be supplemented in order to render it mathematically evident. The proof of God's existence from the concept of the greatest possible being or the most perfect being is incomplete until it is shown first that such a being is possible.

The proposition 'God is', or 'Absolute Being is', is an analytic proposition. The predicate ('is') is contained in the notion of the subject. God is definable as the necessary Being. It would therefore be a contradiction to deny that being belongs to the Being who necessarily is. He must *be*; he must exist, if he is possible. Now, the idea of God implies no intrinsic contradiction. Therefore the idea of the all-great or all-perfect Being is the idea of a Being that is possible. It is the idea of a necessary Being, a Being uniquely endowed with this privilege that he must exist. The idea implies no contradiction, and so the necessary Being is possible. To be possible or to be capable of being is to be endowed by nature with a tendency towards 'the inner possession of the end', that is, a 'tendency towards being'. In God, possible perfection is infinite, and it includes an infinite and irresistible tendency to be, to exist, so that God not only is but necessarily is. There is nothing that can hinder the actualization of the possibility of that which possesses no limitations, no negations and no contradiction. This alone suffices to establish the existence of God *a priori*. Furthermore, if Being of itself were impossible, then all beings by others would also be impossible; and so nothing at all could exist. If God were impossible, then nothing could be possible.

This argument, however, equates a negative possibility with a positive possibility. Since human knowledge is limited knowledge, an absence of discerned contradiction, or in other words, a negative possibility (e.g. 'I don't see why not') is not the same thing as a positive possibility. The positive possibility has to be established *a posteriori*.

Leibniz's views exercised considerable influence throughout the eighteenth century. In Germany, Christian Wolff presented a popular, systematized version of the philosophy of Leibniz which remained the reigning philosophy in the universities of Germany down to the time of Immanuel Kant. In the period of the Enlightenment, the spirit of confidence in an ever-increasing human perfectibility and progress derives its origin from Leibniz's theory that this present world is the best possible of all the possibles that can actually coexist. The whole system of beings (monads) is progressing in an unending self-unfolding and self-development. The goal of history is the 'city of God', a harmonious 'moral order within the natural world' (Gerhardt [1890] VI, p. 622).

Leibniz's system of philosophy, like that of Descartes and Spinoza (and of Wolff subsequently), is a rationalist system of philosophy. Its first premiss is that the whole universe is intelligible and rational. The new mathematical scientific discoveries of the late Renaissance were seen as constant pointers to the evident truth of this premiss. The continued application of the principles of mathematics to astronomy and to the physical sciences had notable success in the discovery of new truths of fact about nature. This success of the mathematico-physical sciences prompted Descartes, Spinoza, Leibniz and other rationalist philosophers to set out on a voyage of discovery in which a whole system of factual information about the world could be deduced from a small number of fundamental, self-evident first principles. They were convinced that the certainty attained in the mathematico-physical sciences arose from carefully reasoned deductions which could never have been possible if Nature were simply chaotic and irrational. Reality is rational; and the conceptual-discursive method is the key to an understanding of its actual structure. The universe is best understood, then, through the medium of certain self-evident first principles which are basically similar to God's own creative ideas. These first principles are virtually innate. The mind has the power of finding these virtually innate ideas and first principles, as natural propensities, dispositions and virtual habits, within itself. It is reason, and not the sensations of the rational animal, that is the real source of human knowledge. The world has an intelligible structure, and human reason must attempt to reconstruct this intelligible, objective structure by a conceptual-discursive or deductive process which re-enacts the self-unfolding of creative intelligence.

One may say, by way of critical evaluation, that epistemological rationalism, in general, undervalues and ignores the contributions of sense-data to the human process of concept formation. It undervalues the role of willing and feeling in the full life of the whole man. It assimilates the ontological causal relation to the mental relation of logical entailment. It attempts to deduce reality and existential propositions from the resources of the mind without recourse to experience. It implies that all contingent propositions (e.g. Caesar crossed the Rubicon; Socrates drank hemlock) are deductions from necessary propositions. This, in turn, implies that the deduction of the existence of the finite being from the ontological principle of all finite beings (namely God) is a necessary deduction. Different emphases on different aspects of these excesses led to different lines of development of pre-Kantian Continental rationalism. Descartes asserted a duality of spiritual and material substances. Spinoza asserted that there is only one substance, the substance of being itself. Leibniz affirmed that there is a plurality of finite beings, each dependent on Infinite Being and independent of all others. For each of these philosophers, reason is the unique source of human knowledge. This excessive emphasis of Continental rationalism soon gave rise to the contrary excessive emphasis of the British empiricists.

19 Empiricism in Britain (I): the seventeenth century

1. Hobbes   2. Locke   3. Philosophy of science
4. The Cambridge Platonists   5. Philosophy of religion
6. Moral philosophy

1. Hobbes. *Thomas Hobbes* (1588-1679), who is frequently called the father of modern analytic philosophy, was a son of the vicar of Westport near Malmesbury, not far from the source of the Thames. As a tutor in the service of the Cavendish and Clinton families he was able to read widely and to meet influential thinkers in Britain and on the Continent of Europe. He was concerned about the dangers of democracy, and about the 'slaughter, solitude' and general shortages which arise from civil war. He was fascinated by the new natural philosophy (of Galileo and others) and the concepts of the new science of motion, and resolved to apply these scientific conceptual schemes to explain the nature and cause of sensation and to explain man's role as citizen in civil society at large. He wrote *The Elements of Law* (1640), *De cive* (1642), *Human Nature* (1650), *De Corpore Politico* (1650), *Leviathan* (1651), *Questions Concerning Liberty, Necessity and Chance* (1656) and *Behemoth* (1668).

According to Hobbes, the knowledge of the ordinary man in the street is a knowledge gleaned from experience. It is not scientific knowledge. Experience is nothing but 'remembrance of what antecedents have been followed by what consequents'. Scientific knowledge, such as that of Galileo or Harvey, is the product of reason. It is reason which gives knowledge of general, eternal and immutable truth. The paradigm of scientific knowledge is geometry.

Geometers start with the definitions of terms or names. Definition is the way to scientific 'knowledge of all the consequences of names appertaining to the subject in hand'. Reason makes combinations of different statements, whose terms have meanings fixed by convention or decision, and then reckons 'the consequences of (these) general names agreed upon for the marking and signifying of our thoughts'. Names are signs of our past and present assembled cognitions concerning 'things' which do or do not exist. We have decided names for such 'things' as a house, the future, the possible, and nothing. Names of this kind can be used in a universal way to denote the

members of a class of things. The term 'universal' is predicated of the
name alone; it is not predicated of any individual and singular thing
designated by the name. The name (e.g. a 'house') signifies directly a
mental representation, a 'conception', or 'fiction', that is, a phantasm
or image. The name has an indirect relation to the reality (e.g. the
actual house) inasmuch as the mental representation, the image, is
itself caused by the reality or body present to the senses.

Science commences then with the explications, or definitions, of
the meaning of names of this kind, and through universal names it is
able to 'conclude universally'. However, it is dealing with names, and
it has no guarantee that its scientific propositions are really applicable
to reality. Its theories are hypothetical and probable. Its reasoning is a
reasoning about abstract 'universals', namely, classes of names such
as 'body', 'motion', 'likeness', 'quantity', 'straightness', joined
together in propositions. These classes of names are conceptions or
fictions which can be explained causally in terms of motions that take
place in the head and persist even after the stimulation of sense organs
by external bodies.

For Hobbes all modes of mental activity are motions that take place
in the body, or more precisely in the head, and for this reason all
modes of mental activity are fundamentally the same. Bodies in
motion outside our own bodies cause motions to occur within us. Our
'perceptions' of external bodies are 'phantasms' which represent the
different ways we experience our internal motions and reactions to
these external bodies. These perceptions linger on, like ocean waves,
as decaying sensations retained within by 'imagination' and
'memory'. Thinking is simply a variation of sensation; motions that
succeeded one another 'in sense' continue to cohere together 'after
sense'. In this way thought can be explained in terms of sensation and
memory. Human thinking is superior to animal thinking in this, that
men are able to form names to mark their sensations and, thus, recall
their sensations. Philosophy, or scientific knowledge, then becomes
possible when man combines words and sentences in speech. The
relation seen to exist between words is based on the relation seen to
exist between the objective motions represented by the words.
Particular experiences lead to formulation of general terms. These
terms do not point to general realities, because there are no such
realities; there are only particular realities. But the terms and
propositions, which are based on particular experiences, do enable
the scientist to 'conclude universally'.

Hobbes' emphasis is on the deductive mathematical method of
ratiocination but not to the extent of excluding the inductive method

from natural philosophy. He recognizes that there are empirical sense-data which form the remote source of the philosophy of man, society and nature. In his *Physics or the Phenomena of Nature*, for example, Hobbes commences with sensible phenomena and he then searches out their possible causes. This approach differs significantly from the wholly deductive approach of the Continental rationalists.

The philosophy of Hobbes is one which combines together the main tenets of nominalism, empiricism and mechanism. He was obsessed, he tells us in his verse autobiography (1672), by the omnipresence of motion. Geometry is the science of simple motions. Mechanics explains the effects of the motions of one body on another. Mental activities are motions in our bodies. The object of thought is bodies in motion. Philosophy concerns itself with the causes and characteristics of bodies in motion: physical bodies, the human body, and the body politic. All causation consists in motion. 'There can be no cause of motion except in a body contiguous and moved.'

Hobbes asserted that causality as we experience it (e.g. if fire warms my hand) is to be explained in terms of the sum of all the conditions required in both agent and patient for the existence of that thing. Within the total or 'entire cause', he distinguished between the '*efficient* cause', which is the sum of all the conditions required in the agent, and the '*material* cause', which is the sum of all the conditions required in the patient, for the production of an effect. If the entire efficient cause is present to the 'patient', the effect follows necessarily from the cause. All such causes are necessary causes. They operate necessarily and mechanically. Philosophy is concerned with necessary causality. It is concerned with the laws of dynamics operating necessarily and mechanically. (This tenet and viewpoint is that of mechanistic determinism.)

Hobbes then applied these same principles of his study of the human body and the body politic. The 'natural' state of man is that of atomic individualism. Individualism is rooted in the natural human passions. The passions are 'motions about the heart' which accompany the 'motions about the head' that arise when external objects affect the sense organs. Several of these different 'motions about the heart', or passions, in different individual bodies, lead naturally to competition, mistrust and the disposition towards a state of war between individuals. In the natural state of war, civilization, peace, rational self-preservation and liberty suffer. Force and fraud become the two cardinal virtues in the state of war. 'Where there is no common power, there is no law, where no law, no injustice.' All suffer.

There are some 'motions about the heart', however, which incline men to seek for peace. Each human body naturally fears being murdered; and each desires 'commodious' living. Rational self-preservation then suggests certain natural 'laws' for peace, namely, certain dictates of enlightened egoistic prudence which lead men to form commonwealths or states. In this regard, the fundamental law of nature is 'to endeavour peace'. The second law is that each divest himself of the liberty to hinder another's right to peace. To achieve this in practice each and all enter a covenant of mutual trust in which each trusts the other 'to perform his part at some determinate time thereafter'. The third law is 'that men perform their covenant made'; not to do so is 'injustice'.

The transition to organized society from the condition of atomic individualism, therefore, is achieved through social covenant. Covenant, when backed by effective force, guarantees individual liberty. Liberty is simply the absence of external hindrance to motion. The process of entering into covenant 'is as if every man should say to every man, I authorize and give up my right of governing myself, to this man, or to this (sovereign) assembly of men, on this condition that thou give up thy right to him, and authorize all his actions in like manner'. Covenants, to be effective, must be backed up by 'the sword'. There must therefore be a government, or common power, backed by armed force and able to punish; and so there arises the 'generation of the great Leviathan...that mortal god to which we owe our peace and defence'. A new artificial person is generated. It is called the Commonwealth or the Sovereign. It has power which is absolute. It may be an individual or it may be an assembly. It may be generated either 'by institution' (by agreement) or 'by acquisition' (by force). It is not a party in the making of the covenant; and so 'there can happen no breach of covenant on the part of the sovereign'. Its power is sovereign power, unlimited and inalienable. In a nation of Christians, it is the Christian sovereign who is the fount, under God, of all jurisdiction and authority. He alone is the final judge of all Christian matters and of all interpretations of Scripture. This is the only effective means of overcoming political and religious dissensions. The Church is subordinated to the sovereign State (this is the theory known as Erastianism). It is only if and when the sovereign loses effective power that the subjects are absolved from obedience; and then a new sovereign can be set up.

Hobbes played a major role in the gradual establishment of political science as an independent 'naturalistic' science. He formulated a system of political philosophy in which the dynamics of power plays the fundamental role. The State is necessary because of the warring passions of man, he says. Absolute power and authority is necessary not for the sake of exalting the sovereign but to promote security and peace among passion-driven individuals. The State is the means for uniting warring individualists. Unity, not popular consent, is the basis of government. Security, peace and strength lie in conformity to the sovereign will. Sovereign power is a demand of human nature. Legal authority is grounded not on tradition but on axioms which express the exigencies of human nature. In this way Hobbes founded his political system of philosophy on his naturalistic interpretation of the needs of human nature. Machiavelli, by contrast, had concerned himself only with the practical methods and techniques of attaining and preserving power. The political theory of Hobbes is a political system of philosophy (even though it is inadequate in many respects). In his own century it pleased neither the Stuart royalists nor the Puritan parliamentarians of the English Civil War. No Hobbist school of mechanistic materialism emerged. Yet the works of Hobbes have never ceased to be studied down to modern times. He was read with sympathy by the utilitarians and many others. Karl Marx spoke of Hobbes as 'the father of us all'. His influence on the history of modern empiricist philosophy should not be underestimated.

2. Locke. *John Locke* (1632-1704) was born at Wrington, near Bristol. His father was a West Country lawyer and a Puritan who fought with the parliamentarians. Locke studied at Oxford, where he found a decadent form of Scholasticism being taught. He interested himself in chemistry, physics and medicine. Subsequently he taught for some years at the university before entering the service of the Earl of Shaftesbury. He was employed at the Board of Trade and became involved in public diplomatic affairs in France and Holland. Locke's principal work is his *Essay concerning Human Understanding*, first published in 1690. He wrote *Two Treatises of Civil Government* (1690), a *Letter on Toleration* (1689) and other material. He died at Oates in Essex in October 1704.

Locke tells us that in discussions with friends at Oxford on 'the *principles* of morality and revealed religion' he concluded that there could be no resolution of the 'doubts which perplexed us' until philosophers tried 'to examine our own *abilities*, and (tried to) see what *objects* our understandings were or were not fitted to deal with'. Locke himself became the first philosopher to devote his main philosophical work to an inquiry into 'the origin, certainty and extent of human knowledge'.

In the first book of the *Essay* Locke deals with the theory of innate ideas as proposed by Lord Herbert of Cherbury (see below), Ralph Cudworth (d. 1688) and others. 'It is an established opinion among some men', he says, 'that there are in the understanding certain innate principles...stamped upon the mind of man, which the soul receives in its very first beginning, and brings into the world with it.' All agree, he points out, that the mind is capable of understanding and assenting firmly to basic mathematical propositions and fundamental principles such as 'what is, is'. These propositions are not found in the thoughts of children. Why then call them 'implicitly innate'? They are not 'stamped' on the mind of babies. They are grasped and assented to only as the mind matures. The theory of innatism is superfluous. The origin of ideas can be explained in a much more simple and empirical way.

The objects that our understandings are fitted to deal with are ideas. Knowledge is restricted to ideas. Ideas arise from experience, either external, through sensation, or internal, through reflection on the mind's operations or activities of perceiving, doubting, willing, believing and so forth. Experience, external or internal, is the fountain of all ideas. The 'empiricist principle', namely, that experience alone is the one and only source of all knowledge, was subsequently adopted as the fundamental 'truth' or assumption of classical British empiricists and modern neo-positivists. They quoted this principle as a justification of their rejection of metaphysics as a knowledge that exceeds experience. They regarded Locke as the real founder of empiricism in Britain.

Locke was not the originator of the theory that our ideas originate in experience. Aristotle, Aquinas and others had held this view previously, but they understood that sensation and sense-knowledge alone are unable to explain universal concepts, judgements, universal propositions and other forms of human knowledge. Thus, for example, the proposition 'All empirical knowledge is true' and the 'principle' that 'experience alone guarantees true knowledge' cannot be established by or deduced from experience alone. Experience, as even Kant himself saw, is possible only on the presupposition of non-experienceable conditions and functions of the human mind. Experience is itself conditioned by foundational factors that exceed experience; and, for this reason, in all forms of human knowing, mere experience is always surpassed. The human knowledge of the *animal* rational animal is always and already the more-than-empirical, human knowledge of the *rational* rational animal.

After having criticized the theory of innate ideas, Locke then propounded the more positive aspect of his investigation. Knowledge is restricted to 'ideas' generated by objects we experience. 'Ideas or perceptions in our minds' represent to us the physical objects which cause these ideas or perceptions. 'Whatsoever the mind perceives in itself or is the immediate object of perception, thought or understanding, that I call idea.' Some ideas are passively received through the external senses or through simple reflection on simple experiences; these are *simple* ideas. Other ideas are composite combinations (e.g. a congregation, the universe) of simple ideas; these are *complex* ideas. Complex ideas may be ideas of simple modes such as the ideas of five, space, succession, duration, time and infinity. The idea of infinity, for example, can be explained empirically as the idea of the confused, incomprehensible, inexhaustible remainder of endless addable numbers. (Thus, it is not at all an 'innate' idea.) Some ideas are ideas of mixed modes such as the ideas of gratitude, beauty, obligation, law and morality. Ideas of this kind come to us, generally, through our having the meaning of these names explained to us. In these different ways all ideas can be explained empirically.

Objects, says Locke, have within themselves certain objective 'primary qualities' such as solidity, extension, figure, motion or rest, and number, which are capable of producing 'sensations or perceptions', that is, 'ideas', in our minds. These primary qualities 'really do exist in the bodies themselves'. Roundness and hardness, for example, really do exist in a hard, round object. But objects also have virtual or 'secondary' qualities or powers such as odours, tastes, colours and sounds, which produce ideas or perceptions in our minds even though the qualities have no exact counterpart in the object. They do not belong to or constitute bodies, except as powers to produce these perceptions in us. They are 'virtual' powers of the object but not real 'primary' qualities of the object itself. In this way Locke sought to distinguish between sensible appearance and objective reality. He failed to see that this distinction is groundless if one also maintains that it is only the 'idea' itself that is 'the immediate object of thought'. There can be no valid distinction of this kind in a representative theory of perception; mental representations are not something more than mental representations.

Our ideas of primary qualities of movement, solidity and so forth obviously presuppose that there must be a something, a 'substance', which is solid and is moving. We do not experience 'substance' itself but we do experience the primary qualities or 'accidents' that cluster together in groups around a 'supposed but unknown' support or substratum which is generally called the substance. The 'idea' of substance lies beyond experience. It is obtained by abstraction, that is, by a separating of some 'ideas' from other 'ideas' that accompany them; or rather, it is a 'supposition' of we 'know not what' as a support of qualities that appear to clump together around an invisible substratum. It is not perceived but it is inferred. Here, as in several other instances, Locke seems to find it necessary to depart from his own empiricist premises.

The real essence of any object, namely, the substratum, can never be known; it can never be 'abstracted' or separated from the particular circumstances of time and place, according to Locke. However, the mind does observe likenesses between the qualities of similar objects, such as similar pieces of silver, and it can then abstract or separate these observable common characteristics in 'general ideas' which are capable of representing more individuals than one. Universality and generality are attributes of these general ideas and of the general terms which signify the general ideas. The complex idea of these common characteristics is the nominal essence. It is this nominal essence, then, and not the real essence (the substratum) which is abstracted.

Our ideas of perceptions do not extend beyond the actual experience which we have had. All ideas come from experience, that is, from sensation and from reflection on sensations or experiences. 'We can have knowledge no further than we can have ideas', Locke says. Knowledge, then, is nothing more than 'the perception of the connexion of the agreement or disagreement and repugnancy of any of our ideas'. But there are three modes of perception or knowledge, namely, intuitive perception, demonstrative perception and sensitive perception. Each of these leads to different degrees of knowledge or representation of objective reality. Intuitive knowledge is the clearest and most certain; we know from intuition, for example, that we exist, and that black is not white, and that a circle is not a triangle. Demonstrative knowledge arises from a disclosure of the mediate deductive processes by which a conclusion can be inferred; we can know, for example, by reasoning, that God exists. Sensitive perception or knowledge merely 'passes under the name of knowledge'; it simply gives us a transient experience of particular sensed qualities clustering together around unperceived 'substances' (objects). Perceptions or 'ideas' express only actual experiences; and universal perceptions or 'ideas' express only 'connexions' between different perceptions or ideas.

If it is true, as Locke says, that we can have no knowledge further than we have perceptions (ideas), what value can be attached to *history* and to the *natural sciences?* The natural sciences and historical propositions, he asserts, attain no more than varying degrees of probability. The mind has a faculty or ability for formulating probable opinions or judgements on things that are not self evident. We judge a proposition to be probably true if it conforms with our observation and experience, or again, if it conforms with the testimony of others. The propositions of history and the natural sciences are of this kind. They are based on experience, and experience simply makes us aware of qualities that are sensed as they are at the time that we are experiencing them. This shows us how limited our knowledge is and how uncertain it is in many areas.

In the third and fourth book of the *Essay*, Locke points out that all our *moral* ideas, like all other ideas, derive from and terminate in simple perceptions (ideas). *Moral* ideas arise on the level of demonstrative perception. Morality, in fact, can really have the precision of mathematics, he says. Things are good or evil only in reference to pleasure or pain. 'That we call good which is apt to cause or increase pleasure, or diminish pain in us... .' This is the objective basis of morality. Moral perception is the perception of good and evil in things pleasant or painful in human behaviour. We discover the rules or laws pertaining to moral good and evil by the light of nature, namely, by our reason. Moral good and evil is 'the conformity or non-conformity of our voluntary actions to some law' which is backed by sanctions. Locke mentions three kinds of laws: the law of (public) opinion or reputation, civil law and divine law. The divine law, promulgated by reason and revelation, is the ultimate criterion of rectitude in human behaviour.

The moral theory of Locke is sketchy and undeveloped. It intermingles partial elements of medieval moral theories, authoritarianism, hedonism and utilitarianism. He did not elaborate his various dicta in Books 2, 3 and 4 of the *Essay* into a unified system of ethics.

Locke expressed his political philosophy in the *Two Treatises of Civil Government* which were published in 1690, not long after the 'glorious revolution' of 1688. These two treatises were destined to become important documents in the subsequent history of liberal thought.

In the first *Treatise*, Locke argued against the view that kings derive their right to rule from divine authority. Sir Robert Filmer had defended this view in his *Patriarcha* (1680). It implied that all men are born in a state of natural subjection to a king who rules by divine right. Having ridiculed and demolished Filmer's thesis, Locke then turned, in *Of Civil Government: The Second Treatise*, to investigate the actual basis of government and the actual source of political power.

Men existed in 'the state of nature' before the advent of government-ruled States, according to Locke. In the state of nature, all men were naturally free and equal; no man was naturally sovereign over other men. In this state, men lived together according to reason, without a common superior, other than God. Reason revealed to men the natural moral law as a universally obligatory moral law binding in conscience. Natural moral law imparts to all men natural rights and correlative duties independently of any government or civil legislation. Reason reveals that no one ought to harm another in his life, health, liberty or possessions. It reveals that each human being, as a creature of God, possesses an intrinsic value. The state of war is a violation of the natural value of the person.

Among the natural rights of man, Locke laid special emphasis on the right to private property. It is a natural right, preceding civil law, that a man is entitled to enjoy the products of his labour as his means of support and well-being. And since there is a natural duty imposed on every father to provide for his offspring there is a corresponding right of inheritance on the part of the offspring.

In order to preserve their property in general, that is, their 'lives, liberty and estates', and to remedy a situation in which every man is his own judge, men enter into a social contract which creates civil and political society. Civil society is thereby empowered to judge men and to defend the natural rights of men. It is desirable that each civil society have a set of written laws and a panel of independent judges to decide disputes and to pass sentence concerning the correct punishment for crime.

Political society must rest on the consent of men. This consent is normally that 'tacit consent' of people who accept the rule of the majority and the privileges of common citizenship. In this light, absolute monarchy is 'no form of civil government at all'. Men give up their liberty, not to enter a state of servitude, but rather, to safeguard their inalienable rights.

Supreme sovereign power is placed in the hands of the members of the legislature as representatives of the majority of the people. Those who administer or execute the law are themselves 'under the law' of the legislature. The supreme power of the legislature is not absolute power. It is a fiduciary power, given in trusteeship, and so, held as a trust, on behalf of the union of persons, the citizens, who constitute civil society. The legislature, like the executive and the judiciary, can be removed or altered if it acts contrary to the trust reposed in it.

Thus if any government endangers the security and rights of the citizens, then that government is in a state of rebellion against the people. It has violated the terms of the social contract from which its trusteeship derives. 'The people shall judge'; and the people have the right to dissolve it. The dissolution is not a dissolution of society. It is simply the dissolving of one particular government so that a new government can be established.

Locke's political theories are full of glaring inadequacies; and yet the broad sweep of these same theories prepared the ground for the popular and democratic governments of the eighteenth and nineteenth centuries. His theory that the state of nature, which preceded the original social compact, was a state of perfect freedom and equality is a theory which is artificial, unhistorical and unreal. It is the theory of a rationalist and liberalist who is attempting to justify the imposition of limitations upon the presupposed unlimited freedom of action of the naturally free individual. However, Locke's general political theory obtained widespread acceptance in his own day. His writings inspired many of the leading minds in Britain, France, America, and to a lesser extent in Germany. Different aspects of his thought were developed by Berkeley, Hume, Voltaire, Montesquieu, the Encyclopedists, Bolingbroke, Jonathan Edwards, Hamilton, Jefferson, Condillac and others. His *Essay* is the source of many of the empirical theories, ideas, methods and problems which have prevailed in British and American 'philosophy of mind' ever since its first publication in 1690.

3. Philosophy of science. *Robert Boyle* (1627-91), who is sometimes called 'the father of chemistry', was born in Lismore Castle in Ireland. In 1654 he built a laboratory in Oxford where he and his research assistants conducted innumerable experiments on the elasticity of air, the conveyance of sound, the expansion of ice, the testing of alkalinity and other similar experiments. They presented their findings in brief scientific papers or 'essays', of the modern type, rather than in general treatises. As a scientific investigator, Boyle implemented in practice the principles that Francis Bacon advocated in the *Novum Organon* (1620). Boyle's success and fame as a physicist, chemist and natural philosopher influenced the thought of other British thinkers, such as John Locke, in calling constantly renewed attention to the latest findings of the empirical, experimental sciences. Boyle emphasized the fruitlessness of *a priori* philosophical reasoning about issues that could be settled only by experiment. He spoke of the alchemical theories of Paracelsus and van Helmont as 'book philosophy'. He himself actually suggested certain physical and chemical theories, such as the corpuscular theory of matter and the kinetic theory of gases. He regarded it as the scientist's task to develop theories that are as clear, simple, and comprehensive as possible, and to subject these theories or hypotheses at once to experimental tests. Theories of this kind ought never to be taken as final and definitive, he said. They should be thought of as 'the best we have but (always) capable of improvement' (*Tracts* [1661]).

The revolutionary thinking of Renaissance physical theory reached its apex in the achievements of *Sir Isaac Newton* (1642-1727). He was born at Woolsthorpe in Lincolnshire; and here, after he had graduated from Cambridge, he formulated the basic features of his theories of 'fluxions' (calculus), motion and gravitation, and the composition of light. His thought dominated the sciences of astronomy, mechanics, mathematics and optics for two centuries. Newton was an outstanding genius, a scientist and mathematician who was idolized in his own age. Alexander Pope, the poet, wrote of him: 'Nature and Nature's Laws lay hid in night; God said, "'Let Newton be," and all was light'.

Newton presented a mechanical interpretation of the world which gave a powerful impetus to the development of the empirical sciences. Many scientists and philosophers accepted Newton's law and theory of universal gravitation as having established the fact that the mechanical laws which hold good on the surface of the earth are valid also throughout the universe.

For Newton, the philosophy of nature studies the 'forces of nature'. It studies the descriptive mechanical laws or principles which govern changes in moving bodies. It starts with empirical observation. It uses mathematics as its principal tool. It aims to take an inductive discovery of mechanical laws and then to give a deductive explanation of all the associated phenomena in the light of these newly discovered laws. These deductions from the inductive discoveries must be subjected to carefully controlled tests with a view to their experimental verification.

Leibniz and other critics maintained that Newton's theories, such as the theory of gravitation, offered no ultimate explanations for the forces of nature which were being investigated. Newton replied *Hypotheses non fingo* ('I feign no hypotheses'). In as far as facts can be accounted for by many different hypotheses, he said, he chose to decline all hypotheses. He seems to have meant that he rejected all unverifiable speculations. He preferred to rely only on what was proved by the facts. In actual practice, however, Newton frequently advanced tentative 'hypotheses' in connection with his own patient, cautious experimental work, as for example in his *Opticks* (1704). He made several suppositions as starting points for reasoning and for further investigation without assuming these suppositions as true. His corpuscular view of light, for example, led to his later view that light has wave properties as well as corpuscular properties. 'Facts' and 'laws' seemed to point to tentative suppositions which focused on specific phenomena which in turn demanded further experimental testing. This approach was accepted by his followers and admirers as implying that in natural philosophy the ultimate criterion is experimental verification, and the ultimate explanation is the mechanical explanation.

4. The Cambridge Platonists. British philosophy in the seventeenth century was predominantly empiricist, utilitarian and naturalistic in character. But it was not universally so. There was another philosophical tradition, less influential, but nonetheless actively present in British thought. This tradition is represented by Lord Herbert of Cherbury, the Cambridge Platonists, Richard Cumberland and others.

Lord Herbert of Cherbury (1583-1648) held that every person has a number of innate 'common notions' or truths implanted in the mind by God and apprehended by 'natural instinct'. There are notions concerning natural religion, morality and law, for example, about which in a general sense all people agree. These common notions give certainty; history and tradition provide only probability. As we have seen, John Locke in his *Essay* attacked Herbert's theory of innate ideas.

The Cambridge Platonists (or 'latitudinarians') were a group of seventeenth-century Anglican moralists, philosophers and clergymen who made 'a public profession of Platonism in the University of Cambridge' (P. Sterry). S. T. Coleridge pointed out that since they read Plato through the eyes of the (Florentine) Neo-Platonists they should be renamed the 'Cambridge Plotinists'. The leading members of this group, Benjamin Whichcote, John Smith, Ralph Cudworth, Nathanael Culverwel and Peter Sterry, were educated at Emmanuel College, Cambridge, which was the intellectual centre of the Puritan and Calvinist branch of the Church of England. Henry More, another leading member, was educated at Christ's College, Cambridge, where there were three factions — the High Church party, the Calvinistic Puritans and the (moderate) Medians. These and other members of the group were influenced by Whichcote's Sunday lectures at Holy

Trinity Church. They shared a common moral and religious attitude of hostility to 'enthusiasm' and fanaticism, admiration for Plato, and confidence in reason. They defended a spiritualist interpretation of the universe as a foundation for the Christian moral life.

Whichcote maintained, against dogmatic Calvinists, that 'to go against Reason is to go against God; it is the self same thing.... Reason is the Divine Governor of Man's Life; it is the very Voice of God.' The world of Platonic thought, with its emphasis on eternal and immutable goodness, offers to the human spirit 'tranquillity of soul, contempt for worldliness, love of truth, concern for rectitude and justice'.

Whichcote criticized Bacon for his view that religion was a matter of faith alone, not reason. Cudworth and More criticized both Hobbes and the Calvinists for their views that morality depended either on the will of the sovereign or on the will of God. They also criticized Descartes' mechanism and the Cartesian divorce of the spiritual from the material world. They advocated a conversion of the mind to the contemplation of cosmic reality in its relation to divine reality. Henry More held that cosmic space is a divine attribute; it is God's sensorium.

Richard Cumberland (1631-1718), a moral philosopher and Anglican Bishop of Peterborough, wrote De Legibus Naturae (1672) as a philosophical refutation of the work of Thomas Hobbes. In this work he attempted to supplement the political and social thought of Grotius by demonstrating that natural laws are founded on 'the nature of things'and not on the commands of sovereign rulers. The natural laws of morality are based on Nature itself. They are eternal and immutable. If one seeks evidence for this, then, the evidence is 'the evidence of sense and experience'. Benevolence is natural to mankind and to brute animals alike, he said. Human instincts lead men to co-operate with their fellow men in society. The 'natural impetus of man' is towards securing the common good; it is not a war of all against all, as Hobbes suggested. 'The common good is the supreme law.' Man is by nature a social being; he secures his own good by the promotion of the good of the whole to which he belongs. This doctrine anticipates the views of nineteenth-century utilitarianism.

5. Philosophy of religion

Isaac Newton was a religious believer who was convinced that the order of the cosmos provides evidence for the existence of God. He asserted that it is God who keeps the stars from collapsing into one mass under the influence of gravitation, and that it is God who maintains the stability of the solar system in spite of the perturbations of planetary motions by other planets. He was impressed by Henry More's argument that space is a divine attribute and that it is the divine sensorium. Newton held that absolute space and absolute duration (time) are manifestations of the divine properties of omnipresence and eternity.

Samuel Clarke (1675-1729), an Anglican clergyman, was a fervent admirer of Newton who had anticipated Newton in declaring that infinite space and duration are the divine properties of omnipresence and eternity. In 1704 and 1705 he delivered two sets of Boyle lectures at St Paul's in London on the Being and Attributes of God. In the first of these lectures he presented a chain of eight propositions connected together in one argument pertaining to the existence and attributes of the divine being. Each proposition was carefully propounded and explained. The first three pertain to the existence of God. 'It is absolutely and undeniably certain that something has existed from all eternity.' Existing things cannot come from nothing. 'There has existed from eternity some one, unchangeable and independent being.' An endless succession of dependent beings could be broken off. 'That unchangeable and independent being, which has existed from eternity without any external cause of its existence, must be self-existent, that is necessarily existent.' The idea of a self-existent, necessary being is the 'idea of a being the supposition of whose non-existence is an express contradiction'. Clarke then went on to establish, in the succeeding propositions, that this Being is infinite, omnipresent, intelligent, free, omnipotent, wise, good and just.

Clarke made a sharp distinction between his own 'reasonable' approach to the philosophy of religion and that of the deists. These deists accepted the Creator God of the natural (traditional) religions while rejecting the idea of any supernatural revelation of divine mysteries. They were rationalists who said they believed in the First Cause of created Nature, 'without the reception of any religion' (Dr Johnson). In his *History of England,* Hume named James Harrington, Algernon Sidney and Sir John Wildman as leaders of deist thought in the seventeenth century. Deism had its roots, however, in a series of earlier movements, such as Unitarianism, anti-Trinitarianism, Erastianism, Arminianism, Socinianism, secularism and anti-clericalism in the sixteenth century.

Lord Herbert of Cherbury received the title of 'the father of English deism', though he never explicitly called himself a deist. He ridiculed Bible-worship, and treated Scripture as ordinary history. His disciple Charles Blount (1654-93) wrote a *Summary Account of the*

Deist's Religion which was published after his death by suicide in 1693. In 1696, *John Toland* (1670-1722) produced his *Christianity not Mysterious: Or, a treatise Shewing That there is nothing in the Gospel Contrary to Reason, Nor above it: And that no Christian Doctrine can be properly call'd a Mystery*. Toland professed himself to be a freethinker, deist, materialist and pantheist. Anthony Collins (1676-1729) published a *Discourse of Free-Thinking* in 1713. Matthew Tindall (1657-1733), who called himself a 'Christian deist' and a rationalist, published his *Christianity as Old as the Creation: Or, The Gospel A Republication of the Religion of Nature* in 1730. This work became known as 'The Deists' Bible'. It castigated priestcraft and repudiated tradition, and asserted that men of status and education should follow only Right Reason. Reason alone is the judge of truth in religion, as elsewhere. This same attitude is present also in the writings of William Wollaston, Thomas Chubb, Henry St John, Viscount Bolingbroke, Peter Annet, Voltaire, Diderot, Benjamin Franklin and other writers of the seventeenth and eighteenth centuries.

William Law (1686-1761), who was a forerunner of John Wesley, argued, in his book *The Case of Reason* (1731), that in the areas of morality and religion, reason is of minor significance when compared to the major role played by historical evidence and holy and devout faith. Bishop Joseph Butler (1692-1752), in the *Analogy of Religion*, pointed out that the deistical objections raised against revealed religion were applicable similarly to natural religion. In religious matters, human difficulties do not constitute disproof. Our knowledge of religious matters, like our knowledge of nature, is probable knowledge. In matters of vital concern we act wisely when we act according to the balance of probability. This applies to religious affairs just as much as it applies to temporal affairs. One does not wait until all difficulties are cleared up.

Henry Dodwell, in his *Christianity Not Founded on Argument* (1742), asserted that all rationalistic approaches to religion merely succeed in spreading infidelity. The religious man believes because he wishes to believe. John Wesley (1703-91) attacked rationalism through his doctrine of enthusiastic evangelism and emotional conversion of soul. David Hume (1711-76) attacked deism and rationalism by his sceptical attack on human intelligence itself. In Britain the Age of Reason came to an end with the advent of Wesley and Hume. Emotionalism, fideism and anti-rationalism triumphed.

6. Moral philosophy. The moral philosophy, or ethics, of Thomas Hobbes derived from his basic vision of man as a natural machine which is essentially egoistic. The self-assertive 'concupiscible part' of man seeks self-advancement, power, gain and glory; the 'rational part' counsels man to shun anarchy, which leads to death in poverty, and to seek peace through covenant. The words 'good' and 'evil' merely name the objects of our desires and aversions. Moral and civil prudence counsel the acceptance of rules that limit the pursuit of goods when it dangerously affects the similar pursuits of our rivals.

The Cambridge Platonists insisted that man's nature is essentially social and not purely egoistic. By way of reaction to Hobbes they restricted the importance of the will and the emotions, and propounded instead a doctrine of ethical rationalism; it is *knowledge* of the good that is normative for the moral conduct of man. Nathanael Culverwel, for example, in his *Light of Nature* (1652) emphasized the accessibility of moral truth to the natural light of reason. The roles of the will and the emotions were almost ignored.

One group of British moralists in the late seventeenth and eighteenth centuries insisted on man's possession of a distinct moral sense. This group tended to see ethics as a separate and distinct subject of study. The main proponents were Shaftesbury and Hutcheson.

Anthony Ashley (1671-1713), Earl of Shaftesbury, admired the Greek ideal of balance and harmony. He took an optimistic and benevolent view of human nature. All men possess a moral sense, a faculty analogous to the aesthetic sense. In the moral man, that is, the man of refinement, integrity and character, the self-regarding impulses and the altruistic impulses or benevolent instincts are balanced and harmonized. Individual happiness and fulfilment are best achieved by the establishment of a harmonious balance between private and social impulses. This approach to moral philosophy was expounded and developed in a more systematic form by Francis Hutcheson (1694-1746) in his *System of Moral Philosophy*, which was completed in 1737. The moral sense, he said, is a natural, inborn sense of moral beauty. It is the perception of pleasure in morally beautiful actions. The primary objects of this moral sense are the benevolent or 'kind affections', desiring universal happiness, that is, 'the greatest happiness of the greatest number'. But this moral sense is also a rational moral faculty because it passes rational judgements about the consequences of actions. The theory was remembered in the history of moral philosophy, however, as the 'moral sense theory', and as one of the harbingers of utilitarianism.

Bishop Joseph Butler pointed out that self-love and benevolence are merely two affections among the many affections of man, and furthermore that man is something more than a mere bundle of affections. Man possesses a superior faculty of reflection, or conscience, which passes judgement on the affections and on the actions which flow from them. Conscience pronounces 'some actions to be in themselves just, right, good; others to be in themselves evil, wrong, unjust'. It is judgement of this kind which distinguishes man from the beasts; it makes man a moral agent. Butler's moral philosophy is Aristotelian for the main part, though he also quotes the *Discourses* of Epictetus with reference to his doctrine of conscience.

The ethical theory of Cumberland, Hutcheson and others, that universal benevolence can produce happiness, was developed further by Hartley, Tucker and Paley.

David Hartley (1709-57), an association psychologist and moral philosopher, maintained that there are certain higher and more valuable classes of pleasure and pain from which we derive our rule of life. Sympathy arises from the pleasures and pains of our fellow creatures; theopathy arises from affections excited by our contemplation of the Deity; and the moral sense arises from our awareness of moral beauty and deformity. These higher pleasures constitute the worthiest object of human pursuit that man can find.

Abraham Tucker (1705-74) and William Paley (1743-1805) taught that men are so constructed that they always pursue their own satisfaction. Nevertheless it is true that universal benevolence is to our long-term, as opposed to our short-term, self-interest. It is in the long run that we will secure our happiness if we follow the fundamental moral rule of benevolence here and now. We are all depositors into a bank of happiness from which we all draw dividends. Benevolence rebounds in universal personal gain. The promotion of the common good is the best means for the promotion of long-lasting individual happiness.

This development of ethical theory along the lines of utilitarian benevolence influenced the thought of Hume, Bentham, Grote, Mill, Sidgwick and other moralists in the nineteenth century. The interest in moral philosophy and ethical problems has remained one of the characteristic features of British thought down to our own times.

20 Empiricism in Britain (II): the eighteenth century

1. Berkeley   2. Hume   3. Reactions to Hume

1. Berkeley. *George Berkeley* (1685-1753), an Irishman of English ancestry, studied at Trinity College, Dublin, before he was ordained to the priesthood in the (Episcopal) Church of Ireland. In 1707, when he became a Fellow of the college, he started to keep a personal record of his reflections on his reading of Locke, Newton, Malebranche and other writers. These early *Philosophical Commentaries* contain the main outlines of his immaterialist, empiricist and phenomenalist metaphysics. Berkeley presented his thought in further detail in his published works, the *Essay towards a New Theory of Vision* (1709), *A Treatise Concerning the Principles of Human Knowledge* (1710), *Three Dialogues between Hylas and Philonous* (1731) and *Siris* (1744). In 1728, he travelled to America to prepare a project for establishing a college in Bermuda, but since the promised Government funds were not forthcoming he returned home in 1731. In 1734 he was made Bishop of Cloyne, Ireland. He retired in poor health in 1752, and died at Oxford a year later.

Berkeley was convinced that those natural philosophers or scientists who were materialists and religious sceptics had been lured into a world of unreal abstractions because they did not seriously reflect on the meaning of the words they were using. They used words such as 'matter', 'mass', 'bodies', 'force', 'gravity', 'energy' and so forth, as if these names denoted existing corporeal substances. A host of insoluble problems had arisen in physics, mathematics, philosophy, theology and in almost every field of study where thinkers had tended to hypostatize their own abstractions. In his *Philosophical Commentaries* (Note 491), Berkeley asserted 'This sprang from their not knowing what existence was and wherein it consisted. This is the source of all their folly. 'Tis on the discovering of the nature and meaning and import of Existence that I chiefly insist.' The failure to examine the meaning of the word 'is' is the most crucial mistake of all mistakes.

Berkeley asserted that when we perceive that something 'is' brown, or 'is' cold, or 'is' a table, the word 'is' means 'is perceived' or 'is perceivable' as brown, or cold, or as a table. The word is merely describing an experience; it is not affirming the existence of an occult corporeal substance or object. In this context, the verb 'is', or 'to be', means 'is perceived' or 'is perceivable'. *'Esse est percipi vel percipere.'* To say that an orange is soft and round and sweet and yellow is to say that it is being perceived as such or that it is perceivable as such by anyone who cares to test it by using his own senses. Here the word 'is' does not mean that a corporeal substance 'exists' yellow or 'exists' round and sweet; it simply means that the orange 'is being perceived' as soft and round, or 'is capable of being perceived' as such by any interested perceiver. Statements of this kind, then, are statements about perceptions; they are not statements about 'matter', or about occult 'substances'. It is belief in such occult material substances that promotes atheism.

Berkeley admired the empirical aspect of Locke's philosophy, but he found that Locke had not been sufficiently empirical. Locke had allowed for the 'existence' of non-empirical 'substrata' (substances) and for a non-empirical distinction between 'objective' primary qualities and sensible secondary qualities. A distinction of this kind is untenable on the part of a consistent empiricist. Berkeley therefore attempted to prune the philosophy of Locke of its non-empirical elements. A properly pruned empiricism states that the world we know is the world we experience; it is our experiences, our perceptions, that are the real objects of our knowledge. In the empirical or phenomenal world to say that something 'is' there, or that it 'exists', is simply to say that it was experienced (perceived) and that it is still experienceable (or perceivable, or sensible). Sensibles, that is, sensible 'things', are simply what perceivers perceive. What then are sensible objects, he asks, 'but the things we perceive by sense, and what do we perceive besides our own sensations or ideas?' (*Principles* 3).

Berkeley does not deny that beings actually exist. They are in fact the creations of the Creator. Berkeley is not really concerned about such beings and the attributes of being. He is concerned simply with the meaning of words, such as 'matter' and 'exists'; and he is concerned that philosophers ought to 'think before they speak' and 'settle the meaning of their words'. 'I take not away substances... I only reject the philosophic sense of the word substance.' 'Let it not be said that I take away Existence. I only declare the meaning of the word so far as I can comprehend it.' He is simply concerned to point out that when the man in the street says that something 'exists' he means simply that something has been experienced and that it is experienceable by perceivers. In other words, the language of common sense is a language of or a talking about experiences. It is empirical. There is a multitude of philosophers and scientists who forget that this is so.

There are philosophers and mathematicians and scientists who use words expressing unreal abstractions ('substance', 'lines', 'angles', 'particles', 'gravity', 'existence') as if these words denoted realities and entities. The only world that ever comes before us is the world of our experience. We know our experiences. We know our 'ideas' or perceptions or sense-data. This is all we know.

Percepts or 'ideas' are perceptions or experiences. We can generalize a percept, that is, a particular image, to make it stand for a number of other similar percepts. Then we have a general idea, a representative image. These ideas are useful in reasoning; but we must be careful not to try to concretize them, or to regard them as denoting some kind of universal entity. This is the mistake that mathematicians and scientists make when they speak of 'numbers', 'triangles', 'matter' and other abstractions, as if these terms denoted some ontological reality independent of experiences. We have no knowledge of entities. We know only percepts or 'ideas', or sense-data.

Ideas are perceptions, and perceptions 'cannot exist otherwise than in a mind perceiving them'. In the everyday language of common sense, ideas which come from without are called sensations, and ideas from within are called thoughts. The 'objects' of the mind are sensations and thoughts. Perceived things are not 'objective' things; they are ideas or collections of ideas. Sensible 'objects' are sensations. Tables and mountains are simply names designating clusters of sensations. The words 'table' and 'mountain' are names which name certain specific contents of the mind. It is humanly impossible to visualize something (e.g. a solitary table) existing absolutely unvisualized: as soon as one visualizes something such as a table, it is no longer unvisualized. To say that something 'exists' is to say that it is visualized or visualizable; and the 'things' that language refers to are invariably particular contents of the mind. The mind knows the contents of the mind; and it knows nothing other than the contents of the mind. The mind knows only its experiences. In this way Berkeley merges together the basic tenets of idealism and empiricism within a theory which he himself referred to as 'the immaterialist hypothesis'.

It is only by reason, Berkeley asserts (*Principles* I, 145-147; *Alciphron* 4, 5) that we know of the existence of God and other minds or selves. The knowledge we have of other minds is not immediate, as is the knowledge we have of our own experiences. I do not see the individual thinking being of Alciphron, for example. I merely perceive 'such visible signs and tokens as suggest and infer' his existence as an active agent similar to myself. I know of the existence of Alciphron or of some other finite self by only a few signs. In the case of God, however, the evidence is far stronger. 'The existence of God is far more evidently perceived than the existence of men; because the effects of Nature are infinitely more numerous and considerable than those ascribed to human agents' (as above).

For Berkeley, the existence of sensible things when not being perceived by finite spirits is an eminent proof of the existence of an infinite spirit who perceives them always. God is the Mind in which perceived things continue to exist even when embodied finite spirits are not perceiving them. God is the creative cause of their existence. Their existence in the divine mind is 'archetypal and eternal'. Their existence in the minds of embodied perceivers is 'ectypal or natural'. This serves to show, once again, that all reality is immaterial, spiritual, and not material. The 'immaterialist hypothesis', according to which we directly perceive clusters of ideas that exist only as perceived, has the merit of not only eliminating scepticism but also of being in accordance with common sense.

The natural world in which we live is a world of divinely perceived and divinely ordered things. It is a world of individual perceptible objects, not a world of hypostatized abstractions. The natural sciences study the order and laws of this sensible world. But the current vocabulary of the natural sciences must be more carefully defined and verified by reference to sensory experience. The sensory world does not present us with ideas of 'material substances', 'absolute space', 'absolute time', 'absolute motion', or of causality and other such misleading abstractions. Thus for example mechanical explanations of the movements of bodies in terms of 'gravity' or 'force' or 'attractions' are simply mathematical hypotheses based on the definitions given to these terms. The terms themselves are not the names of real entities. Similarly, natural 'causes' are simply antecedent signs of what follows them. Fire does not 'cause' wax to melt, but the fire is so regularly followed by the melting that fire is a reliable sign of it as long as 'the Author of Nature always operates uniformly' (*Principles* 107).

The last of Berkeley's philosophical works was *Siris*, which he published in 1744. This work is mainly concerned with the medicinal merits of tar water, but it also develops the theme that the causes of all phenomena must be sought for in the divine activity. Several references are made to the philosophy of Plato and the Neo-

Platonists. The universe is seen as a unified grouping of particular projected thoughts in which Infinite Mind is manifesting itself. This panoramic view of reality emerges as a natural overall vision which gathers together the various strands of his earlier thought. Reality is a manifestation of ideas, of spirit. Things are 'true' and knowable because their very origin is penetrated by spirit. This is the viewpoint of transcendental metaphysical idealism. Berkeley did not develop this viewpoint at length, as in the case of the different philosophies of the nineteenth-century German Idealists. He undoubtedly anticipated the thought of the metaphysical idealists. But the main body of his own writings presents a viewpoint which is, generically, the viewpoint of empirical idealism: the objects of thought are the experienced contents of individual consciousness (*esse est percipi*). Berkeley limited the application of the thesis of empirical idealism, however, to the material world. In this way he avoided the doctrine of solipsism. Matter is an unreal abstraction. Minds and perceptions alone are real. This position can be designated as that of 'immaterial' or a-material empirical idealism.

In the subsequent development of British philosophy, it was the empiricist element of Berkeley's philosophy which proved to be the most influential element. Hume spoke of Berkeley as a great philosopher who made 'one of the greatest and most valuable discoveries', namely, that 'all ideas are nothing but particular ones'. In the nineteenth century Locke, Berkeley and Hume became known as the three outstanding classical British empiricists. In the twentieth century it is Berkeley's use of linguistic analysis which has become a matter of particular interest.

2. Hume. *David Hume* (1711-76) was born in Edinburgh, Scotland. He entered the university of Edinburgh, at the age of twelve, to study Latin, Greek and philosophy. He composed the first edition of his *Treatise of Human Nature* (1739-40) at La Flèche, in France. His empirical approach to the study of human nature stood in stark contrast to the current approach of the Continental rationalists. The treatise was not successful; it fell 'dead-born from the press', he tells us. Hume returned to Britain, where his 'love of literary fame' spurred him on to write *Essays, Moral and Political* (1741-42), *An Enquiry concerning the Principles of Morals* (1751), *An Enquiry concerning Human Understanding* (1751; a second edition of the unsuccessful first *Treatise*), *Political Discourses* (1752), *Four Dissertations* (1757), *Dialogues concerning Natural Religion* (published 1779), and other works. He died of cancer in Edinburgh in 1776.

Hume's philosophy is a philosophy of radical empiricism and phenomenalism leading on to a philosophy of what he designated as mitigated consequent scepticism. The scepticism is mitigated in the sense that 'the strong power of natural instinct' (or irrational sensitive belief) saves it from 'the force of the Pyrrhonian doubt' (*Treatise* I, 4; *Enquiry* 4). (Bertrand Russell, who accepted many of Hume's premisses, said that if there is no 'answer to Hume within the framework of a philosophy that is wholly or mainly empirical', then 'there is no difference between sanity and insanity'. It is 'a desperate point of view': *History of Western Philosophy* 2nd edn, p. 646.)

A Treatise of Human Nature presents the groundwork of Hume's later thought and writings. He conceived the central idea for the treatise in a moment of inspiration ('which transported me beyond measure': letter to his physician in 1734), when he was about eighteen years old. He applied himself to the writing of the treatise 'with an ardour natural to young men' (*ibid.*) for a period of eight years.

Hume's plan was to extend to philosophy in general, and to the science of human nature in particular, what Newton, Galileo and others had accomplished for natural science. His policy was to apply the Newtonian experimental method, and the methodological limitations of Newtonian physics, to the study of man in his cognitive and reasoning activities and in his moral, aesthetic and social life. The empirical findings of psychology, epistemology, logic, conceptual analysis, ethics, aesthetics, social philosophy and politics would be unified together in one great empirical science of human nature.

For Hume, knowledge is obviously confined to the contents of the mind, and the contents of the mind are perceptions. Perceptions are either *impressions*, that is, vivid original perceptions, or *ideas*, that is, less lively versions and reflections of the original impressions. Without impressions there can be no ideas. We can have no ideas of things, or of the world, as distinct from our impressions of them.

In the process which we call *thinking*, ideas group themselves together into recognizable patterns which are brought about by 'some associating quality', or commonly prevailing 'gentle force', which gathers together 'those simple ideas which are most proper to be united in a complex (idea)'. These associative qualities in ideas are: resemblance, contiguity (in time or place), and 'causal' relation between ideas. Thus, for example, one house is easily associated with a similar, neighbouring house, built in the same year by the same builder. Ideas of this kind are naturally related by the natural force of association. Ideas of memory, similarly, are preserved as ideas in their remembered order and position. Other ideas, however, are freely arranged, as in the case of poetry and its poetic similes. In this case, comparisons are made at will, without mental compulsion. Mathematical and philosophical relations are of this kind. One can compare, for example, degrees of quality, or proportions in quantity, and the relations of contrariety and causation.

The relation of cause and effect has a very special role to play in all of the experimental sciences, and so it merits a special (phenomenological) analysis, according to Hume. If we observe fire heating water, we have (sense) impressions of fire and heat and water but no impression of causality. What is the origin then of the idea of causality? Between A, the cause, and B, the effect, there are the relations of contiguity, priority and constant conjunction, but none of these relations imply that there is a 'necessary connection' between cause and effect as commonsense and belief seem to indicate. No individual object A implies the existence of another object B. It is only by experience that we infer a necessary connection between one object and another. It is only through experience that a 'habit of association' is established by the repeated occurrences of A and B. (In this account no mention is made of induction.) 'The foundation of our inference is the transition arising from the accustomed union.' A cause, considered as a natural relation, can be defined as 'an object precedent and contiguous to another and so united with it that the idea of the one determines the mind to form the idea of the other, and the impression of the one to form a more lively idea of the latter'. It is custom or habit that determines the mind to associate, for example, fire and melting wax, or the moon and rising tides. A cause, considered as a philosophical relation, can be defined as 'an object precedent and contiguous to another, and where all objects resembling the former are placed in like relations of precedency and contiguity to those objects that resemble the latter'. Through custom or habit the mind develops a propensity to associate cause A with effect B. The idea of necessary causal connection is the idea or image in consciousness of the original impression, the given propensity to associate.

Hume's analysis of causality is thoroughly phenomenological and empirical. It leads him to the conclusion that the causal relation of ideas does not arise from an intuitive examination of our ideas; it arises from a (non-rational) sensitive propensity to associate ideas of impressions that are constantly conjoined. The principle of causality, then, is neither self-evident nor intuitively known nor capable of demonstration, according to Hume. Nevertheless all our information about what is happening beyond our immediate experience is based on causal reasoning; and if the causal relation has no foundation other than a propensity to associate ideas, then the validity of all our knowledge, scientific and non-scientific, is completely undermined. All thought and all reasoning is no more than a 'species of sensation', as Hume himself came to conclude eventually. In the final chapter of Book I of the *Treatise,* Hume seems distinctly frightened of the sceptical consequences of a doctrine of thoroughly consistent empiricism. All science must be based on belief, then, and no belief can be based on reason. All science must survive in an atmosphere of prevailing scepticism.

Hume's scepticism about the conclusions of the empirical sciences derived in large part from his reduction, in practice, of the causal relation to what previous philosophers had understood as an indicative sign relation. (Thus, for example, sailors regard a red sky at night as a sign, though not an explanation, of fine weather expected next day.) In other words, Hume had reduced induction from causes to induction from signs. In so doing he reduced scientific explanation to mere prediction with probability. His scepticism derived in part, then, from his failure to elaborate any doctrine of signs and from his failure to differentiate between the different kinds of induction.

Hume rejected Locke's representative theory of ideas. If the primary data of knowledge consist of nothing but representations, and if our thoughts are merely copies of these representations, then there is no way in which we can verify how accurate the sense-representations may be, and there is no way in which we can form ideas about the real world apart from our sense-impressions of it. Knowledge is empirical: it is knowledge of impressions of sense and of impressions of reflections which stem from 'ideas' (images) of impressions of sense. It is not knowledge of the material *world*; it is knowledge of *impressions*. Berkeley had already shown that corporeal substances are merely hypostatized abstractions, but Berkeley should have gone further and applied the same phenomenalistic interpretation of substances to immaterial spiritual substances, such as 'minds', as well as to 'matter'. The ideas of substance, material or immaterial, according to Hume, 'is nothing but a collection of simple ideas (images) that are united by the imagination and (that) have a particular name assigned them'. The function of the name (e.g. 'mind') is to recall the collection of images united in the imagination. Thus, there is no mind to have ideas, and there is no hope that the ideas represent the world to us. Knowledge, scientific or otherwise, is knowledge of collections of impressions having particular names assigned to the collections.

Knowledge of impressions is either empirical knowledge of 'matters of fact' or *a priori* knowledge of 'relations of ideas' (images). This distinction is also called the distinction between 'probability' and 'knowledge' (cf. *Treatise* I, 3; *Enquiry* 4, 1). It is the distinction which exists between contingent truths (e.g. one town is five miles or eight kilometres from another town) and *a priori* necessary truths (as in mathematics). Empirical 'matters of fact' can be discovered by observation and non-demonstrative inference based on the relation of cause and effect. These empirical 'facts' or 'probabilities' can always be conceived to be false without contradiction. *A priori* knowledge of 'relations of ideas', as in Euclidean geometry, can be discovered by intuition and by demonstration. It is knowledge of the relations of 'resemblance, contrariety, degrees in quality, and proportions in quality and number'. The relations involved in causation, identity and spatio-temporal relations are not *a priori* 'relations of ideas'; they are not known by intuition or demonstration and they are not *a priori* 'necessary truths'.

Even though we cannot know anything other than perceptions we still continue to believe in the existence of bodies as existing apart from our perceptions. Credulity is a natural propensity. Belief in the existence of bodies and in the uniformity of nature cannot be supported by cogent demonstration; and yet our everyday actions are grounded on such beliefs. What, then, is 'belief'? Belief or opinion, Hume says in the Appendix to the *Treatise*, is a 'lively idea associated with a present impression' but it has an element of steadiness, firmness, force and solidity which differentiates it from poetical imagination and superstition. Belief, as in the case of the beliefs which arise from education, is 'something felt by the mind, which distinguishes the ideas of the judgement from the fictions of the imagination. It gives them more force and influence; it makes them appear of greater importance; infixes them in the mind; and renders them the governing principles of all our *actions*.' Thus, belief can be described only in terms of feeling; and it is in our *actions*, in conduct, that our steady feeling of belief is manifested. In actual everyday human life it is natural belief and not critical reason that prevails and that should prevail. Reason cannot tell us how to live. Natural belief has therefore its own important role to play in human life.

The human mind, Hume tells us (*Treatise* I, 4, 6), 'is a kind of theatre where several perceptions successively make their appearance'. There is no simplicity in the stream of perceptions at any one time, nor is there identity in the perceptions at different times. It is 'the successive perceptions only that constitute the mind'. There is no continuous self-identity. It is merely the power of memory that gives the propensity to believe in the continuous identity of 'self' by a kind of fiction. Hence arises the illusion of the permanent self and permanent selves. The 'mind' is merely the name given to the collection or the stream of perceptions.

Hume applied the same line of argumentation to the questions which are raised in the philosophy of religion. The traditional arguments for the existence of God as presented by Clarke, Butler and others, rely on some version of causality. However, a causal relation can be established only in so far as there is an observed constant conjunction; and there is no possibility of observing God at all. The argument from design, for example, argues that from the presence of order and design in the universe one can conclude to the existence of a designer. But this inference is uncertain because 'the subject lies entirely beyond the reach of human experience'. The world is a sublime mystery, beyond reason and beyond philosophy. We do know certain 'matters of fact' but from matters of fact we cannot infer further facts. For this reason it can be said that the religious hypothesis is a 'useless' hypothesis (*Enquiry* 11, 110; *Dialogues concerning Natural Religion*). The order of the universe is simply an empirical fact and we cannot infer from it the existence of any other 'fact' such as the existence of any kind of God. The existence of God is certainly a matter of widespread personal 'belief', but for the empirical philosopher it is a matter of academical consequent scepticism.

In the *Treatise* (I, 4 and 7) and in the first *Enquiry* (section 12) Hume presented his general attitude with regard to *scepticism*. He held that the 'antecedent' form of scepticism as used in Descartes' method of doubt has some modicum of merit only as a general counsel to try to attain unprejudiced impartiality in the process of philosophical enquiry. Mitigated consequent scepticism is the form of scepticism which Hume himself practised and advocated. Doubt as to the certainty and extent of our knowledge is based on, and derives from, an examination of our faculties. Careful examination reveals to us the unfitness of our mental faculties to present us with reliable factual knowledge concerning the external universe, space, time, existence, matter, causality, God, minds, self, and other such areas of speculation. This need not necessarily lead, however, to the utter despair of extreme (Pyrrhonian) consequent scepticism. A form of scepticism mitigated by the natural beliefs of 'common life', methodized and corrected, may be admitted as durable, useful, and capable of permitting the kind of rich intellectual life evidenced at play in the science of man.

Hume regarded all of these topics, however, as merely (preparatory) groundwork preparing the way for his study of the 'immense depths of philosophy' which still lay before him (of *Treatise* I, 4, 6). He was now ready for the attempt to understand the moral and political life of mankind by analysing and studying the empirical data, the human passions and elementary beliefs, which operate in man's practical ethical and political life. 'Moral philosophy is in the same condition as astronomy before the time of Copernicus.' He now sought to do for ethics what Newton had done for natural science.

The fundamental fact about ethics, for Hume, is that moral approval and moral disapproval, that is, moral judgements of good and evil, arise from a special sort of feeling rather than from the judgements of reason. Reason does play a role in our subsequent discussions about ethical decisions; it concerns itself only with the truth or falsehood of matters of fact and relations of ideas. But the irresistible feeling of approbation or blame is a special sort of irresistible feeling of pleasure or displeasure which is aroused only by human characters and human actions. It is this irresistible 'moral sentiment' or feeling which decides moral questions; and the sentiment is actuated only by what is pleasant or unpleasant, or by what is felt to be useful or pernicious, either to its possessor or to others affected by it. Thus, for example, the 'viciousness' which we associate with the poisoning of a child lies not in the child, nor in natural chemicals, but in the sentiment of strong disapprobation which we project on to such an action. In this case the 'matter of fact', that is, 'the object of feeling,... lies in yourself, not in the object'.

However the irresistible sentiments of moral approval and disapproval are not just relative and subjective matters of individual taste, according to Hume. It is man's capacity for sympathy, or fellow-feeling, that explains why different men unanimously praise or blame the same actions. Human sympathy, as for example in the case when we feel concerned about a suffering fellow human being, provides us with a common and impartial standard eliciting uniform approval or disapproval. Virtue then can be defined as 'whatever mental action or quality gives to a (sympathetic) spectator the pleasing sentiment of approbation; and vice the contrary'. The reason why qualities such as temperance, prudence, patience, constancy, industry and justice excite universal approbation is that these qualities are agreeable and useful to all who are served by these qualities of character or action. 'Everything which contributes to the happiness of society, recommends itself directly to our approbation and good-will.' It is this combination of sympathy, disinterested benevolence, and utility which 'accounts for the origin of morality'. In this respect one can say that Hume is a forerunner of the utilitarians.

Hume devoted special attention to explaining the virtue of justice. The principles of justice are commonly opposed to sentiment and to expedience. He held that this does not disprove his theory of virtue. Because of human rapacity men in society enter into an agreement or convention to 'abstain from the possessions of others'. This artifice or scheme is analogous to that of men pulling the oars of a boat. The convention of justice towards all reflects the self-interest of each member who desires security of person and property. Each shares the uneasiness of the others by sympathy. Thus, '*self-interest* is the original motive of the establishment of justice: but a *sympathy* with public interest is the source of the moral approbation which attends that virtue' (*Treatise* III, 2, 2). Public utility is the sole reason, therefore, why the social virtues of justice, equity, and fidelity, that is, the performance of promises, win our moral approval. These virtues, like all other virtues, depend on felt utility.

Organized society came into existence because of men's felt need to enhance their security, increase their ability, and augment their power. The sense-appetite between the sexes is 'the first and original principle of human society' (*ibid.*). The first rudiments of government in human society probably originated in the authority enjoyed by the captain or tribal chieftain in times of war between different societies. The foundation of the institution of government, and of the duty of allegiance to government, is the advantage or utility it procures to society 'by preserving peace and order' and by promoting social projects for the common good. If the advantage and utility of allegiance to civil government ceases at any time then the obligation to allegiance also ceases. In cases of oppressive tyranny, rebellion is justified. Matters of this kind are matters of fact. They are capable of being built up to form a science of politics. This science, like other empirical sciences, can attempt to formulate explanatory hypotheses, general maxims, and common sense predictions.

Hume's political theory succeeds in eliminating any *a priori* theorizings and hypotheses which are not confirmed by empirical facts. He attaches little importance for example to the social contract theories of the rationalists. He substitutes instead the basic images of felt-needs, utility, advantage and public benefit. The rational animal shares many of these felt-needs and empirical advantages, in a general way, with the higher species of animals in the animal kingdom. But the weakness of Hume's moral and social philosophy is that it attempts to explain the human being and human action on a level that does not transcend this sensitive, empirical level. His philosophy is a philosophy of pure empiricism, pan-phenomenalism and scepticism. It reduces mind as well as matter to felt-phenomena. Its fundamental principle is that experience, or felt-phenomena, is the sole guarantee of knowledge that is true knowledge. It fails to see that this fundamental principle itself cannot be established on the basis of felt-phenomena or experience alone. Thus, for example, the proposition that 'All experiential knowledge is true' cannot be deduced from nor explained by experience alone. To do this, a more adequate philosophical anthropology is needed. Thus, the radical weakness of Hume's 'science of human nature' derives from the radical (root) weakness of the severely restricted philosophy of empiricism and phenomenalism which underlies and narrowly entrenches the very science which he is attempting to build up. The weakness of Hume's *science* of human nature is its lack of an adequate *philosophy* of human nature, or in other words, its lack of an adequate philosophical anthropology.

Hume's logical and consistent development of the line of thought of the British empiricists led to the destruction of empiricism itself as the sole foundation of philosophy and science, and knowledge in general. It attempted to undermine and negate the principles by which general laws can be known from the observation of a limited number of particular instances. It was incapable of saving itself from Pyrrhonic scepticism except through the proposal that commonly accepted beliefs, none of which can be grounded in reason, should be accepted in practice as everyday guides for human behaviour. This total subversion of necessary and universal truths and principles awoke Immanuel Kant from his 'dogmatic slumber', and gave rise in Scotland to the 'philosophy of common sense'.

3. Reactions to Hume. *Adam Smith* (1723-90), the author of *The Wealth of Nations* (1776), was a Scottish professor of moral philosophy who was a good friend of David Hume. As a student in Glasgow, Smith attended the lectures of Francis Hutcheson. In his *Theory of Moral Sentiments* (1759), Smith rejected Hutcheson's theory of the moral sense and substituted the natural feeling of sympathy as the source of a range of feelings which provide a foundation for virtue. 'Whatever is the passion which arises from any object in the person principally concerned, an analogous emotion springs up at the thought of his situation, in the breast of every attentive spectator.'

Smith, like Hume, maintained then that moral approbation and disapprobation can be referred ultimately to the operation of the sentiment and mechanism of sympathy. He devoted the greater part of his attention to the study of moral sentiments and moral psychology. He then presented only a brief resumé of moral philosophy in the last seventh of his work. Historians have pointed out that his work is that of a psychological analyst rather than that of a moral philosopher.

Richard Price (1723-91), a Welsh dissenting preacher and moral philosopher, wrote *A Review of the Principal Questions in Morals* (in 1758, 1769 and 1787) in which he anticipated the absolute moralism of Immanuel Kant. Price held that our approval and disapproval of actions, that is, our judgements of right and wrong, depend on the good pleasure of our Maker who created us in a certain way. If the Maker had pleased, he might have made us pleased or displeased with other actions, even those contrary to the actions which now please and displease us. However, it has actually pleased the Maker to act as he has done, and, this being so, right and wrong are immutable, and they are independent of man's mind. Right and wrong are real characteristics of the different natures of different actions. Moral ideas are derived not from a moral sense but from the understanding. It is the understanding that is the moral faculty. Man as a rational being ought to act simply as reason commands. Right actions must be done simply because they are right. Human happiness depends on human 'rectitude'. This view is close to that of Kant.

Thomas Reid, the originator of the Scottish philosophy of common sense, acknowledged the French Jesuit *Claude Buffier* (1661-1737) as his precursor. Buffier attempted to refute Descartes' alarming assertion that we know primarily the modifications of our own minds, by appealing to the authority of the common sense and common consensus of mankind, and spoke of common sense as a God-given, natural inclination or 'simple disposition to think in a certain way and with a certain conjecture; for example to affirm, while we are sensing them, that exterior objects exist' (*Traité des premières vérités*, 1717). Those who imagine that they are rejecting the 'first truths' of common sense conduct themselves in practice, like other men, in conformity with these first truths.

Thomas Reid (1710-96), of Aberdeen, was a Presbyterian minister who became professor of moral philosophy at Glasgow in 1764. By way of reaction to the consequences of the empiricism and scepticism of Berkeley and Hume, he wrote *An Inquiry into the Human Mind on the Principles of Common Sense* (1764), *Essays on the Intellectual Powers of Man* (1785) and *Essays on the Active Powers of Man* (1788). He held that the representative theory of perception, thought and memory leads inevitably to the erroneous view that the contents of consciousness are the only objects of knowledge. It is the common conviction and belief of mankind, however, that the objects of perception are objective realities and not subjective impressions.

The common-sense knowledge of the ordinary man is a complex estimative knowledge. His knowing perception of an actual tree, for example, includes sensations, conceptions, estimations, beliefs and judgements as part of the very nature of that perception. The common sense is a common estimative power (of knowing) which is an intrinsic part of the constitution of human nature. In matters of common sense which lie within 'the reach of common understanding', 'Every man is no less a competent judge than a mathematician is in a mathematical demonstration' (*Intellectual Powers* VI, 4). The philosopher, then, is not in a better position than anyone else to make pronouncements on bed-rock matters of common sense, such as the existence of a material world, the personal identity of one's own being through time, the freedom of one's own will, and the existence of other minds. These are basic first principles and truths of common sense. They cannot be made more evident than they already are by any attempt to derive them from deductive proofs. Their intrinsic self-evidence becomes specially apparent through the evident absurdity in opinions contrary to the dictates of these first principles of human thought and everyday conduct.

Reid's way of speaking of 'common sense' brings to mind the passing references of the earlier thirteenth-century Scholastic philosophers to the internal sense which they called the *vis aestimativa* or the human *vis cogitativa*. Reid seems to have rediscovered the importance of the role played by this internal human sense and to have analysed at greater length the contributions of this sense to everyday 'common' thought and behaviour.

Reid's followers George Campbell (d. 1796), James Beattie (d. 1803), James Oswald (d. 1803) and Dugald Stewart (d. 1828) came to be regarded as leading representatives of the Scottish School of Common Sense. Stewart's writings helped to spread the influence of the common sense school of thought in France and America. Thomas Brown (1778-1820), professor of moral philosophy at Edinburgh, accepted the main tenets of the common sense school even though he thought that Reid was not sufficiently analytic. His own analytical procedure, however, was influenced by the form of empiricism which became prevalent in France after the time of Condillac. Sir William

Hamilton (1788-1856) attempted to fuse together the main doctrines of Reid and Kant. He spoke of the 'sovereignty of common sense' while also maintaining the 'relativity of knowledge'. This amalgam of different views brought his later thought close to the empirical view that the objects of perception are subjective, even though this was a theory that he himself wished to reject. His fusion of the doctrines of Reid and Kant proved to be an unstable compound.

Immanuel Kant pointed out that Hume himself might fairly lay claim to having as much natural sound sense as Beattie and the other members of the Scottish school. These men thought they were reacting against the phenomenalism of Hume, he said, by trying to prove (to Hume) a doctrine which Hume himself had always believed and by assuming as true the very central point which Hume doubted. No one doubts that psychological beliefs and personal convictions arise from different sensations and sensitive apprehensions. This is not a problem. The main question is: is the mind capable of obtaining universal, necessary, 'scientific' knowledge about experienced matters of fact? And if so, how does the 'scientific' mind function?

The critical philosophy of Kant, though profoundly influential on the development of different facets of nineteenth-century thought, did not provide an obvious solution to the problem raised. It did not deliver a death-blow to the philosophy of common sense. New defences of a more critical form of common sense appeared later in the works of C. S. Peirce, Henry Sidgwick, G. F. Stout, Bertrand Russell, C. D. Broad, G. E. Moore, Norman Malcolm and other philosophers down to our own times. But Kant's objections against the Scottish school are equally applicable still to these later and more critical forms of the philosophy of common sense.

21   The Enlightenment

1. The growth of the philosophy of history. The philosophy of history is regarded as that branch of philosophy which looks upon human history as the subject-matter of philosophical reflection. It seeks to discover in the process of events of human history an overall meaning or significance which transcends the understanding of history achieved by ordinary historical research work. Whether a special, transcendent understanding of human history is attainable through philosophical reflection is a matter which leaves itself quite open to dispute. Nevertheless several such attempts have been made by different philosophers down through the ages.

Plato and Aristotle formulated socio-political theories concerning the manner in which varying forms of government have characteristically succeeded each other in patterned historical cycles in the city-states. However, they did not develop this speculative interest in history into an overall philosophical understanding of human history as following universal and necessary laws. Augustine in the fifth century A.D., and Bossuet in the seventeenth, were two philosopher-theologians among many others who viewed all historical events in the light of a continuous, divine providential action which is wonderfully and mysteriously fulfilled in and through the human operations and events of history.

Giambattista Vico (1668-1744), a professor of rhetoric at the university of Naples, presented a revolutionary theory of history and social development in his *Scienza nuova* (in 1725, 1730 and 1744). He pointed out that while Grotius, Samuel Pufendorf and Hobbes had made valuable contributions to legal, political and social theory, nevertheless, their use of hypostatized abstractions such as 'natural law' and 'social contract' had lead to major distortions in their historical perspective. They had presumed that human nature is static and unchanging and that the perspectives, feelings and mentality of pre-historical mankind were essentially similar to those of contemporary human beings. History has been made by man, and man can be understood only historically. The philosopher of history must emancipate himself from the assumption that men have always seen themselves and the world in the way that men do today. We can learn about the modes of consciousness of earlier, developing communities through a critical discernment and imaginative recapturing of their mental attitudes as found in their language, and in their myths, fables, legends and traditions handed down from early times. In these early 'poetical periods of human history', mythological narratives and animistic personifications, for example, were not at all regarded as extravagant fictions, as they are today. These narratives and representations present us with the speech and thought in which our remote ancestors directly apprehended the world around them and in which they attempted to enrobe their experiences with imaginative and intelligible meaning. 'Fables are the first histories of these gentile peoples.' Fables can be profoundly revealing and informative, if interpreted with intelligent understanding.

Vico incorporated this theory into his wider 'cyclical' (*corsi e ricorsi*) theory of historical development. Human societies and ethnic groups pass through certain distinct stages of growth and decay. The first beginnings of civilization likely started in places of natural shelter and food supplies where families settled together under the leadership of a patriarchal father-figure. This was the 'religious' phase, 'the age of the gods', when families revered the burial grounds of their ancestors and worshipped the deities. The second stage of development emerged in the 'heroic' age, 'the age of the heroes'. Different patriarchal families formed alliances in order to cope with the challenges arising from internal factiousness and the external aggression of 'lawless vagrants'. Weak vagrants, widows and children took refuge as serfs or slaves under the earlier, 'patrician' settlers. Oligarchies arose and society became rigidly divided into the patrician class and the plebeian class, as in the case of the early history of Roman civilization. The later descendants of these oligarchies have consistently opted for a life of intemperate licence and irreligious intellectualism. The third stage is the 'democratic' phase, 'the age of men', which is engendered by class conflict. The plebeian class has usually attained a status of democratic equality in which a legal system protects its interests and rights. These free democratic republics have eventually become corrupt, anarchic and decadent. The cycle ends through either invasion and conquest from without or disintegration from within. There is a reversion to primitive barbarism; and then the cycle begins again.

Vico believed that these patterns which are discernible in history are ultimately attributable to the work of divine Providence, even though it is man himself, as child of God, who is the author and maker of his own history. Thus Providence moulds the various details of human history into a wider, meaningful mosaic which is not the product of human forethought and planning. In this, Vico anticipated the subsequent theories of Hamann, Herder and Hegel. Vico's writings, however, were generally ignored until a different intellectual climate arose under the influence of German Romanticism in the nineteenth century.

The *Baron de Montesquieu* (1689-1755), in his personal notes, indicated indirectly that Vico's ideas exercised an influence upon his own philosophy of history and his comparative study of society, law and government. Like Vico, Montesquieu attempted to ascertain the principles which underlie the historical development of peoples. In his work *De l'Esprit des lois* (1748), Montesquieu attempted to discover the rational basis for the existence of the laws and the legal systems which are actually in operation in various states. He undertook to examine the 'spirit' of different bodies of law in relation to the geographical and climatic conditions which moulded the economic conditions, the national temperament and religious attitudes of different peoples. He concluded that each of the different political societies of history may be seen as an imperfect embodiment of one or other of three 'ideal' types of society, namely, the republican, the constitutional monarchical, and the despotic forms of political society. Each of these forms of society has its own distinct 'spirit' which gives rise to a certain type of legal system. Thus, the legal 'spirit' will lay emphasis on a community 'spirit' of either civic virtue, or honour, or fear, in the three different 'ideal' forms of society. Montesquieu favoured a liberal constitution of the English type in which there is a separation of legislative, executive and judicial powers, as a safeguard against despotic use of power. His empirical and comparative sociological surveys exercised an influence on political thinkers in both America and France prior to the American (1776) and French (1789) Revolutions.

The *Marquis de Condorcet* (1743-94) published his *Esquisse*, or *Sketch for a Historical Picture of the Human Mind*, in 1794. He sought to apply the attitudes and methods of the physical sciences and probability theory to social questions. In this way he hoped to establish a new social science making use of the calculus of probabilities in order to provide an intellectual foundation for a rational political and social order. Men must be freed from the empire of instinct and passion; and the empire of reason must be restored in social affairs. History demonstrates the power of reason and calculation in the ongoing progress of the mass of the people in their social life. He distinguished nine periods of human liberation, growth and revolutionary progress from barbarism to enlightened civilization as preparatory to indefinite human progress throughout future ages. The primitive period of hunters and fishers was followed by the pastoral period, and then by the agricultural period, the Grecian period, the Roman period, the Crusades, the printing period, the Renaissance and the age of the science of Nature and man. Future progress towards a greater liberty and equality of rights will inevitably result from continuing education, rational enlightenment, political reform and moral formation. He looked forward optimistically to the advent of a democratic, secularist and scientific civilization and to a future which promised indefinite progress to the succeeding generations of mankind. Condorcet's thought expresses typically the outlook of the period of the 'French Enlightenment'.

2. **The French Enlightenment.** The 'Age of Reason' is a term frequently applied to the thought and writings of the seventeenth and eighteenth centuries together. In this case, the seventeenth century is seen as the age of the specialist, rationalist philosophers or the 'Age of Rationalism'. The term 'Enlightenment' is then used to indicate the spread of the Age of Reason, Nature and Progress to a relatively large educated public in the eighteenth century.

In the first half of the eighteenth century, on the Continent of Europe, the educated public acquired the characteristic ideas and attitudes of the Enlightenment from a group of popular writers, literary figures, journalists, and men of 'wit' who are generally called *les philosophes*. They were popularizers and propagandists of the attitudes of the Age of Reason rather than systematic philosophers. They include writers and conversationalists such as Voltaire, Fontenelle, Bayle, Montesquieu, Maupertuis, Vauvenargues, Condillac, Helvétius and others. They popularized among the educated public the recent achievements of mathematics, astronomy, physics and 'natural philosophy'. They brought about the 'reception of Locke' on the Continent, making Locke's social contract theory and theory of knowledge acceptable in educated social circles which had already accepted Newton as a leading hero of the new culture.

The *philosophes* were concerned to free the scientific study of the social and political life of man from theological and metaphysical presuppositions. The Christian Churches and their churchmen were regarded as arresting and corrupting influences in an age of scientific enlightenment. Voltaire said of the Catholic Church, 'crush the infamous thing' (*ecrasez l'infâme*). Human reason must overthrow not only the shackles of faith and revelation but also the burdens of irrational customs and ossified traditions which had accumulated during the dark period of the feudal Middle Ages. All men are naturally moral and 'good' if freed from the pall of illiterate ignorance. The progressive present is far superior to the unnaturally repressed past. The future opens up opportunities undreamed of in the cramped confines of the past. It is in this sense that the eighteenth century was seen as the century of Reason, Nature and Progress.

Pierre Bayle (1647-1706), in his famous *Dictionnaire historique et critique* (1697), expressed the view that the autonomous moral individual does not need religious belief in order to live a virtuous life. Bernard de Fontenelle (1657-1757) held that positive knowledge and scientific explanation is now taking the place of the mythological explanations of phenomena given in earlier epochs. Pierre-Louis de Maupertuis (1698-1759) combined a teleological and hylozoist explanation of Nature with an empiricist and sensist explanation of mathematical and mechanical principles. François Marie Arouet (1694-1778), known as M. de Voltaire, was a resolute defender of freedom of expression for *philosophes* and for freedom of action of enlightened monarchs from clerical influence. The Marquis de Vauvenargues (1715-47) proposed a utilitarian interpretation of morality and emphasized the social and 'passionate' character of human moral behaviour. Claude-Adrien Helvétius (1715-71) propounded a doctrine of environmentalist psychological behaviourism. He denied that there are innate inequalities among men; and he held that the same environmental, educational causes will invariably produce the same behavioural effects. He advocated, then, a system of universal public education for the moral improvement and general happiness of mankind. 'Education can do all.'

Étienne Bonnot de Condillac (1715-80) wrote a treatise on sensation, *Traité des sensations* (1754), for which he became famous in his own times. He attempted to demonstrate that all psychical phenomena are nothing more than transformed sensations. He asked his readers to think of the case of people who are born blind and deaf; or, to go further, imagine a man, a living statue who has no sensation other than the sense of smell. The whole psychical life of this 'statue-man', his attention, his 'I', his memory, judgements, perceptions, images, ideas, desires, hopes, hates, loves and reflections would all be necessarily built upon his sensations of smelling. All his mental operations would merely be transformations of his sense of smell. It is in this same manner that all our psychical phenomena are merely transformations of our sensations of smell, touch, hearing, taste and sight. Condillac then attempted to show how the perception of phenomenological exteriority arises. If there were a similar 'statue-man' who had no sensation other than the tactile sensations of his own felt muscular movements (such as his own felt breathing), and if this statue-man were to press his hand on his own chest he would experience two feelings of solidity, resistance and exclusion, one in the hand and one in the chest. But if he were then to touch some object other than his own body he would experience not a double contact but a single contact. A comparison of these two different tactile experiences would be sufficient to elicit the man's awareness of the outward world of the non-ego. This awareness of exteriority can then become the basis for the transformation of this discovery into the notions of matter and space as transformed sensations. Condillac's explanation of the perception of phenomenological exteriority was developed in a significant way by Destutt de Tracy, Maine de Biran, and the *idéologues* of the nineteenth century.

The thinkers of the first half of the eighteenth century can be classified as moderates who did not bring their criticism of the existing social and political order to bear on any radical reform of the whole social and political environment. The thinkers of the second half of the century, however, after the time of the *Grande Encyclopédie*, edited by Diderot and d'Alembert, were more radical and more committed to total reform of all the existing institutions.

Denis Diderot (1713-86) was a deist who later became an atheist and finally a naturalistic pantheist. He denied the existence of any spiritual soul or freedom of choice. Nevertheless, he propounded at the same time a doctrine of ethical idealism. Jean le Rond d'Alembert (1717-83) separated natural ethics from theology and metaphysics. He held that metaphysical assertions cannot express certain knowledge. Ethics, like the other sciences, must make use of a positivist methodology. These two authors, who saw themselves as 'enlighteners', worked together for several years as co-editors of the *Encyclopédie*. The first volume of this 23-volume work appeared in 1751. It was quickly recognized as a controversial, indispensable, revolutionary publication which embodied the knowledge, opinions and ambitions of an enthusiastic generation of progressive authors and free thinkers.

Paul Dietrich Thiry, Baron d'Holbach (1723-89), was a wealthy patron and contributor who wrote more than four hundred articles for the *Encyclopédie*. His salon in Paris and his country residence of Grandval were regarded as the principal social centres of the enlightened *philosophes*. In *Le Système de la Nature* (1770) d'Holbach presented a comprehensive, systematic defence of atheistic materialism. This work came to be regarded as the Bible of Atheism. Holbach held that man is entirely a product of material nature which constitutes the whole of reality. Nature is the sum of matter and motion. Matter is self-created and eternal. All is governed by a necessary and irreversible chain of causes and effects. The terms 'virtue' and 'vice' are simply descriptive labels assigned to actions favouring or hindering the mutual happiness of society and the individual. The term 'God' is a non-denotative, meaningless term. Goethe criticized d'Holbach as depriving Nature and life of all that is precious. Professor Réné Hubert said of the influence of d'Holbach and his friends that their views endowed France with its dogmatic village atheists (*d'Holbach et ses amis*, Paris, 1928).

Julien Offroy de la Mettrie (1709-51) and Pierre-Jean Cabanis (1757-1808) sought a materialistic and mechanistic explanation of the cosmos, nature, and human behaviour. Cabanis held the view that just as the stomach is a machine for digesting food, so too the brain is a machine for digesting impressions, by 'the secretion of thought'. The brain secretes thought as the liver secretes bile. 'Les nerfs – voilà tout l'homme.' A similarly crude expression of materialism is found in the man-machine theory of La Mettrie's *L'Homme Machine* (1784). Thought is strictly a function of the human physical mechanism. Man's physical life can be explained in terms of sensations. The brain has its own 'thought muscles' just as the leg has its 'walk muscles'. These thought muscles are developed by education.

The *philosophes* in general aimed at freeing the scientific study of man from theological and metaphysical presuppositions. They were not free, however, from other presuppositions and value judgements of their own. They assumed that human progress would result inevitably from the progressive rationalization of man emancipated from the irrational forces of civil and ecclesiastical authoritarianism. The liberated spirit of a scientifically enlightened society of mankind would inevitably advance towards ever higher levels of human morality and virtue. They regarded themselves as enlighteners who were sponsoring a movement which would tend inevitably towards the realization of the ideals of the Age of Reason. They were convinced that man's betterment, happiness and welfare rested in man's own hands. They believed ardently that this could be attained through the extension of the 'scientific' outlook to the field of human psychology, morality and man's social life. They contributed in this way to the formation of a mentality which brought about a different organization of society, and a naturalistic outlook which became widespread in the nineteenth and twentieth centuries.

3. Reaction: Rousseau. *Jean-Jacques Rousseau* (1712-78) reacted strongly against the 'enlightened' view that 'the restoration of the arts and sciences has contributed to the purification of (social and moral) manners'. He regarded the artificially 'mannered' behaviour of refined European society as a depraving deviation from the natural conditions of human existence. His attacks on the corrupting effects of Western civilization met with strong opposition not only from the *philosophes* but also from the established institutions.

Rousseau was born of Calvinist parents in Geneva. He had little formal education. He was apprenticed first to a notary and then to an engraver, abandoned these apprenticeships and served for a time as a lackey. He was befriended and protected by Madame de Warens of Chambéry with whom he stayed happily for some years. During this time he studied enthusiastically under his own direction. Subsequently, he published a *Discourse on the Arts and Sciences* (1750), a *Discourse on the Origin and Foundation of Inequality among Men* (1758), a *Discourse on Political Economy* (1758), *Julie, ou la Nouvelle Héloïse* (1761), *Émile* (1762), *Contrat social* (1762), and other works. Several of these publications were criticized by the *philosophes* and condemned by the civil and ecclesiastical authorities. During the last fifteen years of his life, Rousseau sought refuge with different friends in different countries, oppressed by the thought of universal persecution. He saw himself as a man of warm heart, deep affection and sensitive emotion; he nevertheless quarrelled violently with all who befriended him. His intolerant and suspicious temperament made social adjustment difficult. His friend Edmund Burke said of him that his life was regulated by vanity. David Hume, who befriended Rousseau in England, regarded him as a man of high-pitched sensibility who 'has only *felt* during the whole course of his life'. When Rousseau died at Erménonville in 1778, suicide was suspected, though his death was probably caused by uraemia.

Rousseau was convinced that the artificial conventions and polite restrictions which gilded the ruthless calculating egoism of those who lived a life of luxurious idleness thwarted the mature development of their authentic human nature. Conventional society, priding itself in the restoration of the arts (including the theatrical arts), is a society which has lost its innocence and authentic openness. It is a hypocritical, deceitful way of life totally lacking in natural virtue. It is the unhealthy excrescence of a proud life of unjust and unnatural inequality based on power, privilege and wealth.

In the earlier, more rudimentary forms of primitive society, as in the case of the Spartans and the Germanic tribes, men were more open-hearted and sincere, according to Rousseau. Subsequent progress in the arts and sciences, as in the case of Egypt, Greece and Rome, produced luxurious living and generated effeminate weakness. Man in the primitive state of nature is naturally good. Primitive man had an inborn feeling of compassion for others and a worthy self-esteem. He led a happy, isolated existence in the forests, satisfying his basic natural appetites without difficulty. He was self-sufficient and untouched by modern man's anxiety neuroses. The era of the first rudimentary social communities was the golden age of humanity. It was the era of natural human equality. It was the era which existed before the usurpation of private property divided men into the rich and the poor, and before political institutions gave permanent legitimacy to the rule of the powerful over the weak. A vestige of this unspoiled simplicity and innocence can still be seen in small republics such as Geneva by way of contrast to the large monarchical states of Europe which have travelled furthest along the road to human perdition.

Rousseau sought a cure for the malady of modern civilization in a new method of education which would foster the growth of human sensibility, reason and imagination, and in a reform of political society which would ensure civic freedom and human equality. He was convinced that even though men of power are wicked, yet man himself is good. *Émile* is, for the main part, a philosophical treatise on the goodness of human nature. It is set in a rural environment where the child is allowed to grow, without inhibition, from infancy to maturity, in accordance with his own developing needs and in accordance with 'the natural progress of the human heart'. Bookish learning is to be eschewed and early education is to be based on direct contact with the world of natural physical objects. The early judgements of the child must be formed not through words or abstractions but through sensations and feelings. The child's early relationships with other children and adults are to be based on natural sensibility rather than on reason.

Each and every man must be allowed to develop his most fundamental impulse of natural self-love (*amour de soi*), or worthy self-esteem. This is not at all the same thing as overweening pride (*amour propre*) which destroys compassion and the human self-esteem of one's fellow men. It is simple folk, those who have found their freedom in their social expression of natural passion, close to nature, and least corrupted by artificial civilization, who are best able to intuit and feel what is virtuous and right and what is vicious and wrong. It is only the simple folk who can say: 'I see God everywhere in his works; I feel him within myself'.

Nature is the whole realm of being originally created by God. It is God himself who guarantees its goodness, unity and order. The sensitive man develops a deep 'feeling for nature' and a spiritual bond with the whole spiritual order which manifests itself outwardly in the natural objects and forces of the physical universe. There is in man a 'divine instinct' which forms the basis of man's moral existence. God gave man 'conscience to love the good, reason to know it, and freedom to choose it'.

Man's God-given nature is good. Nature intended man to live a life of moral goodness. It intended him for social life. With the growth of sensibility, reason and imagination, the young person embarks on a way of living which involves relations with his fellow human beings. The mature human being is the social human being aware of his natural fellow feelings and obligations to others who are his kin. In his social contacts with others, man's innate natural goodness and sympathy for others leads to a growing awareness of the common good and the need for all to live in harmonious relationship together. Natural goodness leads to virtuous living. Goodness subordinates itself to the growing demands of human conscience, social morality and natural virtue. Social living, through the individual's participation in the 'common unity', confers on man a new rational unity which gradually replaces the instinctive self-sufficiency of his primitive state.

The mature social man participates willingly and freely in the formulation of the community ordinances and laws which express the general feeling and the general will of the community. In obeying the community ordinances he willingly aligns his own will with the community will for the common good. In obeying a State law he is obeying an expression of the general will which represents the real will of his own best judgement and reason. The virtuous community-man is the man who conforms his will to the general will of the general community. The virtuous citizen is the one who aligns his will with the general will of the State. The State, in turn, is part of 'the great city of the world... whose general will is always the will of nature'.

Rousseau's *Contrat social; Principes de droit politique* is basically a philosophical discussion of civic freedom and political right. It is concerned primarily with the fundamental principles on which true government, irrespective of factual particular forms of government, must be based. Government must never subjugate justice and political right to utility and political expediency. Civic freedom and equality must be secured for each and all. The only valid basis for a community way of life that respects the requirements of human freedom is that this community or political society must be the result of a free association, or social pact (*contrat social*), of intelligent human beings who deliberately choose to form the particular type of political society to which they agree to give their willing allegiance. In this way, each one uniting with all obeys his greater self and continues to be as free as ever before. Each one agrees to give himself not to sectional interests but to the general will which is always directed towards the general good.

The 'general will' is a 'real force, superior to the action of any particular will'. It is the objective embodiment of man's higher moral nature. Through willing obedience to a superior moral law which he prescribes for himself, the individual escapes from the bondage of appetite and achieves as an intelligent being the true freedom which arises from response to the call of reason and conscience. In this way the mature citizen finds fulfilment in a community experience of fraternity and equality with other citizens who willingly live in accordance with the same ideal. They become a body politic, a corporate self, or public person, in which each acquires a higher form of liberty and in which each actualizes his individual self more fully. It was in this way that the corporate moral being, the State, was brought into existence.

In the State, sovereignty of the body politic is 'nothing less than the exercise of the general will'. The sovereign is the whole moral body of the citizens, exercising the general will. Sovereign and subjects are simply the same people in different respects. The sovereign, the new organic entity or 'public person', wills the common good. The legislature of the whole body politic expresses the general will and in doing so it expresses the real, superior will of each and all to strive for the common good. The body politic was brought into existence by the social contract and it can be dissolved at any time that the assembled citizens agree to dissolve the compact. The sovereign people may delegate the executive function of the state to a head of state, a prince, or a government, which then becomes the agent or officer of the people in a monarchical or aristocratic or republican type of executive State government.

The general will infallibly wills the common good. But this general will, in practice, has to be embodied in specific concrete laws. Rousseau points out that, for the legal formulation of particular laws, the sovereign people will normally employ a wise law-framer or trained 'legislator' who will enlighten them on what is the common interest in particular instances. If the general will is to attain concrete expression in law, the sovereign legislative assembly must be careful to prevent any partial factions or self-interested parties, such as a fanatical priestly party, from interfering with the legal expression of the general will. Those who try to promote particular group interests and refuse to submit to the general will and the common good threaten the state with anarchy and dissolution. They are to be regarded as irresponsible individualists, like criminals, who forfeit their right to be considered as responsible human beings. They are to be subjected to compulsion for their own sake. In this way they (or he) 'will be forced to be free', really free. If safeguards of this kind are kept, then the majority vote will inevitably express the general will of the assembly.

The State executive power, or government, is merely the ministerial instrument of the sovereign legislative body. It is concerned with the daily administrative application and enforcement of the universal law enacted by the sovereign legislative power. The government, and the entire body politic, like the human body, tend naturally to degeneration. A clear separation, by various constitutional devices, of the executive power from the legislative power will serve as an effective means to preserve the body politic and its government in a healthy condition over a long life-span.

Rousseau's reformist ideas and his lively and colourful literary style were perfectly adapted to the tastes and opinions of many of his contemporaries in France and Europe. The influence of his thought and writing was widespread. The revolutionaries of 1789 looked on Rousseau as the father of the French Revolution, and voted a statue to commemorate his name. Rousseau's writings inspired the work of Robespierre, who embodied Rousseau's notion of 'being forced to be free' in the applied political doctrine of 'the despotism of liberty'.

Rousseau did not make a philosophical analysis of the idea of the 'general will' nor attempt to specify the modality of its reality, and did not delve deeply into the problem of the relation between the individual and the State. His notion of the 'general will' of the State was sufficiently suggestive and ambiguous, however, to evoke different interpretative responses. Thus for example, it prompted

Kant to develop a doctrine of the autonomous rational will or practical reason; and it prompted Hegel and the Hegelians to develop a doctrine of the State as an organic moral being whose will may perhaps be articulated through the medium of some charismatic national leader. Rousseau's emphasis on sensibility and intuition, similarly, exercised a powerful influence on subsequent French and German thought and literature.

4. The German Enlightenment. The first important thinker of the German Enlightenment or *Aufklärung* was *Christian Thomasius* (1655-1728). He was the son of Jakob Thomasius of Leipzig, an Aristotelian philosopher who had taught philosophy to Leibniz as a young man. Christian Thomasius held that philosophy should concern itself in a practical way with man, his nature, and his needs, and that university education should be practical and worldly rather than pedantic and scholastic. It should help to train administrators, courtiers, and diplomats for the State, and be regarded as a useful instrument for promoting the common good and the temporal happiness of the individual. The exercise of reason should be directed to jurisprudence, law, ethics, and the promotion of the social public good. Thomasius himself embraced the enthusiastic religious views of the Pietists in Germany and his philosophy soon became the official philosophy of the Pietist movement. Man can be rescued from his moral powerlessness by divine grace alone. Man finds meaning and purpose not in metaphysical abstractions but in personal faith and prayerful interiority.

The chief representative of the second phase of the German Enlightenment and the most prominent rationalist philosopher of the *Aufklärung* was *Christian Wolff* (1679-1754) who, on Leibniz's recommendation, was appointed professor in the university of Halle and elected to the Berlin Academy. In 1743 he became chancellor of the university, and in 1745 a baron of the Holy Roman Empire.

Wolff was a gifted systematizer who simplified, synthesized, and further elaborated some of the key principles in the thought of Leibniz and the late Scholastics. He developed a complete, rational, deductive, system of philosophy which was divided into ontology, rational psychology, cosmology, and rational theology (theodicy). He was the first to write philosophy extensively in the German language. He helped to make philosophical studies available to German readers and ensured that his own books were suitable for instruction and use in the German schools and universities. Like Leibniz, he postulated the existence of unextended simple substances whose harmonious actions are described in terms of pre-established harmony. However, it is frequently said by historians that he lacked insight into the profounder thought of Leibniz, and failed to express its real spirit. Wolff's primary importance lay in the fact that he provided a widely accepted school-philosophy for the German universities until the advent of the critical philosophy of Immanuel Kant.

Martin Knutzen (1713-51), the teacher of Immanuel Kant, was a Wolffian philosopher and a Pietist who attempted to reconcile Wolff's theory of pre-established harmony with the Pietist doctrine of physical influence. He was one of the first philosophers in Germany to accept and teach the Newtonian theory of gravitational attraction as a real force. Kant accepted this view and then attempted to give the *Metaphysical Foundations of Natural Science* in general.

Alexander G. Baumgarten (1714-62) was a Wolffian philosopher and aesthetician whose Latin handbooks on metaphysics, ethics and practical philosophy were widely used in German universities. Kant, who regarded Baumgarten as a noteworthy metaphysician, adopted Baumgarten's *Metaphysics* and *Practical Philosophy* as textbooks for his own courses and lectures in philosophy at Königsberg. Baumgarten regarded aesthetics as the branch of empirical psychology which studies the faculty of sensible knowledge; and he regarded 'gnoseology', that is, theory of knowledge, as combining together aesthetics and logic.

Baumgarten regarded 'sensitive representations' as not only being representations in the senses but also being associated with human feelings, of which the faculties of knowledge and rational will are cognizant. A beautiful poem, for example, is a well-formed sensitive discourse which awakens a lively, but indistinct and 'confused' human feeling. The artist adds feeling to reality in the process of creating a world which is a felt-world. His area of concern is that of reliable sensible knowledge of truths and things made perfectly lively. Baumgarten's stress on the importance and relative independence of the 'inferior' faculty of human sensitive knowledge foreshadowed and influenced Kant's doctrine of the special, independent function of sensibility in human knowledge.

Gotthold Lessing (1729-81) was a German dramatist and critic whose widely read writings disseminated an influential literary expression of the spirit of the *Aufklärung*. In his book *The Education of the Human Race* (Berlin, 1780), Lessing presented views which anticipated the theories of the 'post-Christian' positivists and the liberal philosophers of religion of the nineteenth century. He held that the role of religious belief in the historical process is a relative, evolving role and a transient state in the advance of humanity towards maturity. He presented a *New Hypothesis concerning the Evangelists considered as merely Human Historians* (1784) in which he pioneered the work of critical study of the Bible as a collection of several different literary works. He sought to encourage among the educated people of his times an attitude of critical enquiry which would lead them away from impersonal disinterestedness concerning religious matters and towards enthusiastic engagement and personal involvement in historical research.

In summary, the Enlightenment, or the Age of Prose and Reason, while often manifesting negative, anti-metaphysical and anti-religious aspects, also manifested the more positive and programmatic aspect of promoting the study of the human experimental sciences and of promoting the creation of new and more rational forms of social and political life. The thinkers and writers of this era placed emphasis on the role of enlightened reason in their attempt to understand man scientifically in his psychological, moral, religious, and social life. Their views differed noticeably, however, from those of the Rationalists. They were influenced considerably by the empirical thought of Locke and Newton. They strove ardently, like Hume, to extend the secular, scientific outlook to the study of psychology, morality and social life. They endeavoured to separate ethics from moral theology and metaphysics. They wished to set up the science of morality as an independent science having its own autonomous area of jurisdiction, freed from theological and metaphysical presuppositions. Reason, 'free thought', and empirical research, must replace the traditional role of authority and the former emphasis placed on *a priori* speculation. They believed confidently in the power of enlightened reason to promote the betterment of man and the progress of society. They rallied enthusiastically to the clarion call of 'Progress'.

In their efforts to free the scientific study of man from theological presuppositions and rationalist *a priori* speculation, the enlighteners were not free, however, from other value-judgements and presuppositions of their own. They desired to reconstruct society according to what were believed to be the demands of reason, and they felt that this reconstruction could be easily achieved once men were brought to see it in the light of reason. Their unquestioned belief in progress and human perfectibility frequently involved an arrogant disregard or contempt for history and tradition, and an angry impatience with existing institutions, as contrary to reason and natural law. They looked to enlightened despots, such as Catherine of Russia, Frederick the Great of Prussia, Charles III of Spain, Maria Theresa and her son Joseph II in Austria, and the Marquis de Pombal in Portugal, to use their near-absolute powers to bring about reforms consistent with the contemporary theories. They assumed that progress consists in the progressive rationalization of man and in man's progressive emancipation from traditional institutional forms of beliefs and repressions. Mankind would then advance in morality and virtue. In this way they formed their ideals concerning man and society, and they then believed optimistically in human progress as a movement towards the realization of those ideals of their own age. Previous ages were regarded as not really enlightened. In fact some centuries were ignored and written off as 'Dark Ages'.

The following generation, which came to maturity in the early years of the nineteenth century, rejected the ideals and scientific aspirations of the previous generation of enlighteners. Wordsworth, for example, regarded the writings of Voltaire as the 'dull product of a scoffer's pen', and he advocated that the 'barren leaves' of science and art be closed up so that the human heart could open itself to the mysterious call of Nature herself. One more new age had dawned, one in which the rationalistic, positivistic, optimistic beliefs of the 'barren' enlighteners were abandoned with contempt.

5. Reaction: Hamann, Jacobi, Herder. *John Georg Hamann* (1730-88), of Königsberg, who was known as the 'Wise Man (Magus) of the North' attacked the pretentiousness of the *Aufklärung* and the tyranny of 'omnicompetent' discursive Reason. In his *Socratic Memorabilia* (1759), he made use of the figure of Socrates, the hero of the Enlightenment, to call upon the enlightened enlighteners to make a philosophical confession of ignorance instead of making philosophical pretensions to knowledge. Hume's scepticism illustrated quite well the bankruptcy of Reason, a hypostatized abstraction. Man is a creature of flesh and blood; and reasoning is simply one activity among many activities of the human organism. Inspiration and genius are seldom if ever manifest in the arid works of rationalists and scientists; they are eminently evident in the language, music and imagery of the poets.

In his essay *Metacritique of the Purism of Reason* (1784), Hamann argued against the belief that Kant had ever demonstrated that reason can be separated from sense experience. 'The entire capacity to think rests upon language.' Thus, for example, space and time are language symbols or mental symbols which can never be demonstrated to be 'pure' and empty of sense experience. Space and time are not empty, passive, receptive forms of sense intuition. They are active forms of language, or symbols. The philosopher must see and study 'space' and 'time' as language, and not as subjective forms sundered from reality. 'Language is in the very middle of reasoning's misunderstanding of itself.' Language has the capacity to hypostatize and create reified abstractions and other illusions which may appear *a priori* and necessary. There is an obvious need therefore for a philosophy of language.

Friedrich H. Jacobi (1743-1819), like Hamann, was a major critic of the critical philosophy of Kant, and a leading representative of the philosophy of sentiment, feeling and faith. He subjected the thought of both Spinoza and Kant to severe criticism. He said of Kant's *Critique of Pure Reason*: 'We cannot enter the Critique without assuming the existence of things-in-themselves, but we cannot retain this assumption upon leaving the *Critique*'. The reason for this is that we cannot know things by the 'objective' scientific mind. We can know things only by a cognition determined by the individual ego. If the Kantian position wishes to be consistent, then, it should deny any objective reality existing independently of cognition and it should resolve the object completely in subjective presentations of our minds. A consistent Kantianism would then be a doctrine of pure subjective idealism. In this case, the only reality would be the ego. Jacobi rejected Kant's phenomenalism and empty formalism. He held that genuine faith, which is an affair of the heart (*Gemüt*), must be completely separated from discursive reason and philosophy. Faith is an inner illumination of man's higher reason (*Vernunft*). It is this higher reason which gives man an immediate intuition of things as they are in themselves, the existence of God, the existence of the external world, immediate apprehension of supersensible reality, and moral values. Faith plays a role of primary importance, therefore, in everyday human life, since even the certainty of the existence of things in themselves is based on faith. Hume had recognized this fact. Belief in the reality of sensed things commands the same kind of certainty that one attains through an act of revelation. It is a certainty we are aware of, but cannot explain rationally.

Johann Gottfried Herder (1744-1803), general-superintendent of the Lutheran clergy at Weimar, was influenced at first by the thought of the Enlightenment but then reacted against its rationalistic strictures. He singled out for criticism four areas in which the *Aufklärung* had made important, erroneous assumptions: in psychology, language, art, and history.

Eighteenth-century 'faculty psychology', such as that of Christian Wolff, split up the human mind into a number of different compartments, or faculties, which it then proceeded to hypostatize or personify as 'the reason', 'the will', 'desire', 'the judgement', 'sensation', and so forth. This tendency to personify abstractions is particularly clear in the work of Immanuel Kant. Faculty psychology also tended to split up the human being into body and soul. But perceiving, feeling, reasoning, wanting, and so forth, are simply activities of one, whole, human being whose psychological and physiological aspects are one at every step. The inner man, with all his dark forces, stimuli, and impulses, is simply one; and the activity of reasoning must *not* be regarded as a superior 'Agent' intent upon subordinating to its own control other spheres of human activity.

Language, the human activity of communicating, similarly, must not be considered in abstraction from the many human activities in which it is involved. Thinking, for example, is inward speaking, according to Herder. Thinking essentially involves language whether interiorly, without utterance, or exteriorly, in vocal utterance. The power to reason ('inward speaking') is developed in the child as a consequence of the child's training in the use of significant signs ('thinking aloud'). A mastery of significant signs (*Merkmale*) is a prerequisite of all logical thought. Language is an essential attribute of man. Man can be defined as a rational animal, or as an animal capable of using significant signs (language). From the viewpoint of the historical development of the vernacular language of any people, human language in its infancy has always expressed passion; in its youth it expressed itself poetically, in its manhood it developed literary prose, and in its old age, as in the case of the language of *les philosophes*, it always leads to arid pedantic accuracy. Herder advocated a constant creative use of the vernacular language, and called attention to the spontaneous natural genius evident in national folk-poetry as a source of inspiration for a continually developing poetic literature of the future.

With regard to the domain of aesthetics and art, Herder pointed out that several of the *Aufklärung* writers spoke of personified 'taste' as an innate and constant faculty which dictates a uniform standard of beauty acceptable to all men at all times. This approach to aesthetics and art totally ignored the historical approach to the study of art. At different times in history there are different environmental and psychological factors that influence artistic creativity and aesthetic appreciation. Historical conditions mould and shape contemporary artistic conceptions. The empirical historical data of art are significant and anthropologically important expressions of historical personalities as they emerged in particular places and times. Poetry, art, ballads and folk songs are the natural and primary expressions of the human psyche of the times. In this matter the thinkers of the *Aufklärung* got lost in a quagmire of unhistorical, rationalistic speculation. Herder's own insistence on the significance of folk songs and on the important role of vernacular language in the national cultural and aesthetic heritage exercised a great influence on the Dionysian *Sturm und Drang* ('Storm and Impulse') movement of German thought and literature.

Herder's *Ideas for the Philosophy of the History of Mankind* (1791) presented many original and imaginative suggestions for the reinterpretation and understanding of the human past. His approach is similar to that of Giambattista Vico, who died in the year Herder was born (1744). Each different culture must be understood from within, according to its own spirit and complex unity, by means of painstaking research into all the available data such as popular fables, folk songs and poetry. Research into the history and cultures of China, India, Egypt, the Jews, Greece and Europe reveals that the life-cycle of each culture, like that of a biological organism, is governed by natural forces and laws of active growth and decline. Each culture is unique and unrepeatable. It must be considered in and for itself. The research-historian must avoid 'foisting any (pre-conceived) set pattern upon it', and aim at achieving a sympathetic understanding of a people's way of life 'from within'. He must avoid making judgements which derive from some external and supposedly superior standpoint.

Each culture has grown and developed as a distinctive human response to the combination of environmental conditions existing in a particular time and place. The human achievements of that particular society are to be interpreted and assessed in relation to the cultural milieu to which these achievements belong. Each community should respect the culture of other communities while remaining true to its own. Each community should preoccupy itself unceasingly with the formative education of its youth if it is to preserve itself from sinking into cultural decline and social decay. Divine providence is at work in history, and it works in and through human and social action. Man's God-given 'potential' humanity becomes a realized, perfected humanity through the humanizing activities of language, cultural education, the arts, and the sciences, in the social history of the times. It is for this reason that the history of each nation and people must be studied, and understood, non-judgementally and 'from within'. This conception of history exercised an important influence on the historians and historiography of the nineteenth century.

22 Kant (I): Kant's critique of theoretical thought: on experimental knowledge and metaphysical synthesis

1. Kant's life, and pre-critical writings. *Immanuel Kant* was born in Königsberg (now Kaliningrad in the U.S.S.R., but at that time a German city), the son of Pietist parents. He studied the current tradition of speculative metaphysics and became a member of the university of Königsberg in 1755. In 1770 he was appointed to the chair of philosophy that had been held by his teacher, Knutzen. He was known as a successful lecturer, an interesting conversationalist and a charming host. He was a self-disciplined, hard-working author who produced an impressive succession of eminent philosophical works. He travelled little, never married, and died aged nearly eighty at Königsberg in February 1804.

Knutzen stimulated Kant's interest in Newtonian physics; and Kant's early writings and lectures were devoted to the physical science of his time. For several years Kant regarded the physical world as a Newtonian mechanical system of bodies operating in accordance with mathematically formulated laws. In the world of 'the starry heavens above' a rigorous causal *determinism* reigns. However, Kant had a deep reverence not only for 'the starry heavens above' but also for 'the moral law within'; and in the domain of morality it is not determinism but *freedom* that reigns.

In his early, 'pre-critical' years, Kant turned mainly to the rationalistic form of metaphysics, presented in the textbooks of Baumgarten and Wolff, to explain to his students the rational grounds for 'the moral law within', the nature of free judgement and choice, the existence of God, and the immortality of the soul. However, he encouraged the students to think for themselves. He criticized the textbook arguments for the existence of God and proposed a new intellectual basis or rational ground for a demonstration of God's existence.

In his book *The Only Possible Ground for a Demonstration of God's Existence* (1762), Kant maintained that the existing ontological, cosmological and teleological arguments for the existence of God were inadequate. The ontological argument, he said, presupposes that existence is a predicate. The teleological argument indicates that there is a divine intelligent ordering of the material universe without indicating that this 'ordering' involves any creaturehood dependency. The only possible ground, then, for a demonstration of God's existence, according to this early work of Kant, lies in an argument that the existence of God is implied as the rational and existential ground of all *thinking*.

'Thinking', or in other words the whole world of *thought*, is a given, experienced fact, or datum. Metaphysics can start with this datum. It can describe and analyse it. It can then ascertain the immediate certain judgements to which the descriptive analysis of consciousness, or thinking, as a datum gives rise. Consciousness, or thinking, points to the existence of God as the ground of all thinking. The inner experience of 'morality', or moral obligation, similarly, is a given fact. A descriptive analysis of this datum can give rise to certain judgements about freedom and immortality. In this way, 'inner experiences' become the starting point for metaphysics. One can therefore respect and accept the authority of science while also respecting, and grounding in experimental data, the universal judgements of morals and metaphysics.

2. The conception of the critical philosophy and the general problem of theoretical philosophy.
Some few years before 1770, Kant's confidence in the power of human reason to move with certainty in the realm of metaphysics was shaken by his recent acquaintance with the sceptical arguments of Hume. Kant now began to regard the metaphysical speculations of Wolff and the rationalists about the nature of reality beyond experience as 'dogmatic', non-empirical, speculations. He confessed that it was the objections of David Hume that 'first interrupted my dogmatic slumber and gave my investigations in the field of speculative philosophy quite a new direction'. Hume had undermined the foundations and the whole

edifice of rationalism. The bounds of experience, according to Hume, are also the bounds of all knowledge. Arguments which appear to extend and advance the frontiers of experiential knowledge by means of inductive inference and the notion of causality are 'dogmatic', non-empirical arguments which merely tell us about our human beliefs and expectations without actually extending our existing empirical knowledge. Kant appreciated that if this argument were true, then we could never have knowledge of any reality beyond our immediate experience. Universal knowledge, such as Newton's scientific knowledge, would be nothing more than confident human expectation and belief. However, Kant was also convinced that the striking success of Newtonian physics was not at all explained by the scepticism of Hume's form of British empiricism. Hume had failed to make a critical appraisal of the real bounds of empirical sense-knowledge and of human scientific and moral knowledge. There was therefore a need for a new critical philosophy which would make a critical appraisal of empirical sensory knowledge and of human intellectual knowledge. The fundamental, 'critical' problem for contemporary philosophy was therefore whether such a thing as philosophy, or metaphysics, was possible at all or not.

In 1770 Kant presented his inaugural Latin dissertation as professor *On the Form and Principles of the Sensible and Intelligible World*. In this dissertation Kant divided all human knowledge into sensitive knowledge and intellectual knowledge. In sensitive knowledge he distinguished between the *matter* of sensitive knowledge, namely the random sensations produced by sensible objects, and the *form* of sensitive knowledge, namely the 'pure intuitions' of space and time which co-ordinate the sensations and thereby make sensitive knowledge possible. 'Space', he said, 'is not something objective and real... but subjective and ideal, like a form (*schema*), issuing by a constant law from the nature of the mind, for co-ordinating among themselves everything externally sensed.' Space as the receptive form of external sensibility, and time as the receptive form of inner sensibility (of simultaneity or succession of sensations), are *a priori* co-ordinating forms of sensible intuition whose immediate, singular and co-ordinated presentations of the object bring the faculty of knowing immediately into relation with the object. Space and time are pure, singular, human intuitions in which all sensible objects are co-ordinated and intuited, or sensitively thought (*sensitive cogitata*). They are subjective conditions of the passive intuitions of the receptive human senses. They are subjective forms of the sensibility, and pure intuitions.

Sensitive knowledge, then, arises from the sensible objects presented to the mind when the random sensations or impressions (the matter) are co-ordinated in the pure intuitions of space and time (the form) within the sensing or experiencing subject. Knowledge of this kind is knowledge of the phenomenal world of experience.

Intellectual knowledge, however, is not knowledge of the phenomenal world of experience. Intellectual knowledge, such as human metaphysical knowledge of the soul and God, is knowledge of things as they are (*sicuti sunt*). It arises on the occasion of an 'inner experience' (of moral obligation, of purposiveness, of thinking, of the sublime) which is not a direct intuition. On an occasion of this kind human intellection or thought produces from within its own intrinsic nature non-empirical concepts (of necessity, reality, substance, and so forth) which give rise to intellectual knowledge of the intelligible world, just as sense-phenomena can give rise to human knowledge of the sensible world. This intellectual kind of knowledge, however, is not immune from error. The objects of thought (such as God and soul) transcend the senses. A critical philosophy must guard itself against applying to supersensible realities any concepts (such as causality) which are applicable only in the sphere of sensitive knowledge. The metaphysics of the dogmatic rationalists has erred gravely in this regard. Knowledge of supersensible realities must be grounded on thinking, that is, on the world of thought itself, and not on the world of sense perceptions.

3. The first *Critique*. In a letter to a friend (2 September 1770), written only two weeks after his public defence of the dissertation, Kant said that there were certain sections of his work which 'by reason of my indisposition (or ill-health) I was unable to work out to my satisfaction'. He mentioned in a later letter (to Marcus Herz, 21 February 1772) that, since he had not satisfactorily explained in the dissertation how the understanding's representations are related to the object 'without being in any way affected by it', he was now writing a new work which would give 'the key to the whole secret of metaphysics'. The new work, with a theoretical and practical part, was to have the title of 'The limits of sensation (*Sinnlichkeit*) and intellection (*Vernunft*)'. Kant was now attempting to evaluate, and determine the limits of, the two different forms of human knowledge, one attained through the medium of sense-apprehension, and the other attained in a non-sensory, intellectual, comprehension of the realities postulated by the practical problems and issues of moral decision and action.

Kant had planned to write one short work 'On the limits (bounds) of sensation and intellection' which he hoped 'will be published in about three months', but as he continued to face the problems arising, he found it necessary to cover the material in three volumes, the last of which was published eighteen years later in 1790. These three volumes on the bounds of sensibility and reason were entitled the *Critique of Pure Reason (Vernunft)*, published in 1781, the *Critique of Practical Reason (Vernunft)*, published in 1788, and the *Critique of Judgement*, published in 1790.

The human understanding in its normal operations, and the natural sciences in their formulation of general conclusions and laws, provide us with different kinds of universal propositions and judgements which do not arise 'out of experience' even when they 'begin with experience'. They arise in the faculty of rational judgement and not in the faculty of sensation. 'If one desired an example from the sciences', says Kant, 'one needs only to look at any proposition in mathematics. If one desires an example from the commonest operations of the understanding, the proposition that every change must have a cause can serve one's purpose.' These judgements of the human understanding can be understood only when the relationship of the terms (of the judgement) to the object are understood. In a judgement concerning reality, the subject and the predicate are diverse representations of the object, and the judgement brings this diversity of representation into synthesis. The subject of the judgement is a representation of the object in function of the sensibility; and the predicate of the judgement is the representation of the object in function of the forms of understanding. The sensible representation and the intellectual representation are brought into synthesis (S is P), in a synthetic judgement. The objective reference of the sensuous presentation (*Vorstellung*) presented no great problem to Kant. The main problem arose concerning the objective reference of our intellectual representations in any (scientific) judgement.

The judgements or statements of the physical sciences are judgements which express universal, necessary propositions. Universal, necessary knowledge of this kind does not arise *a posteriori*, directly from the singular intuitions of the senses; it is *a priori* knowledge. Thus, for example, the scientist, and we ourselves, can know *a priori*, antecedently, that every event must have a cause and that mathematical propositions are necessarily and universally true *a priori* in relation to all possible experience. Necessity and strict universality of this kind cannot arise from simple experience. It would appear, then, that the cognitive faculty supplies from within itself certain *a priori* elements, or pure conditions for knowing, on the occasions when sense-impressions are present in the faculty of sensibility. The critical problem is therefore the problem of *a priori* knowledge. Thus the question now is: What are these *a priori* elements, or pure conditions for knowing, which enable the scientist and ourselves to make synthetic judgements *a priori*? This is the main problem which Kant deals with in the first of the three critiques, the *Critique of Pure Reason (reinen Vernunft)*.

Kant's 'synthetic judgements *a priori*' are more readily understood in terms of his distinction between different types of judgements. An 'analytic' (or explicative) judgement, such as 'triangles have three angles' or 'peaceful resisters shun violence', is a judgement in which the predicate concept is included within the subject concept, as analysis will normally disclose. An analytic judgement does not require verification by experience; its sole criterion is the law of contradiction. A 'synthetic' (or amplicative) judgement, such as 'peaceful resistance is quite effective', is a judgement relating a subject concept with a predicate concept not included within the subject proper. The validity of such a judgement depends on its 'ground'. A synthetic judgement is said to be *synthetic a posteriori* if the relation between subject and predicate is given only in and through factual experience (e.g. that certain vegetables grow ripe in eight weeks). A synthetic judgement is said to be *synthetic a priori* if the predicate concept is not contained analytically in the subject concept and yet the judgement is characterized by necessity and strict universality, as, for example, in the judgements 'every event must have a cause', and 'the world must have a beginning'.

Universal, necessary (that is, *a priori*) synthetic judgements lie at the heart of mathematical science, natural science, metaphysics and ethics. Thus Kant's central question: 'How are synthetic *a priori* judgements possible?' lies at the heart of four specific problems, dealt with in the *Critique of Pure Reason*. These four problems are: first, how is pure mathematical knowledge or science possible?; second, how is pure physics possible?; third, how is a natural disposition to non-empirical thinking possible?; and fourth, is it at all possible for metaphysics to be a science? The answer to each of these problems depends on the answer given to the key problem: How are synthetic *a priori* judgements possible?

4. Sense-intuition and intellectual functions. Kant maintained, in the *Critique of Pure Reason*, that synthetic *a priori* truths can be seen to be possible only if it can be shown that human knowledge is dependent upon certain concepts which are not empirical in origin but which have their origin in human intellection.

The first major division of the *Critique of Pure Reason* is entitled 'The Transcendental Aesthetic'. It deals with the *a priori* intuitions and principles of sensible experience. Here Kant attempts to show that *a priori* considerations form the basis of human perception or sensibility. Space and time are the *a priori* foundations of sensibility. All objects of perceptions are necessarily located within space and time. No objects can be deprived of space and time and still remain perceptible. Space and time are presuppositions of sense-experience. They are *forms* of intuition distinct from the *contents* of sense-experience. Kant had dealt with this theme previously in his dissertation of 1770. There he had pointed out that the object, as object of the senses, must necessarily conform to the constitution of our faculty of intuition. Kant was aware that this viewpoint was a revolutionary viewpoint, analogous to that of Copernicus. It is the object that is conformed to the operations of the mind in the act of knowing, not the mind to the object.

In the second major division of the *Critique*, Kant then proceeded to consider the *a priori* conditions of human thought or intellection. 'There are two sources of human knowledge, namely sensibility and understanding. Through the former, objects are *given* to us; through the latter, they are *thought*.' In each case we are aware of or know the object as our structured minds permit us to know it. We know things as we are, and not as they are in themselves.

Thought, in its operation of synthesizing, unifying, and understanding our experiences, operates according to its own logical rules for categorizing the contents of sense-experience. It subjects these contents to its own pattern of questions, in a way similar to a barrister's questioning of a witness, or a doctor's questioning of a patient. The mind organizes, relates together, classifies, and unifies the sense-data by making various kinds of judgements as it engages in the act of interpreting the world of sense. Kant argued that the mind has twelve such forms of categorization of sense-data, and he called them the categories of the understanding. The judgement's twelve different ways of relating data together are simply the twelve formal differences of the logical functions of the judgement. Some judgements are *quantitative* in form, namely universal, particular and singular judgements; others are *qualitative* judgements, affirmative, negative, or infinite; others centre on *relationships*, namely categorical, hypothetical or disjunctive judgements; others are *modal*, namely problematic, assertoric and apodictic judgements.

The judgement's classifications or categorizations of sense-experiences correspond to these twelve logical functions of judgement. Thus the manifold of experience is judged and categorized in terms of the quantity, quality, relation and modality of the different sense-experiences. When we judge experiences in terms of quantity we classify them as being one, or many, or a totality; when we make qualitative judgements we have in mind that the objects either are, or are not, or in a limited way; when we make a judgement of relation, we think of the data in terms of either substance and accident, or cause and effect, or agent and patient; and when we make a judgement about the modality of the object we judge the data to be either possible or impossible, either existing or non-existing, and either necessary or contingent. It is through judgements and categorizations of this kind that the mind strives to synthesize further and unify at a higher intellectual level the world of manifold sense-experiences. We could have no intellectual knowledge, or understanding, of objects without these ordering principles or categories of the understanding. The categories, then, are necessary, subjective conditions for our having any intellectual knowledge of objects given to us through our faculties of sensation.

The section of the first *Critique* dealing with the categories, or pure principles of understanding, is entitled 'The Transcendental Analytic'. It analyses the transcendental, or non-empirical, aspect of human experiential knowledge; in other words, it analyses the human *condition* of experience without attending to any particular matters experienced. The following section then gives a 'transcendental deduction', that is, a non-empirical justification of the application of the categories to objects. Kant justifies the application in the following way. He says that objects must be thought of in order to be known. Objects cannot be thought except through the categories of thought; and so objects cannot be known except through the categories. No mere stream of unconnected sense-representations can be called intellectual knowledge. There must be synthesis, and synthesis is the work of understanding (*Verstand*). The understanding's work of synthesizing is not possible except within the unity of consciousness. The manifold of perception is incapable of being thought unless perceiving and thinking are so united in one thinking subject that a consciousness of self as thinking is capable of accompanying all representations.

Experiential knowledge implies a unity of the self. If there were no unity between the several operations of the mind, perceptions, images, memories, conceptions, syntheses, judgements and so forth, then there would be no unity of experience, and no unity of knowledge. Our unified grasp of the world around us is attained in the unifying activity of a single consciousness, or non-experienced, transcendental ego which Kant calls the 'transcendental unity of apperception'. This ego is called transcendental in the sense that it is not experienced directly even though it is necessarily implied by our actual experience. A unified self is implied by our unified consciousness of the world around us. 'Unity of consciousness precedes all data of intuitions.' The transcendental unity of apperception, and the transcendental unity of conscious perceiving and thinking within one subject, one self-consciousness, are permanent *a priori* conditions of any experience of any object. They are *a priori* conditions of the possibility of all experience.

5. The schematizations of the imagination and the principles of understanding. The power of imagination is, for Kant, a constructive power whose operations are constantly exemplified in science, invention and philosophy. Kant had recourse to the imagination as a mediating power which subsumes the manifold data of intuition under the categories, the logical functions of the understanding. Just as, in the case of the scientist, picturesque, imaginative, schematized models (of light-waves, or planetary systems, for example) are used to assist the logical functions of the scientist's understanding of particular data, so too, the imagination formulates schematic procedures by means of which the pure categories of the understanding are applied to the manifold of sensuous intuitions. Imagination does so by determining the temporal conditions under which a pure category, such as that of cause or of substance, is applicable to particular appearances, or, in other words, temporal phenomena. It is imagination, working with the pure form of time, which produces imaginative schematizations through which sensations are subsumed under the functions of the understanding. In this way, imagination connects sense and understanding.

Imagination is the power which connects sense and understanding in such a way that a synthesis results. Imagination brings about the connection, but it is only the *understanding* that is able to make explicit the principles on which the connecting proceeds. 'To bring this synthesis to concepts is a function which belongs to understanding, and it is through this function of the understanding that we first obtain knowledge properly so called' (*Critique* 2nd edn, 103), The understanding produces *a priori* certain principles of understanding (*Verstand*) which state the possibility of experience of objects. These principles are *a priori* rules for the objective use of the categories. They are principles or propositions which must be true if our experience of the world is to be what it is.

The first general principle of understanding corresponds to the three categories of *quantity*, and states: 'All (sensuous) intuitions are extensive (extended) magnitudes'. It is because this is so that synthetic *a priori* geometrical and mathematical propositions are applicable to experience. Thus, for example, 'I cannot represent to myself a line, however short, without drawing it in thought, that is, generating from a point all its parts one after another' (*Critique* 2nd edn, 203). The second general principle corresponds to the categories of *quality*, and states: 'In all appearances, the real which is an object of sensation has intensive magnitude'. Thus, it has a measurable degree of (perhaps increasing, or decreasing) intensity. This enables us to apply mathematics to sensations, and to make predictions about future perceptions or intuitions. The third general principle, corresponding to the schematized categories of *relation*, states: 'Experience is possibly only through the representation of a necessary connection of perceptions'. It tells us that change of appearance implies permanence of substance, that all changes imply causal relation, and that there is causal interaction or reciprocity between substances. Finally, there are three principles which correspond to the three categories of *modality*. The first states that the only existent that can be subjected to the formal conditions of experience is an existent which is really possible within empirical reality. The second states: 'That which is connected with the material conditions of (sense) experience is real'. The third states: 'That which, in its connection with the real, is determined by universal conditions of experience, is (exists as) necessary'. These three principles contain Kant's explanation of the notions of possibility, actuality, and necessity from the critical point of view. Thus, for example, a two-sided figure enclosing a space is not a real possibility, even though its concept is not self-contradictory, because a figure of this kind does not accord with the formal conditions of intuition. These principles of the understanding give the 'ground' for the possibility in principle of a pure mathematical science; and since mathematics is applicable to nature, they also give the 'ground' why a pure science of nature likewise is possible in principle. Pure empiricism does not provide an adequate theory of knowledge nor any 'ground' for a pure mathematical science or a pure science of nature. An *a priori* theoretical justification of Newtonian physics becomes possible, according to Kant, only if the standpoint of the Kantian Copernican revolution is accepted. While many subsequent philosophers did not accept this latter viewpoint of Kantian critical idealism, they nevertheless gave credit to Kant's work as calling attention to the inability of any doctrine of pure empiricism to provide a comprehensive theory of knowledge or a sound basis for science.

6. Empirical knowledge and critical idealism.

Empirical knowledge, Kant says, has its sources *a posteriori*, that is, in experience. 'Empirical knowledge is a compound of that (matter) which we receive through impressions, and that (form) which the faculty of cognition supplies from itself, sensuous impressions giving merely the occasion' (*Critique*: Introduction). The faculty of cognition supplies from itself the pure categories and pure principles of understanding. These categories and principles are valid for, and applicable to, objects of sense only. They are applicable only to phenomena. If there happens to exist any 'pure' *a priori* 'knowledge altogether independent of experience, and even of all sensuous impressions', then the categories and principles of understanding are not applicable to knowledge of this kind. They 'serve only to make *empirical* knowledge possible'. The categories can give no help therefore to the metaphysician who thinks about God, soul and cosmic reality. Metaphysical thought of this kind does not begin with sensuous impressions or experience and so it cannot give rise to empirical knowledge.

Empirical knowledge is knowledge of phenomena, or 'objects as known', or appearances, according to Kant. The known world is not independent of consciousness as such, but it is given as independent of particular consciousness. Thus known objects are not simply private objects. They are given, at least in their spatial aspects, as common to many observers. Nevertheless, empirical knowledge is knowledge of phenomena; it is not knowledge of noumena, according to Kant. Human intuition is sense-intuition, he says. We have no faculty of pure intellectual intuition into realities of things as direct objects of intellectual insight. Thus we cannot know noumena, that is, realities as they are in themselves, 'abstracting from our mode of intuiting them'. We readily believe in the existence of some particular 'thing' in itself, or noumenon. But human empirical knowledge is necessarily knowledge of phenomena; and the categories, one of which is existence, apply only to phenomena. Thus human understanding (*Verstand*) is incapable of knowing things as they are in themselves, apart from our sense-intuitions. No 'knowledge' of noumena is possible, therefore, according to Kant's critical philosophy.

Kant called his critical philosophy, on different occasions, critical idealism, or problematical or transcendental idealism. He uses these different terms to denote his fundamental doctrine that knowledge is a synthetic, relational product of the activity of the transcendental unity of apperception, the transcendental ego. Transcendental knowledge of empirical matters is possible, while transcendent knowledge is not. The word 'transcendent' applies to whatever is beyond possible experience; it simply connotes the unknowable. The word 'transcendental' applies to the *a priori* human condition of experience. Human experiential knowledge and scientific knowledge is, in this sense, transcendental knowledge. But transcendental knowledge is always knowledge of phenomena or 'known objects', and not knowledge of 'matter' itself or of things in themselves (noumena). Thus, the critical philosophy is an idealist philosophy. Its central doctrine is the epistemological doctrine of transcendental idealism. It teaches, in brief, that knowledge is a synthetic, relational product of the transcendental self.

Kant had a deep reverence for the 'starry heavens above' and for the 'moral law within'. He was convinced that the 'noumenal' speculations of the rationalists and the sceptical criticisms of the empiricists merely served to undermine the foundations of science, morality and religion. The issues raised involved the deepest interests of all mankind. He was convinced that critical idealism was the only philosophy which was capable of presenting a theoretical explanation and justification of scientific thought concerning 'the starry heavens above', and of human thought concerning 'the moral law within'. He seemed to be totally unaware that a philosophy of critical realism, or in other words a 'philosophy of being', provided a 'realist' solution to the problem of knowledge, a solution based on the apprehension and affirmation of being or the real. He regarded critical idealism, then, as the only possible answer to the scepticism of empiricism on the one side and the dogmatism of rationalism on the other. It is not the case, however, that one must accept a doctrine of idealism if one wishes to avoid the errors of extreme rationalism and pure empiricism.

7. Metaphysics' function as 'censor' of error. 'Metaphysics', says Kant, 'forms properly that department of knowledge which may be termed, in the truest sense of the word, philosophy.... That, as a purely speculative science, it is more useful in preventing error, than in the extension of knowledge, does not detract from its value; on the contrary, the supreme office of censor which it occupies, assures to it the highest authority and importance' (*Critique* 2nd edn, 860).

Kant shows metaphysics or philosophy at work as 'censor', preventing error, in his critical examination of rational psychology, speculative cosmology and philosophical theology.

(1) Rational psychology, of the Cartesian-Wolffian kind, is not, and cannot be, an empirical science, he says. The principal reason why this is so is that the transcendental ego of pure self-consciousness can never become an object of (sensuous) intuition. If the unity of apperception, that is, the 'I' that is aware (or the ego of the 'I think') is ever regarded as a substance subsumed under the categories, then this view leads inevitably to the various paralogisms, the logically fallacious syllogisms, of dogmatic rational psychology. This does not apply, of course, to empirical psychology, which studies only the empirical ego. The empirical ego is reducible to successive states and is given as an object in time; it can therefore become an object for study in empirical psychology.

(2) Dogmatic speculative cosmology, similarly, can never become an empirical science, Kant asserts. It attempts to use the idea of the totality of phenomena, that is, the 'world', as a means of extending our empirical knowledge of reality. But the idea of the world as a totality of phenomena is a transcendental idea, and no new empirical knowledge can arise out of an idea of this kind. The illegitimate use of a transcendental idea in this way will lead inevitably to contradictory propositions, or antinomies. It is not to be wondered at, then, that one speculative cosmologist may adduce several cogent arguments in support of his view that 'the world has a beginning in time and is limited also in regard to space', while another speculative cosmologist may give several cogent arguments in support of the opposite view, that 'the world has no beginning and no frontiers in space, but is infinite in respect of both time and space'.

We may also find one cosmologist arguing consistently that 'every composite substance in the world is constituted of simple parts, and there does not exist any substance which is not either simple in itself or composed of simple parts', while another may argue equally consistently that 'no composite thing in the world is constituted of simple parts and there is no place where any simple thing exists'. The one treats noumena as though they were phenomena and the other treats phenomena as though they were noumena. Again, one cosmologist may argue that 'the causality of the laws of Nature is not the only causality from which natural phenomena can be derived, since, to explain them, it is necessary to assume another form of causality, causality through freedom', while another may argue that 'there ̶i̶s̶ no freedom; in the world everything happens solely according to the laws of Nature'. Kant's suggested solution to this antinomy is that man is noumenally free and phenomenally determined. A fourth antinomy arises when we find one speculative cosmologist arguing that 'there belongs to the world, either as a part or cause of it, something existing as an absolutely necessary being' while another may argue that 'there does not exist, anywhere, any necessary being as the cause of the world, either in this world o̅r̅ out of it'. One view is maintained by dogmatic rationalists and the other by dogmatic empiricists or materialists. The critical philosophy avoids these antinomies, Kant suggested, by limiting empirical knowledge to the world of phenomena while opening up the world of noumenal reality through practical thought based on moral experience.

(3) Philosophical theology, likewise, can never become an empirical science, according to Kant. The transcendental Ideal, or the transcendental idea of God, lies beyond the proper field of application of the categories of understanding. For this reason it is impossible to demonstrate empirically either the existence or the non-existence of God. Metaphysics, or philosophy, occupying as it does the 'supreme office of censor', can once again provide a useful service in pointing out the errors present in the traditional, alleged proofs for the existence of God.

'All the trouble and labour bestowed on the famous *ontological* or Cartesian proof of the existence of a supreme Being from concepts alone', Kant says, 'is trouble and labour wasted.' Any attempt to include existence in the definition of God is simply an attempt to define God into existence. If anyone denies the existence of God he is not simply denying a predicate of a subject, he is annihilating in thought both the subject and all predicates of that subject; and furthermore, in doing so he does not involve himself in any logical contradiction. According to Kant, every existential proposition is synthetic, and can be denied without contradiction. The ontological argument is in reality nothing more than a verbal exercise.

The *cosmological* argument assumes that if anything exists (and I myself do exist), then an absolutely necessary being must also exist as the adequate cause. The error of this argument, says Kant, is that it makes use of the principle of causality, and the *a priori* category of causality has 'no meaning and no criterion for its application save only in the sensible world'. This argument, like the ontological argument, fails to bridge the gap between our idea of a necessary, perfect being and an empirical demonstration of its existence.

The *teleological* or physico-theological argument argues from the existence of finality and design in the universe to the existence of God as creative cause. Kant points out that this proof could at most establish the existence of an intelligent architect of the world. It does not establish the existence of a creator of all that exists.

Critical philosophy, in its role as 'censor', is able to establish, therefore, that it is impossible to extend empirical knowledge through the use of empirico-deductive arguments revolving around ideas (of the self, and the world, and God) which are non-empirical ideas. Empirical knowledge can neither establish nor disprove the existence of the ego, or the world, or God. Empirical knowledge is totally confined to the sphere of phenomena. The ideas of God, world and self are ideas of pure reason (*Vernunft*). Critical philosophy can now move forward to investigate, positively, the important role that these three ideas play in the systematic arrangement of all of our thought.

8. Metaphysics as speculative, regulative thought. Human thought has a natural tendency, an ineradicable and irresistible impulse, Kant says, to unify and give systematic arrangement to all human experiences and cognitions. For this reason, man has a natural disposition to metaphysics or philosophy. Human thought (*Vernunft*) seeks by its very nature to unify the empirical cognitions of the understanding. It becomes occupied with 'the cognitions of the understanding that are presented to it, for the purpose of receiving the unity of a rational conception, that is, of being connected according to a principle'. The systematic connection which reason gives to the empirical cognition of objects of the understanding, through the use of the transcendental regulative ideas of reason, brings about a unity of experience which is 'indispensable to reason, advantageous to the understanding, and promotive of the interests of empirical cognition'.

The three regulative ideas or forms of totality that we naturally tend to think about when we try to unify all our experience are the idea of the self, the idea of the cosmos, and the idea of God. These ideas are produced not by experience but by pure reason alone. They are ideas of totality which correspond to no object in our experience, but they are ideas we naturally make use of in our attempts to achieve a coherent synthesis of all our experience. In brief, they are transcendental, regulative ideas of pure reason.

Empirical psychology, in its task of bringing together the feelings, emotions, desires and various psychological activities we are aware of to form a unified total scheme, is assisted by the transcendental idea of the ego as a single fundamental power, a permanent being. The unity of apperception, which Kant also calls the 'I think', is the ultimate condition of all experience. It is the logical focus to which all experience relates. Experience is experience for a subject. The ego recognizes thoughts and feelings as *my* thoughts and feelings. This ego of the 'I think' is a logical requirement of all experience. It is simply 'a bare consciousness which accompanies all concepts, ... a transcendental subject of thoughts' (*Critique* 2nd edn, 404). It is a consciousness which is a *thought*, not an *intuition* (*ibid*. 157). Thus the subject referred to is not given empirically as something substantial. It is a 'representation "I"... which is in itself completely empty' (*ibid*. 404). It is simply a regulative idea produced by pure reason as a means for synthesizing into a unity the varied psychological activities relating to the logical subject of experience.

The second regulative idea of merely speculative reason is the concept of the *world* as a totality. 'World, in the transcendental sense, signifies the absolute totality of the content of existing things.' The idea of the cosmos, and cosmological ideas such as the idea of nature in general, the idea of the beginning of the world, and the idea of the limit of the world, or matter, or the real in space, are regulative principles which can serve as rules that prescribe how we ought to proceed in dealing with any absolute totality of series of conditions of given phenomena. Ideas of this kind have a vital regulative function in the scientific quest. They posit a systematic unity to the world and thereby stimulate scientists to look for connections in nature. Thus, for example, a scientist may look for the connections in nature between the gravitational movement of falling apples and the gravitational movements of orbiting planets.

The third regulative idea is the idea of 'God', or being as a totality. This idea merely formulates the command of reason that all connections in the world be viewed as if all these connections had their source in one total, all-embracing being as the supreme and sufficient cause. This idea presents an 'all-sufficient ground... in relation to which we so employ our reason in the field of experience, as if all objects drew their origin from that archetype of reason'. 'We ought not to deduce the phenomena, order, and unity of the universe from a supreme intelligence, but merely draw from this idea of a supremely wise cause the rules which must guide reason in its connection of causes and effects' (*Critique* 2nd edn, 699). This idea of an ordering, purposeful and wholly rational God will suggest to the scientist and astronomer, for example, that the world is rationally constructed and that experimental inquiry will be rewarded with the discovery of new scientific laws at work in nature.

Kant accepted physics as the ideal of science, and Newton as its ideal expositor. He accepted wholeheartedly the fundamental correctness of the Newtonian scientific world-view. This view was expressed in scientific propositions, synthetic *a priori* judgements, for which pure empiricism and dogmatic rationalism had no explanation. To explain how the mind sees necessary connections in objects empirically given, Kant proposed his revolutionary 'Copernican' doctrine that known objects conform to the mind in the process of being known. We know things as we are. Known objects are objects subjected to the *a priori* categories of the human understanding. The human mind or reason (*Vernunft*) has a natural disposition for synthesizing at a level of unification which is higher than that of the multiple categorizations of the understanding (*Verstand*). Man's natural disposition to philosophy enables him to unify the 'technical' cognitions of the understanding under the architectonic ideas of the totality-in-unity of the thinking subject (ego) and the totality-in-unity of the cosmic series of all phenomena (world), both of which are unified, in turn, under the unity of the absolute 'ground' and condition of all objects of thought in general, namely, the idea of the being of all beings (*Critique* 2nd edn, 414). This 'rational cognition on the basis of pure conceptions is properly nothing but metaphysics' (*ibid*. 864).

9. General comment. Kant regarded the objective datum as a 'pure diverse', a random inflow of scattered impressions, lacking all internal structure and intelligibility, and incapable of being a fertile source of determinate knowledge. Under the influence of Hume's phenomenalism which grounded necessary judgements in 'habit', Kant focused his attention on the universalizing and 'informing' structures of the knowing subject. In the process of doing so he depreciated the objective datum. He saw no possible intermediary form of intellectual activity between that of an intuitive intelligence, creating its object, and that of an informing intelligence, imposing intelligible forms on sensed objects. He completely overlooked and ignored the possibility of abstracting intelligence. Thus, in the Kantian 'reconstruction' of knowledge, the value and function attributed to the objective datum is so reduced that the weight of reconstruction must be borne almost exclusively by the activity of the knowing subject. The epistemological principles posited by Kant are the principles of a critical idealism which is also a philosophy of subjectivism.

The critical philosophy of Kant gave rise almost immediately to the transcendental idealism of his successors (Fichte, Schelling, Hegel), for whom the primacy of the subject became absolute, and for whom being is totally subordinated to thought. It gave rise more recently to an important group of modern idealists for whom 'to know is to posit being'. Cognition came to be regarded, then, as an activity which posits, produces, or constructs its object, rather than a submission to and an assimilating and affirming of the real.

23 Kant (II): Kant's critiques of practical thought and discerning judgement: on morality, religion and discernment

1. Practical reason or rational will   2. The moral postulates, and religion   3. The aesthetic judgement and the teleological judgement   4. Purposiveness or finality in the universe   5. Kant's *Opus Postumum*   6. General comment

1. Practical reason or rational will. Human thought (*Vernunft*) is concerned not only to formulate theories about *things*, such as 'the starry heavens above', but also to make practical judgements and decisions concerning human life and *behaviour* in accordance with the dictates of 'the moral law within'. Thought, or pure reason, finds application, therefore, in both theoretical discursive knowledge and in practical rational knowledge, according to Kant. The *Critique of Practical Reason (Vernunft)* deals with the practical or ethical functions of rational thought in its production of moral decisions or choices in accordance with universal moral law. This application of human thought to practical behaviour has rational and voluntary aspects and thus it can be called indifferently either practical reason or rational will. It is the ultimate ground and source of the practical principles of the rational moral law.

In the theoretical philosophy of the first *Critique*, Kant had started with the 'fact' of empirical science with its universal and necessary laws. In the practical philosophy of the next *Critique*, Kant started with another kind of 'fact', equally undeniable, namely the moral fact. The fact of morality with its universal and necessary laws and duties, reaching out to all men without exception, like the fact of empirical knowledge, raises an important query concerning the *a priori* conditions required in man in order to explain this fact or make it possible. Moral laws and judgements, such as 'Thou shalt not bear false witness against thy neighbour' or 'We ought to tell the truth', have qualities of universality and necessity which indicate that they are *a priori* laws and judgements whose basis must be sought *a priori* in the concepts of pure reason. Once again as before, says Kant, an adequate explanation of the *a priori* conditions of human morality will be found not in the *matter* of the fact of morality but rather in the *form* of those universal and necessary laws which impose moral obligation. Moral law is experienced as duty, obligation or rational necessity. It is experienced as a 'thou ought' which implies 'thou canst'. Without this moral 'ought', Kant insists, man would never know himself to be free. The moral 'ought' provides proof of something unconditioned, free uncaused activity.

No 'thing' is good or evil. These designations, good and evil, properly apply only to an acting will. And the acting will is designated as good without qualification only when it acts for the sake of duty. 'The good will is good, not because of what it causes or accomplishes, not because of its usefulness in the attainment of some set purpose, but solely because of the willing, that is to say, it is good of itself.' A will is a good will when it wills for the sake of duty. The rational will is rational when it strives to do what it ought to do. The truly moral act is the one which is done for the sake of the moral law and not the one which is done for some secondary, interested motive. Duty must be done for duty's sake; only thus is a moral action a pure moral action. The good will is the will which acts for the sake of duty.

To act for the sake of duty means to act out of reverence for universal law. This can be translated into terms of the concrete moral life through the principle of duty, namely, 'I am never to act otherwise than so that I can also will that my maxim should become a universal law'. One's actions should not be motivated by selfish desires. Practical reason commends us to rise above selfish maxims. The objective principles of morality are essentially universal. The moral 'ought' is a moral imperative which is universal and categorical. It commands actions, not as means to any end, but as good in themselves.

The truly moral imperative is a universal categorical imperative which is seen to apply instantly to all rational beings. It commands an action as objectively 'necessary of itself without reference to another end'. It is an apodictic practical principle, commanding that the maxims serving as our principles of volition should conform to universal law. The categorical imperative may be formulated thus: 'Act only on that maxim through which thou canst at the same time will that it should become a universal law', or it may also be formulated as 'Act as if the maxim of thy action were to become, through thy will, a universal law of nature'. Kant says, by way of example or illustration, that a person in financial difficulty must not become a borrower if he knows that he would be unable to keep his

promise to return borrowed money in a definite time, since, if a law
obliging the making of such impossible promises were universally
obeyed, everyone would simply ridicule the making of all such
promises as vain pretences.

A person must never be used simply as a means to an end. A
person, a rational being, is an end in itself, having absolute intrinsic
worth. 'Rational nature exists as an end in itself.' This affirmation of
the absolute worth of the individual leads to 'a second formulation of
the categorical imperative which says: So act as to treat humanity,
whether in thine own person or in that of any other, in every case at
the same time as an end, and never merely as a means'.

The rational will, that is, the good will, must be regarded as the
autonomous source of the law which man recognizes as universally
binding. In this way, each person through his own autonomous act
of will legislates the moral law in a way which is regarded as binding
on all. The will of a rational being is directly autonomous; in other
words, it is a law unto itself. This principle of the autonomy of the
will leads to a third formulation of the categorical imperative: 'So act
that the will could regard itself at the same time as making universal
law through its own maxim'. It is this free and independent
autonomous will which is then 'the supreme principle of morality'.
In a kingdom or systematic union of rational beings of this kind,
each person is at once member and sovereign and end. The
members, taken together, constitute a law-making sovereign kingdom of ends.

The categorical imperative, therefore, affirms and points to three
basic moral insights or conceptions, namely the universality of the
moral law, the supreme worth of the rational person, and the
freedom or autonomy of the will. The idea of freedom is a practically
necessary condition of morality. The fact of obligation implies
freedom as a condition. Though we cannot prove empirically that we
are free, nevertheless the idea of freedom, as the condition under
which alone a categorical imperative is possible, is postulated as a
practical necessity for the moral agent.

2. The moral postulates, and religion. It is impossible to
present any empirical demonstration, based on phenomena, Kant
says, that God exists, or the soul is immortal, or the will is free.
Nevertheless, we are intellectually compelled to assume, as a practical necessity for moral action, that man is free, God exists and the
soul is immortal; and, because we are intellectually compelled, we
are thereby intellectually authorized to assume that it is so.

The first postulate of practical reason is freedom, or autonomy. The will is free; for the moral law, in saying 'thou oughtest', implies that *thou canst*. Freedom and moral action are so inseparably united that 'one may define practical freedom as the independence of the will of anything but the moral law alone'. A person could not be responsible if he were not able to respond freely to a moral categorical imperative. One and the same human action can therefore be from one point of view, the action of a phenomenal being determined by historical time-conditions, and yet also be, from another point of view, free and independent of empirical time-conditions. The visible, and yet free, human action is seen, at one and the same time, as historically determined and yet noumenally free. It is the action of a nonempirical, free, and active self.

The second postulate of pure reason in its practical or moral use, according to Kant, is immortality. The moral law commands us to strive for perfect good. This implies an indefinite, unending progress towards the ideal, namely integrity, wholeness, holiness. 'But this endless progress is possible only on the supposition of the unending duration of the existence and personality of the same rational being which is called the immortality of the soul' (*Critique of Practical Reason* 220).

The third moral postulate for Kant is the existence of God as the condition and ground for the *a priori* necessary synthetic connection between virtue (sanctity) and happiness, the degree of happiness being exactly proportioned to the degree of virtue according to the conception of law. We cannot conceive the possibility of the perfect good being realized except on the supposition that a wise and good Creator exists. 'It is only from a morally perfect and at the same time all powerful will... that we hope to attain the highest good which the moral law makes it our duty to take as the object of our endeavour.'

The moral fact, thus, guarantees and requires the existence of three noumenal realities, our liberty, our immortality and God. These three postulates correspond to the three transcendental Ideas of Pure Reason: God, the self, and the world. Nature or the world is a phenomenal manifestation of noumenal reality. Moral law demands that we conceive God as creating and sustaining Nature for a final moral end, that is, the full development and happiness of man as a moral being in a realized or fulfilled kingdom of ends.

This correspondence of postulates with ideas unifies all metaphysics. The closeness of the transcendental ideas to moral certitude confers on the ideas of God, self and the cosmos an extrinsic certitude which suffices to transform these regulative ideas into true, objective, metaphysical theses. These theses are the ground of the science of metaphysics or philosophy.

Though the idea of God is founded, for Kant, on the moral fact and not on religious belief, nevertheless, moral metaphysics provides a rational basis for religious reverence. God is not only the regulative Ideal which unifies all science, he is also the sovereign creator who assures the perfect accomplishment of the moral order by harmonizing duty, sanctity and happiness. Thus every human action performed to accomplish duty becomes thereby an action which fulfils the divine will. In this way 'morality inevitably leads to religion'. But this approach to religion also makes 'religion within the limits of reason' to be the only admissible form of religion; and a philosophy of religion of this kind must necessarily confine itself in content to the content of moral philosophy. Kant himself respected that form of religious piety which avoided undue reliance on dogmatic credal formulas and opened itself instead to a constant awareness of the divine presence.

3. The aesthetic judgement and the teleological judgement. The wonder, the beauty and sublimity of Nature, seen as the vast domain for the full development and happiness of men, as moral beings in a realized kingdom of ends, forms the overall theme of Kant's third critique, the *Critique of Judgement*. In this third *Critique*, Kant provides a principle of connection between the first *Critique*'s world of natural necessity (Nature) and the second *Critique*'s world of freedom (noumenal reality). Judgement, in the sense of cultivated sound judgement, 'mother wit', discernment, or 'sound understanding' (cf. *Critique of Judgement* Preface, 5) mediates between theoretical understanding (*Verstand*) and practical reason (*praktischen Vernunft*), and provides a ground or principle of unity for free, moral action within the law-governed cosmos.

The scientist, for example, aims at constructing a system of interrelated laws by bringing particular observations, through induction, under particular laws, and particular laws under more general laws. Now, 'the faculty of judgement in general is the power of thinking the particular as being contained in the universal'. The scientist's faculty of judgement guides him to think of the phenomenal world as an intelligible unity, intelligible to our faculties. He continues his inquiries under the guidance of the concept that a superior, noumenal intelligence adapts the cosmic system to our cognitive faculties in such a way that we view the phenomenal world (Nature) as being to us an intelligible purposive whole. He is guided, therefore, by the principle of the purposiveness or finality of Nature. This principle is a transcendental principle of the faculty or power of discerning judgement; it derives from the *a priori*, subjective, regulative idea of purpose in nature.

The concept of purposiveness in the world enables us to look upon Nature as a phenomenal manifestation of noumenal reality. 'Thus the faculty of judgement makes possible the transition from the domain of the concept of Nature to that of the concept of freedom.' Nature is the phenomenal manifestation of noumenal reality: it is the phenomenal (physical) field which renders possible the expression of the purposive causality of the noumenal (moral, spiritual) order. (This theme inspired Fichte's concept of Nature as a field for moral activity.)

When the power of 'discerning' judgement pronounces some thing, such as a symphony or a statue, to be beautiful, Kant calls this a pronouncement of 'the judgement of taste'. A proposition of this kind does not express an empirico-categorized concept or item of knowledge. Rather, it pronounces that a 'feeling' of aesthetic or artistic enjoyment is present in our appreciation of the captivating beauty of the thing of beauty. The thing of beauty is seen as giving contemplative satisfaction, without reference to appetitive desires; and it is universally claimed as giving contemplative satisfaction to all who behold and enjoy it. The beauty of the object is 'the form of the purposiveness of the object, so far as this is perceived without any representation of a purpose'. Thus, a beautiful statue or a beautiful flower evokes in us a feeling that its form embodies purposiveness and meaning even though we may not actually know its purpose or meaning. The claim that something is beautiful in itself, and that it is an object of aesthetic satisfaction to all who behold it, presupposes that there is in all of us a universal sense of discernment, or common aesthetic sense, as the necessary condition of the universal communicability of aesthetic pronouncements. It can be called the sense of beauty, or the cultivated, sound judgement of taste.

The judgement of the sublime resembles, and yet differs from, the judgement of the beautiful. The beautiful pleases through its form and its bounds; but the sublime is found when a formless object is represented as boundless (absolute *magnum*), that is, 'great beyond every standard of the senses', even though its totality is present in thought. Thus, for example, we judge the sight of a particular mountain range or a storm at sea, or 'thunderclouds piled up the vault of heaven', to be sublime; but the sublime is a feeling which the contemplation of these objects of nature provokes in us and not a quality inhering in those objects themselves.

The teleological judgement similarly resembles, and yet differs from, the aesthetic judgement. The aesthetic judgement declares that the purposiveness of Nature, represented in an object of beauty, is the ground of feelings of pleasure to all, without any mediating concept. The teleological judgement (as, for example, that 'wings are for flying' or 'the eye is for seeing') judges that a given object fulfils a conceived purpose or end of Nature, without attending to any of the feelings of the subject. The teleological judgement is a logical expression of the power of judgement corresponding to the transcendental *logic* of the *Critique of Pure Reason*, just as the aesthetic judgement is an expression of the power of judgement corresponding to the *aesthetic* of the *Critique of Pure Reason*.

4. Purposiveness or finality in the universe. Kant was specially interested in the inner finality of Nature. Finality in Nature is said to be inner natural finality when the natural purpose of the object (e.g. the ear is for hearing) is seen as lying within the object considered as an organic whole. Relative or external finality is that form of finality in which one thing is seen to serve or protect something else. A problem arises, however, concerning how it is possible to judge that an object embodies within itself a purpose of Nature. What are the requisite conditions for making an absolute teleological judgement about the inner natural finality of an object? Kant suggested, in a preliminary way at first, that 'a thing exists as a purpose of Nature when it is cause and effect of itself'. Thus, for example, a tree produces itself as an individual tree, in a process of self-production. The various parts of the tree, such as the leaves, are produced by the tree; and yet these same parts, which also conserve the tree, are so interrelated that they produce the whole organism by their causality. Each part exists by means of all the other parts; each exists for the sake of the others and for the whole; and each part acts reciprocally with the others in their activity of producing each other. A product which is a self-organizing being of this kind can be called 'a purpose of nature', or a product endowed with inner natural finality. The heuristic principle or maxim, therefore, for judging internal natural purposiveness in organized beings is as follows: 'An organized product of Nature is one in which everything is reciprocally end and means'.

The heuristic principle for judging of internal natural purposiveness is grounded on an *a priori* principle, the regulative Idea of a purpose of Nature. Nature is viewed as adapted *a priori* to the aim of the empirical system of knowledge. Biology, botany, medicine and empirical science in general are being continually developed on the presupposition, or 'sound understanding', that Nature is an interconnected totality or system of empirical laws which is already adapted to the end or aim of a factual systematizing of our empirical knowledge. The scientist's search for these particular empirical laws is a function of his reflexive power of judgement. Nature's formal adaptation-to-end is the *a priori* of the reflexive power of judgement. Judgement, in other words, presupposes that nature is adapted to the aim of the empirical system of knowledge. A scientist's discovery of one or other of the mechanical or empirical laws, sought by his reflexive power of judgement, is always accompanied by a feeling of satisfaction or pleasure that the inner natural finality of the object is found to be actually all that it ought to be.

Kant maintained that once teleology is found in nature in organic things it is right and legitimate to extend the idea of purpose of nature to other things and to nature as a whole. A natural thing which is an end can itself be a means to something else. Thus, plants become nourishment to animals. Inorganic things can be means to organic beings. Rain, sunshine and minerals are means for organic growth. These are instances of external adaptation-to-end or external finality.

When the teleological principle is extended to inorganic things and to the whole cosmos, nature, 'the complex of phenomena', is viewed in a new way as a system of ends. In this natural system everything is seen as an interconnected totality in accordance with the law of finality. In this light the scientist judges in fact that nothing in nature is aimless, and so he systematizes in a teleological way the natural data which the categories systematize according to mechanical causality. He analyses the processes and structures of nature (e.g. eyes) according to mechanical laws but under the light of a teleological viewpoint (e.g. that eyes are for seeing). He subordinates the mechanical principle to the teleological principle. He brings together those elements in nature which form teleological units, and, having done so, he then applies the mechanical principle to these teleological units and their teleological processes. In this procedure of scientific inquiry the laws of nature do not influence practical reason's *a priori* laws of freedom even when freedom is exercising an important influence on nature. The teleological power of sound judgement subordinates nature and our understanding (*Verstand*) of nature to pure reason (*Vernunft*) and its concept of final causality. In this way the reflective power of judgement overcomes the opposition between theoretical and practical reason, and it synthesizes the two forms of human thought in a 'sound understanding' of nature as if it is realizing the concept of final causality.

Human thought of every kind finds its unification then in the regulative idea of a purpose of nature, the concept of finality. We judge nature as if its products were brought to fulfilment by final causality. We do so because it is impossible for us to think of them otherwise than as depending on final causality. Our intellects are not intuitive intellects; they cannot intuit the whole as determining the part. Our discursive intellect simply makes use of the teleological principle in its attempt to overcome its own limitations in thinking of organic matter in the way that an intuitive intellect would do so.

In summary, both the aesthetic representation of the finality of nature and the logical representation of the finality of nature enable us to conceive nature as a possible field for final causality. Supersensible noumenal reality is implied by aesthetic experience and by experience of inner natural finality in cerain products of nature. Practical reason postulates the existence of God and justifies belief in his existence. Reflective judgement enables us to see nature as realizing the concept of final causality. Moral law demands that we conceive God as creating and sustaining the universe for a final *moral* end. This moral end can only be the full development and happiness of men as moral beings in a realized kingdom of ends. Human happiness finds its realization, then, in the final harmonization of the phenomenal or physical order and the noumenal or moral order. The final purpose of nature is the development and happiness of man. 'If the world only consisted of lifeless or irrational beings the existence of such a world would have no worth whatever, because there would exist in it no being with the least conception of what worth is... . The real existence of rational beings subject to moral laws can alone be regarded as the final end of the existence of the world' (*Critique of Judgement* 449-450).

5. Kant's *Opus Postumum*. Kant attempted to explore the limits of sensibility (*Sinnlichkeit*) and rationality or discerning thought (*Vernunft*) in order to discover and determine how human consciousness should be constituted for (scientific) knowledge to be possible. He was prompted to do so because of his admiration for the discoveries of the experimental sciences and because of the evident inadequacies and antinomies of modern empiricism and modern rationalism.

Under the influence of the phenomenalism of Hume, which woke him, he said, from his dogmatic (rationalist) slumber, Kant began his *Critique* with a presumption that the datum which presents itself to human consciousness is a purely diverse datum lacking internal structure and intelligibility. This irrational datum is what is given in the senses. The datum consists in the impressions or modifications affecting the senses. The intuitive representation, present in the senses, is but the senses modified or affected. It does not constitute knowing because it is not yet consciousness of an object; nevertheless, 'without (this sensible) intuition all our knowledge would lack objects and would be entirely empty' (*Critique of Pure Reason* 2nd edn, 87).

Irrational sensible intuition provides knowing with the impressions or modifications affecting the senses. Understanding then categorizes, synthesizes and objectivizes what is intuited by the senses. The function of the understanding is limited to objectivizing the data of the senses. This function is discursive or expatiating in character; it is not intuitive. 'Human knowing is a knowing through concepts, not intuitive but discursive' (*Critique of Pure Reason* 2nd edn, 92).

To become an object of knowing, every content must be objectively represented in consciousness; each content must be referred to the original unity of apperception. In this way it becomes the object-in-me, or the object as known. The irrational real is regarded, therefore, as not knowable in itself. It is the subject which constitutes it as the 'other', the object, and makes it knowable. To know a datum is to make an *object* of it by imposing on it *a priori* forms, according to Kant.

The act of knowing is expressed in the judgement which is a synthesis of subject and predicate. The *subject* of the judgement is the representation of the object as function of the sensibility. The *predicate* of the judgement is a further representation of that representation of the object as function of the understanding alone, at a higher level than that of the senses. This explains why, for Kant, all knowing is necessarily and merely a knowing of what is represented directly and positively in the senses.

Kant's phenomenalist presumption led him, therefore, to view the act of knowing as a constructive action, the result of a synthesis, in which consciousness 'informs' and objectifies a datum which of itself would be formless. The 'diverse' unknown, received in the senses, is informed and objectified by the *a priori* forms of sensibility and the *a priori* categories of the understanding in such a way that it becomes an 'object' of sensory intuition and intellectual conception. Knowledge is regarded, then, as a *production* or a *construction* of the object, rather than as a contemplation or assimilation of the real.

Kant strove strenuously to avoid the logical pan-phenomenalist consequences of the phenomenalist presumption which lay at the foundation of his critique. For this reason he minimized the value of the irrational 'pure diverse' and sought to explain the universality and necessity of scientific knowledge in terms of the subject's *a priori* objectivization of the datum. All knowing is knowing of the 'object', the 'other', opposed to self. The 'other' is known as other in relation to the original unity of apperception which objectivizes it in relation to itself. Knowing is a subjective synthesization and objectivization of diverse data deriving from a 'thing-in-itself' which lacks internal intelligibility.

Kant did not advert, apparently, to the fact that the distrust which he showed for the 'thing-in-itself' could be extended with ease also to his various *a priori* forms and categories and schemata, none of which possess any 'phenomenal' quality. He focused his attention on the *object* of knowledge, in the sense of 'the other' opposed to self. He conceived knowing essentially in function of object. In so doing he failed to rise above the dichotomy of subject and object and therefore failed to arrive at the discovery of knowledge as the assimilation of being (the real) subjective or objective.

Kant was aware that he had not satisfactorily solved the problem of reconciling the two different realms of the objective and the subjective, or the realms of physical necessity and moral freedom. He attempted to develop further the leading ideas of the *Critique of Judgement* in additional incomplete note-jottings which were published as the *Opus Postumum* after his death. In these abbreviated jottings he attempted to reconcile the two realms of physical necessity and moral freedom through a reconsideration of the way in which they are reconciled within man himself. The human being is noumenon and phenomenon. Human nature has a dual aspect, and yet human consciousness is a unity. Man possesses the consciousness of his existence in the world in space and time. Human thought dynamically projects the dual aspects of man's nature in the two regulative ideas of God and the world. Man is the microcosm which thinks and projects the macrocosm. But he is also a microcosm in which the two noumenal, macrocosmic realms of freedom and necessity are reconciled. They are reconciled within consciousness, that is, within the moral consciousness of man himself.

These ideas, which were not developed further in the unfinished manuscripts, indicate implicitly that Kant's thought was gradually veering towards a form of transcendental idealism in which reality and thought were one within the transcendental ego. Kant's explicit intention in these notes, however, was to attempt to reconcile within man's unified consciousness (of beauty, purposiveness and morality) the two different realms of spiritual freedom and physical necessity which lie within the totality of all that is real. He was not prepared to advance the view, expounded by his followers, that it is the subject of knowledge which 'posits' the objective world of nature. Thus, in 1799, he disassociated himself publicly from Fichte's doctrine that it is the subject which 'posits' nature, even though, at this stage, Kant himself was beginning to use a vocabulary which is similar to that which one finds in Fichte's *Wissenschaftslehre*. Kant was not prepared, then, to go so far as to advance the view, as his immediate disciples did, that if it is the subject of knowledge which constructs the 'object' of knowledge, then it follows logically that it is the subject of knowledge which posits the objective world of nature.

6. General comments. Kant is widely regarded as one of the great philosophers of all time. Many students of philosophy have continued to find rich stimulation in his fertile and versatile thought. The Kantian system, however, was a rich amalgam of incongruous elements, and it is not surprising that it disintegrated quickly after its original formulation. The phenomenalist and agnostic aspects of Kant's thought exercised a profound influence on the positivist currents of thought in Europe and America. Schopenhauer based his doctrine of voluntarism on Kant's distinction between phenomena and things-in-themselves. Lotze's teleological idealism was greatly indebted to Kant's *Critique of Judgement*. Fichte, Schelling and Hegel transformed Kantian idealism, with its sceptical attitude towards the thing-in-itself, into a doctrine of transcendental idealism. Fries, Liebmann, Lange, Vaihinger and others developed several of the psychological and pragmatic implications of Kant's thought. In France, the 'phenomenological neo-criticism' or 'phenomenism' of Charles Renouvier was strongly influenced by the critical philosophy of Kant. In Germany, the critical method was revived in the neo-Kantian movement and in the work of Husserl, Heidegger and Cassirer. In Britain and America, Caird, Green, Bradley, Bosanquet, Howison, Royce and other idealists found their primary source of inspiration in Kantian idealism, though they interpreted Kant mainly through Hegel's eyes. In Italy, Spain, Russia, Sweden and Argentina, different facets of Kantian and nineteenth-century idealism were developed by Croce, Gentile, Unamuno, Ortega y Gasset, Lossky, Boström, Aznar and others. It is not surprising, then, that the nineteenth century as a whole, after Kant, came to be known as the Age of Idealism.

24 Absolute idealism

1. Post-Kantian idealist systems. Fichte, Schelling and
Hegel regarded themselves as Kant's disciples and spiritual successors. They carried forward and refined the metaphysical tendencies
latent in Kantian idealism, and developed it into consistent, though
different, forms of absolute idealism.

Idealism in general, as opposed to materialism (or 'naturalism'),
is that philosophical point of view which maintains that mind and
spiritual values are fundamental in the totality of all that is. In a
philosophy which is essentially a philosophy of mind, being is seen as
ultimately mind (*Geist*), spirit or transcendental subject.

Kant reacted against rationalist metaphysicians such as Leibniz
and Wolff who had assumed that the human mind is capable of
discovering all the secrets of ultimate reality. He pointed out that
human knowledge is severely limited by the fact that the human
mind is structured in such a way that it is incapable of proceeding
beyond a categorizing and synthesizing of sense-phenomena. The
human mind cannot attain knowledge about reality-in-itself. It can
never know any particular thing-in-itself. It can know phenomena
but not noumena.

Fichte and the German idealists quickly recognized the inconsistencies in Kant's thought. Noumena do exist, according to Kant,
and they are apparently the cause of our experiences of sensation,
even though we can know nothing other than phenomena, and even
though the categories of 'existence' and 'cause' do not in any way
apply to noumena but only to phenomena. Kant's references to
noumena were seen as inconsistent with the basic principles of his
own critical idealism. He had attempted to ascribe existence to
unknowable entities which were entirely beyond experiential knowledge. It is self-contradictory to speak of knowing something about
what is altogether unknowable. The concept of the unknowable

noumenon was seen, therefore, as having no adequate foundation or place in a consistently idealist philosophy of mind.

Fichte, Schelling and Hegel welcomed that aspect of Kant's thought which called specific attention to the elements of activity and spontaneity in human knowledge and human volition. This spontaneous free activity was explained in terms of a unitary transcendental self which knows known objects posited by the self and opposed to the self. They asserted that mind is incapable of knowing unknowable entities. It can know only the actually knowable; and for mind or spirit or self the actually knowable is all that is. What can be known and what can be are one and the same thing. What we know when we know is thought-reality, real thought; and ultimate reality is ultimate Thought, Absolute Reason.

The physical universe, according to the German idealists, is not the product of the individual, finite mind. It is a universe which is in a state of process, and this process is the process of the self-manifestation of infinite reason. The visible, extra-mental world is the product of thought. It is the self-manifestation of the activity of absolute mind (*Geist*), intelligence or spirit unfolding and presenting itself in the finite world. In man's philosophical reflection on the universe, the universe becomes aware of itself. Philosophical reflection is the self-reflection and self-knowledge of the Absolute; and because it is so, philosophical reflection is therefore capable of retracing the stages of evolution of self-expression of infinite mind. This evolutionary viewpoint of mind unfolding itself in the universe provided the opportunity for each of the German idealists in turn to elaborate a unified and systematized doctrine concerning the universe and its history.

2. Fichte. *Johann Gottlieb Fichte* (1762-1814) was the son of a humble ribbon-maker of Rammenau in Saxony. His remarkably retentive mind brought him to the notice of a Baron von Miltitz who decided to adopt him and send him to school. In 1780 he graduated from school with distinction, and he registered as a student of theology at Jena. His studies soon directed his interests to the study of philosophy. He was impressed by Lessing's emphasis on the vital importance of creative spiritual endeavour, and was influenced in a lasting way by Spinoza's reflections on the supreme happiness which is to be found in the intellectual love of Nature, infinite substance, but he was inspired most of all by his study of the moral philosophy of Immanuel Kant.

Fichte was appointed professor of philosophy at the university of Jena in 1794, and professor and dean of the philosophical faculty of the university of Berlin in 1810. He published several important works, which include the *Basis of the Entire Theory of Science (Wissenschaftslehre*: 1794), the *System of Ethics* (1798), *The Vocation of Man* (1800), *The Closed Commercial State* (1800), *Characteristics of the Present Age* (1805), and *Addresses to the German Nation* (1808). He died of typhus in January 1814, at the time of the German national struggle against Napoleon.

Anyone who is conscious of his own activity, Fichte pointed out, is conscious at the same time of his own self-consciousness. The person who knows anything at all is conscious of himself as knowing something. The self which is experienced is the empirical self. Consciousness of self leads to the further discovery, by intuition, that the activity of intelligence itself within oneself is not the same activity as the experience of the empirical self. It is pure intelligence itself, or in other words, the transcendental ego, active within oneself, that makes synthesis, or judgement, or knowing, possible, as for example when one says 'I feel warm, and I know that I know I feel warm'. The empirical or psychological ego that *experiences* itself as feeling warm is not the transcendental ego, or pure intelligence-in-itself, which is active within oneself.

Philosophical speculation of the mechanistic and materialistic type is totally incapable, Fichte said, of explaining intelligence in itself. It asserts dogmatically, without any possibility of proof, that it is the thing-in-itself which determines the subject in every act of knowing; it invariably reduces intelligence to a mere epiphenomenon. What the mind knows, however, is the data, or presentations, of consciousness; it does not know any non-presented 'thing-as-such'. The mind is conscious in a special way of its freedom as revealed in moral experience. It is capable of reflecting on the activities of intelligence-in-itself active within oneself. The only form of philosophical speculation which can do justice to evidence of this kind is a philosophy of mind *(Geist)* or spirit, and not the dogmatic asseveration of mechanistic materialism.

For Fichte, then, it is not the so-called 'object' that posits the subject in the act of knowing; rather, it is intelligence itself which posits its object. And the intelligence which posits the totality of all that is, or all that is knowable, is boundless intelligence, life, self-activity, absolute mind itself. (Goethe's *Faust* expresses this same viewpoint in the words: 'In the beginning was the Act'.).

Absolute mind, or the transcendental ego, is the creative source of all that is. It is the self-explanatory source of its own being. It is the pure transcendental ego whose affirmation, *'Ich bin'*, 'I am', posits or creates in an unreflective, original, unconscious way its own existence. In positing its existence, it opposits its existence to itself in such a way that there arises a limited experiential knowledge of itself as conscious of experiencing its (posited) being, namely, its non-self. In other words, self-consciousness arises as a synthesis of the original affirmation or thesis ('I am') and the antithesis or opposition between the ego and the posited non-ego. In brief, the 'I' affirms that 'I am', and in doing so there arises the self-consciousness which is present in the fact that I know I am conscious that I am. This dialectic of thesis, antithesis and synthesis is the work of intelligence-in-itself within me and within all who are conscious in the way that I am conscious that I am. Around this central viewpoint, which he called the viewpoint of Transcendental Egoism, Fichte elaborated and systematized the entire corpus of his philosophical work.

The transcendental ego is not a being, according to Fichte. It is an activity, intelligence-in-itself, immanent in empirical consciousness. It produces Nature, that is, the object of knowledge, through the productive power of creative imagination. It is an activity which is an unending and limitless striving to be all that it is capable of being and to know consciously all that it is capable of knowing. It posits Nature, the non-ego, as an instrument, a field, for moral self-realization and self-possession. Man experiences this infinite impulse in his insatiable urge to be all that he ought to be. In human consciousness, the Absolute is conscious of itself as a boundless activity striving for self-possession and moral self-realization, in the limitless spontaneity of unending free activity.

The transcendental ego, then, is the free, wilful activity of intelligence in itself which becomes conscious of its unending self-activity in the consciousness of man. Within man, the lower natural impulses of man as an object of nature, and the higher spiritual impulses of man as a subject of consciousness striving for self-fulfilment, are ultimately one impulse to self-activity for the sake of self-determination, freedom.

Freedom, or self-determination, is freedom to actualize one's objective essence. It is freedom to be all that one can be and ought to be. It is the freedom to be ideally oneself, the freedom to be integrally human. It is therefore freedom within obligation: the obligation to 'be yourself; be human'. The fundamental principle of freedom can be stated in various ways: Be what you ought to be; Fulfil your vocation: Act according to your conscience; Strive unceasingly to pursue the ideal; Commit yourself to the godly life; Act according to your best conviction of your duty; Always fulfil your moral vocation. Through self-determination and self-commitment of this kind, 'Divinity itself enters again into thee, in its first and original form, as life, as thine own life, that thou shouldst live and (that thou) wilt live' (*Die Anweisung zum seligen Leben*).

Fichte saw the dutiful will as the will of man's true self striving unceasingly towards self-realization. In every moral action, man's higher spiritual impulses mould his nature by resisting his lower natural impulses and arousing his nature to manifest 'spirit'. In this way man achieves an ever more loyal dedication to his spiritual ideals. The moral life is the life of free, dutiful endeavour, devoted to the pursuit of one's vocation to be truly human.

The vocation to be human implies the acknowledgement of other human beings, and their vocation and claims and rights. Each and all live in a social institutional milieu. Each should endeavour to secure for each and all, in society and in the nation, the necessary external conditions of socio-economic self-reliant operation. Thus, for example, in a state which is a 'closed commercial state', where imports and exports are strictly regulated by the government, surpluses and scarcities can be avoided, and a carefully planned division of labour can ensure employment for all, according to Fichte. 'Man becomes man only amongst men.'

Man is capable of rising above natural impulse to the 'blest life' (*seligen Leben*) through his fulfilling his moral vocation. Moral vocation is divine vocation. Moral obligation points to God as moral legislator and all-holy Life, pure activity itself, above subject and object, above thought. The moral order is the divine order. God is that living and active moral ordering which is infinite dynamic Will and creative Life. 'This Will binds me (*religio*) in union with itself'; it is the ground of moral vocation and true religion. It is infinite Life, infinite Will, transcending comprehension. It exteriorizes itself in the object of consciousness, the world. The world is, then, an image or picture or schema of the Absolute manifesting itself in consciousness as the object of consciousness. Dynamic panentheistic idealism is therefore, fundamentally, a matter of practical faith in infinite Life, infinite Will, and infinite Intelligence or Light, transcending human comprehension.

Fichte's work is, from one point of view, a leading example of German absolute idealism in the early part of the nineteenth century. From another point of view, however, it differs significantly from the work of the other German idealists, in foreshadowing the basic ideas of later existentialist and pragmatist thought. Fichte's constant emphasis is on the striving self and on the definitive importance of action, that is, wilful moral action, as definitive of self. His thought passes from the metaphysical and idealist level to the moral level, and from the moral to the pragmatic, the existential and the spiritual. He saw a predominant sinfulness as one of the leading 'characteristics of the present age' (1804-05); but he also believed that the eternal 'spirit' present in this epoch would lift up the level of human existence, through a fervent renewal of moral and religious life, to a higher level of 'truly living life, begetting of itself other life' in a brighter and more truly human future.

3. Schelling. *Friedrich W. J. von Schelling* (1775-1854), son of a Lutheran pastor at Leonberg, studied at the theological seminary at Tübingen, where he became friendly with two older students, G. W. Hegel and the poet J. Hölderlin. In 1798 he was called to a professorship at Jena, where he became a colleague and friend of Fichte.

Schelling's thought focused in a special way on the relation between the infinite and the finite and on the transcendental ego's process of self-objectification. The development of his philosophical thought, however, passed through a succession of four (or more) different phases.

In his first period of philosophizing, under the influence of Fichte, Schelling attempted to explain how the totality of nature emerged from the absolute ego. He pointed out that Spinoza, in his attempt to explain the relation of the infinite and the finite, had tended to absolutize the non-ego, that is, Substance, Nature, or absolute Object. Fichte tended, with more notable success, to absolutize the subject, by explaining the finite self as a manifestation of infinite free activity. In this first period Schelling had already begun to work himself free from Fichte's thought, and to develop an independent position of his own.

In his second period, Schelling held that the philosopher must transcend the epistemological distinction between subjectivity and objectivity, and seek to understand everything on the higher level of the absolute, where all things are seen in their ultimate identity. In his *Ideas towards a Philosophy of Nature* (1797) Schelling found the common ground of objective, material nature and the subjective, spiritual ego in the activity of force, experienced in its dual aspects of attraction and repulsion. Force, experienced as attraction towards the inner world of sensation, is objective matter, or nature. Force, experienced as repulsion, thrusting outward from within, is subjective ego, or spirit. The proper study of the higher speculative sciences, therefore, is force. Force is pure activity. Nature is infinite self-activity realizing itself unceasingly in finite matter. Speculative physics is capable of retracing systematically the stages of the process by which ideal Nature, *Natura naturans*, expresses itself in existing nature, *Natura naturata*. Ideal nature posited the lower levels of existing nature as a foundation for the subsequent emergence of the higher levels of organic life. The pure activity, or force, present in all levels of existing nature, is an unlimited activity which checks itself by objectifying itself in the different finite levels of the phenomenal world. Each new movement of repulsion or expansion brings forth a counter-movement of attraction or closure and a new form of self-objectification of the infinite Absolute. This explains the phenomena of mass, light, magnetism, electricity, chemical processes, life, reproduction, sensibility and other such different levels of natural phenomena in the natural world. In this light, the so-called opposition between the mechanical sphere and the organic sphere disappears. It is one and the same pure activity which objectifies itself on different levels of self-arrested movement; and thus nature as a whole is a unified, self-developing, super-organic unity. Nature is a gradual self-unfolding of the eternal Idea. It is a super-organism which has within itself an organizing principle which makes it an organic system. This organizing principle has frequently been spoken of as a 'world-soul'. It is simply infinite self-activity, energy, or force, realizing itself unceasingly in the phenomenal world.

Schelling explained his philosophy of nature further, through insights gained from the Kantian and Fichtean philosophy of knowledge, in his *System of Transcendental Idealism* (Tübingen, 1800). The transcendental ego, in which the intelligence and the will are identical, is pure unlimited self-activity. Kant had spoken of things-in-themselves as at the limits of knowledge. Schelling spoke instead of the consciousness of the non-ego as the limit of self-activity. To become its own object of consciousness, the ego limits its unlimited activity by setting over against itself its production of the non-ego. This production of the non-ego is an unconscious and necessary production. In the first main epoch or stage of the history of emerging consciousness the material world is produced as the unconscious activity of Spirit. On a second level the ego becomes conscious of the object on the level of sense. The third level culminates in the ego's recognition of itself as active, free intelligence. On this level the ego becomes conscious of itself as will, that is, as self-determining or self-realizing activity in conformity with the categorical imperative of moral law. Human history can be described as the development of human freedom in accordance with moral necessity. History is a human drama in which men are simultaneously actors and authors of the drama.

It is in art, in the creative production of a work of beauty, that intelligence becomes completely self-conscious, according to Schelling. The whole universe is a work of art created by aesthetic intelligence. Creative art is the goal towards which all intelligence moves. The creative work of art is the finite manifestation of the infinite Absolute. The creative artistic genius is the vehicle of a power which acts in an inspirational manner through him. The finished product of the artistic genius becomes a crystal-clear revelation of the beauty and the nature of the Absolute. The same power which acts without consciousness in nature, acts through the consciousness of the artistic genius. Aesthetic intuition is intuition of the infinite. The work of art is an intimation and an expression of the divine.

The third stage of the development of Schelling's philosophy was expounded in his published *Vorlesungen* (course of lectures, 1803), which emphasized the undifferentiated identity of the philosophy of nature and the philosophy of knowledge. All reality arises from the infinite and undifferentiated Absolute. In the Absolute, the real and the ideal, the objective and the subjective, are one. In absolute intelligence-in-itself, or Reason, there is a lack of difference between the subject and the object, and so Reason itself is not actually conscious. Intelligence-in-itself attains actual self-consciousness only in and through human consciousness, whose immediate object is the world. Schelling spoke of the Absolute as the vanishing point of all difference and distinction. Hegel compared this viewpoint wittily with 'the night... in which all cows are black'. Schelling saw that his critics were not satisfied that the philosophy of identity solved all the problems involved, and he decided to develop fresh lines of thought.

The fourth phase of Schelling's thought may conveniently be called the 'existentialist' phase. This phase is represented in his Berlin lectures on 'Mythology' and on 'Revelation', published posthumously in his collected works (Stuttgart, 1856-61). He saw his earlier work as being too 'rational'. It had not sufficiently allowed for the element of the 'irrational' clearly present in the history of mankind. This live, irrational element is intimated and evoked in the myths and religions of history. The philosophy of religion which underlies mythology and natural revelation sees God as the eternal, ungrounded abyss, on which all that is finite is grounded. The abyss is forever alienating itself from itself; and its alienation from itself gives rise to a cosmic fall from reality, that is, from the abyss. The origin of the finite world (*natura naturata*) is to be found in this cosmic fall, which is a breaking away or an 'existence' (a standing-out) of the finite from the infinite (Schelling had read the works of Jakob Boehme). The conscious rises up like a spark from the vast unconscious; and the conscious is also deeply aware of the vast unconscious from which it arises. Throughout history, man has attempted to evoke the profound depths of the unconscious in symbolic language and in myth-making and religion. Mythology has its own system of archetypal key-ideas and its own *a priori* structure of psychic activity, analogous to the structures of the Kantian heritage. The symbols of mythology and religion are capable of pointing to the deep wounds and dreads of human consciousness, and capable of healing these wounds with a gentle, 'understanding' touch. This aspect of Schelling's work suggests and anticipates themes of a similar kind which were developed further in existentialist thought, and in the work of Jung, Freud, Tillich, Cassirer and others. This final phase of Schelling's thought was for the main part, however, ignored by his contemporaries and followers.

The aspects of Schelling's thought which proved influential among his contemporaries and followers were primarily his views on the philosophy of Nature, on the philosophy of Art, and, in the case of F. Von Baader (d. 1841) and F. Schleiermacher (see next chapter), on the philosophy of religion.

4. Hegel's system of philosophy.

Georg W. F. Hegel (1770-1831) was born in Stuttgart and educated at Stuttgart Gymnasium before going to the theological school at Tübingen university (1788-93), where he studied theology, philosophy and the classics. He accepted a professorship of philosophy at Jena in 1805, at Heidelberg in 1816, and at Berlin in 1818. His writings include the *Phenomenology of Mind* (1807), *Science of Logic* (1812), *Encyclopedia of the Philosophical Sciences* (1817), *Outlines of the Philosophy of Right* (1820), and collected lecture notes on aesthetics, religion and history, published by his students after his death in a cholera epidemic in 1831. A group of his students published his collected works in nineteen volumes (1832-40).

For Hegel, all objects of knowledge are the products of mind. The existing universe is the product of Absolute Mind. The Absolute is not, however, as Schelling had asserted, the *source* from which nature (object) and spirit (subject) proceed; rather, it is the Absolute its very self, or Idea, which *becomes* successively nature and spirit. It is an infinite dynamic process of infinite evolving activity. All becoming is simply a development of Thought, Mind; and all being is Thought realized. The life of self-thinking Thought is a self-developing process of self-actualization. The Absolute is the totality of all reality; and the totality is a teleological process of self-unfolding and self-development. All that is is rational, and all that is rational is real. Reality is the self-manifestation of infinite reason; and infinite self-thinking Thought actualizes itself in the historical process.

The work of philosophy, according to Hegel, is to reconstruct and make clear the teleological process which is immanent in nature. Philosophy is capable of undertaking this reconstruction because the philosophical reflection of humanity is self-thinking Thought's knowledge of itself. The absolute comes to know itself in and through the human spirit. The work of philosophy is therefore to pursue the historical process of development of Thought or Idea in-itself, through its stage of development outside-itself, in Nature, towards its development for-itself, in Mind (*Geist*) or Spirit. This first great triad, of Idea, Nature, and Spirit or Mind, suggests and gives to us the fundamental, basic division of philosophy into the philosophy of the pure Idea (Logos, Logic), or Metaphysics, the philosophy of nature, and the philosophy of mind. These three studies give us a complete reconstruction, in conceptual form, of the self-actualization or life of the Absolute.

Hegel's first major philosophical work was his *Phänomenologie des Geistes* (*Phenomenology of Mind*) in 1807. In this work he gave an account of the various stages or forms of experience of human consciousness, from simple sense-awareness or sense-perception, to the supreme, philosophical form of knowledge, absolute knowledge, or philosophy. Hegel presents the first phase of the history of consciousness as the naive phase of sense-certainty concerning our acquaintance with immediately given sensible objects. This phase gives rise dialectically to a second phase, namely, social self-consciousness, or social consciousness, in which the mind confronts other minds as members of a common society. In this phase of history, class-consciousness emerges, and consciousness of seniority and inferiority, lordship and serfdom, the ascendent and the dependent. The third phase of the dialectical history of consciousness is the phase of reason where mind finally sees in all things nothing other than the conditions of its own rational subjectivity; all things express rational spirituality. At the level of Reason, the philosopher experiences his consciousness or thought as a finite, participating moment in the innermost life of the infinite Spirit, self-thinking Thought. From the philosophical point of view, according to the *Phenomenology*, the course of history is an organic process of embodiment or incarnation of the Absolute Mind.

In his two volumes of *Logic* (1812-16) and in his *Encyclopedia* (1817), Hegel presented his mature thought concerning the philosophy of Idea, Nature and Mind. In the science of logic (*logos*), which is in effect the science of metaphysics, speculative reason penetrates the inner essence of pure thought about thought. Logic is absolute Thought's knowledge of its own essence. Thought is the Absolute knowing itself as the totality. It reveals itself as dynamic Idea, Logos, Spirit or Rational Will. Logic or metaphysics studies this dynamic Logos or Idea disclosed in Nature and in the working of the human mind. It can do so because philosophical thought is itself a dialectical process, just as the Absolute, and Nature, too, are dialectical processes.

Speculative philosophy, or logic, apprehends the present and the actual in its exploration of the rational. From our experiences of the actual, it deduces the categories that describe the Absolute. Human thinking moves forever onward; it explores and advances. In doing so it encounters difficulties and contradictions. But contradiction acts as a positive spur, a moving force, to further human reasoning. Thus, for example, human thought recognizes something, at first, as simply being. But being in general is featureless and indeterminate. It is seen, in fact, Hegel says, to be absolutely formless and negative. As wholly featureless and indeterminate it merges into the concept of non-being. In this way the concept of Nothing is deduced from Being by way of antithesis. The mind then moves from a consideration of the category or concept of Nothing to a reconsideration of the category of Being, and it finds that in the category of Becoming there is a synthesis in which any being-in-becoming is seen to be both in being and also not yet in being. Thus the original thesis and its antithesis find their unity in a higher synthesis, in the concept or category of Becoming. Again, in a similar dialectical process the mind moves forward from the idea of the being of any datum to the antithetical notion of its essence or limitation in being in the light of the relations seen to exist between it and other beings. The mind then overcomes the inadequacies of these two categories of indeterminate being immediately given and the essential features of differentiated particular being, in a new synthetic understanding of the Idea or Notion of the totality of that particular being as having an importance in and for itself.

For Hegel, thought is a systematic creative process. This exploratory creative movement of thought invariably encounters contradiction; and contradiction acts as an additional moving force for further
progress in human reasoning. All thought expresses itself in triads (of
thesis, antithesis and synthesis) each of which has its own triadic
structure, each member of which has, in turn, a further triadic
structure of its own. It is in this sense that the thought-process is a
dialectical process. It is a progressive process constantly moving
towards the discovery of the truth of all things through the discovery
of their relation to the whole, the Idea.

Nature, according to Hegel, is the Idea, that is, Rationality, in
external form. 'Absolute freedom goes forth freely out of itself
(ex-ists) in Nature.' The infinite Absolute has its life and being in and
through finite particular things. It exists only in and through its
finite, transitory, external manifestations. Inner Thought, Logos,
exists only in and through its outer manifestation in existing Nature.
The outer manifestation is a dynamic, but inadequate expression, of
the dynamic inner Idea. It is a Fall (*Abfall*) from the Idea, just as any
work of art is invariably an inadequate expression of the artistic idea
which it embodies. The Idea does not have a separate existence
distinct from its embodiment in the world, the totality. Existing
Nature is a moment in the dynamic, ongoing life of the Absolute, the
Totality, ultimate reality.

The Absolute Idea, which goes forth out of itself in Nature, returns
to itself in the sensitive, conscious, and self-conscious, finite
individuals which participate at different levels in its own inner
thought. In this process of return to itself it manifests itself as Mind.
At the point of transition from Nature to Mind there is the sensing
and feeling subject called the soul. The sensitive soul, without
reflective self-consciousness, is subjective spirit on its lowest level.
The next level is that of consciousness or awareness of any object.
Self-consciousness, or consciousness of the subject, is a higher level of
subjective spirit. It is capable of rising to a still higher level of
universal self-consciousness in which it recognizes both its oneness
with and its distinction from other selves. The Greeks and Romans
were conscious of these levels of consciousness. With the advent of
Christianity, a further manifestation of the Idea entered the world:
the individual as such was seen as possessing an infinite value.
Rational will existing for itself, as free will and free intelligence, is
now seen as destined to the highest freedom of theoretical and
practical spirit. The philosophy of history now discovers the inner
meaning of history in the key concept of the 'realization of freedom'

in the life of the Absolute. Man in himself is destined to the highest freedom, because the Absolute is realizing its own freedom in the rational free will of man.

5. Hegel and the objective embodiment of Spirit. Just as Nature is the objective embodiment of the Absolute Idea, so too, for Hegel, objective Spirit is the embodiment of subjective Spirit. Absolute Spirit manifests itself subjectively in the minds of individuals; and subjective Spirit manifests itself objectively (and ordinarily) in the social institutions of the family, civil society and the State. Absolute Spirit also manifests and embodies itself in an eminent way in art, religion and philosophy. For Hegel, therefore, social institutions, art, religion and philosophy are not simply creations of mankind; they are objective manifestations of the historical dialectical movements of rational reality.

The free subject expresses his rational will, or 'will as free intelligence' when he appropriates material things as his property and as his right. He can freely relinquish his right over his property or his labour by contract (e.g. by a contract of sale or exchange). When contract of wills is negated there is wrong, fraud, and crime. Crime entails punishment as a cancellation of wrong.

Wrong-doing or crime entails an oppositing of self-centred particular will to the principle of rightness, that is, the rational, social or common will, or the rational free will as such. This opposition is overcome when the particular will conforms itself to the moral rational will, the individual will as it ought to be. This is accomplished in a triadic movement from right, to morality, and finally to social ethics.

Ethical life is the life of social ethics; it is lived in the family, civil society and the State. Life in the family and life in society are united in the higher reality of life in the State, where all find differentiated universality. The State is the highest expression of rational will. It is an organic unity existing in and through its members. It is a 'divine' and objective embodiment of Spirit. It expresses the general will, the real will of the individual.

World history is the self-unfolding of Spirit. Will as free intelligence operates in human history. History is the process whereby World Spirit comes to explicit consciousness of itself as free intelligence, in and through the spirit of a people, a State. In each State or nation the spirit of the nation must work out its own form of political constitution at its own historical level of maturity and development.

Absolute Spirit actualizes itself as concretely existing self-thinking Thought only in and through the human mind or spirit. It does so when the human spirit rises up to that level of self-consciousness in which it frees itself from personal limitation and becomes a moment in the life of the Absolute's knowledge of itself as the ultimate and all-embracing totality. On this higher plane, subjective Spirit and objective Spirit synthesize together as one, and Spirit is reflectively conscious of itself as infinite. On this higher level of self-consciousness, the Absolute actualizes its developing self-knowledge and apprehends itself in and through human art, religion and philosophy.

In an outstanding work of art, spiritual content and sensuous form interpenetrate in a beautiful embodiment of an ideal. Spirit manifests itself to itself, for example, in architecture, sculpture, music, drama and other works of creative artistic beauty. This is true of early Egyptian and Oriental symbolic art even though it allowed the sensuous element to predominate. In the classical art of ancient Greece, the sensuous and the spiritual fuse harmoniously. In Christian and Romantic art, the Spirit overflows the sensuous in a sensible portrayal of the infinite value of the self and its inner life.

Art is unable, however, to convey profound spiritual truth and so it points beyond itself to religion. Art manifests Absolute Idea merely in the form of an object of sense. Religious thought is an activity of thought (not sense) which clothes Thought in imagery and representation of a special ('religious') kind, as for example in the popular idea or image of the creation of the world by God. Religious imagery of this kind expresses truths, and actual revelations of the Absolute, as adequately as the popular mind has been able to grasp them. Religion occupies an essential place in ordinary human life, and through it men come into contact with the divine.

It is only in philosophy, however, that man discovers the Absolute in all the stages of the universal dialectic. Philosophy contemplates the eternal truth, God, and the unfolding of God, in terms of logical sequence. Religion draws men close to God through pictorial thought. The human being needs both. But it is in philosophy that man becomes rational and self-conscious. The philosopher appreciates his own key position in a universe that is rational and organic. He discovers that the universe itself has become conscious of itself transitorily in the absolute self-consciousness of man. In this light, the history of philosophy is seen as the process of development of the Absolute's self-consciousness in the mind of man; it is a movement of divine self-knowledge coming to think itself in time.

The Hegelian system of thought united all branches of knowledge in a brilliant synthesis which was dominated by the dialectic of the Idea. In this system, reality is the thinking idea, mind. In the unity of consciousness, mind, Hegel distinguished consciousness of liberty, subjective mind, and the manifestation of this liberty in the products of the human mind, such as law, morality, politics, theology and literature, that is, objective mind. Hegel's encyclopedic system assigned to every form of reality its proper place in the process of the self-development of Absolute Thought. This Hegelian system had a widespread influence not only in systematic philosophy but also in Lutheran dogmatic theology, in the social, political and juridical sciences, and in literature, historiography, ethics, aesthetics and other areas of human thought. Theologians split themselves into right-wing (Christian) Hegelians, and left-wing (pantheistic) Hegelians. Feuerbach, Marx and Engels made use of the Hegelian dialectic in their revolutionary revision of the Hegelian theories of society and history. Hegel's influence underwent a temporary eclipse in the middle of the nineteenth century, but subsequently his influence in Europe and America became greater than ever.

25 From Schleiermacher to Nietzsche

1. Schleiermacher   2. Reaction against metaphysical
idealism   3. Schopenhauer   4. The Young Hegelians
5. Dogmatic materialists   6. Kierkegaard
7. Neo-Kantianism   8. Inductive metaphysicians
9. Brentano   10. Nietzsche

1. Schleiermacher. *Friedrich D. E. Schleiermacher* (1768-1834) was an outstanding professor of theology at the university of Berlin, and a renowned preacher at the Holy Trinity Church in Berlin, at the time that Hegel was a professor of philosophy in the university. His first published work *On Religion: Speeches to Its Cultured Despisers* (1799) earned him a nation-wide reputation nine years after his ordination. In this and other works on the philosophy of religion Schleiermacher made a critical analysis of the personal and societal manifestations of the religious and ethical dimensions of human life.

Human reason, Schleiermacher pointed out, operates only in individual human beings, each having his own particular inclinations, temperament and talents, historically conditioned by the family, nationality, language, communities and institutions of which each individual is the offspring. Nature and nurture affect individual human reasoning. In this setting each individual becomes endowed with his own life unity, or inalienable personal identity, in which his feeling, thinking and doing are seen as three forms of consciousness which constitute his total personal self-consciousness. The personal identity of each is wholly original and unique. But, if it is not to remain undeveloped, inchoate, confused and immature, it must immerse itself in social and religious relationships in which it inherits and endows, receives and bestows, the rich heritage of social human culture.

Man is relatively dependent on his fellow men and on other creatures within the world. Man is absolutely dependent on God, the infinite Totality. A pervasive and arresting confusion inhibits human consciousness whenever this two-fold dependency is not sharply and clearly distinguished. Religion is a determination of a particular human experience or feeling, namely, that of being an absolutely dependent being in the vital relation of oneself to God. In this relationship, the individual is utterly dependent for the entire constitution of his own unique existence.

The human experience of oneself as a receiver being, totally dependent upon God for one's inner being, is identical with the human experience of one's uniqueness and personal identity in being. It can be called equivalently 'immediate self-consciousness', or 'God-consciousness', or the feeling of being absolutely dependent, or an immediate consciousness of an 'existence-relationship' between the totally dependent and the Absolute.

The sense of total dependency, which is the religious sense, always manifests itself in some particular social and historical form. This is true of historical Christianity, as well as of the other great religions of history. Christianity, like other religions, necessarily bears the stamp of its founder. It is Christocentric, both inwardly, in the inner piety of the Christian, and outwardly, in its social and institutional aspect. The Christian must appropriate to his self-consciousness his relation of total dependency on Christ the redeemer, who then becomes the centre of the individual's inner religious-consciousness. For the Christian, then, his Christianity has not only its external history as an institution, it also has a personal inner history in the self-consciousness of the Christian. In a similar way all the other great religions bear the stamp of their founders. Their devotees steep themselves in the spirit and in the genius of their founder rather than in abstract formulated dogmas.

2. Reaction against metaphysical idealism. Towards the middle of the nineteenth century there was a partial reaction in Germany against the thought of Hegel and against metaphysical idealism in general. The speculative idealists came to be regarded by some thinkers as fanatics for totality who were inflicted with Faustian yearnings for the infinite. Immanuel H. Fichte (d. 1879), Hermann Ulrici (d. 1884) and Christian H. Weisse (d. 1866) opposed Hegel's 'pantheism' and proposed a doctrine of theistic idealism. Others proposed different forms of reconstruction of Kantianism. They were aware of difficulties present in the Kantian position (concerning phenomena and things-in-themselves, morality and religion, moral law and sentiment, and the relationship between the different faculties) which prompted their attempts to reconstruct Kantian philosophy.

Jakob Fries (1773-1843) emphasized the analytical, descriptive and methodological aspects of Kantian critical philosophy as against the speculations of the absolute idealists. He attempted to restate and reconstruct the Kantian critique of speculative and practical reason as a programme of 'psychic anthropology', in the sense of psychological or phenomenological self-observation. Friedrich Beneke (1798-1854) insisted that logic, ethics, metaphysics and philosophy of religion should be based solely on a science of psychology which is inductively established. Johann F. Herbart (1776-1841) studied under Fichte but was unable to accept Fichte's psychology and Fichte's doctrines concerning the ego. He regarded philosophy as an activity of reworking (*Bearbeitung*), elaborating and clarifying concepts by logical or conceptual analysis; he viewed psychology as the mechanics of the mental life of sensations and ideas. At the university of Berlin, Schopenhauer, who regarded Hegelian philosophy as the product of a clumsy charlatan, chose to give his lectures at the same hours as Hegel. His experiment, however, was unsuccessful and his audience soon dwindled away. Hegelian philosophy remained dominant in spite of the reaction of several opponents and critics against it.

3. **Schopenhauer.** *Arthur Schopenhauer* (1788-1860) was born in Danzig (now Gdansk in Poland) and educated in France, England, Switzerland and Austria. He admired Plato and venerated Kant, but he heaped scorn and contempt on Fichte and Hegel at a time when they were held in high esteem. It was only towards the end of his life that Schopenhauer began to attain some of the recognition for which he yearned.

In his doctorate dissertation *On the Fourfold Root of the Principle of Sufficient Reason* (1813), Schopenhauer maintained (like Kant) that the principle of sufficient reason (or causality), as used or rooted in the four different areas of physics, epistemology, mathematics and wilful behaviour (metaphysics), is capable of referring only to the phenomenal world of our mental presentations or ideas (*Vorstellung*), and not to the noumenal world of things-in-themselves. For this reason 'the world' which is known is the phenomenal world of mental presentations or ideas. The noumenal world is not known. The (known) world is 'idea' or representation; and this is true even when the objects of which we are conscious are our own bodies. Every object known is a known (mental) object.

Schopenhauer developed this viewpoint further in his major philosophical work, *The World as Will and Idea (Vorstellung)* (1819). Our intimate awareness of ourselves, self-consciousness, has two facets. I am aware of myself as an *object* among objects, but I am also interiorly aware of myself as a dynamic, self-moving being whose behavioural activities directly express my blind, irrational impulse or *will* to be, to exist. It is this dynamic, instinctive will to be what I want to be that gives itself the phenomenal body known as my body. My known body is simply objectified inner will. Dynamic impulse or will makes use of my abstract concepts, knowledge, intellect, reason and representations as instruments for satisfying its practical, biological, bodily needs. The intellect is the servant and appendage of wilful desires.

The known world, known to me, is 'idea' or representation (*Vorstellung*). In other words, the known world is the phenomenal world. The noumenon behind this phenomenon is Will. Reality, thing-in-itself, that which properly is, Being, is primordial Will. The world is the appearance of one eternal, craving Will to be; all things are simply mirrorings of the Will. Will manifests itself everywhere, in all things. It manifests itself in the impulse by which the magnetic needle turns to the magnetic pole. The Will-to-live manifests itself in the instincts of insects which deposit eggs where the emerging larvae will find food, and in the human drive to foster the family and preserve the species. The Will to be is one, universal metaphysical Will. It is that which is experienced within ourselves as the Will to live. It is blind impulse, eternal becoming, endless striving, never fulfilled. It focuses itself in the sexual urge. It is tortured Will, never satisfied, and forever at variance with itself. The world of tortured Will is hell. All is stress, conflict and tension. Each man is the demon of another: *homo homini lupus*. This is necessarily so because of the metaphysical nature of the rapacious Will. Philosophy or metaphysics, therefore, must necessarily be a philosophy of metaphysical pessimism. The evils present in our lives are fundamentally ineradicable. They are merely the reflection of the aggressive and libidinous urges rooted in our very nature. Mankind in general is doomed to an eternal round of torment and misery.

There are two ways of escape, however, from the slavery of the tormented Will, according to Schopenhauer. The first way of escape is through the medium of art. Aesthetic contemplation, or will-less perception, of the beautiful provides man with a temporary form of escape from his tension and torture, and from 'the penal servitude of willing'. In the enjoyment of artistic experience 'we keep the sabbath of the penal service of willing'. We experience this restful release, for example, in our immersal in great literature, or in works of genuine art, or in the totally absorbing world of music. For Schopenhauer, it is music above all that speaks 'the universal imageless language of the heart'. In contemplating the sublime, as Plato saw, man is freed temporarily from the servitude of rapacious self-assertion.

The second way of release from the slavery of the impetuous will is the more permanent way pursued by the saint. It is the way of asceticism, holiness, mortification and self-denial. The saint turns away from all forms of rapacious self-assertion and becomes detached from everything. He overcomes wild egoism and restless covetousness. He turns away from 'life'. In death he attains the final goal of total denial of the 'Will to live'. The just and compassionate man is capable of seeing through 'the veil of Maya'; he sees through the illusory character of the phenomenal world. He sees his fellow creatures and all things as homogeneous with his own being and nature. He identifies himself with others in the final stage of a mystical 'turning of the will' which involves a total 'abolition' of his previous personality. This is the way of the Buddhist ideal of desirelessness as a means for allaying the will. It is the way of the ascetics and the mystics of all times. Mystical insight, ineffable and indescribable, enables the saint to transcend the will and the world. In this way, the will, having produced intelligence in the morally good man, has actually created the possibility of its own negation in a calm, sympathetic and abstinent life. The saintly man destroys within himself, by all means, the 'Will to live', insatiable self-assertion.

Schopenhauer replaced Fichte's transcendental Ego and Hegel's transcendental Idea with his own transcendental Will. His doctrine that the World is Will and Idea may be called a doctrine of transcendental voluntaristic idealism. The emphasis in his philosophy, as in theirs, is upon the ultimate 'subject' which posits all objectively. The subject which determines the object is a 'transcendental subject'. It is a unitary infinite, eternal, blind Will. Being is ultimately determined by Will (panthelism). Schopenhauer was deeply disappointed and resentful at the lack of recognition he felt to be his due throughout the major part of his life. It was only towards the end of his life that Schopenhauer's writings began to be read with interest in Britain, Russia and the United States. In Europe, his writings influenced the trends of thought of Nietzsche, Burckhardt, Wundt, Vaihinger and Wittgenstein.

4. The Young Hegelians. After the death of Hegel, some of his followers, such as K. Göschel (d. 1861), J. Rosenkranz (d. 1879), J. Erdmann (d. 1892) and E. Zeller (d. 1908) insisted that the real is rational, and that Christianity and Hegelian philosophy are basically in agreement on questions arising currently in the field of religion, culture and politics. They tended to support the status quo, and came to be known as the conservative 'Hegelian Right'. Others however took the opposite position, and tended towards a radical, critical reinterpretation of the current politics, religion and bourgeois culture. They were known as 'left-wing Hegelians' or 'Young Hegelians'. Thus, for example, A. Ruge, D. F. Strauss (d. 1874), L. Feuerbach, B. Bauer (d. 1874), and Karl Marx insisted that rational structures alone have substantial reality, and that the current alienated state of social, religious, and monarchical political existence must yield, by its own inner necessity, to new rational structures of free human existence. The monarchist, Christian, bourgeois order must be assaulted if alienated man is to attain social, religious and political freedom.

Arnold Ruge (1803-80), in the different editions of his *Jahrbücher* (*Yearbooks*), from 1839 to 1844, pointed out that the 'spirit of the age' demanded not constitutional monarchy nor liberal democracy but economic and political socialism. The ultimate measure of any philosophical theory is its timeliness or adequacy in articulating the spirit of the age. The philosopher's task is to make history by changing the institutions.

Ludwig Feuerbach (1804-72) maintained that Hegel's philosophy had degraded man, the senses, and the material world, even though Hegel had apparently denied all transcendence. There is an essentially religious spirit concealed in Hegel's thought. This hidden religious element must be expunged in the interests of the 'philosophy of the future'. Truth, reality and sensibility are identical. Only a sensible being is a real, true being. Thought is a product of nature. Man belongs to the essence of Nature, and Nature belongs to the essence of man. 'The body in its totality is my ego, my existence itself.' Man is the culmination of the natural process. 'Man is what he eats.' Religion is the projected dream which expresses the dim consciousness that man has of his own infinite nature. The sciences of anthropology, psychology and physiology can assist man to raise this truth to a clear awareness that 'the consciousness of God is nothing but the consciousness of the species'. The absolute is humanity itself made concrete in interpersonal relations. In ths way, Feuerbach derived a doctrine of metaphysical materialism out of Hegelian philosophy, and in doing so he 'placed materialism on the throne again', as Engels proclaimed. Feuerbach transformed absolute idealism into materialistic humanism, and prepared the way for the dialectical materialism of Marx and Engels.

Karl Marx (1818-83) and *Friedrich Engels* (1820-95) produced the influential *Communist Manifesto* in 1884. This document pointed out that 'man's ideas, views and conceptions, or in a word, man's consciousness, changes with every change in the conditions of his material existence, in his social relations and in his social life'. From this 'simple fact' they deduced that the material conditions of life provide the explanation for all other human activities, political, religious, artistic and philosophical. The manifesto called on the workers of the world to unite in the struggle against corrupt institutions which had their economic base in bourgeois capitalism. It advocated revolutionary 'changes in the modes of production and exchange' as a preparation for the coming of international socialism and the eventual withering away of morality, philosophy, law, and the State.

Marx was not interested in the construction of a Marxist philosophy. He considered that the baneful influence of the reign of philosophy over men's minds was drawing to a close. He sought to free the study of history, economics and sociology from all religious prejudice and philosophical speculation, and to plot the course that humanity was likely to follow in the next stage of history. His major work *Das Kapital*, of which he was able to publish only one volume, was primarily intended as a study of history and economics; Engels constructed the second and third volumes of this work from Marx's posthumous papers. This work proposed that goods were exchanged at prices or rates which depended on the value of the labour embodied in the commodities or goods; in other words, it proposed the labour theory of value. The monetary value of the labour invested in goods is invariably worth more than the merely subsistence wage paid to the labourer; and the difference in the financial amounts involved is appropriated by the capitalist in a capitalist society. This system however has within itself the seeds of its own destruction; it is self-liquidating. It will be succeeded historically and necessarily by a socialist system where all labourers are producers in a rational society which has no wages, no class-distinctions, no punishment and no State. This is so because the laws at work in history are the laws of historical materialism. The economic substructure and the technical factors in the mode of production of the material conditions of human existence necessarily determine the course of all other human activities, cultural superstructures and social institutions.

Engels developed this doctrine of historical materialism pertaining to human society into a doctrine of dialectical materialism concerning the nature of the universe as a whole. In Nature, all is movement, contradiction, change, development. All of reality is governed by the same dialectical laws. Water changes into steam or into ice abruptly, metals melt and liquefy, chemicals combine and explode, or are suddenly transformed. Alterations in the quantity of a thing are often accompanied by a sudden alteration of its characteristics. New qualities emerge in matter, and they do so in a 'leap'. Sudden qualitative change is a natural characteristic of the universe as a whole. New qualities emerge from quantity. This can be expressed as the law of the transformation of quantity into quality. There are two other laws of dialectics mentioned by Engels. The law of the interpenetration (or unity and struggle) of opposites explains change in terms of the overcoming of certain forces by other opposing forces; and the law of the negation of the negation explains development in terms of competitive destructive forces that usher in a better state of affairs, as in the case where capitalistic expropriators are themselves eventually expropriated. The buried grain of barley is negated in a 'deathless death' which reproduces new life thirty-fold. The emergence of sudden new social forms, for example, is as natural as evolutionary adaptation in an environment which is tense with the clash of opposites. New forms of life and thought are born. Tension, conflict and revolt give rise to new economic substructures which then give rise to new social superstructures, as Marx had pointed out. Human agency can actively speed up this dynamic dialectical process.

It was Engels' understanding of Marx's thought that came to be known as Marxist philosophy, or dialectical materialism. Dialectical materialism distances itself from 'vulgar' mechanical materialism which identifies thought with mechanical brain processes. Mechanistic materialism is regarded as incapable of explaining the emergence of qualitatively new forms of life from more primitive simpler forms. Dialectical thought attempts to understand changing things in the total network of opposing relationships existing between things in the process of change. Dialectical thought alone can explain the emergence of qualitative novelty from matter, in the Marxist view.

There is a fundamental ambiguity, however, in this Marxist explanation. It endeavours to wed together a doctrine of radical materialism and a vision of free, dialectical, revolutionary thought aiming at a goal. Left to itself, Marxism tends naturally to develop further along several different and divergent lines of thought. This divergence is held in check today only by Lenin's (1895) doctrine of total loyalty to a non-deviating *partiinost* (partisanship, or Party spirit), and by the vast political power of the collectivist (communist) Party leaders. The doctrine of *partiinost* considers man as one who has meaning and purpose only as a member of the collectivity or community. The collective is regarded as the absolute; and for the absolute, one of its primary concerns is to establish and defend the absolutizing of itself. In the collective, or 'mass', the special nature and value of the human person is dismissed, and the members of the collective are required to live and die for those (economic, material) values which the collective declares to be its first concern. This deification of the chosen value is regarded as overthrowing without question any pre-existing or alternative order of values. The divergent lines of thought present within the Marxist philosophy (of Marx and Engels) are held in check, then, by a further doctrine which is known as the doctrine of Marxism-Leninism, a doctrine of undeviating Marxist *partiinost*.

5. Dogmatic materialists.

At the end of the eighteenth century, the scientific discoveries of J. Priestley in England and A. Lavoisier in France concerning chemical substance and their interactions effected a revolution in the science of chemistry. The science was soon extended to cover the processes of life. In 1828 the synthesis of urea was achieved, and biochemistry came to be regarded as merely one of the branches of the general science of chemistry. The lively interest in biochemistry gave rise to a wave of dogmatic or extreme *materialist* explanations of life and thought processes. Heinrich Czolbe (d. 1873) attempted to explain sensory qualities and consciousness as products of the motion of atoms. Karl Vogt (d. 1895) said that the brain secretes thought as the liver secretes bile. J. Moleschott (d. 1893) summed up his doctrine of materialist monism in the phrase 'No thought without phosphorus'. Ludwig Büchner (d. 1899) held that force and matter are fundamentally the same thing, and that the universe is eternal 'matter with its properties, or movements'. Views of this kind enjoyed a widespread popularity.

The State-controlled German universities of the mid-nineteenth century fostered an official (semi-Hegelian) philosophy as a defence against social and political reform. The German materialists attempted to free scientific inquiry from the control of Lutheran orthodoxy and political intolerance; and their presentation of a materialist philosophy at that period had political, social and scientific implications. Their writings had a widespread influence and several of their books went through many editions. They pointed out that theological answers should not be given to scientific questions. They protested against duty-centred, puritanical views of morality, and advocated instead a form of utilitarian hedonism. They were frequently criticized for promulgating doctrines which were regarded as subversive of received morality. They stood in the centre of several storms of controversy. Their movement, however, did not present any profound philosophical thought, and they are not now regarded as having made any major contribution to the history of philosophy.

6. Kierkegaard. The Dane *Søren Aabye Kierkegaard* (1813-55) reacted strongly against the type of Hegelian philosophy taught in his student days at the university of Copenhagen. It ignored the self-realization of the free individual through personal self-commitment in undetermined free choice. The individual needs to find 'a truth which is true for *me*, to find the idea for which I can live and die' (*Journal*). He protested against the submergence of the individual in the collectivity. The individual must not be content to think, feel and act as a semi-conscious member of a crowd, with a weakened sense of responsibility. He must become more truly his individual self by acting resolutely on his own principles of conduct, especially in relating himself to God as Thou.

Kierkegaard explained his 'existentialist' views in his publications *On the Concept of Irony* (1841), *Either/Or: A Fragment of Life* (1843), *Fear and Trembling* (1843), *Concept of Dread* (1844), *Stages on Life's Way* (1845), and *Concluding Unscientific Postscript* (1846). In these and other writings, Kierkegaard maintained that each individual constitutes himself as the individual he is, through his undetermined choice of one mode of existence rather than another. Choice is the core of all human existence. The 'existing individual', as opposed to the one drifting along asleep in a crowd, commits himself towards a chosen end which he actively strives to attain. On the religious level, the act of 'existing' is a constant striving towards God.

A man's first stage of awakening is that of aesthetic consciousness in which he experiences only the desire to enjoy, like Nero, the whole range of emotive and sense experience. His incessant craving for one pleasure after another, however, leads him in the end, through boredom and tedium, to the threshold of despair. The individual who is an 'existing individual' is then prepared to choose seriously and passionately the ethical way of life, rather than the aesthetic or hedonistic way of life. The ethical way represents the second stage of human awakening. It is the way which is followed, for example, by the responsible married individual. The 'existing individual' now experiences or feels 'the intensity of duty in such a way that the consciousness of it is for him the assurance of the eternal validity of his being' (*Either/Or* II, 223). He accepts moral standards and obligations as governing his personal ethical behaviour. This inevitably gives rise, within the individual, to the sense of sin and anxiety or dread. The guilty man knows that 'he himself has brought guilt into the world, (and) has himself lost innocence by guilt'. The omnipresence and the burden of dread, whose object is Nothing, 'a nothing which is able only to alarm' and to haunt every man, leads the individual on towards the third stage, the religious stage of human awakening. Knowledge comes through the consciousness of sin. In a moment of decision a man's life can be changed. The individual becomes acutely conscious of his bad will as something for which he is responsible, and yet which he did not originate. In the third stage, then, the individual chooses, in a blind leap of faith, to affirm his personal relationship to God, his Saviour. Faith is a leap of the will, a passionate self-commitment to a transcendent Thou. It is a passionate affirmation and appropriation of the objectively uncertain, a constantly repeated self-commitment to the personal, absolute Thou.

Kierkegaard's protest against submergence in the collectivity, and his insistence on the importance of personal self-commitment in faith, exercised a powerful influence on several aspects of the existentialist movement and on important currents in modern Lutheran thought. In these circles, Kierkegaard came to be known as the 'Danish Socrates'. He never lost sight of the fact that the philosopher remains an 'existing individual', an ethically engaged and personally involved thinker, standing out from the lethargic crowd in a life of dynamic self-commitment through free choice. Kierkegaard's books and writings were ignored after his death, and forgotten for the remainder of the nineteenth century. They were rediscovered at the close of the century, published collectively in Copenhagen in fourteen volumes (1901-06), and translated into German three years later. From this time onwards the writings of Kierkegaard have exercised a stimulative effect not only on the 'existentialists' but also on the thought of several professional theologians and philosophers of the twentieth century.

7. **Neo-Kantianism** began with the publication of Otto Leibmann's *Kant und die Epigonen* at Stuttgart in 1865. The clarion-call of this book, 'Back to Kant', became famous, and several of the German universities adopted the new trend. They sought to avoid the extremes of absolute idealism on the one side and dogmatic materialism on the other. They were convinced that philosophy could be a science only if it adopted once again the method and general spirit of Immanuel Kant. Several different schools of thought now

gave their attention to an exact analysis of the exact words of Kant's texts. The different schools differed widely in their teachings and emphasis; and the quarrels between the different universities became notorious. Members of one school (or party) opposed and blocked the appointments and promotions of members of any other school (or party).

The Marburg school, led by *Herman Cohen* (1842-1918) and *Paul Natorp* (1854-1924), concentrated in a special way on the 'fact of science' and on the unending history of *science* 'as this elaborates itself'. Philosophy is the theory of the principles of science and of all culture in general. The logical (and *a priori*) foundations of mathematical physics, ethics, aesthetics, psychology, law and the natural sciences lie in the intelligence alone. These foundations are independent of all experience. The phenomenal world is the real world and it is the realm of ideas. The world is the creative act of thought.

The Heidelberg school (or the Baden school), led by *Wilhelm Windelband* (1888-1915) and *Heinrich Rickert* (1863-1936), concentrated in a special way on the philosophy of *values*. The criterion of truth is to be found in those values which ennoble, elevate and civilize man. Axiological criteria are more fundamental than, and prior to, epistemological criteria. The members of this school concentrated their attention, therefore, on the development of a Kantian categorization of historical and cultural experience, and on attaining a more profound understanding of the cultural sciences, which deal with history, art, morality and institutions.

Wilhelm Dilthey (1833-1911), like the neo-Kantians of the Heidelberg-Baden school, distinguished the *human* sciences (such as psychology, philosophy, religion, art and literary criticism) from the *natural* sciences. The natural or physical sciences are concerned not with the particular individual but rather with universal propositions, general laws and causal explanations; *explanation* is the characteristic method of the physical sciences. The human or cultural sciences, by way of contrast, seek an *understanding* of the different particular aspects of the spiritual life of man and their objectivizations in history. Thus, art seeks to understand a particular master artist; history seeks to understand a particular warrior-king. Attention is directed to a particular concrete individual in his unique unrepeatable particularity. Here the power of 'understanding' appears as the only adequate method for entering into a 'hermeneutic' (exposition) of the meaning of historical individuals and events. Dilthey rightly emphasized the peculiar characteristics of each historical event, but in doing so he ignored the distinction which exists between temporal cultural changes and a supra-temporal philosophical system of values. Thus he arrived at a doctrine of relativistic historicism which contends that the current stage of cultural development exercises a decisive influence on the (current, relativized) norm of truth. History is then seen as wholly conditioned by time and culture, and as properly understood only by some form of life philosophy or pragmatism.

The neo-Kantians in general seemed to accept the view that one can philosophize with Kant or against Kant but one cannot philosophize without Kant. They also accepted Windelband's view that 'To understand Kant is to go beyond Kant'. They passed on Kantian elements of thought to the next generation, but they themselves had ceased to be a dominant force in German thought by the end of the First World War (1914-18).

8. Inductive metaphysicians. In the latter half of the nineteenth century, there was a further group of independent German scientists-and-philosophers who maintained that the concerned scientist must go beyond the scientific view of the world into the domain of metaphysical reflection. This group entered the domain of philosophy, then, through their speculations on one or other of the empirical sciences. Their metaphysical speculation is closely attached to their experimental studies and for this reason one may justifiably speak of their speculative thought as an inductive form of metaphysics.

Gustav T. Fechner (1801-87), professor of physics at Leipzig, was a pioneer in experimental psychology. He sought to refute the hypotheses of materialistic metaphysics through the presentation of empirical evidence for his doctrine of panpsychism. He maintained that plants have a mental life, and that mind and matter are simply alternative ways of construing one and the same psychological phenomenon or reality. His experimental studies in psychophysics were directed towards the confirmation of his doctrine of panpsychism.

Rudolf H. Lotze (1817-81) was a doctor of medicine and instructor at Leipzig university who subsequently became professor of philosophy at Göttingen. He maintained that the biologist and experimental psychologist must try to confine their explanations of organic nature, as far as they can, to the mechanical type of explanation, even though they will also find facts of experience, in biology and psychology, which severely limit the applicability of the mechanical view. The total culture of man, however, embraces art and value as well as science, and so every rational being, the scientist included, has a natural urge to make philosophical reflection on purposiveness and values in the life of man and the universe.

It is through human experience and not through human thought, according to Lotze, that we have direct awareness of pleasure and pain, harmony and contradiction, good and evil, beauty and ugliness, worth and unworth. Feeling, or love, is the ultimate arbiter of the value or worth of anything. It is the experience of ultimate goodness which drives man towards a more profound comprehension of human life and the cosmos. It reveals to man that Nature or the world is an organic unity; the world is in some sense psychical; things are in some sense psychic entities; and all things are immanent in God. God is expressing himself in the world for the progressive realization of a moral ideal, a spiritual value or end. The causal nexuses and mechanisms which the sciences discover everywhere in Nature are simply the regular means by which God achieves his ends in the cosmos. This psychic view of cosmic mechanism, Lotze said, is a reasonable inference which is rationally preferable to any explanation proffered by any materialist view of cosmic mechanism; it explains the presence of feeling, purposiveness and values in the world. The mechanical laws of nature serve to realize ends in a universe which owes its creation to an act of love.

Wilhelm Wundt (1832-1920) was an experimental psychologist, physiologist and philosopher, who based his general *System of Philosophy* (1889) on a voluntaristic interpretation of human psychology. He was specially interested in cultural 'folk psychology' or 'psychology of peoples' (*Völkerpsychologie*; 1904). He encouraged social psychologists to investigate the psychical energies which underlie the sociogenetic development of speech, language, myth, religion, law, social custom, social structures and arts as 'objective products of the collective intellect' of a people, tribe or nation. It is these psychical energies and their objective products which together manifest the spirit or soul of a people. He advocated, furthermore, that social psychology study the evolution of the concept of universal humanity in the products of universal religions, universal science and in the formation of universal human rights. The human race is a totality of graded volitional unities of peoples and cultures in which the universal spirit of humanity is gradually emerging and tending towards the spiritual unification of mankind.

Each of these philosopher-scientists was impelled towards philosophical speculation through problems which arose for them in their areas of scientific specialization. They were convinced that reflection on the world known to science leads rationally to the formulation of metaphysical theories. This inductive approach to metaphysics is exemplified also in the work of Henri Bergson (see below, Chapter 29), Rudolf Eucken (1846-1926), Hans Driesch (1867-1941), and other thinkers of the twentieth century.

9. Brentano. *Franz Brentano* (1838-1917), who taught at Würzburg and Vienna, is generally acknowledged as the founder of the phenomenological movement. He left the Dominican order, the priesthood, and the Church in 1873, but his thought continued to be influenced by his studies in Aristotelian-Thomistic philosophy. He published several historical works on the philosophy of Aristotle. As a teacher he exercised a lifelong influence on his students Kasimierz Twardowski, Alexius Meinong, A. Marty, C. Stumpf and Edmund Husserl, and indirectly through them on philosophers such as Max Scheler and Nicolai Hartmann.

In his *Psychology from the Empirical Standpoint* (1874 and 1911), Brentano presented descriptive psychology or 'descriptive phenomenology' as a scientific inquiry into psychical acts or acts of consciousness as concerned with 'intentional' objects contained within the acts themselves. Every 'mental' act, such as hearing, seeing, sensing, thinking, judging, inferring, loving, and hating, includes its intentional objective within itself. Consciousness is necessarily consciousness of some content or objective of consciousness. Descriptive phenomenology is concerned with the object of consciousness but not with its ontological nature and status as existing or not existing extra-mentally. It prescinds from 'existence' and considers the mental phenomenon itself as an 'inexistent' objective. The psychical act is an *intentional* 'reference to a content', or 'direction upon an object', prescinding from problems pertaining to existence. The subject-matter of empirical psychology, then, is this intentionality of consciousness.

Brentano classified mental phenomena according to the three different ways in which psychical acts are 'directed upon' their objects. The first type of intentional reference is that in which ideas, thoughts or presentations (*Vorstellungen*) are simply 'present to consciousness' or 'before the mind' without any question arising as to their truth or falsity. The second type, or classification, is that in which an *intellectual* stand is taken in a non-propositional judgement which either recognizes or rejects the object. Thus, for example, the different judgements in which mermaids are rejected and dolphins are accepted are non-propositional judgements. The word 'exist' in the affirmation 'dinosaurs exist' is simply a synsemantic term that is used to express the act of judgement; the intellectual stand is taken with reference to the object alone, and not with reference to 'the conjunction of an attribute of existence with the object'. One simply affirms that one acknowledges or recognizes dinosaurs. The third type of intentional reference is those in which one takes an *emotional* or voluntaristic stand with regard to the object, expressing love or hate, pleasure or displeasure, pursuit or avoidance in reference to the object.

Brentano based his theory of logical truth and his theory of moral rectitude on the second and third classes respectively of mental phenomena. In his book *On the Origin of Our Knowledge of Right and Wrong* (1889), he says that in the case of acts of the first class (simple presentations) none can be called either correct or incorrect. In the case of the second class (nonpropositional judgements), however, one of the two opposed modes of relation, recognition and rejection, is correct and the other incorrect. Again, in the case of the third class, of the two opposed modes of relation, love and hate, being pleased and being displeased, one of them invariably is correct and the other incorrect.

We arrive at the general concepts of correct judgement and correct emotion, Brentano says, just as we arrive at the concepts of what it is to be red and what it is to be coloured, by contemplating actual instances of these concepts. We learn, for example, that knowledge is good, or that every enrichment within the realm of ideas is good, by contemplating actual instances of enriching knowledge. We aspire to certain apodictic certainty and we attain it by reflection and reasoning. We have apodictic certainty that a triangle not only may have, not only has, but *must* have its angles equal to two right angles. To say, then, that something, such as knowledge, is good is to say that it is impossible to love knowledge incorrectly; it is apodictically to reject incorrect lovers of knowledge. Similarly, to say that something, such as parricide, is bad is apodictically to reject incorrect haters of parricide. The correctness of loving (e.g. knowledge) and hating (e.g. parricide) is objective in that it arises from the contemplation of the contrast between actual cases of emotions that are 'qualified as correct' with cases of emotions that are not, and in that it is impossible for one person to love correctly what another hates correctly or to love incorrectly what another hates incorrectly.

A true judgement, Brentano tells us, is one that cannot contradict an evident judgement. Truth pertains to the judgement of one who asserts what the person who judges with evidence would assert. Truth is characterized, then, by reference to evidence. Directly evident actual judgements are known as being evident by contemplating instances, such as judgements of 'inner perception' (as when I judge that I am now judging in a certain way), and judgements of reason or insights (as when I judge that three things are more than two things). Judgements of 'outer perception' (of the external world), by way of contrast, are not at all evident in this way. We believe they are true and worthy of our confidence when we find that they do not contradict any evident judgement. Nevertheless, they are 'blind' judgements, not based on direct evidence.

On the basis of his theory of judgement, Brentano proposed a revision of the four Aristotelian types of proposition according to quality and quantity (A, E, I, O), and he proposed also a corresponding revision of the theory of the syllogism. The proposition 'All S are P' (e.g. All men are mortal) is normally used to express a two-fold judgement, namely, the acceptance of Ss that are Ps, and the rejection of Ss that are non-Ps. He suggested that the proposition 'All S are P' (A) be revised to read 'There is no S which is a non-P'; that 'No S is P' (E) read as 'There is no S which is a P'; that 'Some S are P' (I) read as 'There is an S which is a P'; and that 'Some S are not P' (O) read as 'There is an S which is a non-P'. All the valid moods of the categorical syllogism were then revised and rewritten in terms which are in accord with the theory of nonpropositional judgements.

Two philosophical movements, of similar nature, issued from the teachings of Franz Brentano. One culminated in the phenomenology of Edmund Husserl. The other movement, as represented by Alexius Meinong and his disciples, developed a general theory of objects which included both existent and 'inexistent' objects. The doctrine for which Brentano was specially remembered, however, was that of the intentionality of consciousness.

10. Nietzsche. *Friedrich W. Nietzsche* (1844-1900) was born in Röcken, in Saxony. His father and grandfathers were Lutheran ministers. At school he excelled in religion and in Greek and German literature. At the universities of Bonn and Leipzig he specialized in the classics and philosophy. He was fascinated by the epic poems of Homer, the tragedies of Aeschylus, the *Theogony* of Hesiod, and by their stories about the turbulent creation of the universe, the passionate histories of the gods, and the tragic legends concerning the gods' relations with earthly women.

Nietzsche's first book, *The Birth of Tragedy from the Spirit of Music* (1872), defended the view that Greek tragic drama had its origin in the imposition of Apollonian restraint, harmony and style on the frenzied dance festivals of the Dionysian cult. Greek culture had faced up to the fears and terrors of history and nature, and had achieved 'the sublime as the artistic conquest of the horrible'. The dark and surging forces of passionate life had been harnessed, enformed and beautified in an uplifting, ennobling work of creative art. The suprahistorical dramatic character rises up from a sea of encircling nihilism. The Greek formula, then, for the transformation of human life is the fusion together of the Dionysian and Apollonian power-sources present within human nature.

From 1873 to 1876, Nietzsche published four 'untimely meditations', or *Thoughts out of Season*, in which he attacked the collectivist mentality of the German State (Reich) and Church. State and Church deify success, and idolize the factual, as a means of intimidating men into total conformity to 'government, public opinion, or majority of numbers'. The free individual must, on the contrary, realize his 'true self'. This true self is 'immeasurably high above you, or above what you usually take for your ego'. One must see oneself as a suprahistorical (*überhistorisch*) individual 'for whom the world is finished in every moment'. Salvation does not come with 'ten new years'. It is the individual's 'now' that is of major importance. 'Be yourself.' Now! Be individual! Be original! One is raw; one must *become* original, now.

Nietzsche developed these themes further in his later works *Human, All-too-human* (1878), *The Dawn* (1881), *The Gay Science* (1882), *Thus Spoke Zarathustra* (1883), *Beyond Good and Evil* (1886), *Towards a Genealogy of Morals* (1887), *The Twilight of the Idols* (1889), *The Antichrist* (1895), *Ecce Homo* (1908), *The Will to Power* (1901-06), and other writings. He had planned to write a book called *Revaluation of All Values* as his main work, but he collapsed in January 1889, and was insane throughout the remainder of his life.

The fundamental conception in Nietzsche's major works is that of the will to power. The universe is the manifestation of universal power, energy, force. Organic functions such as appropriation and assimilation, for example, are manifestations of the universal, self-assertive will to power. 'Striving for excellence is the striving to overwhelm one's neighbour.' Even the slave seeks power. He 'hates to serve'; he resents being enslaved, and he takes revenge on his masters with an inactive imaginary revenge. All that each wants is wanted for the sake of power. The will to power in characters such as Nero (and all 'weak characters without power over themselves, who hate the constraint of style') expresses itself in the desire to burn

Rome and to subjugate all others. On the other hand, the will to power manifested in the literature, art and philosophy of the great poets and dramatists is a sublimated will to power embodied in the persons of those who are masters of themselves and masters of their creative media of self-expression. All the admirable heroes of past history are invariably dynamic passionate men of outstanding intelligence, who rose above the resentments and dishonesties of their times, mastered their powerful passions and channelled them creatively into deeds and works which have perennial form and style.

The decay of belief in God in modern times and the decay of the life-denying ethic of Christianity have reached the point where one can now affirm, according to Nietzsche, that 'God is dead'. This opens all the gateways for man's creative energies to develop fully in *this* world. 'At last, the sea, our sea, lies open before us.' The atheistic, aristocratic, masterly man must now be creator of all his own values. The approaching era of atheistic nihilism and dreadful ideological wars will clear the way for the emergence of a higher type of human being, the noble, demi-godlike overman (*Übermensch*) or superman. Common 'Man is something to be surpassed... Superman is the goal'.

Superman will emerge when superior individuals have the courage to revalue all values and 'live dangerously' at the highest level of masterful intellectual and emotional power. They will reject traditional morality in the name of honesty and accuracy, and create their own values. They will be noble embodiments of ardent affirmations of life, giving style to their character, and looking upon themselves as creators rather than creatures. They will cast aside all aspirations towards otherworldliness, and immerse themselves joyfully in the creative tasks of the here and now. They know that the present moment does not abide, but they know too that the present moment returns eternally in an eternal recurrence. They are men who cry 'encore' to a cosmic play played over again a countless number of times. Their attitude is a 'yea-saying attitude' to the joy of living, and to the creative challenge of the recurring moment. Their whole thought is at the service of life. Their whole being is a manifestation of joyful affirmation of 'the Will to Power, which is precisely the Will to Life'.

Nietzsche's writings have interested and influenced different readers in different ways. These writings are in many instances a dramatic expression of the personal, tense, spiritual crises of modern 'post-Christian' man. Some have been impressed by Nietzsche's critique of traditional morality, others by his phenomenological analysis of accepted values, or by his psychological analyses of 'herd-morality', 'resentment', 'sublimation', and other themes. Many of his writings are a loosely-connected assembly of random jottings in the form of aphorisms, which came to mind at different times, especially during long solitary walks. Different selections of these aphorisms, by different readers, lead to varied interpretations of Nietzsche's thoughts. In some respects Nietzsche is a penetrating and prescient thinker; in other respects he is astigmatic and purblind. He criticized the ultimate foundation of the morality of his time as a morality of slavish Christian meekness which aimed at repressing the resentment of vassals and minions against their congenital superiors, and at reappraising the weak and the sick as having a fabricated kind of pre-eminent value. He rejected what he called the Christian slave-morality of humility and brotherly love as mere masks of a sickly compassion for the impotent and the unsuccessful.

Nietzsche glorified biological values, and he resented any subjugation of these values to other Christian, human or rational values. For this reason, contemporary historians suggest that Nietzsche may well be regarded as a nineteenth-century herald and prophet of certain transvalued world views (*Weltanschauungen*) which are accepted with respect in the international commercial and political world of the twentieth century. Thus, for example, power-wielding multinational corporations, armaments dealers, and tax haven commercial bankers can, without censure, promote business and pragmatic valuations which are entirely divorced from higher ethical and social valuations. It is in this sense that Nietzsche may be seen as a nineteenth-century prophet of a twentieth-century revaluation of human values.

Nietzsche rejected the subordination of organic, vital and sensory values to social, spiritual and religious values. He saw in Socratic philosophy the fateful turning-point of Greek thought from myth and instinct to a life-destroying 'rationality'. His contention that every existent is ultimately a blind drive for life places his philosophical thought in the wider school of 'life philosophy' and metaphysical irrationalism.

26 Nineteenth-century philosophy in Britain

1. The utilitarian movement. Utilitarianism as a philosophical doctrine received its classical formulation in the writings of Jeremy Bentham, James Mill and John Stuart Mill. The general 'principle of utility' had been formulated previously, in a theoretical way, in the writings of John Locke, David Hume, William Paley and others. Locke had asserted that 'what has an aptness to produce pleasure in us we call good, and what is apt to produce pain in us we call evil'; and Paley had asserted that the will of God with regard to the goodness or badness of any action may be found by inquiring into its 'tendency to promote or diminish the general happiness'. The rightness and wrongness of actions is determined therefore by the goodness and badness of their consequences. Bentham and Mill applied this theoretical and explanatory principle to the practical problems of their own age, and in so doing they provided British thinkers with an attractively simple moral philosophy and an effective programme for legal, penal, and political reform.

Jeremy Bentham (1748-1832) accepted Hume's identification of value with utility as a practical philosophical base on which to found a simple but thorough programme for the rationalization of law and morality, that is, of public and private principles of conduct. The utilitarian measure of value, and its associated theory concerning human motivation, indicated what kinds of conduct should be prohibited and what kinds of sanctions would be required to make the prohibitions effective. Thus, the legislator who wishes to deter antisocial forms of conduct needs only to attach to these forms of conduct sufficiently dissuasive penalties.

Bentham, who was a reformer rather than an outstanding philosopher, wrote several papers, in which he advocated universal suffrage, annual parliaments, constitutional reform, abolition of the monarchy and aristocracy, codification of the law, the foundation of new universities, and several other reforms which were thought to be 'radical' at the time. He based his arguments in favour of these reforms, firstly, on the (hedonist) theory that every human being naturally seeks to attain pleasure, happiness, or good, and to avoid pain, or evil, and secondly, on the (utilitarian) theory that the welfare of the community is synonymous with the greatest happiness or utility of the greatest number of people in the community. The calculus of this greatest pleasure is dependent on the intensity, duration, propinquity, fecundity, certainty and purity of the pleasure, and on the extent, or number of people affected. To augment and secure maximum happiness of this kind, it is best that legislation and government should be under the control of the people in a democratic state.

James Mill (1773-1836) was a disciple and close associate of Bentham, and one of the leaders of the growing utilitarian movement in Britain. He wrote influential articles in the *Encyclopædia Britannica*, the *Westminster Review*, and other journals and chronicles, in which he applied Benthamite principles to such subjects as government, colonies, education, associationist psychology, prisons, jurisprudence and liberty of the press. In his main philosophical work *Analysis of the Phenomena of the Human Mind* (1829) he attempted to explain all mental phenomena in terms of associationist psychology. He praised Bentham for applying reductive analysis in morals and politics. He believed ardently in the empiricist and utilitarian principles he professed, and he educated his eldest son, John Stuart Mill, at their home in London, with a rigorous intellectual education in accordance with these same principles.

John Austin (1790-1859), professor of jurisprudence at the university of London, applied Benthamite utilitarian principles to the philosophy of law. He defined positive law in coercive terms as a rule set for subjects by a sovereign in a politically independent society; and he claimed that legal obligation arises out of the subject's fear of the sanction. *David Ricardo* (1772-1823) applied Benthamite principles to economics. He held that the common well-being of society, and general harmony of competitive interests, is best attained in a *laissez-faire* free competitive market. These and other Benthamites became a powerful political force which succeeded in accomplishing several of the legal and political reforms that Bentham had originally suggested.

2. John Stuart Mill (1806-73) was initiated into the utilitarian circle of radical reformers by his father James Mill, who was widely regarded as a lieutenant of Jeremy Bentham in the utilitarian movement. At the age of twenty, however, he began to re-examine the doctrines in which he had been raised. He found in poetry, in art and in Saint-Simonian literature (see Chapter 28, section 3 below) an education of the feelings that helped to balance the rigorous intellectual education he received from his father.

J. S. Mill defended the utilitarian ethic and the principle of greatest happiness against widespread attacks and objections that it was a philosophy of egoism and mere expediency. (Thomas Carlyle, for example, attacked Benthamite ethics as a 'pig philosophy'.) In the course of his defence, however, Mill altered the entire foundation on which Benthamist utilitarianism rested. He pointed out that the *qualitative* aspect of happiness and pleasure is an empirical fact which is as empirically factual as the *quantitative* factor considered by Bentham. Man is not just a pleasure-seeking and pain-avoiding unit. The nature of man is such that it is, in fact, better for an individual to be a human being who is dissatisfied than to be a pig wholly satisfied, and that it is better to be a Socrates dissatisfied than a fool, or rascal, or dunce satisfied. The estimation of pleasure, therefore, should not be supposed to rest on *quantity* alone. Rather, human happiness and fulfilment arises through the full use of man's higher faculties. This does not at all entail a philosophy of egoism, since 'the happiness which forms the utilitarian standard of what is right in conduct, is not the agent's own happiness, but that of *all* concerned', or, in other words, it is the greatest happiness of the greatest number of those concerned. Man is by nature a social being, and the firm foundation of utilitarian morality is to be found in the social and 'conscientious feelings of mankind'. 'To do as one would be done by, and to love one's neighbour as oneself, constitute the ideal of utilitarian perfection.' This viewpoint is very distant from that of the Benthamist calculus of quantitative pleasure. The emphasis is on the social nature of man; and the conception of 'happiness' is closer to that of Aristotle than it is to that of Bentham.

The principle of social utility demands civil *liberty*, according to Mill, so that every man be free to attain happiness through the full use of his human faculties. An individual's liberty can rightfully be constrained only in order to prevent his doing harm to others. There are certain areas of human freedom, consequently, which cannot rightly be denied, namely, freedom to believe, freedom of 'tastes and pursuits', 'freedom to unite, for any purpose not involving the harm of others', and freedom to express one's views in the public market-place. It is a matter of major importance for all men's long-range interests that in these areas the freedom and rights of the individual be protected from governmental coercion and from 'the tyranny of the prevailing opinion and feeling', that is, from 'the tyranny of the majority'. These human freedoms and rights are best preserved in democracy with proportional representation to safeguard the rights of minorities.

Mill presented a comprehensive restatement of the current philosophy of experience and the utilitarian doctrine in his widely acclaimed publication *A System of Logic* (1843), which was adopted as a text at both Oxford and Cambridge. In this work, Mill showed that a philosophy of experience is not committed to the sceptical form of Humean 'empiricism', and that, with care, certainty may be attained in a scientific form of inductive reasoning. A philosophy of this kind is a viable alternative, he said, to German idealism, naive 'common-sense' realism, and slovenly generalization; and it is capable of providing a philosophical foundation for the development of society along liberal lines.

In the *Logic*, Mill asserts that the only *particulars* of which we can speak significantly are those we are acquainted with through experience. Terms denote particulars. 'All inference is from particulars to particulars.' Syllogistic or deductive reasoning does not infer particulars, or particular statements, from general statements. It is a form of reasoning or argument which relates inductive conclusions to inductive generalizations. Mathematical knowledge is no exception to this. All mathematical propositions are synthetic and based on experience; and the necessity associated with mathematical conclusions is simply a psychological necessity. The ultimate axioms of mathematics are generalizations from what we have always experienced. Inductive generalizations are possible through the use of the methods of agreement, difference, joint agreement and difference, concomitant variations, and the method of residues. These are inductive methods of experimental inquiry used for the discovery of causal relations between phenomena. Inductive inference is based on the principle of the uniformity of nature; and the principle of the uniformity of nature is itself a principle which is established by 'non-scientific', inductive arguments based on induction by simple enumeration. In the social sciences, where experimentation is largely impossible, the basic laws and methods are those of associational psychology. Social dynamics attempts to explain the historical sequences of social conditions as these are influenced and changed, for example, by exceptional, gifted individuals.

In his *Examination of Sir William Hamilton's Philosophy* (1865), Mill presented his views concerning the foundations and nature of our knowledge of bodies and of minds. He asserted that, although he did not accept the theology of Berkeley, he would nevertheless define matter, 'like all Berkeleians' (phenomenally), as 'a permanent possibility of sensation'. Material things, objects of the mind, are sensations or sense-data. Actual sensations are transient; but the mind, by reason of its expectations, inevitably thinks of the permanent possibilities of sensations as abiding physical objects. The mind itself is 'a series of feelings' which is inexplicably aware of itself as a series; and 'aware of itself as past and future'. This series (or mind) has evidence of the existence of other series (or minds) by inference from overt forms of bodily behaviour not related to mine, that is, from other permanent possibilities of sensations not related to the series which I call my mind. In this way one can avoid the spectre of solipsism without sacrificing the doctrine of phenomenalism, he thought. Mill, however, did not seem to be conscious of the further spectre, or difficulty, that if 'bodies' are analysed in terms of 'sensations', and if the mind is aware of these 'sensations' only through its own sensations, then one must either adopt a doctrine of solipsism or abandon one's doctrine of phenomenalism. Mill was an effective spokesman for the liberal view of man and society. Nevertheless he cannot be ranked among the greatest philosophers. The empiricist and phenomenalist bases of his philosophy provide no secure foundation for the ontological or realist assertions which emerged constantly from his widely respected practical judgement.

3. Empiricists and positivists. The British empiricists of the nineteenth century continued and developed further the traditional trend of thought of their predecessors in the seventeenth and eighteenth centuries and of their more remote precursors, the nominalists of the late Middle Ages. Thus *Alexander Bain* (1818-1903) presented a more thoroughly developed elaboration of the associationist theory of mind by extending it to the emotive and volitional aspects of human nature. He held that the muscles, such as those of the eye, have within themselves an inherent spontaneity or 'preparation of act' such that their expectation of a stimulus is inseparably associated with preparations for a spontaneous reaction to the stimulus. The eyes, for example, close spontaneously when glare is painful. This spontaneity is inseparable from 'will', just as 'preparation to act' is inseparable from 'belief' and expectation. Bain was the founder of the quarterly review *Mind* (1876-), which has become one of the most influential journals of philosophy in the world. *Henry Sidgwick* (1838-1900), of Cambridge, elaborated and developed the ethical intimations of Mill in his 'common-sense' theory that the doctrine of utilitarianism needs to be supplemented by the adoption of the intuited and self-evident principles of benevolence and justice. He professed himself to be 'a utilitarian... but on an intuitional basis'. Sidgwick, like Bain, provided basic financial and administrative support for *Mind* during its first twenty-five years of production.

Charles Darwin (1809-82) gathered a large quantity of biological data during the famous voyage of the *Beagle* (1831-36). He then spent a further twenty years shaping his formulation of an evolutionary hypothesis. In October 1838, Darwin read the *Essay on Population* (1803) by Thomas Malthus. He was impressed by its observations on the human 'struggle for existence'. This suggested to Darwin, and also to the naturalist Alfred Wallace (1823-1913), the key idea of 'natural selection' which, Darwin said, is simply 'the doctrine of Malthus applied with manifold force to the whole animal and vegetable kingdoms'. In July 1858, Darwin and Wallace presented a joint communication to the Linnaean Society in which they explained the phylogenetic changes in the structure and behaviour of organisms in terms of natural selection or survival of the fittest in the struggle for existence. The biological variations which make the survivors to be the 'fittest' were affirmed to be fortuitous. This evolutionary hypothesis was quickly recognized as a revolutionary hypothesis which evidently challenged, and weakened, or perhaps demolished, the ancient hypothesis of the fixity of the species. Darwin provided a wealth of biological data for his theory of evolution in *The Origin of Species* (1859) and *The Descent of Man* (1871).

Thomas Huxley (1825-95), an agnostic, accepted Darwin's 'most ingenious hypothesis' concerning natural selection as 'a very important factor' in the production of species. He maintained that the theory of evolution had to be extended to the cosmos as a whole, that is, the totality of phenomena, if its scope was not to be unnecessarily restricted. Evolution, however, and its 'gladiatorial theory of existence', did not explain the existence of man's moral sense. 'The ethical progress of society depends, not on imitating the cosmic process,... but in combating it.' Nature and morality are at war with each other. Man's moral sense condemns 'ape and tiger methods'. Morality involves going against the evolutionary process. To explain the existence of this moral sense, Huxley invoked a doctrine of ethical intuitionism which seemed strangely at variance with his other views.

4. Herbert Spencer (1820-1903) employed the evolutionary principle to interpret the entire range of biological, social and mental phenomena. He devoted thirty years of his life to the formulation and execution of a plan to apply the idea of development (or 'progress') as a first principle to all the fundamental principles of biology, psychology, sociology and ethics. His *System of Synthetic Philosophy*, in ten volumes, was presented for publication in series from 1862 to 1893.

Spencer aimed to interpret life, thought and society in terms of matter, motion and force. Time, space, matter, motion are all based on the experiences of force; they are based on the consciousness of muscular tension. It is experiences or phenomena of this kind which provide the subject-matter of both science and philosophy. The different sciences aim to unify knowledge in their own different fields of study. Philosophy aims to unify all knowledge. Philosophy makes explicit the fundamental concepts and assumptions, such as time and space, which are involved in all thought. Thus for example, philosophy makes explicit the concept of matter as the concept of co-existent positions which offer resistance. 'The abstract of all sequences is time. The abstract of all co-existence is space.' Force, or rather the experience of force, muscular tension, is the 'ultimate of ultimates'.

Political society, the State, according to Spencer is a super-organism, a whole, which exists for the liberty of its individual members. He opposed all forms of statist socialism and was a firm believer in the principle of *laissez-faire*. Each and every society exists solely for the benefit of its members. Society's essential duty is the defence of the citizen's individuality. Socialism or collectivism necessarily leads to (totalitarian) despotism. The free individual must fight vigorously to ward off 'the coming slavery' and bureaucracy of the omnicompetent State. Man's best safeguard against socialist despotism and State control lies in his support of voluntary organization. For free committed individuals, mutual aid and co-operation in voluntary organizations fosters the evolution of social consciousness and opens up new pathways to human progress.

Spencer's philosophy was influential throughout the nineteenth century. The vision of indefinite human progress was shattered, however, by the injustices of *laissez-faire* capitalism in highly industrialized communities and by the horrors of war in the late nineteenth and early twentieth centuries. The principle of evolution itself was seen to be too general; it did not permit any scientific prediction, and was incapable of falsification. Every change could be interpreted, *post factum*, as a step in the evolutionary process. Spencer's writings are no longer influential, but his prodigious attempt to unify all human knowledge in the light of one architectonic principle assures him a respected place in the history of philosophical thought.

5. Newman. *John Henry (Cardinal) Newman* (1801-90) was a nineteenth-century philosopher of religion and Christian apologist whose works belong to the written tradition of British churchmen who contributed to philosophical thought. Before his conversion to Catholicism he was a tutor at Oriel College and vicar of St Mary's, Oxford. His philosophical background, apart from his study of the ancient classics and the 'Christian wisdom' of the Greek Fathers of the Church, was to a large extent that of British empiricism. He had studied Francis Bacon, Locke, Newton, Butler, Hume, Voltaire, the Scottish philosophy of common sense, Paley, Paine, Dean Mansel, and the logic of Archbishop Whateley and J. S. Mill. He was specially interested in the subject of reasonableness of assent, plausibility, and argument by analogy. He wished to present a phenomenological analysis of the spontaneous movement of the mind culminating in a reasonable, personal assent and response to the living presence of God.

Newman pointed out that there are several important areas of human life in which man gives an assent which is a reasonable assent to matters which are not logically demonstrable. It is not demonstrable, for example, that our senses are trustworthy, or that there is an objective external world with which our senses put us in contact. These beliefs are nonetheless reasonable beliefs; and even the scientist reasonably assumes the objectivity of the sensed world. The jurist, the art critic, the historian, the military strategist, the biologist, and the religious enquirer make use of a 'concrete', personal form of informal reasoning in dealing with individual situations which require personal discernment and personal estimation of what is the case, and of what is to be done. Each human being is constantly faced with moral choices and practical decisions that require a personal concrete assessment of the matter at hand, the circumstances, the means, and the end in view. 'This power of judging and concluding when in its perfection, I call the Illative Sense.' (It may be seen as a rediscovery, on Newman's part, of the human *vis aestimativa* or *vis cogitativa* of the medieval Scholastics.) Newman maintained that this power of 'judging and concluding' is a definite feature of our intellectual activity, and that a theory of mind of this kind is actually more empirical than that of John Locke. It is this same power of 'judging and concluding' which is active in that living belief in God which is present in the man who has a lively sense of moral obligation. Religious belief, based on human conscience, is a belief grounded on factors of human nature which are as real as the powers of perceiving and reasoning. Religious assent, based on the voice of internal authority imposing obligation in matters pertaining to the rule of right conduct, is *reasonable* assent.

The belief in God with which Newman is primarily concerned is a real assent to God as a present living reality. Real assent, like real apprehension, has immediate reference to persons and singular things. Notional assent, like notional apprehension, has reference to abstract ideas or universal terms. Real assent to God involves personal commitment to God; it influences a person's whole life and conduct. The form of inference, then, with which Newman is mainly concerned is a practical 'concrete' inference. It is one in which there is a movement of the mind estimating the evidence and data given in experience to a real assent to God himself as the rational explanation and providential source of the accumulation of imposing evidence presented to us in our everyday experience, and especially so in the experience of the living command of conscience.

Conscience, according to Newman, invites every individual to attain a personal insight into the momentous implications of his awareness of the inner imperative; it opens his mind to 'the ubiquitous presence of one Supreme Master'. It is the individual himself who must make his own personal appropriation of this truth in a real assent to the 'Supreme Power, claiming our habitual obedience'. Each must make his own personal encounter with the lord of conscience, and surrender personally to God himself, the immediate, present and final goal of our whole being and our love.

The empiricists of the seventeenth and eighteenth centuries had emphasized the solitary and momentary experience of the individual perceiver. Newman widened the whole panorama of human experience to include the social, historical and developmental aspects of the ongoing experience of mankind. In his *Essay on the Development of Christian Doctrine* (1845) and in *The Idea of a University* (1873), Newman pointed out that the social growth and development of ideas and institutions depends in practice on the interpretative activity of many minds, judging, suggesting relationships, evaluating, testing, developing and gradually working out the practical implications and different facets of complex ideas, complex realities, and institutional forms. We see this at work in the history of kingdoms, economic policies, religious doctrines, scientific hypotheses and philosophical theories. In all cases of healthy growth of ideas and social institutions there is a common pattern of development which invariably manifests seven aspects or criteria of genuine development. There is an evident preservation of principles which are socially influential, a continuity in the dynamic functioning of these principles, a capacity within the principles to assimilate new data, a logical sequence in their organization of complex social processes, an anticipation of their own future trends, a conservation of their past achievements, and a manifestation of their timeless vigour. Newman applied his study of the dynamics of human thought and his theory of development especially to the development of Christian doctrine, the political constitution, the ideas of civilization, and the university as the vital centre for determining the future direction of human history.

The recent growth of interest in Newman's *Grammar of Assent* and other writings has coincided with the contemporary growth of phenomenological analysis, preoccupation with self-commitment and personal appropriation of truth, and interest in the philosophy of religion. Newman's thought is still regarded today as a source of valuable insight and inspiration.

6. Objective idealism. The assumptions which lay dormant in the radical empiricism and phenomenalism of Locke, Hume and Mill were not adequately exposed or replaced by the ethical theories of moral sentiments or by the Scottish philosophy of common sense. A more profound critique of these assumptions was provided by the importation and adaptation of Kantian critical philosophy and Hegelian idealism in Britain in the latter part of the nineteenth century.

In the early phase of the idealist movement in Britain, the poet Samuel Coleridge (d. 1834), William Hamilton (d. 1856), J. F. Ferrier, John Grote, Thomas Carlyle, T. H. Green and E. Caird spoke of mind and things as expressions of one spiritual reality. They were objective idealists who regarded the subject-object relationship as grounded in spiritual reality. The whole world is the manifestation of spirit. In an age of growing agnosticism and materialism, these objective idealists advocated ethical, social and political theories which emphasized the self-realization and perfecting of the free, human personality.

Thomas Carlyle (1795-1881) spoke of the world as a veiled manifestation of supersensible reality, 'the living visible Garment of God'. *J. F. Ferrier* (1808-64) maintained that the material universe, as object, is unthinkable except as existing as an object for a subject, the divine mind. *John Grote* (1813-66) held that the (scientific) attempt to attain a rational understanding of the universe implied the belief that the universe is the rational creation of an absolute mind; and the rational attempt to act morally in the world implied, similarly, the belief that the universe is morally ordered by an absolute moral governor. One's primary duty in a universe of this kind is the duty of personal self-development within the ambience of one's station in life.

Thomas H. Green (1836-82), of Oxford, presented a thorough criticism of the first principles of British empiricism, in his introduction to an edition of the works of Hume (1874). Popular British philosophy, like that of the ancient Sophists, owed its apparent success, Green said, to certain basic assumptions which were never subjected to critical examination. It assumed, for example, that there was no difference between image and concept, that truth could be attained through simple introspection, and that there was a continuing self-identical subject of consciousness even though no empiricist theory had room for any such reality. Empirical theory, such as that of Hume, reduces human knowledge and the mind's activities to an inexplicable series of phenomena. It leads inevitably to scepticism.

Nature, according to Green, is a complex system of related phenomena; and these complex related phenomena are impossible apart from the action of an infinite intelligence, an eternal consciousness. Nature is the product of the synthesizing activity of a single spiritual mind, an infinite eternal subject. Nature is simply the correlative eternal object which is constituted by the eternal subject, God. Nature is the product of mind. Within nature, the individual human being participates in the general spiritual life of humanity, which, in turn, participates in the life of eternal consciousness. Infinite intelligence is reproduced progressively in the finite mind through the sentient human life and moral activities of the human organism.

Green applied the basic principles of his metaphysical theory to moral and social philosophy in his *Prolegomena to Ethics* (1883). Human actions spring from conscious motives, he said, and a motive is 'an idea of an end, which a self-conscious subject presents to itself (as good), and which it strives and tends to realize'. The ultimate aim of moral action in general is the 'common good' of each and all. The end of each particular moral act is the attainment of 'human perfection', self-realization. Moral perfection or virtue is something permanent and social; it differs radically from momentary and private pleasure, the utilitarian end. The 'good' for man consists in the harmonious actualization of his human potentialities. Society is a moral necessity for human self-realization. The function of political society, the State, is to create and maintain the conditions for the good life, human self-realization. The State exists to promote the common good, the welfare of society as a whole. It does so through social legislation, removing those obstacles created by private sectional interests, and thereby enabling all citizens to develop themselves, in freedom, as human beings.

Edward Caird (1835-1908), a lifelong friend of T. H. Green, sought to reconcile the oppositions between subject and object, religion and science, inclination and duty, reason and desire, freedom and determination, in a higher unity. The larger the part played in knowledge by the mind's synthetic activity, the more adequate that knowledge is. Objects of knowledge are only partial aspects of the ideal whole towards which reason points. Subject and object and all opposition emerge from a higher principle of enveloping unity which we call God. This higher principle, 'the source of being to all things that are', is 'the ultimate unity of our life and of the life of the world'. A philosophy of reconciliation of this kind, reconciling all antagonisms in a higher unity, brings about a spiritual harmony which, in turn, renders possible the highest achievements of the human spirit.

7. Bradley. *Francis Herbert Bradley* (1846-1924), a Fellow of Merton College, Oxford, devoted his life to philosophical writing. His main works were *Ethical Studies* (1876), *Principles of Logic* (1883) and *Appearance and Reality* (1893). In these works he pointed out that philosophy rests on an initial act of faith that ultimate reality is a seamless whole, a totality which is free of all contradictions. All 'things' are only appearances of the Absolute. Contradictions emerge only through the inadequacy of human thought. His doctrine may be classified as a doctrine of absolute idealism incorporating within itself subsidiary doctrines of fideism, monism and partial scepticism.

Bradley's *Ethical Studies* criticized the ethical doctrines of Mill and Kant. The end of moral action is self-realization, the realization of a general state of good will, and not mere pleasure. Ethical behaviour is not involved in an abstract, empty formalism. It has objective content. To be moral, I must will the objective world of 'my station and its duties'. Morality is an endless striving to overcome the bad self, ill-will within oneself. It is a ceaseless effort to identify one's private will with the universal will (of society or the State) and thereby to realize one's true, socialized self in the social organism. The ideal, namely identification with the ideally good, can be attained only in a supra-ethical sphere, the sphere of religious consciousness. It is in the sphere of religion that man can realize himself as a member of an infinite whole. The self is a being that can be itself only by transcending itself through identification with the ideally good.

Bradley's *Principles of Logic* applied his dialectical analysis to the problems of inference and judgement. The proposition and the inference are concerned with reality; they assert that something is or is not the case. Every judgement (e.g. 'S is P') is a reference of ideal content (universal ideas) to reality; it asserts that 'Reality, the universe as a whole, is such that S is P'. Inference presupposes judgement and ideal contents, which, in turn, presuppose generality and universality. One can argue from 'some' to 'all' only if one can surmise that the particulars share some universal character. For this reason, the empiricist account of inductive knowledge is to be rejected as totally inadequate. Knowledge does not advance from particulars to universals or from particulars to particulars, as Mill had suggested, because thought does not start with knowledge of mere separate and independent particulars. All judgement and inference is possible only on the basis of universals, that is, abstract 'ideal contents', which are related to the existing reality to which the judgement refers. Thus, for example, one can say that the nature (or reality) of space is such that a four-cornered circle is an impossibility. Empiricist logic is radically wrong, therefore, in its fundamental presupposition that knowledge advances only by the association of images. Logic is concerned not with images, or psychical facts, but with meanings, abstract ideal contents, related to reality.

Bradley's *Appearance and Reality* (1893) and *Essays on Truth and Reality* (1914) assert that there is an immediate feeling-experience or awareness of reality, 'a knowing and a being in one', and that metaphysics tries to recapture and think this felt-experience of reality at the higher level of intellectual comprehension of the nature of reality itself. The direct experience or sentience of known-being being-known gives us an inkling about the nature of being, or reality, itself. The apparent units, or represented 'things', of the sense-world, and their various sensed qualities, constitute in our minds the world of appearance. This world of appearance, if regarded as the world of reality, gives rise only to insoluble philosophical puzzles. Thus, for example, both the primary and the secondary qualities of apparent, perceived things are simply perceived appearances; and the alleged difference between qualities is merely one of appearance. Space, time, external 'objects' and even the perceived self are all re-presented, sense 'perceptions' or mere appearances. They cannot disclose the nature of reality as contrasted with appearance. The world which thought constructs on the basis of appearances is merely an ideal world and not the real world.

Immediate experience is the key to our knowledge of reality, according to Bradley. In immediate experience we have experiential knowledge of reality as a whole which is diverse and yet one. Reality is consistent and harmonious; it is not self-contradictory, as appearance is. Reality is one. This characteristic also differentiates reality from appearance. Reality or being is 'a single and all-inclusive experience'. Immediate consciousness of reality is 'a knowing and a being in one'. One can know reality only in a direct experience, and the expansion of this experience, once begun, cannot stop short of absolute reality itself. Reality is comprehensive and includes all that is. It is not a plurality of independent reals, unrelated to other reals. Plurality and relatedness are but aspects and features of one reality; all that is in being is one. Reality, the one, the absolute, is directly known in immediate experience. This experience does not fall short of thought; it transcends discursive thought. It is a vague and indistinct but nevertheless direct experiential knowledge of being itself. It provides the nucleus for conceptual and philosophical knowledge of the nature of reality.

Reality or being does not remain unmanifested, according to Bradley. The real appears in what exists. Existence is the mode of being of the phenomenal world. Reality, like truth, and perfection, admits of degrees. A whole scale of degrees of reality manifests itself in the phenomenal world. Thus, organic matter has more reality than inorganic matter; and in the scale of degrees of reality or perfection in general 'the more that anything is spiritual the more it is veritably true'. The human mind finds satisfaction in the measure of coherence and comprehensiveness it attains in its effort to understand the world. Reflection on the degrees of mental satisfaction gives rise to corresponding distinctions between degrees of truth. Every human judgement contains some degree of truth and some degree of one-sided partiality with reference to the fullness of truth. Human error and evil can be accounted for in terms of degrees of reality and degrees of removal from the perfection of reality.

Reality is one. It is absolute, ultimate reality. Reality 'is not personal' but rather 'suprapersonal', since within it there are merged into unity all the distinctions found in personality. It is preferable not to speak of it as 'God', Bradley asserts, because the term 'God', in ordinary speech, has been given a special meaning. The absolute is not a being distinct from others; it is ultimate reality itself, a self-consistent whole in which all differences are merged into an inclusive unity.

Bradley regarded all 'things' and appearances as mere elements which are adjectival to the all-inclusive reality-experience. Conceptual knowledge attains no further than mere appearances. All constructions of thought are constructions of mere appearances. This sceptical doctrine concerning concepts must necessarily extend to Bradley's central concept of reality. Bradley was fascinated by the concept of the one true Reality which the phenomenal world veils, but his scepticism must be allowed to extend necessarily and logically to his concept of the real also. He presents a valuable insight concerning the experience of reality, but his scepticism concerning thought does not allow him to develop adequately a conceptual knowledge of reality based on this experience of reality.

8. Bosanquet. *Bernard Bosanquet* (1848-1923) was a British idealist philosopher who was more Hegelian and less sceptical than Bradley. He maintained that each individual builds up his own mental construction of reality from his own perceptions, and that, for each individual, the world is therefore the individual's own world. Logic is the science which analyses this process of mental construction. Every judgement and inference arises from insight into the system and the sub-systems of systematic connections of this world. Particular judgements are seen to be true as cohering with other truths in the whole system of systematic connections which constitute the wholeness of truth. Human thinking, in general and as a whole, enters ever more deeply into a profounder comprehension of reality through further insight into the sub-systems of the world. Human knowledge is constructed by definite processes which are common to every individual intelligence. Thus, despite private mental constructions of reality, a common objective world is presented in consciousness.

For Bosanquet, reality is a concrete universal individual, or unified whole; it is the absolute, the Universe. Reality or being is an infinite experience of harmonious wholeness, existing in and through its individual elements. Individuality or wholeness is attributed to human beings, but only in a secondary sense. The human being can attain self-realization, uniqueness and wholeness only through breaking out from its self-enclosedness, and through immersing its self in a greater whole, a higher level of reality, where it experiences self-transcendence and union with '*the* individual, the Absolute', the divine, reality itself. This general principle finds a particular application in the individual's immersal of his self in 'the common self or moral person of society'. Societies are concrete universal individuals to a fuller degree than solitary individuals can be. Society, and the State, has a refining, civilizing influence on the individual; it 'hinders hindrances to the best life or common good'. Intelligence is manifested in society to a greater degree than it ever could be in any particular individual. In society men become a 'commonwealth' for the common weal or common well-being of each and all. In obeying the General Will the individual obeys his own rational nature. In obeying the rational whole, the individual attains self-mastery, wholeness, self-realization and freedom.

Bosanquet faced a difficulty, however, in his efforts to explain how the State can do no wrong. He held that war, conquest and confiscation are concepts of a different type to the concepts of murder, illegal entry and theft, since they apply to beings of a different type. A State falls short, rather than does wrong, 'by the degree of its failure to cope with the duties of a state'. The General Will wills only the general good. Moral criticism can be directed in practice only against the morally responsible State agents. One might well regard this latter assertion as an obvious truism. Bosanquet's difficulty arises, it would seem, from his attempt to apply the criteria of personal morality to concepts of the State and the General Will as hypostatized and personified entities.

Leonard T. Hobhouse (1864-1929), a sociologist and philosopher, pointed out the inconsistency in Bosanquet's and Hegel's theory of the General Will and the State. Political obligation is merely one of the expressions of moral obligation: the latter must not be reduced to the former. 'To confuse the State with society and political obligation with moral obligation is the central fallacy of the metaphysical theory of the State.' If Bosanquet did not wish to place the political decisions and actions of the State beyond moral criticism, then his theory of the General Will would have to be revised.

9. Personal idealism. At the close of the nineteenth century and in the first quarter of the twentieth idealism had become a powerful force in the universities of the English-speaking world. Empiricism, utilitarianism and hedonist individualism were held to have been finally discredited. The idealist movement turned away, however, from Bradley's emphasis on the impersonal nature of reality, and it tended instead to combine together idealist and *personalist* interpretations of the ultimate nature of reality.

A. S. Pringle-Pattison (1856-1931), of Edinburgh, was an idealist who insisted on the uniqueness of the individual *person*. 'I have a centre (a will) of my own... which I maintain even in my dealings with God Himself.' Human and divine self-consciousness must not be identified. The idealist must recognize that there is a real self-consciousness in God, and that there is a relative independence of the human person. Personality is the highest value within the field of our experience. Nature is a progressive manifestation of the divine, and yet there is no merging of all into the One. Nature is analogous to a symphony or a drama in which individual performances succeed one another in a single process which is a unified whole. Personal uniqueness is the key to the nature of being or reality.

John M. E. McTaggart (1866-1925) maintained that ultimate reality is spiritual. It is a system or society of selves or persons related by love. The universe is a plurality of minds whose perceptions form the content of selves. He understood this in a way which excluded space, time and material objects from reality as merely 'misperceived' mental contents. Reality consists entirely of individual minds and their contents. All substance is spiritual.

James Ward (1843-1925), of Cambridge, pointed out the inadequacy of the associationists' mechanical and atomistic account of the psychological aggregation of sensations and images. He proposed an alternative explanation based on a biological model. The 'presentations' or contents of consciousness are not discrete objects; they are partial modifications of a total 'presentational' continuum. The contents of consciousness form a continuum; and each 'presentation' is an experience of the active subject of consciousness. All entities in the universe possess a psychical aspect. Every entity is an active centre, interacting with others, in a way which is analogous to social interactions. On this basis, Ward constructed a philosophy of theistic idealism and a theory of panpsychic pluralism which is similar to that of Leibniz but allowing interaction between entities.

Hastings Rashdall (1858-1924) was a personal idealist who held that there is no matter apart from mind. Individual minds are produced by a personal eternal Mind (God), 'in which and for which everything that is not mind has its being'. The well-being of the person is the goal of all personal action. Actions are to be judged by their tendency to produce the greatest good for human beings. Traditional hedonistic utilitarianism must be replaced by 'ideal utilitarianism' which respects the quality of the moral act as well as the consequences of the act.

F. C. S. Schiller (1864-1937), who taught philosophy in both Britain and America, was a personal idealist who maintained that our world is a construction of our active minds. All that exists for us is the bits of matter we see, the particular acts we perform, and the personal thoughts we think. What we call real is that personal selection we make, and evaluate as personally important, from the indeterminate, formless chaos around us. It is the mind that posits reality in an intellectual construction of what is real and important to oneself. All values are simply acts of personal valuation. This was the basic insight of Protagoras, namely, that man is the measure of all things.

These different formulations of personal idealism, in general, placed emphasis on personality as the highest value within the field of our experience. The central polemic of the personalist idealists was against materialism, mechanism and hedonist utilitarianism. It is personality, and not matter or sense-pleasure, that provides the key to the nature or reality. Reality, however, is not monistic, as the absolute idealists had maintained. Human beings and realities are many; they are not mere appearances. The empirical sciences were looked upon as providing valuable support for the theory of plurality of entities. British idealism in general, however, gradually gave way, in the universities, before the new realism propounded by Moore and the trenchant criticism of idealist thought presented in the work of Bertrand Russell.

27 Idealism and pragmatism in America

1. The early writers   2. The Transcendentalists and the
Hegelians   3. Josiah Royce   4. Personal Idealism
5. Pragmatism: C. S. Peirce   6. William James
7. John Dewey

1. The early writers. The Calvinist 'middle' or secondary
schools of Continental Europe, Britain, and the American colonies in
the sixteenth and seventeenth centuries relied heavily on the popular
polymath or encyclopedic textbooks of the Calvinist logician *Petrus
Ramus* or Pierre de la Ramée (1515-72), and his disciple *Johann H.
Alsted* (1588-1638). These works rejected traditional Aristotelianism
and professed to follow instead a methodized form of Plato's dialectic.
They became popular textbooks in the early Puritan communities of
New England, and influenced the thought of the early American
Puritan Platonists.

Jonathan Edwards (1703-58), the most outstanding of the
theologian-philosophers of colonial America, was known as a 'philosophizing divine' and a Puritan sage. His theological works in defence
of Calvinism abound in 'philosophizing' reflections on religion, the
arts, the sciences and philosophy itself. The world of the senses is an
apparent universe created by God as a means for drawing the mind,
under the influence of divine illumination, to contemplation of the
spiritual world, that is, the real world, and to an awareness of God
who is Reality, Being itself. The visible universe has only a mental
existence. Colours are not in things, he asserts, just as pain is not in a
needle. The universe exists primarily in the divine mind and
secondarily in our minds through divine communication of successive ideas. Bodies are only 'shadows of being', exhibiting the divine
mind and will. They are the fascinating traces of God in nature.

Samuel Johnson (1696-1772), first president of King's College
(Columbia University), became one of George Berkeley's devoted
disciples after paying several visits to Berkeley in Rhode Island. He
blended together Berkeley's philosophy of immaterialism with various ideas suggested by the works of Peter Ramus and Puritan
Platonism. The world of the senses, or sensible reality, is simply a
system of ideas communicated to human minds by God as copies of

the archetypal ideas in the divine mind. All ideas are ectypes of the divine archetypes. The writings of Berkeley, Clarke and the English divines influenced Johnson eventually to reject Calvinist predestinationism and join the Church of England. Johnson, like Edwards, read the works of Bacon, Locke, Newton and Hutcheson. Both men attempted to synthesize ideas from the Platonic tradition already present in American thought, and the 'new philosophy' of the British empiricists.

At the time of the onset of the American Revolution (1775-83) many of the colonists were inspired by the empiricist, deistic and liberal ideas and ideals of the Age of Reason. *Benjamin Franklin* (1706-90) was a deist who enjoyed the company and friendship of Hume, Price, Voltaire and the *philosophes*. He accepted democracy to the extent that it would yield good government. He propounded the Aristotelian doctrine that government exists to promote the good life by securing conditions of order for the peaceful exercise of individual initiative. Thomas Paine (d.1809), Elihu Palmer (d.1805), Ethan Allen (d.1789), Thomas Jefferson (d.1826) and their circle of friends were deists and enthusiastic students of science and enlightened liberal thought, who argued that the human rights to life, liberty and the pursuit of happiness constitute the foundation of social justice.

John Witherspoon and Samuel Stanhope introduced Scottish common-sense realism to Princeton, and under the presidency of James McCosh (d.1894) Princeton then became an influential centre of the Scottish philosophy. Francis Wayland (d.1865), president of Brown University, Noah Porter (d.1892) in his early years at Yale, and several other lecturers promoted a philosophy of common-sense realism in the American colleges and universities. They held that the mind seizes its objects intuitively and directly and that first principles and fundamental truths can be derived from these self-evident intuitions.

2. The Transcendentalists and the Hegelians. *Ralph Waldo Emerson* (1803-82), as leader of the New England Transcendentalists, writer, and editor of the *Dial* quarterly review, attained an international reputation as America's leading sage, seer, and man of letters. Emerson, Frederic Hedge, William Channing, Bronson Alcott, George Ripley, Theodore Parker, Henry Thoreau, Orestes Brownson, Samuel Longfellow, and others at Concord and Cambridge, Massachusetts, came to be known as the 'Transcendental Club'. The thought of this group may be regarded as a nineteenth-century continuation of the earlier thought of the Puritan Platonists and

Jonathan Edwards, but it derived additional support too from the works of Coleridge, Carlyle, Wordsworth, Goethe, Fichte and Schelling. They rejected the empiricism of Locke as a form of scepticism, and they rejected the age of rationalism as being too pedestrian. They maintained, in general, that each individual may confidently rely on his own intuitions and may avail himself of limitless powers once he places his trust in the Infinite that streams through his own personality. Their writings expressed an articulate, Romantic outcry against the narrow rationalism, Puritanism and conservatism of their fathers. Emerson characterized the 'Transcendentalist' as one who displays a predominant 'self-reverence' or 'tendency to respect his intuitions'. Their wide range of individual interests and enthusiastic activities touched every aspect of American cultural life in the mid-nineteenth century. They regarded the spontaneous activity of the creative artist as the ultimate achievement of civilization.

Among the German immigrants who fled to America after the armed rebellion of 1848 in Germany there were several writers who were interested in sponsoring the translation and study of the writings of the German idealists. In St Louis and Cincinnati several of the new immigrants and native Americans found in Hegel a philosophy of progress, cultural synthesis and practical idealism admirably applicable to the westward movement of the American Frontier. Henry Brokmeyer (d.1906) and William Torrey Harris (d.1909) founded the Kant Club in St Louis in 1858 and the St Louis Philosophical Society after the American Civil War (1861-65). Harris became the editor of the influential *Journal of Speculative Philosophy* (1867-93). The members of the Philosophical Society were called the St Louis Hegelians. They presented Hegelianism as a consistent world view whose practical applications to ethics, religion, art, politics, law and education were in eminent accord with contemporary needs and the future destiny of the United States of America. The St Louis circle concentrated in particular on the dialectical analysis of current issues in politics, culture and education. Their doctrines spread rapidly throughout the Midwest and to New England. All temporal and material objects, they maintained, derive their being from consciousness; and the only reality absolutely real is mind. This expression of idealism, or philosophy of mind, became the dominant philosophy of the age.

3. Josiah Royce (1855-1916), of Harvard, a prolific author, was the leading American spokesman of the idealist tradition in philosophy. He called his philosophical viewpoint that of absolute voluntarism or absolute pragmatism.

Royce was convinced that the proper task of philosophy is to uncover the basic nature of the real through a study of the nature of experience and knowledge. Philosophy seeks to discover the exact relation between the knowing activity and its matter through concentration on the knowledge process. In *The World and the Individual* (New York, 1902), Royce expressed the problem of Being as the problem of explaining what thought and reality must be like if thought is to attain genuine knowledge of reality. In this work he rejected the classical theories concerning Being and presented his own thesis that reality is the individual fulfilment of a purpose; to be is to be the determinate fulfilment of a wilful or purposeful idea. Thus, for example, the idea of Plato, the writer of dialogues, and the idea of Aristotle, nicknamed the 'Reader', aim at or focus upon the unique individual realities they intend. Plato and Aristotle are the external meanings of ideas (internal meanings) or purposes, which concentrate upon these specially selected and determinate objects of thoughts. The idea in the mind of an artist or painter selects and 'intends' its object. The object is the full realization, or unique fulfilment of the purpose expressed by the original idea. The inner meaning aims at the external meaning (the object) and the one is judged to be true or false by reference to the other.

Royce saw the whole universe as the external expression of an absolute system of divine purposeful ideas. The divine ideas, or archetypes, are a partial fulfilment of the plan of action of the divine will. Being is embodied plan, or purpose fulfilled. Now, within this externally expressed universe, according to Royce, I recognize myself as a conscious intelligent individual; and my mind has its own world, 'my world', the embodiment of my will and my interests. I have ever-present evidence also of the existence of others like myself who are the source of new ideas presented to me. Each of us is a unique expression of the divine purpose or plan of action; and each one embodies or expresses himself in turn in his 'own' world. Through social intercourse we become aware of ourselves as a sharing community of selves. Each becomes conscious of the triadic relationship of 'my fellow and Myself, with Nature between us'. We become conscious of ourselves as a plurality and as a community. We are a plurality of finite realities each of which is what it is in virtue of its fulfilling the purpose of the Absolute Self.

To explain how many realities arise as external expressions of the Absolute Experience (God), Royce introduced the concept of a self-representative system. A self-representative system is one that represents or expresses itself as well as all the other items that it represents. Absolute Experience expresses itself externally (as Being or Reality) in expressing the actual infinity of finite realities which it also expresses and represents. Being is like a mirror of the universe which includes itself among the infinity of items reflected and expressed. The Absolute Self is a self-representative system of this kind. Each individual reality is an expression of the self-representative system. Hence Being or Reality is an actual infinite which is a unity of the one, the many and the infinite.

Royce elaborated further this theory of the unity of the one and the many by introducing the concept of the community of interpretation, in his last major work *The Problem of Christianity* (1913). Self-interpretation is achieved through social interaction. Others help me to interpret myself to myself. Self-knowledge, like all other forms of knowledge, is mediated through signs; it does not arise intuitively. Human beings, in their different political, legal, economic, moral and religious communities, come to know themselves through the purposes and activities of these communities. In these communities they become engaged in interpreting the meaning of things through an infinite system of signs. The Christian community, like the universal Beloved Community, for example, aims to assist the individual, through love, to overcome his engrossing self-centredness. It enables him to devote himself to charity, love of others, through a constant deepening and renewal of community living. In the Beloved Community, God as Spirit or Interpreter bonds together a multiplicity of selves in a spiritual community of loyalty and love. The religious experience of the community has a metaphysical basis in the presence of the Absolute Experience expressing loyalty and love in the loyalty and love experienced by the members of the Beloved Community, the community loved as a person. In willing love, men overcome their separation, and act in concert. They come then to realize that God himself as 'Loving Will', similarly, gathers the whole process and variety of the universe into a single experience which is appreciated and willed in an Eternal Now. Thus, for example, when one appreciates a musical composition one grasps the form of the whole even as the individual notes are heard successively. In a similar way, Royce pointed out, God grasps the whole universe in one eternal act of appreciation even as he appreciates each individual present in the whole. It is only in terms of absolute experience, in which all things are present and understood, that any finite experience can be comprehended.

Royce applied his doctrine of voluntaristic idealism to almost every branch of philosophy. He applied it to ethical and social morality in his well-known *Philosophy of Loyalty* (New York, 1908). Here he propounded the principle of loyalty to loyalty as the basic moral law. 'The true categorical imperative is to be loyal to loyalty.' One must devote oneself to a freely chosen cause or goal which aims to extend the spirit of loyalty and love in social life. This principle upholds the autonomy of the will while pointing to self-realization as the final good. It combines the insights of both Kant and Hegel, according to Royce. Through loyalty to an ideal life-cause, and through that loyalty to one's community which extends the spirit of loyalty in the Beloved Community, one's own will becomes an embodiment of the divine will; one finds self-realization in one's self-chosen vocation within the Beloved Community, the community which helps one to interpret and to know oneself.

The theory of absolute idealism is one which, in considering the total realm of being, presents mind, consciousness, experience, ideas and the ideal as the primary reality. In this sense it stands in opposition to any theory of materialism. Absolute idealism is capable of being interpreted and presented, as in Royce's case, in a theistic sense. The Absolute is then understood as personal, eternal and infinite consciousness or experience in which all finite things are immanent. Consciousness is primary. Reality is secondary. Reality is the external embodiment of inner experiences or ideas. Royce interpreted the inner ideas, capable of external embodiment, as partially fulfilled purposes, or as unfulfilled plans of action. They intend action, that is, pragmatic, practical embodiment; and action of this kind is accomplished by the fiat of the divine will. Royce therefore spoke of his form of absolute idealism as absolute pragmatism or absolute voluntarism. This theory stands in close relation, in several aspects, to the heritage of transcendental Scholastic realism even though it regards reality as secondary. It is directly opposed to materialism, not to realism. Its weakness lies in its failure to see consciousness, will, purpose, experience and action as modes of being. The term *consciousness*, for example, refers to an abstract concept, an abstraction, derived from the *reality* of a 'conscious-being being-conscious'; being conscious is a form or mode of being. Thus, it is being that is primary. Royce's philosophy is not, therefore, a philosophy of being as being; and it lacks an adequate theory of the analogy of being. It is primarily a philosophy of (absolute) mind or experience.

4. Personal Idealism. In the last quarter of the nineteenth century (1875-1900) almost every professor of philosophy in the United States was an idealist of one form or other. Among the eminent supporters of idealism were George Sylvester Morris (d.1889), professor at Johns Hopkins and the university of Michigan, George H. Howison, professor at the university of California, Borden P. Bowne at Boston, J. E. Creighton at Cornell, and the professors at Harvard, Princeton, Yale, Wellesley and other universities. The idealists continued to remain in the majority in the universities until about the time of World War I (1914-18). Their versions of idealism differed considerably, even though all agreed on the primacy of mind and spirit over matter. At the turn of the century, several of the idealists professed different forms of *Personal* Idealism, a doctrine in which emphasis was placed on the separateness and intrinsic worth of individual persons.

George H. Howison (1834-1916) maintained that absolute idealism, including that of Royce, logically involves the merging of everything finite in the Absolute. He formulated instead a system of ethical pluralism which he called 'Personal Idealism'. The universe is a community of self-active beings, minds or spirits, each having within itself the self-explanatory source of its own activity. God attracts each free self towards an ideal harmonious unity of free spirits in himself; and the self's response to God is entirely its own activity. God's creative action on the human spirit is that of final causality, and not of efficient causality. No self-determining being is dependent on any other being of any kind for its existence or for its activity. Reality is a republic of self-active, self-defining spirits, all moving towards an Ideal, a common goal, exemplified in the loving activity of God, 'changelessly attentive to every other mind'.

Borden P. Bowne (1847-1910) defended the view that the universe is a system or society of relatively autonomous persons created by a supreme cosmic Person, God. Nature may be thought of as the energizing of this cosmic Person. It is God willing in accordance with rational principles. God is the unified, dynamic ground of nature. He is transcendent to nature and yet also immanent in relation to it. The 'common world' of thought and action is a phenomenal, experienced world, organized by finite knowers who interact with the structures of the real world in accordance with the cognitive nature, the dynamic categories and purposes of finite knowers. The world as commonly known is a world which persons construct on the basis of their impressions of the reality beyond their thought. God placed man within a world order that sets divine limits to his freedom of action while giving him ample opportunity for self-realization and fulfilment. The universe, therefore, is a realm of persons united by God's purposive action in nature and united in a moral unity created by the free response of mankind to the loving call of the cosmic Person. The universe is the expression of a community of minds with a supreme Person at its head.

James Edwin Creighton (1861-1924) called his system of thought objective or speculative idealism. Philosophical inquiry, he said, must begin with 'the standpoint of experience', and the dynamic co-ordinates of experience are mind, nature and other selves. Mind by its very nature is in touch with reality by direct intuition. Reality is a system of individual entities in which each has a role to play as a significant function of the purposeful whole. Thus, for example, since there are no isolated selves totally removed from society, the objective idealist will be primarily interested in the overall significance and role of the moral activities and the social institutions of a society of selves within the totality of Nature as the all-embracing human environment. Similarly the philosophy of Nature will study the significance of the specialized world of the scientist in reference to the wider totality of all experience. The work of philosophical reflection exists in and through a society of selves. The intellectual life is essentially a social venture. For this reason Creighton and his colleagues in Cornell emphasized the social, co-operative aspect of philosophical thought. They emphasized, for example, the important role of philosophical dialogue, philosophical associations, and philosophical reviews.

5. Pragmatism: C. S. Peirce. *Charles Sanders Peirce* (1839-1914), the founder of pragmatism, was a brilliant systematic philosopher whose writings cover almost all fields of philosophy. He started his philosophical career in 1857 by attempting to combine the Transcendental Analytic of Kant with Platonic idealism. His views underwent considerable change as he grew older, and for this reason there are several unresolved ambiguities which arise from the different tendencies of the different stages of his developing thought. His work nevertheless shows the general outlines of an impressive system of creative thought. His eight volumes of *Collected Papers* were published posthumously (1931-58).

Peirce maintained that the totality of all there is may be classified or categorized in a three-fold ontological classification. Firstly, there is sensed matter, the object of sensation or feeling, and the object of the science of cosmology. Each sensed object is given in sensation as having a phenomenal 'suchness', or quality, which leads us to classify it as red, or wet, or as such and such. This is called the category of Firstness. The second category is that of the immediately experienced 'thisness' or 'thatness', or *haecceitas*, of other individuals, minds, or wills, in dyadic opposition to oneself. This is the object of the science of psychology. It is called the category of Secondness. The third category is that of mediation, thought, rationality, representations, abstractions, laws of behaviour, generalities, or forms. The pure abstract attribute, the Platonic Form in the mind of God, is the object of theology. This is the category of Thirdness.

Peirce made several attempts to define the relations between these three categories. In his early papers he held that the ideas in the mind of God which are archetypes of created objects are given a material embodiment in the objects of human experience, and that these ideas are then derived by the human mind from those objects by a process of abstraction. In this case, all phenomena and all concepts are representations of the transcendental objects, and the human act of knowing (the intuitive judgement) is a synthesis formulated by an interpreting representation, or mind. All synthesis, all knowledge, involves the sign relation, and the 'signhood' present in an act of knowing has a three-fold reference: reference to an object, reference to abstraction, and reference to an interpretant. This prompted Peirce to make a serious study of the sign relation and its three classes of referents as applicable in turn to terms, propositions and arguments. He made a number of major discoveries in the logic of sign relations which anticipated the work of Whitehead and Russell. These discoveries in the new logic led subsequently to his formulation of the belief theory of inquiry and the pragmatic theory of meaning.

Peirce presented his 'belief' theory of inquiry in a context of biological evolution. An organism that wishes to survive must develop habits of following general rules of behaviour that prescribe how the organism should act if it is to satisfy its needs. Habits of behaviour, when thoroughly adopted, may be called habitual behavioural *beliefs*. Inquiry is the process by which the organism passes from an irritating state of uncertainty and doubt to a pleasant state of stable belief concerning the expected satisfaction of is needs. Thus, an organism's belief concerning a particular object permits the inquiring organism to predict the experiences it will have if it should act towards that object in a particular way. Kant had entitled belief of this kind 'pragmatic belief'. This theory of inquiry provided the basis for Peirce's pragmatic theory of meaning.

Peirce regarded pragmatism, or the pragmatic method of inquiry, as a principle or method of scientific definition. It is primarily a formal method of clarifying confusions in conceptual statements. The chief use of the pragmatic method is to ascertain the meaning of difficult, abstract, intellectual concepts. 'Consider what effects, that might conceivably have practical bearings, we conceive the object of our conception to have, then, our conception of these effects is the whole of our conception of the object.' To say, for example, that something is 'fragile' means that 'if we were to strike it, it would snap or shatter'. If any idea does not represent some such conceivable experimental procedure and consequence then it is without meaning. Significance lies in the relation to ends habitually expected. The meaning of a term, therefore, is not an embodied abstraction, nor an indwelling quality that the term connotes. Meaning pertains to behaviour; or more precisely, meaning is given by the behaviour of the object under all circumstances. In the case of scientific inquiry the set of (behavioural) laws specifying inquiry, the habits of behaviour or stable beliefs sought by inquiry are in fact the laws of science.

The problem which Peirce now faced was the problem of whether the three references of signs (things, minds, and abstractions) are real or not, and how they can be known. In 1868, in the *Journal of Speculative Philosophy*, he presented a theory of cognition and a theory of reality which were, in effect, theories of subjective idealism. He said that, in the flood of neural stimuli given as stimuli pouring in upon our senses, we come to detect relations between some of the stimuli and to interpret those particular stimuli as having a common referent. We conceptualize this referent and we acquire a more complete knowledge of it as time progresses. The process of further inquiry and learning is endless; it is never complete. The real is inexhaustible. We now assume that the referent caused our experience of it, even though it was necessarily our experience which came first and our notion of the object which came later. We postulate that an object exists because it gives coherence to our experience. Nevertheless, the object exists as an object of thought even when we think it real. It is thought of as being independent of any particular mind and as representing what would be agreed upon by an ideal community of investigators if enquiry were to go on always, for ever. If inquiry concerning the independent object goes on for ever, then our hypotheses about it will tend to converge towards a final true description. The object is understood to be real then because inquiry converges. It is a permanent possibility of sensation. Thus, reality consists in the convergence of inquiry; and the three classes of referents can be known by scientific enquiry.

In or about 1880, a new problem arose for Peirce: the problem of counter-factuals. If the real is a permanent possibility of sensation then there are real possible sensations; but pragmatically, possible sensations are equivalent to actual sensations. Real possible sensations are therefore pragmatically meaningless. The theory that the real is a permanent possibility of sensation does not prove that phenomenalism is realistic; rather, it ends necessarily in subjectivism. Thus, in 1885, Peirce abandoned this view, and formulated a new objective idealist view instead.

From 1885 onwards, Peirce taught the doctrine that our immediate perceptual judgements place us in direct phenomenal contact with the observable world. Percepts are intuitively synthesized from neural stimuli in a process which is unconscious. They give rise to immediate, indubitable, perceptual judgements, such as 'soft thing here now'. A perceptual judgement, even when past, remains eternally indubitable. It is the original and the ultimate evidence statement. It is the starting-point of all knowledge. It gives a direct report of phenomenal observation of data which must be accepted as given. The data include generality (e.g. 'soft', 'softness') because the perceptual judgement or proposition has a predicate which is general. Thus, the ontological aspects of the three categories of 'suchness', 'thisness', and generality, are empirically observable and given. They are the external referents of our perceptual judgements. They can be shown to be present and given in experience. Peirce saw that this reformulation of his theory of cognition postulated also a reformulation of his theory of reality.

The world, Peirce declared in his later papers, after 1885, contains organic continua. Reality itself is a continuum, an organism, containing within itself real continua. He called this his doctrine of *synechism*, and he indicated that he would like to have his whole system of philosophy called by this name. The continuum is that of which every part is of the same nature as the whole. Reality is a continuum. Thus, there is no dualism, for instance, between mind and matter; each is of the same nature as the whole, reality itself. Peirce spoke of this doctrine as a modern form of Scotistic or Scholastic realism. Different individuals, according to Scotus, share a general, intelligible feature, or a 'common nature', which is individualized in numerically distinct ways in each. Generality is present in each of the real continua; and each continuum contains within itself unactualized possibilities, that is, further generalities.

Each continuum, each inquiring organism, continues to seek to escape from doubt to find belief. Reality is an evolutionary continuum. All of reality, the universe, is an evolving organism, possessed of habits. Our laws of nature are simply descriptions of these habits of the universe; and all our experiences of the external world are experiences of some state or behaviour of the organic universe.

The universe, in the beginning, was a primal chaos, an undifferentiated continuum of pure feeling, or 'firstness', without order, according to Peirce. It evolved from homogeneity to heterogeneity, that is, from unordered lack of habit to relatively stable habitual behaviour, from chance to law and order. The universe evolves by means of the development of habit. Objective orderliness in the universe corresponds to a state in which habit is strong. As order or habit increases, intensity of consciousness or dyadic wilfulness decreases. Mind or volition that is hidebound with complete regularity and habit we regard as dead matter. Thus, cosmic evolution progresses from a state of tychism or absolute chance towards a state of complete rationality and order, in which feeling and action are subjected to belief. The evolutionary end sought by the cosmic process is concrete reasonableness, or, in other words, the realization of rationality in the concrete. Man co-operates in this process through deliberate or self-controlled rational action, that is, through ethical conduct. The whole universe, an inquiring organism, works by a common process, therefore, to a common end, *concrete reasonableness*; and it is the duty of man to aid that process by scientific inquiry and by the complete subjection of disordered feeling and doubt to belief-habit, or knowledge. In this way, man co-operates in the cosmic process moving towards an ever-fuller embodiment of reason and civility in the universe. The cosmic goal is a cosmic community-end. Peirce spoke of it as cosmic 'agapasm', or universal love.

Peirce's search for a systematic interpretation of reality through conceptual analysis and clarification of meaning pushed him inevitably towards a doctrine of metaphysical idealism. He commended Schelling's analysis of the nature of matter, and he stated that the theory of objective idealism is the only intelligible theory of the universe. He wanted to combine his strong personal tendency to logical analysis of the meaning of concepts with a speculative concern for a unified interpretation of all that is. He found himself in an idealistic or rationalistic impasse which was close to that of Kant and the great German idealists. He strove resolutely to present a realist view of reality through the medium of further clarification of conceptual and relational thought. His thought is not grounded in a doctrine of the intelligibility of being itself, and so its constant logical tendency is not towards realism but towards objective idealism.

6. William James (1842-1910), professor of philosophy at Harvard, sought to overcome the conflict between what he called the 'tough-minded', scientific, mechanistic view of the world and the 'tender-minded', religious, humanistic view. His many publications included *The Will to Believe* (1879), *The Varieties of Religious Experience* (1902), *Pragmatism* (1907), *The Meaning of Truth* (1909), *A Pluralistic Universe* (1909), and *Essays in Radical Empiricism* (1912). In these works he spoke of human intelligence as an active, selective agent of adjustment whose function is to guide action. To determine the meaning of beliefs and to test their truth, he maintained, one should look to the effects of beliefs in action.

In *Radical Empiricism* and *A Pluralistic Universe*, James said it is impossible that our abstract ideas should ever be identified with concrete exterior objects. Ideas, then, do not reflect the thing-in-itself. Only that which comes from experience can be accepted as worthwhile knowledge; and the world given to us in our active, selective experience is a world of heterogeneous elements which form some sort of assemblage known as 'consciousness'. James therefore proclaimed himself a radical empiricist and a pluralist. There are no transcendental elements in knowledge. The things which compose the world are multiple, individual, and independent, and they cannot be considered as simple modes or phenomena of any unique and absolute reality. The plurality of objects is cosmological and not simply epistemological.

Radical empiricism is concerned not only with the multiple things of experience, James asserts, but also with the experienced relations between things. It is concerned with the relations expressed in language by prepositions, copulas, and conjunctions (such as 'between', 'unlike', 'before', 'is', 'then', 'but', 'on') which are given in the flow of immediate experience, just as truly as the distinct sensations designated by nouns and verbs. These experienced relations and things possess a continuous, concatenated structure. They are given as an interconnected plurality, and not as a monistic unit. Experience is a continuous whole; it is not atomistic as Locke and Berkeley had maintained. It is a continuum out of which certain elements are actively selected in accordance with the exigencies of life. The grouping of these selected elements is called consciousness.

The truth relation, according to James, is a relation between our ideas and the rest of our experience. It is not something found in the outside world. It is something effected by man. True ideas are those which 'work', which 'lead' to success, and which give various kinds of satisfaction. To be true, ideas, such as scientific ideas or hypotheses, must prove consistent with other ideas conformable to existing fact, and subject to experimental corroboration and validation. '"The true" is only the expedient in the way of our thinking, just as "the right" is only the expedient in the way of our behaving. Expedient in almost any fashion; and expedient in the long run and on the whole.' To say that something is 'useful because it is true' and 'true because it is useful' have exactly the same meaning. This was James's pragmatic theory of truth.

Peirce, like Dewey and other pragmatists, was unwilling to accept the subjectivism of James's interpretation of pragmatism. It is one thing to say that a scientific theory is useful for making certain predictions and quite another thing to say that a belief is useful for giving emotional satisfaction. For Peirce, pragmatism is primarily a formal method of clarifying confusions in conceptual statements; it is a theory pertaining to meaning and not a theory of truth. In 1905 Peirce decided to change the name of his own theory from pragmatism to pragmaticism, in order to dissociate himself from James's way of developing pragmatism into a theory of truth.

In *The Will to Believe*, James made use of the pragmatic method in his defence of the right to believe. The belief of which he speaks is primarily moral belief or belief in the efficacy of action, but it applies also to religious belief. Every new scientific hypothesis is initially unwarranted. The scientist who daringly tests his hypothesis must wilfully risk to believe his own hypothesis sufficiently to move him to test it. Belief is a risk. It must continue to justify itself. It must address itself to the tribunal of experiment. This exercise of the will to believe has important applications in other areas of life too. It applies for example to the hypothesis that men are free. When there is a genuine option, 'of the forced, living and momentous kind', between two hypotheses which have no compelling evidence, then it is entirely in accord with scientific taste if one chooses the more economical and elegant hypothesis. It is our passional nature in this case which will decide our option when we actually exercise our will to believe.

James applied the pragmatist method to the issue between the two different hypotheses of theism and materialism. Looking 'retrospectively', the pragmatist philosopher cannot choose between the two positions. Considered 'prospectively', however, in relation to the expectations that the two positions promise, and other things being equal, the pragmatic method leads to a slight 'edge' in favour of theism, according to James. 'The drift of all the evidence we have seems to me to sweep us very strongly towards the belief in some form of superhuman life with which we may, unknown to ourselves, be co-conscious.'

F. C. S. Schiller (see above, Chapter 26, section 9) pointed out that the fundamental attitude of both William James and himself, as pragmatists, is the attitude that it is man, and not some kind of Absolute, that is the measure of all experience and the maker of the sciences. The pragmatist strives to re-humanize the universe. Truth is relative to human desires and aims. Truths are human valuations. To recognize something as true or false is to recognize it as useful or useless to man. In a Darwinian world, truths are beliefs which we must take account of if we are not to perish; they are beliefs which have survival value. A belief is true when it has been verified that it 'works' for man, the measure of all experience. By way of criticism, however, we may say that this attitude takes no account of what is the final goal of man. Peirce said that he abandoned the term pragmatism because William James and his followers had interpreted pragmatism to mean that to think is simply to plan action and 'that the end of man is action'. The pragmatic theory was originally intended instead as 'a theory of logical analysis, or true definition' and not as a theory concerning the nature of truth. True propositions possess a quality or property which useful falsehoods do not. Utility can be a sign of truth but it is not the (formal) constitutive cause of truth.

7. John Dewey (1859-1952), founder of the famous Laboratory School for children at Chicago University, and a member of the faculty and emeritus professor of Columbia University, was the most influential of all the American pragmatists. He was a prolific writer who continued to produce many books and articles even after his retirement in 1929. He was deeply interested in problems of value and of human conduct, of society and education. He called his philosophy 'pragmatic instrumentalism'.

Dewey's early philosophic formation was influenced by his tutors H. A. P. Torrey, G. S. Morris and C. S. Peirce, and by his interest in the writings of T. H. Huxley and the neo-Hegelians. He drifted away quickly from the Hegelian influences of his early graduate years, but he retained a permanent interest in the emphases on change, process, experience, and dynamic, organic interaction which had been of primary interest to him in his early Hegelian studies.

In his work on *Experience and Nature* (1925), Dewey maintained that nature consists of a variety of actions and transactions which can be grouped together logically on three evolutionary plateaus or levels. These levels of natural transactions are the physicochemical, the psychophysical and the level of human experience, the latest to evolve. Within nature the transactions are continuous with each other, even though each plateau has its own distinctive characteristics. Man is involved in continuous transactions with the whole of nature, and because his experience of these transactions is all-inclusive he can come to understand them through systematic inquiry.

Within man's immediate or 'primary' experience of the transactions at work in the situations in which he finds himself there arise conflicts that initiate inquiry. Reflective, 'secondary' thinking serves to solve the problematic situation. Thinking is a mode of adapting to the challenges of the environment. Conscious processes are transactions of the living organism in response to problematic situations. Thus, for example, if a person experiences that the roof is leaking, this initiates a process of inquiry as to how the problem can be solved. Man becomes enmeshed in conflicts with his material environment and he strives dynamically for practical solutions. He is a dynamic biological organism who struggles for survival. Active thinking and doing are intimately related in man's attempt to adjust and survive in his environment. Thinking is not a quest for eternal truth. It is a natural biological power whose function is instrumental in solving problems. One should therefore reject 'spectator' theories of truth and adopt instead an 'instrumentalist' theory of intelligence and knowledge as organically oriented to inquiry and to problem-solving.

All thinking, Dewey asserts, commences with a perplexed or confused situation and ends in 'a cleared-up, unified, resolved situation'. Inquiry is 'the controlled or directed transformation of an indeterminate situation into one that is so determinate in its constituent distinctions and relations as to convert the elements of the original situation into a unified whole' (*Logic*, p. 104). In so far as we use our intelligence to reconstruct these situations successfully we achieve a reconstructed experience which Dewey called a consummation. Aesthetic experience is a heightened consummation in which aesthetic qualities dominate. Reconstructed experiences are qualified by their integrity, harmony and aesthetic joy. Thus, through successful social reform, for example, life for all men can become funded with enriched meaning and increased aesthetic quality.

The true function of philosophical thinking lies, according to Dewey, in its 'being directed to resolving indeterminate or problematic situations by effecting changes in the environment and in man himself'. The philosopher can examine the existing beliefs and values and ideals of a given society, with its social and moral conflicts, and can indicate new possible ways of dealing with these conflicts. He can do this through a transferral of the 'experimental method from the technical field of physical experience to the wider field of human life'. The function of philosophy is to be found, then, in its development of a general logic of inquiry and a general theory of experimental method for reconstructing particular problematic situations. The basic principles of instrumental logic are not eternal principles. They are principles which are 'generated in the actual process of man's active relation with his environment'. In each problematic situation the hypothesis that objectively transforms the problematic situation is the true one, the verified one. 'The true means the verified.' Knowledge is that which is warranted by inquiry. Thus, 'the hypothesis that works is the true one', and true knowledge is 'warranted assertibility'. There are no absolute, incorrigible, first truths that are given or known with certainty. All claims to truth must be subjected to the methods of inquiry of instrumental or experimental logic. Inquiry, however, is a perpetually self-corrective process; and so we must continually submit our knowledge claims to the public test of a community of inquirers in order to clarify, refine and justify them.

Dewey showed, in numerous books and articles, how the theory and method of pragmatic instrumentalism might be put to practical use in different social problematic situations. He applied instrumentalist thought to problematic situations arising for the human organism in the educational, social and political environment, and in areas of human action which evoked religious attitudes or called for moral evaluation. Practical solutions for all of these problems can be found, Dewey asserted, in the application of the experimental method of naturalistic empiricism.

The function of social and political philosophy, Dewey said, is 'to criticize existing institutions in the light of man's development and needs and to discern and point out practical possibilities for the future to meet the needs of the moment'. The test for all such institutions is 'the contribution they make to the all-round *growth* of every member of society'. Personal and social evil arises as the product of the 'inertness of established habit'. Evil can be overcome through the reform of society's habits, its habits of response and its habits of thought. Human impulses are highly flexible and can be organized into new established ways, or new habits, of interacting with the inertness of the outmoded culture. Change of this kind is best achieved not through the efforts of revolutionaries but through the energetic and patient efforts of intelligent reconstructors and educational reformers.

Education is the most important factor of all in the remoulding of useful, creative habits in society. The educational process must be in practice a process of active, intelligent inquiry. It is not simply a preparation for future living; it is itself a process of living. It is its own end. The human mind is a problem-solving instrument. The education community, the school, must become an experimental, problem-solving community. The purpose of this community is 'the all-round *growth* of every member' of the community. Education is the key to social improvement and to the growth of man as a dynamic biological entity.

'Growth itself is the only moral end', that is, '*growth* in the sense of the dynamic development of harmoniously integrated human nature'. There is no absolute, eternal 'realm of values'. Values are constituted by the evaluating activity of the process of inquiry, a process stimulated by a problematic situation. Values are discovered the way facts are discovered, namely, in experience. Behaviour is said to be 'good' when the consequences are satisfactory. The seat of value is located in human desire and its satisfaction. Desires must be submitted to the critical power of intelligence so that the consequences of the satisfaction of desire can be carefully considered. Value is synonymous with the satisfactory solution of the problem reflected by desire. 'Good consists in the meaning that is experienced to belong to an activity when conflict and entanglement of various incompatible impulses and habits terminate in a unified orderly release in action.'

Dewey rejected absolute values and yet he assumed that all 'growth' or evolutionary development has intrinsic worth independently of any condition. Growth itself is then regarded as an absolute value. Similarly he assumed that there is an absolute demand upon intelligence forcing it to overcome unresolved problematic situations. He does not examine the foundations of his value judgements concerning the worth of growth and action. His strength lies not in his naturalistic empiricism but in his application of intelligent, estimative, practical judgement to contemporary moral, social and educational problems.

28 'The human condition': philosophy in France (I)

1. The traditionalists   2. The eclectics   3. Social reformers in France   4. Comte   5. The positivists 6. Durkheim   7. Philosophy of science

1. The traditionalists. In the writings of the French philosophers, one finds a closer relationship between philosophy and literature and art than in the writings of British philosophers. Social, political, educational and aesthetic problems have always continued to be live issues for French thinkers. Descartes published works in mathematics and physics, Voltaire wrote epic poetry, Rousseau wrote novels, and other French philosophers interested themselves in current social problems and in the fine arts. Several of these men held no university posts, and their interests frequently focused on 'the human condition' reflected in social and political life. Their approach to philosophy is determined not only by its inner logical structure but also by a vigour which arises from ardent resistance to trends of thought which they actively oppose. The Encyclopedists opposed absolute monarchy and ecclesiastical authority. Rousseau's admirers opposed the rationalists. The traditionalists opposed anarchic individualism. Each of their systems of thought derived its ardour, to a notable extent, from the fact that it was a philosophy of resistance.

The philosophy of traditionalism was a philosophy of history and a political programme developed by those who regarded the French Revolution as a disastrous event, destructive of French traditions and ungodly in character, and a product of the anti-authoritarian and ultra-individualistic *philosophes* who strove to substitute anarchic individualism for social stability.

The philosophy of Comte Joseph de Maistre (1753-1821) and Vicomte de Bonald (1754-1840) was formulated in explicit reaction to the anarchy of individualism. Society is not an aggregate of individualists united artificially through a social compact. Man is essentially social. Common language and tradition enshrine common reason and common sense. National traditions and historic institutions have served as the instruments of divine providence. The Church is a divine institution. 'No human institution has lasted eighteen centuries', de Maistre wrote in *Du Pape* (1821). The authority of the Church is binding not only on its avowed members but also on all men. The rationalist doctrine of the sovereignty of the democratic people is a pernicious theory which fosters disorder and anarchy. The scoundrels and criminals of the French Revolution were unwitting instruments of divine providence to punish sin and to regenerate the nation. The remedy for the widespread disorder in society lies in a restoration of the Christian monarchy and in an acceptance of the sovereignty of the infallible Pope. These traditionalists, then, were professedly royalist and ultramontanist or papalist in their sympathies. In political and ecclesial society, as in the family, power naturally belongs to the head of society, they said, and this power is ultimately derived from God.

Pierre Simon Ballanche (1776-1847) maintained that an understanding of the philosophy of history can arise only from an insight into the designs of God in every historical event. The people, like the members of any family, should be permitted to voice their aspirations so that the sovereign might countenance and legitimize those aspirations that are seen to be good and just.

François René de Chateaubriand (1768-1848) wrote glowingly on the gifts Christianity had endowed on European culture. A set of beliefs which has increased the beauty and goodness of human culture, as Christianity has, must necessarily be true.

Felicité Robert de Lamennais (1782-1854) held that no man can conscientiously assent to his own private deductions if these are not in harmony with the traditional opinions of Christendom and human civilization. Each man can find certainty and the solution to his personal problems in faith, authority, general consent and common sense. It is God himself who is the author of the common consent of mankind. Trust in private opinion is eccentric madness. Each and all must submit to tradition to avoid the divisive effects of sectarianism.

The traditionalists in general asserted that a certain primitive revelation by God has been handed down over the ages through the medium of language. Man should place his faith in this traditional revelation, since personal deduction fosters only social division. Faith alone ensures certainty. (This view was condemned by the Church authorities.) Traditionalism magnified the accidental difficulties which individual reason meets in attaining truth. It declared reason to be ineffectual and powerless. It looked to tradition as an exterior basis for truth. Philosophizing was declared to be impossible until the philosopher first assented to the primitive revelation of God handed on by means of language and common sense. The traditionalists failed to see that the starting point of all thought and philosophy must necessarily be an immediate experiential knowledge and affirmation of being.

2. The eclectics. Royer-Collard and Cousin advocated a *juste milieu*, a sane middle course between extremes, in political affairs and in the educational presentation of philosophical ideas. They selected preferred ideas from different philosophical systems and collated them in a loose combination of insights without fusing them into a single organic unity of systematized thought. Cousin spoke of himself as an eclectic who aimed to select and fuse 'the best in each philosopher'. Cousin, Royer-Collard and Jouffroy came to be known as the French eclectics.

Pierre Paul Royer-Collard (1762-1845) introduced into France, and popularized, the philosophy of common sense of Thomas Reid. He was a professor of philosophy at the Sorbonne, a member of the Chamber of Deputies, and the leader of a political group, the 'Doctrinaires', who advocated a compromise between absolute and constitutional monarchy. He believed that in politics, as also in philosophy, *in medio stat virtus*, 'virtue stands in the middle'. He presented the philosophy of common sense as a *compromise* between Condillac's sensationalism and de Maistre's authoritarian traditionalism. In active perception, as distinct from sensation, the perceiver makes common-sense judgements that there is a causally active permanent self and that there are really existing physical objects. The existence of the self and the external world is judged and affirmed by a spontaneous act of the human mind. Royer-Collard did not deal with the objection that a judgement of this kind may express simply a common-sense belief.

Victor Cousin (1792-1867) was an effective and eloquent lecturer in Paris who became an authoritative minister of public instruction, director of the École Normale, and a member of the Institut de France. He maintained that in each particular century, the civilization and philosophy of the age drew its distinctive character from the predominant idea of the century. This predominant idea, assisted by other affiliated ideas 'playing a secondary but real role', expresses itself in the philosophy, religion, science, art, morals and all human concerns of the epoch. He was convinced that the main human concern and human need of nineteenth-century France was moderation and rational eclecticism in the political sphere as also in the philosophical sphere. The valuable elements of sensualism, common sense, idealism and interior mysticism needed to be welded together. These are the elements of which nineteenth-century thought is composed. They can be harmoniously welded together under the predominant idea of God as necessarily manifesting himself both in the physical world and in the sphere of finite selves. 'Philosophy, as the highest development of human reason, aims to know the finite and the infinite and their mutual relations; it is thus, by right, the rule and source of all truth.' Rationalistic empiricism provides a sane middle course between the extremes of Catholic traditionalism and agnostic sensualism.

Théodore Simon Jouffroy (1796-1842), professor of philosophy at the Collège de France, translated into French the main works of Dugald Stewart and Thomas Reid. He maintained that common sense, that is, the collective wisdom of the race, alone possesses the totality of truth, and that individual men can never possess the whole answer to problems concerning truth, beauty and goodness. Philosophers are mouthpieces for the societies and cultures in which they live. They must assist men to understand their dependency on the totality of individuals and to strive to form a unified fraternal community. He combined a marked scepticism towards individual philosophical systems with an ardent belief in the principles of common sense as representing the collective and pre-philosophical wisdom of the human race. 'The integration of the common and the individual is an ideal towards which mankind moves.'

3. Social reformers in France. In the first half of the nineteenth century there were a number of social philosophers in France who attempted to bring about pragmatic social reconstructions which would involve a reformation of the structure of society. These social reformers made a significant contribution to the development of political theory in a way which influenced subsequent socialist thought, even though they were branded by Marx and his followers as utopian idealists.

Claude-Henri de Rouvroy, Comte de Saint-Simon (1760-1825), was a social philosopher who is regarded as the founder of French socialism. He pointed out that the transformation which had overtaken European society since the feudal period can best be explained in terms of the emergence of a new dominant class which came into conflict with an older established class. The conflict issued in new forms of political organization and in a new class-ideology adapted to the interests of the socially and economically dominant class. The feudal society of the Middle Ages began slowly to disintegrate when scientific ideas were introduced from the Islamic world, and when the new class of industrialists, merchants and artisans began to arise. The monarchy aligned itself with the nobility, not with the rising producer class. Violent revolution became inevitable.

The rising class of the nineteenth century, Saint-Simon said, is the class of manufacturers and artisans aided by scientists. The new rulers are the scientific administrators and the captains or managers of industry. The economic interests of the working managers of industry coincide with those of the industrial workers in a successful, united industrial class. It is economic interests which bind the industrial class together in a peaceful society. Furthermore, the common interests of the industrial class in different nations provide a sound basis for international human solidarity. Saint-Simon pointed out that a new science was needed to study the social organism, man-in-society, on a positive, scientific basis. He suggested that the new science be called 'social physiology'. Comte, who acted as Saint-Simon's secretary and collaborator for seven years, suggested that the new science be called 'sociology'.

In 1830, two of Saint-Simon's disciples, S. A. Bazard and B. P. Enfantin, founded the *Globe* newspaper, and other disciples founded the journal *Le Producteur* to propagate the numerous lines of thought which had been suggested by Saint-Simon. These ideas aroused widespread interest. Marx and Engels, like Comte, derived stimulus from Saint-Simonianism. Marx, however, maintained that Saint-Simon did not see that there is a basic conflict between the interests of the self-governing bourgeois industrialist and the unprotected proletarian worker. This conflict leads necessarily to class-warfare, Marx asserted, not to utopian fraternalism.

François Marie Charles Fourier (1772-1837), of Besançon, was a social critic who was acutely aware of the dehumanizing influence of industrial society. His *New Industrial and Social World* (1829), and other works, denounced the appalling conditions of the exploited masses, and charted a new social structure of socialist phalansteries or societies in which families own property, work and live in a self-sufficient form of community life. Fourier, like Rousseau, blamed the unnatural repression of the natural passions (such as the human need for variety, friendship, ambition, love, and family feeling) for the discord, selfishness and disharmony which infected 'civilized' established society. Too many people were leading enslaved, alienated, repressed, unhappy lives. He suggested a social reorganization of independent phalanxes of about sixteen hundred men, women, and children, of different abilities and temperaments. Each person would then have full opportunity to develop his natural talents and passion to the full in his own community or phalanx. He suggested that experimental co-operative societies be established, having shareholders whose shares would be in proportion to their talent, capital and labour. Fourier's importance lies not in his proffered solutions but in his acute observations concerning the frustration and alienation of industrialized society.

Pierre-Joseph Proudhon (1809-65), also of Besançon, was a social philosopher who advocated syndicalism, mutualism, egalitarianism, industrialism, fraternity, and 'anarchy' in the sense of economic managerial administration without authoritarian government of man by man. In his first important work *What Is Property?* (Paris, 1840), Proudhon said that private property of the kind that allows the exploitation of the labour of others may be defined in a word as 'theft'. This is especially evident in the case of ownership of land by those who do not work the land. Human independence requires that each man control the land or tools he can use. Ownership of property that one does not work destroys human equality. On the other hand, communism destroys independence. Property and communism must therefore give way to 'anarchy' or liberty. In an anarchical society, without a master or sovereign, the producers bind themselves together economically by a network of free contracts. In a world-wide working-class organization, with its own mutual credit systems, economic organization makes governmental administration unnecessary. Anarchist revolutionism aims to ensure that there will be 'no more government of man by man through the means of accumulation of capital'. It aims to establish an egalitarian industrial regime.

Proudhon developed his social philosophy further in his anarchist newspaper *Le Représentant du peuple* (1848) and in his *General Idea of Revolution in the Nineteenth Century* (1851), *On the Federal Principle* (1863), and other works. He advocated libertarian socialism as opposed to the authoritarian socialism of Marx. In the ideal libertarian society, based not on laws but on contracts, producers' associations and federations of associations would replace the structures of centralized State government. Centralized State government will be allowed to wither away. It will be replaced by structures which arise freely through fraternal co-operation, and anarchy or mutualism. Industrial functions will take over from political functions. Banks will become people's co-operative banks. Frontiers will be abolished. Communes, industrial associations and flexible federations will replace national states. More attention will be paid to the education of the workers and apprenticeship training in a wide variety of skills, and to the profitable use of leisure.

Proudhon had a considerable following among the workers of Paris, and his disciples played a leading role in the foundation of the first International Workingmen's Association in 1864. He associated in Paris with Marx, Bakunin and other revolutionary theorists. Marx wrote two works attacking Proudhon's views in 1846 and 1847. Mikhail Bakunin (1814-76), a collectivist writer and revolutionary leader, and Alexander Herzen (1812-70), an editor, essayist, and social philosopher, were important disciples of Proudhon. Later forms of anarchist communism (Kropotkin), anarchosyndicalism (Pelloutier), and pacifist anarchism (Tolstoy and Nieuwenhuis) were largely influenced by Proudhon's doctrines. Bakunin acknowledged explicitly that 'Proudhon was the master of us all'.

4. Comte. *Auguste Comte* (1798-1857) is known generally as the father of 'positive philosophy' and as the leading exponent of classical positivism. His period of studies of modern science and technology at the École Polytechnique (1814-16) provided him with the model of his conception of a new organization of society ordered by an elite group of scientist-leaders. As a student, Comte studied the *idéologues* (see Chapter 29 below), Condorcet, Hume, Adam Smith and current political economists. In 1818 he became secretary to Saint-Simon. He adapted some of Saint-Simon's ideas concerning a science of human behaviour but developed them in his own way. From 1826 onwards, he gave lectures on his positivistic philosophy to a private audience composed of physiologists, psychologists, mathematicians and several of the outstanding thinkers of his time. These lectures were re-edited in Comte's major work, the six-volume *Course of Positive Philosophy* (1830-43).

Comte's positive philosophy arose from his historical study of the development of the sciences, astronomy, physics, chemistry, and biology. Each of these sciences has gone through three historical stages of development: a theological stage, a metaphysical stage and a positive stage.

In the theological stage of the sciences men found the ultimate causes of events in superhuman wills. This stage went through three sub-phases of growth. In the animist or fetish phase men regarded each object as having its own will or spirit. In the polytheistic phase, men believed that many divine wills imposed themselves on objects. In the monotheistic phase, they conceived one God as imposing his will on objects. This theological stage of the growth of the human mind has generally been associated with a militaristic social order and with absolute authority, as in the Middle Ages.

The metaphysical or second stage of the progress of the human mind is that of the transformation of the theological wills into metaphysical abstractions such as gravity, nature, vital principles, ether, attraction, energy, and other similar reified concepts. This stage of human progress is associated with radical criticism and with the proclamation of abstract rights and the reign of law, as in the Age of Enlightenment.

The positive or third stage is that of the mature scientific mind which concerns itself not with final wills and first causes but with positive, factual knowledge of the observed universe as it appears relative to ourselves. In this positive, scientific stage the study of the 'laws of relations of succession and resemblance' are seen as the correct object of man's research. Dogmatic assumptions are now replaced by positive facts, according to Comte. This positive stage of human progress is associated with the development and organization of industrial society in a rational, scientific manner.

Having presented his interpretation of the historical development of the sciences, Comte then presented his views on their classification and methodology. The six (or seven) fundamental sciences, in logical order of succession, he said, are mathematics, astronomy, physics, chemistry, physiology-biology, and social physics or sociology; later he added ethics, which he thought of as a positive study of man's overt social behaviour. The simplest and most general or abstract science is mathematics. Astronomy presupposes and depends on mathematics. There can be no effective physics before astronomy, or biology before chemistry. The least abstract, sociology, presupposes and depends on physiology-biology. Other sciences are simply branches or applications of the seven basic sciences. These seven are independent, fragmented sciences. Positive philosophy attempts to unify them.

Positive philosophy achieves a doctrinal synthesis of the seven independent sciences by relating them one by one to humanity and to the needs of man as a social being. Philosophy has also the practical aim of effectively achieving a reorganization and renovation of society through a deepening knowledge of the sociological laws at work within society.

The sciences all share the common scientific method of comparing and co-ordinating observed phenomena (facts) through the formulation of descriptive laws. In addition to this common method, each of the independent sciences, in the process of its historical development, perfects its own special procedure and technique or method, by a logic proper to itself. Sociology too develops its own special procedure; and like the other basic sciences, it makes occasional use of mathematics with a view to obtaining greater precision.

The two major branches of sociology, according to Comte, are statics and dynamics. Social *statics* is the study of the political-social systems in relation to the existing level of civilization. It studies these cultural systems as functioning cultural wholes. Thus, for example, it studies the division of labour, social role-playing, government, and co-ordination of human effort in different societies. Social *dynamics*, on the other hand, studies social progress, or the development of order. It studies the progressive advance of different political organizations. It studies 'the three natural ages of humanity', that is, the three successive theological, metaphysical and positive stages of man's intellectual development. A scientific positivist elite, aware of the laws of social dynamics governing human development, can accelerate the development of industrial society through intelligent social planning and through effective socio-political action.

Comte favoured benign paternalistic government by positivist philosophers and by scientific social management. He had little sympathy for democracy or alleged natural rights of individuals. His emphasis was on society and humanity, not on the individual. He proclaimed confidently that a moral regeneration of mankind would inevitably accompany the development of a society based on science, industry and a total concern for the welfare of humanity.

The new focus of worship and devotion in the regenerated positivist society is to be eternal Humanity itself, according to Comte. Humanity, the 'Great Being' *(le Grand Être)*, will take the place occupied formerly by the Supreme Being in primitive theological thought. A new positivist religious system, having its own high priests of science, its own saintly benefactors, its own temples, comminations, commemorations, and social sacraments, is to replace the old theological institutions, the former Catholic system. Comte himself became the high priest of a new religion which had its own holy days, its calendar of positivist saints, and its own positive nontheistic catechism. The new religion enjoined everyone 'to live for others'. It relied especially on women and the large numbers of the proletarian poor to soften the selfish character of the property-owning capitalists. In this way the managers of industry would be humanized, and class conflict would wither in a positive society where everyone lives for others. Karl Marx read Comte's views in 1866 and judged them 'trashy'.

Comte acknowledged that his theory of the three stages cannot accommodate the detailed facts of history, and he was prepared to recognize a measure of overlapping between the various stages. It is nonetheless true that he attempted to reconstruct history from the viewpoint of the polemic needs of his positivist polity. His descriptive reconstruction is not neutral. There is a certain fitting of favourable facts into a general interpretative scheme. He presupposes that positivism is the absolute terminus of historical development, and makes no allowance for the possibility of any post-positivist intellectual development. His law of the three stages appears to be not so much a positive, falsifiable, scientific hypothesis as the expression of a convinced belief or the expression of a teleological philosophy of history in the light of which the historical data have to be interpreted. His interpretation of history is, in brief, the interpretation of a staunch partisan positivist. Nevertheless, Comte did make a noteworthy contribution to philosophy and to the philosophy of history. He prepared the way for the development of a new science, sociology, which would study not only the functioning interrelations of men in society but also the dynamic development of these interrelations in the course of human history.

5. The positivists. The most widely known direct disciple of Comte was *Émile Littré* (1801-81), compiler of the famous *Dictionnaire de la langue française* (1872). He devoted several articles to the propagation of Comte's positivism but then broke away from the orthodox Comtean school in 1852. He rejected Comte's efforts to append ethics to the list of fundamental sciences. 'Morals... does not belong to the objective order.' He rejected Comte's introduction of the 'subjective' method of relating the objective sciences to Humanity, an abstract collective being which was proposed as an object of cult. He advocated a return to the original positivist epistemological theory of Comte's *Course*, and a pruning away of religious and teleologico-historical accretions from the verifiable scientific core of pure positivist philosophy. The positive philosophy has its foundations not in non-verifiable 'absolute entities' but in matter and the forces immanent in matter. He rejected the religion of humanity as an antiquated mysticism.

Pierre Lafitte (1823-1903) accepted the totality of Comte's thought, including his political doctines and the religion which Comte called 'humanism'. Lafitte succeeded in spreading the cult beyond France, into Great Britain, Sweden and Brazil. The members of the sect took an active part in the revolution which brought independence to Brazil in 1891, and erected a large temple to humanity at Rio de Janeiro. The cult extended into Chile with George Lagarrigue. Pierre Lafitte became the high priest after Comte; and he was succeeded by Charles Jannole in 1903.

Joseph E. Renan (1823-92), of the Académie Française and the Collège de France, declared that his religion was 'the progress of reason, that is to say, of science'. He was deeply impressed by Hegel's writings on the development or evolution of consciousness, and he was strongly influenced by the views of working scientists, such as the chemist Marcelin Berthelot, who were his friends. He attempted to expand the horizons of scientific rationalism and positivism by incorporating into it his views on the development of rationality out of instinct, and on the progressive realization of ideal consciousness (Science, Reason, God) in history. The historical development of the human mind is the key to the universe; and this development is manifested in the historical evolution of languages, religions, and the natural sciences. Thus, the study of the development of the human and natural sciences is the study of the progressive realization of complete, ideal consciousness on earth. New scientific discoveries are new revelations of the divine. The furtherance or progression of science (knowledge) is the great religious task of mankind. The goal of the universe is the attainment of the full measure of beauty and morality of which the complete development of consciousness is capable. The immanent ideal, realized at the end of the process, is ideal consciousness, or in other words, Reason, Science, God. The scientist must face his task, then, with a spirit of religious dedication, seeking revelation of the divine. It was for this reason that Renan declared that his religion was 'the progress of reason, that is to say, of science'. He sought to introduce a naturalistic religious outlook into the fundamentally positivist trends of his thought. In the last years of his life, however, he found that his 'religion of science' did not satisfy his needs. His writings gradually began to show a marked tendency towards scepticism and irony, even though he retained his faith in science or knowledge as man's ultimate goal.

Hippolyte-Adolphe Taine (1828-93), professor at the École des Beaux-Arts, had absolute faith in the ability of the positive sciences to resolve all problems of man and the universe without the help of any other possible source of truth, such as supernatural revelation. Everything, including man and all the products of his activity, admits of a purely naturalistic explanation. The laws of art, literature and history are purely natural laws; and the proper methods of art, literature and history are scientific methods. 'Virtue and vice are products, like vitriol and sugar.' Works of literature and art can be explained entirely in terms of the influence exerted by the basic forces of race, environment, and the pressure of the past on the present, and of the application of the dominant faculty *(faculté maîtresse)* of the artist to the operation of these basic forces. The 'creative genius' of which some people speak is simply a metaphor referring to a world of intangibles which the scientific mind rightly ignores.

Taine himself had a dominant desire to unify and organize all forms of scientific knowledge in a well co-ordinated system. He found in the writings of Spinoza and Hegel a definite orientation and a central principle of supreme unity which enabled him to formulate his own basic theory. This theory has two fundamental postulates: firstly, the positivist postulate that we attain only sensible, experiential facts; and secondly, that each science has its own unifying law, unifying the various facts which constitute the science. Taine proposed that since the only objects which are proportioned to our intelligence are the facts of sensible experience, then the ideal of the positivist philosopher is to disengage, by (isolating) abstraction, the unifying and explanatory law of each science as a means towards attaining eventually the unique and supreme law which unifies all the sciences.

Nature, or the universe, is for Taine an assemblage of facts or phenomena which are simply a manifestation of the Eternal Axiom, the Supreme Law, which people call God. These phenomena of nature are all referable to mechanical local movement, so that their supreme law must be basically a determined, mechanical law. The universe is one, rational, law-ordered system, a unitary totality governed by the immanent activity of a Supreme Law or cause. The human mind has a power of abstraction, that is, isolating abstraction, which enables man to separate and formulate the causes, forces and laws which are factually present in factual events. It has the ability, furthermore, to analyse groups or sets of laws with a view to extracting the most primitive and basic elements of the universe, the first causes. Metaphysics is the search for first causes.

Taine's vision of the universe is not derived from empiricism. It is a metaphysical 'vision', similar to that of Spinoza and Hegel. Like Spencer in England, Taine in France was known as the metaphysician of positivism. His works were influential in France; and yet he had no disciples, since unlimited confidence in the omnicompetence of science had already begun to wane in the last decades of the nineteenth century.

6. Durkheim. *Émile Durkheim* (1858-1917), professor of social science at Bordeaux, and later professor of education and sociology at Paris, was the first to teach social science at a French university. He is regarded as the founder of the Sociological school of positive philosophy, though he himself recognized Comte as the founder of the science of sociology. He wrote important works on *The Division of Labour in Society* (1893), *The Rules of Sociological Method* (1895), *Suicide* (1897), *The Elementary Forms of the Religious Life* (1912) and lecture courses on sociology, philosophy and education which were published posthumously.

In these works, Durkheim maintained, firstly, that society is an entity *sui generis*, specifically distinct from the individuals who compose it, and, secondly, that there is no successful means of studying moral and social phenomena other than that of positive scientific observation. The study of the moral and social life of man, then, constitutes a special positivistic science, namely, sociology, whose object, society, is a unique reality distinct from all other realities.

The sociologist studies social phenomena (facts) and their interrelations in the same empirical and objective manner in which the physicist studies phenomena. He studies social phenomena, such as the social morality and religion of a given social group or tribe, as exercising social pressure or constraint on the individual. Durkheim defined a social phenomenon or fact as a feature of a given society, or a general way of acting, which could be regarded as exercising a constraint or social pressure on individuals. He regarded social phenomena such as language, art, currency, law, literature and division of labour as expressions of the collective consciousness of the distinct entity, society. Each specific society defines concretely how its members, men and women, are expected to follow definite traditional patterns of behaviour. The outlook of a Hindu woman, for example, is largely formed by her social consciousness, through language, of a whole system of categories, beliefs and value judgements assimilated from the society which nurtures her. Each obeys the voice of society and assimilates 'the essential traits of the common type'.

'Morality exists', Durkheim says, 'because society needs it; but it takes the form of the voice of society demanding obedience because it is the voice of society.' Morality is a social phenomenon which originates in society. Moral obligation arises from the constraining voice of collective consciousness. In this sense, the voice of conscience is the voice of society or the voice of 'God'.

The science of ethics is an empirical science, according to Durkheim. It deals with those social facts in which social constraint is exercised on the individual by the collective consciousness. In the modern world, as society becomes more advanced, collective ideals tend to become more abstract, and thus the area of personal freedom grows. In modern industrial and commercial occupations, a large part of human life is passed without ethical guidelines or rules. There is need then for formulations of new codes of professional or 'occupational ethics'. New patterns and codes of moral behaviour are demanded by the new, 'real' voice of society, in contrast to the dated, outmoded voice of the older society. The empirical science of ethics can give valuable assistance in the formulation of new codes of moral and social behaviour; and the need for this assistance is evident especially in modern times, he affirmed, when religion, the primary form of collective consciousness, is a receding phenomenon.

Durkheim attempted to constitute moral science on a basis of positivistic principles. If social facts are governed by necessary laws, however, then there can be no morality of human actions or reactions just as there can be no morality of chemical reactions. The concept of positivistic morality involves a contradiction. There are few if any conclusions of positivistic morality which are capable of being scientifically demonstrated in the way that positivistic science demands. Several views propounded by Durkheim, such as his ideal of moral 'health' and social 'sanctity', and his recommendation for the re-establishment of corporations as a remedy for the excessive liberty granted to modern states, were not grounded in positivistic principles; and other sociologists of the positivistic school rejected them. His advocacy of views of this kind gives evidence of his desire to return to a morality based on sound reason rather than build on a morality searching for a foundation in the principles of positivism.

Lucien Lévy-Bruhl (1857-1939), professor at the Sorbonne, was influenced by the thought of Comte and Durkheim. His *Ethics and Moral Science* stressed the need for an empirical study of the adaptation of different moral ideas to the social structures of different groups. He collected a wide range of anthropological data from various anthropological reports. On the basis of these findings he maintained that there is a difference in kind between the pre-logical, mystical and emotional mentality of primitive peoples, and the logical, empirical and scientific mentality of more recent times. Thus, for example, the members of a totemic group may see themselves as a continuum of occult spiritual powers emanating from their totem rather than as a series of distinct individuals forming a social group. There is need for a scientific collection of historical, sociological and anthropological data, from which it may be possible to develop some useful guidelines for the future. This work might well be performed by sociologists and anthropologists. The positivist philosopher should then concentrate on the analysis of moral notions and on the interpretation of these notions in a strictly naturalistic way.

7. Philosophy of science. Reflection on the natural sciences had an important place in the thought of several French philosophers. Descartes had hoped to find, through the use of the geometrical method, a few simple principles and rules which would guide all scientific inquiry. Comte looked forward to the day when engineers and mathematicians would replace priests and philosophers. The positivists in general sought to attain the general principles common to all the sciences and wished to use these scientific principles as guides to human conduct. Others devoted their attention to making an evaluation or critique of the experimental sciences themselves; and these can more evidently be said to have specialized in the philosophy of science.

Claude Bernard (1813-78) was a professor of physiology whose many discoveries in experimental physiology were awarded several scientific prizes. He published an *Introduction to the Study of Experimental Medicine* (Paris, 1865). In this work, he undertook an investigation into the nature of scientific, experimental method, that is, the method of the construction and empirical testing of verifiable hypotheses. He regarded crude empiricism, which observes and experiments at random, as merely a first step in the direction of advanced experimental method. He regarded the operation of absolute determinism as an absolute principle for the working scientist: a certain set of conditions (a cause) invariably produces the same phenomenon (an effect). Tentative scientific hypotheses and theories are necessary guides for rational experimentation, but they are products of human reason and must be subjected constantly to laboratory experimentation and criticism. They are always provisional and subject to revision or replacement by other theories and hypotheses which are more all-embracing. This attitude anticipated to some extent Karl Popper's view that falsifiability by observation is the criterion of the empirical and scientific character of any theory (see Chapter 33, section 5 below).

Jules Henri Poincaré (1854-1912) was a mathematician and philosopher of science who, like Claude Bernard, criticized the positivist doctrine that perceptual data alone are the stuff of science. Positivism seemed totally incapable of explaining the role of creative imagination in the formulation of scientific hypotheses. He asserted, like Bernard, that the formulation of the proper scientific questions depends on the creative imagination of the questioner. The scientist has a distinctly creative contribution to make to the so-called 'positive facts'.

Poincaré pointed out that the working scientist distinguishes in actual practice between experiment, mathematical reasoning, convention and hypothesis; he does not in practice confuse conventional axioms or principles with experimental laws. The working scientist proceeds with a belief in a general order in the universe, and aims to discover as much as possible of the order of the universe. He aims to express in mathematical formulae the discovered relations between things. In the process of comparing, experimenting and measuring, scientists accept certain conventions because experiment has shown them to be useful and convenient. Thus, for example, scientists accept Euclidean geometry as a convenient conventional way of dealing with bodies which we compare and measure by means of our senses. This does not imply that Euclidean geometry is true and that Lobachevskian or Riemannian or other non-Euclidean geometries are false. One does not ask if kilometres are more true than miles; they are simply different conventions, or 'definitions in disguise'. One can speak consistently of light as travelling in Euclidean non-straight lines or as travelling in non-Euclidean straight lines. Consistent alternative geometries are possible because their axioms or principles have been found in experimental work to be useful conventions. The three principles known as Newton's laws of motion helped to clarify the concept of force, acceleration, mass and momentum. Principles of this kind are general conventions or definitions which are not open to experimental refutation. Principles are simply conventional postulates. Experimental laws, however, are not conventions; they are open to revision in the constant pursuit of generality in nature.

Physical theories, Poincaré says, are devices which enable us to connect and predict phenomena. They do not attempt to describe some reality in all its details. They aim to be predictive, suggestive and 'fruitful'. One theory may be superseded by another theory which is more fruitful than the first. Different concepts having different suggestions are used in the old and the new theories even when both theories use the same differential equations. The old theory is not refuted. It is simply rejected by a more suggestive, useful, and fruitful theory. In some cases the two theories, old and new, may be retained as useful for dealing with different ranges of phenomena. A theory is 'convenient' rather than 'true'. Scientific theories, then, are *conventions* that depend on the scientists' free choice between alternative ways of describing or 'imaging' the natural world. This approach to the critique of the sciences is known as Poincaré's Conventionalism.

Gaston Milhaud (1858-1918), like Poincaré, denounced the scientific dogmatism of crude empiricism. Creative scientific thought needs to be liberated from the obstacles imposed on it by the dogmatism of Comte. There is an element of reason in the construction of scientific theories. We see evidence of this is the *philosophes géomètres* of ancient Greece (the pre-Socratics: see above, Chapter 1) and in the history of modern scientific thought. Positivism is outmoded. Creative thought is not determined by either external or internal necessities, even though, in the construction of scientific theories, this creativity of the human mind is always guided by rational decision.

Pierre M. M. Duhem (1861-1916) did valuable research work in thermodynamics and also in the history of scientific cosmology, mechanics and physics. He regarded metaphysics and science as highly respectable studies which concern themselves with different aspects of reality. Metaphysics is concerned, for example, to understand and explain the grounds of human freedom. Scientific theories do not explain reality. They are representative, not explanatory.

The construction of a scientific theory commences, Duhem says, with mathematical representations, or symbols of observable, measurable properties. It represents felt-warmth, for example, in Centigrade pointer-readings. It then connects a series of these measurement symbols in a small number of propositions, or principles, or hypotheses, which serve as convenient formulae for facilitating particular deductions. It proposes, for example, that momentum be regarded as the product of mass and velocity. It then combines a series of these hypotheses or principles, according to the rules of mathematical analysis, into wider, more all-embracing (algebraic) formulae, which represent in a satisfactory way a group of experimental laws. It finally translates these symbolic operations back into new physical terms and statements about the physical, measurable, properties of bodies. It may speak, for example, of the physical 'wave motion' of light.

A scientific theory is a useful representation of the investigated reality, Duhem asserts, but it is not an 'explanation' of the ontological nature of light or electricity or any other such reality. It is a model representation, not an ontological explanation. Nevertheless, we find, in practice, he says, that many theories have been garnished with picturesque 'explanatory', pictorial elements. It is these 'explanatory' elements that disappear when an older theory is replaced by a better theory. The part of the theory which survives, and which is common to both old and new, is the representative part, namely, the mathematical symbols, principles, and formulae. In summary, 'A physical theory is not an explanation. It is a system of mathematical propositions, deduced from a small number of principles, which aim at representing (and classifying) as simply, as completely and as exactly as possible a set of experimental laws.'

Theories permit prediction, and prediction is empirically testable, Duhem points out. If a theory is falsified, it must be modified or perhaps abandoned. A series of particular verifications does not prove conclusively the truth of the hypothesis. Science advances not so much through particular verifications as through the elimination of previously held hypotheses. The failure of a prediction indicates that there is something wrong with the hypothesis or with some other hypothesis within the same general theory or with some other theory that has been assumed. The negative instance indicates that something is wrong but it does not identify the element which should be rejected. Hypotheses and laws are slowly and painfully evolved by a process of testing and modification. They are not the products of sudden creation and they are not the conclusions of inductions in the sense of generalizations from observations. They arise from interpretations of symbolic representations of phenomena, and each such interpretation has equally acceptable alternatives. Each and all are provisional idealizations whose predictions stand in need of further testing and constant modification. The process is slow and ongoing.

29 'The human condition': philosophy in France (II)

1. The *idéologues* and Maine de Biran   2. Indeterminism, neo-criticism and idealism   3. Spiritualism   4. Bergson's metaphysics   5. Bergson on morality and religion

1. The *idéologues* and Maine de Biran. The theories of Condillac and Locke had not given a satisfactory solution to the problem of the objectivity of knowledge, nor had they given really close attention to what one actually perceives to take place when one speaks and judges and acts voluntarily. Destutt de Tracy and the *idéologues* concluded from this that the only valid approach to a correct understanding of the workings of the human faculties and to the development of a science of human nature is through the use of the method of attentive immediate self-observation.

Destutt de Tracy (1754-1836) coined the term 'ideology' as a name for his analysis of the contents of consciousness ('ideas') into the sensory elements of which he believed them to be composed. Among these ideas there is one, namely the idea of touch, which gives us evidence of the existence of a reality outside ourselves. Our desire to penetrate something is annihilated by a feeling of resistance which forces us to conclude that there is a resisting object. There is an element of activity, therefore, in consciousness. Condillac had placed major emphasis on the passive aspect of knowledge, the passively received sensations. But there also seems to be present among our faculties an active power of composing, judging and analysing our sensations, memories, judgements and desires. Consciousness is therefore active as well as passive. De Tracy and his friends Pierre-Jean-George Cabanis (d.1808) and the Comte de Volney (d.1820) gave their attention to the analysis of the contents of consciousness. They came to be known as the *idéologues* or ideologists, the analysers of the contents of consciousness. They advocated their mode of analysis and study of conscious processes as a substitute for metaphysics.

Pierre Laromiguière (1756-1837) disagreed with Condillac concerning the mind's passive reception of sensory material impressed on the mind by external causes. This theory did not account for the activities of the understanding and the will. The three activities of the understanding are attention, comparison and reason; and the corresponding activities of the will are desire, preference and freedom to act. These powers are essentially active, and so the soul is not simply a passive recipient of sensory stimuli. Seeing is distinct from looking, and listening is distinct from hearing. The task of philosophy, then, is that of discovering the origin of the different contents of consciousness.

F. P. Gonthier Maine de Biran (1766-1824), prompted by the *idéologues*, carefully exploited the phenomenon of human *activity* in the process of knowing. His work gave rise to a new movement (called 'spiritualism') in French philosophy of the nineteenth century. He accepted de Tracy's account of our experience of resistance as one which necessarily presupposes an active power or faculty of *motilité* or moving. But he concluded that the *idéologues* had failed to exploit adequately this idea of human activity as willed effort meeting with resistance. Inward felt effort, he proclaimed, reveals the existence of the active agent, the active ego.

Man has an interior sense *(sens intime)*, Maine de Biran said, by which he senses the 'flow' of life as a primary inner experience. This lived experience is an important source of knowledge. It differs from the 'objective' experience of the outward-oriented senses. It reveals our experience of willed effort or willed bodily movement *(effort voulu)*. We have a directly felt experience, for example, of our willed movements of our organs of speech, and of hearing ourselves speaking. This is not one of the passively received external 'impressions' of the type to which Condillac confined his attention. An active perception differs from a passive impression. Impressions grow vague and dull through habituation, and learning diminishes. We grow accustomed to the clouds, for example, and we are minimally impressed. Learning is closely linked, however, with willed effort and active perception; knowledge is continually enriched through inward experience.

De Biran pointed out that a descriptive analysis of the immediate data of consciousness manifests the self as experiencing itself in willed efforts of which it feels itself subject or cause. In the willed effort of speaking I experience myself as speaking. The consciousness of one's activity is also a consciousness of oneself. The ego apprehends itself as a self-identical causal agent, an active ego, in the relation in which willed effort encounters a succession of resistances. Thus, one has a direct apprehension of the causal efficacy of oneself as a phenomenal subject which is aware of its personal identity. We inwardly perceive or experience this phenomenal or experienced ego and we have a spontaneous natural tendency to believe in it as an abiding meta-phenomenal or noumenal ego. Reflexive psychology, or metaphysics as the science of 'interior phenomena', thus makes a critical reflection on the phenomena or facts or data of the interior sense (*sens intime*); and it pronounces that the ego which apprehends itself as a free causal agent is the phenomenal, experienced ego, not the noumenal ego. It pronounces that the conscious ego is conscious of itself as active cause and not as soul-substance. There is however a natural, spontaneous movement of the mind to believe that the active agent is the phenomenal manifestation of the noumenal, substantial soul. This movement is a movement of spontaneous belief rather than a movement of inductive inference. The idea of the permanent soul is the idea of an object of well-grounded belief rather than an idea arising from inductive knowledge. The belief is solidly grounded on the immediate inner experience of the ego as an active agent of causal activity or efficacy.

The philosophical approach of Maine de Biran can be expressed briefly, and in terminology of a later age, if we say that descriptive phenomenology and analytical epistemology provide a basis for critical, reflective epistemology, which, in turn, provides an introduction to metaphysics. De Biran did not create a developed philosophical system, nor did he have any school of disciples. Nevertheless he exercised a very stimulating influence on the 'spiritualist' current of thought which one finds in Ravaisson, Lachelier, Fouillée, Boutroux, Ollé-Laprune, Guyau, Bergson, Blondel and other French thinkers.

2. Indeterminism, neo-criticism and idealism. The writings of Cournot, Renouvier, Hamelin and Brunschvicg reflect disagreement with the positivism of their own day and with earlier French rationalists. These philosophers rejected several aspects of Kant's critical philosophy, and they conducted critical inquiries of their own into the foundations of human knowledge. (For Brunschvicg, see Chapter 31, section 2 below.)

Antoine Augustin Cournot (1801-77), mathematician, economist and philosopher, rejected dogmatic rationalism and dogmatic empiricism. He held that knowledge is a function of reason. The senses make only a limited contribution to knowledge. Thus, for example, they help to restrain reason from over-extended speculation. The conclusions of one's reasoning require a continuing appraisal. This is particularly evident in the conclusions of the established sciences. All principles must be continually appraised not only to determine their grounds but also to determine the range of their legitimate applications. Reasoning (and knowledge) extends beyond the limits of the senses, and it frequently needs to be confronted again with the contributions of the senses. These sense-contributions, however, do not furnish the criteria of knowledge, nor do they furnish the basis of reasoning. What we know through reason are the relations between phenomena; and our knowledge of these relations is always revisable in principle. The astronomer's knowledge, for example, is real and always subject to revision. The astronomer seeks to discover the order in phenomena, and at the same time it is the astronomer's reason that introduces order and classification into things. It is when the objective order and the subjective order are in accord that there is knowledge. This is true of all the sciences.

There are three basic concepts which all the established sciences have in common, according to Cournot. These concepts are order, chance and probability. *Order*, as the objective reason of things, relates to the nature of things. Order as the subjective reason relates to the means through which we apprehend the nature of things. *Chance*, like order, is an objective feature of the nature of things. A chance occurrence is one in which there is an unpredictable conjunction of two or more independent series of events. Thus, for example, an unpredictable collision is an unpredictable concurrence of independent causal chains, and the resulting events are contingent, unpredictable and fortuitous. The events have causes but the disordered sequences cannot be formulated in a predictive set of laws. There is in the universe an irreducible element of indeterminacy. The scientist has to accept the fact that order and contingency, continuity and discontinuity are equally real. Man cannot attain ultimate, certain truth about nature, but he can approach this truth by continually increasing the probable truth of his statements. He can make some predictions, for example, on the basis of the calculus of probabilities. Mathematical probability is applicable to those situations in which the number and relative frequency of various possibilities can be numerically determined. Philosophical *probability* involves an appraisal of the rational cogency of evidence in situations where the weight of probabilities wins the acquiescence of reasonable persons even though the relevant evidence never attains demonstrable certainty. Human life is continuously and inescapably replete with probabilities of this kind. Cournot applied probability theory to economics and other sciences. He is generally regarded today as one of the founders of econometrics.

Charles Bernard Renouvier (1815-1903) used Kant's thought as a basis from which to launch a personalist form of philosophy which was frequently critical of Kant. He denied the existence of all transcendental entities, such as the noumenon, the thing-in-itself, and the absolute. His philosophy has been called 'phenomenological neo-criticism'. It gave a new direction to neo-criticism by basing it on three independent theses, namely, finitism, freedom, and phenomenal reality.

Renouvier's denial of the existence of any infinite was based on his understanding of mathematics and on his belief that an infinite number was a contradiction in terms. All is finite, including space, time and 'absolutes' of any kind. Each individual is a separate, distinct, finite entity, just as each cardinal number is finite, distinct and separate from all others. Each human being is distinct, free, and incapable of being absorbed into any 'absolute' mind or into a general group-consciousness.

Freedom is a datum of moral consciousness, Renouvier says. Each individual experiences himself as a free moral agent, a responsible human person. He experiences the obligation to be as he ought to be (*devoir être*), and to do his duty (*devoir faire*), and to ascertain that things are as they ought to be through human agency. Each feels obliged to realize his higher self in his character and conduct, and each believes that his happiness depends on this realization of his higher self. The secret of human happiness lies in personal freedom. It is through free judgement and choice that we rise above the beasts. We recognize the humanity of our fellows in their rational, moral actions, and we respect their humanity and their freedom. This emphasis on personal happiness, rationality, and freedom influenced all of Renouvier's attitudes and reflections on Kant, Comte, idealism, determinism, State, Church, and God. He spoke of God, for example, as a finite, limited, and free guarantor of human freedom; and he urged his readers to turn to Protestantism as the religion which championed individual conscience.

Renouvier disagreed with Kant's division between the speculative reason and practical reason, between knowledge and belief, and between noumena and phenomena. Phenomena are simply things as appearing or capable of appearing. They are simply whatever we perceive or make judgements about. Perceived things are not appearances of anything other than themselves. The phenomenal and the real are the same. Perceived things are things perceived by the whole perceiver, the whole person. Similarly, in the case of the whole person as a knower, all knowledge is personal knowledge; and in all personal knowledge there is an intervention of personal will. Human certitude always involves human belief and the will to believe. The whole person is involved. This is true, likewise, of moral action. Morality arises not from duty for duty's sake but from the free action and self-expression of the whole person. It is in this direction that all the basic insights of Kant's philosophy should have been developed.

The world around us, Renouvier says, is a world in which there is given a plurality of existing things. They are known as related, just as numbers are known as related and ordered. Relation is the most general of all categories since nothing can be known except as related. We categorize all things in terms of the relations discovered within the framework of our personal consciousness. We are conscious of our acting as a cause, of seeking ends, making sensory discriminations, quantitative and qualitative, occupying different spatial positions and evolving through moments of time. We categorize all other realities too in terms of the same (nine) categories—relation, number, position, succession, quality, becoming, causality, finality or purposiveness, and personality. All are forms of relation, as discovered within consciousness. All are based in things as perceived and judged by us, that is, in the phenomenal world. It is a world in which plurality, time, novelty, indeterminacy, chance, freedom, purposiveness and personality really exist. It is a world in which there are no absolutes or infinites, and all is finite.

Octave Hamelin (1856-1907) declared himself a disciple of Renouvier. He found stimulus in the phenomenological neo-criticism of Renouvier for the development of his own idealist metaphysics. In his *Essay on the Principal Elements of Representation* (published 1907) he presented a more systematic dialectical deduction of Renouvier's table of categories, in order to develop them into a complete and self-contained rational system. The synthesis of being and nonbeing, as thesis and antithesis, is relation, namely, that which consists in interdependence. From the basic category of relation which is 'the simplest law of things', Renouvier deduced, by antithesis, that which is essentially independent, number. Number and relation are synthesized in time. Space, whose parts are separate, simultaneous and reversible, stands in antithesis to time. The antithesis of space and time is transcended in (quantitative) motion, whose opposite, quality, is unaffected by it. Motion and quality are synthesized in *altération*, which is the modification or change of quality. The antithesis to change is (perpetual) specification, the class or species. Causality, or specific change, arises from the interaction of specification and *altération* in beings which share the world with other beings. The antithesis to specific change or efficient causality is a principle of persistent immanent finality. Personality is the synthesis of causality and finality, expressed as free becoming and free choice in a self-sufficient active system, or conscious self. In this way, Hamelin brought the realm of contingent occurrences and the realm of personal freedom and consciousness within an idealistic dialectical system in which incomplete abstraction works dynamically towards its specification and fulfilment in concrete and individual consciousness. The subject's knowledge, then, is simply 'a putting into action by the subject of his potentialities'. Hamelin's philosophy, in spite of its neo-Hegelian overtones, belongs to a long (Cartesian) tradition of French thought, which shows a predilection for psychological analysis and the affirmation of human liberty.

3. Spiritualism. Maine de Biran's reflection on the human spirit's inner experience of the ego as an active agent of causal efficacy, and on the active spontaneity of the human will, gave rise to a movement which was called the 'spiritualist' or voluntarist movement in nineteenth-century French thought (a term not to be confused with Spiritualism as a religion). Ravaisson, Lachelier, and a number of other French thinkers down to the time of Bergson maintained that philosophy must commence with a study of our immanent, lived activities and not with passive sensations which are presumed to be caused in us by material forces. This movement was regarded as a return to the genuine traditions of French philosophy, and as a reaction against the materialism, determinism and positivism of more recent trends of thought.

Jean G. P. Ravaisson-Mollien (1813-1900), in his *Report on Philosophy in France in the Nineteenth Century* (1867), maintained that Maine de Biran was quite right in using the experience of the inner activity of the ego or will as the proper starting point of philosophical reflection. Scientific studies of the external world cannot tell us anything about the rich inner world of thoughts, aspirations, felt-needs, and human dreams. It is within man that man will find the key to the nature of reality. There is a sharp distinction, he said, between the world of space or matter and the world of spontaneous life and growth, the world of 'nature'. Material things can be adequately described by the laws of necessity in the theorems of physics, and they can be adequately classified and known through the categories of diversity and quantity. Living things, however, he says, in his study *On Habit* (1838), possess a unity of a kind which we discover within our own nature. It is an 'organic' unity and not just an arithmetical compilation. Life cannot exist without a material world, and yet we find that as life develops and as we mount the branches of the tree of life there is an ever-increasing spontaneity and complexity and a steady alienation from matter. We are capable of making an active effort to escape from the limitations of matter.

Ravaisson received his philosophical training in Munich under Schelling; and his view of Nature is similar to that of Schelling. Creation is a kind of cosmic fall. The material universe is the effect, the self-diffusion, and self-manifestation of 'an ultimate reality which gives of itself in liberality'. Mental activity and spiritual phenomena can be understood only when they are viewed in the light of 'the goal-directed upward movement of life, both at the infra-conscious and conscious levels'. In the goal-directed upward movement of life, Nature, which is slumbering spirit, is returning to God. Henri Bergson was Ravaisson's most distinguished student, and one can understand Bergson's life philosophy all the better in the light of Ravaisson's thought.

Jules Lachelier (1832-1918) referred to his own philosophy as 'a spiritualist realism', akin to the neospiritualism of Ravaisson. He rejected the naive attitude of crude materialism and positivism, that scientific measurement techniques provide our only real knowledge of all aspects of life. He accepted the objectivity of Nature, the world in which the mechanical laws of necessary causality operate; but he maintained that the ultimate explanation of Nature is to be found in the fact that reality or being is ultimately determined by thought or spirit operating in Nature. This viewpoint is similar to that of Schelling's objective idealism.

In his doctorate thesis *On the Foundation of Induction* (1871), Lachelier pointed out that the problem of induction is that of explaining how the mind (e.g. of the scientist) draws certain universal laws and conclusions from a limited number of observed cases of connections between phenomena. It implies, he says, that we are confident of the reign of necessity in Nature, and that necessary connections, or laws of nature, are to be found there. The necessary relations, operative among natural phenomena, and expressed by the law of efficient causes, can be explained only in terms of a form of unconscious but logical thought diffused throughout nature. It presupposes also that we are aware of ordered individual phenomenal objects (such as stable chemical molecules, and living organisms) co-ordinated into groups or 'wholes' in order to form complex recurrent unities. These functioning wholes (or whole phenomena) contain within themselves the reason for the organization of their parts. They operate according to the law of final causes. Thus, 'the possibility of induction rests on the double principle of efficient causes and final causes', or, in other words, on the double principle of mechanical necessity in nature and purposive holism in nature.

The existence of innumerable purposive wholes in nature, Lachelier says, reveals the functioning of unconscious thought in nature. Immanent final causality is a controlling force which reigns and rules within the world of mechanical causality. Every phenomenal reality is a manifestation of force which expresses spontaneous tendency towards an end. This insight into the universal purposiveness of nature, or unconscious thought at work in nature, changes our whole concept of the world. It reveals that 'every being is a force, and every force a thought which tends to a more and more complete consciousness of itself'. The world is a self-manifestation of thought or spirit. Absolute thought which operates unconsciously in Nature is one and the same as the thought which comes to self-awareness in and through man. The spiritual realist, therefore, sees reality, or the world, as 'a thought which does not think, suspended from a thought which thinks itself'.

Alfred Fouillée (1838-1918) attempted to reconcile and harmonize the values of naturalistic thought, on the one hand, and those of spiritualistic or idealistic thought, on the other. The world of ideas and the world of physical forces and objects are linked together, he said, in *idées-forces*, creative thought forces (or mind-energy). Mind is an efficient cause of physical action, and in human action there is intrinsic freedom. Every idea has within itself an active tendency to self-realization. Every idea is a force having a potential for realizing itself in action. This is especially and evidently true of the idea of freedom. The idea of freedom is an *idée-force* which tends to self-realization; and the greater the realization, the more the human being is free. Moral ideals too are *idées-forces* having an attractive power which invigorates moral action. Fouillée developed this theory of thought force in several works such as *Liberty and Determinism* (1872), *The Evolution of Thought Forces* (1890), *The Psychology of Thought Forces* (1893), and *The Ethics of Thought Forces* (1908).

Émile Boutroux (1845-1921), a pupil of Lachelier at the École Normale, concerned himself primarily with making a critical evaluation of the contributions of science while placing these contributions in a wider metaphysical framework. His doctorate thesis on *The Contingency of the Laws of Nature* (1874) defended the view that there is a radical contingency and basic discontinuity in nature of such a kind that it is impossible to explain all of nature merely in terms of the mechanical laws that govern matter. The contingency of the laws of nature has its ultimate explanation in the contingency of nature itself.

Scientific observation, Boutroux says, does not by itself reveal necessity, or necessary causal relations, in nature; it merely reveals that relatively invariable relations exist between phenomena. Scientific laws are useful, but they are always schematic, simplified, approximate and provisional. They are contingent, predictive generalizations. Scientific theories and hypotheses are schematic, provisional, and subject to modification and replacement. Human reason makes and breaks hypotheses and moulds of thought in its creative, pioneering quest for knowledge. In this sense, reason itself is discontinuous.

The discontinuity of nature is evident, according to Boutroux, in the distinctly separate levels of material, instinctive and thinking beings which we find in nature. The order of nature is not one of permanence and identity. Cosmic and biological evolution produces constant novelty and qualitative difference. Each higher level of being displays a new element not apparent in its predecessor, and not deducible from it. Nevertheless, historically, the one emerges from the other. In the universe, therefore, there is continuity as well as heterogeneity and discontinuity. The whole of reality is suffused with varying degrees of spontaneous upward thrust towards an ideal. The energy and forces incarcerated in matter are embryonic tendencies which become progressively free and creative in the higher forms of life. Creative teleological processes are at work in all of nature.

All of reality, Boutroux says, is a hierarchy of different levels of teleological tendencies towards ideals, ranging from the physical and mechanical forces present within so-called 'inanimate' matter up to the ideal spiritual perfection in God. All of reality is suffused with spontaneity and mind. There is no essential difference between the animate and the inanimate. There is no irreconcilable conflict between the scientific spirit and the religious spirit. The ideal life of active mysticism is one in which the different attitudes and spirits are harmonized in a rich unity. Bergson's doctrine of the upward thrusting *élan vital*, and his respect for the ideal life of active mysticism, are all the more readily placed in historical context if one recalls that Bergson was a student at the École Normale when Boutroux was teaching there.

Marie Jean Guyau (1854-88), Fouillée's stepson, wrote *A Sketch of Morality Independent of Obligation or Sanction* (1885), *The Non-Religion (L'Irréligion) of the Future* (1887), *The Origin of the Idea of Time* (1890) and other works. He attempted to reconcile positivism and vitalism in a doctrine of cosmic, creative life force. In the evolving universe, there is an infra-conscious life urge, or will to live, which brings forth successively higher forms. At the level of conscious life, a conscious idea is simply a momentary, luminous expression of this infra-conscious dynamic will to self-welfare, self-maintenance, self-intensification and self-expansion. The dynamic will or life urge is the cause and the goal of all action, whether instinctive or conscious. For this reason, the principles of ethics must be seen as arising from the life urge. 'Life at its most intensive and extensive' is the spring of all action. It is the principle or fount of morality.

The life force, Guyau said, is an impulse to creation. It expends itself, for example, in creative sexuality. In man, it becomes a vital moral impulse, impelling him to act according to his 'highest' thought. It gives rise to strong natural feelings of obligation; 'I can, therefore I must'. It impels the human being to be human, and to pursue the good and the beautiful in a moral atmosphere of human brotherhood. 'The moral ideal is to be found in human co-operation, altruism, solidarity, love and brotherhood.' It gives rise also, when thwarted, to strong feelings of guilt, 'falsehood in action', and self-betrayal. Intellectual development and reflection, which are important factors in human progress, tend 'to inhibit purely instinctive and animal-like behaviour'. The problem of morality, then, is that of reconciling inhibiting reflection with the spontaneous life force. This reconciliation is effected in a channelling of the vital moral impulse into acts which accord with man's 'highest' thought and ideals.

It is the universe which is the source of life, according to Guyau; and religious feelings are feelings of reverence for, and dependence on, the universe. The future has no place for dogmatic religion. Authoritarian religious institutions inhibit the intensification and expansion of life. The man of the future will reject the doctrine of vicarious redemption and will affirm himself as his own saviour. His salvation lies in a channelling of his life force into actions which accord with his ethical idealism. Guyau's philosophy is similar in some respects to that of Nietzsche; but it differs from Nietzsche's thought in its emphasis on ethical idealism, human liberty and human solidarity and brotherhood. His life-philosophy is closer to that of Bergson and the French 'spiritualists' than it is to that of Nietzsche.

4. Bergson's metaphysics. *Henri Bergson* (1859-1941) was born in Paris of Anglo-Polish Jewish parents. He showed brilliant talents for mathematics and the sciences but opted to specialize instead in literature and philosophy. He was a professor at the École Normale, and later at the Collège de France. He held this latter post until 1921, when ill health obliged him to retire. His published writings include works on *Time and Free Will: An Essay on the Immediate Data of Consciousness* (1889), *Matter and Memory* (1896), *Introduction to Metaphysics* (1903), *Creative Evolution* (1907), *Mind Energy* (1910), *Duration and Simultaneity* (1922), *The Two Sources of Morality and Religion* (1932) and *The Creative Mind* (1934). In these works Bergson treated in an original, artistic and imaginative way several of the themes associated with the writings of the earlier French neospiritualists. In his early years, he tells us, he was much attached to the philosophy of Spencer, and in his later years he felt attracted towards the mystical element in the writings of Plotinus. He was elected to the French Academy in 1914, and received the Nobel prize for literature in 1927.

The central insight which lies at the heart of all of Bergson's thought is the insight that actual ongoing reality is not a series of discrete entities, conceptualized in static intellectual ideas, but a continuous activity of ongoing being in a process of becoming; and it is intuited in a lived experience of duration.

The difference in the viewpoints of the mathematico-physical sciences and metaphysics, according to Bergson, is readily seen in their different viewpoints concerning the reality which is called 'time'. The abstract, mathematical 'time' of the mathematical-minded scientist is a spatial representation or model of time represented as an extended, homogeneous medium capable of division into standard units of measurement, such as months, hours and seconds. This physical theory of time, like other physical theories of light, heat or the atom, is a useful, picturesque fiction, or imaginative model, which enables the mind to correlate a large number of observations into a schematic, logical synthesis. Abstract, mathematical time is symbolized by the letter t, and is useful in algebraic formulae such as those which deal with the unit or interval $t_2 - t_1$. Mathematical time is a useful, reified abstraction.

Metaphysics concerns itself not with this abstraction but rather with the flowing, irreversible ongoing reality of beings existing in a continuous state of coming to be other than they were. Real time is intuited directly in one's own lived experience of duration in being. It is 'known' in the sensed 'flow' of life as a primary inner experience. The abstract, spatialized notion of time is the product of one's conceptualizing intelligence. Lived time or duration is actual becoming intuitively experienced. Being-in-becoming, reality, is encountered in intuition, not in spatialized abstractions. The sciences are concerned with the measurability and control of matter. Metaphysics is concerned with duration, evolution and becoming; it is concerned with reality itself. Science relies on reductive analysis and abstracting intelligence. Metaphysics relies on immediate consciousness of reality as it is experienced and lived. Neither should be depreciated. Each can receive valuable assistance from the other. But this can begin to happen only when one adverts to the fact that scientific time is not pure time; measured time is not real duration.

It is the abstract, spatialized conception of time, Bergson said, that provides the determinist with a notional, picturesque foundation for his arguments against the possibility of human *freedom* of action. The determinist images and misrepresents the situation of choice as one in which a succession of previous, distinct states determine how we move along a spatial-like path of points of time. There are occasions when we act unauthentically like stereotyped automata. But there are some occasions when our whole personality is the spring and source of spontaneous action, experienced as the life of the whole self in action. In fully human acts of this kind we experience freedom in action. This direct experience of being free is not negated, or explained away, by the reductive analysis of the associationist psychologist who speaks of 'motives' and 'character' as determining choices. Motives and character are hypostatized abstractions which have no substantial existence of their own. Concepts of this kind are, once again, products of reifying, spatializing intelligence; they are picturesque abstractions.

It is by direct experience that we know the reality of freedom and the reality of time. It is by direct experience too, Bergson says, that we know our *bodies* and that we know them to be centres of action. We know our bodies from the outside by perception and from the inside by affection or sensation. We know too that being conscious is something different from being a body with physical brain activity. This difference is evidently seen in the two different kinds of memory we experience, and, again, in the two different kinds of perception.

One kind of memory is a sensory-motor mechanism which has all the characteristics of corporeal habit. The sense-memory mechanism comes into action as a response to an appropriate stimulus, as in the case of a parroted reproduction of words or sounds. The other kind of memory, possessed by man alone, is wholly spiritual. 'Pure memory', or remembrance, is the ability to recall to oneself and to recognize a past event in its totality as pertaining to oneself. 'Consciousness signifies, above all, memory.' Pure memory retains the whole of our past, stored in the form of memory-images in the infra-conscious area of the mind. These memories are retained in the mind. They are not stored, or located spatially, or registered mechanically, in the neurons of the brain. Complex perceptions are recalled in a single memory and not in a multitude of different images. In the recollective process the brain plays a role analogous to that of a telephone exchange. It inhibits the multitudinous memory-images of the mind and admits to conscious recollection only those selected memory-images required for a contemplated action. In this way, on an occasion of action, body, as a centre of action, and mind are related in a convergence in time. The convergence of body and mind for action can be understood in temporal, but not spatial, terms. It cannot be explained in terms of a parallelism existing between a series of conscious states (represented spatially) and a series of brain states. It can be grasped only in the experience of what occurs at the moment we consciously initiate an action, a movement of active becoming, in the centre of action, the body.

Our perception or sensory apprehension of the external world, Bergson says, provides us with a familiar instance of consciousness or mind at work in the body as a centre of activity. Apprehension through one or more of the senses involves an actual presence of the external object to the sense-organs. Sensory apprehension or pure perception is a utilitarian, selective, sensory contact with an object by way of response to the promptings of a need or tendency. It is a form of (reflex) action rather than a form of cognition. It arises in the nervous system; and the role of the nervous system is to facilitate action. It selects those images that have a possible bearing on actions, and it enables the organism to select a course of action that will serve its needs. The objects surrounding an organism have many potential effects on the possible actions of the organism. The organism adapts to this situation by 'reflecting' possible lines of action from its body to the surrounding objects. This enables the organism to anticipate the potential effects on action and to select the course of action that will serve its needs. The object or the world perceived is the real physical object or world related to the organism's tendencies and needs. Pure perception is the 'reflection' of the body's virtual or possible action upon the object, or of the object's possible action upon the body.

As man ascends the stages of the evolution of organic life, and moves into the sphere of consciousness and freedom, Bergson says, the area of possible action grows, and the subjectivity of perception, oriented to action, also grows. Man's actual perception is now 'wholly impregnated with memory images which complete it while interpreting it'. Recollection and perception, though radically different, now interpenetrate each other. Actual human perception is a synthesis of 'mind *(esprit)* and matter'. Mind and matter, soul and body, are united for action; and the union is not spatial. It can be understood only in terms of time or duration. Spirit is not an epiphenomenon of the brain, nor is it a function of the brain. Spirit as turned to action depends on the body, the instrument of action. But mind or spirit differs from body as radically as recollection differs from pure perception, even when they are united for action in the selective act of perception. Damage to the brain or to the body may inhibit action; but body damage should not be thought of as damage also to the mind or spirit in itself. The ongoing human reality is both spirit and matter, combined, not spatially but temporally, in human duration. Consciousness signifies, above all, recollection; and recollection is the point of dynamic interaction of mind and matter, soul and body, which are coexistent and interdependent.

The world we come to know through perceptual acts, Bergson points out, is a world which appears to be relatively stable. Conceptual thought regards reality as constituted of stable, discrete things which seem to exist without change over long periods. The human capacity for conceptual or rational thought is referred to as the intellect. This capacity like all other human capacities is a product of the evolution of the human species. Man is a tool-making and instrument-using social animal who invented language to promote community of action. Language as an instrument of communication stimulated the development of rational, conceptual thought, which in turn influenced the formation of language. Language and thought are instrumental to action. They dissect reality into separate objects to facilitate communication and to promote community of action. The conceptual dissection of reality is a pragmatic device useful for action in everyday life and in the sciences. The conceptualizing intellect deals with reality as if it were three-dimensional, and it 'carves up' its spatialized reality into distinct, static entities in the interests of action. It translates growth, evolution, time and even reality itself, cinematographically, into a series of static 'frames', 'stills', points, or instants, in order to understand ongoing reality in terms of immobile units; and it always does so to promote the interests of action. Scientific knowledge, for example, is directed towards the prediction and control of events. The orientation of the senses and of abstracting intelligence is always practical. 'Our intelligence is the prolongation of our senses.'

Ongoing reality and becoming, however, are not adequately captured or known through the device of static conceptual dissection, according to Bergson. Analytic intellect moves around the object. It is only intuition which enters into its reality. Reality is cosmic and dynamic. Cosmic reality or being is a dynamic, creative activity which expresses itself in, and is at work within, all that is. The experience of our own duration in being is an intuition of the creative activity of the cosmic vital impulse (*élan vital*) at work within all things including ourselves. We participate in the intimate nature of this creative activity; and we grasp it intuitively in a lived experience of our own continuity in becoming, our own evolving reality, and our own free creative activity. 'To think intuitively is to think in duration.' Intuition yields knowledge of reality or being; and so it is of profound importance for philosophy. In the case of the self, intuition is an immersion in the indivisible and continuous flow of one's own consciousness; it is an immediate grasping of duration, ongoing being, and becoming. In the case of the ongoing reality of external objects, that is, things in the making, intuition is an activity 'by which one is transported into the interior of an object in order to coincide with what is unique and inexpressible about it'. This act demands concentration of thought. The insight attained is impermanent. The intellect, however, can suggest concrete ideas, comparisons, metaphors and images to evoke and suggest what cannot be expressed. Insight of this kind is not a private, solipsistic affair, limited to a favoured few; it is a general property or ability of all thinking minds.

The key to the understanding of cosmic evolution, Bergson says, is the cosmic vital impulse, or *élan vital*, a dynamic force which is at work within all things. It is this original impetus, operating in nature, that causes the variations and the emergence of new species. The explosive activity of the creative *élan vital* encounters the resistance of the recalcitrant forces of matter, and in overcoming this resistance develops new lines and new levels of evolution. This creative activity, in the course of its development, has split up into three concurrent but divergent tendencies, namely, the three tendencies towards plant life, instinctive life, and intelligent life. In plant life, the features which predominate are insensible growth and immobile reproduction. In animal life, mobility and (sense) consciousness predominate. In some animals, instinctive (intuitive) life is dominant, as in the case of certain insects. In other animals, animal intelligence in different degrees becomes the dominant characteristic. Instinct is a faculty of constructing and using organized instruments, such as feelers, which are integral parts of the body. Intelligence is the faculty of making and using unorganized instruments, or artificial tools, with a view to acting on the surrounding environment; it too is oriented to action. In man, reflective consciousness emerges, and it splits up at once into human intelligence, or intellect, which analyses and categorizes things in order to achieve active control of matter, and human intuition which is 'instinct become disinterested, conscious of itself, capable of reflecting on its object and of enlarging it indefinitely'. Intuition is oriented to life, and to free creative activity.

The vital impetus does not generate energy of its own, Bergson says, and its direction is not predetermined. It makes use of physical forces and 'engrafts on to the necessity of physical forces the largest possible amount of indetermination'. Thus, indetermination, contingency and creativity have always characterized the history of evolving life. The appearance of man was not predetermined. Creative evolution might have produced some other being with a similar self-reflective consciousness. Nevertheless, it now seems evident that it is man 'or some other being of like significance which is the purpose of the entire process of evolution'. The mechanistic and materialistic interpretation of cosmic evolution in terms of natural selection and random variations failed to explain what it was that had driven the earliest, simple, living things, well adapted to their environments, on to higher and more complex levels of organization, despite the more and more dangerous risks involved. It failed to explain ongoing creative activity. Its failure derives from the fact that the findings of the physical sciences must be supplemented by the findings of metaphysical intuition, namely, that there is a creative, original life impetus that pervades the whole evolutionary process. Evolution, in brief, is creative evolution, and the appearance of man, 'or some other being of like significance', is the *raison d'être* of life on the earth.

Bergson's concept of the cosmic *élan vital* at work within the evolving levels of nature bears some resemblance to Schelling's concept of 'the soul of the world', and to the (*animus* or) *anima mundi* of ancient philosophy. The fundamental insight at the heart of Bergson's philosophy bears an even stronger resemblance to Aristotle's insight concerning *energeia* or *entelecheia*, the purposive activity of being-in-a-state-of-becoming immanent within all things 'physical'.

5. Bergson on morality and religion. In his book on *The Two Sources of Morality and Religion*, Bergson points out that the difference between intellect and intuition is reflected in the two sources of morality and in the two sources of religion. The first source of morality is the pressure of social necessity or social obligation. The voice of duty is the voice of the individual's particular 'closed society', or tribe, or authoritarian social group. Social pressure is exercised on the members of the self-centred social group with a view to the maintenance of the closed society's cohesion and life. Spontaneity and freedom are reduced to a minimum. As in the case of the instinctive social life of bees and ants, the origin of this sense of obligation in man is infra-rational. Nature uses social obligation to secure society's cohesion and preservation. Conformity becomes the prime duty of the members of the group. As civilization progresses, the human intellect begins to distinguish between necessary rules of social conduct and traditional conventions which are no longer necessary or useful. Ethics arises when the intellect looks for reasons to support the necessary rules of conduct.

The second source of morality, Bergson says, is the human aspiration towards higher modes of life. It is the call of the good, the appeal of moral idealism. The ideal of universal love proclaimed by and embodied in the life of a great saintly, moral hero, draws human beings by way of attraction and appeal. This open and dynamic morality is of supra-rational origin, and it is different in kind from closed morality. It is characterized not by social pressure but by a creative vital impetus or 'emotion' within the will.

In the actually existing societies as we know them, the two types of morality, open and closed, coexist and mingle together and interpenetrate each other, according to Bergson. Human reason 'tends to introduce universality into the closed morality and obligation into the open morality'. This gives rise to tension. The intellect formulates necessary laws for all people. Intuition induces ideal aspirations and provides creative emotional power to embrace new modes of life. Human living is empowered to move from a consideration of one's immediate group to a consideration of the larger field of humanity. A future unification of all human society is capable of being achieved, then, either by the triumph of a closed world-imperialism or through man's free response to the highest ideals as mediated through graced and gifted persons.

The two types of religion, corresponding to the two types of morality, are static and dynamic religion. Static religion, the religion of social conformity, is ceremonial and disciplinary. It protects the individual, by means of myths, against the depressing thought of death; and it protects the social group against dissolution through its invocation of the continuing presence and authority of the tribal deities and ancestors. This infra-intellectual attitude survives in a weakened form in even technically advanced societies—in their war-prayers, for example.

Dynamic religion, on the other hand, is in its very essence mysticism. 'The ultimate end of mysticism is the establishment of a contact,... a partial coincidence, with the creative effort which life manifests.' The great mystic continues and prolongs the divine action in the world. The mystic is aware that there is an immanent creative energy operative in the world and he sees the nature of this creative energy as love. He sees the universe as 'a machine for the making of gods', a deified humanity, as transformed through divine love. In the actual religions of the world there is an intermingling of static and dynamic religion. Static religion may be regarded as the crystallization, brought about by a rational process of cooling, of what mysticism had poured hot into the human soul. The ideal is that static religion be transformed once again into dynamic religion.

Jacques Maritain in his book *Bergsonian Philosophy and Thomism* has pointed out that there are two 'Bergsonisms', one of fact and the other of intention. Bergson, in fact, denied concepts as ways to attain reality, and he affirmed the purely utilitarian value of conceptual knowledge as an instrument for the domination of matter. This aspect of Bergson's system did not escape from the shackles of Kantianism, scientism, idealism and positivism which Bergson regarded as enslaving an entire century of philosophical reflection. The other aspect of Bergson's system is the constant quest to keep in close contact with the reality of life and of being-in-becoming. This quest brought his system of thought near to several aspects of Aristotelian and Thomistic thought. At the close of the nineteenth century, Bergson appeared as the spearhead of the vitalist philosophy of life. The influence of his thought and vision was widely diffused. But no Bergsonian school of thought emerged among his disciples, and in recent years his general interpretation of the reality of duration and becoming has been overlooked and overshadowed by other currents of thought.

30 Nineteenth-century thought in other countries

1. Italian philosophers. In nineteenth-century Italy, Spain, Latin America, Russia, Scandinavia, and other countries of the time, the philosophical genius of these different nations was revealed primarily in those thinkers who tried to synthesize the dominant thought patterns of their epoch and the rigorous methodology of German, British or French thought. In Italy, for example, Francesco Soave (1743-1806) adapted to Italian problems and publicized the ideas of Locke, Condillac and the *idéologues*; G. Sigismondo Gerdil (1718-1802) found inspiration in the works of Malebranche; Gian Domenico Romagnosi (1761-1835) and Melchiorre Gioja (1767-1829) adapted Bentham's statistical study of social problems and the planning of social reforms; and thinkers in the second and third quarters of the century made an independent and critical use of the prevailing ideas of German thought. The Italian philosophers, in general, frequently regarded the problems of moral and political philosophy as the central issues of philosophical thought.

Pasquale Galluppi (1770-1864) rejected the 'scepticism' of Kant and the sensationalism of Condillac. He adopted a form of critical empiricism which resembled the (Scottish) common-sense realism as used by his friend Victor Cousin and the French eclectics. The starting point of philosophy, he said, is the immediate apprehension which the existing ego has of itself, in every act of consciousness. The synthetic activity of the understanding is simply a putting together again of the real elements already united together in nature. Our direct experience of obligation testifies that we are at one and the same time free and also obliged by the necessity of the moral good. Our innermost sense affirms our duty to follow as free human beings the dictates of the natural moral law.

Antonio Rosmini-Serbati (1797-1855) reacted strongly against all the 'mundane' forms of empiricism and idealism of his times, and formulated an original system of philosophy which his contemporaries regarded as evidently influenced by the thought of Maine de

Biran. The primary source from which he drew his inspiration, however, was the tradition of Augustinianism and Italian Platonism. Rosmini's system of philosophy is one which radiates outward from a basic intuition of reality as known in the light of the idea of being. The being or reality encountered directly in this intuition constitutes the knowing subject ontologically and existentially, and explains both its mode of acting and its manner of being.

The idea of being, Rosmini says, is present, at least implicitly, in the thinking of every other idea; and it alone can be thought without reference to any other idea. No knowledge is possible except through the idea of being. Nevertheless, knowledge of the actual world of determinate subsistent forms is attained only through intellectual perception, or in other words, through sentient perception infused by the idea of being. The unitary, sentient and intelligent subject lays hold sensibly of a reality in a concrete act of knowing which is simultaneously a sentient and intelligent knowing of an intellectually perceived entity. Conscious awareness of any reality is a synthesis of physical sensation and an intellectual intuition of the being given to the entity by the action of God. In this way the idea of the entity's being has entrance into the sensation, and the sensation has entrance into the idea of the entity's being. Sensation is the vehicle of the form or limitation in being; and human sensation is always infused by the idea of the constitutive being given to the entity. The entity is known not by intellectual vision, nor by pure sensation, but by intellectual perception in which both are related in a vital union.

Rosmini asserted that man has a sixth sense, or rather, a primary, fundamental sentiment or intuitive sense of his own immanent being. It is one's inner being that constitutes self and that draws into a subsistent unity the sensitive, intelligent and volitional aspects of the subject's complex life. This fundamental sentiment is a continuous experience of one's being or existing; and it involves a continuous relationship to a corporeal term, the body. It gives us consciousness of our corporeal existence, and it justifies the classical doctrine of man's composition of body and soul.

One finds in the idea of one's inner being, Rosmini says, the criterion not only of truth but also of moral goodness. The moral imperative can be formulated simply as: Be faithful to being. Follow the light of reason. 'Incline the will towards Being.' In other words, one must recognize in practice and in action what one has recognized speculatively about the integral unity of the whole self. One must strive to be the integral being that one knows one ought to be.

Self-realization is achieved through one's moral efforts to be true to one's being. If one is not faithful in action to what one knows one ought to be, then an intolerable hiatus arises between the speculative and the practical orders; and one experiences this intolerance psychologically in a depressing sense of remorse. If one's moral life is to be faithful to one's being, then one's life must necessarily be an examined life (*vita reflessa*). The most important pursuit in life is the realization of the developed person. This fundamental principle has profound importance for moral philosophy, political philosophy and the philosophy of education.

Fidelity to being, Rosmini says, demands that we give to each his due. The concepts of justice and personal development are basic concepts which affect every aspect of moral, social, political and educational theory. Human rights have their locus in the human being. The function of civil society is simply that of regulating the mode of the enjoyment and exercise of human rights. The function of a State government is that of achieving a balance between the *common good* of each of the members of society distributively considered and the *public good* of the social body considered analogically as operating like an organism. Political society does not have a substantive character. It does not originate rights. It is simply a principle regulating the modality of the enjoyment and exercise of human rights. School authority, similarly, and the process of education find their *raison d'être* in the growth and integration of the free realized person. The guiding principle of all educational effort is to be found in a respect for the human person as the vehicle of divine light and of God-given being. This became the guiding principle too of Rosmini's Institute of Charity, devoted to education and missions.

Vincenzo Gioberti (1801-52) was a priest, philosopher and statesman who was active in the movement for the unification of Italy. He held that the first science (*protologia*) or most fundamental form of knowledge is that of the *creative act* 'and of the ideal formula which expresses it completely'. All other sciences are secondary sciences (*deuterologia*) constructed by reflection on the basic intuition of creative Being creating created beings. The ideal formula which expresses this insight is, in brief, *Ens creat existentias*, 'Being is creating existents'. The first term of this formula, Being, expresses the absolute idea, the absolute substance, and the creative cause. The second term, the creating activity, expresses the type of relationship existing between the absolute and the contingent as relative to the absolute. The third term, existents, expresses the multiplicity of contingent substances, dependent causes and relative ideas. It expresses the fact that the products, namely all real and ideal existents, are simply created things created by creating Being.

Gioberti maintained that all the existents which are present to the human intellect manifest their whole being to the intellect, and they are known as beings by virtue of their being. The intellect, however, assimilates from them only the idea of being-in-itself. The being which is present to the mind, then, is being itself. From this datum, the mind coproduces or 'concreates' its object of thought in conjunction with the creative act which is giving being both to the datum and to the intellect itself. It is the *being* of the datum that is known by the mind. Being is the *primum datum* and the *primum notum*. However, our intellectual knowledge of objective being, while having transcendental extension, is nevertheless confused and indeterminate. It is an intuition of being which can know the particular existent only in conjunction with sensible experience of the existent, present as 'this' or 'that' to the senses. The existent is experienced sensibly as present, and known intellectually as being.

The ideal formula pertaining to creative activity, expressed in full, is, Gioberti says: 'Being is creating existents, and existents are returning to Being'. It is the task of philosophy in history to bring the whole of history to a clear awareness of itself as expressing the activity of Being. Being expresses itself in thought, in light, in life, in language, culture, politics, conscience, law, religion, in all that exists, and all that is active. Everything experienced is an imitation, a *mimesis*, standing-out, alienated from its source in Being. Everything known is known as a limited sharing, a *methexis*, or finite participation in absolute Being. It is the task of metaphysics, and of the moral and political philosopher, to show that all of history, language, religion, culture and society exists in a state of alienation until it is seen as grounded in Being. Human thought must return every existent to its ground in Being. The movement of all philosophic thought is a *palingenesis*, a returning of every existent thing to its original roots in Being. This viewpoint concerning the nature of reality is frequently classified as the viewpoint of Ontologism. It presents a philosophical outlook which can be readily compared and contrasted with the fundamental viewpoints of Malebranche, Vico, Bruno, Scotus Eriugena and Plotinus. It blends together in an original synthesis several of the insights of Italian Platonism, early medieval Neo-Platonism, high Scholasticism, and the *Scienza nuova* of Giambattista Vico.

Carlo Cattaneo (1801-69) can, with some justification, be called the first of the Italian *positivists*. He was a contemporary of Comte and shared the same sociological concerns as Comte. Like his teacher, G. D. Romagnosi, Cattaneo pursued a 'positive' method of empirical, phenomenological inquiry as related to the well-being of society. He contended that the experimental method, which unites scientists and philosophers, must supersede metaphysics, which divides them. The philosopher must work, like the scientist, to change the face of the earth for the good of mankind. All thought must have in view social action. Social psychology must replace individual psychology if the science of psychology is to be of benefit to mankind. This programme of social action was carried on into the twentieth century in the sociological works of Vilfredo Paredo (1848-1923).

Roberto Ardigò (1828-1920) was an Italian positivist (and non-practising priest) whose theories were influenced even more by the writings of Spencer than by those of Comte. He maintained that naturalistic, scientific knowledge is the only possible kind of knowledge. Each of the individual sciences has its own distinct object such as matter, life, mind, or society, as a special object for investigation and study. The science of philosophy concerns itself with 'phenomena of thought' such as logic, aesthetics, ethics, law and economics. It concerns itself with the ulterior region of indistinct matters lying outside the distinct specializations of the individual sciences; and, as such, it can reasonably be called 'peratology'. Philosophy studies that which is not yet known distinctly. It studies the incessant natural (evolutionary) process or passage from the indistinct to the distinct. It studies 'conscience', for example, as a sociological phenomenon which emerges from a progressive interiorization of repeated sanctions that anti-social acts bring into operation because of the customary reactions of society. Ardigò continued to defend his positivistic views in the university of Padua even when, in the closing years of the nineteenth century, idealism became the dominant form of philosophical thought in the majority of the Italian universities.

Bertrando Spaventa (1817-83) was an Italian Hegelian philosopher, intellectual liberalist and political journalist, who renounced his priestly office a few years after ordination. He made use of the Hegelian dialectic to propound a view which gave a prominent position to traditional Italian thought in the historical evolution of European philosophy. He maintained that the true disciples of Bruno, Vanini, Campanella, Vico and other great Italian thinkers were not the Counter-Reformation churchmen of the seventeenth and eighteenth centuries, but rather Spinoza, Kant, Fichte, Schelling and Hegel. Bruno prepared the way for Spinoza, and was the father of modern idealism. Campanella laid the foundations for modern rationalism and empiricism. Vico anticipated the achievements of later German thought. Modern thought, therefore, started in Italy; and it came to its final fruition in the philosophy of Galuppi, Rosmini and Gioberti. The fruit of all European speculation from Descartes to Kant is to be found in the thought of these great Italian thinkers, when rightly interpreted and understood. Spaventa termed this conception the 'circulation of Italian philosophy'. He regarded this theory as one which provided a philosophical foundation for the liberal, political thought of the Italian patriot. Absolute Being or Thought has gradually attained consciousness in the different stages of thinking which emerged in the minds of these positive, phenomenalist and idealist philosophers. Spaventa's views became very influential in Italy, and exercised a lifelong influence on the (Fascist) philosophy of 'actual idealism' of Giovanni Gentile, who was assassinated in Florence in 1944.

Antonio Labriola (1843-1904) taught Hegelianism in the university of Rome. He became a convinced Marxist in the last decade of the nineteenth century. His *Essays on the Materialistic Conception of History* (Paris, 1897) and *Socialism and Philosophy* (Rome, 1897) presented the first philosophical exposition and systematization of Marxist thought by a university professor of philosophy. He maintained that there is an objective dialectical process immanent in the movement of history. History progresses by contradictions; and socialism is an inevitable product of the current contradictory tensions in capitalist society. He regarded the study of historical materialism as offering an objective, scientific method of historical research similar to the methodic research of Charles Darwin. He advocated an inflexible adherence to scientific, orthodox, Marxist method. Labriola and his followers have exercised an extensive influence on academic circles in Italy down through the twentieth century.

In the second half of the nineteenth century in Italy, a new interest arose in the original writings of the Scholastics of the high Middle Ages; and a neo-Scholastic movement was launched. Canon Vincenzo Buzzetti of Piacenza (d.1824) advocated the study of the original sources of medieval literature, art and thought. The new interest grew into a movement mainly through the research work of a group of Jesuit scholastics, Serafino Sordi (d.1865), Domenico Sordi (d.1870), Matthew Liberatore (d.1872), Giuseppe Pecci (the brother of the future Leo XIII), S. Tongiorgi (d.1865), D. Palmieri (d.1909), and J. Cornoldi (d.1892). Other priminent figures in the movement were Canon G. Sanseverino (d.1865), Cardinal T. Zigliara (d.1893), the

Spanish Cardinal Z. Gonzalez (d.1894) and two German scholars, J. Kleutgen (1811-83) and Albert Stöckl (1832-95). The encouraging encyclicals of Pope Leo XIII gave added impetus to the movement, and it spread to all countries of the world at the turn of the nineteenth and twentieth centuries (see Chapter 36, section 4 below).

2. Philosophy in Spain. In Spain, the sixteenth to eighteenth centuries came to be known as the golden age of Spanish Scholasticism. Suárez's presentation of Thomism flourished in philosophy and theology. The doctrine of divine *praemotio physica* of all secondary causes was taught in all Thomist circles. Thomism was proclaimed as representing the *philosophia perennis* of the West, and recent movements of British, French and German thought were ignored and dismissed as products of Ockhamism and other *subtilitates anglicanae*. Spanish philosophy chose to reign in splendid and haughty isolation from other movements of European thought.

In the nineteenth century, *Jaime Balmes* (1810-48), a Catalan priest and journalist, was distressed at the lack of philosophical discussion in Spain. In his popular work on logic *El criterio*, and his *Fundamental Philosophy* (four volumes), he presented an eclectic system which shows the influence of Descartes and several of the 'moderns', even though he extols the works of Aquinas above all others. He recognized the importance of the epistemological or critical problem, and suggested, by way of solution, a form of common-sense intuitionist philosophy, comparable to that of Vives and Thomas Reid. He wrote a four-volume work also on *Protestantism Compared with Catholicism in Their Relations with European Civilization* (1842-44) in which he argued that there had been a long tradition of culture founded on religious unity, which the Protestant Reformers had betrayed, and to which Catholic Spain had remained loyal. Balmes showed an acquaintance with 'modern' thought in his determined opposition to its errors.

In 1843, the new university of Madrid named a doctor of canon law, *Julián Sanz del Río* (1814-69), to be professor of the history of philosophy. He was sent first, however, to Germany to study the latest European currents of thought. At Heidelberg, del Río met Hermann von Leonhardi and some other disciples of an obscure pantheistic philosopher, Karl C. F. Krause, who had died in 1832. Del Río became fascinated by the mystical and spiritualistic theories of Krause, and he travelled to Brussels to interview Heinrich Ahrens and other Krausian disciples. He quickly learned all he could about the life and thought of Karl Krause.

Krause had come under the influence of Fichte and Schelling at Jena. In his book on *The Archetype of Humanity* Krause claimed that he was the true spiritual successor of Immanuel Kant. He called his general theory 'Panentheism'. God or Absolute Being is one with the world even though not coterminous with it or exhausted by it; the relationship is that of whole and part. Divine Reason is organically distributed throughout the realm of individual human minds. Historical man has now passed through the stages of boyhood and youth, and is on the threshold of maturity. As humanity comes of age, world citizenship, philanthropy, and tolerance become the human norm and rule. The unification of all mankind is at hand.

Del Río fell under the spell of a form of thought which attracted little attention in Germany. He returned to Spain, and, as Minister of Culture, spread the philosophy of 'Krausism' in lectures and books which presented free adaptations of the original works of Krause. He translated into Spanish Krause's work on the archetype (or prototype) of humanity, and published it in Madrid in 1860. Del Río was condemned by the traditionalists in Church and State, and was dismissed from the university in 1868, but Krausism continued to flourish in Spain as a form of rationalist cult for fifty years afterwards.

Krause himself had joined the Freemasons in 1805 and used the movement to propagate his ideal of a world society. The Spanish Krausists formed into a similar brotherhood which engendered boundless confidence in the perfectibility of man and in the coming of a better world. It allied itself in politics with the liberal Catholic movement for social progress and greater freedom of expression. It advocated enlightened rationalist religion instead of credulous, dogmatic religion. It inspired enthusiasm and optimism rather than philosophical discussion. It ceased to be an active movement, however, in the second decade of the twentieth century, when other social movements provided more definite and specific programmes for social action, and when Spain began to have a wider acquaintance with contemporary European thought.

3. Latin America. In Latin America, as in Spain and Portugal, Scholastic philosophy reigned unchallenged in the first quarter of the nineteenth century. In the second and third decades of the century, however, the different nations attained independence, and the new social conditions gave rise to an interest in the writings of the French Enlightenment, and to an interest in the works of the *idéologues*, the eclectics and the positivists. The philosophers of Latin America adapted the ideas of these French thinkers in their reflections on themes such as liberty, freedom, intuition, values, change, and dynamic action in which they were specially interested.

Alejandro Deusta (1849-1945), of Peru, was influenced at first by the philosophy of Karl Krause, and later by the philosophy of Henri Bergson. He was specially interested in the liberty and spontaneity which is conciliated with sensation and emotion through the mediation of an ideal order created by the imagination. Art is the graceful expression of this 'conciliation imaged by the artist and translated by means of adequate or expressive forms'. Dynamic liberty is, above all, creativity and novelty. Realized in order, it manifests itself as grace. It is sovereign and free from all external norms in the aesthetic domain. Aesthetic value is 'the value of values', according to Deusta. Most of his writings were done after his retirement from San Marcos University because of age, and they belong to the philosophy of the twentieth century.

Raimundo de Farias Brito (1862-1917), of Brazil, found intellectual stimulation in the works of Schopenhauer, and later in the works of Bergson and the French spiritualists. He held that metaphysics and religion can assist man to withstand the constant threats of suffering, moral disintegration, social anarchy, and despair. Modern philosophy, however, with its tendency to phenomenalism and scepticism, seems incapable of providing the necessary truth and knowledge that will assist man to confront his crisis. Farias Brito turned at first, in *The Finality of the World* (1895), to a philosophy of idealistic monism and a correlated naturalistic form of religion, for sustaining truth and conviction. Later, under the influence of French spiritualism, he formulated his main system of thought, *Philosophy of Spirit (espírito)* (1912-14). In this work, he pointed out that in our experience of our existence we have an experiential knowledge of existential reality; we know what it is 'to be', and we are conscious of ourselves as knowing it. Conscious introspection reveals both the data of consciousness, and also consciousness itself, as constituting existential reality. Man is understood to be essentially conscious spirit; and this truth leads on logically to the postulation of ultimate transcendent (or divine) spirit.

Enrique J. Varona y Pera (1849-1933) of Havana, Cuba, was a philosopher and statesman who dominated Cuban intellectual life in the last quarter of the nineteenth and the opening decades of the twentieth century. As a positivist and determinist he denied that man is free; and as a revolutionary he fought for the political freedom and cultural independence of Cuba. He adapted the main trends of French positivism and British empiricism to the political, social and cultural life of his country and his times. He said that, though man is not free, a developed intelligence enables man to understand, tame and direct nature's causal determination; and this is equivalent to overcoming nature and its determination. The human organism, however, is dependent on its social environment in a way similar to the dependence of the biological organism on its natural environment. In this light, human morality is seen as conformity with social solidarity. Man is sociable and through his being sociable he becomes moral. The conscious adaptation and accommodation of the individual to the social milieu gives rise to that form of individual behaviour which is called moral behaviour. Morality, then, is simply conformity with social solidarity. Varona was Secretary of Public Instruction in Cuba at the close of the century, and, later, Vice-President of Cuba from 1913 to 1917.

José Ingenieros (1877-1925), of Buenos Aires, Argentina, was a positivist philosopher who had studied medicine and psychiatry, and had lived for some years in Germany and Switzerland. He maintained, like the Italian positivist Roberto Ardigò, that even though naturalistic scientific knowledge is the only possible kind of certain knowledge, metaphysics has as a valuable area of study those 'inexperiential' matters pertaining to the natural world that the natural limitations of the senses and of measurement techniques exclude at present from their own areas of immediate concern. Thus metaphysics concerns itself with the problems of metabiology, metacosmology and metapsychology. It formulates revisable hypotheses and theories concerning, for example, the origin of life, the possibility of life on other planets, and the purpose of life. It studies the inspiring ideals and values formulated by the creative imagination of outstanding, idealistic men, and conserved in the minds of the mediocre mass of mankind. These values and ideals are always relative to the age. They are a challenge to a lively, vigorous philosophy. They are hypotheses for the perfecting of human life; and they are tested in the tensions of the evolutionary process of life.

In the writings of the twentieth-century Latin American philosophers Antonio Caso and J. Vasconcelos of Mexico, Alejandro Korn and F. Romero of Argentina, E. Molina Garmendia of Chile, C. Vaz Ferreira of Uruguay, and Miguel Reale of Brazil, one finds a common concern and continued interest in the same themes of human freedom, dynamic action, liberation, intuition, order, spontaneity, change, and ideal heroic values as in the writings of the philosophers of the nineteenth century.

4. Philosophy in Russia. In Russia, during the eighteenth and nineteenth centuries, the authorities of Church and State maintained strict control over the orthodox teachings of the Russian universities and theological seminaries. With few exceptions, critical independent thinkers earned their livelihood in the world outside the schools and universities. They were a non-academic intelligentsia who wrote with a passionate and often immoderate intensity on social, political, literary, cultural and philosophical topics, in an atmosphere charged with personal risk to all who hoped to change the established order. They regarded themselves as concerned not with doctrinal or theoretical truth *(istina)* but with what is right-and-just *(pravda,* justice-truth). They sought practical justice in individual and social life.

The Russian Tsar (Czar) Peter the Great acquainted himself with Western methods to modernize his country. He opened the port and capital of St Petersburg (now Leningrad) as a 'window upon Europe'. Catherine II (1762-96) invited Diderot to the Petersburg court, and announced that she desired to rule 'rationally' as a 'benevolent despot' in the spirit of the Enlightenment. The works of Voltaire and the Encyclopedists, and their attitudes of rationalism and scepticism, enjoyed widespread popularity. After Napoleon's invasion of Russia, Russian interest in Western values and ideas turned towards Germany. The writings of Schelling, Kant, Fichte and Hegel were enthusiastically circulated, often in manuscript translations because of Tsarist censorship. The teaching of philosophy and its liberal ideas was forbidden after the 'Decembrist' rising of constitutionalists in 1825; and for fifty years afterwards students were initiated into philosophy privately in informal discussion circles. In these discussion circles they turned in a special way to Hegelianism and to the philosophy of the French social reformers.

Alexander N. Radishchev (1749-1802) spent five years at the university of Leipzig in Germany, where he read widely in current French philosophy. On returning to Russia he used the social contract theory and the principles of natural law to justify a severe critique of serfdom, autocracy, censorship and Russian social institutions. He combined metaphysical speculation on man and the immortality of the soul with moral and social criticism of man's inhumanity to man. He aroused the anger of the Russian nobility, and was exiled to Siberia. His combination of metaphysical reflection and pioneering social criticism provided an influential precedent for several Russian philosophers and social critics who followed him.

Several Russian thinkers in the early part of the nineteenth century such as A. S. Khomyakov (1804-60) and I. V. Kireyevski (1806-56) were religiously Orthodox and politically conservative Slavophiles. They regarded Western Europe as having abandoned its heritage of Christian wisdom and its 'Golden Age' reconciliation of faith and reason. Western thought had abandoned itself to the excesses of egoistic individualism and to a soul-destroying quest for comfort and security. It had fragmented man because of its proud addiction to one-sided, sceptical rationalism. They saw Holy Russia as a potential saviour of Christian civilization, destined to redress the human tragedy that had overtaken the spiritual life of the West.

Other thinkers in the early part of the nineteenth century, however, insisted that if Russia wished to modernize its medieval economy and feudal structures, and if it wished to acknowledge the freedom and dignity of the human individual, then it would have to break out of its isolation and take its rightful place in the family of civilized nations. Several in this group were students of Hegelianism who, in time, either abandoned Hegelian thought or moved instead towards Feuerbach and the Hegelian left.

V. G. Belinski (1811-48), in his Hegelian period, spoke of the State as sacred, and of society as superior to the individual. In 1841 however he turned from Absolute Idealism to the writings of the French socialists and developed a philosophy of ethical personalism. *A. I. Herzen* (1812-70) similarly moved away from Hegelian impersonalism and 'bourgeois' socialism. He admired the attitude of respect for the human person which he said he found in the Russian peasant and the village commune.

Mikhail Bakunin (1814-76) used the Hegelian dialectic to turn Proudhon's theory of mutualism into a doctrine of 'dialectical nihilism'. He advocated violent revolution as a means to establishing collectivist anarchism. Bakunin, N. G. Chernyshevski (d.1889), D. I. Pisarev (d.1886) and others professed themselves to be radical nihilists who sought the total annihilation of the existing economic, political, cultural, religious, social order. The necessary means, however drastic and violent, would be justified by the 'good' end of revolution and social transformation of every aspect of society. They saw their mission as that of the Titans shaking the mountains of age-old evil. 'The urge to destroy is also a creative urge', Bakunin asserted. 'Let us put our trust in the eternal spirit which destroys and annihilates only because it is the unsearchable and eternally creative source of all life.' Bakunin was sent to exile in Siberia, but escaped, through Japan and the United States, to Western Europe, where he joined the International Workingmen's Association and challenged the power and policies of Karl Marx.

The recurrent emphasis in Russian literature on the human needs and ideals of the common people *(narod)* gave rise in the 1870s to the Populist phase of Russian thought. *P. L. Lavrov* (1823-1900) and *N. K. Mikhailovski* (1842-1904) regarded the goal of history as the physical, moral and intellectual development of the individual. They maintained that 'critically thinking individuals' who have already attained development of this kind owe a debt to the common people whose toil has given these individuals the leisure and resources needed for self-cultivation. The Populists developed an agrarian socialist programme which stressed the village commune as the foundation of a new socialist order which would bypass the evils of capitalism. Modern industrial society, with its division of labour, ignores all moral evaluations and disregards the feelings and aims of the ordinary common man. It stunts the growth of the individual. The peasant village commune, by way of contract, fosters co-operation rather than industrial competition. Every autonomous moral individual must be allowed to rely on his own active energies for the promotion of his moral ideals. In this way alone can right-and-just truth *(pravda)* be actualized in historical life. Failure to act in the presence of the suppression of another's human growth is unjust and immoral. The intelligentsia must speak out on behalf of the fundamental needs and the legitimate aspirations of the common man. This view was supported by B. N. Chicherin (1828-1904), mayor of Moscow, and professor at the university. Man is an end in himself, a 'bearer of the Absolute'; he must not be 'treated as a mere instrument'. It is 'not society, but individuals that think, feel and desire'. It is the individual who is the 'foundation stone of the entire social edifice'. It is 'a monstrous notion' that society is some kind of high organism, an 'all-devouring Moloch', whose function is 'to make mankind happy by putting it in chains'.

Philosophical themes of a similar kind were presented dramatically in some of the great Russian novels and literary dramas of the nineteenth century. *Fëdor Dostoyevsky* (1821-81) presented a vivid dramatization of the conflict of freedom and the totalitarian order in *The Brothers Karamazov* (1879-80) and other novels. In *The Devils* (or *The Possessed*; 1871-72) he called attention to the totalitarian tendencies of the Russian radicals, and warned Russia of the dangers inherent in the use of a 'utilitarian' calculus whose principles would be used to justify the excesses of inhuman totalitarianism. The dignity and value of human beings, including those who are criminals and prisoners, is absolute and inviolable. The moral quality of human actions is not judged according to a calculus of happy consequences. Russia has a historic mission to bring to the West its message of salvation-in-suffering. *Leo Tolstoy* (1829-1910) extolled the virtues of voluntary poverty, manual labour, and ascetic self-discipline. He was revered by his compatriots as the 'living conscience' of Russia. He maintained that social institutions can be improved only through the reformation of men's hearts. The human heart must be freed from subjection to the law of violence and brought under the reign of the law of *agape*, the law of love. The evil in social institutions arises from the evil in the human heart. It is the heart that must be reformed.

In the universities, the professors of philosophy were, in general, expositors of previous systems of thought rather than critical, independent thinkers. *Vladimir Solovyov* (1853-1900) was a professional philosopher who was an exception to this general trend. He left the academic world in 1881, however, because of the restrictive controls of government and university authorities over philosophical views propounded in the universities. Solovyov was influenced by the later religious thought of Schelling. His theosophical speculation and his profoundly religious thought show a marked affinity of spirit with that of Schelling. He was an original thinker, however, and not a disciple of anyone. He attempted to make an 'organic synthesis of religion, philosophy and science in the interests of the integral life'. His philosophy of religion exercised a lasting influence on almost all of the leading Russian religious thinkers of the twentieth century.

5. Poland. In Poland, the Scholasticism of the Counter-Reformation was the dominant form of philosophy in the seventeenth century and in the first half of the eighteenth century. This resurgent form of Scholasticism was taught mainly in the schools and colleges staffed by the Jesuits.

In the later part of the eighteenth century and the beginning of the nineteenth century (during which time Poland, partitioned between three empires, no longer existed as a country), the works of Wolff, Bacon, Locke, Condillac, the physiocrats, the Encyclopedists, the Scottish philosophy of common sense, and Kant were translated into Polish and popularized by writers of the Polish Enlightenment. It was an age of lively polemics in political and social thought which gave rise to two unsuccessful uprisings in 1830 and 1863, and also to a prophetic philosophy of history which was called Polish Messianism.

The Messianist doctrine, in general, announced the advent of a new epoch of freedom and justice for all in a commonwealth of free people.

Philosophy, animated by the spirit of the Polish nation, was regarded as having a special messianic role in the task of changing and transforming society. Polish philosophy was said to have a messianic mission to change the world and not just interpret it. This doctrine was frequently combined with various adaptations of Hegelian dialectic, or with different forms of theistic and personalistic metaphysics. These, in turn, gave rise to a variety of suggested methods, specific aims and prophetic forecasts concerning the new epoch which was about to dawn.

Josef M. Hoene-Wroński (1778-1853) proclaimed that a scientific unification of human knowledge would bring about a universal rule of reason and a rational transformation of world-society. August Cieszkowski (1814-94) developed a religiously inspired modification of Hegelianism which emphasized practical action as leading to the imminent 'fulfilment of philosophy'. The poets J. Słowacki (d.1849), Z. Krasiński (d.1859), and A. Mickiewicz (d.1855) transformed Messianism into a national gospel-proclamation of moral regeneration.

Polish 'positivism' replaced Polish Messianism after the second uprising of 1863. The emphasis of the positivistic social reformers was placed on practical economic improvement, popular education, and the gradual reconstruction of society. In this 'positivist' phase of social reform, J. Ochorowicz (1850-1917) and other positivists were influenced mainly by the works of Comte and J. S. Mill.

At the turn of the century, *Kazimierz Twardowski* (1866-1938) made important contributions to epistemology, philosophical anthropology and the philosophy of science, which influenced several later trends of twentieth-century Polish and European philosophy. Twardowski studied philosophy under Franz Brentano in the university of Vienna, and was appointed professor of philosophy at the university of Lwów in 1895. He initiated regular meetings of philosophers in Poland, and encouraged among the members a common acceptance of rigorous standards of professional excellence. He became the founder of the Polish school of logicians which was to play a prominent role in the development of mathematical logic. Twardowski defended introspection or 'psychological investigation' as a source of knowledge, and he spoke of 'descriptive psychology' as the basic philosophical science. He introduced a sharp distinction between the (mental) *content* of the mental act and the (non-mental) *object* of the same act. His general theory concerning objects of thought anticipated the theories of the realist branch of twentieth-century phenomenology, and the later trends of Husserl's transcendental idealism. Twardowski's reflections influenced Meinong, Husserl and the Viennese conceptual analysts, and through them much of early twentieth-century philosophy.

6. Scandinavian philosophers. Scandinavian or Nordic philosophy, in Sweden, Finland, Norway and Denmark, in general reflected the dominant trends of 'modern' philosophy. Towards the end of the seventeenth century, Cartesian philosophy was the dominant form of thought in all the Nordic universities. In the eighteenth century, Locke, Hume and Kant influenced the philosophical trends of thought. This gave way in the nineteenth century to the influence of Schelling, Hegel and German idealism. Søren Kierkegaard of Denmark (see above, Chapter 25) propounded a different, intensely personal philosophy, but this exercised little influence on nineteenth-century Nordic thought. Kierkegaard's writings influenced the religious commitment of Harald Höffding and others, but his recognition as a major philosopher came with his 'rediscovery' by German philosophers in the first decades of the twentieth century.

Niels Treschow (1751-1833) was Norway's first professor of philosophy at the new university of Oslo (1813). He defended a monistic form of philosophy which was strongly influenced by Spinoza and Leibniz. The Absolute One, or God, produces the manifold of evolving individuals and 'stands in the same relation to the manifold produced by it as does our mind to its thoughts, feelings and decisions'. God is transcendent, eternal and independent, above all evolving things, while also immanent within them. His nature is manifest in our consciousness, which 'pictures' him. The natural history of man is part of the history of the whole manifold of evolving nature produced by the One. Man has developed and evolved gradually from some pre-human individual in which the specifically human dispositions potentially inhered. Each man is the one concrete individual that he is. His so-called 'body and soul' are simply two aspects of his individual reality seen from the different viewpoints of the inner and the outer sense. The individual can be fully grasped only by the One, since he alone grasps the idea which expresses all the states of the evolving individual. Treschow had to give up his chair after one year in Oslo university to accept a post in government service. Hegelianism was introduced into the university shortly afterwards by Martin Möller (1794-1838).

Henrik Steffens (1773-1845), who was of Danish and German descent, was born in Norway. He studied natural philosophy under Friedrich Schelling at Jena, and lectured on natural philosophy and anthropology at Halle, Breslau and Berlin. In his *Contributions to the Inner Natural History of the Earth* (1801) he introduced a form of speculative philosophy which was strongly influenced by the pantheistic thought of Spinoza and by the world-soul hypothesis of Schelling. Nature is creative, and the historical development of nature from inorganic to animate, organic forms is governed by a divine purpose. The summit of the natural creative process is the production of free individual human personality or spirit.

Christopher Jacob Boström (1797-1866), of Uppsala university, like Hegel, dominated Swedish intellectual life throughout the entire nineteenth century. Boström, who is often referred to as Sweden's Plato, was an original thinker, a spiritualistic 'rational idealist', whose philosophy was influenced by the works of Plato, Leibniz, Berkeley, Schelling and Hegel. He argued that being is immaterial, and that nothing but minds and their perceptions exists. Any thought or assertion pertaining to reality implies a relation between consciousness and its data. The only feature which consciousness and the objects of consciousness have in common, as a basis for a relationship between the two, can be consciousness alone. The object of consciousness is simply a feature of consciousness. Conscious reality is real consciousness. Reality and consciousness are one.

Particular minds and particular perceptions, Boström says, are forms of consciousness or reality. Conscious reality or self-consciousness itself can be likened to a 'substance or stuff of which everything ultimately consists'. The spatio-temporal world of a particular person's experience is simply the way in which the different forms (or 'ideas') of reality, the different entities-in-themselves, appear to that person, because of the imperfection of his particular perceptive faculty. The different entities-in-themselves, that is, the different forms (or 'ideas') of being, which underlie the appearances, are limited forms of reality itself, which is nonspatial and nontemporal. They are different 'ideas' of reality that form a series which contains a maximal 'idea', God. (Boström uses the word 'idea' in Plato's sense, as meaning a distinct form of being.) Each of the limited forms or units of being contains within itself the preceding forms (from which it has evolved), and does not contain or perceive the succeeding forms. Each limited 'idea' perceives the whole system imperfectly. Infinite real consciousness alone has a perfect perception of the whole system; and infinite consciousness (God) does not conceive of reality through the medium of space and time but as it really is, a system of units or forms of being. The understanding of this 'ideal' world of being is the goal of human thought. In Swedish academic circles in the latter half of the nineteenth century, Boströmianism and Hegelianism reigned without serious challenge from any other school of thought.

Harald Höffding (1843-1931), of Copenhagen, Denmark, abandoned Christianity as a student after reading Kierkegaard's works. He became an agnostic. In 1868 and 1869, during a period spent in Paris, he studied the works of Comte, Spencer and the French and English positivists. These works aroused in him a lasting interest in the philosophical outlook of liberal humanists. He became convinced that human welfare and progress were inseparably connected with the progress of scientific knowledge. In his *Outlines of Psychology* (1881) he placed special emphasis on the dynamic aspect of psychology, that is, on the will, conation, endeavour, urge, need, demand and desire. His *Ethics* (1887), which is a system of welfare ethics, presented the utilitarian principle, of the greatest happiness of the greatest number, as the fundamental value. His *Philosophy of Religion* (1901) claimed that the foundation of all religious feeling is the desire to believe in the existence of values. He published a *History of Modern Philosophy* (2 volumes, 1894-95) in which he presented the epistemology of Spinoza, Hume and Kant in a particularly favourable light. Fifteen years later he propounded his own theory of knowledge in *Human Thought: Its Forms and Problems* (1910). He spoke of his theory as that of 'critical monism'. He maintained that the world of reality as a whole is unknowable; however, we may believe that conscious experience and its unity provide us with data that give us some knowledge of the ideal aspect of reality.

Höffding's works were translated into several languages and became popular textbooks in the different branches of philosophy. His reputation was world-wide in the opening decades of the twentieth century. In Denmark he was regarded as the leading Danish thinker, and he was honoured with many outstanding awards. As a result of his work, Danish philosophy became less dependent on German philosophy, and Danish thinkers began to adapt prominent elements of French and English thought to the Danish philosophical trends of the twentieth century.

PART FIVE

CONTEMPORARY PHILOSOPHY

31 Positivism and idealism: continuity and change

1. 'Modern' philosophy and contemporary philosophy
2. Idealism   3. Life-philosophy   4. Neo-positivism

1. 'Modern' philosophy and contemporary philosophy. Francis Bacon and René Descartes are traditionally regarded as the fathers of 'modern' philosophy; and Immanuel Kant is similarly regarded as the apogee of 'modern' thought. Bacon and Descartes saw themselves as breaking away from the decadent Scholastic thought-patterns of the fifteenth and sixteenth centuries and making a new start in a new form of philosophy, free from theological presuppositions and free from the cluttering accretions of late medieval Scholastic tradition. Philosophers of the period 1600 to 1900 and up to the First World War (1914-18) were content to regard themselves as *modern* philosophers. Philosophers of more recent times, however, wish to differentiate their thought from that of the *modern* period; and they regard contemporary philosophical investigation as attempting to transcend the subjectivist thought-patterns of the Age of Reason and the Age of Idealism. They speak of twentieth-century philosophy not as modern philosophy but rather as contemporary philosophy.

Contemporary thought may be said to be at one in its rejection of all forms of subjective idealism. It investigates definite problems of our own era and takes account of certain novel attitudes and stances. It is pluralist, pointing out the differences in the various levels of being, and emphasizing the plurality of self-subsistent beings. It is realist, actualist, and personalist. The human person and human activity are, in the main, the centre of philosophical interest. This does not imply, however, that contemporary philosophy is one single school of thought or a single distinctive tendency. There are several different movements: empiricist, linguistic, idealist, vitalist, phenomenological, existentialist and metaphysical. For this reason present-day philosophy is rich, lively, and variegated.

The emphasis on novelty and change must not be allowed, however, to become an overemphasis on novelty to the exclusion of continuity in thought between so-called modern philosophy and contemporary philosophy. Contemporary idealists and neo-positivists present a developed and updated form of the idealism and positivism of the eighteenth and nineteenth centuries. Existentialist thought applies to contemporary times several themes found in Kierkegaard's works, which were written in the 1840s. The life-philosophy of Henri Bergson spans several decades of both the modern and the contemporary periods. There is significant change and novelty, but there are also many strands of continuity.

2. Idealism. The first quarter of the twentieth century was a time of strenuous philosophical activity. It was a transitional period in which idealist and empiricist movements of thought, with roots in the previous century, continued to grow alongside more contemporary tendencies. British and American idealism continued to exercise a dominant role in Anglo-Saxon thought during the lifetimes of Josiah Royce (d. 1916), George H. Howison (d. 1916), Francis H. Bradley (d. 1924), Bernard Bosanquet (d. 1923), and John M. McTaggart (d. 1925). At the same time, however, other points of view opposed to idealism were being vigorously developed. Moore, Russell, Wittgenstein, the new realists, and the critical realists revolted against idealism; and, in the second quarter of the twentieth century idealism had ceased to be an influential movement in British and American life. In Germany, France and Italy, however, idealism continued to be an influential philosophical movement until the Second World War (1939-45), when it apparently became a thing of the past. Idealism and neo-Kantianism gave way either to phenomenological, existentialistic and metaphysical schools of thought, or to philosophical concerns about modern logic, the philosophy of language, and the methodology of science.

Twentieth-century idealists, like their nineteenth-century counterparts, were convinced that mind or spirit is something utterly different from matter and cannot be reduced to it. They maintained that knowledge is not merely a passive reception of images. It is not simply a mirror which reflects what is there. Kant had seen that the mind approaches the world with concepts and presuppositions of its own. Knowledge is a spontaneous free activity of synthesizing and interpreting. Mind, spirit, knowledge and freedom are fundamental realities which cannot be explained in terms of reductive materialism and mechanistic determinism. Philosophical idealism, then, is not opposed to realism but is radically opposed to materialistic naturalism. Mind and spiritual values have not simply emerged from material things and processes, and they are not reducible to them. They are fundamental realities in their own right and they take first place in the total realm of being.

Benedetto Croce (1866-1952), an Italian philosopher and prolific writer who lived most of his life in Naples, applied the fundamental tenets of his *Filosofia dello Spirito* ('philosophy of spirit'), in particular, to the spheres of aesthetics, literature, logic, economics, ethics and cultural history. No reality exists apart from the spirit, according to Croce. All individuals are only transitory 'moments' or elements of one reality whose different 'moments' are comprehended within the world, the unity of spirit. Subject and object, singular and universal, theory and practice, philosophy and history, are united within the world, which is the evolutionary manifestation of the pure Absolute, the mysterious goal which the cosmos has not yet reached.

Croce's background and interests were predominantly literary. He thought of aesthetics mainly in terms of literary and poetic products, uniquely individual entities, created in the universal, conceptual medium of language, spiritual expression. In 1903 he founded the literary and intellectual journal *La critica*, for which he himself wrote many articles. In 1904 he became an editorial adviser to the publishers Laterza of Bari, through whom he exercised an important influence for many years on the literary and academic world.

Croce's philosophy, like that of Kant, is a philosophy of rationalistic conceptualism. It stressed the universality and necessity of conceptual knowledge; but, by way of contrast with the (Scholastic) theory of abstraction, it finds the foundation of this necessity in the *a priori* functions of the mind rather than in things and their essences or natures. It asserts that the universal has existence only in the concept, and it denies that there is anything at all in reality that corresponds to universal concepts. Universal concepts are simply instruments for the logical division and ordering of reality. Croce asserted that there are only two ways of knowing, namely, the intuitive or aesthetic way and the conceptual or logical way of knowing. The first way pertains to the senses and has the singular individual thing as its object. The second way is rational and refers to universals; its sole function is to link together sensuous intuitions of the eternal stream of events.

There are four modes or ways in which the activity of spirit manifests itself, according to Croce. Aesthetic activity is theoretical activity with reference to singulars; logical activity refers to universals. Economic activity is practical activity with reference to individual aims; moral activity refers to the universal good. Philosophy is to be divided then into four sections which correspond with these four modes of the appearance of spiritual reality.

Aesthetics is the science of sensuous intuitive experience, the primitive nonconceptual form of cognitive experience. It is the science of lyrical creative expression, communicating cosmic, non-conceptual emotions and moods. It is the activity of the spirit revealing itself in personal experience and in the evolving history of the human spirit.

Logic is the science of pure judgement or pure synthesis of concept and intuition, two manifestations of one and the same spirit. Reality is spiritual. The real is the logical, the rational, the truly 'scientific', the historical. Knowledge is historical knowledge, based on historical, perceptual judgements. Logic is the transcendental pure critique of the natural sciences. The natural sciences, metaphysics and religion are of interest only in so far as they are steps, or 'moments' of the spirit, by which the spirit ascends towards true science, the philosophy of the spirit. This philosophy is not separated from the evolving history of the human spirit. It is concrete and historical. History is identical with philosophy and philosophy with history. Reason is historical reason.

Economic volition, the primitive form of practical activity, arises from the blind urge of organic life or vitality. It involves theoretical activity. The calculation of economic utility is a rational process and it involves historical judgement. Economic action is the first, primitive form of action. It aims at what is useful, economically and politically. Moral activity is distinguished from it by aiming at the whole, the universal good. It overrides private inclinations and orders man towards a universal and spiritual end. In moral activity, economic judgements and moral judgements, while distinct, are combined in a higher synthesis within the realm of the spirit. It is a synthesis which brings with it a sense of 'harmony with the Universe'. Moral activity is that superior form of human activity in which the spirit exhibits spontaneity, self-possession and individual uniqueness. Moral awareness is the final all-embracing awareness of the spirit in its wholeness, that awareness of spirit which transforms philosophy into the Philosophy of Spirit.

Léon Brunschvicg (1869-1944), who held a professorship at the Sorbonne in Paris, declared like Kant that the exterior world is unknowable and that cultural history and the mathematical sciences can be understood only in terms of the creative role of thought or spirit. He sought then, through philosophical inquiry, to grasp the mind's activity in the history of mathematics, metaphysics and science. Progress in science and in moral insight throughout history has always consisted of a questioning of the apodictic truth of the classical, traditional principles, and a bringing to birth of novel and unforeseeable relations through the inventiveness and creativity of the mind. The mind is creative. Any doctrine of pure empiricism is shown to be utterly inadequate in the light of the brilliant inventiveness and spontaneous creativity of the intelligent scientist. The mind or spirit creates new forms; and in so doing it comes to know itself in and through its own creation.

In his doctoral thesis *The Modality of Judgement* (1897), and in *The Progress of Consciousness (conscience) in Western Philosophy* (1927) and other works, Brunschvicg maintained that an object which was beyond knowledge would be for us equivalent to nothing. Knowledge constitutes a world which is for us the known world. Beyond it there is nothing. It is within consciousness itself in fact that any distinction between subject and object, or between internality and externality, arises. Any judgement of perception, for example, involves subject and object, or interiority and exteriority. But the form of 'exteriority', as Fichte saw, is simply a restraining activity that the mind imposes dialectically on its own creative freedom, its 'interiority'. Our world is the world of knowledge, the world of the mind; we can know no other.

The main object of thought, Brunschvicg said, is not the concept but the spirit's own activity; and philosophy can be defined as an intellectual activity attempting to become conscious of itself. In childhood, the human spirit passes through the acousmatic age, the age of externality, when the spirit accepts what issues from the voice of authority. The age of full maturity is that of the mathematician, the man of rational science, as the Pythagoreans, Socrates and Descartes discovered. All of history reveals a continuous progress of consciousness towards its perfect fulfilment in reason, whose prototype is found in the science of mathematics, the highest level of knowledge yet reached by human thought. Mathematical knowledge, as evidenced in scientific progress, however, is something more than a triumphant breakthrough of intellect. It is an exemplification of mankind's growing self-understanding. The history of scientific progress is the history of 'the progress of consciousness (*conscience*)'. It is the history of the progression of the human spirit's self-understanding towards refinement of conscience and moral autonomy. The progress of consciousness and conscience in Western philosophy bears witness to humanity's spiritual unification. Mankind is moving towards self-identification through the communion of shared intelligence.

Galileo renounced the primacy of the earth in the theoretical sphere. We must do the same in the moral sphere, Brunschvicg asserted. The world of science is the progressive creation of the human spirit ever moving towards unification, intelligibility. In the moral sphere too the human spirit moves towards a unification; it moves towards the interrelations of justice and love. The human spirit, by reflecting on its own creative power in independence of all else, creates not only its scientific and aesthetic values but its moral values as well. A religious attitude to scientific investigation reveals to us that God is whatever enables us to live the life of the spirit. Modern man is the modern savant who immerses his spirit in universal science. He is one who becomes to himself his own rule of truth and morality. He is one whose activity of spirit achieves complete unity in consciousness.

Brunschvicg was a major figure in French academic life for nearly half a century. He was regarded as the inheritor and synthesizer of two great currents of French historical thought: the tradition of critical inquiry into the foundations of human knowledge as undertaken by Cournot, Renouvier and Hamelin, and the current of thought which made special use of the method of attentive self-observation as manifested in the work of the *idéologues*, Maine de Biran, Ravaisson-Mollien, Lachelier, Fouillée, Boutroux, Guyau, and the French 'spiritualists' (see above, Chapter 29, section 3).

In Germany, *Ernst Cassirer* (1874-1945), a representative of the Marburg school of neo-Kantianism, and *Bruno Bauch* (1877-1942), of the Heidelberg-Baden school, presented a developed and updated form of neo-Kantian philosophy. (See above, Chapter 25.) Cassirer pointed out that recent advances in non-Euclidean geometry, relativity theory, quantum mechanics, language science, and the cultural (moral) sciences indicated that the Kantian synthetic *a priori* principles of the understanding are not static and unchangeable. He then wrote several works on the nature of symbolic representation and the philosophy of culture, in which he aimed to extend Kant's static critique of the organizing principles of natural science and morality into a dynamic critique of the organizing principles of the human mind in all its continually developing aspects. Bruno Bauch, in his chief work *Truth, Value and Reality* (1923), attempted to synthesize all neo-Kantian thought. The Marburg school had given primary attention to Kant's first *Critique of Pure Reason*, and the

Baden school to the second *Critique of Practical Reason*, whereas it is Kant's *Critique of Judgement*, with its emphasis on the purposiveness or finality of nature as oriented to the development and happiness of man, that presents the summit vision of Kantian thought. Truth, value and actuality are transcendental interconnecting relations or attributes of all of evolving reality. There is continuous evolution in the material world and in the world of thought; and all of evolving reality is permeated with purposiveness and finality.

In Britain, *Robin George Collingwood* (1889-1943), archaeologist and Waynflete professor of metaphysical philosophy at Oxford (1935-41), was the only effective defender of idealism in the second quarter of the twentieth century. In his *Speculum Mentis* (1924) and other early philosophical works, Collingwood accepted the idealist viewpoint. He regarded theories of archaeology and the mathematico-physical sciences as presenting merely abstract, hypothetical suppositions, and philosophy alone as yielding unfettered knowledge. A few years later he abandoned this earlier view. In *The Philosophy of History* (1930) and the philosophical writings of his middle period, Collingwood accepted the findings of science and history as presenting genuine knowledge about the physical world. The object of philosophy, then, by way of contrast, is the being that comprehends all being, the *ens realissimum*, of which all finite beings are appearances.

In his last years, from 1937 to 1943, Collingwood proposed a historicist view of philosophy. The task of philosophy is that of eliciting the absolute presuppositions which underlie the complexes of questions and answers formulated by different peoples at different times. Philosophical investigation is historical investigation of men's ultimate and largely unacknowledged principles. Philosophy seeks to ascertain what is absolutely presupposed in a given society and to ascertain how one set of absolute presuppositions has come to be replaced by another. Most people in a given society are quite unconscious of their absolute presuppositions; and any gradual change in absolute presuppositions is not a conscious change. Changes of this kind come about because of internal strains. When metaphysicians uncover or discover these absolute presuppositions, they must refrain from criticizing their pseudo 'truth' or 'falsity'. The presuppositions are not answers to questions, and truth or falsity belongs only to answers to questions. Metaphysics is simply a historical science, therefore, whose task is that of uncovering absolute presuppositions. It has its practical applications in such different 'forms of experience' as art, science, religion, ethics and politics.

Political life, for example, is fundamentally a process in which a non-social community is transformed into a social one. Civilization is a process whereby a community undergoes a change from a condition of relative barbarity to one of civility. This is the theme of *The New Leviathan* (1942), Collingwood's last book before his death (after a series of strokes) in 1943.

In America, *Brand Blanshard* (b. 1892), Sterling professor of philosophy at Yale, presented a philosophical standpoint which he originally regarded as the standpoint of idealism but which he later spoke of as that of rationalism. In his first major work *The Nature of Thought* (1939), Blanshard sifted carefully through the arguments of many alternative schools concerning the nature of mind and thought in order to show the special merits of an idealistic view of knowledge. He saw his task as that of 'vindicating (immanent and common) reason against recent philosophical attacks' by empiricists, behaviourists, logical positivists, pragmatists, linguistic analysts and other persistent antirationalists. In an age when he found philosophers having nothing better to do than to raise doubts as to whether knowledge is possible, Blanshard wrote with a convinced sense of mission in support of his fundamental thesis: 'Thought is that activity of the mind which aims directly at truth'. When engaged in thinking, a person seeks fulfilment as a rational being by endeavouring to reach beyond himself and embrace something which is transcendent to thought, namely, the nature of things as they are. Thinking is problem-solving. Ideas are halfway houses on the road to reality. Ideas are potentially what they represent. They stand in relation to things as acorns stand in relation to oak trees. Thinking seeks the mind's goal and fulfilment in truth. Reality possesses coherence; thought strives for coherence. There is a perennial philosophy which, down through the centuries, has discovered that 'through different minds one (coherent) intelligible world is in the course of construction or reconstruction, and that the secret of sound thinking is the surrender of individual will to an immanent and common reason' in a communion of shared intelligence.

After his retirement from Yale in 1957, Blanshard commenced a three-volume work which would bring together material originally presented in his Carus and Gifford lectures. The first volume on *Reason and Analysis* (1962) asserted that antirationalist movements such as logical positivism, logical atomism and linguistic philosophy suggested criteria of meaning which broke down under closer inspection. They aimed to distract the mind from real facts and real necessities that are metaphysically significant. An analytic procedure based on the ordinary use of words would prove to be far more richly productive if it were to be placed at the service of a psychology of human thought and a reason-founded ethics. The second volume of the series, *Reason and Goodness*, was published in 1961. It carefully examined the different moral schools of the twentieth century in order to show the unique merits of a rationalist view of moral life and moral judgement. It traced out the dialectical interplay between the demands of reason and the demands of feeling (or love) throughout the history of ethical theory. It offered elaborate critiques of moral subjectivism and ethical emotivist theories which do not and cannot adequately depict or explain the rational temper of the moral sage. In the final volume, *Reason and Belief* (1975), Blanshard reflected on the role of reason in the religious and ethical area. He challenged the religious irrationalism of Kierkegaard, Brunner and Barth and their sundering of faith from reason. He criticized Catholic apologists as presenting doctrines, pertaining to miracles, for example, which were irreconcilable with the scientific rule of causality as interpreted by the uniformity of nature. It is scientific thought that is the paradigm of rational thought. The universe is indifferent to good and evil. The moral life has its throne in the human mind. It is their personal dedication to reasonableness or to the rational temper that unites religiously moral men in a communion of shared reason. It is in this sense that Blanshard's work is a twentieth-century development of earlier forms of (scientific) rationalism.

3. Life-philosophy. The early writings of Henri Bergson, William James and Wilhelm Dilthey struggled successfully against the dominant hold of positivism and idealism on nineteenth-century thought. These writers in their own different ways attempted to explain all reality in terms of life, becoming and growth, rather than in terms of mechanism, rationalism or idealism; and their writings gave rise in the twentieth century to different schools of irrationalist, empiricist life-philosophies.

Édouard Le Roy (1870-1954) succeeded Bergson as professor of philosophy at the Collège de France in 1921. He acknowledged that his own thought was deeply indebted to that of Bergson. He maintained that the criterion of truth is not rationalist coherence, nor utilitarian use, but rather life itself, dynamic and self-developing. Intuition alone is the instrument of genuine knowledge. In practice, the fundamental criterion of truth is that one should have lived it, and lived it with authentic moral and religious concern. Scientific knowledge, with its pragmatic expression of facts and theories, is

purely conventional and devoid of inner significance. It is an arbitrary
mental construct, a formal word game, designed to meet our needs
and to facilitate effective action in pursuit of those needs. It distorts
reality in the interests of practical action. It is the creator of its own
universe. Reality is a continuous flow of happenings and experiences;
it can be grasped by intuition alone.

Maurice Blondel (1861-1949), of the university of Aix-en-Prov-
ence, defended an activist psychology and a voluntaristic metaphysics
which sought to transcend the two extremes of intellectualism and
pragmatism. Philosophy, in its quest for truth, must turn from
abstract thought and look to the whole man-of-action, his feeling,
willing, thinking, living, if it is to grasp human experience in all its
fullness and richness. Action of this kind is not a blind drive. It
always includes thought; and thought can attain its goal only in as far
as it remains closely associated with such action. Blondel's philosophy, then, unlike other expressions of contemporary life-philosophy,
is not anti-intellectualist and irrationalist.

The main emphasis of Blondel's philosophy is on the basic dynamic
orientation of the dependent and exigent human spirit to God. There
is an immanent dialectic within dynamic action itself. The basis of
this dialectic is the constant gap between action and its realization.
Permanent dissatisfaction arises from the inability of human action to
attain an ultimate fulfilment of the totality of human demands within
the domain of action of the whole living person. The demands of
action point beyond the realm of the phenomenal and the human to
the realm of the supraphenomenal, the Transcendent. A philosophy
of this kind becomes a philosophy of immanence, that is, a reflection
on the basic dynamic orientation of the active thinking and willing of
the human spirit to God. In a philosophy of immanence, the approach
to being and reality is made through the philosophical method of
immanence, namely, through critical reflection on the active
subject's dynamism of thought and will as manifested, for example,
in the genesis of morality, science and philosophy. A philosophy of
immanence shows the insufficiency of the natural order to provide
man with the beatitude to which he aspires; and in doing so, it points
beyond itself to an opening-out of the mind and will to the absolute
activity of the Transcendent. As soon as the whole man becomes
aware of his dynamic orientation to the Transcendent he is necessarily
faced with a fundamental option or choice between uniting his own
will to the divine will, on the one hand, and seeking to be
self-sufficient and autonomous, without God, on the other. It is
through union of total human action with the divine activity that

human nature is perfected. A philosophy of immanence, then, which allows itself to be open to Christianity and to the Transcendent, opens the horizon of the human spirit to the ultimate goal of human thought and will. It opens the human spirit to the free self-revelation and self-communication of the divine. Many aspects of Blondel's thought anticipated themes which were given special emphasis in the works of later existentialist thinkers.

Several twentieth-century thinkers have been influenced by the historicism and 'philosophy of life' (*Philosophie des Lebens*) of Dilthey (see above, Chapter 25, section 7). At the university of Berlin, *Eduard Spranger* (1882-1963) and other disciples of Dilthey formed a Diltheyan historicist school of thinkers who devoted themselves to varied aspects of *Lebensphilosophie* ('life-philosophy'). For these historicists, the study of human, spiritual development is not confined or restricted by rational procedures or by the methods of natural science. Its range encloses the totality of human experience with its irreducible variety. This emphasis gave rise to a radically irrationalist interpretation of human experience, and to a relativist interpretation of all valuations and moral principles as being the product of particular individuals living at a particular time in a particular place and hemmed in by the limited horizons of their age. This radically relativist, historicist approach was given notable articulation in Oswald Spengler's *The Decline of the West* (Munich, 1918-23).

Ludwig Klages (1872-1956), German psychologist and philosopher, promulgated a form of biologistic philosophy, or life-philosophy, which conceived of becoming as a broad flow of vital elements. He became a major spokesman of a generation of intellectuals who dedicated themselves to the repudiation of cerebral civilization in the name of instinctive life, and to the repudiation of reason in the name of primitive vitality. Mind destroys vitality. It is the adversary of all that is natural, instinctive, loyal and valuable. We must return to the world view of Pelagianism, that is, to a primitive-unconscious form of instinctive living that is free from stifling mind.

German life-philosophy, historicism, Bergson's philosophy of *élan vital*, and American and British pragmatism (see above, Chapter 27) emphasized movement, becoming and life rather than mind or matter. The proponents of these different forms of 'life-philosophy' were, in the main, resolute empiricists and irrationalists. They overcame the stranglehold of 'modern' scientistic rationalism. They presented a one-sided, anti-idealist, but vitalistic, organic and concrete view of reality; and in so doing they opened up new possibilities for new movements in contemporary thought.

    4. Neo-positivism. *Ernst Mach* (1838-1916), an Austrian physicist and philosopher, is widely regarded as the father of logical positivism and as the 'real master of the Vienna Circle' (P. Frank). He developed the empiricism of Berkeley and Hume into a philosophy of radical empiricism, and then applied it to the facts, laws and theories of modern science. In *The Science of Mechanics* (1883) and *The Analysis of Sensations* (1906, 1914) Mach maintained that the mind knows nothing beyond its own sensations, and that scientific theory is simply a device for predicting the course of our sensations of things. All sciences have one and the same subject-matter, namely, sensation. The basis and origin of all scientific knowledge is sense-experience. Our 'world consists only of our sensations'. In mechanics there can be no *a priori* mathematical demonstration or proof that can tell us anything about the world that sense-experience cannot tell us. It is sense *verification* rather than proof that is the appropriate method for establishing scientific conclusions. Scientific laws are general, summary descriptions of phenomena. Their main function is to summarize past experience and to assist prediction. The only scientific hypotheses or theories that are admissible are those that can be tested in sense-experience. The statements of atomic theory, and any other such pseudo-scientific theory, referring to what is in principle unobservable, are not descriptive statements; and for this reason they cannot be placed among the conclusions of the sciences. Scientific theories are mathematical models for 'facilitating the mental reproduction of facts'. They are valuable only in so far as they lead us to observed *descriptions* of observed phenomena. It is scientific description that constitutes scientific explanation. For this reason Mach steadfastly refused to believe in the existence of the physico-chemical atoms of contemporary atomic theory.

    Jules Henri Poincaré (see above, Chapter 28, section 7) made significant contributions to the philosophy of science and in doing so he showed up some of the inherent difficulties and weaknesses present in Mach's account of scientific 'explanation'. The formulae or laws expressing mathematically the discovered relations between things are open to revision in the constant pursuit of generality in nature. Theories are 'convenient' rather than 'true'. One theory, or imaginative, suggestive model, may be superseded by another theory which is more 'fruitful' than the first. Theories, then, are (analytic) conventions that depend on the scientist's free choice between alternative ways of 'imaging' or explaining the natural world.

In Vienna in 1907, the mathematician Hans Hahn, the economist Otto Neurath, and the physicist Philipp Frank, came together in an informal group to discuss the philosophy of science. They accepted Mach's general doctrine that science is basically the description of experience, but they were convinced that Mach had not sufficiently emphasized the central role of mathematics, logic, and explanatory theories in the philosophy of science. They drew on the work of Poincaré to supplement the general doctrine of Mach and in doing so they anticipated the main themes of logical positivism. It was in 1922 that the growing 'Vienna group' became the internationally known 'Vienna Circle' *(Wiener Kreis)* under the leadership of Moritz Schlick.

Moritz Schlick (1882-1936), of Berlin, had studied physics under Max Planck. As associate professor at the university of Rostock he published a series of works in which he elaborated new criteria for scientific knowledge. These publications attracted widespread attention. Following the work of Poincaré and Einstein, Schlick re-examined the assumed synthetic *a priori* character of the general laws of physics. He concluded that these laws are conventions or analytic propositions, and that there are no synthetic *a priori* propositions. All propositions are either analytical or empirical; and empirical knowledge is 'knowledge of sameness', or similarity, of sense-data, and of ordered relationships of empirical phenomena. Scientific knowledge seeks to know the relations between physical *magnitudes*; metaphysics must be denied the status of scientific knowledge.

In 1922, at the instigation of the members of the Vienna group, Schlick accepted a call to the chair of philosophy of the inductive sciences at the university of Vienna. He soon manifested personal and intellectual gifts which fitted him to be the natural leader of a large, co-operative discussion circle. The members of this 'Vienna Circle' included professional philosophers, mathematicians, psychologists and sociologists. Visiting scholars from the United States, Germany, England, Australia, Poland, Norway and Sweden took part in the discussion sessions. They constantly refined, in their discussions, the neo-positivist methods of the Vienna School of thought and they did so with an enthusiasm which gave rise to a wide-ranging profusion of positivist writings. The circle organized a series of congresses which made its tenets familiar to a wider world. It took over the philosophical journal *Annalen der Philosophie* and renamed it *Erkenntnis* ('Knowledge'). In the mid-1930s, however, the political situation in Europe was deteriorating, and the Vienna Circle began to disintegrate

as a group or sect. Several of the members went to England and to the
United States. The meetings were discontinued after the death of
Schlick in 1936; and logical positivism as a philosophical movement
was quickly absorbed into the contemporary movement of international logical empiricism. But the influence of its thought, especially on English linguistic philosophy, persisted long after the Circle
itself had dissolved.

In an age when the majority of German-speaking philosophers
were still committed to one or other form of German idealism, the
relatively small Vienna Circle wished to destroy the claim of these
idealist philosophers to have ideal access to knowledge and truth. The
logical positivists rejected idealism and all forms of transcendental
metaphysics as incapable of verification and as devoid of significance.
It is nonsensical to assert or to deny, for example, that there is an
external world which is independent of our experience, or that the
Absolute is beyond time or that there is a 'realm of values' over and
above the world of experience. Statements of this kind lack 'cognitive
meaning'. They do not convey information. They are 'meaning-less'.
No experience of any kind could possibly serve to verify assertions of
this kind. 'The meaning of a proposition is the method of its
verification.' The meaning of a proposition consists in whatever
observations or experiences show whether or not it is true.

Mathematical and logical propositions which are consistent with all
observations were admitted as meaningful by the logical positivists.
Propositions of this kind are analytical and tautological. They can be
proved or disproved from definitions alone. They explicate the
meanings of terms. They say nothing about how things actually are in
the world. Theological and metaphysical propositions are not of this
kind. They attempt to make unverifiable assertions concerning the
creation of the world, the nature of reality as a whole, and so forth.
Non-tautological propositions of this kind, in principle unverifiable
by any observation, are *ipso facto* devoid of (scientific) meaning. They
are neither true nor false; they are simply meaningless (unscientific).
All arguments either for or against them are equally pointless.
Philosophy can become scientific only at the cost of becoming purely
analytic.

Logical positivism relied heavily on its key principle, the verifiability principle, which was not itself a verifiable scientific proposition. This gave rise to a set of problems with which Schlick, Neurath,
Carnap and their colleagues had to grapple. How can the verifi-
cationist theory of meaning be formulated satisfactorily? What form
of analysis of experience will hold intersubjectively, to ensure

common agreement concerning any particular (scientific) statement? What kind of meaningfulness and testability is in question?

The members of the Vienna Circle were now concerned that the principle of verifiability threatened to destroy not only metaphysics but science and history as well. All scientific laws and historical propositions might be said to be meaningless in as far as they are not conclusively verifiable by observation. In an effort to save scientific laws, Schlick adopted a suggestion put forward by F. P. Ramsey. General propositions, of the form 'all As are B', are in fact 'variable hypotheticals'. They are not authentic propositions having truth value. They are rules or formulae for judging, for example, that if something is found to be an A then it will be judged to be a B: 'if something is A then it is B'. Schlick suggested that scientific laws should be regarded not as statements, then, but as rules or formulae or 'inference licences' (Ryle) permitting us to pass from one singular statement (A) to another singular statement (B). Otto Neurath and Rudolf Carnap pointed out, however, that, in practice, attempts are made in science to falsify scientific laws, and so these laws are statements and not rules: one does not attempt to 'falsify' rules.

In the latter part of the 1920s, the Vienna Circle began to replace the notion of 'verifiability' with the notion of 'confirmability' or with the notion of 'testability'. A proposition has meaning only if it is possible to test or confirm it. It has meaning if true propositions can be derived from it. This weaker re-formulation, however, seemed to re-admit as meaningful several of the metaphysical statements which the Circle from the beginning had endeavoured to outlaw. The controversy concerning the formulation of the requisite principle was never satisfactorily concluded. Empiricists in general began to turn away from the dogmas of logical positivism. They turned instead towards the less rigid forms of conceptual and linguistic analysis. (See Chapters 32 and 33 below.)

32 Twentieth-century thought in Britain and America (I)

1. Moore's method of conceptual analysis   2. Russell's method of reductive analysis   3. Russell's moral and social philosophy   4. Realists, neo-realists and critical realists

1. Moore's method of conceptual analysis. At the beginning of the twentieth century, George Moore and Bertrand Russell led a revolt against the dominant idealist philosophy which reigned in the British universities during their undergraduate years. They argued that the evidence of common sense and the findings of the physico-mathematical sciences point to the fact that the world consists of different realities of different kinds and that it is not in fact true that all of reality is mental or ideal. Idealism must therefore give way to realism.

The new trend towards realism may be said to have commenced in 1903 with Russell's *Principles of Mathematics* and Moore's *Principia Ethica* and *Refutation of Idealism*. The groundwork had already been laid, however, in an article on the nature of judgement which Moore published in *Mind* in 1899.

George Edward Moore (1873-1958), of Cambridge, was strongly attracted to the views of F. H. Bradley and Kant in his early formative years. However, in his 1899 article 'The Nature of Judgement', and in other early articles, he proposed the doctrine that mental acts and their objects are separate entities, and that the unique relation between the knowing subject and the known object makes no difference to the nature of the object known. Each thing is what it is and it is not definable in terms of its relations to a knower or indeed to anything other than itself. 'Everything is what it is, and not another thing' (*Principia Ethica*, quoting Bishop Butler). An analysis of statements such as 'I perceive X', or 'I think of Y' designate an act of consciousness and different objects which are related to but distinct from the act of consciousness. Each reality is perceived and known directly, and each is known as distinct from all others. The object of a sensation is distinct from the act in which it is sensed, even though the sensed object is sensed directly. The acts of sensing objects and conceiving objects are identical with realities sensed and conceived. One might perhaps rephrase this statement by saying that the act of sensation is that of a sensed being's being sensed, and that the act of conceiving is that of a conceived being's being conceived. Known things are one and the same as things known. In knowledge, reality is known directly. This understanding of the nature of knowledge is founded on a philosophy of common-sense realism, according to Moore.

Moore pointed out in *A Defence of Common Sense* (1923) that there are certain common-sense propositions which we all accept and know to be true. I know, for example, that there exists a living human body which I call my body, and I know that there are other people, each of whom regards a certain living body as his own body. I know too that the earth exists and has existed for several years, and that the earth and corporeal things are external to the mind. Moore then contended that one of the main functions of the philosopher is that of analysing and defining some of the complex concepts used in common-sense propositions of this kind. In several of his articles and lectures he devoted himself to the practice of phenomenological, clarificatory, conceptual analysis, a form of analysis in which he attempted to pick out and name the essential constituents of complex concepts and complex objects.

In a series of essays, starting with *The Status of Sense-data* (1914) and ending with *Visual Sense-data* (1958), Moore's interests focused in a special way on the analysis of perception and on problems concerning our knowledge of the external, material world. He maintained that a sufficient proof of the existence of an external, physical object is given if one can indicate one or more such objects. Thus for example one can indicate that 'This is a chair', and 'Here is a coin', and 'This is a hand'. No special philosophical proof can be found as an addition to the existing evidence we already have concerning the chair, or coin, or hand. The philosopher can however make a valuable contribution by making a philosophical analysis of a proposition such as 'Here is a coin, or an extra-mental physical object'. A proposition of this kind is a deduction from two simpler propositions, namely, 'I am perceiving THIS' and 'THIS is a coin'. The 'THIS' which is directly apprehended is a 'sense-datum' or a 'sense-content'. The sense-content is not identified with the physical object and it is not identified with the perceiving or the seeing. If we look at a red book and a blue book we see rectangular red and blue patches, or 'sensibles', as the immediate objects of direct perception. When two people look from different angles at a penny standing on its edge, or at a bicycle wheel, they perceive their shapes differently. One can then question whether these two different groupings of 'sense-data' are or are not part of the objects which are being perceived, and whether different sense-data can exist anywhere when they are not objects of perception. If we stare at a lighted electric lamp for a little while and then close our eyes, the after-image which we see, Moore tells us, is a specimen of the sort of thing he means by a sense-datum. A common-sense view of the world enables us to know with certainty, he asserts, that there are external, physical, material objects, but an analysis of this proposition leads to the problem of how we know that there are physical objects to which the sensible sense-data are related. Moore did not succeed in solving problems of this kind, but he made a significant contribution to philosophical thought in his various phenomenological analyses of sense-perception in general.

Ethics provided a second area of philosophical inquiry to which Moore devoted special attention. In this field, he maintained that the central problem was that of the definition of goodness: 'What is good?'; 'What is goodness in itself?'; or 'What is good if quite alone?' He came to the conclusion that it cannot be defined. It is a simple, unique and indefinable notion. 'The notion "good" has no definition because it is simple and has no parts'. It is unanalysable and indefinable. Some philosophers have attempted to define it in terms of pleasure, utility, self-realization, or God's commands. Attempts of this kind commit 'the naturalistic fallacy'. They attempt to convert a mere fact of nature into a value. They equate 'is' (fact) with 'ought' (value). Goodness cannot be equated with any natural property. It is a non-natural, though objective, intrinsic quality which we can recognize in at least some objects. We can recognize what things possess the quality of being good even though we cannot define that quality.

In 1942, Moore considered that C. L. Stevenson's non-descriptive, emotive theory of ethics (namely, that terms such as 'right', 'wrong', 'ought' and 'good' have merely emotive meaning) may be partly right. 'I am inclined to think that this is so, but I am also inclined to think that it is not so, and I do not know which way I am inclined most strongly.'

Moore felt unable to explain his views concerning the nature of the good satisfactorily. His philosophy was not a philosophy of being, and he found himself incapable, therefore, of viewing the good as one of the transcendental properties of being. He failed to see that everything is intelligible and intellectually desirable, or good, in so far as it is being. His strength lay in his detailed phenomenological analysis of perception and of ethical notions rather than in ontology, the science of 'being as being'. His actual use of analysis of this kind had an important influence on the analytical methods of practical philosophizing which have come to dominate the schools of philosophy in British and American universities in recent decades.

2. Russell's method of reductive analysis.

Bertrand A. W. *Russell* (1872-1970), who was privately educated as a boy, entered Trinity College, Cambridge, where he studied mathematics and philosophy from 1890 to 1894. Throughout his long and eventful life he held a variety of university posts, interspersed with several other pursuits in the literary, educational and socio-political fields. He is especially renowned for his work in mathematical logic. He published *A Critical Exposition of the Philosophy of Leibniz* (1900), *The Principles of Mathematics* (1903), *Principia Mathematica* (with Whitehead; 1910-13), *The Problems of Philosophy* (1912), *Our Knowledge of the External World* (1914), *Introduction to Mathematical Philosophy* (1919), *The Analysis of Mind* (1921), *The Analysis of Matter* (1927), *The Scientific Outlook* (1931), *An Inquiry into Meaning and Truth* (1940), *Human Knowledge: Its Scope and Limits* (1948), *Logic and Knowledge* (1948), *My Philosophical Development* (1959), and several other works.

In 1898 Russell reacted strongly against the idealism of Bradley and Hegel which had attracted him in his earlier years. In his *Principles of Mathematics* he expressed a form of all-embracing realism which equated meaning and referents. He believed that all terms when used meaningfully refer to real entities, perceptible or imperceptible. Thus, for example, points of space, numbers, and instants of time are existent entities. He soon realized however that there are terms (such as 'the average family') which do not refer to existent entities, even though we find it useful to speak as if they did. Terms of this kind, he said, are logical constructions which are reducible, or translatable, into terms or statements about more basic, unproblematic entities. Constructions out of known entities are preferred to logical constructions and inferences which introduce problems concerning the existence and status of unknown things.

Russell's early fame rested on two main contributions which he made to logic in the first decade of the twentieth century, namely, the theory of descriptions and the theory of types. Russell pointed out that there are certain denoting phrases ('*the* man') containing descriptions ('the man in the moon') which seem to refer to non-existent entities, and are nevertheless part of a meaningful sentence. A sentence such as 'The present King of France is bald' is meaningful even though it has no referent. The putative act of reference is eliminated when one analyses the sentence into a claim concerning existence and a conditional proposition: 'There is a unique individual ruling France, and if someone rules France then he is bald'. This analysis reveals that the sentence is false, and, as false, can be said to be meaningful. Russell used the term 'incomplete symbol' to refer to any denoting phrase containing a description which appears to refer to a non-existent entity. (The German logician Gottlob Frege [1848-1925] met the same difficulty by distinguishing two kinds of meaning, the sense [*Sinn*] and the denotation [*Bedeutung*] of a term or phrase. Thus, 'Scott' and 'the author of *Waverley*' have the same denotation [an individual man], but not the same sense. 'The King of France' has a sense but no denotation.) Analysis of this kind is reductive analysis; and reductive analysis is capable of showing that the grammatical form of a sentence (such as 'I saw nobody in the class-room') is not the same as its logical form, and that the grammatical subject or object is not necessarily the real logical subject or object.

Russell formulated his theory of types as a solution to a paradox generated by the notion of a class of classes which includes itself as a member. Some sets or classes appear to be members of themselves and some not. The set of horses, for example, is not a member of itself, whereas the set of non-horses seems to be a member of itself; again, the class of dogs is not a dog, but the class of classes is a class. A question then arises as to whether or not the class of all classes that are not members of themselves is a member of itself. If yes, then the answer is no. If no, then the answer is yes. An answer of any kind seems to involve a self-contradiction. This paradox had an important influence on the subsequent development and understanding of set theory and the logic of classes. The problem raised is basically the problem of self-reference. Russell proposed his theory of types as a solution to the paradox. Classes whose members are ordinary objects are first-type or first-level classes. Second-type classes are those classes whose members are first-type classes. Thus, for example, the class of horses and the class of sheep are first-type classes which are, in turn, members of a higher, second-type class of animal classes. A statement referring to other statements must be of a higher level or type than the statements that it is about. The paradox disappears when we realize that it is obvious nonsense to say of a class either that it is or it isn't a member of itself. The class of all first-type or first-level classes which are not members of themselves is a second-type or second-order class. No class is a member of itself. There can be no class of *all* classes; there can only be a class of all classes of a given type.

The theory of descriptions and the theory of types have important applications in the construction of different systems of mathematical logic free of contradiction. Thus, for example, in the sphere of classes (or set theory), individuals are regarded as type one, classes of individuals are of type two, and classes of classes of individuals are of type three. This later led to the further realization that many antinomies or paradoxes (as, for example, the *Liar*: a liar said of himself 'I am now lying'. Was he lying?) are not logical but semantic antinomies. They arise from a confusion of language with metalanguage and with metametalanguage. (Cf. F. P. Ramsey, below, Chapter 33, section 5.)

In 1912 Russell decided to apply the method and techniques of reductive analysis to the problems of philosophy. In *The Problems of Philosophy* (1912), *Our Knowledge of the External World* (1914), *The Analysis of Mind* (1921), and *The Analysis of Matter* (1927), he applied the method of reductive analysis and its principle of parsimony to our knowledge of physical objects and to our knowledge of self or mind. 'Wherever possible, logical constructions are to be substituted for inferred entities.' Empirical concepts are to be substituted for non-empirical concepts. 'Substitute constructions out of known entities for inferences to unknown entities.' With this principle in mind Russell attempted to show that physical, scientific entities can be construed as a complex structure of undeniable data of perception. A building or a tree, for example, can be regarded as a system of all the actual and possible sense-experiences that would be regarded as present in perceptions of that building or that tree. Physical objects, then, are regarded as complex structures of data of the sort given in sense-perception. The perceiver perceives directly the end product of a complex causal chain of physical and physiological events in the brain of the perceiver. Thus, it is of events in our brains that we are directly aware; and known objects are logical constructions from these brain events.

Similarly, the subject or self or mind, Russell maintained, is a logical construction or logical fiction or a 'description'. It is not an entity with which we can become acquainted: it is an assemblage or class of particulars. Ordinary everyday language makes legitimate reference to subjects and objects which are simply grammatical subjects and objects of sentences. The grammatical level of language, however, should not be confused with other levels where language is used for a different purpose and in a different context. There is no warrant for believing in the existence of a subject of awareness, a self, which performs acts. This 'subject' is simply a logical construction of a complex of brain events of which we are directly assured by our experience. Thus, 'self' and matter, mind and body, consist of events which are neither spiritual nor material. William James had expressed this viewpoint as that of neutral monism. Thus, if I am touching a stone, the perception (event) is both a mental and a physical event in a unified experience. If this experience is grouped with other experiences which are said to be experiences of that stone, the logical construction is that of a stone. If the experience is grouped up with still other experiences and memories the logical construction is that of a mind. Mind and matter are simply different forms of arrangement of the same elementary components. 'Both mind and matter are logical constructions out of particulars which are neither mental nor material but neutral.' Everything we know about minds can be expressed in terms of sensations and images without assuming the existence of any entity called mind.

Russell made a serious effort to apply the method of reductive analysis also to the ontological aspect of logical constructionism. In 1918, prompted by insights which arose from his conversations and correspondence with Wittgenstein (see below, Chapter 33), he gave a series of lectures on the philosophy of logical atomism. In these lectures and in an article on logical atomism written for *Contemporary British Philosophy* in 1924, he spoke of the isomorphism of the structure of an ideal language and the structure of reality. A description of the world presented in an ideal language would provide an account of what the world is like because of the identity of structure between the ideal language and reality. Reductive analysis of the conditions necessary to give a sentence a definite meaning reveals that ordinary molecular sentences must be compounded from fundamental atomic units of meaning. These atomic units of meaning arise from direct acquaintance with the basic entities whose relations make up the states of affairs in the non-linguistic world. They are the names, of, or terms for, particular sense-data, properties of sense-data, and relations between sense-data. Names and terms of this kind are capable of being combined into atomic sentences in which one or more named entities have predicated of them a single property ('This is yellow') or relational term ('This is behind that'). Simple, irreducible names and terms of this kind are combined in simple atomic sentences which state a minimal fact about a momentary content of sense-experience. They are sentences which can be verified or falsified by a single experience.

Logical atomism assumes then that reality consists of a plurality of ultimate events or facts which are discernible in a single moment of experience, and that knowledge is dependent on experienced facts as data of immediate experience. The simple objects in the world of common sense (stones and trees) are complicated complexes of atomic facts of different kinds. Russell knew, however, that generalizations such as 'All men are mortal' cannot be explained in terms of compounds of large numbers of atomic sentences alone; nor can intensional sentences expressing belief ('He believes he will win'). Similarly, logical atomism does not explain how we can understand words such as 'is' and 'the' which seem to provide us with the logical framework of sentences. Logical atomism in its extreme form was found to be untenable; and subsequently both Russell and Wittgenstein abandoned it.

In *Human Knowledge: Its Scope and Limits* (1948), Russell sought to find and formulate the minimum principles required to justify scientific inference and generalization. He approached this problem from the viewpoint of a query concerning the nature of the universe: what must the universe be like if the inferences and successful predictions of the empirical sciences are to be theoretically justified? The scientist, for example, assumes that nature has some permanent or semi-permanent patterns of behaviour of such a kind that he can make a special application of the mathematical theory of probability to these patterns of behaviour. He makes general assumptions about the way in which nature works, and then having found certain properties always associated together in the past infers that it is probable that he will find them always associated together in the future. What, then, are these general assumptions or 'postulates' which provide the human mind with probabilities concerning the patterns of behaviour of nature?

There are five 'postulates', or extra-logical principles, or general assumptions which underly scientific generalizations concerning the patterns of behaviour of nature, according to Russell. The first postulate is that of quasi-permanence: given any event A, it frequently happens that an event (a person, or a thing) very similar to A occurs in a neighbouring place at a neighbouring time. The second is the postulate of separable causal lines: it is frequently possible to form a series of events such that from one or two members (or events) of the series we can infer something about all the other (more distant) members. The third is the postulate of spatio-temporal continuity: when there is a causal connection between non-contiguous events, there will be found to be intermediate links in the causal chain such that each link is contiguous to the next. The fourth is the structural postulate: when a number of structurally similar complex events occur around a centre (like spectators around a stage) from which they are not widely separated, it is generally the case that all belong to causal lines having their origin in an event of similar structure at the centre. The fifth is the postulate of analogy: given two classes of events A and B, and given that, whenever both A and B can be observed, there is reason to believe that A causes B, then if, in a given case, one of these classes of events (A or B) occurs but we cannot observe whether the other occurs or not, it is probable that it has occurred or does occur. For Russell, this latter postulate of analogy can justify belief in other minds.

Russell recognized and acknowledged the limitations and inadequacy of pure empiricism as a theory of knowledge. From one group of empirical events, one cannot infer with empirical certainty the occurrence of any other group of events. Scientific prediction cannot be theoretically justified on the grounds of empiricism alone. The five postulates, or general assumptions, required to justify nondemonstrative scientific inference and generalization about the world cannot be proved by empirical arguments, since these postulates are the very principles on which the validity of such arguments rests. However, even though Russell acknowledged the inadequacy of pure empiricism as a theory of knowledge, he found himself unable to transcend it or to replace it with a more adequate theory of knowledge and reality.

3. Russell's moral and social philosophy. Russell devoted considerable time and attention to ethical, social and religious topics; and his ethical and socio-political theories developed and changed throughout the course of his life. His early essay on *The Elements of Ethics* (1910) defended a viewpoint closely akin to that of his friend G. E. Moore in *Principia Ethica*. Goodness is regarded as an intrinsic, objective, indefinable property of certain things. 'Good and bad are qualities which belong to objects independently of our opinions, just as much as *round* and *square* do.' Genuine differences between people's judgements in regard to intrinsic goodness and badness are primarily differences concerning means to attain some good end.

He changed his views a few years later, after reading G. Santayana's *Winds of Doctrine* (1913); and in subsequent works he presented an ethical theory which he acknowledged to be a form of 'the doctrine of the subjectivity of values'. This later viewpoint was expounded in his *Principles of Social Reconstruction* (1916), *What I Believe* (1925), *Outline of Philosophy* (1927), *Religion and Science* (1935) and other works. 'All human activity springs from impulse and desire.' There is 'no property analogous to truth that belongs or does not belong to an ethical judgement'. If different men differ about values, 'there is not a disagreement as to any kind of truth, but a difference of taste' (*Religion and Science*, p. 238). Good and bad are derivative from desire and aversion. Any argument given for or against a moral opinion, as, for example, that 'Racial discrimination' or 'Cruelty' 'is evil', is a persuasive expression of one's own attitude in a manner which is designed to change other people's desires. 'The person who says A is good is wishing others to feel certain desires. He will therefore, if not hindered by other activities, try to rouse these desires in other people if he thinks he knows how to do so' (*Reply to My Critics*, p. 724). 'I should interpret "A is good" as "Would that all men desired A"' (p. 722). Judgements of value of this kind cannot be proved true or false: they are simply persuasive devices in the optative mood, designed to change other people's minds. When his critics pointed out the intrinsic weakness in this subjectivist theory of values, Russell acknowledged that the criticisms had his entire approval. 'I can only say that, while my own opinions as to ethics do not satisfy me, other people's satisfy me still less' (p. 724). He found his own views argumentatively irrefutable, but nevertheless incredible, and he acknowledged that he did not know the solution. He felt unable to answer the question: 'But what (ultimately) are "good" desires? Are they any more than desires you share?' He seems to have been attracted to the idea of intrinsic goodness and badness, but was not aware of any way in which this idea could be derived from the empirical form of philosophy which he had espoused.

In *Power: A New Social Analysis* (1938), Russell applied reductive analysis to the laws of social dynamics. All human activity springs from impulse and desire. Love of power is the desire to produce intended effects upon the outer world, whether human or non-human. Power is the basic concept in social science; and the basic task of social science is the task of revealing the laws of the transformation of power. He condemned, however, in *The Theory and Practice of Bolshevism* (1920) the worship of 'naked power' for its own sake as he saw it practised in the Soviet system. He was appalled on the occasion of his visit to Soviet Russia (1920) to discover an entire nation which seemed to be 'one vast prison in which the jailors were cruel bigots'. His personal desire and recommendation was that power be used 'to promote social co-operation, not in one group as against another, but in the whole human race'. Social organization, as also effective world organization, should not be aimed at as an end in itself, but as a means to the promotion of the good life with a view to facilitating the harmonious development of the human personality.

If, however, disagreement about values indicates simply 'a differ-ence of taste', in what sense can one's personal desire and recom-mendation be said to be 'better' than the desires of the power-wielding militarist? Russell said that an important difference is seen to exist between purely personal desires and 'impersonal' desires. Thus, for example, a monarch who says 'Monarchical government is better than republican forms of government' and desires that nations profit from monarchical government regardless of his own personal gain, uses the word 'better' in its properly moral sense. The object desired is universal and not purely personal. The wish is personal, but what it desires is universal. It is in this sense that those philosophers who laid stress on the 'universality' of moral principles were emphasizing the essential difference between personal and 'impersonal' desires. Russell did not explain however, why the 'universal impersonal' is 'better'; and he was not prepared to consider any 'non-empirical' explanation.

Russell regarded religion and religious belief as belonging to the infancy of human reason and to a stage of development which mankind is now outgrowing. Religion will fade and die out as people begin to solve their social problems. There is no evidence for or against the existence of God. The Christian God has no more and no less likelihood of existing than the Olympian gods of Greece or the Norse gods. Belief in gods is a comforting belief in hypothetical entities, akin to the belief in elves or fairies. Religious feelings do not give evidence concerning the existence of anything outside our emotions. Religious emotion plays a valuable role in the formation of a religious attitude of serious concern about life. It fosters fine 'spirit', the principle of impersonal feelings, and enables us to transcend merely personal satisfaction. It fosters altruism, human welfare and social co-operation. Religious organizations, however, have normally fostered religious beliefs which are based primarily and mainly on fear. They have promoted religious wars, and have had in general a baneful influence on human society. Religious feeling has some value. Religious organizations have none.

Russell was convinced that the function of philosophy is that of applying reductive (logical) analysis to obscure but basic notions such as subject, object, mind, and non-demonstrative inference, notions which have tended to obfuscate all of our empirical knowledge. Philosophy aims to discover the objective truth concerning the ultimate nature of reality. It keeps alive interest in enigmatic questions, such as those pertaining to purposiveness in the universe and the ends of life. In doing so it broadens our mental horizons and provides a stimulating impetus towards further scientific research and definite knowledge. Russell, however, in applying reductive analysis and the law of parsimony to the order, unity and continuity of the universe reduced it to a logical, human construction or fiction. He reduced all knowledge to logical constructions founded on the end-products of a complex causal chain of physical and physiological events in the brain of the perceiver. He was unable to transcend the severe limitations of empiricism as a theory of knowledge. He eliminated, in practice, every method for the acquisition of knowledge other than the method of reductive analysis. He championed the tenets of rationalism, empiricism and non-religious humanism even though he recognized and acknowledged the limitations and inadequacies of these different theories. He was unable to transcend the limits of the empirical and subjectivist school of philosophy which he had adopted as his own.

4. Realists, neo-realists and critical realists. At Cambridge university the realist movement inaugurated by Moore and Russell was continued and extended by C. D. Broad, A. C. Ewing and the Cambridge realists in general. *Charlie Dunbar Broad* (1887-1971) regarded sense-data as private objects interposed between the perceiver and the unobservable physical world. The physical world is the remote causal ancestor of our sensations, he maintained. The question concerning the isomorphism of the properties of sense-data and physical properties is one which cannot be settled without further scientific evidence.

At Oxford university, *Thomas Case* (1844-1925), while supporting the idealists in their criticism of materialism, defended a mediate realist view that the existence and nature of physical things are inferred mediately from sense-data. Sense-data arise as modifications of the nervous system caused by a world of real things existing independently of sense-data.

John Cook Wilson (1849-1915), Wykeham professor of logic, was a sharp critic of absolute idealism. Like G. E. Moore at Cambridge, Cook Wilson tended to select particular problems for thorough analysis, and to view these problems from the vantage point of common-sense claims to knowledge. Knowledge can be exemplified but not explained or defined. We are aware of what knowledge is by actually knowing some thing. We perceive extended physical objects as existing independently of the act of perception. Physical objects possess the power to produce the sensations of secondary qualities in the subject. For this reason, it is untrue to say that knowledge *makes* the object or to say that it terminates in a *copy* of the object. The idealist and the representationist theories of knowledge must therefore give way to a moderate realist theory of knowledge.

H. A. Prichard (1871-1947), a disciple of Cook Wilson, maintained that knowledge is *sui generis* and cannot be defined or 'explained'. Knowledge and belief are altogether distinct and cannot be mistaken for each other. We know directly and infallibly whether our state of mind is that of knowledge or of belief. The known is independent of our knowledge of it. Things must exist if there is to be knowledge of them. Secondary qualities, however, do not exist independently of a percipient subject.

Henry H. Price (b. 1899), in his major work on *Perception* (1932), analysed philosophers' claims to perceive objects in the external world. Perceivable 'objects' include not only material things but also rainbows, flames, shadows and other perceivable entities. A question arises as to how far perception is a genuine source of form of knowledge ('Is this a dagger that I see before me?': *Macbeth*, II, i). Is perception a private sensory experience? Do sense-data constitute an impenetrable veil of appearance between the perceiver and the external world? Price pointed out that the representative theory of perception and the causal theory of perception both assume that external objects stimulate us into experiencing private sense-data. They assume that we are never directly aware of the (public) external objects themselves. In this case, it becomes impossible to know anything about the existence or nature of such objects, or to know that they are causing us to have sense-data. All talk about assumed external objects is reducible to talk about our own actual or possible private sense-data. Views of this kind lead logically to the doctrine of phenomenalism: material objects are simply 'permanent possibilities of sensation'. Price agreed, with Russell and others, that what we directly know are sense-data, but he rejected both the representative and causal theories of perception. He pointed out that material things have causal powers beyond their abilities to cause sense impressions in the perceiver. Price's work on perception gave a powerful impetus to further discussion of sense-data at Oxford and other universities.

In the United States of America the realist revolt against idealism in the early decades of the twentieth century was given special prominence in two movements or schools of thought known as 'new realism' and 'critical realism'.

Ralph Barton Perry (1876-1957), of Harvard, attacked idealist philosophies in an influential article entitled 'The Ego-centric

Predicament', in the *Journal of Philosophy*, vol. 7, No. 1 (1910). He maintained that the idealists had confused the statement that 'everything which is known, is *known*' with the statement that 'everything which *is*, is known'. Objects of knowledge and experience are capable of being related to consciousness or mind without being dependent on that relationship for their existence. In the same year (1910), Perry, W. P. Montague, R. B. Holt, W. T. Marvin, W. B. Pitkin and E. G. Spaulding established themselves as an organized neo-realist movement when they published 'The Program and First Platform of Six Realists' in the *Journal of Philosophy*. The same authors later published a volume of essays in 1912 under the title *The New Realism: Co-operative Studies in Philosophy*.

Perry and the new realists wrote several books and essays in which they defended the view that the world, in lending itself to being known, does not thereby become simply a part of the knower. The world is not exhaustively defined by the relationship of being known. Particulars persist independently of our consciousness of them. They also defended the view that universal ideas are real, and that real particulars and universals are apprehended directly. Knowledge through intermediaries (copies or mental images) is subordinate to direct or presentative knowledge.

The new realists disagreed among themselves however on several other issues, particularly on the nature of mistaken perceptions, illusions, hallucinations and other such phenomena. Is a table, for example, which looks round to one perceiver and elliptical to another both round and elliptical? Is a mountain which looks green to a perceiver standing nearby and blue to a perceiver standing at a distance both green and blue? Are shapes, colours and other qualities possessed by the object at its own location, but perceived in a way which is subject to the perspective or viewpoint of the perceiver? In fact, do objects intrinsically possess shapes and colours and other such qualities at all? Holt and Perry asserted that since percepts in consciousness are identical with their immediate objects, then false percepts, like true percepts, are 'real'. Montague asserted that false percepts, illusions and hallucinations exist objectively; but he maintained that they have no causal force. This reply did not answer objections and queries which arise concerning our different perceptions, for example, of a staff partly submerged in water. The replies of the neo-realists in general did not satisfy the queries of the critical realists.

In 1920, some of the leading critical realists published a joint volume of *Essays in Critical Realism: A Co-operative Study of the*

Problems of Knowledge. The contributors were George Santayana, A. O. Lovejoy, Roy Wood Sellars, C. A. Strong, J. B. Pratt, Durant Drake and A. K. Rogers. They agreed with the neo-realists in rejecting idealism, but they disagreed with the neo-realists' rejection of representationalism. They were convinced that what is directly given in perception is a datum from which the perceiver may know indirectly of the existence of physical objects, by inference. A theory of critical realism of this kind, they maintained, had the advantage of enabling us to explain error in perception by attributing it to the psychological state of the perceiver.

In expounding this doctrine, however, they were not in full agreement concerning the nature of the immediate datum of perception. Santayana, Strong, Drake and Rogers held that the immediate data of consciousness are 'essences' which exist only as exemplified. These essences or abstract characters have a distinct ontological status, independent of both the object and the mental states in which they are present as data. Lovejoy, Sellars and Pratt, on the other hand, denied the doctrine of essences and held that the data in perception are the mental existents or particular ideas of the moment (not independent entities). Each group agreed that the existence of physical objects is inferred, and each group had then to face the serious epistemological problem of how this inference could be justified. A representationalist theory of knowledge seems to immerse the knower for ever in the world of 'representation'. Lovejoy admitted that one cannot 'prove' the existence of physical objects. One can say with justice then that both neo-realism and critical realism gave rise equally to serious epistemological difficulties.

33 Twentieth-century thought in Britain and America (II)

1. Alexander 2. Whitehead 3. Wittgenstein
4. American naturalism 5. Logical positivism
6. Philosophy of language

1. Alexander. *Samuel Alexander* (1859-1938), who was born in Sydney, Australia, was the first Jew to be elected a fellow at Oxford or Cambridge. He was a realist metaphysician who was professor of philosophy at the university of Manchester from 1893 to 1924. His major work *Space, Time, and Deity* (1920) was based on his Gifford lectures delivered in Glasgow in 1915. He rejected representationalism and constructed a metaphysical world-view similar to that of Spinoza, but influenced by the idea of evolution, empirical psychology and the realism of Moore and Russell.

For Alexander, metaphysics is the science of being and its essential attributes. The basic feature of all experience of reality is its spatio-temporal character. Ultimate reality, the basic matrix of all things, is space-time. Space and time, or the spatial aspect and the temporal or durational aspect of reality, together constitute one reality, Nature, an infinite continuum of pure-events, happenings, or point-instants. Empirical things are simply organized groupings or complexes of these smallest instances of spatio-temporal motions. The *nisus* or creative tendency of the motions of the organized complexes produces qualitatively new syntheses, or 'emergents', in a hierarchy of genuinely new qualities, each of which may be regarded as a higher 'divinity' above the lower. In the history of the universe, four levels so far have emerged, namely, motion, matter, life and mind. These four levels can prepare the basis for a fifth level yet to come, a 'deity', or next highest emergent quality, which the universe is engaged in bringing to birth. The universe of space-time, *Deus sive Natura*, can be thought of, then, as 'pregnant' with emergent qualities: it is being-in-becoming, or reality in 'divine' process. The religious sentiment, which is an empirical fact, may be regarded as the felt-experience of beings who are caught up in the *nisus* of a universe striving to produce the quality of deity.

Alexander played an important role in the realist reaction against the idealism which had been prevalent during his early years in university life. In 1914 he wrote an influential article on 'The Basis of Realism' which was published in the *Proceedings of the British Academy*. He held that knowledge, generally, is contemplation of an object where there is a relation of 'com-presence' or togetherness between a mind and an object which is an object in an independent world. The thing known is what it is whether it is known or not. Sense-data are simply perspectives of things which are known directly. Illusions, too, are perspectives of the real world, referred mistakenly by the mind (the judgement) to a context to which they do not belong. The categories of substance, cause, number and relation are not conceptual frameworks imposed on the world by the mind. They are real categories discovered or discerned in the world. 'Universals' too are discerned in the world. They are persistent plans of configurations of motions in space-time. They are patterns or habits which determine actual events. They manifest persistent identities of such a kind as to warrant our calling them real 'habits' of space-time.

2. Whitehead. *Alfred North Whitehead* (1861-1947), who was born at Ramsgate in Kent, was a philosopher and mathematician who worked mainly in Cambridge, London and Harvard. At Cambridge his most distinguished pupil was Bertrand Russell, who collaborated with him, from 1900 to 1912, in the writing of *Principia Mathematica*. In this three-volume work, which attempted to prove that mathematics could be deduced from premisses of formal logic, Whitehead concentrated mainly on the mathematical section and Russell on the philosophical, but in such a way that the whole work was one of complete collaboration. Whitehead's other main works of philosophical interest were *An Enquiry concerning the Principles of Natural Knowledge* (1919), *The Concept of Nature* (1920), *Science and the Modern World* (1926), *Symbolism* (1928), *Process and Reality* (1929) and *Adventures of Ideas* (1933).

Whitehead considered that contemporary physics demanded a new philosophical reflection on the world as presented in modern science. He developed a philosophy based on creative processes and events rather than on the Newtonian scheme of the material world as composed of atoms and objects each occupying a position in absolute space at an absolute time.

In his works on the philosophy of nature Whitehead maintained that natural science must necessarily present an account of the content of sensation. The physical world is that which is observed in perception through the senses. Nature must not be 'bifurcated' into an apparent world of phenomenalistic sense-data, pure 'patches of colour', or Humean 'impressions of sensation', on the one hand, and a causal, scientific world of non-apparent moving particles which give rise to perceptions and appearances, on the other. Mathematical and scientific concepts, such as concepts of points and lines, can be defined in terms of things and sets of events given directly in experience. Points and lines, for example, can be defined in terms of volumes extending over other volumes which can be perceived.

The most primitive mode of perception, Whitehead says, is that of environing realities pressing in upon us. It is a visceral feeling, a kinaesthetic organic sensation. An organic perception, or percipient event, is an actual occasion of active interaction between the whole organism and its whole environment. Organic sensation of this kind is 'perception in the mode of presentational immediacy'; it is 'perception in the mode of causal efficacy' mediated through organic experiences of the percipient's body. An organic sensation of a red event, for example, may have an irritating affective tone among nerve-racked people and bulls. This gives rise to a paradox for philosophy even though it is fairly obvious to common sense. Reality is that which is given in organic perception of this kind. There are no static concepts in the world. We must be careful to avoid the fallacy of misplaced concreteness which gives rise to reified abstractions of 'things' such as matter, force, gravity and substance. Reality is a network of ongoing, extended, organic, spatio-temporal events. Our experience is that of ongoing reality with spatio-temporal spread. This ongoing passage of nature can be divided into events whose constituents are not reified atomic abstractions but happenings which can be described as events extending over other events.

Whitehead rejected the Cartesian and phenomenalist tradition which regarded the subject-object dichotomy with its emphasis on intellect and understanding as the obvious foundation of knowledge. The subject, he said, is a later, 'emergent' datum in the organism. The primitive datum is the organism's complex of sentient experiences. The primitive experiences are sense-receptive experiences rather than sense-perceptions. The world is received as a complex of feelings. In this early stage of sense-reception it is feeling that is pervasive. The foundational datum is sympathy, or feeling in another and feeling conformally (in conformance) with another. The environing universe is received in this initial phase as a complex of feelings and is disclosed as a system of 'vector feelings'. In this (non-phenomenalist) causal view of perception, the functioning of the physiological organism is crucial.

The primitive kinaesthetic sensation, Whitehead says, is a sensation of coalescence, or concrescence, a growing together with the environing realities pressing in upon the organism. There is a primitive 'prehension' or 'grasping' of the concrete facts of relatedness on a level of sensation which is more basic than that of conscious apprehension. The universe of the organism is prehended or grasped in a series of actual occasions which, in their own process of becoming, synthesize their relations to other actual occasions. In this way there arises a 'concrescence of prehensions', a sensed unity of actual occasions. Some of these unities are prehended or grasped as 'nexus' or 'societies' of actual occasions, structured by subsocieties, in real actual unities that endure. They are not merely actual occasions; they are enduring societies of actual occasions. They are prehended as real actual things (such as stones or animals). They are prehended as enduring 'societies' or, in other words, as organisms.

Whitehead called his philosophy 'the philosophy of organism'. He defined his notion of organism as 'the concept of unities functioning and with spatio-temporal extensions'. The biological sciences are regarded as studying the larger units or organisms in nature as systems of smaller units with their own inner structure. The physical sciences are regarded as studying the smaller organisms or unities. The philosophy of organism replaces the traditional philosophy of substance. The method of descriptive generalization, applied to descriptions of enduring dynamic processes, replaces the method of deduction, applied to morphological generalizations about static structures. Only a philosophy of organism can provide an adequate understanding of a universe in which 'fields' of energy, process, dynamic actualization, interdependence, and continual creativity are disclosed as the primary data of immediate experience. The universe is one of becoming, flux and perishing. 'All things flow.' Each actual entity is essentially a process of self-creation, or self-development. Each is a 'prehending' entity in active interaction with its whole environment. Each selects and rearranges the material provided by its surroundings, just as each, in its own turn, becomes material for the next generation of actual entities. Each shapes the activities of the environment into a new creation. Each in being itself at this moment is nevertheless a continuation of the antecedent world. The universe is thus a unified dynamic process, a plurality in unity, which constantly manifests creative advance into novelty. The process of concrescence exhibits a pre-established harmony in which all prehensions are contributive to universal cosmic order.

God is differentiated from all other actual entities in that he alone is not occasioned by anything. The most decisive expression of a metaphysics of theism, Whitehead said, is that given in the Galilean origin of Christianity. God is not an Aristotelian unmoved mover exhibiting no concern for the process of the universe nor is he the Caesar-like figure of medieval theology. He is the God of love, the *lure* for feeling, the 'object of desire'. He is the principle of concretion whereby actual processes take their rise. God does not create other actual entities; he provides them with an initial impetus to self-creation. God is a particular outcome of self-creativity, the drive to self-realization. He is the chief exemplification of the philosophy of organism. In his primordial nature he is unlimited or infinite potentiality. In his primordial nature he is not only an envisagement of all the eternal objects (the pure potentials) by reason of which actual entities are determined or defined in their subjective determining forms, but also an appetition for their actualization. In his consequent nature, which is the consequence of the reaction of the world upon God, the 'epochal' happenings of the world are 'objectified' or sympathetically re-enacted in his own self-formation. In this context, Whitehead seems to think of God, by analogy with the self, as a unity of feelings, enjoyments, hopes, regrets, valuations of alternatives, decisions, satisfactions – all of them subjective reactions to the epochal happenings of the world as active in his own nature. His unity, or being, is his process of shaping this welter of material into his own consistent pattern of feelings. His enjoyment is what he is in his active shaping of the activities of the universe into a new creation, which is himself at this moment (cf. *Modes of Thought*, p. 228).

The natural theology of Whitehead has given rise, during the past four decades, to a prolific movement of thought which has come to be known as Process Theology. This movement finds a rich mine for further exploratory thought in the writings of Bergson, Alexander and Whitehead, and in Teilhard de Chardin in more recent years. It has given rise to a special journal, *Process Studies*. Several books and articles have been written on 'the new natural theology' and 'the Whiteheadian doctrine of God' by John B. Cobb, Charles Hartshorne, Bernard M. Loomer, Bernard E. Meland, Schubert M. Ogden, W. Norman Pittenger, Walter E. Stokes, Henry N. Wieman, Daniel D. Williams and several other philosophers and process theologians. In these works reality is seen as a temporal process. We live in a world that is being born instead of a world that is. The categories of becoming and activity replace the categories of being and substance;

and special emphasis is laid on creativity, the emergence of novelty and the organic interdependence of all things. Whitehead's thought has also had a deep influence on recent studies in logic, general biology, and social theory.

3. Wittgenstein. *Ludwig J. J. Wittgenstein* (1889-1951), who was born in Vienna, studied with Russell at Trinity College, Cambridge, and in 1939 succeeded Moore in the chair of philosophy. *Tractatus Logico-Philosophicus* (1921; English translations 1922 and 1961) was his only book published during his lifetime. Out of a mass of philosophical writings, some books, notebooks and notes (*Zettel*) have been published posthumously. The most important of these is *Philosophical Investigations* (1953), a work which criticizes and rejects the logical atomism of the earlier *Tractatus*. Both works, however, manifest Wittgenstein's abiding preoccupation with the scope and limits of language.

In the *Tractatus Logico-Philosophicus*, Wittgenstein attempted to trace the limits of what could be stated explicitly and to point to a realm that cannot be stated explicitly but can only be depicted or shown. In doing so he attempted to preserve an extensionalist logic by propounding a doctrine of logical atomism. He was convinced that language is simply a representing medium, a means of conveying the state of things as they are in the world. The complex totality of facts, or situations, or states of affairs in the world may be analysed, theoretically, into a series of mutually independent atomic facts. The world is made up of atomic facts, facts which are incapable of analysis into more elemental facts. Atomic propositions are related to atomic facts as 'pictures', or models, or representations of these facts. In atomic pictures of this kind there is a one-to-one correspondence of elements between picture and thing pictured, and there is a common arrangement of these elements, that is, a common structure or 'logical form'. All our propositions consist of such pictures. All genuine propositions are truth-functions of elementary propositions; their truth-values are entirely determined by the truth-values of their constituent atomic propositions.

Wittgenstein was impressed by a magazine account of how a motorcar accident was represented in a law court by means of small model cars and model dolls. The models could be manipulated to 'show' or project different accounts of what took place. 'A proposition', similarly, he said, 'is a model of reality as we think it to be' (*Tractatus* 4.01). 'In a proposition a situation is, as it were, put together experimentally' (4.031). A proposition is a logical picture of a possible fact. It represents the possibility of the existence and non-existence of atomic facts. It does so through its form of representation of a fact, that is, through its sense. Propositions do not state or express the form of representation of facts; they 'show' it. 'The proposition *shows* how things stand, *if* it is true.' Thus, for example, if we say 'a is larger than b', we can explain to another person what we mean by 'a' and 'larger' and 'b'. We then expect the other person to *grasp* the meaning of the combination. We cannot explain further what the combination means; the combination *shows* its meaning. Whatever can be said can be said clearly, but not all that is understood can be said; it can only be *shown*. There is a realm of the unutterable, the inexpressible, the metaphysical, the unthinkable, which appears to be the foundation of all language and all thought. In some inexpressible way we grasp this foundation of all thought. It is mirrored in our thoughts, but it cannot be the object of thought. It is what cannot be said but can only be shown. This distinction between what can be said in propositions and what cannot be said but can only be shown is the 'cardinal problem of philosophy', according to Wittgenstein.

A large part of the *Tractatus* is taken up with a discussion on the apparent exceptions to the 'picture' theory. Tautologies and contradictions, for example, do not seem to be reducible to pictures in the required sense. They are, strictly speaking, 'nonsensical', even though they help us greatly to gain deeper insight into how language actually functions. Any tautology, such as 'It is either raining or not raining', is true, and any contradiction, such as 'It is both raining and it is not raining', is false, for all possible states of affairs. They 'say nothing' about the world. They have no sense; they *show* us nothing. However, the truth of a tautology is certain; the truth of a contradiction is impossible; and the truth of all other propositions is possible. Hence, the truth-functions (T,F,P) of any group of elementary propositions (p,q,r,s) may be arranged in a serial arrangement which forms the basis for a theory of probability. In a suitable notation, such as that of a truth table, concerning a proposition (p) that is a truth function of other propositions (q,r) 'we can recognize the formal properties of propositions by mere inspection of the propositions themselves', without any knowledge of the formal principles of logic.

In the final section of the *Tractatus*, Wittgenstein asks: what, then, is philosophy? Philosophy has two tasks, he tells us. One of its tasks is to show that every proposition is a picture of a fact. The other is to show that philosophy is not a theory but an activity, a process of clarification, in which we try to delimit thoughts which are obscure and confused. There *is* a realm about which one can *say* nothing. For this reason, there can be no propositions of ethics, aesthetics or metaphysics; their realm is that of the 'transcendental', the 'mystical' (6.421, 6.45). 'Whereof one cannot speak, thereof one must be silent' (7).

For several years after finishing the *Tractatus*, Wittgenstein abandoned philosophy for other pursuits (as a schoolteacher, and later as a gardener's assistant in a monastery). During these years he came to see his previous account of language in terms of logical atomism as seriously defective. One cannot argue from the logical structure of language (even if the language is an ideal language) to the nature of the world that grounds the meaningfulness of this language. He decided then to change his approach and to concentrate on the way in which the meaning of terms in ordinary language is a function of their use. 'Let us look and see what *is* the case, what language-users actually do with their language.' He abandoned his previous 'picture' analogy, with its representationalist one-to-one correspondence of elements, and replaced it with 'tool' and 'game' analogies instead.

From 1929 onwards, at Cambridge, Wittgenstein devoted himself once again to the philosophy of language. He began writing his *Philosophical Investigations* in 1936. These investigations, or remarks, or 'sketches of landscapes', as he called them, were completed, in three parts, in an isolated cottage on the west coast of Ireland in 1949. He now conceived language as an activity involving the uses of words as tools. Language may be compared to a collection of carpenter's tools, each with its own function and technique of use. It may also be compared to a range of games (football, Ludo, chess), each with its own appliances and rules and objectives and criteria of success and failure. Each linguistic move, like each games move, can be judged as successful or not, and permissible or not, only as a move within a particular game. Each new language game *(Sprachspiel)* embodies a new 'form of life'; it is not merely a rearrangement of what was there before. There is nothing common to all games, or to all language games; they are not united by any essence. Words are not labels for things. The meaning of a word (such as 'This') or the meaning of a sentence (such as 'This is clear') arises in its 'use', its 'employment', its 'application'. The word or sentence has its sense only in the particular circumstance in which it is used to do something, in the special 'surroundings' in which it is a meaningful move in a particular language game. 'Look at the sentence as an instrument, and its sense as its employment' (section 421). It is the employment, the activity, that is fundamental. The emphasis, then, is on activity and not on previously fixed meaningful 'pictures'. Meaning is *not prior* to use. Conceptual analysis must give way to concern for linguistic use.

Wittgenstein maintained that it is our agreement, or human practice, that fixes the meaning of the rules, defining their content, within the 'surroundings' of the present, particular language game. Thus a sentence (such as 'This is clear') spoken within its own special context might perhaps be deciding some issue, or expressing a sensation, or asserting something, or asking, or repeating, or intending, or expecting something, and so on. A precise and mutually acknowledged meaning emerges because customary ways of doing things, or agreed rules, are being followed in practice. The meaning is present in the particular 'use' of words in particular circumstances in which customary guidelines are being followed. For this reason, language is essentially social or public. A 'private language' would be impossible to develop. It would have no criterion for distinguishing between rules correctly used and rules merely apparently kept, and so it could have no genuine rules at all. Thus, for example, Pyrrhonic scepticism or solipsism is entirely ruled out by the absence of genuine rules, and hence of genuine language in which it could be (privately) formulated.

Wittgenstein's contention throughout the *Philosophical Investigations* is against conceptual analysis. It is against the idea that the meaning of a word is a meaning which the speaker thinks or feels privately. He was convinced that this mentality concerning the meaning of words lay at the heart of all philosophical contentions and problems. Philosophical investigation, in general, is not a study of 'inner processes'. It is an activity, or form of life, in which the investigator attends to the actual use of 'public' terms such as 'think', 'feel', 'see', 'understand', 'remember' as revealing a 'complicated network of similarities overlapping and criss-crossing' in the novel uses and moves of each language game. Philosophical problems arise when philosophical speech ignores 'public' use of language and goes on 'private' holiday into an analytic world of introspective private processes. Philosophical problems are best resolved, not by answering them, but by showing that they involve confusions concerning the use of language, confusions in which language is thrown out of gear. The treatment of a philosophical question, then, is like the treatment of an illness. The philosopher who attempts to 'describe' his state of mind in the way he 'describes' his room needs to 'call to mind the differences between the language games' (section 290), and he must learn to 'reject the grammar which tries to force itself upon him here' (304). To understand is to master techniques, forms of life, modes of action, to which our attention is directed when language is used. The use of language is a form of life in which the complex criss-crossing similarities of patterns of action must not be obscured and confused by the over-simplification of some grammatical fiction.

Wittgenstein's early thought was selectively used and developed in a positivistic way by the logical positivists of the Vienna Circle. His university lectures and later works have had a powerful influence on the development of linguistic philosophy in English-speaking universities throughout the world down to our own times. Atomism has given way to contextualism.

4. American naturalism. In the late 1930s in America the realist contention concerning the independent reality of physical objects had ceased to be an important issue, and naturalism replaced realism as the dominant trend of thought. Naturalism as a general philosophical theory directs its interest to the principles of (physical, biological) nature, and regards all that is specifically human (such as history, thought) as an extension of the biological order. All phenomena can be explained by natural causes. Cognitive claims can be established only by the logico-empirical method of science.

The biologically oriented psychology of William James and John Dewey left a strong impression on their disciples and followers. We see this influence present, for example, in the thought of George Santayana (see below, Chapter 36, section 2) and Ernest Nagel. Santayana, in his early work *The Life of Reason* (1905-06), asserted that the philosophy of history implies no providential plan of creation or redemption but is simply 'retrospective politics'. Historical events are explained in terms of causal laws. The rise and development of reason is in reality an extension of the order already achieved in organized matter.

In 1944, John Dewey, Ernest Nagel, Sidney Hook, George Boas and others published an important collection of essays entitled *Naturalism and the Human Spirit*. The contributors in general maintained that the conditions of man's life are continuous with the rest of nature. The scientific method is continuous with the operations of thought used in ordinary life and is capable of studying social phenomena, consciousness and everything that exists. No transcendent, intuitive, metaphysical method is needed to deal with uniquely human phenomena. In his essay in this collection, and in several other independent works, Ernest Nagel (b. 1901), John

Dewey professor of philosophy at Columbia University, maintained that mental events are aspects of the organization of human bodies and that they are contingent upon the organization of human bodies. Events, qualities, and processes are dependent, similarly, on the organization of spatially and temporally located bodies. There are no occult forces or disembodied spirits directing natural events, and there is no personal immortality when bodily organizations disintegrate.

The interest in nature, and in man-in-nature, was broad enough to permit several approaches and hence several types of American naturalism to emerge. George Woodbridge (1867-1940), a colleague of Dewey at Columbia, spoke of his own realism and naturalism as reaffirming in modern terms some basic themes of Aristotle's metaphysics. Morris Raphael Cohen (1880-1947) argued, against idealists, positivists and pragmatists, that logical arguments and logical connections belong to a rational order whose invariant relations have an ontological basis in the objective order of reason and nature. These invariant relations of logic and science belong to 'the eternal present'. Roy Wood Sellars (b. 1880), in *Evolutionary Naturalism* (1969), and other works, contended that all non-materialistic types of naturalism are inadequate. 'Life is not a nonnatural force coming from outside, but a term for the new capacities of which nature has found itself capable.' On the other hand Vincent C. Punzo's *Reflective Naturalism* (1969) developed a reflective form of naturalism that took cognizance of Dewey's reflective valuing of all modes of experience. The experienced tendencies of human nature are seen as open to the influences of the theistic dimension as well as to the influences of the community of nature and mankind.

Several of the American naturalists gave special attention to the problem of value and valuation, and to problems concerning moral values as an aspect of the wider problem of the nature of values in general. Ralph Barton Perry (see above, Chapter 32, section 4), of Harvard, maintained that 'Any object, whatever it be, acquires value when any interest, whatever it be, is taken in it'; and he defined interest as that which is characteristic of instinct, desire, will, feeling, and all their states, acts and attitudes of expectancy. All men speak of some objects of interest as being 'better' or 'worse' than others. In this way moral valuation emerges. Men recognize that integrated or harmonized interests, effected through 'reflective agreement' between the personal and the social will, lead to a state of 'harmonious happiness'. This moral criterion, which excludes hatred and personal aggrandizement, is universally applicable to everybody's interest. It is one that men are capable of adopting and one by which they are capable of being governed since it agrees with human nature and the circumstances of human life.

Clarence Irving Lewis (1883-1964), also of Harvard, propounded a similar naturalistic theory of value and valuation. In his *Analysis of Knowledge and Valuation* (1946) Lewis maintained that value is simply an aspect or mode of the given, the sense-presentation; it is the given as gratifying or grievous. A gratifying subjective experience is intrinsically good. Objects of experience are extrinsically good (or bad) according to their capacity to produce experiences which are satisfying (or unpleasant). The ultimate test of goodness is 'the long-run satisfaction of our needs in general'. In this light, the basic rational (categorical) imperative may be formulated as: So think and so act that later you will not be sorry. Value judgements are confirmable in the same way that other empirical judgements are confirmable. This emphasis on value and valuation as having meaning only within the world of empirical scientific knowledge is pervasive in the writings of the American naturalists.

5. **Logical positivism.** Logical positivism or 'scientific empiricism', which was first developed by the 'Vienna Circle' in its co-operative discussion meetings in the 1920s, began to be influential in Britain and America in the 1930s. Moritz Schlick, Rudolf Carnap, Otto Neurath and other leading exponents of the ideas of the group thought of themselves as continuing a nineteenth-century empirical tradition which was closely linked to British empirical thought. Wittgenstein's *Tractatus Logico-philosophicus* (published in German in 1921) had a remarkable influence on the deliberations of the discussion circle, where it was accepted as being a logical development of British empiricism. The Vienna neo-positivists in general maintained that all meaningful sentences must be either analytic or synthetic. Analytic sentences contain no factual information, and they are either true (tautologies) or false (contradictions) by reason of their logical form alone. Synthetic, or empirical, sentences are factual reports of some observations or generalizations based on empirical observations. Synthetic propositions are meaningful to the extent that they can be verified. Since metaphysical and theological statements did not fit into any of these categories they were dismissed as meaningless ('non-sensical') pseudo-statements.

For a sentence to have 'factual', 'descriptive', 'literal' or 'cognitive' value (as when one affirms that 'water boils at 100°C'), the logical positivists maintained, it must be empirically *verifiable*, namely, by reference to empirical observations. In 1930, Friedrich Waismann formulated the neo-positivist Principle of Verifiability in these terms: 'Anyone uttering a sentence must know in which conditions he calls the statement true or false; if he is unable to state this, then he does not know what he has said. A statement which cannot be verified *conclusively* is not verifiable at all; it is just devoid of any meaning.' This came to be known as the requirement of 'strong verifiability'. The meaning of a sentence lies in its logical possibility of verification; the meaning is given by the experience that would verify it conclusively.

Several objections quickly emerged, however, against this 'strong' formulation of the principle of verifiability. Universal statements of scientific laws (covering an unlimited number of instances) are not conclusively verifiable; are they therefore devoid of any meaning? Is the principle of verifiability itself either analytic or empirically verifiable, and if not, in what sense is it meaningful? Statements about the experiences of other people and statements about past and future events are not conclusively verifiable. Denials of existential statements (for example, 'infra-red things do not exist', as a denial of 'infra-red things do exist') are not verifiable according to the requirements of 'strong', conclusive verifiability; are they therefore never meaningful? Objections of this kind led Schlick, Ayer and others to reformulate the principle of verifiability in terms of 'weak' verifiability. Each of the attempted reformulations, however, seemed unavoidably to allow metaphysical statements too as being meaningful. The formulators were then left with a choice between formulating the principle in a way which would apparently bypass their anti-metaphysical convictions or allowing the principle to retain its plausibility in modes of expression which would be sufficiently vague.

In the mid-1930s, Carnap, Reichenbach, Frank, Feigl, Hempel, Tarski and other leaders of the movement fled from political or racial persecution to the United States. There they found that their teachings were gradually winning widespread approval in different university departments of psychology, ethics, jurisprudence, and the natural sciences.

In Britain, *Frank Plumpton Ramsey* (1903-30) was one of the first philosophers to expound the early teachings of Wittgenstein. He propounded what has been called the redundancy theory of truth. To say that 'It is true (or false) that Caesar was (or was not) murdered' means no more than to assert the basic proposition 'Caesar was (or was not) murdered'. To say that a proposition is true ('p is true') means no more than to assert the proposition ('p') itself. The assertion of truth is an assertively redundant expression. The traditional notion of truth as a property or relation is, therefore, misguided. P. F. Strawson refined this theory further into the 'performative theory of truth', namely, that the function of 'It's true that' is to agree with, accept, endorse or 'ditto' the basic proposition ('p') itself; it is a performance of an endorsing action and not a formulation of a statement. Neither of these theories took into account Dewey's theory of 'That's true' as expressing warranted assertibility.

Alfred Jules Ayer (b. 1910), Wykeham professor of logic at Oxford, did his early philosophical studies in Oxford and Vienna. He introduced logical positivism to Britain in his Oxford lectures in 1933 and in his first book *Language, Truth and Logic*, published in 1936. This work made an immediate impact on British philosophers, and became one of the most influential works in mid-century British philosophy. It attacked, with uncompromising and revolutionary vigour, all metaphysical statements and the mistakes of much of traditional philosophy; and it did so in language which is a model of elegance and lucidity. In the preface to the first edition, the author acknowledged that the views he advocates derive from Russell, Wittgenstein, Hume and the logical positivists of the Vienna Circle; and in the introduction to the second edition he acknowledged that his theory of philosophy as equivalent to contextual definition was over-simplistic and needed to be amended. Like Carnap and the logical positivists in general, Ayer identified philosophy with analysis and analysis with linguistic concerns. Linguistic analysis of this kind eschews all forms of conceptual or ontological definition. In their later works, however, both Carnap and Ayer modified their previous views about analysis and their formulations of the principle of verification in ways which would unavoidably admit as meaningful the particular kinds of philosophical and theological views and statements they endeavoured to outlaw.

Ayer, like the other logical positivists, wished to bring about a unification of knowledge, or a unification of the sciences, through the creation of a common scientific descriptive language. He accepted the language of science as a paradigm of meaningful language. In this light he discounted or dismissed other forms of language as possessing only expressive-evocative significance. He spoke of value statements in ethics and aesthetics as being simply 'emotive' statements. They failed to attain the status of the paradigm language of science; they are simply expressions of emotion with imperative overtones. Wittgenstein, by way of contrast, pointed out that there is no one language game which is the paradigm or model language to which all other language games must conform. No particular form of language is privileged except for a specific purpose. The uses of ethical terms can be understood only within the context of an ethical 'language game' which expresses a unique form of life. Empirical verifiability has a legitimate role to play in the field of scientific hypotheses. Outside that particular role it may not be used as a general criterion of meaning, nor as a yardstick for ascertaining what is meaningful and what is 'nonsense'. Granted the complexity of language, the narrow concept of 'meaning', as visualized by the logical positivists, is seen to be grossly inadequate. Some recent philosophers, such as W. V. O. Quine and N. Goodman, are convinced that this inadequacy derives from a still more basic inadequacy, namely, the questionable dichotomy between analytic and synthetic statements, or Hume's dichotomy between logical and factual statements. This highly questionable dichotomy is one which underpins all of Ayer's thought and the thought of the logical positivists in general.

Karl Raimund Popper (b. 1902), professor of logic and scientific method at the London School of Economics, pointed out in *The Logic of Scientific Discovery* (1935, 1959) that it is *falsifiability* and not verifiability that is the essential criterion for the scientific character of discourse, and is the hallmark of science. No scientific theory is ever conclusively verified, no matter how many tests it has survived. Our present scientific knowledge is simply that body of theories which have so far, in history, survived all sustained and systematic attempts to falsify them. There have been, down through the course of history, metaphysical theories which have been historically important and meaningful. Falsifiability distinguishes empirical theories from nonempirical theories; it does not distinguish the meaningful from the meaningless. Scientific knowledge commences with an imaginative conjecturing of hypotheses; this is something that cannot be subjected to rules. It proceeds by a sustained and systematic exposure of the consequences of these hypotheses to the risk of empirical falsification. Scientific theories eventually become provisionally acceptable by successful submission to empirical tests. It is salutary to remember that, in the history of science, not even the well-attested and widely accepted Newtonian physics has proved permanently immune from further scientific revision.

In *The Open Society and Its Enemies* (1945), *The Poverty of Historicism* (1957), and *Conjectures and Refutations* (1963, 1974), Popper applied his theory of 'scientific knowledge as a free creation' to man and society. He did so in the form of an attack on the deterministic theory of historicism, the theory that there are general laws of historical development that render the course of history inevitable and predictable. The future course of human history is not predictable, as Hegel and Marx suggest. Predictions, as in the case of eclipses, are possible only for systems that are 'well-isolated, stationary and recurrent'. In human society, one of the major factors determining personal and social development is human decision with regard to human response to particular situations. Our contemporary technological society could not, even in principle, have been predicted a century ago. Human choice, response and responsibility lie within individuals. No historicist (a Plato, Hegel or Marx) can ever have sufficient grounds to warrant an assertion that society must necessarily develop in a particular direction whether its members want it so or not.

Ordinary scientific method can be applied to society, to particular isolable aspects of the whole, just as it is applied to nature, Popper says. Social science can seek to discover laws that explain the unintended consequences of human action. There are no laws, however, that govern and determine the whole system; and so there is no valid foundation for total revolutionary reconstructions of the entire social order. Social reform proceeds by piecemeal social engineering. In this light, the crucial problem of politics is that of devising institutions that will minimize the risks of bad rulers. The main question is not who should wield power but how the misuse of power is to be prevented.

6. Philosophy of language. Philosophical analysis as practised by the British and American realists ended with logical positivism and with the widespread repudiation of analysis as the proper method of philosophy. In the 1950s the new generation of young philosophers turned away from contextual definition, conceptual analysis and reductive resolution, and towards the conception of philosophy as an activity which strives to describe and elucidate, through language, difficult and basic expressions relating to reality. John Wisdom, Susan Stebbing and others questioned the feasibility of reducing statements about physical objects to statements about sense-data. Wittgenstein pointed out that it is an illusion to think that language 'pictures' have meanings which are named by terms that state the facts. Isolated words and sentences, independently of their use, do not refer to or name anything. There is no ideal language, and hence there are no ideal expressions to analyse. Philosophical analysis gave way then to linguistic philosophy. It is now through the complexities of language that extra-linguistic reality is approached. The meaning of any expression is governed by and found in, or is interpreted as, the rules, conventions, regulations and habits which govern the actual uses of the expression. The aim of philosophy therefore is the elucidation of the logical grammar of any such expression. Philosophical activity expresses itself in descriptions of the actual workings of ordinary language. Thus, for example, the meaning of 'induction' or 'cause' or 'good' or 'mind' is best pointed out in one or the other of the many uses of these words. If one is clear about the various uses of such words as 'evidence' or 'reason', for instance, then the traditional pseudo-problem concerning induction can be 'dissolved' in the process of bringing into the open the confusions that gave rise to a pseudo-question. Elucidation of the uses of these words dispels the temptation to think in terms of treacherous analogies; and in doing so it dispels the temptation to ask the original question.

The Oxford 'philosophers of ordinary language', notably Gilbert Ryle and J. L. Austin, unlike Wittgenstein, did not regard philosophical paradoxes as conceptual disorders or 'diseases' awaiting philosophical cure. They regarded them as convenient points of entry into the philosophical activity of setting out the complex, deviant, nonstandard logics of the philosophically crucial terms of ordinary speech. The philosopher must constantly return to what people say and do, and to how they vivify and enact their signs; and he must then map out and set out the 'logical geography' or 'rational grammar' of the living, variant logics of informal ordinary speech.

Gilbert Ryle (1900-76), Waynflete professor of metaphysical philosophy at Oxford, wrote a wide range of philosophical articles, each of which focused on a specific issue, such as 'Systematically Misleading Expressions', 'Negation', 'If, So and Because', 'Feeling', 'Pleasure', 'Predicting and Inferring', 'Use, Usage and Meaning', 'Ordinary Language', and similar related themes. In these articles, Ryle, like Wittgenstein, regarded philosophical investigation as the activity of dispelling conceptual confusions arising from our unconscious inclination to construe grammatical similarities and differences as indicative of logical similarities and differences. Linguistic philosophy enables us to map the extension, the boundaries and roles of interrelated concepts in such a way that we come to see better the 'logical geography' of our conceptual system and the logical errors of category mistakes.

In his book *The Concept of Mind* (1949), Ryle said that to suppose that the mind is a ghost mysteriously embodied in a machine is to commit the category mistake of confusing the logic of discourse about bodies and things with the logic of discourse about minds. There is no such 'thing' as mind comparable to a thing called body. It is a *person* that thinks or knows or chooses. To speak of a person's mind is to speak of the person's propensities to behave in certain ways. Words such as 'think' and 'know' and 'aspire' are disposition words indicating that, under certain circumstances, certain modes of performance would be evidenced. Ways of acting which by analogy with 'physical processes' and 'physical acts' are called 'mental processes' or 'mental acts' are simply *ways* of acting, or dispositions, which are not themselves acts. A man's knowledge of himself, like his knowledge of other persons, comes simply from observing his own *behaviour*. Ryle said he had no wish to be branded as a philosophical behaviourist, even though he acknowledged a certain debt to the philosophy of behaviourism.

(Arthur) John Wisdom (b. 1904), who succeeded Wittgenstein in the chair of philosophy at Cambridge, was deeply influenced by the thought, and the change in thought, of Wittgenstein. In an early series of five articles entitled 'Logical Constructions' (1931-33), Wisdom argued that certain entities (such as material objects, or the average family) are 'incomplete symbols' or logical constructions out of more fundamental 'atomic' elements (such as sense impressions) and that statements about these entities can be translated into statements about more unproblematic or ultimate sense-data. Thus, statements about the Danish nation are translatable into statements about Danes. The task of the philosopher (the 'logical atomist') is that of analysing complex statements into 'atomic statements' which are logically and epistemologically fundamental. 'The philosophical intention is clearer insight into the ultimate structure.'

In his essay on 'Philosophical Perplexity' (1936) and his book on *Metaphysics and Verification* (1938), however, Wisdom, like his mentor Wittgenstein, abandoned the earlier reductionist programme and presented a new conception of the nature of philosophy and of language. Philosophical queries arise out of a dissatisfaction with certain 'kinds of statement', or 'categories of being', implicit in our ordinary language. There are concealed likenesses and differences between statements about material objects and statements about sensations. These linguistic likenesses and differences give rise to philosophical claims that certain material-object statements 'mean the same thing' as certain complex sense-datum statements. Philosophical investigation must bring out in full the relevant likenesses and differences that are concealed by, or implicit in, our ordinary way of talking and categorizing. Insight and clarity with regard to alternative categorizations can then allay the dissatisfaction that was expressed in the disquieting philosophical query. On this point Wisdom regarded his own approach as differing from that of Wittgenstein. Wittgenstein represented philosophical queries 'as merely symptoms of linguistic confusion'. Wisdom represented them 'as also symptoms of linguistic penetration'.

Max Black, an American analytical philosopher, was born in Baku, Russia, in 1909. He studied at Cambridge, and was profoundly impressed by the thought of Ludwig Wittgenstein. He lectured subsequently at Cornell University, where he became professor of philosophy in 1954. In 1964, Black published an extensive and renowned study, *A Companion to Wittgenstein's Tractatus*. This work contains, in addition to an exegesis of the *Tractatus*, several critical expository essays on the principal topics encountered in the text. Black also wrote several philosophical essays and articles which were collected and published in three volumes: *Language and Philosophy* (1949), *Problems of Analysis* (1954) and *Models and Metaphors* (1962). These essays in analytical philosophy focus on several of the themes which are prominent in Wittgenstein's later work. The conception of language as a mirror of reality is radically mistaken. The task of linguistic philosophy is that of bringing to light the presuppositions and implications underlying the 'loose' use of language rules in the formation of language utterances, such as, for example, assertions, denoting phrases and definitions.

John Langshaw Austin (1911-60), White's professor of moral philosophy at Oxford, was convinced that the many subtle distinctions which are enshrined in ordinary language provide an insight into important distinctions that have been observed in the world around us. He was convinced that the basic task of philosophical investigation is that of carefully elucidating and clarifying the forms and concepts of ordinary language, in the tradition of countless philosophers from Socrates to G. E. Moore. He made a meticulous application of the methods and standards of a scholar of classical texts to contemporary discussions. He applied these methods, for example, in a special way to the language of perception, illusion, delusion, and the illocutionary forces which lie within certain locutionary acts, as clear instances of the philosophical importance of the nuances of ordinary language.

In several of his published articles, and in his 1955 Harvard lectures, published posthumously as *How to Do Things with Words* (Oxford, 1962), Austin pointed to the significance of performatory utterances (such as 'I promise'), namely, speech acts which are in themselves the performance of an action. A locutionary act, that is, an utterance (saying words) having a sense and a reference, as for example that 'The window is open', may in some cases be also a performance of an illocutionary act of making a hint, or promise or exclamation, expressing the speaker's (perhaps unfavourable) attitude in such a way that he succeeds in performing the perlocutionary act of positively influencing (or embarrassing) his audience to do something about it. Illocutionary forces of this kind are frequently present in ordinary speech acts.

In his lecture-series *Sense and Sensibilia* (published posthumously in 1962), Austin examined the arguments of A. J. Ayer, H. H. Price and others with reference to perception, sense-data, illusions and sense appearances. He examined the use of words such as 'looks', 'seems', 'appears' in arguments pertaining to 'illusions' arising from sticks placed in water, dreams and after-images. He found that the uses of these particular words were not carefully studied or correctly described. Illusions are confused with delusions. A straight stick in water does not look like a bent stick out of water, because we can see the water. The complex uses of words are oversimplified. The ordinary man who sees rainbows, shadows, and mirror images does not believe or assert that all his perceptions are perceptions of material things. Philosophers err in attempting to give a single account of all forms of perception and all forms of perceptual error. This is an area in which philosophical error arises from empirical error. It is an area in which scientific investigation, and not philosophy, may be able to lead to greater enlightenment and understanding.

Willard V. O. Quine (b. 1908), professor of philosophy at Harvard, and a follower of the logical positivist Rudolf Carnap, has been the most influential empiricist in recent American philosophy. In *Methods of Logic* (1950), he elaborated a system of logic similar to that of Russell but differing from the logic of Russell in as far as Quine's system is one in which singular terms can be eliminated. In two well-known articles, 'On What There Is' (1948), and 'Two Dogmas of Empiricism' (1951), which were reprinted in his book *From a Logical Point of View* (1953), Quine presented a slogan criterion and a criticism of analytic statements which gave rise to widening circles of discussion, controversy and debate. He presented his slogan, 'To be is to be the value of a variable', as a criterion for distinguishing between realists and nominalists. He cast doubt on the notion of analyticity in an effort to rid philosophy of the dogmatic programme of reductionism and of its fixed notion of cognitive synonymous meanings. He sought to promote a nominalist philosophy of language which would eliminate the postulation of unnecessary entities, 'meanings', and synonymy.

Quine, like Nelson Goodman (b. 1906), avoided speaking of 'classes' (non-individual abstract entities) and emphasized the thesis that language is extensional. Thus language is regarded as being built up of variables and an indefinite set of predicates (one-place and many-place predicates) such that complex sentences are related to atomic sentences by truth-functional relationships and by quantification.

According to Quine, there is no statement that depends for its truth on a direct confrontation with experience. Thus it is not any factual component but rather the linguistic component that constitutes the sentence. No sharp precise boundary can be drawn, then, between analytic and synthetic statements or between logical statements and factual statements. The distinction is, at most, a relative distinction between statements which are either more or less deeply entrenched in some relatively close-knit system of connected statements, as in the case of a system of logical statements or mathematical statements. Systems of this kind resemble an interconnected web in which no part is immune from revision and in which each revision (in the light of experience) affects more than one part. Single sentences, isolated from a system, have no meaning; and, within one or more systems, a single sentence can always be regarded as meaning a multitude of different things. In *Word and Object* (1960) Quine called this thesis the thesis of the 'indeterminacy of radical translation'. Any statement can be held to be true no matter what is observed, provided that adjustments are made elsewhere in the system.

In his later works, *Set Theory* (1963), *Philosophy of Logic* (1970) and *Roots of Reference* (1973), Quine made several noteworthy contributions to set theory, linguistic translation of ontic commitments, and regimentation of ordinary language. However, his sustained objections to meanings, necessity, and accounts of analyticity that depend on the notion of synonymy have been the most discussed part of Quine's work.

Stuart Newton Hampshire (b. 1914), Warden of Wadham College, Oxford, in his book *Thought and Action* (1959), brought together into a systematic comprehensive theory several of the detailed conclusions of previous linguistic investigation. Hampshire acknowledged a certain distant indebtedness to the broad systematic outlook of Spinoza, Jean-Paul Sartre and Maurice Merleau-Ponty for prompting and encouraging his own concern to bring together views in the theory of knowledge, ethics, aesthetics, metaphysics and the philosophy of mind. The world cannot be analysed and expressed in terms of sense-impressions alone. Language and thought present objects and persons as identifiable persistent realities. Self-consciousness, or the subject's sense of identity, is dependent on the subject's awareness of being a physical agent in a physical environment. It is in communication with other persons that self-knowledge arises and grows. Personality is expressed through will and action as well as through contemplative understanding; it is not coterminous with intellect alone. Man is an essentially active being. He perceives the world through bodily interaction with it, even more than through disengaged aesthetic contemplation. He is conscious of his continuing identity and the passage of time by way of the flow of his intentions. Human activities must be understood historically or genetically, that is, as rooted in the person's early experiences and unconscious memories. Human freedom is achieved through a growing knowledge of the semi-conscious factors that make conscious intentional action ineffective, and through knowledge of means of modifying these factors. It is on a comprehensive view of human nature, of this kind, that any comprehensible system of ethics must be grounded.

Peter Frederick Strawson (b. 1919), Waynflete professor of metaphysical philosophy at Oxford, and formerly a leading advocate of 'ordinary language philosophy', succeeded in restoring (descriptive) metaphysics as a philosophical undertaking not unrespectable for British thinkers. The groundwork for his book *Individuals: An Essay in Descriptive Metaphysics* (1959) had been laid, in part, in an earlier article 'On Referring' (*Mind*, 1950), and in his *Introduction to Logical Theory* (1952). In these earlier linguistic works Strawson pointed out that Russell's theory of descriptions fails to see the important distinction that must be made between presupposition and entailment, and between sentence and statement. It is this failure which underlies the 'bogus trichotomy' of true, false, and meaningless sentences. One must not disregard the difference between a sentence and the particular use of that sentence in a specific context. A sentence of the form 'The f is g' (e.g. 'The king of France is bald') may refer to an 'entity' which the speaker *presupposes* to exist, without stating or asserting that the entity actually exists. Something is asserted ('S is P'); but what is asserted does not *entail* that the referent, the subject noun phrase, or the 'entity', exists. Reference and presupposition is to be distinguished from entailment. A sentence of this kind can be meaningful or meaningless. It is not the sentence, however, but the statement (or assertion) made, in using the sentence, that is capable of being characterized as true or false. Statements of the form 'The f is g', or 'All fs are gs' have existential presuppositions and these are capable of being true or false. The statement that 'The king of France is bald' is neither true nor false; it is one of its presuppositions that is false, namely, the *presupposition* that there is such a king, since France is a republic and it has no king.

Shortly after the publication of his *Introduction to Logical Theory*, Strawson's interest began to focus on the broad field of phenomenological description or descriptive metaphysics rather than upon the specialized philosophical investigation of ordinary language. He now attempted to 'lay bare the most general features of our conceptual structure'. He did so in a work which was subtitled 'An Essay in Descriptive Metaphysics' (1959). In this work, which he called *Individuals*, Strawson, like Kant, examined the general structure of thought about the world. He concentrated on the relations between particulars and universals, subjects and predicates, reference and predication, as a means towards understanding the preconditions for the identification of particular objects in speech. He concluded from this study that from the viewpoint of particular identification, material objects are the 'basic particulars' in relation to which all spatio-temporal and non-spatio-temporal objects are identifiable.

In this work, Strawson attacked the Cartesian notion of 'person' as implying duality of mental substance and corporeal substance intimately connected. He also attacked the contemporary serial theory of consciousness, according to which states of consciousness are not ascribed to anything at all. Each of these views is seen ultimately as being incoherent. Strawson suggested that the concept of person is a 'logically primitive concept such that both predicates ascribing states of consciousness and predicates ascribing corporeal characteristics are equally applicable to a single individual of that single type'. The concept of person is a primitive concept. It is not a composite concept made up of the concept of mind and the concept of body. States of consciousness and physical states or physical properties are ascribable to one and the same public thing, namely, a public person. In this way, Strawson, while using a frame of reference and method which is similar to that of Kant, arrived at an understanding of the nature of the person which resembles that of Aristotle. This understanding of the nature of the person may be seen also in Strawson's commentary on aspects of Kant's thought, *The Bounds of Sense* (1966).

Strawson distinguished between 'descriptive metaphysics' which 'is content to describe the actual structure of our thought about the world' and 'revisionary' (or critical judgemental) metaphysics which attempts to show that the described structure of our thought about the world is the correct structure, or better than rival structures. *C. O. Evans*, in *The Subject of Consciousness* (1970), went beyond Strawson by unifying the (phenomenological) themes of self-awareness, attention, intentionality, and Strawson's theme of public-person reference. The self as an experiencer is seen as persisting, unprojected consciousness, experiencing and knowing the world of consciousness, without becoming an object of consciousness. *D. M. MacKinnon*, in his Gifford lectures, *The Problem of Metaphysics* (published 1974), examined moral and poetic tragedy and its portrayal of man's ethical and religious life to discover a model of how to use language in ways that are 'revisionary', and not merely 'descriptive' of our categorization of the universe. *T. E. Wilkerson*'s *Minds, Brains and People* (1974) presented a further facet of revisionary metaphysics. Personal traits such as purposeful intentional activity, and refraining from certain activities, and intentional engaging in valuational ceremonies, cannot be accounted for totally in terms of philosophical physicalism. A distinct philosophy of persons is required. *John Eccles*, a neurosurgeon, who collaborated with Sir Karl Popper in a 'revisionary' work on *The Self and Its Brain* (1977), said in his Gifford lectures, *The Human Mystery* (published 1979): 'It is my thesis that we have to recognize (our) unique selfhood as being the result of a supernatural creation of what in the religious sense is called a soul'. In his later years, A. J. Ayer decided to concede, with reference to the metaphysician, that after all 'there may be good reasons why he says the strange things he does'. In conclusion one might say that metaphysics, whether 'descriptive' only or 'revisionary' also, became once again in the 1960s and 1970s a respectable (or a not-unrespectable) philosophical enterprise even within the field of the philosophy of language.

34 Phenomenology

1. The rise of phenomenology   2. Husserl   3. Scheler
4. Ingarden   5. Merleau-Ponty

1. The rise of phenomenology. Phenomenology and life-philosophy (or vitalism) were two different movements of twentieth-century thought which brought about a radical break with earlier 'modern' thought. Life-philosophy emphasized (biological) vitality, life, becoming and growth. Husserl's phenomenology emphasized the data of consciousness, the phenomena that manifest themselves immediately in the field of consciousness.

The origins of phenomenology may be traced back to the teachings of Franz Brentano and his doctrine of intentionality. (See Chapter 25, section 9, above.) Images, concepts, knowing and willing acts are 'intentional' in the sense that they 'mean' or intend something. They are oriented to an object or objective (such as a centaur, for example); and each signified object itself, as an imagined, thought, admired, hated, inferred or willed object, possesses an 'intentional' existence in the mind. Each possesses this intentional existence in the mind irrespective of its possible, extra-mental, or real existence in itself. For Brentano, intentionality of consciousness is the subject-matter of empirical psychology.

Brentano had several pupils who developed and applied his Aristotelian-Thomistic-based doctrine of intentionality in their own particular areas of speciality. *Kazimierz Twardowski* (see above, Chapter 30, section 5), professor of philosophy at the university of Lwów, developed a Brentanist descriptive psychology in which he distinguished between the contents of consciousness and the objects of the mental acts. *Alexius Meinong* (1853-1920), of Graz, a disciple of Brentano, defined 'content' as that attribute of the mental act that enables attention to be directed towards an object; and he defined 'object' as that towards which a mental act can be directed. An object may be an existing object, or a possible object, or an impossible object. A round square, for example, has the character of being-such-and-such *(Sosein)*, being round and square; but it is an impossible object, since it has a contradictory nature or character *(Sosein)* which precludes its existing *(Sein)*. Thus, a statement such as 'The mountain I am thinking of is golden', or 'The round square that I am thinking of is round and square', is a *true* statement about a non-existent object; it is a *Sosein* statement and not a *Sein* statement. The totality of objects of this kind extends far beyond the confines of what is merely real (and so it extends beyond the confines of Russell's theory of descriptions). Meinong suggested that a further analysis of objects of this kind might well throw light on several of the well-known logical paradoxes. It was in this general climate of thought, inspired by Franz Brentano, that Edmund Husserl, the most eminent of Brentano's pupils, became the principal architect of the phenomenological method of philosophical analysis.

2. Husserl. *Edmund Husserl* (1859-1938) began his academic career as a mathematician, but he decided to devote himself to philosophy when he attended Brentano's lectures (1884-86). He taught philosophy in Halle, Göttingen and Freiburg-im-Breisgau, where Martin Heidegger was one of his pupils. He devoted himself with utmost moral fervour to the pursuit of complete clarity and understanding, and in so doing he won the adherence of a large school of eminent followers, in Germany and throughout the world.

Husserl's first major work *Logical Investigations* (*Logische Unter-suchungen*, 1900-01) focused attention on the foundations of logic. It presented a thorough critique of nominalism, positivism, relativism and 'psychologism', the view that logic is reducible to the empirical natural science of psychology and its empirical laws of association. Logic is not concerned with the psychological succession of real psychical acts. It is concerned with what is thought; or, it is concerned with 'the meant' (*gemeint*), the intended, the sphere of meaning. Meanings can be universal, whereas things such as psychical acts are all individual, particular. Particular things can be imaged or imagined; universal meanings cannot. What we imagine when we think of a universal mathematical proposition, for example, is of no importance to the ideal universal content, the meaning, of the proposition. Locke and Hume and their successors attempted to hypostasize ideal objects such as universals by erroneously treating them as generalized, schematic images. They attempted to reduce logical laws to probable, empirical generalizations, comparable to the rules or inductive generalizations of the empirical sciences. But logical laws are not merely probable, inductive, changeable empirical rules. They are *a priori* and ideal. They belong to an entirely different order, the order of meaning. Philosophy, like logic and mathematics, is a nonempirical, *a priori*, autonomous science. It is concerned, for example, with concepts which are important in logic, such as 'meaning' and 'judgement'. It deals with the intentionality of all mental acts. It is a purely descriptive, nonempirical science which describes observable phenomena by means of direct perception or insight (*Anschauung*, 'a looking at'). It can be called phenomenology in as far as it deals directly with the integral phenomena given in immediate experience.

From 1913 to 1930, Husserl, as editor in chief, worked with a large group of phenomenologists who published their studies in the *Jahrbuch für Philosophie und phänomenologische Forschung (Annual for Philosophy and Phenomenological Research)*. Moritz Geiger (1880-1937), Alexander Pfänder (1870-1941), Oskar Decker (1889-1959), Edith Stein (1891-1942), Adolph Reinach (1883-1916), Roman Ingarden and Max Scheler were well-known members of this new school of philosophy. They adopted as their slogan '*Zu den Sachen!*' ('To the things!'). This slogan exhorted the members of the group to shun doctrinaire presuppositions and to investigate with care the evidence manifested by and in the phenomenon or object or example that is being inspected. Hume's phenomenalism, for example, was the product of his doctrinaire assumptions concerning the function of nouns and the referents of concepts. His view that human beings and physical objects are nothing but collections of their sensory qualities was not the product of an unprejudiced examination of the actual nature of men and women and objects. The phenomenologist, as opposed to the phenomenalist, examines and then describes phenomena as they present themselves, studiously avoiding assumptions, prejudices and presuppositions of any kind while doing so. *Zu den Sachen!* Shun all presuppositions! Attend to what is there! The truth of the resulting phenomenological statement depends entirely then on the accuracy of the description of the phenomenon examined and explicated.

Thus, for Husserl and the phenomenologists in general the word 'phenomenon' is applicable to that which is apparent or manifest to our consciousness. The ultimate source of all statements is a 'seeing' of the things immediately given in consciousness (without any effort to decide whether the thing that is there is a reality or an appearance). The phenomenological method consists in pointing to what is given and elucidating it. It elucidates it by pointing to the necessary and invariant features, the essential structure, or 'essence', of the object.

Several schisms arose within the phenomenological movement, however, because of disagreements about the set of conditions necessary for an object to be a phenomenon. Husserl, with the support of Pfänder, Reinach and Scheler, maintained that objects may be regarded as phenomena only after we have 'bracketed' or suspended our belief in the existence of the objects. The intuition of essences is not at all the same thing as a simple seeing of objects of sensory observation. All judgement in regard to the ontological or existential status or reference of the phenomena, the objects of consciousness, must be suspended. This does not imply a methodical Cartesian *doubt* about existence. It is simply a phenomenological *epochē* or 'bracketing' of existence, a suspension of judgement with regard to the ontological status of the object. Attention is then directed simply and solely to the essential structure of the phenomenon or object. It is quite irrelevant whether the object described exists or not. The object has become an 'example', an illustration, having evidential functions; and the truth of the phenomenological statement depends entirely on the accuracy of the description of the example.

Through the use of (arbitrary) 'free imaginative variation', Husserl said, we can discover which features of an example are accidental and which features are necessary and invariant. By adding or deleting one or other predicate contained in the description we can discover those predicates which do not affect the essential features of the kind of object exemplified in different examples. In this way the 'essence' or the necessary and invariant features of a given kind of thing can be discovered through the use of free imaginative variation of different predicates and different examples. The statements resulting from this procedure are phenomenological nonempirical statements about the essential structure of the inspected phenomenon.

Phenomenological philosophy, therefore, Husserl maintained, is a reflective enterprise. It reflects about the essential features of arbitrarily chosen examples of a given phenomenon. After reflection, a statement is made about the necessary conditions for any object's being an example of the phenomenon on which the phenomenologist is reflecting. The statement is a statement about the necessary relations between the properties of some particular example or examples of a certain kind of thing; and it is a statement in which we do not consider whether the description refers to an existing object. The truth or falsity of the description is independent of sensory, empirical observation, in the sense that it is not immediately preceded by sensory observations of existent objects.

The phenomenological descriptions which Husserl has in mind are primarily descriptions of those kinds of activities which we perform with ease in everyday life (in the *Lebenswelt*) but which we find difficult, or not easy, to describe. How would one describe the action of 'lying', for instance, and how would one describe the making of a mental restriction, as distinct from the telling of a lie? How would one describe the activity of valuing, or owing, or stealing, or hoping or being angry or being unjust? If one methodologically 'brackets' detailed existing cases, and if one reflects instead on clear examples (and counter-examples) of what people would regard as obvious illustrations of 'lying' or 'stealing', then one is in a position to discover and see the essential features, or 'essence', of these activities. One might then be in a position to state that one sees lying as the use of a word, sign or action in a way which expresses the contrary of what one thinks or wills (usually in order to deceive others), and that one sees 'stealing' as being the secret taking of a thing against the reasonable will of its owner. These particular descriptions, even though they are not those of Husserl himself, may nevertheless serve to illustrate what Husserl was doing when he applied the phenomenological method to phenomena and to the phenomenological method in order to discover the 'essence' of a phenomenon and in order to discover the 'essence' of the phenomenological method itself.

As a result of his own reflections on phenomena, Husserl concluded that statements about phenomena are statements about the essential features, or essences, which are intuited or seen, as a result of bracketing existence, in acts or activities which are invariably intentional acts. Statements about perceiving, thinking, fearing, doubting, hoping, expecting and other similar activities are statements about intentional acts. A sentence such as 'The victim believed that her guardian angel had saved her sanity' presents a complete description of an intentional act of belief. It indicates the tetradic relation of the subject, the action, the object, and the manner in which the object is related to the subject's action. The truth of a statement of this kind, describing someone's intentional act, depends solely on the accuracy of the description of the act, and it does not permit any inference concerning the existence or nonexistence either of the object of the act or of anything pertaining to what the act is about. The existence or nonexistence of the object cannot be deduced from the true description of the intentional act. This characteristic may be regarded as an essential feature, and, indeed, a criterion, of all coherent and intelligible acts (and series of acts) that are purely *intentional* acts.

The proper object of phenomenology, Husserl said, is the pure *eidos*, the essence, or the necessary and invariant features of intentional acts such as believing, meaning, judging and so forth. This *eidos* can be attained only through an *epochē*, or suspension of judgement, or act of detachment, with regard to certain elements of the given; and no further interest is taken in these separated detached elements. The process of bracketing is one of phenomenological reduction and there are three different types of reduction. The historical reduction or *epochē* sets aside historical presuppositions, such as those of nominalism, psychologism, phenomenalism and the assumptions and abstractions of the natural sciences. The eidetic reduction sets aside the individual existence or nonexistence of the illustrating object. The third reduction, the 'transcendental reduction', which takes up an important place in Husserl's later works, consists in a bracketing of all that is not a correlate of pure consciousness of essences. This requires further explanation.

In his *Cartesian Meditations* and *Paris Lectures* (published posthumously, 1950 and 1964), Husserl explained that the act of detaching himself from all except his own pure consciousness enabled him to discover himself as the ego, the life of pure consciousness within which and through which the contents of consciousness, the objects of his world, in their entirety, exist. Within the field of consciousness, the ego contains the world. Thus, I cannot think, live, experience, value or act in any world other than the world which is in some sense in me; and this world, my world, derives its meaning and truth from me. Husserl now found that he was led back *(re-ductus)* to the conscious self as the centre of reality. He had discovered that it was only through his pure ego, his conscious self, that any reality had any possible validity and made any sense to him. It is the constantly present ego, pure awareness, that is the consciousness and source of all its own objects and their meanings. All objects of thought manifest themselves as entirely determined by the structure of thinking itself. The whole of reality is now seen to be a stream of experiences in which intentional objects are presented to a pure reference point, consciousness. Consciousness itself however is not a real subject. It is a logical subject whose acts are only intentional relations. There is a bipolarity within consciousness just as there is in every intentional experience. Thus consciousness has two aspects: 'being conscious of' *(noēsis)* and the 'consciously known' *(noēma)*. The consciously known is not contained in the *noēsis* as a real part of the *noēsis*; it is constituted as an object by *noēsis*. It is because this is so that the *noēma* can be grasped and described in an immediate ideation or intuition of essence. The logical subject is present to the intentional object, which, by its essence, is present to the pure subject, the transcendental ego.

At this stage Husserl had now made a transition over to a form of transcendental idealism which resembled that of the neo-Kantians.

Unlike the Marburg neo-Kantians, however, he continued to recognize the existence of a plurality of existent subjects; and he maintained that the world is what it is, not for any isolated transcendental individual but for an intersubjective community of transcendental individuals. The abstract world of science can be understood only after we have studied the ordinary world of common experiences, the *Lebenswelt*. The study of the lived world is the primary task of phenomenology. This doctrine is one of pluralist transcendental idealism. It was a doctrine which did not commend itself to the other members of the school of phenomenology, and Husserl did not persuade his colleagues to use the phenomenological method along his own idealistic lines.

Husserl's work contains a vast store of penetrating and subtle analyses; and the phenomenological method which he created is now widely used by philosophers. His philosophy, however, did not develop into a full metaphysics or philosophy of being. It is basically a philosophy of essence. It failed to ask or to study the key questions about being and existence, and about the relationship of the existent to the world of phenomena. It 'bracketed' and ignored existence, and it confined its attention to the work of descriptive epistemology and to the philosophy of 'essence'.

3. Scheler. *Max Scheler* (1874-1928), who was born in Munich of German and Jewish parentage, was a man of intense emotions, brilliant speculative ability, and outstanding originality of thought. As a student and *Privatdozent* at the university of Jena he was deeply influenced by the spiritualistic-idealistic life-philosophy of his teacher Rudolf Eucken, and by the writings of Nietzsche, Dilthey and Bergson. In 1907 he accepted a teaching post in the university of Munich, where he met Franz Brentano (before Brentano's death in 1907), and joined the Husserl circle of phenomenologists. He quickly became a leading exponent of the phenomenological approach to fresh, new thinking on the problems of psychology, ethics, and religious and social philosophy. During the period of his maturity, when he continued to be a personalist, a theist and a Christian, he wrote several of his most important works, *Ressentiment* ('Rancour'; 1912), *On the Phenomenology and Theory of Sympathy and of Love and Hate* (1913), *Formalism in Ethics* (1916), *On the Eternal in Man* (1921), an apologia on his conversion to Catholicism in 1920, *The Nature of Sympathy* (1923), and *Sociology* (1924). At this time, Scheler went through a restless emotional and religious crisis. He abandoned Christianity, repudiated theism, and focused his interests on anthropology and the natural sciences. He then wrote *The Place of Man in the Cosmos* (1928), *Man in the Age of Equalization* (1929), and other works, in which he maintained that man is the unique site or locus of the realization of the divine. This phase of his thought was not adequately amplified before his death in 1928. Scheler is remembered today mainly for the personalistic reflections of the mature period, prior to his emotional perturbation and religious crisis.

Scheler applied phenomenological analysis to the phenomenon of '*knowing*' and he concluded that knowledge is to be interpreted instrumentally as a social, historical, and biologically adaptive form of behaviour. There are three types of (instrumental) knowledge. Inductive knowledge, or scientific knowledge, is rooted in the urge for dominion, mastery and technological control. It is knowledge of particulars, and of the accidental (*zufällige*) or contingent nature of things. Particular scientific predictions aim to give man power over nature, society and history. Knowledge of forms or essences, or 'first philosophy' (Aristotle), is a different type of knowledge. It is knowledge of the universal; it is knowledge of the essences and categories of being. Knowledge of this kind is motivated not by domination but by love of knowledge. It is acquired, through the medium of eidetic reduction, by observing even a single (real or imaginary) object, and, so, is logically independent of any process of induction. It is true *a priori* knowledge of reason. It is the foundation of science and the starting point for metaphysics. Metaphysical knowledge is knowledge of being itself, and of liberation and salvation. Knowledge of metaphysical reality does not begin, however, with the study of objective being. It begins with philosophical anthropology and its study of the being of man; and this study is possible only through a synthesis of the first two types of knowledge. Metaphysics then becomes meta-anthropology. The study of man is the primary source of access to God. Man is a *microtheos*, God in miniature, a co-creator with God. Man shares in the divine nature. He senses this in his inner drive of sympathy and love towards oneness with the cosmos. Human liberation and salvational knowledge of God is achieved through the committed conjunction of one's personal activity to the creative activity of God within oneself and within the universe.

The phenomenological method shows that *values* are the intentional objects of feelings. Just as colours are given directly to vision, Scheler said, so too, values are given directly to intentional feeling. The feeling nature of man is found to be included within the constitution of human consciousness. Values are discovered as the *a priori* grounds of cognitive emotion. They are not at a remove from objects, as Plato had thought. They are essential properties of objects that warrant our designating the objects good or goods. They are objective essential properties or essences given to immediate intuition.

There is a hierarchy of objective values, all open to our intuitive inspection. These values may be classified in an ascending scale of four classes, and there is nothing subjective about this ordering. There are values of sensible feelings, some pleasant, some unpleasant. There are values of vital feeling, or values of life, some noble, some common and coarse. There are values of the spirit, spiritual values, cultural values, political, scientific and aesthetic values, beautiful and ugly, correct and incorrect, just and unjust, and the spiritual value of pure knowledge of truth. Finally there are religious values, values of the holy and unholy. To be ethical is to implement one or more of these values, each of which has an ethical dimension. Questions and problems concerning moral obligation arise when a conflict of values arises. Moral obligation is that imperative of human nature which binds us, in such a situation, to take as the order of priority of incentives the values as they are ordered in the objective value hierarchy itself.

Love and sympathy are the sole means by which we gain an intuitive insight into moral reality. Sympathy respects the unique subjectivity of the other in the personal encounter with the other. It is therefore more than a mere understanding of another's emotion, or a contagious experience of his feeling, or a feeling of fused at-one-ness with him. Sympathy recognizes, meets and respects the unique subjectivity of the other human existence in a genuinely interpersonal encounter. Love is the *sine qua non* for sympathy because love, in fact, is not a feeling at all. Love or hatred is always love or hatred for a person as reality. The sum of values attached to the beloved person does not present an adequate account for the 'unaccountable' love of the concrete person of the beloved. Love is a movement in which the concrete valued one achieves the highest possible value ideally destined for the loved one. The striving to exalt the beloved is a striving which also exalts the lover. God is revealed as the supreme source of love. It is God who endows the person with his love, his ground of being. Love of God is a participation in God's love for the world; it is a love which enables man to love the world in God.

Relativistic theories attempt to identify love with altruism, which is an abstraction. Nineteenth-century humanitarians, socialists and egalitarians spoke of love as love of humanity, or as love of the other as other, another abstraction. They then identified it with the urge to improve and help others. These altruistic, sentimentalist theories are structures which conceal their anti-metaphysical bases. They are based on resentment, rancour, and hatred of higher values, and fundamentally, of God. An attitude of envy towards those who are the bearers and messengers of higher values, afraid to expose and satisfy its actual motivation directly, attempts to rationalize and excuse itself under a cover of egalitarian, humanitarian abstractions which are a fundamental denial of love. Love is never love for a value; it is always love for a real person, a person as reality. At its highest pitch it is the love of God. Any other 'love' is counterfeit.

A phenomenological analysis of the phenomenon of *personality* reveals to all who consider it attentively that the person is neither a soul-substance, nor object, nor pure spontaneity. The person is revealed only in its actions. The whole person is committed in each personal action. It also varies in each action, and it does so without exhausting its being in any one of its actions. It is not simply the sum of all its acts. It is given, rather, as the concrete unity of activity within the matrix of all-encompassing being. The person, the unity of activity, is revealed in the actions. The entire realm of these actions is spiritual, and so the person, the unity of activity, is essentially spiritual. This spiritual unity of activity is a new principle, not found elsewhere in nature; it is totally different from nature. It is given as a unity of activity which is capable of abstracting essence from existence, and it is also given as a determinable reality capable of being determined by the objective nature of things. The fundamental sign of the human spirit is given in the ability to separate essence and existence, or in other words in the act of ideation.

The spiritual being and activity of the person, Scheler says, is rooted, or grounded, not only in the private reality of the individual person but also in the shared reality of membership in a common body, or community. Each human being is endowed with a private and a common personality-factor *(Gesamtperson)*. The 'common person' within the individual may achieve social union with others through slavish conformism and infectious mass-imitation, or through the experience of sharing the same things together *(Miterleben)*, or through an artificial unity arising from the previously shaped links of institutional society *(Gesellschaft)*, or it may achieve social union through participation in the religious community of the church or the culture-community *(Gemeinschaft)* of the nation. Without community *(Gemeinschaft)* of some kind there can be no real society *(Gesellschaft)*; and without the 'common person' there would be no foundation for social structures.

The phenomenology of religion reveals that man is constantly in search of an infinity. This infinity has traditionally been called God. Man is a God-seeker *(Gottsucher)*, a searcher for God. Man is the creature who prays. He is the 'person', the image of the living God, constantly striving towards the living God. This search leads man to a numinous experience of God as *ens a se*, being in itself, ultimate Personality. God is disclosed in terms of the divine attributes of infinite and absolute being, goodness, power and holiness. The God of religious phenomenology is a living God, ultimate spiritual Personality. In this light man is to be understood in terms of man's 'theomorphism'. Man's experience of his creaturehood is an experience of direct contact with the source of his being. He experiences himself as absolute nothingness without God, and as 'infinite dependence'. He is called to respond religiously; and he finds he is responsible, he is able to respond. If he responds authentically he faces and encounters God. If he refuses to respond authentically he faces and encounters a substituted idol. Auguste Comte, for example, professed to worship the humanity of *homo naturalis* as his adopted *grand être*. Religious acts and ritual rites well up from within man's deepest nature, in contrition, self-immolation, faith, reverence and prayer. God calls man to respond to God in faith; and God responds to this faith by revealing himself to man as ultimate Personality. Religion and belief are the products within man of the workings of a personal God. All knowledge of God is knowledge through God who calls man to respond, and then reveals himself to man.

During the last four years of his life, after a time of moral and emotional crisis, Scheler began to turn away from Christianity, Catholicism and theism. He now insisted that the higher values and levels of being are weaker than the lower ones. Primitive, inorganic, unconscious urges, blind to ideas and essences, are powerful sources of energy. Nature will out. It is the sciences that present us with some of the most important facts about man. Biology, experimental psychology, economic geography, climatology and ethnography help us to understand the material conditions of man's environment. However, there is still a spiritual aspect within man; and the sociology of knowledge studies the influence that the material aspect has upon this spiritual aspect of man.

From the viewpoint of the social role, or sociology, of knowledge, Scheler said, there are five contemporary varieties of philosophical anthropology, or in other words, five theories of man. The theomorphic, religious view of man is one which derives principally from Jewish and Christian sources. The excessively rationalistic view of man as *homo sapiens* derives mainly from ancient Greek sources. The naturalistic, positivistic and pragmatic theory of *homo faber* regards man merely as a large-brained animal capable of using symbols and tools. The pessimistic theory of 'decadent man' views man as imprisoned in an egocentric state of pathological mega-lomania. The fifth conception of man is that of the Superman (*Übermensch*) as depicted in Nietzsche's *Also Sprach Zarathustra* and the *Ethik* of Nicolai Hartmann.

In this final phase of his philosophical career, Scheler returned once again to some of the lines of thought which had influenced his first, original trends in philosophy. He had been influenced in a profound way by his admiration for the works of Nietzsche, Dilthey, Bergson and life-philosophy. Though this aspect of Scheler's thought was developed only in part, it nevertheless accounts for Ernst Troeltsch's apt title for Scheler as 'the Catholic Nietzsche'.

4. Ingarden. *Roman Ingarden* (1893-1971), a Polish phenomenologist, and professor of philosophy at Cracow, used the phenomenological method and analytical descriptions of Husserl to formulate a moderate realist system of philosophy which avoided the epistemological inconsistencies of Husserl's final phase of transcendental idealism. Ingarden pointed out that a work of art, such as a poem, which depends for its existence on the significance with which its creator endows it, is a work which transcends the act of its creator. It is a work which continues to exist in its material shape after its creation. There is a necessary connection between the mode of being of the work and its formal structure. The activity of deciphering the significance (of the poem), expressed by physically perceptible signs, requires the existence of a second intentional act on the part of the admirer. The work of art therefore possesses many different strata harmoniously orchestrated towards the creation of the overall 'poetic significance' of the work. For this reason a work of art is called a purely intentional object.

There is a phenomenologically perceptible difference, Ingarden said, between the existent and its existence. Existence is not that which exists, and it is not an attribute or property of the existing object; it is that by means of which something exists. We must differentiate between the real existence (or actuality) of something, the possibility of something, and the ideal existence (or plan) of something. There are different modes of existence or being. The different modes of being, in turn, are also distinct from the particular existential moments of these different modes of being. What we grasp in the object is its variety of particular existential moments, its actually being this and being that and being such and such. It is these existential moments that are the key to our understanding the object.

The moments of being may be divided into four basic pairs. A thing is either existentially autonomous, when it has its existential foundation in itself and is immanently determined in itself, or heteronomous, if it is not autonomous. A thing is either existentially original, that is, incapable of being produced in its essence by any other object, or derivative, if it is not original. A thing is either existentially separate, not requiring in its essence another coexisting support, or 'inseparate', if it is not separate. Finally, a being is either existentially self-dependent or existentially contingent. The only object which does not require for its existence some other existentially separate object is an existentially self-dependent object which is also an existentially separate object. Existential contingency involves separate objects which require for their existence other existentially separate objects.

Ingarden wrote more than a hundred phenomenological mono-graphs and works on different aspects and problems of aesthetics, epistemology and ontology. Several of these problems had perennial roots in Aristotelian and Scholastic philosophy. Many of Ingarden's analyses are all the more clearly understood in the light of traditional Scholastic distinctions, as for example between the principles of determination (*quo est, quo est tale*), the principle of determinability (*potentia*), and the principle of causal dependency in being (*causa*). Ingarden's main work *The Controversy over the Existence of the World* (1946-66) makes use of the phenomenological method in an effort to resolve the controversy between idealism and realism concerning the nature of the world and our relation to it. His approach to a solution is closely akin to that of contemporary neo-Scholastic thought.

5. **Merleau-Ponty.** *Maurice Merleau-Ponty* (1908-61), pro-fessor of philosophy at the Collège de France, was a phenomenologist and philosophical psychologist whose thought focused in a special way on man as 'body-subject' in dialogue with the world and with other 'body-subjects' or persons. He wrote *The Structure of Behaviour* (1942), *Phenomenology of Perception* (1945), *Sense and Nonsense* (1948), *Signs* (1960) and *The Visible and the Invisible* (published 1964). In these and other works, Merleau-Ponty pointed out that man is not a dualistic composite of body and spirit. The live human body is

a conscious being-in-the world, a subject which is in dialogue with the world. Its encounter with the world and with other conscious beings is a contingent and nonconceptual encounter. Every perceptual experience, every encounter, carries with it an essential reference to a world that transcends consciousness. Phenomenological description aspires to depict manifestly the referential and self-transcending character of our immediate perceptual encounters. Perception, and not conceptual thought, holds primacy of place as a mode of access to the real. The human mode of being-in-the-world presents an original and unique perceptual relationship to the world that is not adequately explained by scientific psychological theories (of the behaviouristic and Gestalt types) which attempt to represent perceptual experiences as quantitative or qualitative effects produced in the mind by the action of extra-phenomenal physical causes. Again, it is not explained by the sense-datum theory of perception, a theory which strips 'pure' sensations of any transcendent reference to the objects of the world.

The human body is not just an object among objects. The phenomenal body as we live it is an incarnate subject involved in its milieu, the world. It is in constant encounter and dialogue with the world, and it has its own understanding of the world. The subject is not an entity hidden away inside the body; it is the body itself, the body-subject. All levels of knowing are based on the 'life-world', the realm of perception in which we continue to live. The body as lived or experienced is not the physical 'objectified' body of the experimental psychologists. It is not just one more body in the abstract world of mechanical reciprocal causality and blind responses to external stimuli. On the pre-conscious level of perceptual behaviour there is a continual dialogue, a lived dialectical relationship between the human organism and its global environment. In this dialectical relationship, the environment or milieu, as a term in the relationship, takes on new forms and meanings correlative to the aptitudes and abilities of the subject. Edibles become food for the subject. The meanings of things are determined not only by the object but also by the subject in this lived dialogue between the incarnate subject and the world, its environment. Rivers and trees become obstacles, or tools, for the subject. Man is born into a world of historical and cultural objects (villages, bells, streets, spoons, and churches), through which he experiences 'the near presence of the other under a veil of anonymity'. The small child has a pre-reflective perception of its mother in the dialogue of their perceptual behaviours. It discovers that it is not the other; others appear as other subjects. It finds itself in a historical and cultural situation where objects are already clothed with meaning. In the human being's act of becoming aware of reality, reality or the world becomes visible to itself in and through man. Man's awareness of nature is nature's awareness of itself. Being or ultimate reality-in-itself is invisible. Being is the foundation which grounds both subject and object. It is the invisible dimension of the visible structures of the world. Within this visible world man's freedom is never absolute. Man's exercise of freedom is conditioned by a pre-existing situation; it is always 'situated' in the real world around him.

35 Existentialism

1. Existentialist philosophies in general. The existentialist philosophies of Kierkegaard, Heidegger, Sartre, Marcel, Jaspers and others focus attention in a special way on what are now commonly called the 'existential' problems of man, namely, on the meaning of life, death, choice, destiny, authentic existence, self-creation, self-transcendence and similar related themes. The existentialists, in general, are preoccupied primarily and dramatically with human existence in the world, and this from a special point of view, that is, from the viewpoint of man's genuine ability to transcend the influence and weight of the past, the viewpoint of human freedom of choice. They see man as a defiant, free individual who, even though he is a part of nature, a unity in a collectivity, a being in the world, nevertheless 'ex-sists' or stands out from his grounding in nature and from submersal in the collectivity. Like the popular conception of Luther, standing out before the emperor and his Elector-princes and archbishops at the Diet of Worms, the 'existing' individual asserts: 'Here stand I. I can not otherwise. So help me God. Amen.' The authentically free individual stands up against all that appears to threaten his personal responsibility and his unique existence as a self-creating subject. In this type of dramatic 'existential' situation, the term 'existence' is restricted in its connotation to that specific mode of being of man which can be called 'ex-sistent' (or 'out-standing') individual existence.

The thought patterns of the different existentialist philosophers are diverse, and for this reason the term 'existentialism' is one which is applicable to a certain attitude or outlook, and to a historical movement of thought, rather than to a particular philosophical system or doctrine. The systems differ, but, nevertheless, the prevalent attitude to the free, 'existing' individual has brought about a common concern and interest in certain themes which pertain to the individual's choice of his destiny. These key themes are: the dramatic shock of the existential experience; the individual's insertion into the world; his subjectivity and intentionality; and the individual's free choice of his own destiny.

Kierkegaard had pointed out that there are experiences of crisis in life when the human being grasps in a traumatic way important truths about human nature. Stress on the traumatic existential experience is a common characteristic of all existentialist writings. Everyday conventional experiences are thought of, by way of contrast, as complacent forms of unthinking self-deception. Jaspers found this awakening experience in the experiential awareness of the brittleness of being, the fragility of our existence. Heidegger found it in man's continuous awareness of his 'propulsion towards death'. Sartre found it in the thinking man's nauseating awareness of the absurdity of human existence. True knowledge of reality, these existentialists say, is not achieved through notional knowledge but through experiential knowledge arising from an awareness of generalized anxiety, dread, futility, contingency, and nervous confrontation with an unmade future. Each of the different forms of existential thinking bears the stamp of a basic existential experience of this kind. The existentialists acknowledge clearly that their philosophies originate in a personal experience of the frail, contingent, human mode of being.

Hegel and other metaphysical rationalists of the nineteenth century had regarded the universe as a total system within which the individual could find fulfilment by subordinating his private will to the general will. Kierkegaard and other rebelled against this conception of man as a docile anonymous one who lives out a stereotyped role within an engulfing whole. Dostoyevsky stressed the unpredictable character of every form of collectivity, whether in society or in nature. Heidegger asserted that, though man is thrown down helplessly into the here and now, nevertheless, human existence so dominates the things of the world that it endows them with their meaning and truth. The existentialists in general spoke of the individual as 'inserted' into the world and into society. The individual faces a determinate situation where mundane objects exist opaquely *in* themselves *(en soi)*. He is aware of himself however as a conscious and free agent who exists *for* himself *(pour soi)*. He freely makes his concrete situation. The individual is in fact his own concrete, personal situation. It is in concrete situations of an extreme kind, when he confronts anxiety, guilt, despair, and the spectre of death, that the individual becomes aware of his true self. The self has a specially close and necessary connection with other individuals. It is this connection with other selves, each in his own personal situation, that gives existence the personal quality of 'communication', 'me and thee', or 'togetherness'.

Sartre asserted that if other people view me as an intentional object of their own perceptions, beliefs and emotions, then they view me as other than I am. The object of their perception and belief is an intentional object, internal to their own perception and belief. To myself I am not an intentional object. I am pure subject. This view of man as pure subjectivity is a characteristic feature of the existentialist philosophies in general. Man is not a singular appearance of an absolute One, nor a manifestation of a universal life process, nor is he an internal objective pole of an observer's act of consciousness. The individual experiences himself as subject. When this subject is viewed or loved or hated as an object, then it is viewed and loved and hated as something other than it really is. Knowledge of the subject is not achieved by an understanding of an object but through the experiencing of 'existence' in every moment of existential awareness.

Man creates himself freely. Man is his freedom, the existentialists say. Existence is an ongoing human process. It is always becoming; it never actually is. It is a self-creative pro-jection, and it is essentially the same thing as personal temporality. Existence is the ever ongoing possibility of free choice. It is choice that brings one's nature into being. All my actions and even my decisions not to act imply choices. In the domain of morality and religion I am free to act or not to act and I am free to choose the criteria which I decide to employ. No phenomenological analysis of my free actions can ever present a deterministic or causal explanation of acts which are seen to be responsible and free. I am a being who is a being-in-the-world. I am not a self-enclosed ego of the Cartesian type. I am not an abstract epistemological subject. I am 'open' to other individuals and to the world. I am a free, self-creating and self-transcending subject. I am a being-in-the-world, standing out from the background of the world, and capable of taking my destiny in my own hands and shaping it with authentic freedom. This is the existentialist view of man's call to true 'existence'.

2. Heidegger. *Martin Heidegger* (1889-1976), who was born in Baden, began to study philosophy as a Jesuit novice. In 1916, under the supervision of Husserl, he wrote a thesis on categories and signification in the philosophy of John Duns Scotus. In 1927, when he was professor at Marburg, he published his greatest and most influential work *Sein und Zeit: I* (*Being and Time*, Part 1). The opening paragraph of this work announces the mission and fundamental task of the philosopher in these words: 'it behoves us to pose anew the question concerning the sense of being *(dem Sinn von Sein)'*. He dedicated this work to Husserl. In 1928 he succeeded Husserl in the chair of philosophy at Freiburg-im-Breisgau, and he continued to teach there until 1946. Heidegger also wrote *Kant and the Problem of Metaphysics* (1929), *What is Metaphysics?* (1929 and 1951), *An Introduction to Metaphysics* (1953), *What is Philosophy?* (1956), *Essays in Metaphysics: Identity and Difference* (1957), and several other works in which he continued his life-long phenomenological investigation of human 'being' as a necessary preliminary to the investigation of being itself. Existential analysis, or a hermeneutics of existence, is regarded as an introduction to ontology, and to philosophy and the sciences in general.

Being and Time: I presents, firstly, a phenomenological description of man's inauthentic, everyday existence. It then presents an account of how man is capable of achieving authentic existence. Man's existence becomes authentic when man creatively affirms the present as the opportune time for that kind of resolute, decisive action through which the future is faced courageously.

Human being, or existence, Heidegger says, displays three fundamental aspects: facticity, existentiality, and forfeiture or fallenness. Facticity or factuality is a term used by Heidegger to express the fact that man finds that he has been thrown into the world which is now his own world, without consultation, and that he has been abandoned to the chance factors which have already constituted him. Thus, I am always already cast into a world which is *my* world even though it is not of my making. My world is mine to appropriate and assimilate freely; but I am already begun and I have a past through which I have been defined and shaped. Human being or existence is seen, then, as *Dasein*, being present here, or being present there; it is already factually being-in-the world. Each man is what his heredity and environment have made him.

The self of each person is also submerged in the everyday world of passing moods, daily chores, escapist activities, petty gossip and the flight of the self from itself. Human being is being-in-the-world, but the world around man is man's own world. It is not a world of Cartesian *res extensae*. It is a world of tools, opportunities and handy materials, for human use and application; as in the case of a hammer actually hammering, the world is revealed in man's primitive experience as a world of utensils or instruments in actual use. Tool-things are always 'for' something. They are characterized by their handiness; and handiness has human existence for its condition.

They are utensils, having owners and users. They are handy and
they are for our handling. This handy world can also be conceptually objectivized in an epistemologically secondary and derivative
way. One's world, like one's hammer, can be viewed secondarily or
abstractly as a detached physical object, in abstraction from its
active use. It then becomes the object of a theoretical, scientific
construction, formulated and defined in terms of measurements,
pointer readings, and abstract descriptions. It becomes an adjacent
world, a world of objective things viewed as 'being-beside' oneself
and being 'near at hand'. It is important to remember that this is a
later (and largely sterile) construction. One must constantly return
to the original data of immediate experience and describe these data
as they manifest themselves in their primitive disclosure. One must
return repeatedly to the world of *Dasein* and to the foundational
experience of 'being-in-the world' of ongoing personal projects, as
distinct from the derivative notion of 'being-beside' extended
substances and things. Man is not revealed or given as an island
isolated from the world. Man discovers himself as already immersed
within a world of preoccupation with utensils and of concern for
others like himself. As in the case of being in business, or being in
love, being in the world implies being involved, being creative,
questioning, observing, inquiring, applying, fostering, producing,
sacrificing, undertaking, being active, being preoccupied, and being
concerned. Being-in-the-world, in this sense, is constitutive of
man's being.

Being preoccupied (with one's environmental region) differs from
being concerned (with one's communal region). The model relationship of human existence in regard to a tool is that of practical
preoccupation. The model relationship of human existence in regard
to another human existence is that of personal concern. However,
even though being human is essentially being-with-others (*Mitsein*),
man frequently degrades himself into an unauthentic 'anonymous
one' who transforms others into objects or things with which he is
pragmatically preoccupied rather than personally concerned. The
depersonalized 'anonymous one' abrogates personal commitment,
responsible decision and striving for excellence. He lowers himself to
the level of *Das Man*, the 'average' depersonalized individual who
thinks and feels and acts as the general public does. The fallenness of
human being, or *Dasein*, manifests itself particularly in the
movements of public gossip, reiteration of clichés, curiosity for news
as providing momentary distraction, and in the ambiguity of mind
which lacks singleness of purpose.

Facticity and fallenness are two of the structural elements in the ontological constitution of *Dasein*, being human. The third structural element is existentiality. Facticity expresses primarily man's rootedness in the *past*. Fallenness *(Verfallen)*, or forfeiture, expresses man's submersion in the preoccupations and distractions of the *present*. Existentiality or transcendence expresses man's disclosure of that personal existence which he *can* become. Man experiences freedom and responsibility to transform his world and to redefine himself in his concern for others. Through the act of appropriation he can make his real world his own. Human being, *Dasein*, grasps the possibilities of its situation as a challenge to its own power of becoming what it is freely capable of becoming. It reaches out beyond itself and aims at what it is not yet. It strives to understand and appropriate its world, and it strives to create and become its authentic self. Existentiality, self-transcendence and self-projection are temporally rooted in *futurity*. The existential man understands himself as moving into a future that is personally controlled.

Having presented a phenomenological description of man's everyday, *inauthentic* existence, Heidegger's *Being and Time: I* then proceeds to give an account of how man can achieve *authentic* existence through the medium of courageous decisive acts which resolutely face personal dread, death, nothingness, conscience, guilt, finitude, responsibility, freedom and destiny.

Human being is capable of uprooting itself from petty, everyday self-betrayal and of gazing upon man's life in its entirety. In doing so it gazes necessarily on life's dreaded ending in death. Human life in its entirety is life facing death. Human being then knows itself as 'being-unto-death'. Dread *(Angst)*, unlike fear, has no definite, nameable object. Dread confronts man with his irredeemable finitude. Its source is nothingness. Nothingness cannot be objectivized or conceptualized. It can be experienced and pre-objectively disclosed through dread, or free-floating anxiety. Dread brings *Dasein* face to face with radical human *finitude* and the threat of human *meaninglessness*. It reveals man's basic predicament, namely, 'being-to-death'. The temporary distractions collapse. Trusted supports vanish. Significant attachments become insignificant. Shackles fall away, and one becomes free to appropriate oneself totally in a free affirmation of one's radical being-to-death. I can now affirm and make my own the only event which is uniquely, authentically mine: my being-unto-death.

Conscience is the lonely voice by which human being calls itself out from petty distractions to the lonely avowal of its own responsibility for being itself. It is the call to deroot oneself from forfeiture and to follow the path towards authenticity. It is the call to escape from enslavement and to face resolutely one's own inner capability. It is the call to self-appropriation. It calls me to actualize my possibilities. In choosing some of these possibilities, however, I must always sacrifice other possibilities. In actualizing one possibility I become guilty of not actualizing another. I cannot exist without acting and yet every action implies exclusion and guilt. Guilt is an irremovable quality, an inevitable and irreducible determinant of human being. It is a determinant of man's finite existence, a structural implication of his finitude and nothingness.

The lonely will, burdened with irremediable guilt, and driven by dread to face the prospect of its inevitable dissolution, is nevertheless capable of resolute, courageous action in which it can attain its proper freedom. Resolution is the indispensable condition for authentic existence. In resolute choice, *Dasein*, human 'presence', appropriates his unique past, anticipates his unique future, and integrates his past and future in a creative affirmation of the present as the opportune time for decisive free action.

Human being or 'presence' exists in time. But human or existential time is not quantitatively-measured, irreversible, clock-time. Human presence, as time, is being-unto-death. *Dasein* and its existentiality are rooted in futurity. Thus, my cares and concerns are primarily oriented to the future. Nevertheless, the time that is my time, my life-span, is an ecstatic unity. My past, future and present are inseparable phases of the care-structure of my existence. In a present act of resolute choice, my past is still real and my future is *already* real. In reaching out decisively to the future, human being assimilates freely, as its own, the past history from which emerges the responsibility of the present moment.

It is in this way that human presence attains its destiny. Resolution enables *Dasein* to become whole. In resolute decisive action, past and future are co-present, the present is raised out of forfeiture, and human being becomes unified, authentic and whole. Death, guilt, conscience, freedom and finitude now dwell together in an authentic present. In dread and silence, *Dasein* has now come face to face with his own nothingness and has decisively shaped his own life in the moment of confrontation and encounter. He achieves integrity at that moment when he apprehends himself in his temporal and historical movements, acknowledges past and future possibilities, and appropriates himself as radical being-unto-death in a resolute choice which involves the whole of his being. Through resolute affirmation of his being, a radical being-unto-death, he achieves his destiny, authentic freedom, authentic existence, authentic presence.

In *Being and Time: I*, Heidegger presented a phenomenological analysis of human existence from the viewpoint of its temporal and historical character as an introduction to an apprehension of the meaning and structures of Being itself. He aimed to found a universal phenomenological ontology on the basis of this hermeneutics of human existence. He did not produce the second section of *Being and Time*, however, and he turned his attention instead to particular facets of his wider quest to apprehend Being itself. Thus, for example, in *What is Metaphysics?*, *An Introduction to Metaphysics* and *Holzwege* ('Woodpaths'; 1950) he spoke of man's true quest or vocation as that of seeking, in a world darkened by enshrouding distractions, the holy Ground of Being itself, through which all things are. We live in an age of co-ordinated research into technological tasks which call for engineering inventiveness rather than ontological insight into our true calling. We are called to be seers and pastors of Being; but we are fallen out of Being and have made ourselves manufactures, consumers, and collectors of gadget-things instead. Our world is darkened by our forgetfulness of human being and by our forgetfulness of what Being itself is. We have become rootless units floating complacently in the mediocre mass. We must learn again to open ourselves to what is, and to stand within an openness to all that is. Like the poet and the prophet who speak of a world seen in the 'illumination of Being', we too must set out on the track of the holy. The path to the holy is the path to healing and wholeness. We too, like them, can learn to name the holy and speak of Being. Heidegger did not develop this quest further into a philosophy of religion. One has to turn to other thinkers, Rudolf Otto, Martin Buber, Paul Tillich, or Rudolf Bultmann, to find a theological development of this numinous vein of thought.

3. Sartre. *Jean-Paul Sartre* (1905-80) was a French philosopher who studied at the Sorbonne and then under Husserl at Freiburg. He wrote several philosophical works and existentialist novels and plays, and at the end of World War II emerged as one of the leaders of left-wing Paris intellectuals. He maintained that Marxism and existentialism complemented each other in their critique of social institutions and in their aim to promote human freedom in a context of political liberty. Sartre's numerous works include *The Transcendence of the Ego* (1936), *The Imagination* (1936), *La Nausée* (*Nausea* or *The Diary of Antoine Roquentin*; novel; 1938),

Outline of a Theory of the Emotions (1939), *The Psychology of the Imagination* (1940), *L'Être et le néant* (*Being and Nothingness*; 1943), *The Roads of Freedom* (three novels; 1945-49), *Huis Clos* (*In Camera*; play; 1945), *Existentialism and Humanism* (1946), *Situations* (1947), *Critique of Dialectical Reason* (1960), *Les Mots* (*Words: reminiscences*; 1963), *The Idiot of the Family* (1972), *Situations* (1976) and several other works. He accepted the term existentialist philosophy as a correct designation of his system of thought.

For Sartre the basic datum of phenomenological analysis is pre-reflexive consciousness of existent objects such as tables, chairs, walls, windows, people, and so forth. I have an immediate pre-reflexive awareness of the presence of these various things. My consciousness or awareness posits these objects as transcending itself; and in this sense my consciousness is transcendent or non-immanent. It is a consciousness of a transcendent something towards which it reaches out intentionally. The wall or table is given and posited as existing out there in that place, in exterior space. It is not at all given as a content immanent in my consciousness. Thus, it is a brick wall that I perceive and not a mental representation of a wall. It is the solid, existent, transcendent, opaque thing in itself which is the real object of my intentional act.

Sartre maintained, therefore, that Husserl erred when he 'bracketed out' existence and treated all objects as purely immanent. Descartes erred too in starting his analysis with an act of reflexive consciousness in which the self-enclosed ego is constituted as object. Reflexive consciousness is not first-order consciousness; it is a reflection on pre-reflexive consciousness. The self which arises in reflexive consciousness is a derivative and fugitive self, dynamic, non-stable and boundlessly free. It is discovered as one pole of the bipolar act of knowledge. The subjective pole and objective pole, the ego and the transcendent object, arise in correlation. To isolate the subjective pole of an act of knowing and to treat it as an isolated datum is a mistake. Consciousness is consciousness of itself only insofar as it is consciousness of a transcendent object. Thus, if I think of myself as thinking of Peter, then this reflexive act is not the same as the pre-reflexive act of thinking of Peter. It is only when I turn my own consciousness of Peter into an intentional object that the self is posited in a reflexive act. The basic datum, however, is immediate pre-reflexive awareness of Peter.

The being of Peter or of the brick wall evinces a transphenomenal character, according to Sartre's phenomenological ontology. It is the primordial being itself that appears; and it is given as completely independent of the fact of its appearing. The being, in the totality of its aspects and manifestations, never becomes wholly translucent to consciousness. It is a transcendent being which is never exhausted by any of its particular phenomenal aspects. But the transcendent thing is not given as a Kantian noumenon or 'thing-in-itself' concealed behind the phenomenon or appearances. The appearances of a wall embody the full reality of the wall. It is the full reality itself that appears. All phenomena overflow themselves, suggesting other phenomena yet to be disclosed, and the known being is co-extensive with the whole of its phenomenological manifestations. This points to a fundamental distinction between the being of things and the being of their appearing. The transphenomenal and the phenomenal, even though co-extensive, are none the less distinct. The object of consciousness is distinct from consciousness. An important question arises therefore as to the nature of this fundamental rupture in being: what is the relationship between the transcendent object and consciousness; what is the relationship between 'being-in-itself' *(l'en-soi)* and 'being-for-oneself' *(le pour-soi)*?

The being of things, 'being-in-itself', is rigid, immobile, deterministic, and already complete in itself. Devoid of potency and becoming, it simply *is*. It is absolutely contingent, wholly given, and without any reason for its being. It is roughly equivalent to the inert world of objects and things. 'Uncreated, without reason for being, without connection with any other being, being-in-itself is superfluous *(de trop)* for all eternity.' The world simply is, it is in itself, and it is what it is. It has no ultimate ground for existence. It is inexplicable, absurd. Apart from consciousness, the world is simply gratuitous, opaque, nebulous, undifferentiated being-in-itself. If consciousness picks out a rock from this background, as ballast, for example, then this rock's differentiation from the undifferentiated background is the work of consciousness. Consciousness differentiates the object as a handy instrument and negates the background. It is consciousness then that makes things appear as distinct.

By way of contrast, 'being-for-oneself' *(pour-soi)* is forever incomplete, fluid, vacuous and lacking in determinate structure. It corresponds to the being of human consciousness. Now, since every thing which is existing must be a thing-in-itself, Sartre concludes that this different type of being, *le pour-soi*, can only be *not* thing-in-itself. It is therefore non-being, nothingness *(le néant)*. It *is not*. Thus, human being, being-for-himself, consists in nothing. This can be shown in the human ability to receive negative answers to questions. Thus, for example, if one discovers that the spare tyre is missing from the car, or that one's friend Peter is not in the restaurant, then one learns also how 'negative realities' *(des négatités)* come into the world through man. Non-being can appear in this particularized or local form within the world only because human consciousness constitutes itself as 'not thing', or as *other* than its physical environment, its body, its past, and indeed every thing in the world about it. Like an empty chamber or cavity within a vegetable, consciousness creates a hole within being-in-itself; and being-in-itself then becomes the horizon or 'world' that surrounds this inner focus of negation. Being-for-itself derives from being-in-itself through an original nihilation *(néantisation)*; it constitutes a nihilation of being-in-itself. It makes its appearance as a nothingness which 'lies coiled in the heart of being, like a worm'. The source of the power of nihilation remains inexplicable and mysterious. The 'for-itself' simply finds itself *there*, an irreducible and ultimate datum, different from the absolute fullness of the surrounding 'in-itself'. Sartre does not refer to Augustine's conception of evil as a privation of the good, a tendency towards nothingness within a being which is its host; nevertheless his analysis of *le néant* as found at the heart of being is one remarkably similar to that of St Augustine.

It is through human being that nothingness comes into the world; and it is human freedom that occasions this nothingness. Freedom is in fact the 'nature' of man, since there is no difference between human being and being-free. Consciousness of freedom is disclosed in anxiety or dread. The feeling of anguish is our experience of freedom. 'It is in anxiety that man has consciousness of freedom, or if you prefer, anxiety is the mode of being of freedom as consciousness of being; it is in anxiety that freedom, in its being, is in question of itself.' Thus, nothingness, freedom and anxiety are inter-related structural determinants of human being. Man flees from the dread of his own nothingness. He seeks to escape from his freedom, his future, and even from his past. He cannot escape from dread, and from his dread of freedom, however, because man *is* his dread.

Human being, in the face of freedom, can adopt one or other of two contrary attitudes. Man can attempt to conceal his freedom from himself by a variety of pretences, excuses and rationalizations; or he can accept his freedom and his sole responsibility for his acts. Those who attempt to conceal their freedom from themselves, by asserting their belief, for example, in some form of psychological determinism, succeed only in providing the conditions which make possible the movement of 'bad faith' *(mauvaise foi)*. Bad faith is a form of semi-self-deception which makes use of freedom in order to deny it. It produces a paradoxical internal duality of consciousness, in which consciousness, while giving secret recognition to its freedom, thinks of itself as an irresponsible being-in-itself, a thing. In 'bad faith', one attempts to conceal the truth from oneself. Thus, for example, a woman who allows her hand to be caressed by an amorous suitor, while pretending not to notice that she is doing so and postponing a decision about her relationship to the suitor, stages a flight from responsible decision, hides the truth from herself, and enters into a state of 'bad faith' with herself. The alternative is to acknowledge one's dreaded freedom and to recognize and accept that one is wholly responsible for one's own acts; one is not a thing.

Sartre condemns the adoption of an attitude of 'bad faith'. He condemns any attempt by human consciousness to 'objectify' itself and look upon itself as an inert determined thing-in-itself. His whole approach to ethics is based on the distinction between the two life-attitudes of irresponsibility and responsibility, of covert 'bad faith' and free self-appropriation. Man must not try to blame everything on his parents or his past. Man's existence necessarily precedes his essence; he first exists and then becomes what he freely decides to be. He makes his own character, or essence. His destiny lies in his own hands. The for-itself escapes the determination of inert being-in-itself and is essentially free. It 'projects' its own ideal goals and seeks to overcome the restrictions of the environment. It escapes from itself as already made by its past and aims at itself as something to be made. Man is 'condemned' to the anguish of being free, he cannot choose or manage to be not free. His awareness of his responsibility and of his condemnation to be free is manifested in 'anguish' (*angoisse*), the anguish of the free.

A man's actually *operative* ideal is revealed in his *actions* rather than in his publicly professed ideals. A politician, for example, reveals his ideals in his post-election actions rather than in his pre-election avowals. It is what one does that reveals what one is and what one has really chosen to be. Moreover, one's various particular choices, Sartre says, are always particular manifestations of one's basic life-attitude, one's basic original choice (or fundamental option). The 'for itself' makes a certain, original projection of its ideal self in the light of a chosen set of values. These values are revealed in one's actions. The original, fundamental free choice can be changed, but this demands a radical conversion and profound change of one's original option. Underlying all these free options, however, there is an existential human project which belongs to the very structure of the *pour-soi* in its flight towards the being which it will be. Man aspires to be the in-itself for-itself, in one, being and consciousness in one. 'Man is fundamentally the desire to be God.' This desire is doomed to failure. The very idea of God is contradictory. There cannot be a nothing thing, an in-itself for-itself. In striving to be an in-itself for-itself the self can only lose itself as for-itself. Man must therefore reconcile himself to the fact that he is a useless striving, a useless passion. '*L'homme est une passion inutile.*'

The world of the 'for-itself' is not an insulated world experienced in isolation. It is a world in which the 'others' (*autrui*) have already made their appearance. The being of the for-itself is always given as a being-for-others as well. My apprehension of my own being is so structured that it presupposes the existence of other conscious beings. This is manifested especially in the case of feelings of shame. Through the feeling of shame I discover simultaneously the 'other' and an aspect of my being as standing in front of the other. The other reveals the structures of my own being to me; he reveals myself to me. In 'the look' (*le regard*) of the other we find a pre-reflective disclosure of the self and the other. 'Being-watched constitutes me as a being without defence for a freedom which is not my freedom.' The 'look' of the other reduces me to a reified object, a being-in-itself. I experience my freedom as threatened by another who is about to ingest and absorb me into the orbit of his concerns. I can defend and affirm my freedom, in retaliation, by rendering the 'other' into an object; but the other can stage a similar counterattack, and the cycle simply repeats itself. All attempts to absorb the other's freedom, as in the case of love, or to reduce either the self or the other to an object, as in the case of sexual desire, are doomed to failure because I must first recognize my own liberty, or that of the other, in order to suppress it.

Heidegger's general account of *Mitsein* (being-together) needs to be reconsidered, Sartre says, in the light of *le regard*. There can undoubtedly be a consciousness of community togetherness, a sense of 'we', as in the case of a pre-reflexive outburst of applause at a concert or festival. On the level of reflexive consciousness, however, it is conflict, and not *Mitsein*, that is the essence of the relationships between different consciousnesses. Conflict is the original meaning of the experience of 'being-for-others' (or being-an-object-for-others). Reflexive 'we-consciousness' arises only in a situation of confrontation with a group of 'them', the Others. Being a being-for-others implies confrontation with 'them'. The essence of the relationship with others, then, is conflict. Each seeks to dominate the other as a free being, to possess him both as an object and as a free being. This can be seen clearly, he asserts, in the erotic caress.

In his lecture on humanism Sartre speaks of existentialism as nothing other than 'an attempt to draw all the consequences from a consistent atheist position'. The very idea of God as a being-in-itself-and-for-itself is a self-contradictory idea. It is not simply that there is no God; there cannot possibly by a God. There can therefore be no universally obligatory moral law, and there is no set of absolute fixed values. It is man who is the source of all values, and in this, as in other areas, man's liberty is unrestricted. Through the projection of his chosen ends, man is the creator of his own situation and destiny. What man makes of himself depends on the operative ideal which he has freely projected for himself. Any set of values or ethical norms which a man endorses becomes his values precisely because of his own act of choice. Sartre maintained that this meta-ethical theory does not encourage a capricious choice of ethical norms, and does not promote moral anarchy. He held that when one chooses value one chooses ideally for all, and that responsibility for oneself is also responsibility for all. This theory acknowledges that to choose with a sense of responsibility for others is a value; but the theory also has as its first premiss that it is the individual who creates every value through his act of choice. Thus, if one atheistic existentialist chooses to regard social responsibility as a value, and another chooses to regard unrestrained choice, without any sense of social responsibility, as a value, then Sartre's meta-ethical theory is incapable of vindicating any assertion that either of these values is intrinsically superior to the other. This theory has no transcendent values and no universal moral law. It is a theory of unrestricted atomic individualism.

At the end of World War II Sartre became severely critical of the atomic individualism that was characteristic of his earlier moral theory, as expressed in *L'Être et le néant* (1943). In articles written for *Les temps modernes* (1945ff.) and in his *Critique de la raison dialectique* (1960), he pointed out that the moral autonomy of the individual is restricted and qualified by the fact that the individual lives in an exploitative society in an age of scarcity. The dialectic of human antagonism hampers the realization of true moral freedom. He began to consider the original Marxist philosophy as a dynamic, living philosophy through which the new ascending class is coming to consciousness of itself. Stalinism had encrusted Marxist thought within closed, hardened dogmas. But the original, revolutionary concepts of Marxian (rather than Marxist) thought can be humanized and rejuvenated if these concepts are interpreted not in terms of deterministic Nature but in terms of existential humanism. An existentialist Marxism would replace atheistic materialism with atheistic humanism. Through concerted human action, a humanistic revolutionary 'group' is capable of liberating the alienated individual from captive encirclement by the 'practico-inert', namely, dehumanizing machinery and the inert mass of mechanistic human products.

It is scarcity (*rareté*) of goods that underpins the division of men into consumers and sub-consumers, those who have much and those who have little. To overcome scarcity, man invents tools and machines to act on his material environment. All the structures of each society rest on the workers' productivity and their utilization of determinate tools. In a milieu of mechanization and industrialization, however, man falls under the domination of the very machines, tools and wrought matter (*matière oeuvrée*), the 'practico-inert', which he himself has created. In an industrialized society, matter dominates man; and man becomes self-alienated, or estranged from himself. The machines, the practico-inert, determine the serialization and stratification of men into 'collectives' or classes, skilled or unskilled. Individuals become competitive units within a series, a disgruntled queue, in which other units or members are seen as rivals or enemies. This 'anti-dialectic' of man's domination by his own creation, however, can be negated. The class-in-itself is capable of becoming the class-for-itself. The series of alienated 'collectives' can be transformed into a revolutionary, humanistic 'group' who aim at the realization of a new society.

In his early writings, including *L'Être et le néant*, Sartre's emphasis is on the unrestricted freedom, contingency, and anguish of human existence. Human being is regarded as rootless, entirely sundered from nature. Man looks upon 'agglutinant' matter with revulsion and dread. The rootless but free intellectual (seated perhaps in the public café) rejects the routine role-playing and rigidities of the bourgeois household and the kind of society of which it is the paradigm. He creates his own values and aspires to the development of his future possibilities in the direction of his fundamental operative ideal. He aspires to be a totally liberated *pour-soi*, until he relapses at death into the viscous, agglutinant *en-soi* which will finally overwhelm him.

In his later writings, including the *Critique of Dialectical Reason*, Sartre's emphasis is on the concerted human activity of the forward-marching 'group' as it transcends the antagonisms generated by scarcity, the enslaving domination of the 'practico-inert', and the constraining pressures of the general movement of history. The dynamic group works with revolutionary fervour for the realization of a new form of society. History possesses its own intelligible dialectical movement, which, from one point of view, man must necessarily endure; but it is man himself who makes history. The conflict between the *pour-soi* and *en-soi* of the early writings is now replaced, through a dialectical negation of dehumanizing 'collectives' or classes, by the dynamic, existentialist group. Man is capable of transcending his externally imposed enslavement.

There are several differences between Sartre's earlier and later thought, but there is also a discernible continuity. The dialectical relationship between the individual free agent and his threatening milieu remains basically the same. The *Critique*, however, introduces a new, quasi-Hegelian note, in speaking of history as embodying a unified *intelligible* movement of which man himself is the instrument. This view of historical development seems to imply that values are attached to reality through a postulated movement of history that ensures their eventual realization. Sartre did not develop the (apparently teleological) implications of this view.

4. Camus. *Albert Camus* (1913-60) was born in Algeria and studied philosophy at the university of Algiers. He was specially interested in philosophers such as Socrates, Pascal, Spinoza, Kierkegaard and Nietzsche whose method of philosophizing was closely bound to their personal experiences and personalities. In 1940 he moved to Paris and worked with the resistance movement during the German occupation of France. His novels, plays, essays and notebooks *(carnets)* reflected his philosophical concerns. These philosophico-literary works may be divided into three phases of development.

In 1942 Camus published his first novel *The Stranger*, and an essay *The Myth of Sisyphus* which presented a philosophical exposition of moral attitudes closely akin to those depicted in the novel. In these and other early works, Camus maintained that it is impossible to find any significance in the world. The world itself lacks reason. It is irrational, inhumane, and utterly silent. Within the depths of man, however, there is a desperate desire and appeal for *clarity* about the meaning of the world and human history. Man's perception of the meaninglessness of existence gives rise to his feeling that all is absurd. All reason for existing disappears, and one finds it unbearably absurd to live on without meaning in a godless world lacking absolute objective values. Meaningless existence is unbearable; and yet suicide is no solution. Suicide would be an act of resignation or capitulation to the absurdity of the world and human existence.

Human life has worth only when man lives in proud, conscious revolt against the absurd. It is in a life of protest against his destiny that man wins his freedom and adds greatness to his life. The 'atheist saint' chooses to live a life of self-commitment, *engagement*, living life to the full in his irrational historical situation. He chooses to be virtuous by caprice, living his life ardently, as a freedom fighter, for example, or a creative artist, clearly conscious that every cause is also a doomed, futile cause.

Camus explains this attitude further by saying that all is permitted, except a life of crime, which is puerile. Man is an evaluative and purposive being in a world which is unreasonable. He can achieve his full stature by going on living in the face of the absurdity of all that is in existence. He can reject passive despair and attain humanistic transcendence by transforming nihilism into a dynamic revolt against the world's indifferences to man. Revolt of this kind is authentic revolt when it is done in the name of man's solidarity with man. Camus had difficulty, however, in explaining how an ethic of human solidarity emerges naturally from a nihilist philosophy which negates all values.

In 1947 Camus published a novel called *The Plague (La Peste)*, and in 1951, *The Rebel (L'Homme révolté)*, a philosophical essay on the concept of revolt. His emphasis had now shifted from heroic nihilism to heroic humanism. Man must revolt against the human condition, but even more so, he must also revolt against totalitarian man's inhumanity to man. The Jacobin, Nazi and Soviet revolts against the human condition of their times led only to a new terrorist enslavement of man by man, not to a new social order of human fraternity. Nihilist revolt clears away all sham foundations but provides no principles for a humanistic ethic of reconstruction. The rebel must rebel also against political murderers and statist totalitarians of all kinds, Nazi, Marxist or otherwise. This view provoked a sundering of relations between Camus and Sartre. There is no justification of any kind, political or non-political, for the enslavement or the killing of human beings, Camus asserted.

In 1956, in *The Fall (La Chute)*, and in his *Reflections on Capital Punishment* (1960), Camus came to realize that evil does not exist in socio-political institutions as such, except in as far as they are merely articulations of a 'basic duplicity' and inner complicity with evil in the heart of man himself. He decided to abandon political and social action. He saw his philosophy of revolt as concerned fundamentally with moral values, human freedom, social justice, peace, the elimination of violence, and the development of moral responsibility. His revolt was against exploitation, oppression, violence, and suppression of freedom. In this way Camus threw light on the problems of conscience of our times.

In 1957 Camus received the Nobel prize for literature. In 1960 he died in a motor accident in France. The work of Camus, like that of Sartre, by drawing attention to man's situation and destiny in a world regarded as a godless world, drew attention again to the importance of the problem of the existence of God.

5. Marcel. *Gabriel Marcel* (1889-1973), when studying philosophy at the Sorbonne, and teaching philosophy at various lycées, showed a special interest in the works of F. H. Bradley and J. Royce. His experiences in the First World War convinced him, however, that idealist philosophy failed to explain satisfactorily the tragic character of human existence. In an early essay on *Existence and Objectivity* (1925) and in his *Journal métaphysique* (1927), Marcel introduced several themes concerning man as being in the world, the priority of existence over essence, commitment, participation, and being with others, which later became central themes in the works of Jaspers, Heidegger and other existentialist thinkers. In later works such as *Being and Having* (1935), *Creative Fidelity* (1940), *Homo Viator* (1945), *Philosophy of Existentialism* (1949), *The Mystery of Being* (1951), *Man against Mass Society* (1951) and *Problematic Man* (1955), Marcel presented the existing subject, the incarnate being who is already in his world-situation, as the absolute starting-point for all philosophical thought. Each of these works is an intensely personal exploration and communication of a human situation which gives rise to wonder and mystery. Several of his explorations focus on the theme of interpersonal relationships.

In a world which Marcel spoke of as a 'broken', fragmented, or functionalized world, the human being is looked upon as an agglomeration of functions: the citizen, the bus-driver, the husband, the consumer, the clerk, the depersonalized role-player. Man is atomized and collectivized; and, in the process, the world is devitalized. There arises a widespread and pitiful blindness to the presence of 'mysteries'. It is in this functionalizing context that Marcel distinguishes between first reflection and second reflection, and between problem and mystery.

Primary reflection, as exemplified in scientific and technical thought, is characterized as abstract, analytical, universal, objective and verifiable. The scientific questioner is separated from the objective data. The problem being investigated, as in mathematics, is one which can be dealt with in an impersonal way. It can be dealt with by anyone, or by a programmed machine, and the product-solution can be handed on. The individual is not personally involved, and the problem can be addressed in an abstract, detached way.

Secondary reflection, as exemplified in a person's contemplation of the mystery and wonder of his being, is an exploration of the metaphysical significance of a lived, immediate, personal, feeling-experience. It concerns itself with the personal realm of mystery and not with the impersonal realm of the problematic. In dialogue, it opens itself humbly to the revelation of the total presence of the other. Experiences of personal relationship, love, joy, fidelity, faith and hope provide insights into the nature of reality which one cannot obtain on the level of technological primary reflection. Secondary reflection returns to immediate experiences of this kind, and it explores them, so far as this is possible, from within the experiences themselves. It involves the whole being of the questioning subject in such a way that the questioner is never disregarded. The question points then to a 'mystery' in which oneself is involved, and not simply to an impersonal problem about a detached object.

For Marcel, embodiment or incarnation is the 'central given', the absolute starting-point of a philosophy of existence. The primary datum is not myself as a self-insulated ego but myself present in the world as 'incarnated'. My presence, a corporeal presence, is 'mysterious'. I cannot say that my body is something 'I have' or something 'I am'; and yet it is through my incarnation that I participate in being and in the world. As far back as I can remember I have been participating in being, always open to being, and open to others.

We arrive at an understanding of human being especially through the study of human relationships. In the plane of interpersonal communion my openness to 'the other' is an openness to a 'thou'. I become available as a person, 'disponible' to the other. It is on this level that there arise intersubjective relationships of love, fidelity and loyalty, which can be explored from within by second reflection. Thus, for example, a loved one can be present to me, as a 'thou', even when he or she is physically absent or dead. At the centre of the thou-relationship there is a faithfulness (*fidelité*), a creative fidelity, which engenders an 'active perpetuation of presence' of the other. The faithful one commits himself or herself to the loved one in a new and active participation in the sphere of being. In doing so, the faithful one creates himself or herself anew in freedom, loyalty and love.

Human being aspires basically to an absolute self-commitment and to an absolute fidelity and loyalty. This involves the invocation of the absolute Thou, the personal transcendent Absolute, the ground of all being and value, God, who alone makes eternal fidelity possible. Through openness to being and to others, I transcend my egoism and prepare my being, in adoration and prayer, for a personal self-relating to God, the absolute Thou. In this approach to God, fidelity becomes faith, and 'disponibility' becomes hope. Human being, open to the mystery of Being, is overtaken by a new awareness of the eternal fulfilling Presence that he seeks to know. It is only in this way that human being can overcome isolation, tragedy and despair. Man's quest for being is identical therefore with his quest for salvation. The immanence of being in human experience, however, never becomes a consummated possession. It is constantly created anew in every interpersonal relationship of the 'I' with the empirical 'thou' or with the absolute 'Thou' who is God himself.

Marcel's various essays in 'second reflection' and his exploration of 'mysteries' are attempts to open out for us new vistas on the wondrous dimensions of our being. He calls attention to the outward signs of eternity present in every interpersonal relationship. He attempts to reveal to us the *metaphysical* significance of simple, familiar experiences of human existence, human being.

6. Jaspers. *Karl Jaspers* (1883-1969), who was born in Oldenburg in Germany, was a leading existentialist philosopher whose work was deeply influenced by his early training in medicine, psychology and psychiatry. His main works are *General Psychopathology* (1913), *The Psychology of Fundamental Attitudes to Life* (1919), *Man in the Modern Age* (1932), *Philosophy* (1932), *Reason and Existenz* (1935), *Nietzsche* (1936), *Descartes* (1937), *Existenzphilosophie* (1938), *Philosophical Logic: Truth and Symbol* (1947), *The Future of Mankind* (1957), and *The Great Philosophers* (1957, 1961).

In his preface to *Philosophy* and in *Reason and Existenz* Jaspers defined philosophy as the elucidation of *Existenz*. No description of *Existenz* is possible; it can be clarified only by reference to concrete situations. Human being as standing over against the world of existing objects is more than something 'there' *(Dasein)*; it is that being which is essentially the potentiality of its own being. *Existenz* is the freedom of an individual. It is the possibility of decision. Human being 'exists' in this special sense of *Existenz* because he alone is that which he can become in his freedom. I am the *possibility* of my own being. I am never something already made. I am constantly creating

myself, freely realizing my being through my choices. The *Existenz* of
the individual is unique because the possibilities open to each are
unique and personal. What I make of myself is my own unique
creation. My *Existenz* is entirely my own. Reflection on the lives of
men like Bruno, Spinoza, Kant, Schelling, Kierkegaard and Nietzsche clarifies for us the potentialities of human existence. Each of
these attempted to present his own clarification of existence (*Exis-
tenzerhellung*). Each explored man's continual movement towards the
discovery of himself in liberty. Each saw the function of philosophy
as that of opening up the mind to reality and destiny. Philosophy
must be a lived philosophy. It is a personal philosophizing in one's
existential or historical situation. It begins in the attempt to
communicate to another the nature of one's forward-looking, inner
self, one's *Existenz*.

Existenz is the eternal in man, the authentic indefinable ground of
his being. It is mysterious and rich in paradoxes and antinomies. It is
free in its dependence, it communicates in solitude, it is happy even
in grief and progresses even through destruction. It is the dynamic
Dionysian principle, the abyss or dark ground of selfhood, limited by
impenetrable boundaries. Death, suffering, fortune, chance, struggle, conflict, guilt, evil, finitude are some of the most dramatic and
important of the inescapable situations and impenetrable barriers of
Existenz. The world itself provides no ultimate foothold. We
experience the jaggedness, the brittleness and finitude of all being.
'Failure is ultimate.' Death, the source of anxiety, emphasizes the
urgency of living authentically, without pretences, and without
postponements. Guilt, like death, cannot be obliterated. It must be
accepted and borne courageously. Man could have chosen otherwise;
he *is* guilty. His guilt demonstrates the power that his freedom has
over his destiny. Man can face these boundary situations with courage
and integrity, and, through freely choosing them as his own, make
them humanly constructive.

Existenz 'is' freedom. I experience freedom through existential
choice, that is, through deciding to affirm and become myself. My
freedom however is not absolute. It is the reconciliation of necessity
and free choice. My choice is free, but I bind myself by my choice. I
carry out my free choice and accept its consequences. 'I can because I
must.' My freedom is not determined by empirical reality. It is
determined by self-creation at the moment of choice.

Each of my choices carries with it the accumulated weight of
previous decisions. My original first choice (*Urentschluss*), for my
own good (like original sin), bears down on my subsequent history.

That choice eliminated other possibilities and in doing so rendered me guilty. To be responsible now for that choice means to have accepted my guilt. The inherent difficulty of surrendering myself to my authentic existential possibilities and choosing from among them each day leads to anguish and further guilt. Always moving into a future, *Existenz* is burdened with the enduring responsibilities of decisions.

No *Existenz* achieves his humanity in isolation. He survives or lives only in and through others. He comes to an apprehension of the truth of his *Existenz* only through interdependent and mutual communal understanding. Communicated truth is necessarily empirical, relative and changing. As one's situation changes so does the truth about one's situation. But *Existenz* strives to overcome these changes in its 'loving struggle' to communicate to another *Existenz* the innermost meaning of its being. In this light, one can see that existential communication is communication between irreplaceable persons. Existential philosophizing is self-disclosure through authentic, existential communication.

In man's forward movement towards the discovery of his true self in liberty he becomes conscious of his finitude. He becomes conscious, however, not only of his limits but also of his movement towards the transcending of limits. He discovers the Transcendent in the process of discovering himself as a transcending being. He becomes aware of the Transcendent as the enveloping presence, the negatively apprehended complement of finitude and limits. He becomes aware of himself and of his situation as grounded in Being. Transcendence is experienced as the intimation of an encompassing power by which man himself (i.e. 'freedom') exists. The 'encompassing' *(das Umgreifende)* is unknowable, ultimate Being, lying beyond all horizons of determinate being. It is the realm of the numinous, the noumenal, which never makes its appearance as a determinable object of knowledge. Man encounters the Encompassing, the Comprehensive, not within any conceptual scheme but in existential decision and philosophical faith. The godhead remains utterly hidden, unknowable, the absolute unity beyond all categories. It is presented to us only in cypher. The most important task for metaphysics, then, is the reading of cyphers of transcendence.

Cypher is being as presenting transcendence to us. Nature, history, givenness, failure, consciousness, human being, freedom, fragility, finitude, may each be regarded as constituting a cypher for transcendence. Philosophical speculation, like art, is basically cypher-reading. We experience everything as falling into disruption. In the human situation existence itself fails. The illusions of knowledge and philosophy are doomed to failure. The given world, given as permanent, is not permanent; it is not what we think we know it to be. Thus, 'permanent' things are not the standard of value; and the given world is not the absolute. To draw near to the Transcendent, cypher-reading is necessary. Finitude points to Infinity. To philosophize is 'to learn to die'. The cypher-reader learns that the absolute can become visible only when all else is seen as shattered. It is in and through failure that we become capable of encountering Transcendence, Being Itself.

Existential philosophy in general has made a valuable contribution to our appreciation of the independence, uniqueness and dignity of the individual human being. It is through free decision that man takes his destiny in his own hands. It is through *Angst* or anxiety that he experiences nothingness and the shattering of all that is finite. It is through taking hold of himself with fixity of purpose that he achieves authenticity and realizes the fullness of his own being. Existential philosophy does not overcome, however, the Cartesian dichotomy of human and non-human being. It may even be said to exacerbate the dichotomy. It presents a valuable, partial view of reality, but not a full philosophy of being.

36 Philosophy of being

1. Metaphysics, ontology and being   2. Twentieth-
century metaphysicians and ontologists   3. Hartmann
4. Contemporary Thomism   5. Teilhard de Chardin
6. Transcendental method   7. Bernard Lonergan

1. Metaphysics, ontology and being. An adequate
treatment of the numerous twentieth-century philosophers of being
would require several chapters. It is not possible to devote a special
section to this theme in a work which aspires to be a one-volume
history of philosophy. Within the space available we can deal
with the thought of only a few of these philosophers and merely
allude to others who are avowed metaphysicians, ontologists, or
philosophers of being. But we must first consider, however
briefly, some of the numerous meanings which have been given to
the terms 'metaphysics', 'ontology' and 'being' by different
philosophers.

Aristotle (see above, Chapter 5, section 3) defir.ed the philosophy
of nature, or 'physics', as the study of 'those realities that exist by
nature' (animals, plants, and such 'simple bodies' as fire and water),
having within themselves a principle of *kinēsis*, motion, process, or
development. Andronicus of Rhodes, in collecting and arranging
Aristotle's works, is said to have listed some of the treatises 'after
the *Physics*' (*meta ta physica*). Aristotle had thought of this untitled
group of texts as pertaining to first philoso?hy, theology, or
wisdom. Several medieval and modern philosophers regarded the
'metaphysics' as a study of transcendent things transcending nature.
Eighteenth-century *littérateurs* then used the term to refer to all that
is abstruse, otherworldly, and even occult. Positivists used the term
as a term of opprobrium in promoting their 'nonmetaphysical'
positivistic doctrines. The *Metaphysics* or First Philosophy of
Aristotle, however, is simply a study of the first principles or first
causes which underlie all the specialized philosophical disciplines,
such as the science of natural philosophy which confines its interest
to the principles of natural development alone. It is in this sense
that twentieth-century metaphysicians regard all special philosophical sciences (of nature, knowledge, values and so forth) as particular
applications of a general ontology and metaphysics.

Metaphysics or 'first philosophy' studies 'being as being'. It preoccupies itself with the concepts of existence, reality, the ultimate nature of things, and of the world as a whole; and it relies for its conclusions on the effort of reason alone. It endeavours to attain an overall point of view from which we are enabled to see things synoptically. This vantage point arises from a distinctive set of first principles which apply without restriction to all the data of experience. It enables the philosopher to resolve conceptual conflicts through the patient formulation of well-considered terms which enable him to express his vision of the nature of reality. In an age when pure empiricism and positivism are themselves discredited, 'first philosophy' is seen as an exercise which is no longer regarded as reprehensible. The human mind is permitted once again to address itself to the whole of reality. 'Accordingly, we too must grasp the primary causes (or basic factors) of being as being' (*Metaphysics* IV, 1003a30; see also above, Chapter 6, section 1).

Aristotle pointed out that the special sciences make use of the basic concepts of being, beginning, explanatory factor (cause), nature, necessary, power (*dynamis*), the inner activity of being (*energeia*), process or becoming (*kinēsis*), and similar fundamental concepts. They make use of the concepts; but these concepts are not the objects of their inquiries. It is first philosophy itself that has concepts of this kind as the proper object of its inquiries. He then pointed out, with reference to the concept of being, that a being may be a thing or existent in itself, or it may be an accidental being. Furthermore, things may be predicated to 'be' in as many different ways as there are categories. The 'is' or 'is not' in a statement may mean that it is true or false to say that something is so (IV, 1017a31). To 'be' and 'being' may sometimes mean that what is said is true of a thing which is in 'power' (*dynamis*), as when we say it *can see*, or of a thing which is in 'active possession of its end' (*entelecheia*), as when we say it is actually *seeing* something. Aristotle did not speak of being as a name naming a special object or property possessed by everything that is. This was the later view of the extreme realists and nominalists. Abelard and Aquinas returned to, and reaffirmed, the pure Aristotelian tradition. Being is not a predicable; it is not a genus; it is not a property of an essence; and it is not an accident of some realm of (occult) properties. *That* a thing is does not derive from *what* the thing is. To ask 'what is being?' is to assume that being is a 'what', a property, an essence, an accident, a nature, or a genus.

For Aristotle, and also for Aquinas, 'to be' (*esse*) refers to an inner operation, an inner actuality, activity, or act. Thus, for example, for living things, 'to live' and 'to be' are coterminous; in their case, 'being' is 'living' and 'living' is 'being'. In this sense, 'being' is an ongoing inner 'activity' *(energeia)*, which is best expressed in verbs and participles such as 'exists', 'is', 'to be', *esse*, 'being', 'possessing its perfection within itself' *(entelecheia)*, 'inner activity or act' *(energeia)*, and 'existing'. Aquinas pointed out that it differs from the accidental power of operation, or activity, of a constituted thing, by reason of the fact that it is a co-relative constitutive co-principle (with the co-principle of limitation, or *essentia*), *constituting* the finite existent. It is the constitutive co-principle of perfection. In God there is no co-relative co-principle of limitation, and so God may be spoken of as subsisting *'Esse'* or as being 'Being' its very self.

Jacques Maritain, in his *Preface to Metaphysics* and other works, speaks of a (special) metaphysical insight or intuition of being. This cannot be an insight into the essence of being because being does not possess an essence. One may well wonder if Maritain regards this insight as exceedingly rare and accorded to people of particular ability. There seems to be no good reason for speaking of a special intuition of being differing in any notable way from the ordinary explanation given above. Thus, for example, it is by ordinary human discernment that we know that, in the case of living things, *'being'* and living are one and the same. *'Vivere viventis est esse.'* In this case 'metaphysical insight' is a very ordinary phenomenon indeed and need never be implied to be unusual or special. One trusts that in saying so one has not done an injustice to Maritain's thought.

The term 'ontology' was coined by Goclenius or one of the early seventeenth-century Scholastic philosophers. In 1661 Duhamel spoke of ontology as a study which was distinct from that of natural theology. It was regarded as the study of existent finite beings and all that belongs essentially and immediately to them. It was the study of the existent as distinct from the study of God. This view was solidly entrenched in the rationalist writings of Wolff and Baumgarten in the earlier part of the eighteenth century. The rationalists regarded ontology as a deductive discipline, a science of necessary truths akin to geometry in form but having the existent as its subject-matter. This approach gave rise to various 'essentialist' views of the 'nature' of *being*. In the works of N. Hartmann and M. Heidegger the study of the (finite) existent is similarly considered as closed off from the idea of the Infinite. In the works of Sartre the existent is totally separated from consciousness which is regarded as 'nothingness'. These ontologists confine their attention to the analysis of structure in the existent. The metaphysicians, by way of contrast, regard their studies of the special philosophical disciplines (knowledge, nature, values) as resting basically upon their primary study of 'being' and the fundamental concepts of 'first philosophy'.

2. Twentieth-century metaphysicians and ontologists.

Hans Driesch (1867-1941) maintained that the concerned scientist must go beyond the scientific view of the world into the domain of metaphysical reflection. His experimental research work on the blastomeres of the two-cell stage of a sea-urchin egg showed that each blastomere developed into a whole embryo half the normal size. He concluded that a 'harmonious equipotential system' of this kind cannot be accounted for in terms of mechanistic principles. He then devoted his attention to the science and philosophy of the organism, and to the formulation of an inductive and teleological philosophy of being. In a similar way, Oswald Kulpe (d. 1915), R. Eucken (d. 1926), H. Maier (d. 1933), E. Jaensch (d. 1940), E. Becher and others entered the domain of metaphysics through their speculations on one or other of the empirical sciences. (See also Chapter 25, section 8 above.)

Samuel Alexander (1859-1938) developed a comprehensive evolutionary system of philosophy (of space-time) which he claimed to be metaphysics following an 'empirical method'. *A. N. Whitehead* (1861-1947), a mathematician and natural scientist by profession, turned to metaphysics in order to explain the concept of nature, process and reality, and science and the modern world. (See Chapter 33 above.)

George Santayana (1863-1952) in his early works propounded a naturalistic philosophy which postulated a universal reality based on matter. The scepticism of reason, he maintained, is compensated by an animal faith in matter. The world is known through intuitive 'essences' or ideal characters derived from the interplay of objects and organisms. In his later writings he developed this view in a 'Platonist' fashion. Reality reveals itself to consciousness as an infinity of essences subsisting in and by themselves. These essences collectively compose one absolute essence in 'Pure Being' which is common to all essences. Essence is the primary and incontestable mode of being. When an essence is exemplified in the realm of spatio-temporal matter it can be called substance. Matter or substance is knowable only through the essences it exemplifies. This doctrine may be classified as one of transcendental subjectivity. It differs from associated or similar doctrines in as far as it is both a semi-Platonist and a naturalistic system of philosophy.

Heinrich Scholz (1884-1956), who founded the Institute for Mathematical Logic and Basic Research at Munich, maintained that classical Platonist mathematical analysis, and Platonist philosophy in general, as striving for universal knowledge, provide an eminently useful framework and foundation for the theoretical constructions of modern science. Relativity theory, for example, is basically Platonist. Platonism, reinterpreted in the light of Russell's type-theoretical logic, provides an ontological basis for the science of mathematics.

William Ralph Inge (1860-1954) was convinced that the Neo-Platonic philosophy of Plotinus presented an inspired message and a broadly based rational philosophy for the positive thinkers of our own times. It shows us how to take account of universal values as well as of scientific facts.

Alfred Edward Taylor (1869-1945), an authority on Plato, Aristotle and Greek philosophy, argued that for the person who takes moral experience seriously, the values of the moral life point beyond moral experience to the world of religious experience and to a theistic understanding of the nature of reality. The good at which the moral life aims is a non-defective, non-transient, eternal good. This eternal good is attainable by man only through the initiative of the eternal itself, or, in other words, through divine grace. Moral experience leads to God. The grounds for belief in God are found in cosmology, in conscience, and in religious experience. Taylor's interpretation of reality is consistently theistic and spiritualistic.

René Le Senne (1882-1954) and *Louis Lavelle* (1883-1951) were French spiritualistic philosophers and joint editors who published the series of works in the collection 'Philosophie de l'esprit'. They regarded this series as continuing the French traditional study of immanent, lived activities, as found in the works of Maine de Biran and the nineteenth-century spiritualist or voluntarist movement. Le Senne regarded all existents as dependent upon infinite, transcendent Being. Man participates in absolute, transcendent value and also in a world of brute matter. Through each of these he creates himself unceasingly by making these values determinate in his given, concrete situation. According to Lavelle, Absolute Act, or Being, is the infinite source of every individual participated act of being, and the infinite source of all possible forms of limitation of being, from which each particular existent receives its limited, individual and unique act of being. The human participant in being, in pursuit of his vocation and ideal, namely, to 'be human', becomes a co-creator of his maturing spiritual self. Matter, and the 'natural spontaneity' of instinct, in limiting the spirit, offers the resistance necessary for the self to transcend itself. Spontaneity is converted into human freedom through the human spirit's subordination of instinctive spontaneity to reflection and rational discipline. Even in the least significant instants of our daily existence, our vocation is to immerse ourselves in our participated act of being, participate in the Absolute, and 'be human'.

3. Hartmann.

Nicolai Hartmann (1882-1950), who studied under Cohen and Natorp at Marburg, revolted against the neo-Kantian idealist 'School-philosophy' of the German universities. He maintained that one must return not to Kant but to things. What the mind knows, when it knows, is beings, things. Epistemology is based on ontology and not the other way round. The categories to which the philosopher must attend are the 'categories', or, rather, the structures of the world, the different modes or levels of being. The real difference between organic beings and inorganic beings, and the real difference between aesthetic values, consciousness and physical entities is not accounted for by positivism or neo-Kantianism. It is the function of the philosopher, then, to develop a realist ontology rather than to construct one more speculative system of thought. Speculative metaphysics has involved philosophers invariably in insoluble problems. Ontology, the science which studies the different modes of being and the different levels of being within these modes, is capable of attaining genuine knowledge of reality.

The realist philosopher, Hartmann says, must first of all make a careful, descriptive, phenomenological analysis of the different modes of being and levels of beings exemplified in the beings given in experience. This analysis will normally give rise to problems *(aporiae)* which must be unravelled into their strands. Aporetics, as a philosophical method, unravels the contradictions that the analysed facts seem to harbour. It presents them as clear-cut antinomies for further philosophical analysis. The mind can then weigh the pros and cons of apparent solutions and direct its attention to problem-solving. The dialogues of Plato and the works of Aristotle exemplify the use of aporetics as the basic method of their philosophical investigations.

In the act of knowing something there is an ontic relation between the knowing being and the being known. The problem of the relation between subject and object is therefore an ontological problem and not just an epistemological problem. The knowing being and the being known are different structures within the context of being *(Seinszusammenhang)*. It is the function of ontology to investigate the different ways in which things are given as 'being this' or 'being that' or 'being such and such'. Even if the epistemological problem should continue to be an insoluble metaphysical problem, the ontological problem, concerning the actual structures of being involved in any act of knowing something, is one which is conceptually manageable.

Hartmann avoids speaking of 'classes' or kinds of being because these terms may be though of as connoting class-concepts and subjective classifications. He is concerned in a special way with the different modes of being (being such-and-such) and not with mental categories.

A descriptive, phenomenological account of an act of knowing something makes it manifest that the thing experienced or known is experienced as existing independently of its being known. The thing experienced is experienced as actually existing in itself and not simply for us. Knowing, or knowledge, is seen to be a transcendent act. It is not restricted to the subjective pole of consciousness alone. It oversteps consciousness and unites itself to that which is independent of it and exists in itself; it is a transcendent act. The being which is known is not exhausted in its being known by a knower. The relation between the knower and the thing known is an ontic relation between two beings, each of which is a being in itself (*Ansichseiende*). This does not need to be proved to sceptics, critics and idealists. It is given, as the world itself is given, and as the being of another person is given. No philosophical theory can ignore it.

Phenomenological analysis reveals four distinct spheres of being: the sphere of real beings, the sphere of ideal being, the cognitive sphere and the logical sphere. The two primary spheres, of real being and ideal being, may also be designated as modes of being. The sphere of real beings embraces both actual beings and real possibilities. There is an intimate cross-relationship between the real modes of being and the cognitive sphere, and again between the logical sphere and the ideal modes of being. The sphere of ideal being includes universal essences, values, and mathematical being.

Within these spheres of being there are different strata or levels of being. Real beings are found on four levels: inorganic matter, organic nature, consciousness, and spirit (personal spirit, social spirit, and institutionalized spirit). Being known, or, in other words, the sphere of cognition, involves observation, intuitive perception, recognition, and comprehensive knowledge. Logical being, as traditionally understood, divides into concept, judgement and inference.

Hartmann then delved further into the fundamental categories and the modal categories of being, the categorial laws or principles through which the different levels of being are determined. He regarded the traditional distinction between essence and existence as a distinction between two relative factors or moments of a being: the presence '*that* it is' *(Dasein)*, and its presence as '*what* it is' *(Sosein)*. He analysed the content of values and explored the relationship of several values to each other, to the ought and to the real. He explored the problem of the freedom of the human being living in a world of several levels. He concluded that natural determination by the causal laws of nature is not eliminated but, rather, diverted by the intervention of a higher determination, namely, self-determination, which is freedom, or that autonomy of will through which an agent commits himself to the realization of value.

Hartmann's ontology takes the form of an analysis of the structures exemplified in the beings given in experience. He passed over and ignored the crucial question concerning *being* itself or the very *being* of beings. He regarded this as an inscrutable metaphysical problem. He developed an impressive realist ontology of the categories of experienced (finite) beings. But he avoided any enquiry into the 'inner activity' of being which gives every being the perfection of being, and he avoided all reference to the unlimited act of being itself, *ipsum esse subsistens*.

4. Contemporary Thomism, which is grounded on the basic principles of St Thomas Aquinas (1224-72), has been one of the most important philosophical movements of the mid-twentieth century. It is a movement which has several research centres and faculties or institutes of higher studies at its disposal. More than twenty quarterlies and journals of Thomistic philosophy throughout the world have continued to present specialist articles by Thomistic philosophers and to review hundreds of new works each year by members of the Thomistic school of thought.

The Scholasticism of the eighteenth century was a decadent and minor school of thought which for the main part favoured Ockhamism, shunned metaphysics, promoted Aristotelian physics, and wondered about the significance of the mathematico-physical hypotheses of the fledgling new sciences. In the early part of the nineteenth century, several Christian thinkers attempted to adapt a religious interpretation of idealism, traditionalism or ontologism to the problems of their times. Some of these efforts were condemned by the magisterium of the Church. In Italy, as already mentioned in Chapter 30, Serafino and Domenico Sordi, two brothers who became

Jesuits, Giuseppe Pecci, the brother of the future Pope Leo XIII, and Gaetano Sanseverino, with the support of the Jesuit periodical *Civiltà Cattolica*, started a new movement which aimed to restore Thomistic thought and apply its principles to contemporary issues. The movement gathered momentum from the writings and teachings of Professors J. Kleutgen and M. Liberatore, of the Gregorian University, Albert Stöckl (1832-95), and the Dominican Cardinals Zigliara and Gonzalez. In 1879, Pope Leo XIII's encyclical *Aeterni Patris* urged Catholic philosophers to develop Thomist principles in relation to modern needs. He asked all Catholic universities, institutes and seminaries to explore again the riches of the Scholastic tradition, including that of Thomism. Many of the religious orders of the Church, Dominicans, Benedictines, Carmelites, Augustinians, Jesuits and others had already adopted St Thomas Aquinas as 'the prince and master of all' (Leo XIII). Scholasticism quickly revived; and neo-Thomism in particular flourished.

Several of the early neo-Thomists combined a deep respect for tradition with an equally deep hostility to modern errors. They restricted themselves to the traditional point of view and adopted a polemical attitude to several of the mainstream currents of thought of the late nineteenth and early twentieth centuries. This attitude brought about a hostile reaction in many circles against the dogmatic statements of conservative neo-Thomistic thinkers.

In 1880, Cardinal Dechamps, Archbishop of Malines in Belgium, appointed Désiré Joseph Mercier to teach an advanced course in the philosophy of St Thomas at the university of Louvain. Within the department of natural philosophy, Mercier established a laboratory for psycho-physiology and psycho-physics. He introduced a course in criteriology, to study the critical problem of the value of knowledge. He abandoned Latin and expounded Thomism in the vernacular, French. He succeeded in raising the department of philosophy into a higher institute which was empowered to grant degrees in Scholastic philosophy. Several critics at Louvain and Rome feared that the courses in experimental psychology were infected with positivism, and that the various courses in the vernacular made alarming concessions to modern opinions. They succeeded in having the faculty of granting degrees withdrawn, and in having Msgr Mercier summoned to Rome to defend himself. Pope Leo XIII, however, gave his complete agreement to Mercier's methods of presenting an updated form of Scholastic philosophy which stated clearly and faced courageously the full implications of the Cartesian, Humean and Kantian critical problem concerning the value of knowledge; and the faculty of granting degrees was restored to the higher institute. Louvain quickly became an internationally recognized centre for advanced studies in philosophy, attracting students and faculty members from all over the world. It has continued to be a centre of important philosophical research and writing down to our own times.

In Milan, Fr A. Gemelli, the rector of the Catholic University of the Sacred Heart, and a friend and admirer of Cardinal Mercier, supported the programme of the progressive school of neo-Scholastic thinkers. He encouraged the study of experimental psychology, history of philosophy, and gnoseology, or the study of the problem of knowledge. Other Catholic universities and superior institutes quickly followed the progressive neo-Scholastic trend.

Among the many contributors to the development of Thomism in the modern world one may mention a few of the most influential thinkers and writers. *Antonin Sertillanges* (1863-1948) made a special study of the relationship between philosophy and Christianity. He was a prolific writer who applied the fundamental principles of Thomism to a wide range of studies of ethics, the problem of evil, socialism and related topics. *Joseph Geyser* (1869-1948) was a critical realist, and inductive metaphysician, who made a thorough investigation of the principle of sufficient reason; he maintained that it is only through experience that we can discover the meaning of causality. *Réginald Garrigou-Lagrange* (1877-1964) defended the objective validity and transcendental range of human thought against nominalist empiricism and Kantian subjectivism, and against the Bergsonian relativism of Édouard Le Roy. *Pierre Rousselot* (1878-1915) asserted that, according to Aquinas, there is in the will a dynamic orientation of the human spirit, a dynamism of love, which gives rise to the movement of the mind to Being Itself in philosophical reflection.

Joseph Maréchal (1878-1944), of Louvain, published the major part of his influential work on the starting-point of metaphysics, *Le point de départ de la métaphysique*, between 1922 and 1926. In the fifth *Cahier* (Book Five) of this work Maréchal maintained that each known being or thing, known immanently within the field of consciousness, presents a triple aspect: a sensible aspect, a conceptual aspect, and a transcendent aspect which points towards Being itself. The active intellect, in virtue of its innate active dynamism to Absolute Being, attains metaphysical reality, being, in its synthetic elaboration of the being which is known. This idea of the intellectual dynamism of the knowing being (the subject) as oriented to Being itself is virtually present, he maintains, in the thought of St Thomas

Aquinas. It is an idea which can serve to synthesize Kant's severed 'Knowledge' (Understanding, *Verstand*) and 'pure discerning thought' *(Vernunft)*; and in doing so it can also serve to transcend Kantian agnosticism. Kant failed to recognize the *(a priori)* active dynamical tendency of the active intellect to Absolute Being, Pure Act, as its natural entelechy or end on the preconscious and pre-elicitive level. Kant overlooked this Thomistic starting-point of metaphysics, and he failed therefore to make a metaphysical critique of the object. When thought reflects on its own being-oriented (object-oriented) activity it discovers that its innate active dynamism to Being itself is an *a priori* condition of that activity.

In his later notes, published posthumously as the fourth *Cahier* of *Le point de départ de la métaphysique*, Maréchal called attention to the emphasis on intellectual dynamism evident in Kant's *Opus Postumum* and in Fichte's development of Kantian thought. In this fourth *Cahier*, the knowing being's apprehension of its own being, Maréchal says, is a primary fact of consciousness which constitutes 'the sole solid foundation of all philosophy'. This theme anticipates, to some extent, the more thoroughly developed theme of introspective self-appropriation which one finds in the work of Bernard Lonergan. (See below.)

Jacques Maritain (1882-1973), in *The Degrees of Knowledge* (1932) and other works, pointed out that there are several different ways of knowing reality. There are different kinds or degrees of conceptual and discursive knowledge, and there are also different nonconceptual and immediate forms of knowledge. There is a difference, to start with, on the conceptual level, between the conceptual lexicon of the scientist and the conceptual lexicon of the philosopher or ontologist in their ways of speaking of the universe of mobile being. This calls for an empiriological analysis and an ontological analysis of the sensible real, the sphere of the knowledge of nature. This sphere, in turn, differs from the sphere of mathematics which deals mainly with the universe of quantity, and from the sphere of metaphysics which deals with the universe of being as being.

Theoretical physics, Maritain says, is 'a mathematicization of the sensible'. It constructs geometricized universes which are fictional causal entities, or *entia rationis*, with a basis in reality. These enable us to make predictions about nature and to control and master nature, but they do not provide knowledge concerning the ontological structure of nature. This is the work of the philosophy of nature. Philosophy of nature is concerned primarily with the essence of mobile being. It is concerned, for example, to know the nature of quantity, time, space, and the continuum. It is also concerned with the ontological principles which account for the mutability of mobile beings. Metaphysics, finally, works at the purest degree of abstraction. It is concerned with being as being, and it opens up on the immaterial. It is contemplative, not experimental. It reveals to man authentic values and their hierarchy. It provides the highest form of *scientia*, the knowledge of things through their causes.

There are other forms of knowledge which are nonconceptual. One thinks, for example, of the Freudian unconscious of traumatic memories, repressed images and desires, instincts, tendencies and complexes. But there is also a spiritual unconscious, or preconscious of the spirit. In the choice of the good, as against evil, for example, in virtue of the internal dynamism of the will, there is a non-conceptual, pre-reflective form of knowledge. There is also 'knowledge by connaturality' in our knowledge of persons and in our moral convictions concerning the essential inclinations of human nature. In addition, there is 'poetic' or emotional knowledge which tends to artistic expression and creation. One must be careful not to think of knowledge, therefore, as if there were only one kind of knowledge. The mind's reflection on its own activity in knowing things reveals that there are a number of distinguishable ways in which the mind knows reality.

Etienne H. Gilson (1884-1978) was professor of medieval philosophy at the Sorbonne, and later at the Collège de France, and Toronto. He wrote several influential works on Aquinas, Augustine, Bonaventure, Dante, Scotus and on the role of medieval thought in the formation of the Cartesian system. Gilson rejected the assumed primacy of the so-called critical problem concerning the mind's capacity to know. It is in and through the act of knowing something that the mind becomes aware of its capacity to know. For Aquinas, it is the act of existing (*esse*), in the heart of the real, that has primacy within every being and within the act of knowing. We have experiential knowledge of the inner activity, or act, of being. But this inner activity of 'existing' (or, in the case of living beings, of 'living') is not an essence, and so it is not conceptualizable. The act of being or existing is not an essence; it is the act by which the limiting essence exists. It can be grasped only in and through the existing essence as the inner act of existing of the essence. All 'essentialist' philosophies, including neo-Thomistic essentialist philosophies, omit consideration of this act of existence (*esse*). They focus attention on dead mental quiddities and essences sundered from contact with the act of being. All contemporary 'existentialist' philosophies, similarly (of

Heidegger, Sartre and others), focus attention on existence only as an object of a possible phenomenology of human existence. They too omit consideration of the act of existing *(esse)*. They may be regarded as phenomenologies which are still in search of a philosophy of being *(esse)*. The philosophy of being of Aquinas is the authentic 'existential' metaphysics. It is also an authentically philosophical Christian philosophy in which one who is a Christian philosophizes about his religious thought and belief. It is a Christian philosophy, then, which is genuinely philosophical.

5. Teilhard de Chardin. There are a number of Christian thinkers and philosophers whose thought processes have been influenced to a considerable extent by the basic principles of Thomistic thought, but whose finished work cannot be classified as neo-Thomist in the sense in which the works of Sertillanges or Maritain, for example, are said to be neo-Thomistic. Their thought has been influenced by the works of Heidegger or Bergson or other philosophers to as great an extent as it has been influenced by that of Aquinas and other Christian thinkers. We will consider first, however, the entirely independent and original thought of Fr Teilhard de Chardin.

Pierre Teilhard de Chardin (1881-1955) presented an imaginative and original view of the development of the universe which attracted widespread interest among philosophers, theologians and scientists. The world-vision of his *Phenomenon of Man* (1955) and *The Divine Milieu* (1957) is partly philosophical, party scientific, partly theological and Christological, and entirely confident and uplifting. Teilhard saw the history of the universe as a dynamic evolutionary movement in which the basic stuff of the cosmos is continually undergoing irreversible changes in the direction of greater complexity of organization. The developing complexification of non-living nature has given rise to the vast array of organic forms which have appeared in evolutionary history. This dynamic evolutionary movement is one in which spirit has already emerged from non-living nature, and one in which spirit is still moving towards further development. From the beginning, the universe has been a developing whole, in which life and consciousness have been present potentially in matter. Matter is ever pregnant with life and spirit. The evolving whole is a manifestation of the divine. It is a development which is taking place in a Christocentric setting; the setting is that of the cosmic body of Christ.

For Teilhard, every particle of the cosmos has 'a conscious *inner* face that everywhere duplicates the material *external* face'. The mechanistic 'without' of the stuff of the universe has its corresponding 'within'. The birth of the biosphere, the genesis of life, commenced with the emergence of the cell. In the natural history of living things there has been a movement towards the eventual emergence of consciousness and thought, the birth of the noösphere. The noösphere, or thinking layer, forms the unique milieu of man. With the evolutionary convergence of disparate cultures and forms of consciousness into an externally manifested single world culture there arises a parallel psychical concentration in which the noösphere will become involuted in a hyperpersonal focus of consciousness at a point which we may call the Omega point. This hyperpersonal union will be a union of the personal and the collective on the planes of thought and love. At Point Omega evolution will reach the terminal phase of convergent integration. The risen Christ progressively unites all men in love, so that the cosmic Christ eventually becomes 'all in all'. Evolution therefore is a process of hominization and divinization in which individuals become personally enriched in a new body, a one-and-many, in and through Christ. This vision of the noösphere as progressively evolving into the Christosphere inspires Teilhard to hymn the universe.

6. Transcendental method. Several thinkers, philosophers and theologians, have focused attention on the long-standing and contemporary problematic, or difficulty, concerning a subject-oriented philosophy. They have succeeded in evolving a metaphysics of the knowing subject, the knowing being. We may mention by way of example André Marc (1892-1961), A. Brunner (b. 1900), Karl Rahner (1904-84), B. Lonergan (see below), J. B. Lotz (b. 1903) and Emmerich Coreth (b. 1906). The method of procedure used by these metaphysicians is frequently referred to as the 'transcendental method'. Like the transcendental method of Kant it concentrates on the subject's act of knowing; the method is used now however in the service of a philosophy of being. Here we shall attend not to the different systems of thought of these different philosophers but to certain general features which emerge from their use of the subject-oriented method in their study of being as being.

These philosophers begin metaphysics with a descriptive analysis and critical examination of an act of knowledge. The act of knowledge may be of the kind which is evidenced in a simple affirmation (e.g. 'This exists'), or personal encounter, or question, or judgement. Rahner and Coreth assert that, if the science of knowledge is to have an entirely presuppositionless point of departure, then inquiry must commence with the *question*. In reflecting on itself the question becomes the question of the question.

Philosophical reflection on the act of questioning (about anything) shows that the questioner is always striving beyond the horizon of what he already knows (his rudimentary present knowledge) to what he does not know as yet. In a knowing kind of not knowing (nescience), the questioner knows that he knows little about that which *is*. This anticipatory knowledge of what *is* is the condition of the possibility of every question. Every question is directed to 'being', to what *is*. Every question therefore presupposes some previous knowledge of being as such. The aspect under which we know anything is being: we know it as being this or as being that. There is a certain openness to being, or pre-knowledge of being, preceding every question in the human mind. The mind itself provides a background or horizon of being for every question and for every act of knowing and willing. A metaphysics and a knowledge of Being itself is implied in the human being's every act of knowing, willing and questioning. In this way, the subject-oriented or 'transcendental' method facilitates the grounding of philosophy in being, and therefore in the absolute. It points to the unquestionable departure point of the philosophy of being.

7. Bernard Lonergan.

Bernard J. F. Lonergan (b. 1904), a Canadian Jesuit who was until 1984 Distinguished Visiting professor at Boston College, has written widely discussed books and articles on the understanding of understanding, on generalized empirical method as a communal undertaking, and on scientific cognitive self-possession. His writings on *Insight. A Study in Human Understanding* (1957), *Method in Theology* (1972), collected papers, workshops, and lectures have become the focus of a philosophical movement known as the Lonergan movement, or Lonerganism, even though Lonergan himself insists that progress in self-understanding and in cultural and historical consciousness can never be institutionalized.

Lonergan points out that each man and woman, conscious of the abiding imperative to be authentically human, is faced with the challenge of self-actualization, self-mastery, and self-transcendence. The world in which we live is one in which we are constantly pushed and called and pulled to rise beyond that level of rational animality at which we have already arrived. We feel called to exercise further intelligence, reasonableness, and conscientious deliberation. We learn by experience that the eagerly sought goal of our flesh and blood, our sensitivity, our intelligence, freedom, and responsibility is, in short, self-transcendence, a 'falling in love'. The experience of authenticity is best described in terms of self-transcendence of this kind.

The person who is striving towards self-transcendence is ever aware of shortcomings. He is also aware that he is striving to be authentically human. The person who attempts to evade the call to self-realization and self-transcendence busies himself in an attempt to conceal the call from himself. His busyness is inauthentic busyness.

The call to 'be human' is in an important sense a call to 'be understanding'. To be understanding implies something more than to be in possession of a causal explanation of the kind offered by the physico-mathematical sciences; it implies a constant growth in cultural and historical consciousness. Understanding requires an immersion of the whole man into reality. It is necessary then to have an understanding of understanding. It is also necessary to understand whether or not we can really attain an understanding of objective truth.

Empiricists assert that they attain objective truth in the 'world of immediacy', namely, in the immediate data of sense and consciousness. They find it necessary, however, to step over into another world, the world mediated by meaning, occasionally, to explain the meaning of these data. Rationalists, on the other hand, assert that they attain objective truth in the world mediated by meaning, the world of questions and correct answers. They find it necessary, however, to appeal occasionally to the data of sense and consciousness for the subject-matter of their questions and for verifications of their deduced answers. Each of these stances is extremist; and each reneges, in practice, on the original protestation concerning the initial premiss. Neither of these stances does justice to the complexity of the human world of immediacy *and* meaning. The continuing search for objective truth has been hindered rather than helped by the intransigence of these conflicting doctrines concerning the nature of science, certitude and necessary truth. Thus, contemporary thought now turns instead to an investigation of *method*.

For many centuries, the notion of 'science' and the preconceptions of the Aristotelians concerning necessity, truth and certitude, hindered the early experimenters from setting up an appropriate conceptual framework of their own with regard to the general nature or notion of scientific knowledge. The scientist kept looking for (the Aristotelians') true and certain knowledge of causal necessity, and for the necessary laws of nature. They found however that their principles and laws, even when often verified, were never definitively established. The falsification of a hypothesis was definitive; but no series of verifications ever became definitive. The principles and laws of empirical science become ever more probable but never more than probable. Modern scientists (after Einstein, Heisenberg, Planck, Kelvin and Darwin) questioned the assumption that science consists in true and certain knowledge of causal necessity, and that its quest is fundamentally a quest for logical conclusions. Logic certainly plays a role in science but it does so within a scientific, empirical method which includes observation, description, query, discovery, experimentation, verification and revision. The emphasis now is on empirical method. Science is seen to yield not objective truth but the very best available opinion of the day. Definitive, scientific objective truth is not obtainable. What, then, is one to do? Lonergan's suggestion is that we use a generalized empirical method.

In generalized empirical method one takes as data all of one's own conscious activities. All data are envisaged or included: data of sense, data that are expressions of meaning, data of consciousness, objects of consciousness seen as objects of the corresponding operations of the subject, and the subject's operations seen as operating on their corresponding objects. All are seen as related and recurrent operations that yield ongoing and cumulative results, in natural science, in hermeneutics, in history, in common sense.

Generalized empirical method also generalizes the notion of method to include observation, description, discovery, understanding, common sense, grasp of intelligible relationship in the data of sense and consciousness, inquiry, adequate formulation of solutions, reflection, testing, checking, verifying, passing judgement, and commitment. All of these operations are conscious operations that move along dynamically from the spontaneity of sense to the other operations and from one operation on to the next. The operations are infused with intelligence, understanding and reasonableness. All of this is the infrastructure given in consciousness. One must now attend to one's attending, advert to one's intelligence, attend to one's own reasonableness, and advert to one's responsibility and free deliberation. One heightens one's consciousness and objectifies it by '(1) experiencing one's experiencing, understanding, judging, and deciding, (2) understanding the unity and relations of one's experienced experiencing, understanding, judging, deciding, (3) affirming the reality of one's experienced and understood experiencing, understanding, judging, deciding and (4) deciding to operate in accord with the norms immanent in the spontaneous relatedness of one's experienced, understood, affirmed experiencing, understanding, judging and deciding' (*Method*, p. 15). It is in doing just this that one's understanding becomes an understanding of the operations of human understanding. One becomes innerly convinced that one knows. This inner conviction is the fruit of self-transcendence, of being attentive, intelligent, reasonable and responsible. It is the conviction that the norms of attentiveness, intelligence, reasonableness and responsibility have been satisfied.

The world of immediacy presents us with the sensate objectivity of the world already-out-there-now, the firm-set world that bears our weight. The world mediated by meaning and motivated by values demands of us, in the interests of its own different kind of objectivity, that we satisfy the norms of attentiveness, intelligence, reasonableness and responsibility. It is through insight into insight that we approach an ever more adequate formulation of what it is to understand. The real, the objective, is what is to be reached by correct understanding. When attention to understanding ranges over all areas in which understanding is operative, then the overall enterprise arrives at an adequate viewpoint. This viewpoint demands of the understanding-subject a self-appropriation, or cognitive self-possession or self-attention of scientific dimensions. The structured known requires a scientifically structured knowing.

Scientific self-possession is capable, Lonergan says, of mediating a transformation of science and of human living. It can do so, however, only in so far as generalized empirical method becomes both a culturally available scientific technique and a communal undertaking. The use of this technique brings about a change in philosophic and scientific discourse. It effects a genetic shift from cognitive and affective possession of the object by the subject to a self-appropriation of the subject. In the field of the philosophy of religion and theology, self-possession of the subject becomes the self-appropriation of the faithful subject, and continual intellectual conversion through interpersonal understanding becomes continual religious conversion. Religious conversion opens human nature to the grace through which God himself enables the human being to be lovingly (or self-transcendently) and attentively (self-possessively) understanding.

Lonergan summarizes the positive content of his major work in a single affirmation (*Insight*, p. xxviii): 'Thoroughly understand what it is to understand, and not only will you understand the broad lines of all there is to be understood but also you will possess a fixed base, an invariable pattern, opening upon all further developments of understanding'.

BIBLIOGRAPHY

PART ONE

1: The pre-Socratic philosophers

Allen, R. E., and Furley, D. J. (eds), *Studies in Pre-Socratic Philosophy* (2 vols, London/New York, 1975).

Armstrong, A. H., *An Introduction to Ancient Philosophy* (London, 1947).

Barnes, J., *The Pre-Socratic Philosophers* (2 vols, London/Boston, 1979).

Burnet, J., *Early Greek Philosophy* 4th ed. (London, 1930).

Copleston, F., *A History of Philosophy* I, rev. ed. (London, 1947).

de Vogel, C.J., *Greek Philosophy: a Collection of Texts* I, 3rd ed. (Leiden, 1963).

Diels, H., and Kranz, W. (eds), *Die Fragmente der Vorsokratiker* 6th ed. (3 vols, Berlin, 1951-52).

Freeman, K., *Ancilla to the Pre-Socratic Philosophers* (Oxford, 1948). A translation of the texts in Diels-Kranz.

Guthrie, W. K. C., *The History of Greek Philosophy* I-II (Cambridge, 1962-65).

Heidegger, M., *Early Greek Thinking* (New York, 1975).

Heidegger, M., and Fink, E., *Heraclitus Seminar 1966/67* (Princeton, N.J., 1979).

Hussey, E., *The Pre-Socratics* (London, 1972/New York, 1973).

Kirk, G. S., and Raven, J.E., *The Pre-Socratic Philosophers* (Cambridge, 1957).

Lambridis, H., *Empedocles* (University, Alabama, 1976).

Mansfeld, J., and de Rijk, L. M., *Kephalaion: Studies in Greek Philosophy* (Assen, 1975).

Seligman, P., *The 'Apeiron' of Anaximander* (London, 1962).

Solmsen, F., *Intellectual Experiments of the Greek Enlightenment* (Princeton, N.J., 1975).

Wilbur, J., and Allen, H. (eds), *The Worlds of the Greek Philosophers* (New York, 1979).

2: The Sophist and Socratic period

Burnet, J., *Early Greek Philosophy* 4th ed. (London, 1930).

Copleston, F., *A History of Philosophy* I, rev. ed. (London, 1947).

Cornford, F. M., *Before and After Socrates* (Cambridge/New York, 1932).

de Vogel, C. J. *Greek Philosophy: a Collection of Texts* I, 3rd ed. (Leiden, 1963).

de Vogel, C. J. *Philosophia* (Atlantic Highlands, N.J., 1970).

Furley, D. J., and Allen, R. E., *The Beginning of Philosophy* (N.J., 1970).

Guthrie, W. K. C., *The History of Greek Philosophy* III (Cambridge, 1971).

Hussey, E., *The Pre-Socratics* (London, 1972/New York, 1973).

Nahm, M. C., *Selections from Early Greek Philosophy* (New York, 1947).
Sprague, R. K. (ed.), *The Older Sophists: A Complete Translation* (South Carolina, 1972).
Taylor, A. E., *Varia Socratica* (Oxford, 1911).
Taylor, A. E., *Socrates* (London, 1932).
Untersteiner, M., *The Sophists* tr. K. Freeman (Oxford, 1954).
Xenophon: *Memorabilia Socratis Dicta* tr. E. C. Marchant (London/New York, 1923).

3 and 4: Plato

Allen, R. E. (ed.), *Studies in Plato's Metaphysics* (London, 1965).
Armstrong, A. H., *An Introduction to Ancient Philosophy* (London, 1947).
Bambrough, R. (ed.), *New Essays on Plato and Aristotle* (London, 1965).
Benn, A., *The Greek Philosophers* 2nd ed. (London, 1914).
Burnet, J., *Greek Philosophy*, Part I (London, 1914/New York, 1961).
Burnet, J., *Platonism* (Berkeley, 1928).
Copleston, F., *A History of Philosophy* I, rev. ed. (London, 1947).
Cornford, F. M., *Plato's Theory of Knowledge: the Theaetetus and the Sophist* (London, 1935).
Cornford, F. M., *Plato's Cosmology: Timaeus* (London, 1937).
Demos, R., *The Philosophy of Plato* (New York, 1939).
Findlay, J. N., *Plato: The Written and Unwritten Doctrines* (London, 1974).
Findlay, J. N., *Plato and Platonism* (New York, 1978).
Gomperz, T., *Greek Thinkers: A History of Ancient Philosophy* (4 vols, London, 1901-12).
Guthrie, W. K. C., *The History of Greek Philosophy* IV-V (Cambridge, 1975-78).
Hardie, W., *A Study in Plato* (Oxford, 1936).
Irwin, T., *Plato's Moral Theory* (Oxford, 1928).
Jowett, B., *The Dialogues of Plato* 4th ed. (Oxford, 1953).
Klein, J., *Plato's Trilogy: 'Theaetetus', 'The Sophist' and 'The Statesman'* (Chicago, 1977).
Koyre, A., *Discovering Plato* (New York, 1960).
McGinley, J., *Commentary on Parmenides* (Scranton, 1976).
Matthews, G., *Plato's Epistemology and Related Problems* (London/New York, 1972).
Ross, W., *Plato's Theory of Ideas* (Oxford, 1951).
Sallis, J., *Being and Logos: The Way of Platonic Dialogue* (Pittsburgh, 1975).
Stace, W. T., *A History of Greek Philosophy* (London, 1920).
Stenzel, J., *Plato's Method of Dialectic* (Oxford, 1940).
Strauss, L. *The Argument and the Action of Plato's Laws* (Chicago, 1976).
Taylor, A. E., *Plato, the Man and his Work* (London, 1926).
Vlados, G., *Plato's Universe* (Seattle, 1975).
Whittemore, R. (ed.), *Studies in Plato* (New Orleans, 1978).
Zeller, E., *Outlines of the History of Greek Philosophy* (London, 1931).

5 and 6: Aristotle

Aristotle: *The Works of Aristotle* ed. J. A. Smith and W. D. Ross (Oxford, 1910-52).
Aristotle: *Aristotle's Metaphysics* tr. H. G. Apostle (Bloomington, Indiana, 1966).
Aristotle: *Aristotle's Physics* tr. H. G. Apostle (Bloomington, Indiana, 1969).
Aristotle: *The Ethics of Aristotle* tr. J. A. K. Thomson (London, 1976).
Aristotle: *Aristotle's Categories* tr. H. G. Apostle (Bloomington, Indiana, 1979).

Barker, E., *The Political Thought of Plato and Aristotle* (London, 1907/New York, 1959).
Bochenski, J. M., and Lukasiewicz, J., *Aristotle's Syllogistic* (Oxford, 1957).
Brentano, F., *On the Several Senses of Being in Aristotle* (Berkeley, 1976).
Burnet, J., *The Ethics of Aristotle* (London, 1900).
Chroust, A. H., *Aristotle: New Light on His Life and on Some of his Works* (2 vols, London/Notre Dame, 1973).
Copleston, F., *A History of Philosophy* I, rev. ed. (London, 1947).
Grayeff, F., *Aristotle and his School* (London/New York, 1974).
Guthrie, W. K. C., *The History of Greek Philosophy* VI (Cambridge, 1981).
Hintikka, J., *Time and Necessity: Studies in Aristotle's Theory of Modality* (Oxford, 1973).
Jaeger, W., *Aristotle: Fundamentals of the History of his Development* 2nd ed. (London, 1962).
Kenny, A., *The Aristotelian Ethics* (Oxford, 1978).
Marx, W., *Introduction to Aristotle's Theory of Being as Being* (The Hague, 1977).
Morrall, J. B., *Aristotle* (London, 1977).
Mure, G. R., *Aristotle* (London, 1932).
Owens, J., *The Doctrine of Being in Aristotle* 2nd ed. (Toronto, 1963).
Ross, W. D., *Aristotle* 5th ed. (London, 1949).
Sullivan, R. J., *Morality and the Good Life: Aristotle* (Memphis, 1978).
Taylor, A. E., *Aristotle* (London, 1944).
Veatch, H. B., *Aristotle: A Contemporary Appreciation* (Bloomington, Indiana, 1974).

7: Hellenistic-Roman philosophy

Armstrong, A. H., *The Architecture of the Intelligible Universe in Plotinus* (Cambridge, 1940).
Armstrong, A. H., *Plotinus* (London, 1953).
Arnold, E. V., *Roman Stoicism* (Cambridge, 1911).
Bailey, C., *The Greek Atomists and Epicurus* (Oxford, 1928).
Bochenski, J. M., *Ancient Formal Logic* (Amsterdam, 1957).
Copleston, F., *A History of Philosophy* I, rev. ed. (London, 1947).
Dodds, E. R., *Select Passages illustrating Neoplatonism* (London, 1923).

Dudley, D. R., *A History of Cynicism* (London, 1937).
Evans, E. E., *Stoics and Sceptics* (Oxford, 1913).
Findlay, J. N., *Plato and Platonism* (New York, 1978).
Fuller, B. A., *The Problem of Evil in Plotinus* (Cambridge, 1912).
Guthrie, W. K. C., *The History of Greek Philosophy* IV (Cambridge, 1975).
Hicks, R. D., *Stoics and Epicureans* (London, 1910).
Inge, W. R., *The Philosophy of Plotinus* 2nd ed. (2 vols, London, 1923).
Long, A. A., *Problems in Stoicism* (Berkeley, 1953).
Long, A. A., *Hellenistic Philosophy: Stoics, Epicureans, Sceptics* (London/ New York, 1974).
McKenna, S., *The Treatises of Plotinus* (5 vols, London, 1917-30).
Mansfeld, J., and de Rijk, L. M., *Kephalaion: Studies in Greek Philosophy* (Assen, 1975).
Marcus Aurelius: *The Meditations* (London, 1844).
Nichols, J. H., *Epicurean Political Philosophy: Lucretius* (London/New York, 1976).
Proclus: *The Elements of Theology* tr. E. R. Dodds (Oxford, 1933).
Rist, J. M., *Stoic Philosophy* (Cambridge, 1969).
Rist, J. M., *Epicurus: An Introduction* (Cambridge, 1972).
Rist, J. M. (ed.), *The Stoics* (London/Berkeley, 1978).
Sandbach, F. H., *The Stoics* (London/New York, 1975).
Turnbull, G. H. (ed.), *The Essence of Plotinus* (London, 1935).
Wallis, R. T., *Neoplatonism* (London/New York, 1972).
Whittaker, T., *The Neo-Platonists* 2nd ed. (Cambridge, 1918).
Zeller, E., *The Stoics, Epicureans and Sceptics* tr. O. J. Reichel (London, 1870).
Zeller, E., *A History of Eclecticism in Greek Philosophy* tr. S. F. Alleyne (London, 1883).

8: Early Christian philosophy

Arnou, R. (ed.), *De 'Platonismo' Patrum* (Rome, 1935).
Augustine, St: *City of God* tr. J. Healey (2 vols, London/New York, 1945).
Barrett, H. M., *Boethius: Some Aspects of his Life and Work* (Cambridge, 1940).
Boethius: *De Consolatione Philosophiae* ed. G. D. Smith (London, 1925).
Bonner, G., *St Augustine of Hippo: Life and Controversies* (London, 1963).
Bourke, V. J., *Augustine's Quest of Wisdom* (Milwaukee, 1945).
Butterworth, G. W. (ed.), *Origen on First Principles* (London, 1936).
Copleston, F., *A History of Philosophy* II (London, 1950).
Gilson, E., *The Christian Philosophy of St Augustine* (New York, 1960/London, 1961).
Marrou, H. I., *St Augustine and his Influence through the Ages* (New York, 1957/London, 1958).
Mayer, J. E. B. (ed.), *Tertullian's Apology* (Cambridge, 1927).
Meagher, R. E., *An Introduction to St Augustine* (New York, 1978).
Prestige, G. L., *God in Patristic Thought* (London, 1936).

Rand, E. K., *Founders of the Middle Ages* (Cambridge, Mass., 1941).
Rolt, C. E. (ed.), *Dionysius the Areopagite on the Divine Names and the Mystical Theology* (London, 1920).
Sheed, F. J. (tr.), *The Confessions of St Augustine* (London, 1943).
Switalski, B., *Neoplatonism and the Ethics of St Augustine* (New York, 1946).

PART TWO

9: The formation of Scholasticism
Abelard: *Sic et Non: A Critical Edition* ed. B. Boyer and R. McKeon (London/Chicago, 1976).
Algazel: *Algazel's Metaphysics: A Medieval Translation* (Toronto, 1933).
Al-Kindi: *Al-Kindi's Metaphysics* tr. A. L. Ivry (Albany, N.Y., 1974).
Arnold, T. W., and Guillaume, A. (eds), *The Legacy of Islam* (Oxford, 1931).
Avicenna: *Avicennae Metaphysices Compendium* (Rome, 1926).
Bett, H., *Johannes Scotus Eriugena: A Study in Medieval Philosophy* (Cambridge, 1925).
Boer, T. J. de, *The History of Philosophy in Islam* (London, 1903).
Buxton, E. M. W., *Alcuin* (London, 1922).
Carré, M. H., *Realists and Nominalists* (Oxford, 1946).
Cayré, F., *Précis de Patrologie* II (Paris, 1936).
Copleston, F., *A History of Philosophy* II (London, 1950).
Curtis, S. J., *A Short History of Philosophy in the Middle Ages* (New York, 1943/London, 1950).
Efros, I., *Studies in Medieval Jewish Philosophy* (London/New York, 1974).
Eriugena, John Scotus: *Periphyseon: On the Division of Nature* tr. M. Uhlfelder (Indianapolis, 1976).
Gilson, E., *The Spirit of Medieval Philosophy* (London/New York, 1950).
Husik, I., *A History of Medieval Jewish Philosophy* (London/New York, 1918).
Laistner, M., *Thought and Letters in Western Europe, A.D. 500-900* (London, 1931).
Luscombe, D. E., *The School of Peter Abelard* (Cambridge, 1969).
McKeon, R., *Selections from Medieval Philosophers* (2 vols, New York, 1929/London, 1930).
Maimonides, Moses: *The Guide of the Perplexed* tr. S. Pines (London/Chicago, 1963).
Maimonides, Moses: *Ethical Writings* ed. R. L. Weiss and C. E. Butterworth (New York, 1975).
Maimonides, Moses: *Rambam: Reading* tr. L. E. Goodman (New York, 1976).
O'Leary, De L., *Arabic Thought and its Place in History* (London, 1922).
Powell, J. M., *Medieval Studies* (New York, 1976).
Roth, L., *Spinoza, Descartes and Maimonides* (Oxford, 1924).
Runciman, S., *The Medieval Manichee* (Cambridge, 1947).
Schufreider, G., *An Introduction to Anselm's Argument* (Philadelphia, 1979).

Sickes, J. G., *Peter Abaelard* (Cambridge, 1934).

Smith, M., *Al-Ghazālī the Mystic* (London, 1944).

Sweetman, J. W., *Islam and Christian Theology* I (London, 1945).

Taylor, H. O., *The Mediaeval Mind* I (London, 1911).

Webb, C. C. J., *John of Salisbury* (London, 1932).

Wolfson, H. A., *Studies in the History of Philosophy and Religion* (2 vols, Cambridge, Mass., 1973-77).

Wulf, M. de, *History of Medieval Philosophy* (New York, 1952).

10: The thirteenth-century Scholastics: pre-Thomistic thought

Albert, S. M., *Albert the Great* (Oxford, 1948).

Copleston, F., *A History of Philosophy* II (London, 1950).

Coussins, E. H., *Bonaventure and the Coincidence of Opposites* (Chicago, 1978).

Gilson, E., *The Philosophy of St Bonaventure* (London, 1938).

Gilson, E., *The Spirit of Medieval Philosophy* (London/New York, 1950).

Haskins, C. H., *Studies in the History of Mediaeval Science* (Cambridge, Mass., 1924).

Hourani, G. F. (ed.), *Essays on Islamic Philosophy and Science* (Albany, N.Y., 1971).

Mayer, F., *History of Ancient and Medieval Philosophy* (New York, 1950).

Mellone, S. H., *Western Christian Thought in the Middle Ages* (London/Edinburgh, 1935).

O'Donnell, C. M., *The Psychology of St Bonaventure and St Thomas Aquinas* (Washington, 1937).

Quinn, J. F., *The Historical Constitution of St Bonaventure's Philosophy* (Toronto, 1973).

Rashdall, H., *The Universities of Europe in the Middle Ages* (3 vols, Oxford, 1895).

Reilly, G. C., *The Psychology of St Albert the Great Compared with St Thomas* (Washington, 1934).

Scheeben, C. H., *Albertus Magnus* (Bonn, 1932).

Shahan, R. W., and Kovach, F. J. (eds), *Bonaventure and Aquinas: Enduring Philosophers* (Norman, Oklahoma, 1976).

Sharp, D. E., *Franciscan Philosophy at Oxford in the Thirteenth Century* (Oxford, 1930).

Thomson, S. H., *The Writings of Robert Grosseteste* (Cambridge, 1940).

Ulrich of Strasbourg: R. R. Bolgar (ed.), *Classical Influences on Western Thought* (Cambridge, 1979).

Wulf, M. de, *Philosophy and Civilization in the Middle Ages* (Princeton, N.J., 1922).

Wulf, M. de, *History of Medieval Philosophy* (2 vols, London, 1935-38/3rd ed., New York, 1952).

11: St Thomas Aquinas

Aquinas: *The Summa Contra Gentiles* (2 vols, London, 1923).
Aquinas: *Summa Theologiae*, 60 vols (London, 1964-76).
Aquinas: *Selected Writings* ed. M. C. D'Arcy (London, 1939).
Aquinas: *Basic Writings of St Thomas Aquinas* ed. A. Pegis (New York, 1945).

Bourke, V. J., *Aquinas' Search for Wisdom* (Milwaukee, 1965).
Bourke, V. J., *A Guide to the Study of St Thomas* (New York, 1965).
Chenu, M. D., *Towards Understanding St Thomas* (Chicago, 1964).
Chesterton, G. K., *St Thomas Aquinas* (London, 1943).
Conrad of Prussia, *Commentary on De Ente et Essentia* ed. J. Bobik (The Hague, 1974).
Copleston, F., *Aquinas* (London, 1955).
Doig, J. C., *A Historico-Doctrinal Study on the Commentary on the Metaphysics* (The Hague, 1972).
Garrigou-Lagrange, R., *God: His Existence and Nature* (London, 1934).
Gilby, T., *The Political Thought of Aquinas* (Chicago, 1958).
Gilby, T., *Principality and Polity: Aquinas and the Rise of State Theory in the West* (London, 1958).
Gilson, E., *The Christian Philosophy of St Thomas Aquinas* (New York, 1956/London, 1957).
Henle, R. J., *St Thomas and Platonism* (The Hague, 1956).
Klubertanz, G. P., *St Thomas Aquinas on Analogy* (Chicago, 1960).
Maritain, J., *The Angelic Doctor* (New York, 1958).
Maurer, A., *St Thomas and Historicity* (Milwaukee, 1979).
Owens, J., *An Elementary Christian Metaphysics* (Milwaukee, 1963).
Pegis, A. C., *St Thomas and the Problem of the Soul in the Thirteenth Century* (Toronto, 1934).
Persson, P. E., *Sacra Doctrina: Reason and Revelation in Aquinas* (New York/Oxford, 1970).
Pieper, J., *Introduction to Thomas Aquinas* (New York, 1963).
Reith, H., *The Metaphysics of St Thomas Aquinas* (Milwaukee, 1958).
Rommen, H., *The State in Catholic Thought* (London/St Louis, 1945).
Rousselot, P., *The Intellectualism of St Thomas* (London, 1935).
Sertillanges, A. D., *Foundations of Thomistic Philosophy* (London/St Louis, 1931).
Smith, G., *Natural Theology: Metaphysics II* (New York, 1951).
Weisheipl, J. A., *Friar Thomas D'Aquino* (New York, 1974).
Wolfson, H. A., *Studies in the History of Philosophy and Religion* (2 vols, Cambridge, Mass., 1973-77).

12: Thirteenth-century cross-currents

Burke, R. B., *The Opus Maius of Roger Bacon* (2 vols, Philadelphia, 1928).
Copleston, F., *A History of Philosophy II* (London, 1950).
Crowley, T., *Roger Bacon: The Problem of the Soul* (London/Louvain, 1950).

Easton, S. C., *Roger Bacon* (New York, 1952).

Gilson, E., *History of Christian Philosophy in the Middle Ages* (London/New York, 1955).

Hocedez, E., 'Gilles de Rome et Henri de Gand' *Gregorianum* (1927).

Koch, J., *Giles of Rome: Errores Philosophorum* tr. J. O. Riedl (Milwaukee, 1944).

Little, A. G. (ed.), *Roger Bacon* (Aberdeen, 1912/London, 1914).

Mandonnet, P., *Siger de Brabant et l'averroïsme latin au XIIIᵉ siècle* 2nd ed. (2 vols, Louvain, 1908-11).

Marrou, H., *St Augustine and his Influence through the Ages* (London/New York, 1957).

Paulus, J., *Henri de Gand: Essai sur les tendances de sa métaphysique* (Paris, 1938).

Peers, E. A., *Ramon Lull: A Biography* (London, 1929).

Rashdall, H., *The Universities of Europe in the Middle Ages* (3 vols, Oxford, 1895).

van Steenberghen, F., *Siger de Brabant* (Louvain, 1931).

van Steenberghen, F., *Aristotle in the West. The Origins of Latin Aristotelianism* tr. L. Johnston (Louvain, 1955).

13: Duns Scotus

Duns Scotus: *Opera Omnia* ed. L. Wadding and L. Vives (26 vols, Paris, 1891-95).

Duns Scotus: *Philosophical Writings* ed. A. Wolfter (London, 1962).

Duns Scotus: *A Treatise on God* tr. E. Roche and A. Wolfter (Chicago, 1965).

Duns Scotus: *God and Creatures: The Quodlibetal Questions* ed. F. Alluntis and A. B. Wolfter (London/Princeton, N.J., 1975).

Copleston, F., *A History of Philosophy* II (London, 1950).

Day, S., *Intuitive Cognition* (New York, 1947).

Effler, R., *John Duns Scotus and the Principle 'Omne Quod Movetur ab alio Movetur'* (St Bonaventure, N.Y., 1962).

Gilson, E., *The Spirit of Medieval Philosophy* (London/New York, 1950).

Gilson, E., *Jean Duns Scotus* (Paris, 1952).

Grajewski, M. J., *The Formal Distinction of Duns Scotus* (Washington, 1944).

Maurer, A., *Medieval Philosophy* (New York, 1962).

Ryan, J. K. (ed.) *Studies in Philosophy and the History of Philosophy* (4 vols, Washington, 1961-69).

Vier, P., *Evidence and its Function According to John Duns Scotus* (New York, 1947/London, 1951).

Weinberg, J., *A Short History of Medieval Philosophy* (Princeton, N.J., 1964).

Wolfter, A., *The Transcendentals and their Function in the Metaphysics of Duns Scotus* (New York, 1946).

Wulf, M. de, *History of Medieval Philosophy* (London, 1935/New York, 1952).

14: The fourteenth century: William of Ockham
Ockham: *Ockham: Philosophical Writings* ed. P. Boehner (Edinburgh, 1957).
Ockham: *Summa Logicae* tr. M. J. Loux (Notre Dame, 1974).
Ockham: *Theory of Terms* I, tr. M. J. Loux (Notre Dame, 1975).

Boehner, P., *Collected Articles on Ockham* (New York, 1958).
Copleston, F., *A History of Philosophy* III (London, 1953).
Ghisalberti, A., *Ockham* (Milan, 1972).
Gilson, E., *The Spirit of Medieval Philosophy* (London/New York, 1950).
Hawkins, D., *A Sketch of Mediaeval Philosophy* (London, 1946).
Kretzmann, N., *William of Sherwood's Introduction to Logic* (Minneapolis, Minnesota, 1966).
Leff, G., *William of Ockham* (Totowa, N.J./Manchester, 1975).
McGrade, A. S., *The Political Thought of William of Ockham* (London, 1974).
Maurer, A., 'Henry of Harclay' *Medieval Studies* (1954, 1957, 1961).
Moody, E. A., *Truth and Consequence in Medieval Logic* (Amsterdam, 1953).
Moody, E. A., *The Logic of William of Ockham* (London/New York, 1965).
O'Donnell, J. R., 'Nicholas of Autrecourt' *Medieval Studies* (1939).
Shapiro, H., *Motion, Time and Place According to William of Ockham* (New York, 1957).
Webering, D., *The Theory of Demonstration According to William of Ockham* (New York, 1953).
Weinberg, J. R., *Nicolaus of Autrecourt* (Princeton, N.J., 1948).
Weinberg, J. R., *Ockham, Descartes and Hume* (Madison, Wisconsin, 1977).

15: New trends and reactions in the late Middle Ages
Anderson, F. H., *The Philosophy of Francis Bacon* (Chicago, 1948).
Bett, H., *Nicholas of Cusa* (London, 1932).
Bonasea, B. M., *Tommaso Campanella: Renaissance Pioneer of Modern Thought* (Washington, D.C., 1969).
Boulting, W., *Giordano Bruno: His Life, Thought and Martyrdom* (London, 1914).
Bruno, Giordano: *The Heroic Frenzies* tr. P. E. Memmo (Chapel Hill, N.C./Valencia, 1964).
Burckhardt, J., *The Civilisation of the Renaissance in Italy* (London, 1944).
Burtt, E. A., *The Metaphysical Foundations of Modern Physical Science* (New York, 1925).
Butterfield, H., *The Origins of Modern Science, 1300-1800* 2nd ed. (London, 1957).
Campanella, Tommaso: *The City of the Sun* tr. W. Gilstrap (New York, 1952).
Campbell, W. E., *More's Utopia and his Social Teaching* (London, 1930).
Cassirer, E. (ed.), *The Renaissance Philosophy of Man* (Chicago, 1948).

Cassirer, E., *The Individual and the Cosmos in Renaissance Philosophy* (New York, 1963/Oxford, 1964).

Clark, J. M., *The Great German Mystics* (Oxford, 1949).

Connolly, J. L., *John Gerson: Reformer and Mystic* (Louvain, 1928).

Copleston, F., *A History of Philosophy* III (London, 1953).

Dampier, W. C., *A History of Science and its Relations with Philosophy and Religion* 4th ed. (Cambridge, 1948).

D'Entrèves, A. P., *Natural Law* (London, 1951).

Drake, S., *Galileo at Work* (Chicago, 1978).

Drake, S., *Galileo* (Oxford, 1980).

Epstein, J. J., *Francis Bacon: A Political Biography* (Athens, Ohio, 1977).

Foster, M. B., *Plato to Machiavelli* (vol. I of *Masters of Political Thought* ed. E. McChesney Sait) (London, 1942).

Frame, D. M., *Montaigne's Discovery of Man* (New York, 1955).

Gewirth, A., *Marsilius of Padua* (2 vols, New York, 1951-56).

Geymonat, L., *Galileo Galilei* tr. S. Drake (New York, 1965).

Gilson, E., *Christian Philosophy in the Middle Ages* (London/New York, 1955).

Grant, R., *Johann Kaepler* (Baltimore, 1931).

Hopkins, J., *A Concise Introduction to the Philosophy of Nicholas of Cusa* (Minneapolis, Minnesota, 1979).

Jardine, L., *Francis Bacon* (London, 1974).

Jeans, J. H., *The Growth of Physical Science* (Cambridge, 1947).

Kelley, C. F., *Meister Eckhart on Divine Knowledge* (New Haven, Connecticut/London, 1977).

Koenigsberger, D., *Renaissance Man and Creative Thinking: A History of Concepts of Harmony, 1400-1700* (Brighton, 1979).

Kristeller, P. O., *Renaissance Thought: The Classic, Scholastic and Humanist Strains* (New York, 1961).

Kristeller, P. O., *Eight Philosophers of the Italian Renaissance* (Stanford, 1964).

Lindberg, D. C. (ed.), *Science in the Middle Ages* (Chicago, 1978).

Machiavelli: *The Prince* tr. J. B. Atkinson (Indianapolis, 1976).

Michel, P.-H., *The Cosmology of Giordano Bruno* (Cornell, N.Y./London, 1973).

More: *Utopia* tr. J. H. Lupton (Oxford, 1895).

More: *The Complete Works of Thomas More* IV (New Haven, Connecticut, 1965).

Morrall, J. B., *Gerson and the Great Schism* (Manchester, 1960).

Owen, J., *The Skeptics of the Italian Renaissance* (London, 1893).

Paracelsus: *Selected Writings* ed. J. Jacobi (London, 1951).

Popkin, R. H., *The History of Scepticism from Erasmus to Spinoza* (New York, 1964).

Previté-Orton, C. W., *The Defensor Pacis* (Cambridge, 1928).

Randall, J. H., *The School of Padua and the Emergence of Modern Science* (Padua, 1961).

Ridolfi, R., *The Life of Niccolò Machiavelli* tr. C. Grayson (New York, 1963).
Sabine, G. H., *A History of Political Theory* (New York, 1937/2nd ed., London, 1941).
Sarton, G., *Introduction to the History of Science* III (Baltimore, 1948).
Sedgwick, W. T., and Tyler, H. W., *A Short History of Science* (New York, 1939).
Sigmund, P. E., *Nicholas of Cusa and Medieval Political Thought* (Cambridge, Mass., 1963).
Ullmann, W., *Medieval Foundations of Renaissance Humanism* (London/Ithaca, N.Y., 1977).
Williams, G. H. (ed.), *Spiritual and Anabaptist Writers: Documents Illustrative of the Radical Reformation* (London, 1957).
Williams, G. H., *The Radical Reformation* (Philadelphia, 1964).
Yates, F. A., *Giordano Bruno and the Hermetic Tradition* (London/Chicago, 1964).

16: The revival of Scholasticism: Suárez

Cajetan: *On the Analogy of Names* tr. E. A. Bushinski (Pittsburgh, 1953).
Copleston, F., *A History of Philosophy* III (London, 1953).
D'Entrèves, A. P., *Natural Law* (London, 1951).
Descoqs, P., 'Thomisme et Suarezisme' *Archives de philosophie* (4/1926).
Figgis, J. N., *Studies in Political Thought from Gerson to Grotius, 1414-1625* 2nd ed. (Cambridge, 1931).
Hart, H. L. A., *The Concept of Law* (Oxford, 1961).
Lilley, A. L., *Francisco Suarez* (London, 1926).
Midgley, E. B., *Natural Law, Tradition, and the Theory of International Relations* (New York/St Albans, Herts, 1975).
Norena, C. G., *Studies in Spanish Renaissance Thought* (The Hague, 1975).
Nussbaum, A., *A Concise History of the Law of Nations* (New York, 1954).
O'Connor, W. R., 'Molina and Banez' *New Scholasticism* (21/1947).
Scott, J. B., *The Spanish Origin of International Law: Francisco de Vitoria and his Law of Nations* (Oxford, 1934).
Smith, G. (ed.), *Jesuit Thinkers of the Renaissance* (Milwaukee, 1939).
Suárez: *Selections from Three Works of Suárez* (Oxford, 1944).
Trend, J. B., *The Origins of Modern Spain* (New York/Cambridge, 1934).

PART THREE

17: Descartes

Descartes: *Oeuvres* ed. C. Adam and P. Tannery (12 vols, Paris, 1897-1910).
Descartes: *Philosophical Writings* ed. N. Kemp Smith (London, 1952).
Descartes: *The Essential Writings* tr. J. Blom (London, 1974).
Descartes: *Philosophical Writings* tr. G. E. M. Anscombe and P. T. Geach (Edinburgh, 1954).
Descartes: *Meditations on First Philosophy* tr. D. Cress (London, 1978).

Balz, A., *Descartes and the Modern Mind* (New Haven, Connecticut, 1952).
Beck, L. J., *The Method of Descartes* (Oxford, 1952).
Copleston, F., *A History of Philosophy* IV (London, 1958).
Gibson, A. B., *The Philosophy of Descartes* (London, 1932).
Gilson, E., *Etudes sur le rôle de la pensée médiévale dans la formation du système cartésien* (Paris, 1930).
Gilson, E., *Descartes: Discours de la Méthode* (Paris, 1938).
Hooker, M. (ed.), *Descartes: Critical and Interpretative Essays* (London/ Baltimore, 1978).
Keeling, S. V., *Descartes* 2nd ed. (London, 1968).
Maritain, J., *Three Reformers: Luther, Descartes, Rousseau* (London, 1928).
Maritain, J., *The Dream of Descartes* tr. M. L. Andison (London/New York, 1946).
Smith, N. K., *Studies in the Cartesian Philosophy* (London/New York, 1902).
Smith, N. K., *Studies in the Philosophy of Descartes* (London, 1952).
Williams, B., *Descartes: The Project of Pure Enquiry* (London/Atlantic Highlands, N.J., 1978).
Wilson, M. D., *Descartes* (London, 1978).

18: Theocentric thinkers and rationalist systems

Allison, H. E., *Benedict de Spinoza* (Boston, 1975).
Balz, A. G. A., *Cartesian Studies* (New York, 1951).
Broad, C. D., *Leibniz: An Introduction* (London, 1975).
Cailliet, E., *The Clue to Pascal* (London/Philadelphia, 1944).
Cailliet, E., *Pascal: The Emergence of Genius* (New York, 1961).
Carr, H. W., *Leibniz* (London, 1929/New York, 1960).
Church, R. W., *A Study in the Philosophy of Malebranche* (London, 1931).
Copleston, F., *A History of Philosophy* IV (London, 1958).
Davidson, H. M., *The Origins of Certainty: Means and Meanings in Pascal's Penseés* (London/Chicago, 1979).
Guéroult, M., *Malebranche* (3 vols, Paris, 1955-59).
Guhrauer, G. E., *G. W. von Leibniz* (Hildesheim, 1965).
Hallett, H. F., *Benedict de Spinoza* (London, 1957).
Hampshire, S., *Spinoza* (London, 1951).
Hessing, S. (ed.), *Speculum Spinozanum* (London, 1977).
Hostler, J., *Leibniz's Moral Philosophy* (London, 1975).
Joachim, H. H., *A Study of the Ethics of Spinoza* (New York, 1901).
Joseph, H. W. B., *Lectures on the Philosophy of Leibniz* (London, 1949).
Kline, G. L., *Spinoza in Soviet Philosophy* (London, 1952).
Leibniz: *Theodicy* tr. E. M. Huggard (London, 1952).
Leibniz: *Philosophical Works* tr. L. Loemker (Chicago, 1956).
Leibniz: *Philosophical Writings* tr. M. Morris and G. H. R. Parkinson (London, 1973).
McRae, R., *Leibniz: Perception, Apperception and Thought* (Toronto, 1976).
Mesnard, J., *Pascal: His Life and Works* tr. G. S. Fraser (London, 1952).

Mortimer, E., *Blaise Pascal: The Life and Work of a Realist* (London/New York, 1959).

Nadu, P. S., *Malebranche and Modern Philosophy* (Calcutta, 1944).

Parkinson, G. H. R., *Spinoza's Theory of Knowledge* (Oxford, 1954).

Pascal: *Pensées* tr. M. Turnell (London, 1962).

Rescher, N., *Leibniz: An Introduction to his Philosophy* (New York/Oxford, 1979).

Rome, B. K., *The Philosophy of Malebranche* (Chicago, 1963).

Roth, L., *Spinoza* (London, 1929).

Russell, B., *A Critical Exposition of the Philosophy of Leibniz* (Cambridge, 1900).

Saw, R. L., *Leibniz* (Harmondsworth, Middx, 1954).

Shahan, R. W., and Biro, J. I. (eds), *Spinoza: New Perspectives* (Norman, Oklahoma, 1978).

Shahan, R. W., and Biro, J. I. (eds), *Mind, Brain and Function: Essays in the Philosophy of Mind* (Norman, Oklahoma/Brighton, 1982).

Spinoza: *Ethics* tr. W. H. White and A. H. Stirling (Oxford, 1927).

Spinoza: *Chief Works* tr. R. Elwes (New York, 1956/London, 1962).

Wetlesen, J., *The Sage and the Way: Spinoza's Ethics of Freedom* (Assen, 1979).

Wienpahl, P., *The Radical Spinoza* (New York, 1979).

Wilbur, J. B., *Spinoza's Metaphysics* (Assen, 1976).

Wolfson, H. A., *The Philosophy of Spinoza* (Cambridge, Mass, 1948).

Woolhouse, R. S. (ed.), *Leibniz: Metaphysics and Philosophy of Science* (Oxford, 1981).

19: Empiricism in Britain: the seventeenth century

Hobbes: *The English Works of Thomas Hobbes* ed. W. Molesworth (11 vols, Oxford, 1839-45).

Hobbes: *Leviathan* ed. M. Oakeshott (Oxford, 1947/New York, 1962).

Hobbes: *Leviathan* ed. C. B. Macpherson (Harmondsworth, Middx, 1975).

Locke: *An Essay Concerning Human Understanding* ed. J. Yolton (London, 1961).

Locke: *The Locke Reader* ed. J. Yolton (Cambridge, 1977).

Clarke: *The Works of Samuel Clarke* ed. B. Hoadly (London, 1742).

Aaron, R. I., *John Locke* 3rd ed. (Oxford, 1973).

Andrade, E. N. C., *Sir Isaac Newton* (London, 1954).

Aspelin, G., *John Locke* (Lund, 1950).

Brett, R. L., *The Earl of Shaftesbury* (London, 1951).

Cassirer, E., *The Platonic Renaissance in England* tr. J. P. Pettegrove (London, 1953).

Copleston, F., *A History of Philosophy* V (London, 1959).

Cranston, M., *John Locke* (London, 1957).

De Beer, F. S., *Correspondence of John Locke* (5 vols, Oxford, 1976-79).

Dobbs, B. J. T., *The Foundations of Newton's Alchemy* (Cambridge, 1976).

Duncan-Jones, A., *Butler's Moral Philosophy* (Harmondsworth, Middx, 1952).

Fisher, M. S., *Robert Boyle* (Philadelphia, 1945).

Gierke, O., *Natural Law and the Theory of Society, 1500-1800* tr. E. Barker (2 vols, Cambridge, 1934).

Gough, J. W., *The Social Contract: A Critical Study of its Development* (Oxford, 1936).

Gough, J. W., *John Locke's Political Philosophy* 2nd ed. (Oxford, 1973).

James, D. G., *The English Augustans* I: *The Life of Reason: Hobbes, Locke, Bolingbroke* (London, 1949).

Lemos, R. M., *Hobbes and Locke* (Athens, Georgia, 1978).

Muirhead, J. H., *The Platonic Tradition in Anglo-Saxon Philosophy* (London, 1920).

Nagel, E., *The Structure of Science* (New York, 1961).

Oakeshott, M., *Hobbes on Civil Association* (Oxford, 1975).

O'Connor, D. J., *John Locke* (Harmondsworth, Middx, 1952).

Parry, G., *John Locke* (London, 1978).

Passmore, J. A., *Ralph Cudworth: An Interpretation* (Cambridge, 1951).

Putnam, H., *Meaning and the Moral Sciences* (the John Locke Lectures) (London, 1978).

Quintana, R., *Two Augustans: John Locke and Jonathan Swift* (Madison, Wisconsin, 1978).

Rand, B., *The Classical Moralists* (London, 1910).

Ross, R. G. (ed.), *Thomas Hobbes in his Time* (Minneapolis, 1974).

Selby-Bigge, L. A. (ed.), *British Moralists* (2 vols, Oxford, 1897/New York, 1964).

Squadrito, K. M., *Locke's Theory of Sensitive Knowledge* (Washington, D.C., 1978).

Stephen, L., *Hobbes* (London, 1904/Ann Arbor, Michigan, 1961).

Thayer, H. S. (ed.), *Newton's Philosophy of Nature* (New York, 1953).

Tulloch, J., *Rational Theology and Christian Theology in England in the Seventeenth Century* (London/Edinburgh, 1872).

Warrender, H., *The Political Philosophy of Hobbes* (Oxford, 1957).

Watkins, J. W. N., *Hobbes's System of Ideas* 2nd ed. (London, 1973).

Yolton, J. W., *John Locke and the Way of Ideas* (Oxford, 1956).

20: Empiricism in Britain: the eighteenth century

Berkeley: *The Works of George Berkeley* ed. A. A. Luce (9 vols, London, 1948-56).

Hume: *Hume's Philosophical Works* ed. T. Green and T. Grose (4 vols, London, 1874-75).

Hume: *A Treatise of Human Nature* I ed. D. MacNabb (New York, 1962).

Hume: *An Enquiry Concerning Human Understanding* ed. P. Nidditch (Oxford, 1975).

Reid: *The Works of Thomas Reid* ed. W. Hamilton (London/Edinburgh, 1849).

Reid: *Inquiry and Essays* ed. K. Lehrer (Indianapolis, 1975).
Smith: *The Theory of Moral Sentiments* ed. D. D. Raphael (Oxford, 1976).

Bonar, J., *Moral Sense* (London, 1930).
Buffier, C., *First Truths and the Origins of our Opinions, Explained* (London, 1780).
Copleston, F., *A History of Philosophy* V (London, 1959).
Flew, A., *Hume's Philosophy of Belief: A Study of His First Inquiry* (London/New York, 1961).
Foley, V., *The Social Physics of Adam Smith* (Lafayette, Indiana, 1976).
Gaskin, J. C., *Hume's Philosophy of Religion* (London, 1978).
Grave, S. A., *The Scottish Philosophy of Common Sense* (Oxford, 1960).
Hendel, C. W., *Studies in the Philosophy of David Hume* (Princeton, N.J., 1921).
Livingstone, D. W. (ed.), *David Hume: A Re-evaluation* (New York, 1976).
Luce, A. A., *Berkeley and Malebranche: A Study in the Origins of Berkeley's Thought* (Oxford, 1934).
Merrill, K. R. (ed.), *David Hume: Many-sided Genius* (Norman, Oklahoma, 1976).
Morice, G. P. (ed.), *David Hume, Bicentenary Papers* (Edinburgh, 1977/Austin, Texas, 1979).
Olson, R., *Scottish Philosophy and British Physics* (Princeton, N.J., 1975).
Passmore, J., *Hume's Intentions* (Cambridge, 1952).
Pitcher, G., *Berkeley* (London, 1977).
Smith, N. K., *The Philosophy of David Hume* (London, 1941).
Stephen, L., *History of English Thought in the Eighteenth Century* 3rd ed. (2 vols, London/New York, 1902).
Stewart, J. B., *The Moral and Political Philosophy of David Hume* (New York, 1963).
Stroud, B., *Hume* (London, 1977).
Thomas, R., *Richard Price: Philosopher and Apostle of Liberty* (London, 1924).
Todd, W. B. (ed.), *Hume and the Enlightenment* (Edinburgh, 1975).
Warnock, G. J., *Berkeley* (London, 1953).
Zabeeh, F., *Hume: Precursor of Modern Empiricism* (The Hague, 1960).

21: The Enlightenment

Albridge, O., *Voltaire and the Century of Light* (Princeton, N.J., 1975).
Berlin, I., *Vico and Herder* (London, 1976).
Bredvold, L. I., *The Brave New World of the Enlightenment* (Ann Arbor, 1961).
Brinton, C. (ed.), *The Age of Reason Reader* (New York, 1956).
Brunschwig, L., *Enlightenment and Romanticism* (Chicago, 1975).
Cassirer, E., *Rousseau, Kant, Goethe* (Princeton, N.J., 1947).
Cassirer, E., *The Philosophy of the Enlightenment* (Princeton, N.J., 1954).
Cassirer, E., *The Question of J.-J. Rousseau* (New York, 1962).

Charvet, J., *The Social Problem in the Philosophy of Rousseau* (London, 1974).

Clark, R. T., *Herder: His Life and Thought* (Los Angeles, 1955).

Cobban, A., *Rousseau and the Modern State* 2nd ed. (London, 1968).

Copleston, F., *A History of Philosophy* VI (London, 1960).

Croce, B., *The Philosophy of Giambattista Vico* tr. R. G. Collingwood (London, 1913/New York, 1964).

Durkheim, E., *Montesquieu and Rousseau* (Ann Arbor, 1960).

Flint, R., *Vico* (Edinburgh, 1884).

Gillies, A., *Herder* (Oxford, 1945).

Green, F. C., *Jean-Jacques Rousseau* (Cambridge, 1955).

Grimsley, R., *Jean d'Alembert* (Oxford, 1963).

Hampson, N., *The Enlightenment* (London, 1968).

Hazard, P., *European Thought in the Eighteenth Century* (London, 1954).

Hendel, C. W., *Jean-Jacques Rousseau, Moralist* (2 vols, London/New York, 1934).

Hibben, J. G., *The Philosophy of the Enlightenment* (London, 1910).

Hubert, R., *D'Holbach et ses amis* (Paris, 1928).

Lange, F. A., *History of Materialism* (3 vols, London, 1879).

Lemos, R. M., *Rousseau's Political Philosophy* (Athens, Georgia, 1977).

Manuel, F. E., *The Age of Reason* (New York, 1951).

Martin, K., *The Rise of French Liberal Thought* (New York, 1954).

Mason, H. T., *Pierre Bayle and Voltaire* (London, 1963).

May, H. F., *The Enlightenment in America* (New York/Oxford, 1976).

Morley, J., *Rousseau* (2 vols, London, 1883).

Morley, J., *Diderot and the Encyclopaedists* (London, 1923).

Pompa, L., *Vico* (Cambridge, 1975).

Redwood, J., *Reason, Ridicule and Religion: The Age of Enlightenment in England* (London/Cambridge, Mass, 1977).

Richter, M., *The Cosmopolitan Idea in Enlightenment Thought* (Notre Dame, 1977).

Smith, P., *A History of Modern Culture* II (London/New York, 1934).

Smith, R. G., *J. G. Hamann* (London, 1960).

Todd, W. B., *Hume and the Enlightenment* (Edinburgh, 1975).

Torrey, N. L., *Voltaire and the English Deists* (New Haven, Connecticut, 1930/Oxford, 1962).

Vartanian, M., *Diderot and Descartes: Study of Naturalism in the Enlightenment* (London, 1976).

Wade, I. O., *The Structure and Form of the French Enlightenment* (2 vols, Princeton, N.J., 1977).

Wickwar, W. H., *Baron D'Holbach: A Prelude to the French Revolution* (London, 1935).

Wright, E. H., *The Meaning of Rousseau* (London, 1929).

22 and 23: Kant

Kant: *Critique of Pure Reason* tr. N. K. Smith, 2nd ed. (London, 1933).

Kant: *Critique of Practical Reason* tr. T. K. Abbott, 6th ed. (London, 1909).

Kant: *Critique of Judgement* tr. J. O. Meredith (Oxford, 1911).

Kant: *Selections* ed. T. M. Green (London/New York, 1929).

Kant: *Prolegomena to Any Future Metaphysics* tr. P. Carus and H. H. Hudson (New York, 1960).

Kant: *Religion within the Limits of Reason Alone* tr. T. M. Greene and H. H. Hudson (New York, 1960).

Aune, B., *Kant's Theory of Morals* (Princeton, N.J., 1979).

Beck, L. W., *A Commentary on Kant's Critique of Practical Reason* (Chicago, 1960).

Beck, L. W., *Essays on Kant and Hume* (New Haven, Connecticut, 1978).

Bird, B., *Kant's Theory of Knowledge* (London, 1962).

Brittan, G., *Kant's Theory of Science* (Princeton, N.J., 1978).

Broad, C. D., *Kant: An Introduction* (Cambridge, 1978).

Cassirer, H. W., *A Commentary on Kant's Critique of Judgement* (London, 1938).

Cassirer, H. W., *Kant's First Critique* (London, 1954).

Copleston, F., *A History of Philosophy* VI (London, 1960).

Duncan, A. R., *Practical Reason and Morality* (London/Edinburgh, 1957).

Ewing, A. C., *Kant's Treatment of Causality* (London, 1924).

Ewing, A. C., *A Short Commentary on Kant's Critique of Pure Reason* 2nd ed. (London, 1950).

Gregor, M. J., *Laws of Freedom* (Oxford, 1963).

Guyer, P., *Kant and the Claims of Taste* (London/Cambridge, Mass., 1978).

Hartnack, J., *Immanuel Kant: An Explanation of his Theory of Knowledge and Moral Philosophy* (N.J., 1974/Brighton, 1978).

Jones, W. T., *Morality and Freedom in the Philosophy of Immanuel Kant* (Oxford, 1940).

Koerner, S., *Kant* (Harmondsworth, Middx, 1955).

Nell, O., *Acting on Principle: Kant* (New York, 1975).

Paton, H. J., *The Categorical Imperative* (London, 1948).

Paton, H. J., *Kant's Metaphysics of Experience* 2nd ed. (2 vols, London, 1952).

Raschke, C. A. *Moral Action, God, and History in the Thought of Immanuel Kant* (Tallahassee, Florida, 1975).

Ross, W. D., *Kant's Ethical Theory* (Oxford, 1954).

Smith, N. K., *A Commentary on Kant's Critique of Pure Reason* 2nd ed. (London/New York, 1950).

Teale, A. E., *Kantian Ethics* (London, 1951).

Walsh, W. H., *Kant's Criticism of Metaphysics* (Edinburgh, 1975).

Warnock, G. J., 'Kant' in D. J. O'Connor (ed.) *A Critical History of Western Philosophy* (New York, 1965).

Weldon, T. D., *Introduction to Kant's Critique of Pure Reason* 2nd ed. (Oxford, 1958).

Werkmeister, W. H. (ed.), *Reflections on Kant's Philosophy* (Gainesville, Florida, 1976).

Wilkerson, T. E., *Kant's Critique of Pure Reason: A Commentary for Students* (Oxford, 1976).
Willey, T. E., *Back to Kant* (Detroit, 1978).
Wood, A. W., *Kant's Rational Theology* (London/Cornell, N.Y., 1978).

PART FOUR

24: Absolute idealism
Fichte: *Fichte's Popular Works* tr. and ed. W. Smith, 4th ed. (2 vols, London, 1889).
Fichte: *The Science of Knowledge* tr. A. E. Kroeger (Philadelphia, 1868/London, 1889).
Fichte: *The Science of Rights* tr. A. E. Kroeger (Philadelphia, 1869/London, 1889).
Fichte: *The Science of Ethics* tr. A. E. Kroeger (London, 1907).
Schelling: *The Philosophy of Art* tr. A. Johnson (London, 1845).
Schelling: *Of Human Freedom* tr. J. Gutmann (Chicago, 1936).
Schelling: *The Ages of the World* tr. F. de Wolfe Bolman, Jr (New York, 1942).
Hegel: *The Phenomenology of Mind* tr. J. B. Baillie (New York, 1931).
Hegel: *The Science of Logic* tr. L. G. Johnson and L. Struthers (2 vols, New York, 1929/London, 1961).
Hegel: *Philosophy of Mind* [from *Encyclopedia of Philosophical Sciences*] tr. W. Wallace (Oxford, 1894).
Hegel: *Lectures on the Philosophy of History* tr. E. S. Haldane and F. H. Simpson (3 vols, London, 1892-96).
Hegel: *The Philosophy of History* tr. J. Sibree (New York, 1900).
Hegel: *The Philosophy of Fine Art* tr. F. Osmaston (4 vols, London, 1920).
Hegel: *The Philosophy of Right* tr. T. M. Knox (Oxford, 1942).
Hegel: *The Philosophy of Hegel* ed. C. J. Friedrich (New York, 1953).
Hegel: *Encyclopaedia of Philosophy* tr. G. E. Mueller (New York, 1957).

Adamson, R., *Fichte* (London/Edinburgh, 1881).
Aiken, H. D. (ed.), *Age of Ideology: The Nineteenth Century Philosophers* (London/New York, 1957).
Copleston, F., *A History of Philosophy* VII (London, 1963).
Cunningham, G. W., *Thought and Reality in Hegel's System* (New York, 1910).
Everett, C. C., *Fichte's Science of Knowledge* (Chicago, 1884).
Findlay, J. N., *Hegel. A Re-Examination* (London, 1958).
Grégoire, F., *Études hégéliennes* (Louvain, 1958).
Kaufmann, W., *Hegel: Reinterpretation* (New York, 1965/London, 1966).
Lowith, K., *From Hegel to Nietzsche* tr. D. Green (London, 1965).
McTaggart, J., *Studies in Hegel's Dialectic* (Cambridge, 1896).
Mure, G. R. G., *An Introduction to Hegel* (Oxford, 1940).
Mure, G. R. G., *A Study of Hegel's Logic* (Oxford, 1950).

Stace, W. T., *The Philosophy of Hegel* (New York, 1955).

Talbot, E. B., *The Fundamental Principle of Fichte's Philosophy* (New York, 1906).

Thompson, A. B., *The Unity of Fichte's Doctrine of Knowledge* (Boston, 1896).

Travis, D. C. (ed.), *A Hegel Symposium* (Austin, Texas, 1962).

Watson, J., *Schelling's Transcendental Idealism* 2nd ed. (Chicago, 1892).

25: From Schleiermacher to Nietzsche

Schleiermacher: *The Theology of Schleiermacher: A Condensed Presentation of his Chief Work 'The Christian Faith'* tr. G. Cross (Chicago, 1911).

Schleiermacher: *The Christian Faith* (Edinburgh, 1928).

Schopenhauer: *The World as Will and Idea* tr. R. B. Haldane and J. Kemp (London, 1948).

Schopenhauer: *The World as Will and Representation* tr. E. Payne (Indian Hills, Colorado, 1958/New York, 1966).

Feuerbach: *The Essence of Christianity* tr. M. Evans (London, 1881).

Marx: *Capital* tr. S. Moore, E. Aveling and E. Untermann (3 vols, London/Chicago, 1909-26).

Marx and Engels: *Selected Works* ed. C. P. Dutt (2 vols, London/New York, 1942).

Marx and Engels: *Basic Writings* ed. L. S. Feuer (New York, 1959).

Marx and Engels: *Collected Works* (vols 1-50, London, 1975-).

Engels: *Socialism: Utopian and Scientific* tr. E. Aveling (New York, 1892/London, 1932).

Engels: *Principles of Communism* tr. P. Sweeney (New York, 1952).

Kierkegaard: *Complete Works* tr. D. F. Swenson and W. Lowrie (12 vols, Oxford/Princeton, N.J., 1936-53).

Kierkegaard: *A Kierkegaard Anthology* ed. R. Bretall (London/Princeton, N.J. 1947).

Nietzsche: *Basic Writings of Nietzsche* tr. W. Kaufmann (New York, 1966).

Acton, H. B., *The Illusion of the Epoch, Marxism-Leninism* (London, 1955).

Beer, M., *Schopenhauer* (London, 1914).

Berdiaeff, N., *The Origin of Russian Communism* (London, 1937).

Bochenski, I. M., *Soviet Russian Dialectical Materialism* (Dordrecht, 1963).

Bossenbrook, W. J., *The German Mind* (Detroit, 1961).

Brandt, R. B., *The Philosophy of Schleiermacher* (London/New York, 1941).

Brinton, C., *Nietzsche* (London, 1941).

Chamberlin, W. B., *Ludwig Feuerbach* (London, 1941).

Collins, J., *The Mind of Kierkegaard* (Chicago, 1953/London, 1954).

Copleston, F., *Friedrich Nietzsche: Philosopher of Culture* (London, 1942).

Copleston, F., *Arthur Schopenhauer: Philosopher of Pessimism* (London, 1946).

Copleston, F., *A History of Philosophy* VII (London, 1963).

Gardiner, P., *Schopenhauer* (Harmondsworth, Middx, 1963).

Gooch, G. P., *The German Mind* (London, 1945).

Hodges, H., *The Philosophy of W. Dilthey* (London, 1952).

Hollingdale, R. J., *Nietzsche* (London/Boston, 1973).

Hook, S., *Marx and the Marxists* (Princeton, N.J., 1950).

Jolivet, R., *Introduction to Kierkegaard* tr. W. Barber (New York, 1951).

Kaufmann, W., *Nietzsche* (Princeton, N.J., 1950).

Korsch, K., *Karl Marx* (London/New York, 1938).

Lange, F., *The History of Materialism* tr. E. C. Thomas (3 vols, London, 1879-81).

Lea, F. A., *The Tragic Philosopher: A Study of F. Nietzsche* (London, 1957).

Lichtheim, G., *Marxism* (London, 1964).

Lowith, K., *From Hegel to Nietzsche* tr. O. Green (London, 1965).

Lowrie, W., *Kierkegaard* (London, 1938).

Marcuse, H., *Reason and Revolution: Hegel and the Rise of Social Theory* (New York, 1941/2nd ed., London, 1963).

Marcuse, H., *Soviet Marxism* (New York, 1958/London, 1968).

Merz, J. T., *A History of European Thought in the Nineteenth Century* (3 vols, Edinburgh, 1896-1912).

Morgan, G., *What Nietzsche Means* (Cambridge, Mass., 1941).

O'Connor, D. J. (ed.), *A Critical History of Western Philosophy* (New York, 1965).

Tucker, R., *Philosophy and Myth in Karl Marx* (Cambridge, 1961).

Wartofsky, M. W., *Feuerbach* (Cambridge, 1977).

Wetter, G. A., *Dialectical Materialism* (London, 1958).

Zimmern, H., *Arthur Schopenhauer: His Life and his Philosophy* 2nd ed. (London, 1932).

26: Nineteenth-century philosophy in Britain

Abel, R., *The Pragmatic Humanism of F. C. S. Schiller* (London/New York, 1955).

Abel, R., *Humanistic Pragmatism: the Philosophy of F. C. S. Schiller* (New York/London, 1966).

Anschutz, R. P., *The Philosophy of J. S. Mill* (Oxford, 1953).

Bain, A., *John Stuart Mill* (London, 1882).

Boekraad, A. J., *The Personal Conquest of Truth According to J. H. Newman* (Louvain, 1955).

Bosanquet, H., *Bernard Bosanquet* (London, 1924).

Bouyer, L., *Newman* (London/New York, 1958).

Brinton, C., *English Political Thought in the Nineteenth Century* (Cambridge, Mass., 1949).

Britton, K., *John Stuart Mill* (London, 1953).

Broad, C. D., *Examination of McTaggart's Philosophy* (2 vols, Cambridge, 1933-38).

Cassirer, E., *The Myth of the State* (London/New Haven, Connecticut, 1946).

Collins, J., *Philosophical Readings of Cardinal Newman* (Chicago, 1961).

Copleston, F., *A History of Philosophy* VIII (London, 1966).

Cowling, M., *Mill and Liberalism* (London, 1963).

Davidson, W. L., *Political Thought in England: Bentham to J. S. Mill* (London, 1950).

De Beer, G., *Charles Darwin: Evolution by Natural Selection* (London, 1963).

Fairbrother, W. H., *The Philosophy of T. H. Green* (London, 1896).

Froude, J. A., *Thomas Carlyle* 2nd ed. (2 vols, London, 1896).

Haldar, H., *Neo-Hegelianism* (London, 1927).

Havard, W. C., *Henry Sidgwick* (Gainesville, Florida, 1959).

Irvine, W., *Thomas Henry Huxley* (London, 1960).

Jones, W. T., *Masters of Political Thought from Machiavelli to Bentham* (London, 1947).

Leavis, F. R. (ed.), *Mill on Bentham and Coleridge* (London, 1950).

Leslie, S. W., *Political Thought from Bentham to Mill* (London/New York, 1947).

Lofthouse, W., *F. H. Bradley* (London, 1949).

Mack, M. P., *Jeremy Bentham* (London, 1962).

Metz, R., *A Hundred Years of British Philosophy* tr. J. Harvey *et al.* (London, 1938).

Moore, G. E., *Some Main Problems of Philosophy* (London, 1953).

Muirhead, J. H. (ed.), *Contemporary British Philosophy: Personal Statements* (2 vols, London, 1924-25).

Muirhead, J. H., *Coleridge as Philosopher* (London, 1930).

Muirhead, J. H., *The Platonic Tradition in Anglo-Saxon Philosophy* (London, 1931).

Passmore, J., *A Hundred Years of Philosophy* (London, 1957).

Plamenatz, J. P., *The English Utilitarians* (Oxford, 1949).

Richter, M., *The Politics of Conscience: T. H. Green and his Age* (London, 1964).

Russell, B., *John Stuart Mill* (London, 1956).

Seth, J., *English Philosophers and Schools of Philosophy* (London, 1912).

Sorley, W. R., *A History of English Philosophy* (Cambridge, 1920).

Stephen, L., *The English Utilitarians* (3 vols, London, 1900).

Taylor, A. E., *F. H. Bradley* (London, 1924).

Thompson, J. A., *Herbert Spencer* (London, 1906).

Wollheim, R., *F. H. Bradley* (Harmondsworth, Middx, 1959).

27: Idealism and pragmatism in America

Abel, R., *The Pragmatic Humanism of F. C. S. Schiller* (London/New York, 1955).

Abel, R., *Humanistic Pragmatism: The Philosophy of F. C. S. Schiller* (New York/London 1966).

Anderson, P. R., and Fisch, M. H. (eds), *Philosophy in America* (London/New York, 1939).

Barrett, C., *et al.*, *Contemporary Idealism in America* (New York, 1932).

Bentley, J. E., *An Outline of American Philosophy* (Paterson, N.J., 1963).

Bernstein, R. J., *John Dewey* (New York, 1966).

594   Bibliography

Bishop, J., *Emerson on the Soul* (London/Cambridge, Mass., 1965).
Blau, J. (ed.), *American Philosophic Addresses, 1700-1900* (New York/ London, 1946).
Blau, J., *Men and Movements in American Philosophy* (New York, 1952).
Boler, J. F., *Charles Peirce and Scholastic Realism* (Seattle, 1963).
Buchler, J., *Charles Peirce's Empiricism* (New York/London, 1939).
Childs, J. L., *American Pragmatism and Education* (New York, 1956).
Cohen, M. R., *American Thought* (Glencoe, Ill., 1954).
Compton, C. H. (ed.), *William James: Philosopher and Man* (New York, 1957).
Copleston, F., *A History of Philosophy* VIII (London, 1966).
Cotton, J. H., *Royce on the Human Self* (Cambridge, Mass., 1954).
Cunningham, G. W., *The Idealist Argument in Recent British and American Philosophy* (New York, 1933).
Fisch, M. H. (ed.), *Classic American Philosophers* (New York, 1951).
Fleckenstein, N. J., *A Critique of John Dewey's Theory of Nature and the Knowledge of Reality* (Washington, 1954).
Frankel, C. H. (ed.), *The Golden Age of American Philosophy* (New York, 1960).
Fuss, P., *The Moral Philosophy of Josiah Royce* (Cambridge, Mass., 1965).
Gallie, W. B., *Peirce and Pragmatism* (Harmondsworth, Middx, 1952).
Geiger, G. R., *John Dewey* (New York/London, 1958).
Goudge, T. A., *The Thought of C. S. Peirce* (Toronto/London, 1950).
Hook, S., *John Dewey* (New York, 1939).
Knight, M., *William James* (Harmondsworth, Middx, 1950).
Knudson, A. C., *The Philosophy of Personalism* (New York, 1927).
Kurtz, P. (ed.), *The American Philosophers* (New York, 1956).
Kurtz, P. (ed.), *American Philosophy in the Twentieth Century* (London, 1967).
Lovejoy, A. O., *The Thirteen Pragmatisms* (Baltimore, 1963).
Marcel, G., *Royce's Metaphysics* tr. V. Ringer and G. Ringer (Chicago, 1956).
Marett, R., *Ferdinand Canning Scott Schiller* (London, 1938).
Matthiessen, F. O., *American Renaissance* (New York/London, 1941).
Mayer, F., *A History of American Thought* (Dubuque, Iowa, 1950).
Miller, P., *Jonathan Edwards* (New York, 1949).
Miller, P., *Errand into the Wilderness* (Cambridge, Mass./London, 1956).
Morris, L., *William James* (New York, 1950).
Muelder, W. G., and Sears, L., *The Development of American Philosophy* (Boston, 1940).
Murphey, M. G., *The Development of Peirce's Philosophy* (Cambridge, Mass., 1961).
Nathanson, J., *John Dewey* (New York, 1951).

Pochmann, H. A., *German Culture in America* (Madison, Wisconsin, 1961).

Reck, A. J., *Recent American Philosophy* (New York, 1964).

Riley, I. W., *American Thought* 2nd ed. (New York, 1923).

Riley, I. W., *American Philosophy: The Early Schools* 8th ed. (New York, 1958).

Roth, R. J., *John Dewey and Self-Realization* (Englewood Cliffs, N.J., 1962).

Royce, J., *William James and Other Essays* (New York, 1911).

Sanders, C. L. (ed.), *Benjamin Franklin* (Boston, 1955).

Santayana, G., *Character and Opinion in the United States* (New York, 1920).

Schaub, E. L. (ed.), *W. T. Harris* (Chicago, 1936).

Schneider, H. W., *A History of American Philosophy* 2nd ed. (New York, 1963).

Smith, J. E., *Royce's Social Infinite* (New York, 1950).

Smith, J. E., *The Spirit of American Philosophy* (New York, 1950).

Stovall, F., *American Idealism* (Norman, Oklahoma, 1943).

Thompson, M., *The Pragmatic Philosophy of C. S. Peirce* (Chicago/London, 1953).

Townsend, H. G., *Philosophical Ideas in the United States* (New York, 1934).

Van Wessep, H. B., *Seven Sages: The Story of American Philosophy* (New York, 1960).

Wennerberg, H., *The Pragmatism of C. S. Peirce* (Lund, 1963).

White, M. G., *The Origin of Dewey's Instrumentalism* (New York, 1943).

White, M. G., *Social Thought in America* 2nd ed. (Boston, 1957).

Winslow, O. E., *Jonathan Edwards* (New York, 1940).

28 and 29: 'The human condition': philosophy in France

Aiken, H. E. (ed.), *Age of Ideology* (London/New York, 1957).

Alexander, I. W., *Bergson: Philosopher of Reflection* (London, 1957).

Alpert, H., *Emile Durkheim and his Sociology* (New York, 1939).

Andreski, S. (ed.), *The Essential Comte* (London, 1974/New York, 1975).

Bierstedt, R., *Émile Durkheim* (London/New York, 1966).

Boas, G., *French Philosophies of the Romantic Period* (Baltimore, 1925).

Boas, G., *Dominant Themes in Modern Philosophy* (New York, 1957).

Brogan, C., *Proudhon* (London, 1936).

Charlton, D. G., *Positivist Thought in France During the Second Empire* (Oxford, 1959).

Charlton, D. G., and Potts, D. C., *French Thought Since 1600* (London, 1974/New York, 1976).

Chevalier, J., *Henri Bergson* (New York, 1926).

Collins, J., *A History of Modern European Philosophy* (Milwaukee, 1954).

Copleston, F., *Bergson on Morality* (London, 1955).

Copleston, F., *A History of Philosophy* IX (London, 1975).

Crawford, L. S., *The Philosophy of Emile Boutroux* (New York, 1924).

Dondo, M. M., *The French Faust: Henri de Saint-Simon* (New York, 1955).

Evans-Pritchard, E., *Lévy-Bruhl's Theory of Primitive Mentality* (Oxford, 1934).

Frank, P., *Modern Science and its Philosophy* (Cambridge, Mass., 1949).

Gunn, J. A., *Modern French Philosophy* (London, 1922).

Hallie, P. P., *Maine de Biran: Reformer of Empiricism* (Cambridge, Mass., 1959).

Hanna, T. (ed.), *The Bergsonian Heritage* (London/New York, 1962).

Höffding, H., *Modern Philosophers* (London, 1915).

Joll, J., *The Anarchists* (London, 1964).

Kahn, S. J., *Science and Aesthetic Judgement: A Study of Taine's Critical Method* (New York, 1953).

Kennedy, E., *A Philosopher in the Age of Revolution: Destutt de Tracy and the Origins of 'Ideology'* (Philadelphia, 1978).

La Capra, D., *Émile Durkheim* (London/Ithaca, N.Y., 1972).

Lévy-Bruhl, L., *A History of Modern Philosophy in France* (London/Chicago, 1899).

Lévy-Bruhl, L., *The Philosophy of Auguste Comte* (New York, 1903).

Lowinger, A., *The Methodology of Pierre Duhem* (New York, 1941).

Lubac, H. de, *The Drama of Atheist Humanism* (London, 1950).

Lukes, S., *Émile Durkheim* (London, 1973).

Manuel, F. E., *The New World of Henri de Saint-Simon* (Cambridge, Mass., 1956).

Manuel, F. E., *The Prophets of Paris* (Cambridge, Mass., 1962).

Maritain, J., *Bergsonian Philosophy and Thomism* (New York, 1955).

Martineau, H. (ed. and tr.), *The Positive Philosophy of Auguste Comte* (2 vols, London, 1853).

Marvin, F. S., *Comte: The Founder of Sociology* (London, 1937).

Mill, J. S., *Auguste Comte and Positivism* (London, 1865).

Moore, F. C. T., *The Psychology of Maine de Biran* (Oxford, 1970).

Nagel, E., *The Structure of Science* (London, 1961).

Olmsted, J. M. D. and E. H., *Claude Bernard and the Experimental Method in Medicine* (New York, 1952).

Pilkington, A. E., *Bergson and his Influence* (Cambridge, 1976).

Popper, K. R., *The Logic of Scientific Discovery* (London, 1959).

Scharfstein, B.-A., *Roots of Bergson's Philosophy* (New York, 1943).

Simon, C., *Contemporary French Philosophy* (London/New York, 1964).

Simon, W., *European Positivism in the Nineteenth Century* (Ithaca, N.Y., 1963).

Van Duzen, C., *The Contributions of the Idéologues to French Revolutionary Thought* (Baltimore, 1935).

Woodcock, G., *Pierre-Joseph Proudhon: A Biography* (London, 1956).

Woodcock, G., *Anarchism* (Cleveland, Ohio, 1962/Harmondsworth, Middx, 1963).

Wolff, K. H. (ed.), *Émile Durkheim* (Columbus, Ohio, 1962).

30: Nineteenth-century thought in other countries

Berdyaev, N. A., *Dostoevsky: An Interpretation* tr. D. Attwater (London, 1936/New York, 1957).

Billington, J. H., *Mikhailovsky and Russian Populism* (Oxford, 1958).

Boas, G., *The Major Traditions of European Philosophy* (New York, 1929).

Boas, G., *Dominant Themes of Modern Philosophy* (New York, 1957).

Borkenau, F., *Pareto* (London, 1936).

Boström, C. J., *Philosophy of Religion* tr. V. E. and R. N. Beck (New Haven, 1963).

Bowman, H. E., V. *Belinsky* (Cambridge, Mass, 1954).

Burnham, J., *The Machiavellians: Defenders of Freedom* (New York, 1943).

Caponigri, A. R., *A History of Western Philosophy* IV-V (Chicago, 1974).

Carr, E. H., *Michael Bakunin* (London, 1937).

Craufurd, A. H., *The Religion and Ethics of Tolstoy* (London, 1912).

Edie, J. M., *Russian Philosophy* (3 vols, Chicago, 1965).

Fülöp-Miller, R., *Fyodor Dostoevsky* tr. R. and C. Winston (New York, 1950).

Guy, A., *Philosophes espagnols* (Toulouse, 1956).

Ivanov, V., *Freedom and the Tragic Life: a Study in Dostoevsky* (New York, 1957).

Leetham, C., *Rosmini* (London, 1957).

Lossky, N. O., *A History of Russian Philosophy* (New York, 1951/London, 1952).

Macauley, C., *K. C. F. Krause* (Berkeley, 1925).

Masaryk, T. G., *The Spirit of Russia* (New York, 1955).

Pagani, G. B., *The Life of Antonio Rosmini-Serbati* (London, 1906).

Plekhanov, G., *The Materialist Conception of History* (New York, 1940).

Redpath, T., *Tolstoy* (London, 1960).

Ruggiero, G. de, *Modern Philosophy* (London, 1921).

Russell, B., *Proposed Roads to Freedom: Socialism, Anarchism and Syndicalism* (London, 1918/New York, 1919).

Salazar Bondy, A., *Philosophy in Peru, a Historical Study* (Washington, D.C., 1954).

Sánchez Reulet, A., *Contemporary Latin-American Philosophy* (Albuquerque, 1954).

Simmons, E. J., *Leo Tolstoy* (Boston, 1946/London, 1949).

Trend, E. B., *The Origins of Modern Spain* (Cambridge, 1934).

Utechin, S. V., *Russian Political Thought* (New York, 1964).

Venturi, F., *Roots of Revolution* (New York, 1960).

Weidle, W., *Russia Absent and Present* (London, 1952).

Zander, L. A., *Dostoevsky* tr. N. Duddington (London, 1948).

Zenkovsky, V. V., *A History of Russian Philosophy* tr. G. L. Kline (London, 1953).

PART FIVE

31: Positivism and idealism

Ayer, A. J. (ed.), *Logical Positivism* (London/Glencoe, Illinois, 1959).

Copleston, F., *Contemporary Philosophy* (London, 1956).

Crespi, A., *Contemporary Thought of Italy* (London, 1925).
Deschoux, M., *La Philosophie de Léon Brunschvicg* (Paris, 1949).
Donagan, A., *The Later Philosophy of R. G. Collingwood* (Oxford, 1962).
Dumery, H., *Blondel* (Paris, 1954).
Ewing, A. C., *Idealism: A Critical Survey* (London, 1934).
Ewing, A. C., *The Idealist Tradition: From Berkeley to Blanshard* (London/ Glencoe, Illinois, 1957).
Fisch, M. H. (ed.), *Classic American Philosophers* (New York, 1951).
Frank, P., *Modern Science and its Philosophy* (Cambridge, Mass., 1949).
Kohn, H., *The Mind of Germany* (New York, 1960).
Kraft, V., *The Vienna Circle: The Origin of Neo-Positivism* tr. A. Pap (London/New York, 1953).
Kurtz, P. (ed.), *The American Philosophers* (New York, 1965).
Kurtz, P. (ed.), *American Philosophy in the Twentieth Century: A Sourcebook from Pragmatism to Philosophical Analysis* (London/New York, 1967).
Macdonald, M. (ed.), *Philosophy and Analysis* (Oxford, 1954).
Muelder, W. G. (ed.), *The Development of American Philosophy* 8th ed. (Cambridge, Mass., 1960).
Nagel, E., *Sovereign Reason* (London/Glencoe, Illinois, 1954).
Nagel, E., *Logic Without Metaphysics* (Glencoe, Illinois, 1956).
Orsini, G., *Benedetto Croce* (Carbondale, Illinois, 1961).
Passmore, J. A., *A Hundred Years of Philosophy* (London, 1957).
Piccoli, R., *Benedetto Croce: An Introduction to his Philosophy* (London, 1922).
Popper, K., *The Logic of Scientific Discovery* (London, 1959).
Reck, A. J., *Recent American Philosophy* (New York, 1964).
Schilpp, P. A. (ed.), *The Philosophy of E. Cassirer* (Evanston, Illinois, 1949).
Schneider, H. W., *A History of American Philosophy* (New York, 1963).
Smith, C., *Contemporary French Philosophy* (London/New York, 1964).
Tomlin, E. W. F., *R. G. Collingwood* (London, 1953).
Urmson, J. O., *Philosophical Analysis: Its Development between the Two World Wars* (Oxford, 1956).
Warnock, G. F., *English Philosophy Since 1900* (London, 1958).

32 and 33: Twentieth-century thought in Britain and America

Ambrose, A. (ed.), *Wittgenstein's Cambridge Lectures* (Totowa, N.J., 1979/Oxford, 1980).
Anscombe, G. E. M., *An Introduction to Wittgenstein's 'Tractatus'* (London, 1959).
Ayer, A. J. (ed.), *Logical Positivism* (London/Glencoe, Illinois, 1959).
Ayer, A. J., *The Concept of a Person and Other Essays* (London/New York, 1963).
Black, M., *Problems of Analysis* (London/Ithaca, N.Y., 1954).
Black, M., *A Companion to Wittgenstein's 'Tractatus'* (Cambridge, 1964).
Blanshard, B., *Reason and Analysis* (London/New York, 1962).

Bolton, D., *An Approach to Wittgenstein's Philosophy* (London/Atlantic Highlands, N.J., 1979).

Boman, L., *Criticism and Construction in the Philosophy of the American New Realism* (Stockholm, 1955).

Braithwaite, R. B., *George Edward Moore* (London, 1963).

Bunge, M. (ed.), *The Critical Approach to Science and Philosophy* (London/New York, 1964).

Butler, R. J. (ed.), *Analytical Philosophy* (Oxford, 1962).

Carnap, R., *Logical Foundations of Probability* (Chicago, 1950/London, 1951).

Carnap, R., *Meaning and Necessity* 2nd ed. (Chicago, 1956).

Charlesworth, M., *Philosophy and Linguistic Analysis* (Pittsburgh/Louvain, 1959).

Cohen, L. J., *The Diversity of Meaning* (London, 1962).

Cohen, M. R., *American Thought* (Glencoe, Illinois, 1954).

Collingwood, R. G., *An Essay on Metaphysics* (Oxford, 1948).

Copleston, F., *Contemporary Philosophy* (London, 1956).

Copleston, F., *A History of Philosophy* VIII (London, 1966).

Egner, R. E. (ed.), *Bertrand Russell's Best* (London, 1975).

Egner, R. E., and Dennon, L. (eds), *The Basic Writings of Bertrand Russell* (New York, 1961).

Feigl, H., and Sellars, W. (eds), *Readings in Philosophical Analysis* (New York, 1949).

Fisch, M. H. (ed.), *Classic American Philosophers* (New York, 1951).

Flew, A. G. N. (ed.), *Essays in Conceptual Analysis* (London, 1963).

Gellner, E., *Words and Things* (London, 1959).

Gellner, E., *Thought and Change* (London, 1964).

Graham, K., *J. L. Austin: A Critique of Ordinary Language Philosophy* (Hassocks, Sussex, 1977).

Hill, T. E., *Contemporary Theories of Knowledge* (New York, 1961).

Kazemier, B. H., and Vuysje, D. (eds), *Logic and Language* (Netherlands, 1962).

Kraft, V., *The Vienna Circle: The Origin of Neo-Positivism* tr. A. Pap (London/New York, 1953).

Kurtz, P. (ed.), *The American Philosophers* (New York, 1965).

Lawrence, N. M., *Whitehead's Philosophical Development* (London/Berkeley, 1956).

Lazerowitz, M., *The Structure of Metaphysics* (London, 1955).

Leclerc, I., *Whitehead's Metaphysics: An Introductory Exposition* (London, 1958/Bloomington, Indiana, 1975).

Leclerc, I. (ed.), *The Relevance of Whitehead* (London, 1961).

Lee, D. (ed.), *Wittgenstein's Lectures: Cambridge* (Totowa, N.J., 1980).

Lowe, V., *Understanding Whitehead* (Baltimore, 1962/Hemel Hempstead, Herts., 1967).

Luckhardt, C. (ed.), *Wittgenstein* (New York/Brighton, Sussex, 1979).

McCarthy, J. W., *The Naturalism of S. Alexander* (New York, 1948).

Malcolm, N., *Ludwig Wittgenstein* (London, 1958).

Malcolm, N., *Knowledge and Certainty* (London/Englewood Cliffs, N.J.,
1963).

Marsh, R. C. (ed.), *Logic and Knowledge* (London, 1956).

Mayer, F., *A History of American Thought* (Dubuque, Iowa, 1950).

Morawetz, T., *Wittgenstein and Knowledge* (Brighton, 1980).

Muelder, W. G., and Sears, L. (eds), *The Development of American
Philosophy* (Boston, 1940).

Nagel, E., *Logic Without Metaphysics* (Glencoe, Illinois, 1956).

Neurath, M. (ed.), *Selected Papers of O. Neurath* (New York, 1969).

O'Connor, D. J., *A Critical History of Western Philosophy* (New York,
1965).

Palter, R. M., *Whitehead's Philosophy of Science* (Chicago, 1960).

Passmore, J. A., *A Hundred Years of Philosophy* (London, 1957).

Pears, D. F. (ed.), *The Nature of Metaphysics* (London, 1957).

Pears, D. F. (ed.), *Freedom of the Will* (London/New York, 1963).

Pitcher, G., *The Philosophy of Wittgenstein* (Englewood Cliffs, N.J., 1964).

Reck, A. J., *Recent American Philosophy* (New York, 1964).

Rosenfield, L. C., *A Portrait of M. R. Cohen* (New York, 1962).

Saydah, J. R., *The Ethical Theory of Clarence Irving Lewis* (Athens, Ohio,
1969).

Scheffler, I., *The Anatomy of Inquiry* (New York, 1963).

Schilpp, P. A. (ed.), *The Philosophy of G. Santayana* (Chicago, 1940).

Schilpp, P. A. (ed.), *The Philosophy of Bertrand Russell* 2nd ed. (New York,
1946).

Schilpp, P. A. (ed.), *The Philosophy of A. N. Whitehead* 2nd ed. (New
York, 1951).

Schilpp, P. A. (ed.), *The Philosophy of G. E. Moore* 2nd ed. (New York,
1952).

Schilpp, P. A. (ed.), *The Philosophy of C. D. Broad* (New York, 1959).

Schilpp, P. A. (ed.), *The Philosophy of C. I. Lewis* (La Salle, Illinois, 1968).

Schilpp, P. A. (ed.), *The Philosophy of K. Popper* (La Salle, Illinois, 1974).

Schneider, H. W., *A Hundred Years of American Philosophy* (New York,
1963).

Shahan, R. (ed.), *Essays on the Philosophy of W. V. Quine* (Norman,
Oklahoma/Brighton, 1979).

Urmson, J. J., *Philosophical Analysis: Its Development Between the Two
World Wars* (Oxford, 1956).

Walsh, W. H., *Metaphysics* (London, 1963).

Wann, T. W., (ed.), *Behaviourism and Phenomenology* (London/Chicago,
1964).

Warnock, G. J., *English Philosophy Since 1900* (London, 1958).

Weinberg, J. R., *An Examination of Logical Positivism* (New York,
1936/2nd ed., London, 1950).

White, A. R., *G. E. Moore: A Critical Exposition* (Oxford, 1958).

White, M., *Toward Reunion in Philosophy* (Cambridge, Mass., 1956).

Whitehead, A. N., *Process and Reality* ed. D. Griffin (Cambridge, 1929/New York, 1979).

Wilmot, L. F., *Whitehead and God* (Ontario, 1979).

Wood, A., *Bertrand Russell: The Passionate Sceptic* (London, 1957).

Wood, R. E. (ed.), *The Future of Metaphysics* (Chicago, 1970).

34: Phenomenology

Boer, T. de, *The Development of Husserl's Thought* (The Hague, 1978).

Bossart, P. J., *Phenomenological Perspectives* (The Hague, 1975).

Cunningham, S., *Language and the Phenomenological Reductions of Edmund Husserl* (The Hague, 1976).

Elliston, F. (ed.), *Husserl: Expositions and Appraisals* (London/Notre Dame, 1977).

Farber, M. (ed.), *Philosophical Essays in Memory of E. Husserl* (Cambridge, Mass., 1940).

Farber, M., *The Foundations of Phenomenology* 3rd ed. (New York, 1967).

Frings, M. S., *Max Scheler: Centennial Essays* (Pittsburgh, 1965/The Hague, 1974).

Husserl, E., *Ideas: General Introduction to Pure Phenomenology* tr. W. R. B. Gibson (New York, 1931).

Husserl, E., *Cartesian Meditations: An Introduction to Phenomenology* tr. D. Cairus (The Hague, 1960).

Husserl, E., *The Idea of Phenomenology* tr. W. Alston (The Hague, 1964).

Husserl, E., *Phenomenology and the Crisis of Philosophy* (New York, 1965).

Husserl, E., *Phenomenological Psychology* (The Hague, 1977).

Kockelmans, J. L., *Phenomenology: The Philosophy of Edmund Husserl and its Interpretation* (New York, 1967).

Kohak, E., *Idea and Experience: Edmund Husserl's Project of Phenomenology* (Chicago, 1978).

Kwant, R. C., *The Phenomenological Philosophy of Merleau-Ponty* (Pittsburgh/Louvain, 1963).

Kwant, R. C., *From Phenomenology to Metaphysics: An Inquiry into the Last Period of Merleau-Ponty's Philosophical Life* (Pittsburgh/Louvain, 1966).

Lauer, Q., *The Triumph of Subjectivity* (New York, 1978).

Mallin, S. B., *Merleau-Ponty's Philosophy* (London/Yale, 1979).

Mehta, J. L., *Martin Heidegger: The Way and the Vision* (Honolulu, Hawaii, 1977).

Mohanty, J. N., *Edmund Husserl's Theory of Meaning* (The Hague, 1964).

Osborn, A. D., *The Philosophy of Edmund Husserl* (New York, 1934).

Robinet, A., *Merleau-Ponty* (New York, 1967).

Sallis, J. (ed.), *Radical Phenomenology* (Atlantic Highlands, N.J., 1978).

Scheler, M., *The Nature of Sympathy* (London, 1954).

Scheler, M., *Philosophical Perspectives* (Boston, 1958).

Scheler, M., *On the Eternal in Man* tr. B. Noble (London, 1960).

Spiegelberg, H., *The Phenomenological Movement: An Historical Introduction* (2 vols, The Hague, 1960).

Tymieniecka, A. T., *et al.*, *For Roman Ingarden: Nine Essays* (The Hague, 1959).
Welch, E. P., *The Philosophy of Edmund Husserl* (New York, 1941).

35: Existentialism

Barrett, W., *Irrational Man: A Study in Existential Philosophy* (New York, 1958/London, 1961).
Blackham, H. J., *Six Existential Thinkers* (London, 1952).
Brée, G., *Camus* (New York, 1959).
Brock, W., *Introduction to Contemporary German Philosophy* (Cambridge, 1935).
Cain, S., *Gabriel Marcel* (London/New York, 1963).
Camus, A., *The Outsider* (London, 1946).
Camus, A., *The Collected Fiction of Albert Camus* (London, 1960).
Camus, A., *The Essential Writings* ed. R. E. Meagher (New York, 1979).
Caws, P., *Sartre* (London/Boston, 1979).
Collins, M., *The Existentialists* (Chicago, 1952).
Copleston, F., *Contemporary Philosophy* rev. ed. (London, 1972).
Copleston, F., *A History of Philosophy* IX (London, 1975).
Cranston, M., *Jean-Paul Sartre* (London/New York, 1962).
Cruickshank, J., *Albert Camus and the Literature of Revolt* (London, 1959).
Dempsey, P., *The Psychology of Sartre* (Oxford/Cork, 1950).
Desan, W., *The Tragic Finale: An Essay on the Philosophy of Jean-Paul Sartre* (Cambridge, Mass., 1954).
Gallagher, K. T., *The Philosophy of Gabriel Marcel* (New York, 1962).
Grene, M., *Introduction to Existentialism* (Chicago, 1952).
Grene, M., *Martin Heidegger* (London/New York, 1957).
Grimsley, R., *Existentialist Thought* (Cardiff, 1955).
Heidegger, M., *Existence and Being* tr. D. Scott *et al.* (London/Chicago, 1949).
Heidegger, M., *Being and Time* tr. J. Macquarrie (London/New York, 1962).
Jaspers, K., *Man in the Modern Age* 2nd ed. (London, 1952).
Jaspers, K., *Reason and Existenz* (New York, 1955/London, 1956).
Kaufmann, W. A. (ed.), *Existentialism, Religion and Death* (New York, 1976).
Kern, E. (ed.), *Sartre* (Englewood Cliffs, N.J., 1963).
La Capra, D., *A Preface to Sartre* (New York, 1978/London, 1979).
Laing, R. D., *The Divided Self* (London, 1960).
Laing, R. D., and Cooper, D. G., *Reason and Violence: A Decade of Sartre's Philosophy* (London, 1964).
Manser, A., *Sartre: A Philosophic Study* (London, 1966).
Marcel, G., *The Philosophy of Existence* (London, 1948/New York, 1949).
Marcel, G., *The Mystery of Being* (2 vols, London/Chicago, 1950-51).
Marcel, G., *Homo Viator: Introduction to a Metaphysic of Hope* (London/ Chicago, 1951).
Molina, F., *Existentialism as Philosophy* (Englewood Cliffs, N.J., 1962).

Bibliography 603

Murdoch, I., *Sartre: Romantic Rationalist* (Cambridge/New Haven, Connecticut, 1953).
Natanson, M. A., *A Critique of Jean-Paul Sartre's Ontology* (Lincoln, Nebraska, 1951).
Olson, R. G., *Introduction to Existentialism* (New York, 1962).
Onimus, J., *Albert Camus and Christianity* (London/Dublin, 1970).
Ruggiero, G. de, *Existentialism* (London, 1946).
Sartre, J.-P., *Existentialism and Humanism* (New York, 1956).
Sartre, J.-P., *Being and Nothingness* tr. H. Barnes (New York, 1956/London, 1957).
Sartre, J.-P., *The Philosophy of Jean-Paul Sartre* ed. E. D. Cumming (London, 1968).
Schaldenbrand, M. A., *Phenomenologies of Freedom* (Washington, D.C., 1960).
Schilpp, P. A. (ed.), *The Philosophy of Karl Jaspers* (Illinois, 1958).
Schmitt, G., *The Concept of Being in Hegel and Heidegger* (Bonn, 1977).
Spiegelberg, H., *The Phenomenological Movement* II (The Hague, 1960).
Stack, G. J., *Sartre's Philosophy of Social Existence* (St Louis, 1977).
Steller, J., *Jean-Paul Sartre* (New York, 1960).
Thody, P., *Albert Camus: A Study of his Work* (London, 1957).
Tillich, P., *The Courage to Be* (London, 1952).
Troisfontaines, R., *De l'Existence a l'être* (Paris/Louvain, 1953).
Vycinas, V., *Earth and Gods: An Introduction to the Philosophy of Martin Heidegger* (The Hague, 1961).
Wahl, J., *A Short History of Existentialism* (New York, 1949).
Wahl, J., *Philosophies of Existence: An Introduction to the Basic Thought of Kierkegaard, Heidegger, Jaspers, Marcel and Sartre* (London, 1969).
Warnock, M., *The Philosophy of Sartre* (London, 1965).
Wyschogrod, M., *Kierkegaard and Heidegger* (New York, 1954).

36: Philosophy of being
Bochenski, J. M., *Philosophy — An Introduction* (Netherlands, 1962).
Chauchard, P., *Man and Cosmos: Scientific Phenomenology in Teilhard de Chardin* (New York, 1965).
Collingwood, R. G., *An Essay on Metaphysics* (Oxford, 1948).
Copleston, F., *Contemporary Philosophy* rev. ed. (London, 1972).
Copleston, F., *A History of Philosophy* IX (London, 1975).
Corbishley, T., *The Spirituality of Teilhard de Chardin* (London, 1971).
Corte, N., *Pierre Teilhard de Chardin: His Life and Spirit* (London, 1960).
Crowe, F. E. (ed.), *Collection: Papers by Bernard Lonergan* (New York/London, 1967).
Crowe, F. E. (ed.), *A Third Collection: Papers by Bernard Lonergan* (Ramsey, N. J., 1984/London, 1985).
Cuénot, C., *Teilhard de Chardin: A Biographical Study* (London/Baltimore, 1965).

Delfgaauw, B., *Evolution: The Theory of Teilhard de Chardin* (London/New York, 1970).

Evans, J. W. (ed.), *Jacques Maritain: The Man and his Achievement* (New York, 1963).

Fecher, C. A., *The Philosophy of Jacques Maritain* (New York, 1969).

Fox, A., *Dean Inge* (London, 1960).

Gade, J., *The Life of Cardinal Mercier* (New York, 1934).

Gallagher, D. and I., *The Achievement of Jacques and Raïssa Maritain* (New York, 1962).

Garrigou-Lagrange, R., *God, His Existence and Nature* (St Louis, 1934).

Garrigou-Lagrange, R., *Reality, A Synthesis of Thomistic Thought* (London/St Louis, 1950).

Gilson, E., *The Philosophy of St Bonaventure* (London, 1938).

Gilson, E., *Being and Some Philosophers* (Toronto, 1949).

Gilson, E., *The Spirit of Medieval Philosophy* (London, 1950).

Gilson, E., *Christian Philosophy in the Middle Ages* (London, 1955).

Gilson, E., *The Christian Philosophy of St Thomas Aquinas* (New York, 1956/London, 1957).

Gilson, E., *The Christian Philosophy of St Augustine* (New York, 1960/London, 1961).

Gilson, E., *The Spirit of Thomism* (New York/London, 1964).

Gilson, E., Maurer, A. A., and Langan, I., *Recent Philosophy* (New York, 1966).

Hanson, A. (ed.), *Teilhard Reassessed* (London, 1970).

Hartmann, N., *New Ways of Ontology* (Chicago, 1953).

Lonergan, B., *Insight: A Study of Human Understanding* (London, 1957).

Lonergan, B., *Method in Theology* (London, 1972).

Lonergan, B., *Philosophy of God and Theology* (London, 1974).

Lubac, H. de, *Teilhard Explained* (New York, 1968).

McShane, P. (ed.), *Foundations of Theology* (Notre Dame/Dublin, 1971).

McShane, P., *Introducing the Thought of Bernard Lonergan* (London, 1973).

McShane, P., *Wealth of Self and Wealth of Nations* (New York, 1975).

McShane, P., *The Shaping of the Foundations* (Washington, 1977).

Maritain, J., *Introduction to Philosophy* (London, 1930).

Maritain. J., *A Preface to Metaphysics: Seven Lectures on Being* (London/New York, 1939).

Maritain, J., *The Degrees of Knowledge* (New York, 1946/London, 1959).

Maritain, J., *Existence and the Existent* (New York, 1948).

Maritain, R., *Adventures in Grace* (New York, 1945).

Michener, N. W., *Maritain on the Nature of Man in a Christian Democracy* (Hull, Quebec, 1955).

Muck, O., *The Transcendental Method* (New York, 1968).

O'Connor, R. E. (ed.), *Bernard Lonergan: Three Lectures* (Montreal, 1975).

Owens, J., *The Doctrine of Being in Aristotelian Metaphysics* 2nd ed. (Toronto, 1963).

Pears, D. F. (ed.), *The Nature of Metaphysics* (London, 1957).

Phelan, G. B., *Jacques Maritain* (New York, 1937).

Quinn, J. M., *The Thomism of Etienne Gilson* (Villanova, Pennsylvania, 1971).

Raven, C. E., *Teilhard de Chardin: Scientist and Seer* (London, 1962).

Rideau, E., *Teilhard de Chardin: A Guide to his Thought* (London, 1967).

Santayana, G., *The Life of Reason* (5 vols, New York, 1905-06).

Santayana, G., *Realms of Being* (2 vols, New York, 1927-30).

Schilpp, P. A. (ed.), *The Philosophy of G. Santayana* 2nd ed. (New York, 1951).

Speaight, R., *Teilhard de Chardin: A Biography* (London, 1967).

Sprigge, T., *Santayana: An Examination of his Philosophy* (London, 1974).

Taylor, A. E., *Elements of Metaphysics* 2nd ed. (1909).

Taylor, A. E., *Does God Exist?* (London, 1945).

Teilhard de Chardin, P., *The Phenomenon of Man* (London/New York, 1959).

Teilhard de Chardin, P., *Le Milieu Divin: An Essay on the Interior Life* (London/New York, 1960).

Teilhard de Chardin, P., *The Future of Man* (London, 1964).

Teilhard de Chardin, P., *The Appearance of Man* (London, 1965).

Teilhard de Chardin, P., *Hymn of the Universe* (London, 1965).

Teilhard de Chardin, P., *Man's Place in Nature* (London/New York, 1966).

Timosaitas, A., *Church and State in Maritain's Thought* (Chicago, 1959).

Towers, B., *Teilhard de Chardin* (London, 1966).

Tyrrell, B., and Ryan, W. (eds), *Bernard Lonergan: A Second Collection* (London/Philadelphia, 1974).

Walsh, W. H., *Metaphysics* (London, 1963).

Whitehead, A. N. *Adventures of Ideas* (New York, 1933).

Wildiers, N. M., *An Introduction to Teilhard de Chardin* (London/New York, 1968).

Index